INFORMATION TECHNOLOGY *for* HEALTHCARE MANAGERS

NINTH EDITION

INFORMATION TECHNOLOGY *for* HEALTHCARE MANAGERS

Gerald L. Glandon
Detlev H. Smaltz
Donna J. Slovensky

HAP

AUPHA

Health Administration Press, Chicago, Illinois
Association of University Programs in Health Administration, Washington, DC

Your board, staff, or clients may also benefit from this book's insight. For information on quantity discounts, contact the Health Administration Press Marketing Manager at (312) 424-9450.

25 24 23 22 21 5 4 3 2

Library of Congress Cataloging-in-Publication Data

Names: Glandon, Gerald L., author. | Smaltz, Detlev H. (Detlev Herb), author. | Slovensky, Donna J. (Donna Jean), author. | Association of University Programs in Health Administration, issuing body.
Title: Information technology for healthcare managers / Gerald L. Glandon, Detlev H. Smaltz, Donna J. Slovensky.
Other titles: Information systems for healthcare management
Description: Ninth edition. | Chicago, Illinois : Health Administration Press ; Washington, DC : Association of University Programs in Health Administration, [2020] | Preceded by: Information systems for healthcare management / Gerald L. Glandon, Detlev H. Smaltz, Donna J. Slovensky. Eighth edition. 2014. | Includes bibliographical references and index. | Summary: "Healthcare organizations are now focused on big data aggregated from myriad data-producing applications both in and beyond the enterprise. Healthcare leaders must position themselves to leverage the new opportunities that arise from HIT's ascendance and to mine the vast amount of available data for competitive advantage. Where can they turn for insight? Information Technology for Healthcare Managers blends management theory, cutting-edge tech knowledge, and a thorough grounding in the healthcare applications of technology. Opinions abound on technology's best uses for society, but healthcare organizations need more than opinion—they need knowledge and strategy. This book will help leaders combine tech savvy with business savvy for sustainable success in a dynamic environment"– Provided by publisher.
Identifiers: LCCN 2020018798 (print) | LCCN 2020018799 (ebook) | ISBN 9781640551916 (hardback) | ISBN 9781640551923 (ebook) | ISBN 9781640551930 (epub) | ISBN 9781640551947 (mobi) | ISBN 9781640551954 (xml)
Subjects: MESH: Management Information Systems | Medical Informatics Computing | Information Technology | Health Services Administration
Classification: LCC R855.3 (print) | LCC R855.3 (ebook) | NLM W 26.5 | DDC 610.285–dc23
LC record available at https://lccn.loc.gov/2020018798
LC ebook record available at https://lccn.loc.gov/2020018799

The paper used in this publication meets the minimum requirements of American National Standard for Information Sciences—Permanence of Paper for Printed Library Materials, ANSI Z39.48-1984. ♾™

Acquisitions editor: Jennette McClain; Project manager: Theresa L. Rothschadl; Cover designer: James Slate; Layout: Integra

Found an error or a typo? We want to know! Please e-mail it to hapbooks@ache.org, mentioning the book's title and putting "Book Error" in the subject line.

For photocopying and copyright information, please contact Copyright Clearance Center at www.copyright.com or at (978) 750-8400.

Health Administration Press
A division of the Foundation of the American College of Healthcare Executives
300 S. Riverside Plaza, Suite 1900
Chicago, IL 60606-6698
(312) 424-2800

Association of University Programs in Health Administration
1730 M Street, NW
Suite 407
Washington, DC 20036
(202) 763-7283

BRIEF CONTENTS

DETAILED CONTENTS

PREFACE

The challenges of healthcare quality, cost, and access have been with us for more than half a century. Despite the rapid changes in information technology and its application to healthcare problems—and despite healthcare leaders' continuing struggle to come up with economic, political, and technological solutions—the problems persist even today.

With every "fix," we create additional challenges. Developments such as the electronic health record (EHR) as a repository for digital health information and the enhanced ability of providers, payers, and patients to share that information among themselves have appeared as solutions. Prior to the passage of the American Recovery and Reinvestment Act of 2009, which provided significant incentives for both hospitals and physicians to adopt EHRs, movement toward those solutions had been slow, and challenges related to data privacy and security, as well as the sheer cost of the solutions, made some organizations reluctant to implement them. Recently, the new challenges of physician and caregiver burnout emerged as a by-product of significantly increased interaction with automated tools like the EHR. In this era of the Patient Protection and Affordable Care Act (ACA), we are forced again to reexamine and update the use of information technology to support operational, management, and clinical decision-making.

The study of health information technology (HIT) should no longer be relegated to a small subsection of the health administration curriculum. It has become central to all that a healthcare practitioner does and a healthcare management instructor teaches. The chief information officer (CIO) is now part of the senior executive team at most healthcare delivery organizations. Fortunately for those in the field, new information technologies have raced far ahead of their use in healthcare. Such technologies present the CIO and the rest of the leadership team with challenges related to understanding their potential applications and implications, strategically planning their selection and implementation, ensuring that users receive sufficient training on their proper use, and finding a way to pay for them.

To reflect the pervasiveness of information *technologies* in almost every single workflow in a healthcare organization, we have changed the title of this ninth edition to *Information Technology for Healthcare Managers*—HIT has moved far beyond the information *systems* of the past. This edition provides a comprehensive overview of HIT, including the effects of the external environment and government policies on its evolution; the expanded and increasingly complex role of the CIO in orchestrating HIT; the importance of effective HIT governance, project management, and day-to-day HIT service management processes; the types of operational, management, and clinical applications; the growing importance of leveraging data and information via robust analytic capabilities; and the value HIT brings to the healthcare enterprise. The concepts included in the book reflect our broad vision of HIT management as a combination of technology, information, and leadership of staff.

The book is intended for current healthcare management students, as well as practicing healthcare executives and managers. Although many of the readers may not fill a CIO role or be in charge of the HIT function, they will benefit from having a basic understanding of this expanding element of healthcare delivery. The book is suitable for a one-semester graduate or advanced undergraduate course in healthcare IT or informatics. It is also an extensive reference for healthcare managers and others involved in selecting and implementing HIT systems. Links to internet sources are included to provide additional information on the major topics covered in each chapter.

All chapters have been updated to reflect mandates of the ACA and other new federal laws, as well as to discuss the current (and potential future) challenges that HIT leadership and users face. The three sections in this edition address those changes (see the following list). Along with a wholly new chapter on analytics, this edition offers current examples, an updated glossary, and a list of abbreviations.

- *Part I: HIT Strategic Alignment.* The four chapters in this section reflect our view that successfully managing HIT today requires leaders who understand the influence of the external environment, including government interventions and policies. The same can be said about internal HIT activities and strategies. More than ever, achieving synergistic alignment between the HIT strategy and that of the overall healthcare organizations strategy is critical.
- *Part II: Operational Effectiveness.* The five chapters in this section center on the crucial elements that enable HIT to operate effectively and efficiently.
- *Part III: Strategic Competitive Advantage.* The four chapters in this section focus on crucial HIT capabilities that can help deliver value to healthcare organizations. Project portfolio management and a new chapter on analytics are included along with a chapter on HIT value analysis.

Instructor Resources

This book's Instructor Resources include a test bank, PowerPoints, and answers or discussion points for the in-book discussion questions.

For the most up-to-date information about this book and its Instructor Resources, go to ache.org/HAP and search for the book's order code (2418I).

This book's Instructor Resources are available to instructors who adopt this book for use in their course. For access information, please email hapbooks@ache.org.

ACKNOWLEDGMENTS

Developing a text of this scope requires the input and support of a host of individuals. This work, begun by Dr. Charles Austin in the 1970s, continues to be salient today. We owe him, his later coauthor Dr. Stuart Boxerman, and other contributors to this book over the years a substantial debt for initiating the conversation about information systems in healthcare and for ensuring that subsequent editions of the book kept pace with the dramatic rate of change in the information technology (IT) industry and the proliferation of IT adoption models in healthcare organizations. We have a profound respect for the bodies of knowledge accumulated in previous editions and the value these compilations brought to healthcare managers and executives. Many individuals have influenced the content of this book directly, and many more indirectly through conversations and recommendations. We are most appreciative of all our colleagues and associates who supported us through past and current editions.

Dr. Glandon wants to thank Brian Malec from California State University, Northridge, for responding to thoughts and questions along the way. He has a seasoned perspective that kept my thinking on track. I also express my appreciation to individuals who provided assistance in prior editions of the text, to the continuing benefit of the current edition.

Dr. Smaltz also extends his thanks to the members of his former team at the Ohio State University Wexner Medical Center (OSUWMC) for their dedication to continuously improving the practice of HIT management. In particular, Ben Walters and Ron Kibbe provided excellent counsel on IT service management. In addition, Phil Skinner, Benita Gilliard, Kevin Jones, and Jyoti Kamal of OSUWMC, as well as Randy Carpenter, formerly CIO at HealthSouth, all provided sample exhibits and invaluable insight. Thank you to Paul Murphy, formerly at Encore Health Resources and now at the Chartis Group, for his input on the section about the system selection process. Also, John Daniels, formerly at HIMSS Analytics, provided invaluable insights into the EMR Adoption model. Finally, a big thank you to Dr. Stephen Blackwelder, chief analytics officer at Duke Health, for contributing a case study to the chapter on analytics.

Dr. Slovensky extends her thanks to Amanda Dorsey for her thoughtful review and edit of chapter 5.

The responsibility for any errors or oversights in this ninth edition lies entirely with us.

PART

I

HEALTH INFORMATION TECHNOLOGY STRATEGIC ALIGNMENT

CHAPTER

1

CONNECTING THE STRATEGIC DOTS: DOES HEALTH INFORMATION TECHNOLOGY MATTER?

Learning Objectives

1. Define the three fundamental drivers of change to the healthcare system.
2. List and define six major external challenges facing healthcare delivery systems today.
3. Describe the complexity of these interrelated challenges for healthcare and health information technology.
4. Illustrate the history, development, and current state of healthcare information systems.
5. Name and describe the four categories of healthcare information systems.
6. Analyze the six key priorities of healthcare information systems today that will affect their future.
7. Describe the importance of future challenges to management health-care information technologies.

Health Information Technology: The Future Is Now

Healthcare delivery continues to be an information-intensive set of processes. A series of Institute of Medicine (IOM 1999, 2001) studies suggests that high-quality patient care relies on careful documentation of each patient's medical history, health status, current medical conditions, and treatment plans. Financial information is essential for strategic planning and efficient operational support of the patient care process. Management of healthcare organizations requires reliable, accurate, current, secure, and relevant clinical and administrative information. A strong argument can be made that the healthcare field is one of the most information-intensive sectors of the US economy.

Information technology (IT) has advanced to a high level of sophistication in healthcare and other sectors. However, technology can only provide tools to aid in the accomplishment of a wider set of organizational goals. Analysis of information requirements in the broader organizational context should always take precedence over a rush to computerize. IT by itself is not the answer to management problems; technology must be part of a broader restructuring of the organization, including engineering and reengineering of business processes. Alignment of IT strategy with management goals of the healthcare organization is essential. Despite these cautions, effective design, implementation, and management of health information technology (HIT) show great promise (De Angelo 2000; Glaser and Garets 2005; Kaushal, Barker, and Bates 2001; Koppel 2016; Raghupathi and Raghupathi 2014; Wimble and Leroy 2018).

An essential element in successful information systems implementation is carefully planned teamwork by clinicians, managers, and technical systems specialists. Information systems developed in isolation by technicians may be technically pure and elegant in design, but rarely will they pass the test of reality in meeting organizational requirements. On the other hand, very few managers and clinicians possess the equally important technical knowledge and skills of systems analysis and design, and the amateur analyst cannot hope to avoid the havoc that can result from a poorly designed system. A balanced effort is required: Operational personnel contribute ideas on system requirements and organizational realities, and technical personnel employ their skills in analysis and design.

The reality in recent years suggests that careful planning and ample warnings of challenges may not be sufficient. The feature article in the April 2019 *Fortune* magazine summarizes aspects of the failure of electronic health record (EHR) systems to live up to the intended outcome (Schulte and Fry 2019). Their detailed conclusion is that converting healthcare medical information to electronic records intended to make healthcare "better, safer and cheaper"; after the field has spent more than $36 billion on conversion, the digital revolution has failed to deliver. The reasons for the failure are many and complex. The important point is that HIT is only a tool. It does not constitute a silver bullet or easy answer to all problems.

This chapter sets the stage for the remainder of the book, and its last section outlines the book chapters in detail. It begins with an overview of the current healthcare environment as a driver of fundamental changes in HIT. This includes the triple aim of cost, quality, and access, along with six key factors not at the systems level but substantially outside of an individual organization. It then presents a short history of the development of HIT systems and a method of broadly categorizing HIT. This last item becomes a tool for learning about these interdependent systems. The chapter then outlines seven of the many HIT priorities and challenges faced today. It ends with a peek into HIT challenges in the near future.

As you consider these individual items, notice three things. First, the placement of change motivators does not always uniquely fall into a particular grouping. There is substantial overlap and interdependence. Second, a number of common themes appear across categories. Third, some of these presentations are only the tip of the iceberg, and subsequent chapters will delve into them in more depth.

Technological Obsolescence: The Current Challenges in the Healthcare Environment

While nothing is more dangerous than predicting the future, Goldsmith (1980) looked into the future of healthcare in the late 1980s. He foresaw a vastly different landscape for the delivery of care than existed at the time. He documented a number of demographic, secular, and organizational changes that would shape that future. Such changes included the growing elderly population, the decline of the hospital as the center of the healthcare delivery universe, the oversupply of physicians, the expanded role of government in financing healthcare, the shift of financial risk from payers to providers, the expansion of health maintenance organizations (HMOs) in various forms, and problems related to the uninsured. He observed that to address issues such as continuity, linkage, coordination, and accountability, changes in the organization of the healthcare delivery system would be required. One can question the accuracy of specific predictions made in Goldsmith's forecast, but most cannot deny that he was correct in the change in focus. Looking back, it is clear that these issues require added emphasis on improving the management of both healthcare information and its technology.

The complexity and challenges in healthcare delivery are many. To give a sense of the situation, consider that delivery systems today must provide high-quality, timely care that attains full transparency regarding costs and quality; be mindful of growing privacy and security concerns of patients; use personalized medicine as appropriate; adhere to best-practice evidence; and adopt care coordination across settings and time (Wanless and Ludwig 2011). On top of these pressures, with the accountable care organization (ACO) model supported through healthcare reform, delivery organizations may have more financial incentive to implement disease prevention and wellness effectively (Centers for Medicare & Medicaid Services 2020). Further, all of these issues must be addressed in an environment in which technological change makes the innovation of yesterday obsolete today. Professionals in the field need to make an array of good choices, implement those technologies, prepare practitioners to use those technologies, and evaluate their relevance against the next technological advance. For a recent summary of the scale and scope of the challenges, read *FutureScan: Healthcare Trends and Implications 2018–2023* (American College of Healthcare Executives 2018).

To assist the learner in understanding these myriad changes, we present healthcare's current challenges at two levels: the fundamental drivers of change at the systems level and the fundamental societal and sector changes that occur largely outside the control of participants in the delivery system. The fundamental drivers of change for years have been the following: (1) healthcare costs, (2) medical errors and poor quality of care, and (3) access and health disparities. These changes set in motion inescapable transformations that were external to healthcare delivery: (1) health systems change, (2) evidence-based medicine, (3) consumer empowerment, (4) connectedness, (5) transparency, and (6) medical tourism.

Fundamental Drivers of Change

More of this will be covered in chapter 2, but what some have called the golden triangle still applies. Until we can provide cost-effective care that is appropriate, high quality, and accessible to all, all other concerns are means to these ends.

Healthcare Costs

Healthcare costs continue to spiral upward, continuing a trend of the last 50 years. Concern about persistent cost increases—and, more important, the value of dollars spent on healthcare services—appears to drive operational and policy changes. A common belief is that high healthcare costs make the US economy less competitive and have different effects on different segments of the national economy. These contentions can be debated, and few analysts have clear strategies to control costs, but we have seen and will likely continue to see cost control being implemented by government, by private payers, and even by consumers.

The fact that we can control costs has been made more apparent by some recent popular analyses that examine differences in the utilization of services and costs across communities in the United States. Gawande (2009), for example, demonstrates a nearly twofold difference in healthcare expenditures for the Medicare population in communities that are otherwise similar in demographics and objective need for services. The Dartmouth Atlas Project has significant, detailed analyses that clearly demonstrate variation of utilization and costs across regions even after controlling for demographics and behavioral risk factors (see Fisher et al. 2009). It is clear that better data—aggregated and compared across regions—will enable us to investigate the differences further. HIT at the organizational level, shared with regional and national entities, will be called on to address these issues.

Medical Errors and Poor Quality of Care

According to the IOM's 1999 landmark report, *To Err Is Human*, medical errors are a leading cause of adverse health consequences in hospitals. The report estimated that at least 44,000 and as many as 98,000 individuals die in hospitals per year as a result of preventable medical errors. Errors also resulted in greater direct and indirect costs borne by society as a whole. The report stated that "the total national cost associated with adverse effects [of medical errors] was approximately 4 percent of national health expenditures in 1996" (IOM 1999, 41). Further, in 2001 the IOM issued a blueprint, titled *Crossing the Quality Chasm,* designed to help organizations fix the delivery system.

More than ten years after the publications of the IOM reports, unnecessary deaths from medical errors (preventable and otherwise) and poor quality of care were still occurring at a high rate (Sternberg 2012). Even today, Makary and Daniel (2016) report that medical errors are responsible for over 250,000 deaths each year, ranking as the third leading cause of death in the United States. Estimating the number of errors is difficult because no centralized reporting mechanism exists (Doheny 2009). We have seen the costs of poor quality and excessive medical errors, but the solutions to this complex problem are elusive. Having said that, some evidence exists that progress is being made (Berger 2015). A Harvard University study documented specific improvements as part of the mandatory reporting on improvement in healthcare quality. The *National Healthcare Quality and Disparities Report* (Agency for Healthcare Research and Quality 2018) presents some hopeful progress in quality, with substantial gains in patient safety, improvement in patient–provider communication, almost complete use of effective treatment, and enhancement of healthy living.

Access and Health Disparities

The myriad problems arising from the failure of the US healthcare system to provide reasonable access to care have been well documented (Families USA 2012). While better information systems and exchange of information can address these challenges, they cannot directly solve all of them. Dealing with the uninsured will put a greater strain on the collection and reporting of clinical and administrative data at the organizational and system levels. The number of those uninsured is so large that the entire healthcare delivery system will be challenged as we implement policies to expand coverage. Data from the Centers for Disease Control and Prevention (CDC) (Cohen, Terlizzi, and Martinez 2019) suggest that the number of individuals 65 or younger without health insurance was 30.1 million, or about 11.1 percent of the population (exhibit 1.1). That is up from 28.9 million in 2017, or about 10.7 percent of the population under 65. These are both better than the 48.2 million, or 18.2 percent of the population, in 2010. This trend runs

EXHIBIT 1.1
Number and Percent of Population Uninsured: Younger than 65 (select years)

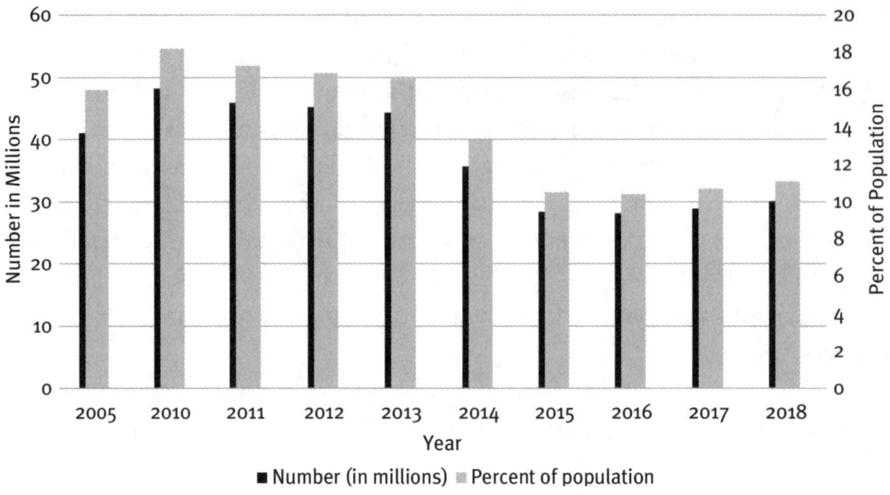

Source: Cohen, Terlizzi, and Martinez (2019).

in the right direction, but the uninsured still present a managerial challenge. However, government data (USHHS 2016) suggest few health disparity measures demonstrated any progress, with the exception of the elimination of racial and ethnic disparities in childhood immunizations and of adverse events associated with procedures.

External Challenges

Beyond the prime movers of change in the healthcare system are a host of system changes that result from or are coincidental to challenges derived from cost, quality, and access. These largely external challenges are associated with key societal and political changes that influence healthcare delivery and by extension healthcare information management systems. These include healthcare system change, evidence-based medicine, consumer empowerment, connectedness, transparency, and tourism.

Healthcare System Change

The fundamental shift in thinking, partially expressed in the Patient Protection and Affordable Care Act of 2010 (discussed in chapter 2), was largely overshadowed by the immediate emphasis on providing access to care for the uninsured population in the United States. Within that massive legislation were the seeds of experiments designed to identify other ways of operating the healthcare delivery system. Elements such as bundled payments, payment for outcomes, ACOs, patient-centered medical homes, and comparative effectiveness research all challenge the conventional fee-for-service payment and focus on the care of an individual patient. These changes will alter the sources of data that information management professionals will be required to identify, collect, store, analyze, and report. All of the challenges we face today will expand with the addition of sources of information and legitimate users of information outside of the normal organizational boundaries.

In the coming years, payment will be more oriented toward the outcomes generated and will cover the costs of a full range of services necessary to treat the patient. Already we are bundling Medicare payments for surgery and postsurgical care. Even broader ranges of clinical services—from presurgical assessments and testing to postsurgical clinical management and rehabilitation—are likely to be paid to a single provider. This expanded episode-of-illness system will fundamentally enlarge the sources of vital data that an organization must process. Because these data cross organizational lines, episode-of-illness systems complicate how the data are linked and aggregated for reporting purposes. Starting in 2012, hospitals are penalized for excessive 30-day readmission rates, so leadership is demanding more information and intervention to make sure that patients are ready to be discharged and that essential follow-up care is provided.

Similarly, our responsibility for providing reasonable cost, high quality, and good access will shift from individual patients to populations. Monitoring and designing interventions to keep people healthy before they show up at the healthcare provider's door require a different type of thinking about data needs. For example, how do providers capture and assist the patient with uncontrolled diabetes living in the community but not yet showing up with out-of-control blood sugar?

Finally, as the government gets more directly involved in changing the system, it will fund research aimed at identification of positive changes. IOM (2009) identified the top 100 funding priorities as a means of guiding government research support. Brief descriptions of the ten priorities from the top quartile are as follows (IOM 2009, 107):

1. Compare the effectiveness of treatment strategies for atrial fibrillation, including surgery, catheter ablation, and pharmacologic treatment.
2. Compare the effectiveness of the different treatments (e.g., assistive listening devices, cochlear implants, electric-acoustic devices, habilitation and rehabilitation methods) for hearing loss in children and adults, especially individuals with diverse cultural, language, medical, and developmental backgrounds.

3. Compare the effectiveness of primary prevention methods, such as exercise and balance training, versus clinical treatments in preventing falls in older adults.
4. Compare the effectiveness of upper endoscopy utilization and frequency for patients with gastroesophageal reflux disease on morbidity, quality of life, and diagnosis of esophageal adenocarcinoma.
5. Compare the effectiveness of dissemination and translation techniques to facilitate the use of comparative effectiveness research by patients, clinicians, payers, and others.
6. Compare the effectiveness of comprehensive care coordination programs, such as the medical home, and usual care in managing children and adults with severe chronic disease.
7. Compare the effectiveness of different strategies of introducing biologics into the treatment algorithm for inflammatory diseases, including Crohn's disease, ulcerative colitis, rheumatoid arthritis, and psoriatic arthritis.
8. Compare the effectiveness of various screening, prophylaxis, and treatment interventions in eradicating methicillin-resistant Staphylococcus aureus in communities, institutions, and hospitals.
9. Compare the effectiveness of strategies (e.g., biopatches, reducing central line entry, chlorhexidine for all line entries, antibiotic-impregnated catheters, treating all line entries via a sterile field) for reducing healthcare-associated infections, including catheter-associated bloodstream infection, ventilator-associated pneumonia, and surgical site infections in children and adults.
10. Compare the effectiveness of management strategies for localized prostate cancer (e.g., active surveillance, radical prostatectomy [conventional, robotic, and laparoscopic], and radiotherapy [conformal, brachytherapy, proton-beam, and intensity-modulated radiotherapy]) on survival, recurrence, side effects, quality of life, and costs.

Clearly, these are comprehensive assessments that will strain even the best data collection, reporting, and analysis systems for healthcare. Further, they give rise to structural changes in healthcare organizations. Healthcare markets continue to change as they face ongoing efforts to manage costs, quality, and access. As these markets—and the major delivery organizations in the markets—adapt, HIT will be required to accommodate these changing needs accordingly.

Market-driven healthcare reform and efforts to increase market competition, initiated in the 1990s, have evolved, but their effectiveness still cannot be fully judged. Wilensky (2006) and Ginsburg (2005) provide historical perspectives on the changing healthcare landscape. They demonstrate that in the mid-1990s, nearly 75 percent of people with employment-based insurance had some form of managed care, and HMOs constituted the largest component. Insurance companies and hospitals poured into this market because of the potential for profits. More recent healthcare outlooks emphasize the need to create financial sustainability in the new economy and experiment with evolving delivery modes, all in response to competitive pressure (Burrill and Beaudoin 2019).

As discussed earlier, the population of uninsured and underinsured US residents is still high, and disease prevention remains an elusive goal in most health plans today. This pressure seems unlikely to subside. Creating an organization and having the leadership in place to assist in meeting these and other challenges are essential. As we discuss in chapter 3, the chief information officer (CIO) role will become even more essential in the future.

Evidence-Based Medicine

Evidence-based medicine (EBM) grew in the late 1990s (Clancy and Eisenberg 1998) and has become mainstream, as indicated by the publication of at least one online EBM journal (*Evidence-Based Medicine for Primary Care and Internal Medicine*, launched in 1995). Landry and Sibbald (2001, 1,226) define *evidence-based medicine* as "an information management and learning strategy that seeks to integrate clinical expertise with the best evidence available to make effective clinical decisions that will ultimately improve patient care." It is a systematic approach to diagnosis and treatment that encourages the physician to formulate questions and seek answers from the best available published evidence. EBM has gained momentum as an important mechanism for improving healthcare delivery. Some even suggested that EBM could become the new paradigm for organizations to follow in providing care; in fact, Moskowitz and Bodenheimer (2011) have proposed the concept of "evidence-based health," which requires the involvement of patients and their communities to expand the EBM model. Widespread implementation of EBM may have bumps. Some have begun to caution against the transition to "evidence," given that the patients' easy access to information that they do not fully understand on the internet may cause pressure for providers (Diamond and Kaul 2008). Recent articles suggest that the level of detail and nuance in the examination of evidence have become extreme (see Roever et al. 2016).

In summary, scholars now recognize the limitation of evidence alone. Djulbegovic and Guyatt's (2017) assessment, however, is that the contributions of evidence in clinical space will be to place medicine on a solid scientific base, to develop hierarchies of evidence, to recognize the role of patient values and preferences, and to develop trustworthy recommendations.

The focus of this book lies between two extreme views in the managerial world. Management of HIT requires focused attention to core operations; thus, the creation, storage, and retrieval of evidence for health management decision-making necessarily involve HIT. This use of HIT, however, is associated with the organization's strategic decisions involving both costs and benefits of HIT spending or other organizational priorities. All of these costs and benefits need to be assessed, and healthcare managers need to develop their skills in using internal health information intelligently and entering into health information exchanges to support their organization's strategic and operational goals (Johnston, Pan, and Middleton 2002; Sidorov 2006; Williams et al. 2012).

Consumer Empowerment

Consumers have become increasingly sophisticated in their selection and use of healthcare services—a fact that is related, in some ways, to the reform of the delivery system. Patients may now be empowered to engage with the care process. Informed by the internet, consumers are seeking medical information and joining in support groups as they interact with physicians and other healthcare providers. Goldsmith stated that "the patient is in charge of the process. . . . The internet has enabled patients to aggregate their collective experiences across disease entities" (Reece 2000).

Although providers express legitimate concerns about clients who may misuse or misunderstand information from the internet, they realize that the trend of internet use by healthcare consumers is clear and irreversible. Herzlinger (2004) has been called the godmother of consumer-driven healthcare on the basis of her book with that title. She argues strongly for the value of expanding the roles of the consumer and patient and provides clear advice to providers, payers, and those influencing policy in this regard. Oravec (2001) suggests that the healthcare system should help develop approaches to empowering consumers to use the internet effectively as one part of a total healthcare strategy, rather than simply warning them about the potential hazards of inaccurate or misunderstood information. Further, the Foundation for Accountability (FACCT 2003) proposed recommendations that arose from health reform meetings held in Jackson Hole, Wyoming, and input from other policymakers. The proposal looked to Congress to establish national information infrastructure, a process for uniformity of systems, and support for implementation. The proposal called for changes in payment and culture that are still being debated as part of healthcare reform. Most important, however, it argued for infrastructure-related developments, including architecture for national health information infrastructure and personal health records (PHRs), mandatory publication of performance data for federally funded projects, support of informed patients through professional licensure and accreditation, and inclusion of health as a major national commitment in education provided from kindergarten through high school.

Evidence shows that the consumer empowerment and involvement movement is growing and is highly integrated with the need for information management in healthcare. (For a comprehensive overview of the history of social networking and social media not applied to healthcare per se, see Boyd and Ellison [2007]). PricewaterhouseCoopers's Health Research Institute (2012) has published results of a consumer participation survey related to healthcare. The findings reveal that age matters in who trusts online health information and shares it on social media information (younger patients are more likely to trust and share). However, young people in poor health are also more likely to engage in health-related social media. Consumers in general are likely to share through social media any (positive and negative) information on the care received, on experiences with medication and treatment, and on specific providers. A post on social media raises expectations for the organization to respond to consumers' requests for appointments and information and to their complaints. Consumers appear willing to seek a second opinion and choose a facility, physician, or health plan on the basis of the information they find on social media. All of this suggests that consumer preferences and managing the information of consumers will be vital to provider survival and raise the demand on HIT professionals to help address these needs.

Concerns about rising consumer populism—as opposed to consumer empowerment—have already been raised as systems struggle to meet rising consumer expectations (Simborg 2010). Empowerment implies that technology and communications enable consumers to play an active and constructive role with their providers to enhance outcomes and satisfaction. Once the internet places unedited information on their hard drives, consumers can subscribe to waves of populist beliefs, often to their detriment. The rationale for consumer empowerment involves a complex set of decisions but also presents significant challenges. Individuals could mitigate costs with appropriate health and wellness interventions because their illnesses, and subsequent costs, relate to lifestyle choices (e.g., overeating, alcohol consumption, smoking) and to other potentially preventable problems. Access to a quality primary care provider (PCP), however, has proven difficult because PCPs are few in number. They also have time challenges: Their time to review the literature, consider the patient's record, and speak with an individual patient is limited. Consequently, individuals can benefit from asserting control over their own healthcare and lifestyles.

Once the internet becomes a factor, Simborg (2010) argues that for HIT, healthy empowerment converts to unhealthy populism. Without high-functioning HIT supporting communication and integration by providers, the patient has the best direct access to health information from the increasingly fragmented provider system. In this case, the argument goes: Who but the individual, then, has the greatest motivation and can most easily aggregate the health information from across the system, incorporate nonprovider medical and health activities into a single location, and assert control over access and distribution of these data? But the problems with this scenario are many.

- Patients most likely wish to build a relationship with a trusted provider—one who is highly qualified, personable, and available over the long term. In addition, when that provider is contacted, they must have access to the patient-controlled medical information, and along with that access will come interoperability and security issues.
- Providers receiving this information will worry that the information has been altered by the consumer or their family or friends. Because of uncertainty surrounding the truth for all medical information, providers consider the source and that requires that the truth of source must be maintained.
- The application of independent clinical decision support in PHRs uncoupled from providers may extend beyond simple rules established. Drug interaction alerts, for example, may be overridden when physicians make purposeful decisions considering the risks and benefits of prescribing potentially interacting medications.
- Synchronizing information between multiple databases is difficult, and providers must keep a medical record of their patients. That need will never go away. Duplication of information between provider- and patient-controlled systems adds to confusion, potential errors, and costs.

Despite these and other concerns, even Simborg (2010) argues there is a need for and value to an independent consumer-based internet system that provides healthcare support and education. These external systems can effectively provide education and decision support tools regarding diet, exercise, smoking, and other lifestyle changes. The future nature and scope of consumer empowerment remain uncertain, but most likely, HIT professionals will be asked to make more information available to patients and to the general population.

With all of this said, consumer empowerment has not advanced as expected by many proponents. The question "will this be the year?" remains. Jones (2019) makes four predictions about this evolution from the business side of healthcare:

1. Consumers will redefine patient empowerment. They will use their experiences from advances outside of healthcare to motivate change within. Look for Amazon, among others, to elevate expectations.

2. Consumers will demand greater empowerment through their employers and through increased pressure on politicians for government reform.
3. Decision support tools will supplant additional information access.
4. Empowerment will drive transparency (see section on Transparency below).

Connectivity

Related to the rise of the consumers and their connectivity is how providers and payers will change the healthcare delivery system and, as a result, HIT needs. Social media needs a series of hosts for transmitting connected information. Not long ago, people relied heavily on the telephone to communicate, but that technology is being supplanted by email, text, tweet, and other mechanisms. This change is central for consumers, especially younger consumers, and is certainly worthy of significant study. As a brief overview, each year many bloggers post the top new technologies related to consumer connectivity and technology. The problem is that these trend articles and their authors often do not survive for long. We have seen Android devices, tablet computers, internet television, low-cost cameras, and many more items enter the market and evolve. Today many of these are old news. As we look to the future, innovation will occur, as summarized by Raiz (2019), in broader categories and not individual products:

- *Connected devices.* Beyond the fancy gadgets currently debuting on the market, we now innovate by enabling these devices to coordinate the information they collect. The focus will shift from access to utility.
- *Healthcare of the future.* The complex structures and processes that constitute medicine will benefit from connected digital technologies. In the future, our institutions will not have walls, as transfer of diagnostic and therapeutic technologies can be done from anywhere. Devices will aid this process, as we begin to gather reliable and valid information from wearable devices performing real-time data collection and monitoring (see chapter 2's section on the Health Insurance Portability and Accountability Act and other privacy and security constraints).
- *Voice technologies.* Today there are an estimated 118 million smartspeakers in the United States, with about 70 percent of users incorporating them into their daily activities. Which applications will survive this evolution are not yet certain, but potential disruptive change exists.
- *Automotive innovation.* Now that self-driving cars are on the road, the car will no longer be just a mode of transport, but a living experience.

- *Artificial intelligence and image recognition.* The ability to identify users digitally has substantial implications for transportation, commerce, finance, and education. While this has potential negative applications, it can evolve as a force for good.

The push toward connectivity has begun to permeate the health provider system as well. A good gauge of how this connectivity will proceed can be seen in a report from the Federal Communications Commission (FCC) (mHealth Task Force 2012). The FCC chair asked leaders to evaluate the opportunities and challenges arising from the widespread adoption of wireless health technologies. The result was the formation of the mHealth Task Force, which examined how patient care can be improved and made more efficient through mobile health, wireless health, and e-care technologies. The task force aimed to make these technologies best practices by 2017; to this end, it identified five broad goals (mHealth Task Force 2012, 1) that drove subsequent actions by the FCC:

> Goal 1: FCC should continue to play a leadership role in advancing mobile health adoption.
>
> Goal 2: Federal agencies should increase collaboration to promote innovation, protect patient safety, and avoid regulatory duplication.
>
> Goal 3: The FCC should build on existing programs and link programs when possible in order to expand broadband access for healthcare.
>
> Goal 4: The FCC should continue efforts to increase capacity, reliability, interoperability, and radio frequency safety of mHealth technologies.
>
> Goal 5: Industry should support continued investment, innovation, and job creation in the growing mobile health sector.

The scope was broad, in that the task force examined nine aspects of mobile technology (mHealth), as seen in exhibit 1.2.

The types of challenges in adopting this technology are the subject of study for government and private specialists. Since the 2012 initiative, the FCC convened a mHealth Innovation Expo in 2013 to showcase mobile health products and solutions. Subsequent to these developments, the FCC began a collaboration with the Food and Drug Administration and the Office of the National Coordinator of Health Information Technology (ONCHIT, sometimes shortened to ONC) to develop strategies and recommendations for a comprehensive regulatory strategy (FCC 2020). As another example, the National Institute of Standards and Technology (2018) has convened a number of integrative forums to address such innovations as cloud computing. These often have strong proponents but also focus on the challenges that new technology presents to cybersecurity.

EXHIBIT 1.2
Nine Aspects of mHealth Activities Evaluated by FCC mHealth Task Force

1. Medical devices that act as remote patient monitors used in clinical, home, mobile, and other environments
2. Mobile medical and general health software applications that allow patients to upload or download health information at any time
3. Medical body area network sensors that capture and wirelessly forward physiological data for further analysis
4. Medical implant devices that allow neuromuscular microstimulation techniques to restore sensation, mobility, and other functions to paralyzed limbs and organs
5. Medical device data systems that allow for the transfer, storage, conversion, or display of medical data through wired or wireless hubs, smartphones, or broadband-enabled products
6. Mobile diagnostic imaging applications that allow doctors the flexibility to send or review medical images from virtually any place and at any time
7. Patient care portals that can be accessed anywhere for self-reporting and self-management
8. Accessible clinical decision support tools that allow doctors to help patients in real time with diagnosis, treatment options, and necessary medical calculations at the point of care
9. Broadband-enabled HIT infrastructure that allows healthcare providers to share rich electronic health information with other providers, regardless of their provider organization and geographic area

Source: Data from mHealth Task Force (2012).

By 2020, these initiatives had begun to evolve (FCC 2020). As evidenced by the response to the FCC's request for public comment, the agency was looking at the following, among others:

- Efforts to develop solutions to encourage broadband adoption and promote HIT
- Incentives and barriers to the deployment of radio frequency–enabled advanced healthcare technologies and devices
- Support of telehealth infrastructure through the FCC's Rural Health Care Programs
- Demonstration of the value of broadband in the healthcare sector to consumers

The following timeline of specific initiatives emanating from the mHealth task force from 2012 suggests substantial effort at improving connectivity to improve health (FCC 2020).

2018

- *Rural Health Care Program funding.* Provided budgetary support for a program to address funding shortages for rural telemedicine services

2017

- *Virtual listening sessions.* Convened virtual listening sessions to facilitate targeted input on broadband-related health issues (including on the gap between rural and urban settings and other digital divide issues)
- *Broadband cancer collaboration.* Signed a memorandum of understanding with the National Cancer Institute to assemble stakeholders of public and private partnerships to address connectivity gap in Appalachia

2016

- *Mapping Broadband Health in America.* Released Mapping Broadband Health in America, a data platform enabling users to examine the linkages between connectivity and health at the county level in the United States

2015

- *Wireless Test Beds Workshop.* Hosted "Promoting Medical Technology Innovation: The Role of Wireless Test Beds" with the Food and Drug Administration

2014

- *Streamline equipment authorization program.* Through the webpage Report and Order, the FCC amended its radio frequency equipment certification rules to further streamline the process for bringing products (including medical devices) to the market
- *Medical Body Area Network.* Via Report and Order, allocated a broadband spectrum specifically for connected wearable medical sensors. Setting aside 2360–2400 MHz, it was first to designate specific connectivity space as the Medical Body Area Network
- *FCC-FDA-ONC Collaboration (FDASIA Health IT Report).* Proposed strategy and recommendations on regulatory framework to promote innovation, protect patient safety, and avoid regulatory duplication
- *Connect2HealthFCC Task Force formed.* Addressed the intersection of broadband, advanced technology, and health to improve access for all
- *Beyond the Beltway series.* Showcased communities that leverage broadband technologies and next-generation communications services to improve access, especially targeting rural and underserved areas

Transparency

The movement to greater transparency has been around for some time (Davis and Collins 2006), but it got a big national push with the federal government's value-driven healthcare initiative. An executive order signed by President George W. Bush (2006) established value-driven care consisting of four cornerstones: (1) interoperable HIT, (2) public reporting of provider quality information, (3) public reporting of cost information, and (4) incentives for value comparisons. This government support added to the growing evidence that the system could improve in a number of ways if consumers, providers, and payers had better information on which to base their decisions. Early efforts in this regard concentrated on price transparency (Deloitte Center for Health Solutions 2018), but a Commonwealth Fund report suggested that price transparency was not in itself an answer to cost problems but could enable the development of the following (Davis and Collins 2006):

- Valid benchmarks of provider performance
- Quality and efficiency reward programs by payers
- Informed choices by patients

The report pointed out, however, that without transparency in outcomes and information on the "total cost" of care, price transparency could not enable consumers to make better choices. As discussed earlier, some broader changes are coming in the future. The American Medical Association, among others, has entered this discussion with detailed initiatives to implement price transparency. For them, it is a means to help patients and physicians make better and more informed choices. Their plan (Robeznieks 2018) consists of eight specific data transparency principles.

1. Healthcare organizations should address patient confusion and poor health literacy by developing resources that help patients understand the complexities of healthcare pricing.
2. The government should require all health professionals and entities to make information about prices for common procedures or services readily available.
3. Physicians should communicate information about the cost of their professional services to individual patients by considering the insurance status of the patient.
4. Health plans should provide plan enrollees or their designees with complete information regarding plan benefits and real-time, cost-sharing information associated with both in-network and out-of-network provider services or other plan designs that may affect patient out-of-pocket costs.

5. Health plans, public and private entities, and other stakeholder groups should work together to facilitate price and quality transparency for patients and physicians.
6. Entities promoting price transparency tools should have processes in place to ensure the accuracy and relevance of the information they provide.
7. All payer claims databases should be supported and strengthened.
8. EHR vendors should include features that assist in facilitating price transparency for physicians and patients.

Increasing transparency puts added pressure on healthcare's data systems to collect and report more data and to ensure all information is accurate and timely.

Medical Tourism

Medical tourism is an important element of the future that will affect HIT. The prospect of US healthcare organizations losing patients to providers in other countries on the basis of price for select procedures or therapies could pose a major challenge. In addition to system effects, the IT world would be made more complicated because these patients would want information about their medical history, tests, and prior procedures to be sent overseas. In addition, when the patients come back home, their surgical case information would have to be returned and then integrated into existing records of any follow-up care. There are many reasons, however, that medical tourism may not make as big an impact as first thought. The inability of average patients to afford long-distance travel to seek care for most clinical problems puts a limit on medical tourism's scale and scope. Further, despite quality assertions and some review by Joint Commission International, the lingering hesitancy by many people to try this trend may keep it at bay for years to come. The future may expand, however—there is even a Medical Tourism Association (2020) with a mission:

- To raise awareness of the high level of quality healthcare available in various countries.
- To promote positive and stable growth of the Medical Tourism and Global Healthcare Industry [sic] with a strong focus on Transparency and Communication.
- To provide an unbiased source of information for patients, insurance companies and employers about top hospitals, their quality of care and outcomes.
- To protect the reputation of Medical Tourism from disreputable hospitals, healthcare providers and medical tourism facilitators which may not have the same level of quality healthcare and standards.

- To serve as one voice for purposes of dealing with government organizations and the media to protect the reputation of the Medical Tourism Association's members.
- To promote and provide a forum for communication and to increase connectivity between patients, healthcare providers and insurance companies.
- To seek out future affiliated industries and technologies that will allow international healthcare providers to operate more efficiently in the global healthcare industry.
- To educate patients, insurance companies, agents, brokers, consultants and physicians from around the world about the growth of medical tourism and the globalization of healthcare.

However, if the notion of medical tourism were expanded to include regional or cross-border travel within the United States, the phenomenon takes on a new level of importance. Reports are still incomplete and the evaluation scale is not clear, but in 2012, Walmart joined a number of large US employers that are contracting with select national delivery systems (known as Centers of Excellence) to provide specialty services to employees and their dependents (Diamond 2012). Lowe's and Boeing are also mentioned in this context, contracting with healthcare organizations with national name recognition, such as Cleveland Clinic, Geisinger Medical Center, Baylor Scott & White Health, Virginia Mason Medical Center, and Mercy Hospital Springfield. The services include spine care, transplants, and heart procedures (Elliott 2012; Zeltner 2019). This innovation will be explained further in this chapter's section on telemedicine.

Historical Overview of Healthcare Information Systems

The evolution of HIT could fill a text by itself, but a brief overview will help you understand where the system began and where it is likely heading. Many fine, classic summaries (e.g., Collen 1995) can help this process, along with newly developed tutorials that effectively tell the history of healthcare information systems in the United States. Exhibit 1.3 presents a list of the specific section of ONCHIT's updated (2020) Health Information Technology Workforce Curriculum Components, a tutorial that discusses the comprehensive history of HIT. It enables interested readers to absorb a broad perspective. Especially important to note in these historical presentations is how the medical education community and professional organizations grew and supported the infusion of HIT into the research and practice communities. For complete information on this and other courses, visit www.healthit.gov/topic/health-it-resources/health-it-curriculum-resources-educators.

EXHIBIT 1.3
Detail of HIT Curriculum Component 5

Component 5: History of Health Information Technology in the US

Unit 1. Evolution of Health IT: The Early Years
Unit 2. Evolution of Health IT: The Modern Era
Unit 3. Evolution of Health IT: The HITECH Act
Unit 4. Evolution of Public Health Informatics
Unit 5. Evolution of Nursing Informatics and HIT Tools Used by Nursing
Unit 6. History of Electronic Health Records (EHRs)
Unit 7. History of Clinical Decision Support Systems
Unit 8. History of CPOE and E-Prescribing
Unit 9. History of Health Information Exchange
Unit 10. History of Privacy and Security Legislation
Unit 11. Software Certification and Regulation
Unit 12. History of Mobile Computing
Unit 13. History of Telemedicine
Unit 14. History of Quality Improvement and Patient Safety
Unit 15. History of Health IT Organizations

Source: Data from ONCHIT (2020).

The first computer systems in healthcare date back to the early 1960s, when a small number of hospitals began to automate selected administrative operations, usually beginning with payroll and patient accounting functions. These systems were developed by analysts and computer programmers hired by the hospitals, and they were run on large, expensive, and centralized computers referred to as *mainframes*. Little attention was given to the development of clinical information systems to support patient care, and the paper medical record was the legal and clinical record of the treatment experience. The growth of medicine as a science that could benefit from systematic collection and analysis of information spurred analysts to expand computer applications to clinical medicine.

The medical record was still a relatively new concept, and standards for the paper version were established and widely adopted only in the 1960s. A few systems were developed for the electronic storage and retrieval of abstracts of inpatient medical records, but these systems contained limited information and were operated on a postdischarge, retrospective basis. The early "computer-based medical record" systems, such as COSTAR and RMRS, were attempts to capture the patients' experience in an easily retrievable manner.

Advances in technology during the 1970s expanded the use of information systems throughout the economy, and hospitals were no exception. These systems eventually became part of other healthcare settings such as clinics, physician office practices, and long-term care facilities. Computers became smaller and less expensive, and some vendors began to develop "applications software packages"—generalized computer programs that could be used by any hospital, clinic, or physician's office that purchased the system. Most of these early software packages supported administrative operations, such as patient accounting, general accounting, materials management, scheduling, and practice management. Eventually, clinical systems were developed as well, particularly for hospital clinical laboratories, radiology departments, and pharmacies (for a description of current applications, see chapter 9).

As the scientific knowledge base of medicine expanded during this period with funding from the federal government, effectively diagnosing and developing treatment for patients began to tax the capacity of providers. Clinical decision support systems, such as MYCIN and HELP, were introduced to assist providers to apply the rules for diagnosis and treatment. While computers helped with retrieval of information, providers found that specialization became essential. Consequently, the collection, storage, analysis, and reporting of the expanding body of healthcare information required professional specialization of the HIT community as well. Organizations for medical records professionals (e.g., American Medical Record Association, which later became American Health Information Management Association), informaticists and researchers (e.g., American Medical Informatics Association), and HIT practitioners (e.g., Hospital Management Systems Society, which later became Healthcare Information Management Systems Society) supported the professionalization and specialization of the HIT workforce.

A virtual revolution in computing occurred in the 1980s with the development of powerful and inexpensive personal computers (PCs)—desktop devices with computing power and storage capacity that equaled or exceeded the large mainframe systems of the 1960s and 1970s. A second major advance in this period was the development of electronic data networks, whereby PCs and larger computing systems could be linked together to share information on a decentralized basis. An increasing number of vendors entered the healthcare software business, and a much larger array of products became available for both administrative and clinical support functions. The use of PCs in physicians' offices, particularly for practice management, became commonplace. This ad hoc proliferation of systems and applications to meet specific clinical and administrative needs contributed to the system integration challenges providers face today.

The 1990s witnessed even more dramatic changes in the healthcare environment with the advent of market-driven healthcare reform and expansion of managed care. Much greater attention was given to the development of clinical information systems and strategic decision support systems to assist providers in achieving a critical balance between costs and quality in the delivery of care. These changes were supported by advances in technology through the use of laptop computers and, today, notebook computers or the iPad. This portable hardware expanded the ability of clinicians and other caregivers to take the data collection tool with them, access information from virtually anywhere, and communicate with others in the care team quickly.

In the 1990s, electronic data interchange and networking were used to link components of integrated healthcare delivery organizations and support enterprise-wide information systems. As a result, healthcare organizations now employ internet technology to support internal communications and external connections with patients and business partners. Similarly, telemedicine applications can link primary care providers at remote locations with clinical specialists at centralized medical centers. These technologies provide potentially better access to high-quality care at reasonable costs.

While hardware and software continued to emerge and to be implemented widely, many began to realize that information systems were being developed in partial isolation. The ability of products to connect and transfer information seamlessly was being impeded by the lack of rigorously defined standards. Consequently, many in healthcare began to call for sector-wide and, ultimately, government standards. Some of the standard-setting organizations today include the following:

- International Organization for Standardization (www.iso.ch)
- American National Standards Institute (www.ansi.org)
- Health Level 7 (www.hl7.org)
- Healthcare Information Technology Standards Panel (www.hitsp.org)
- Current Procedural Terminology of the American Medical Association (www.ama-assn.org)
- Health Information Technology Standards Committee (www.healthit.gov)

As addressed in chapter 2, government got heavily involved in the setting of standards after 2000. For an outstanding review and history of HIT standards, see Collman and Dempster (2013).

Categories of Healthcare Information Systems

Computerized information systems in healthcare fall into four categories: (1) clinical information, (2) operational management, (3) strategic decision support, and (4) electronic networking and e-health applications.

Clinical information systems support patient care and provide information for use in strategic planning and management. Examples include computerized patient records systems; clinical department systems for pharmacy, laboratory, radiology, and other units; automated medical instrumentation; clinical decision support systems (computer-aided diagnosis and treatment planning); and information systems that support clinical research and education.

Operational management systems support non–patient-care activities in the healthcare organization. Examples include financial information systems, payroll, purchasing and inventory control, outpatient clinic scheduling, and office automation.

Strategic decision support systems assist the senior management team in strategic planning, managerial control, performance monitoring, and outcomes assessment. Strategic information systems must draw data from internal clinical and management systems as well as from external information on community health, market area demography, and activities of competitors. Consequently, information system integration—the ability of organizational information systems to communicate electronically with one another—becomes very important.

Healthcare organizations also engage in *electronic networking*, which supports data interchange with external organizations and business partners for such activities as insurance billing and claims processing, accessing clinical information from regional and national databases, communicating among providers in an integrated delivery system, and communicating with patients and health plan members. Many of these applications are web-based *e-health applications*. Computer applications in healthcare organizations are described in detail in chapters 8 and 9.

Challenges for Health Information Technology Today

With all that is going on in the healthcare system as outlined above, it is amazing that there are equivalent and vital challenges faced by HIT today. These often relate to the broader issues outlined in the prior sections but have more direct impact on individual healthcare organizations on a day-to-day basis.

Interoperability

The Health Information and Management Systems Society (HIMSS 2020b) defines interoperability as the ability to connect information within and across the artificial boundaries of organizations with the purpose of improving the health of populations. This ability facilitates access, exchange, and cooperative use of data among stakeholders.

Interoperability provides seamless access to the information that providers need to diagnose and treat individuals. It is not, however, an all-or-nothing concept. There are varying degrees of interoperability:

- *Foundational interoperability* enables one system or application to share data with and receive data from another, nothing more.
- *Structural interoperability* implies a more deeply rooted interchange by specifying the structure or format of data exchange. This specification enables providers to preserve the clinical or operational purpose and meaning of the data. Data exchanged contains syntax, so that it can be interpreted at the data field level.
- In *semantic interoperability*, a system is able to exchange information and to interpret and use that information. It builds on structural-level interoperability with the codification of the data, including standard, publicly available vocabulary, so that the receiving information management systems can interpret the data.
- The term *organizational interoperability* indicates that the exchange encompasses not only the technical components but also clear policy-related, social, and organizational components. These components facilitate the secure, seamless, and timely communication and use of data within and between organizations and individuals.

While these definitions are useful, interoperability has not been widely achieved in the US healthcare system. Most believe that interoperability is a noble goal but that achieving the goal is a long way off (Hammadeh 2018).

Telemedicine

Telemedicine, a newer technology, involves the use of electronic communications and software to provide clinical services to patients without an in-person visit. Telemedicine technology is frequently used for follow-up visits, management of chronic conditions, medication management, specialist consultation, and a host of other clinical services that can be provided remotely via secure video and audio connections. It enables healthcare professionals to evaluate, diagnose, and treat patients at a distance using telecommunications technology. The approach has been through a striking evolution in the last decade and it is becoming an increasingly important part of the American healthcare infrastructure.

Today's telemedicine started over 60 years ago with select providers sharing information using the telephone. It primarily linked physicians treating a patient to specialists located elsewhere. Rural providers, in particular, benefited from the technology. Now, many devices enable video transmission to other clinical locations, patients' homes, and even the workplace.

Although the terms *telemedicine* and *telehealth* are often used interchangeably, there is a distinction between the two. Telehealth includes a broad range of technologies and services for patient care and improvement of the healthcare delivery system as a whole. Telehealth is different from telemedicine because it refers to a broader scope of remote healthcare services than telemedicine. While telemedicine refers specifically to remote clinical services, telehealth can describe remote nonclinical services, such as provider training, administrative meetings, and continuing medical education, in addition to clinical services. According to the World Health Organization, telehealth includes "surveillance, health promotion, and public health functions." Telemedicine involves the use of electronic communications and software to provide clinical services to patients without an in-person visit.

Consumer-Facing Technology

Patient-centered care and patient engagement have become central components of the modern clinical encounter. The National Academy of Medicine defined patient-centered care as "care that is respectful of and responsive to individual patient preferences, needs, and values, and ensuring that patient values guide all clinical decisions" (IOM 2001). Technology, with its array of capabilities to measure data, manage information, and automate processes, plays an integral role in healthcare's ability to adequately respond to patient preferences, needs, and values. Central to fulfilling this role is ensuring that care is delivered in a safe and effective manner. With literally hundreds of thousands of preventable deaths and millions of avoidable adverse events happening each year, the stakes are simply too high not to employ every tool at our disposal to improve patient safety.

Patient-facing technology has the potential to improve quality and safety by enabling patients to take a more active role in their care. It can enable patient engagement and can enhance the evolution toward patient-centered care. HIT can improve safety through standardized documentation, easier access to vital patient information, and standardized communication. Though this age of digital health presents significant challenges (Wachter 2015), engaging the patient through technologies has great promise. A full exposition of these opportunities and challenges can be found in a workshop hosted by the Institute of Medicine in 2015. The major topics of the symposium included consumer-facing technology. What is it, and what are the issues? Participants also discussed health-literate digital design and strategies; catalyzing widespread, informed engagement; and HIT and selected populations.

Imaging

While it would appear that imaging issues have been adequately addressed, the technologies surrounding imaging collection, storage, and retrieval persist. Congdon (2010) summarizes some of the major challenges. First, medical imaging data requirements have exploded in recent years. Along with more patients, more tests, and large-scale storage needs for resultant data, the requirements continue to grow. On-site storage can no longer handle either recent or long-term needs, giving rise to cloud technologies or other remote storage. In turn, cloud technologies give rise to the second challenge, financial and productivity issues. Juggling the storage of information between locations requires trade-offs between ease of access and costs. Cost pressure often leads to less-than-optimal storage solutions. Related to both issues are interoperability challenges specific to imaging. Different tests require use of alternative data storage types and thus make sharing of information a challenge even within an institution. X-ray storage is with Digital Imagining and Communications in Medicine (DICOM), EKGs are stored in PDF, and echocardiograms are in MPG files. Because these are all stored separately, they inhibit interoperability and rapid transition among the files.

Commentators have raised issues surrounding the business challenges associated with imaging (Warner 2020). These include conventional business challenges such as reductions in reimbursement for imaging services and increased competition from other provider entities. In addition, operational efficiency and workflow have become challenges as delays in service and scheduling affect patient satisfaction.

Electronic Health Record Improvements

Care providers continue to struggle to convert to EHRs but most are slowly making that conversion (Simborg 2010). It is not an easy process. Adopters always have a learning curve and, at least at first, experience a loss of productivity. Some abandon the attempt in frustration. The successful ones become comfortable and even facile with their system, to the point where they are as fast using the electronic system as they were with their paper records, if not faster. Providers learn to navigate the system's displays and entry screens so that the process becomes familiar and easy. At that point, they also begin to experience the benefit of electronic availability of patient information coupled with the decision support benefits of expert knowledge. Our goal as a society, given this new electronic world for both care provider and patient, is to maximize the quality of each of their encounters, however brief, whether in person, over the phone, through email, by webcast, or via another mechanism.

Recent evidence (Meeks et al. 2014) suggests that EHRs can contribute to patient safety outcomes. The study intensively examines safety issues in the Veterans Administration healthcare system to uncover sources. They find that errors originated with unsafe technology and unsafe use of technology in a 70:30 ratio. They also find, however, that most problems had multiple and interrelated causes. For example, some problems arise from the display of information in the EHR after software upgrades and modifications and from transmission of data from various components of the system. They recommend that even those with experience in the EHR software should establish a robust infrastructure to enable them to learn from their experiences, correct errors, and upgrade the system.

According to Meeks and colleagues, before each medical encounter, the care provider reviews the patient record, whether paper or electronic. With only 6–15 minutes allotted to each visit, this must be done quickly. If the care provider has an electronic system, there is usually some type of summary screen and the provider knows how to navigate quickly from this to the most recent interval information or other relevant information. Now, imagine the patient handing the provider a printout (or transfer of an electronic copy in readable format) from a PHR at each encounter. These "documents" will vary in volume, content, and format as a result of the myriad contributing systems. If the patient is new to the care provider and there are no previous locally available medical records, handing over such a document will be very helpful. However, the care provider will still have to make the effort to incorporate this information into the organization's own electronic system. Given current time pressures for brief visits, for an existing patient with prior encounters, most care providers simply would not take the time to review the documents in addition to looking at their own records. Nor will they log onto a patient's EHR system to do such a review, except perhaps in emergencies. The workflow for the provider to incorporate external record information into their existing system is formidable from a manual entry perspective—it would be too time-consuming for this to work.

The solution would be to provide an electronic interface between a patient's own copy of their health record and the provider's EHR. This must be done, however, in a manner that allows integration with the provider's existing system so that the new information is incorporated in a seamless manner consistent with the semantics and format of the existing EHR. In that way, the providers do not alter their normal workflow in accessing and navigating the EHR. Otherwise, the electronic copy of the PHR would be no better than the paper copy. If clinical informaticians can achieve the level of standardization to accomplish this degree of interoperability between the multiple PHRs on many different PHR systems and EHRs, then EHRs should be able to do the same among themselves. With the concentration of the EHR market, there are far fewer EHR vendors to deal with. The fragmented PHR market makes standardization a larger challenge, and the same problem impedes interoperability. If that is true, we would be much better off empowering patients by requiring all certified EHRs to provide PHR functions than to encourage untethered PHRs.

Reporting and Analytics

It is difficult to discuss reporting and analytics outside of the context of big data. With sufficient data, we can change healthcare management. Analytics potentially can reduce treatment costs, predict outbreaks of epidemics, and reduce the impact of preventable diseases. Lebied (2018) presents a host of specific applications that, given sufficient data, can make tangible impacts (e.g., predicting patient admissions to improve staffing, providing real-time alerts to providers, enhancing patient engagement with use of smartphones, addressing the opioid abuse crisis, and reducing fraud). The opportunity to reap a full array of benefits from healthcare information expands greatly with the quantity of data.

With opportunity comes challenges, however. Bresnick (2017) summarizes a number of those challenges in the context of analytics and big data. While not surprising or insurmountable, they are vital for the design and use of information systems. Key elements include the following:

- *Data capture.* The essential role of a robust data capture protocol represents the first challenge encountered. Bad data governance processes hamper the veracity of data entering the system. Every data element must have a source; thus, organizations must employ data governance and integrity expertise from those with adequate training to make data capture an asset, not a liability.
- *Cleaning.* Once captured, most data must be "scrubbed" to provide accurate, consistent, relevant, and uncorrupted information. Tools to replace manual cleaning are getting better and will soon also make this process an asset.
- *Storage.* Historically, healthcare managers sought control over security, access, and uptime, and they thus maintained in-house servers. As the magnitude of data has exploded in recent decades, many have moved to the cloud for storage. Advantages include disaster recovery, lower costs at start-up, and easier expansion. Loss of control remains a challenge, however.
- *Security.* Most organizations will employ the obvious security processes, such as antivirus software, firewalls, encrypting when essential, and multifactor authentication. Security, however, rests heavily on the motivation and training of staff involved.
- *Stewardship.* The length of time data must be maintained and the increasing use of data for research purposes suggest that processes for data management—and a person with ultimate responsibility for that function—are essential.
- *Querying.* Because data come from multiple sources with varying rules, standardization has been a challenge. To query a database without intimate knowledge of the idiosyncratic nature of those sources can compromise the query.

Information Security

Security in information systems for healthcare receives significant attention, but problems persist and arguably have grown. Protections have been mandated by federal and state law; chapter 5 discusses security more specifically. For this introduction, we will maintain a broad perspective. First, healthcare data have real value in the market, giving an incentive for hackers to employ creative approaches. HIT professionals must maintain constant vigilance. Roohparvar (2017) talks about making sure that security is a strategic initiative for the organization. This problem is not an IT issue but a system-wide strategic challenge. The sources of vulnerability are many, but insecure mobile devices and email appear to be getting the most attention from IT professionals and consultants. Further, Lord (2018) focuses attention on the need to identify key staff in IT, including a specified leader with security responsibility. Training of all employees on basic security procedures and critical engagement of clinical and business staff in the governance of data are essential. The problems of mobile devices, email, security leadership, and staff training will be major elements of the IT function for years into the future. Governance will be addressed further in chapter 4.

Future Challenges for Healthcare Information Systems

Looking to the future and pulling from some common threads detailed above, we have identified five key challenges for HIT to consider: artificial intelligence (AI), blockchain technology, the cloud, the Internet of Things, and the fourth industrial revolution.

Artificial Intelligence

AI is a branch of computer science that develops machines and software with human-like intelligence, sometimes referred to as *machine intelligence*. As with any evolving technology, analysts create a framework for categorization of AI that includes varying levels: analytical, human-inspired, and humanized AI. Analytical AI embodies cognitive intelligence and effectively describes the world. With it, machines use learning to inform future decisions. Human-inspired AI adds emotional intelligence to analytical intelligence to enable machines to incorporate human emotions. Humanized AI combines cognitive and emotional intelligence with social intelligence in an attempt to enable the machines to be self-conscious and aware of interactions. Success in these developments will enable machines to perform and assist with an unlimited array of medical applications.

An interesting comprehensive study of the state of this art provides strategy for development and a description of a host of applications (Davenport, Hongserneier, and McCord 2018). Historically, providers built their own EHR systems or used open-source products, but today AI can be used to develop useful applications. Most are now narrow in scope but they can address:

- *Data extraction.* Coded data pose extraction challenges, but free text has proven to be a challenge to the development of actionable healthcare data applications. (Free text includes notes describing a diagnosis or treatment option that defy standard methods to convert the text to information.) Several vendors are using AI to review medical notes and index materials.
- *Diagnostic and predictive algorithms.* Google and others have applied AI in the examination of high-risk medical problems such as sepsis to understand better how to anticipate and then how to treat.
- *Clinical documentation and data entry.* Nuance has software to facilitate data entry from diverse sources.
- *Clinical decision support.* Watson, Change Healthcare, and Allscripts have systems that learn effectively based on new data received.

The challenge with these attractive new applications is to integrate them into existing EHR systems. They tend to stand alone currently, but as the technology develops, customers will likely demand, and receive, better integration.

Blockchain Technology

This newer technology has become a topic of discussion, but how it will influence healthcare is not clear. Blockchain is a record of peer-to-peer transactions distributed across participants rather than residing in a single, central location. It consists of interlinked transactions or groups of transactions (transaction blocks) in a digital ledger. Because blockchain has no central authority, its participants view, exchange, and store information safely. For more information on blockchain and its security features, read *Blockchain for Dummies* (Laurence 2019). It offers a promise for cost efficiency and can enhance accountability for health data transactions.

In short, it facilitates compliance with Health Insurance Portability and Accountability Act (HIPAA) privacy and security requirements. Blockchain technology has the potential to facilitate a more widespread collection and sharing of healthcare information. Shiklo (2017) argues effectively that caution related to health information exchange (HIE) hampers implementing advances from much of HIT. Were it more secure, HIE could be the information superhighway (HIMSS 2020a). However, the lack of uniform architecture and standards prohibits open and trusted access to protected health information (PHI). This lack of exchange decreases patient engagement in the healthcare process because patients do not have ownership rights for their data. It minimizes the cooperation among providers, thus reducing healthcare quality and safety, and inhibits efforts to improve population health because the participants do not share necessary information.

The Cloud

Cloud computing, the classic outsourcing of data storage and retrieval, has become a major business in healthcare, with estimates of market potential of $40 billion by 2026 (Acumen 2020). It may be a lower-cost solution to accessible data storage for healthcare organizations that preserves patient information privacy and safety. In addition to privacy and cost, the cloud offers healthcare organizations agility as business needs change. In-house solutions necessitate larger fixed costs for servers and their storage, as well as staff able to manage the data systems.

Cloud computing has no chance of subsiding, but converting your organization to this method can be risky. Confidential data can be leaked, and skeptical patients worry about having their data stored with external vendors. It also puts the healthcare organization at risk should the vendor become financially or operationally unstable. Despite these concerns, the worldwide cloud computing market is expected to expand substantially. Favorable regulation, increased healthcare investments, the widespread use of high-speed internet, government organizations, increased public awareness, and increased demand for regulatory adherence—all represent pressure for greater use of cloud computing in the future.

Internet of Things

To add to the complexity of interoperability challenges, the growing Internet of Things (IOT) will be a challenge for HIT in the future. “Things” are consumer devices that collect and transmit health data, which give providers access to information useful to diagnose and treat a host of medical problems (see Ranger 2018). These devices now have the capacity to connect to healthcare systems and patient records. The myriad sources and transmission of these data to a central system raise security concerns. Harpham (2015) presents this as a dichotomy for HIT leaders. They must provide for important new opportunities but protect against risk. Examples of those decisions include the following:

- *Consumer devices.* Apple Watches and other fitness trackers constitute the first wave of data collection devices that will house potentially valuable information for clinicians.
- *Falling sensor costs.* The rapid reduction in the cost of sensors used to measure heart rate, blood glucose, and other critical diagnostic tools will make these and other devices more accessible to an ever-greater portion of the US population.

- *Finance.* The IOT economy is expected to reach $6.2 trillion in sales by 2025.
- *OMA SpecWorks (formerly IPSO Alliance).* This technical working group consisting of major manufacturers such as Google, Cisco, Intel, Oracle, and others collaborate to develop standards in support of rational proliferation of all electronic devices capable of transmitting or receiving data.
- *BYOD policy.* The "bring your own device" policies have evolved in a haphazard manner, but the field is developing standards that can be implemented more broadly. Employees increasingly want to use their own smartphones and computers for work. Without a policy, it will be difficult to address such concerns as allowing employees to receive and send PHI from their personal devices.

Fourth Industrial Revolution

Forward-thinkers have dubbed our current environment—though it may sound a bit grandiose—the beginning of the "fourth industrial revolution." As we have seen in this chapter, mobile supercomputing, AI and robots, the IOT, neurotechnological brain enhancements, and genetic editing all suggest dramatic change. These and other shifts induce Schwab (2017) to believe we have entered the fourth industrial revolution that will alter how we work, live, and interact. Others agree (see, e.g., World Economic Forum 2019) and, as with past industrial revolutions, life will improve after a period of significant adjustment.

The fourth industrial revolution has a major impact on business, including such elements as customer expectations, product enhancement, collaborative innovation, and organizational forms (Marr 2018). Customers, at the center of the economy, will demand improvements in how they receive service. Digital capabilities enhance physical products and services, all aimed toward increasing their value. More durable and resilient assets arise from use of analytics, and this same information changes maintenance schedules. Doing all of this requires pioneering forms of collaboration to adapt to the speed of product innovation and disruption. Finally, global platforms and other new business models will help organizations respond to these changes, but "talent, culture, and organizational forms" will evolve as well.

Structure of This Book

Healthcare organizations and their leaders operating in the current environment of rapid change must understand the history and evolution of HIT. They also must keep an eye on how the future will likely unfold if they want long-term success. Most important, however, is that they must provide valid, reliable, and secure clinical and administrative information to assist healthcare leaders in making optimal clinical, operational, and strategic decisions. To this end, organizations are developing sophisticated information systems to support clinical and administrative operations and strategic management.

This book is designed to meet the needs of a variety of healthcare information professionals as they strive to support their private and organizational missions. As a result, the chapters that follow address both focused, detailed information needs and broader corporate information needs. We hope that this format is useful to those with clinical backgrounds, technical backgrounds, and business backgrounds. Because such individuals must learn to work together to achieve common goals, it is vital for each not only to gain knowledge to manage their own domain but also to gain a deeper understanding of others' perspectives.

The book addresses the priorities of today by embedding one priority in each chapter:

- *Chapter 2: External Environment.* The strategic direction of any healthcare organization is influenced by the world outside its walls. Gaining a deep understanding of the fundamental forces of change and the ability to observe and anticipate that change is essential to the long-term success of the healthcare information professional. In this chapter, we explore the healthcare triangle of cost, quality, and access because these challenges prompt government and market changes that must be addressed by any organization. We also examine EBM and evidence-based management because these will likely be the mechanism of change in the delivery of healthcare services. The US delivery system operates amid a vast array of government regulations and other interventions that affect cost, quality, and access. This chapter then examines recent government interventions that change the HIT landscape. Our discussion starts with the appropriate role of government and quickly turns its focus on the healthcare reform legislation—the Patient Protection and Affordable Care Act of 2010—and subsequent efforts to repeal it. Finally, the chapter compares domestic with international systems because many aspects of the US healthcare world are and will continue to be influenced by developments in other countries.
- *Chapter 3: Leadership: The Case of the Healthcare Chief Information Officer.* Here, we examine the case of the CIO. To better manage the healthcare information enterprise, organizations need an appropriate structure. The roles of senior HIT managers are different today from those in the recent past, and thus their place within the organization

must change as well. Senior-level HIT managers must become a part of the corporate strategy—both to understand organizational direction and to provide advice on the challenges that direction might impose from the IT perspective. Similarly, HIT professionals must have a different set of skills to maneuver in the new organizational structure. CIOs must have leadership expertise and analytical and strategic thinking skills, and they must also be clinically savvy and technologically sound.

- *Chapter 4: Health Information Technology Governance and Decision Rights.* To take advantage of revised organizational structures and CIO leadership skills, HIT units must incorporate appropriate and effective governance structures. These are the necessary how-to components for ensuring that HIT infrastructure and operations reliably accomplish goals. The growing scale and scope of IT's reach in the delivery system present major challenges to these assurances; thus, the importance of appropriate HIT governance expands accordingly.
- *Chapter 5: Health Information Technology Infrastructure, Standards, and Security.* While leading successful HIT systems do not require an in-depth working knowledge of computer and communication technologies, a basic understanding of the physical and logical structure of information systems and their components is essential. This chapter offers a core lesson, clarifying the differences between hardware and software; providing examples of computer network structures; differentiating operating systems, utility programs, and application software; and exploring telecommunication concepts such as wireless technologies.
- *Chapter 6: Health Information Technology Service Management.* Operation of an HIT department has evolved and now consists of managing a complex set of interdependent elements. Unlike the other components of a healthcare delivery organization, all HIT components must coordinate and communicate effectively, accurately, and securely. Consequently, service delivery and support services are vital to effective functioning. This chapter outlines the challenges of unplanned work and the necessity of implementing a process improvement framework for an organization. It also introduces the concept of an Information Technology Infrastructure Library and its components to assist HIT operations.
- *Chapter 7: Health Information Technology Selection and Contract Management.* In the past, delivery organizations on the frontier of HIT development created their own information systems because integrated options from vendors were not available or adequate. Now, organizations purchase complex, integrated, and expensive HIT

systems from a vast array of vendors. The selection of these systems constitutes a major financial, clinical, and administrative investment by an organization's leadership. The need to identify system requirements and ensure that vendors deliver those specifications in a timely manner requires a systematic approach to selection and contract management.

- *Chapter 8: Applications: Electronic Health Records.* In previous editions, the applications chapter was small and primarily emphasized administrative and financial functions. This edition features two application chapters—chapter 8 is devoted to the EHR, and chapter 9 to management and administrative systems. Chapter 8 outlines the importance of EHRs to the present and future of healthcare organizations. It discusses key capabilities, organizational benefits, costs of adoption, and methods of adoption and implementation. It follows up on meaningful use in the context of the EHR, the electronic medical record, and the PHR. In addition, it discusses related concepts, such as computerized physician order entry, and constraints, such as interoperability.
- *Chapter 9: Applications: Management and Financial Systems.* This chapter addresses the many conventional uses of HIT to support the overall goal of a delivery organization. The enterprise system applications include resource planning, financial management, scheduling, decision support, research, and medical education.
- *Chapter 10: Health Information Technology Project Portfolio Management.* Successful HIT operations require conventional project management expertise. This chapter expands that necessary project management content to include HIT program and portfolio management techniques. The ultimate goal is to reach the synchronized stage of portfolio management. At this level, HIT leadership should regularly evaluate the portfolio with operational unit leaders. The evaluations should include both the risks and returns of the complete HIT portfolio.
- *Chapter 11: Analytics.* Moving from operational effectiveness to achievement of strategic competitive advantage with HIT involves a transformation into a knowledge-enabled organization. Analytics involving big data, machine learning, and a host of other applications relevant to the fourth industrial revolution will be presented. Analytics evolves to become an integral part of the organization, thereby ensuring organizational success today and in the future. The chapter places a great emphasis on "baking in" the knowledge into workflows.
- *Chapter 12: Health Information Technology Value Analysis.* A formal, comprehensive valuation of an HIT system's direct and indirect costs

will help organizations move to the next level of operational excellence. Too often, HIT decisions are based on partial assessments of both costs and benefits, a strategy that may spell doom in cost-competitive future scenarios. State-of-the-art valuation processes from other industries provide a full social benefit and cost assessment tool that will become part of our collective HIT future.

Summary

The management of healthcare organizations can be improved through the intelligent use of information. This requires systematic planning and management of information resources to develop information systems that support patient care, administrative operations, and strategic management. Change is occurring rapidly and persistently in the healthcare field. Major forces of change at the systems level that have a direct impact on the application of IT include (1) continued pressure for healthcare cost containment, (2) concerns about medical errors and poor quality of care, and (3) challenges resulting from limited access to care and health disparities. Other changes that are mostly external to the organization include (1) health systems change, (2) growth in the use of EBM, (3) consumer empowerment, (4) connectivity, (5) transparency, and (6) medical tourism. Within the organization, HIT leadership must address (1) interoperability, (2) telemedicine, (3) consumer-facing technology, (4) imaging, (5) EHR improvements, (6) reporting and analytics, and (7) security. The US healthcare system is in the middle of fundamental change, and HIT plays a role in solving all the system's challenges.

As we look to the future, we see these five primary challenges remaining: (1) artificial intelligence, (2) blockchain, (3) the cloud, (4) Internet of Things, and (5) the fourth industrial revolution. These, too, pose challenges and opportunities for HIT and healthcare leadership.

Web Resources

There are many good sources of information from vendors and consultants regarding the development of healthcare information systems and challenges faced. These are useful but often not totally objective. A number of organizations' websites, however, provide more objective information on the topics discussed in this chapter.

- Agency for Healthcare Research and Quality (www.ahrq.gov) is the health services research arm of the US Department of Health and

Human Services that complements the biomedical research mission of its sister agency, the National Institutes of Health. It is home to research centers that specialize in major areas of healthcare and is a major source of funding and technical assistance for health services research and research training at leading US universities and other institutions.

- US Bureau of Labor Statistics (www.bls.gov) has many components that report varied data regarding the US economy. Particularly, it presents detailed information on consumer prices at the national and state levels.
- Care Continuum Alliance (www.carecontinuum.org) is an organization dedicated to the improvement of population health.
- Centers for Medicare & Medicaid Services (www.cms.gov) offers access to a vast array of healthcare-related information regarding Medicare, Medicaid, research and statistics, and regulations.
- Institute for Healthcare Improvement (IHI) (www.ihi.org) is a not-for-profit organization leading the improvement of healthcare throughout the world. IHI's work is funded primarily through its fee-based program offerings and services as well as through support from foundations, companies, and individuals.
- National Association for Healthcare Quality (www.nahq.org) empowers healthcare quality professionals from every specialty by providing vital research, education, networking, certification, professional practice resources, and a strong voice for healthcare quality.
- National Committee for Quality Assurance (NCQA) (www.ncqa.org) is a private, 501(c)(3) not-for-profit organization dedicated to improving healthcare quality. NCQA has been a central figure in driving improvement throughout the healthcare system, helping to elevate the issue of healthcare quality to the top of the US political agenda. Its mission is to improve the quality of healthcare with a vision to transform healthcare quality through measurement, transparency, and accountability.
- Office of the National Coordinator for Health Information Technology (ONCHIT, www.healthit.gov) is the primary federal agency responsible for coordinating efforts to promote and develop HIT infrastructure. The ONC was created in 2004 via an executive order and codified by the Health Information Technology for Economic and Clinical Health Act. Its aims are to improve quality of care while reducing cost, enhance coordination of care, encourage health information exchanges, and ensure a secure PHR for the US population.

Discussion Questions

1. Because most developers are not clinicians and most clinicians are not developers, what measures are necessary to ensure the development of an effective healthcare information system?
2. What is the golden triangle, and why does it influence healthcare management today?
3. What are the six most important external challenges faced by HIT today, and why do they influence HIT management?
4. What are the five most important future challenges that HIT will face, and why?
5. In what ways may improved HIT assist in continuity, communication, coordination, and accountability of patient care?
6. How can HIT assist organizations in responding to the drivers of IT changes?
7. Define and describe EBM. Are there positive or negative aspects of this concept for the healthcare field?
8. Why is the improvement of clinical information systems a high priority to most healthcare organizations?
9. Identify the most important challenge facing HIT today.
10. Order the following types of healthcare information systems from most important to least important to a healthcare organization, and discuss why you chose this order:
    a. Clinical information
    b. Operational management
    c. Strategic decision support
    d. Electronic networking and e-health applications
11. Discuss how future challenges facing healthcare information systems will change the future of healthcare delivery.

References

Acumen Research and Consulting. 2020. "Healthcare Cloud Computing Market." Accessed February 24. www.acumenresearchandconsulting.com/healthcare-cloud-computing-market.

Agency for Healthcare Research and Quality. 2018. *2017 National Healthcare Quality and Disparities Report.* US Department of Health and Human Services. Published September. www.ahrq.gov/research/findings/nhqrdr/nhqdr17/index.html.

American College of Healthcare Executives (ACHE). 2018. *FutureScan: Healthcare Trends and Implications 2018–2023.* Chicago: Society for Healthcare Strategy & Market Development and Health Administration Press.

Berger, K. 2015. "An Update on United States Healthcare Quality Improvement Efforts." *Inside Health*. T. H. Chan School of Public Health, Harvard University. Published December 22. www.hsph.harvard.edu/ecpe/an-update-on-united-states-healthcare-quality-improvement-efforts.

Boyd, D., and N. Ellison. 2007. "Social Network Sites: Definition, History, and Scholarship." *Journal of Computer-Mediated Communication* 13: 210–30.

Bresnick, J. 2017. "Top 10 Challenges of Big Data Analytics in Healthcare." Health IT Analytics. Published June 12. https://healthitanalytics.com/news/top-10-challenges-of-big-data-analytics-in-healthcare.

Burrill, S., and D. Beaudoin. 2019. "2019 US and Global Health Care Industry Outlook: Shaping the Future of Health Care Trends." Deloitte. Accessed January 15, 2020. www2.deloitte.com/content/dam/Deloitte/global/Documents/Life-Sciences-Health-Care/gx-lshc-hc-outlook-2019.pdf.

Bush, G. W. 2006. "Executive Order: Promoting Quality and Efficient Health Care in Federal Government Administered or Sponsored Health Care Programs." Published August 22. http://georgewbush-whitehouse.archives.gov/news/releases/2006/08/20060822-2.html.

Centers for Medicare & Medicaid Services. 2020. "Accountable Care Organizations (ACOs): General Information." Updated January 6. www.innovations.cms.gov/initiatives/ACO/index.html.

Clancy, C., and J. Eisenberg. 1998. "Outcomes Research: Measuring the End Results of Healthcare." *Science* 282 (5387): 245–46.

Cohen, R., E. Terlizzi, and M. Martinez. 2019. "Health Insurance Coverage: Early Release of Estimates from the National Health Interview Survey, 2018." National Center for Health Statistics. Published May. www.cdc.gov/nchs/data/nhis/earlyrelease/insur201905.pdf.

Collen, M. F. 1995. *A History of Medical Informatics in the United States: 1950–1990.* Indianapolis, IN: BooksCraft.

Collman, J., and B. Demster. 2013. "Managing Information Privacy and Security in Healthcare." HIMSS. Published April. www.himss.org/sites/hde/files/d7/HIMSSorg/Content/files/CPRIToolkit/version6/v7/D01a_History_PSToolkit.pdf.

Congdon, K. 2010. "What's the Biggest Challenge in Medical Imaging?" Health IT Outcomes. Published July 30. www.healthitoutcomes.com/doc/whats-the-biggest-challenge-in-medical-0002.

Davenport, T. H., T. M. Hongsereier, and K. A. McCord. 2018. "Using AI to Improve Electronic Health Records." *Harvard Business Review*. Published December 13. https://hbr.org/2018/12/using-ai-to-improve-electronic-health-records.

Davis, K., and S. Collins. 2006. "Transparency in Health Care: The Time Has Come." Commonwealth Fund. Published April. www.commonwealthfund.org/publications/publication/2006/apr/transparency-health-care-time-has-come.

De Angelo, M. 2000. "Internet Solution Provides Important Component in Reducing Medical Errors." *Health Management Technology* 21 (2): 20–21.

Deloitte Center for Health Solutions. 2018. *State Price Transparency Reporting*. Accessed February 24. www2.deloitte.com/content/dam/Deloitte/us/Documents/risk/us-rfa-state-pricing-transparency-reporting.pdf.

Diamond, D. 2012. "How Wal-Mart May Have Just Changed the Game on Health Care." *California Healthline*. Published October 17. https://californiahealthline.org/news/how-wal-mart-may-have-just-changed-the-game-on-health-care.

Diamond, G., and S. Kaul. 2008. "The Disconnect Between Practice Guidelines and Clinical Practice—Stressed Out." *Journal of the American Medical Association* 300 (15): 1817–19.

Djulbegovic, B., and G. H. Guyatt. 2017. "Progress in Evidence-Based Medicine: A Quarter Century On." *Lancet* 390 (10,092): 415–23.

Doheny, K. 2009. "Deadly Medical Errors Still Plague the U.S." WebMD. Published May 19. www.webmd.com/healthy-aging/news/20090519/deadly-medical-errors-still-plague-us.

Elliott, V. 2012. "Large Companies Try Domestic Medical Tourism." Amednews.com. Published January 9. https://amednews.com/article/20120109/business/301099967/6.

FACCT Foundation for Accountability. 2003. "Innovators and Visionaries: Strategies for Creating a Person-Centered Health System." Markle Foundation. Published September. https://markle.policyarchive.org/index?section=5&id=95522.

Families USA. 2012. *Dying for Coverage: The Deadly Consequences of Being Uninsured*. Published June. https://familiesusa.org/wp-content/uploads/2019/09/Dying-for-Coverage.pdf.

Federal Communications Commission (FCC). 2020. "FCC Health IT Actions and Activities Timeline." Accessed January 13. www.fcc.gov/general/fcc-health-it-actions-and-activities-timeline.

Fisher, E., D. Goodman, J. Skinner, and K. Bronner. 2009. "Health Care Spending, Quality, and Outcomes." Dartmouth Institute for Health Policy and Clinical Practice. Published February 27. www.dartmouthatlas.org/downloads/reports/Spending_Brief_022709.pdf.

Gawande, A. 2009. "The Cost Conundrum." *New Yorker*. Published May 25. www.newyorker.com/magazine/2009/06/01/the-cost-conundrum.

Ginsburg, P. B. 2005. "Competition in Healthcare: Its Evolution Over the Past Decade." *Health Affairs (Millwood)* 24 (6): 1512–22.

Glaser, J., and D. Garets. 2005. "Where's the Beef? Part 1: Getting Value from Your IT Investments." In *The CEO-CIO Partnership: Harnessing the Value of Information Technology in Healthcare*, edited by D. Smaltz, J. Glaser, R. Skinner, and T. Cunningham III, 53–73. Chicago: Healthcare Information and Management Systems Society and Health Administration Press.

Goldsmith, J. A. 1980. "The Healthcare Market: Can Hospitals Survive?" *Harvard Business Review* 58 (5): 100–112.

Hammadeh, M. 2018. "The Current State of Interoperability." HIMSS News. Accessed June 27, 2019. www.himss.org/news/current-state-interoperability.

Harpham, B. 2015. "How the Internet of Things Is Changing Healthcare and Transportation." *CIO*. Published September 8. www.cio.com/article/2981481/how-the-internet-of-things-is-changing-healthcare-and-transportation.html.

Healthcare Information and Management Systems Society (HIMSS). 2020a. "Blockchain 101." Accessed January 13. www.himss.org/library/blockchain-101.

———. 2020b. "What Is Interoperability in Healthcare?" Accessed January 21. www.himss.org/what-interoperability.

Health Research Institute. 2012. *Social Media "Likes" Healthcare: From Marketing to Social Business*. PricewaterhouseCoopers. Published April. www.pwc.com/us/en/health-industries/health-research-institute/publications/pdf/health-care-social-media-report.pdf.

Herzlinger, R. 2004. *Consumer-Driven Health Care: Implications for Providers, Payers, and Policy-Makers*. San Francisco: Jossey-Bass.

Institute of Medicine (IOM). 2015. *Health Literacy and Consumer-Facing Technology*. Washington, DC: National Academies Press.

———. 2009. *Initial National Priorities for Comparative Effectiveness Research*. Washington, DC: National Academies Press.

———. 2001. *Crossing the Quality Chasm: A New Health System for the 21st Century*. Washington, DC: National Academies Press.

———. 1999. *To Err Is Human: Building a Safer Health System*. Washington, DC: National Academies Press.

Johnston, D., E. Pan, and B. Middleton. 2002. *Finding the Value in Healthcare Information Technologies*. Boston: Center for Information Technology Leadership.

Jones, A. 2019. "Will 2019 (Finally) Be the Year of Patient Empowerment?" *Healthcare Business & Technology*. Published January 29. www.healthcarebusinesstech.com/will-2019-finally-be-the-year-of-patient-empowerment.

Kaushal, R., K. N. Barker, and D. W. Bates. 2001. "How Can Information Technology Improve Patient Safety and Reduce Medication Errors in Children's Healthcare?" *Archives of Pediatric Adolescent Medicine* 155 (9): 1002–7.

Koppel, R. 2016. "Great Promises of Healthcare Information Technology Deliver Less." In *Healthcare Information Management Systems: Cases, Strategies, and Solutions*, 4th ed., edited by C. A. Weaver, M. J. Ball, G. R. Kim, and J. M. Kiel., 101–21. New York: Springer.

Landry, M. D., and W. J. Sibbald. 2001. "From Data to Evidence: Evaluative Methods in Evidence-Based Medicine." *Respiratory Care* 46 (11): 1226–35.

Laurence, T. 2019. *Blockchain for Dummies*. New York: John Wiley and Sons.

Lebied, M. 2018. "12 Examples of Big Data Analytics in Healthcare That Can Save People." Datapine. Published July 18. www.datapine.com/blog/big-data-examples-in-healthcare.

Lord, N. 2018. "Healthcare Information Security: The Top Infosec Considerations for Healthcare Organizations Today." *Data Insider*. Posted June 25. https://digitalguardian.com/blog/healthcare-information-security-top-infosec-considerations-healthcare-organizations-today.

Makary, M. A., and M. Daniel. 2016. "Medical Error—The Third Leading Cause of Death in the US." *British Medical Journal.* Published May 3. www.bmj.com/content/353/bmj.i2139.

Marr, B. 2018. "The 4th Industrial Revolution Is Here—Are You Ready?" *Forbes.* Published August 13. www.forbes.com/sites/bernardmarr/2018/08/13/the-4th-industrial-revolution-is-here-are-you-ready/#5f12c2d8628b.

Medical Tourism Association. 2020. "A Global Platform for the Healthcare Ecosystem." Accessed January 13. www.medicaltourismassociation.com/en/index.html.

Meeks, D., M. Smith, L. Taylor, D. Sittig, J. Scott, and H. Singh. 2014. "An Analysis of Electronic Health Record-Related Patient Safety Concerns." *Journal of the American Medical Informatics Association* 21 (6): 1053–59.

mHealth Task Force. 2012. "Findings and Recommendations: Improving Care Delivery Through Enhanced Communications Among Providers, Patients, and Payers." Published September 4. www2.itif.org/2012-mhealth-taskforce-recommendations.pdf.

Moskowitz, D., and T. Bodenheimer. 2011. "Moving from Evidence-Based Medicine to Evidence-Based Health." *Journal of General Internal Medicine* 26 (6): 658–60.

National Institute of Standards and Technology. 2018. "Cloud Computing." Updated March 29. http://csrc.nist.gov/groups/SNS/cloud-computing.

Office of National Coordinator for Health Information Technology (ONCHIT). 2020. "Health IT Curriculum Resources for Educators." US Department of Health & Human Services. Published February 21. www.healthit.gov/topic/health-it-resources/health-it-curriculum-resources-educators.

Oravec, J. A. 2001. "On the Proper Use of the Internet: Self-Help Medical Information and On-Line Healthcare." *Journal of Health and Social Policy* 14 (1): 37–60.

Raghupathi, W., and Raghupathi, V. 2014. "Big Data Analytics in Healthcare: Promise and Potential." *Health Information Science and Systems* 2:3.

Raiz, G. 2019. "What CES Says About the Future of Connectivity." Rightpoint. Published January 21. www.rightpoint.com/thought/2019/01/21/what-ces-2019-says-about-the-future-of-connectivity.

Ranger, S. 2018. "What Is the IoT? Everything You Need to Know About the Internet of Things Right Now." ZDNet. Published August 21. www.zdnet.com/article/what-is-the-internet-of-things-everything-you-need-to-know-about-the-iot-right-now.

Reece, R. L. 2000. "A New Industrial Order for Physicians: A Talk with Jeff C. Goldsmith, Ph.D." *Physician Executive* 26 (1): 16–19.

Robeznieks, A. 2018. "8 Ways to Improve Health Care Price Transparency." American Medical Association. Published September 20. www.ama-assn.org/practice-management/economics/8-ways-improve-health-care-price-transparency.

Roever, L., E. S. Resende, G. Biondi-Zoccai, and A. S. R. Borges. 2016. "Degrees of Recommendations and Levels of Evidence: What You Need to Know." *Evidence Based Medicine and Practice* 2 (2).

Roohparvar, R. 2017. "Why Is Information Security Important for the Healthcare Sector?" Infoguard Cyber Security. Published July 23. www.infoguardsecurity.com/information-security-important-healthcare-sector.

Schulte, F., and E. Fry. 2019. "Death by a Thousand Clicks." *Fortune*, March 18, 56–73.

Schwab, K. 2017. *The Fourth Industrial Revolution*. New York: Random House.

Shiklo, B. 2017. "How Blockchain Can Improve the Health Information Exchange." *Forbes*. Published June 27. www.forbes.com/sites/forbestechcouncil/2017/06/27/how-blockchain-can-improve-the-health-information-exchange/#5fe07891f05b.

Sidorov, J. 2006. "It Ain't Necessarily So: The Electronic Health Record and the Unlikely Prospect of Reducing Healthcare Costs." *Health Affairs* 25 (4): 1079–85.

Simborg, D. 2010. "Consumer Empowerment Versus Consumer Populism in Healthcare IT." *Journal of the American Medical Informatics Association* 17: 370–72.

Sternberg, S. 2012. "Medical Errors Harm Huge Number of Patients." *US News & World Report*. Published August 28. http://health.usnews.com/health-news/articles/2012/08/28/medical-errors-harm-huge-number-of-patients.

US Department of Health & Human Services (USHHS). 2016. "Health, United States 2015: With Special Feature on Racial and Ethnic Health Disparities." National Center for Health Statistics. DHHS Publication No. 2016-1232.

Wachter, R. 2015. *The Digital Doctor: Hope, Hype, and Harm at the Dawn of Medicine's Computer Age*. New York: McGraw-Hill.

Wanless, S., and T. Ludwig. 2011. *Business Intelligence and Analytics for Healthcare Organizations*. Peoria, IL: Ark Group.

Warner, J. 2020. "The Major Business Challenges of Medical Imaging Centers." RX4 Group. http://rx4group.com/the-major-business-challenges-of-medical-imaging-centers.

Wilensky, G. R. 2006. "Consumer-Driven Health Plans: Early Evidence and Potential Impact on Hospitals." *Health Affairs* 25 (1): 174–85.

Williams, C., F. Mostashari, K. Mertz, E. Hogin, and P. Atwal. 2012. "From the Office of the National Coordinator: The Strategy for Advancing the Exchange of Health Information." *Health Affairs* 31 (3): 527–36.

Wimble, M., and G. Leroy. 2018. "Health Information Technology: Promise and Progress." *Journal of Health Systems* 7 (3): 161–65.

World Economic Forum. 2019. "Health and Healthcare in the Fourth Industrial Revolution: Global Future Council on the Future of Health and Healthcare, 2016–2018." Published April. www3.weforum.org/docs/WEF__Shaping_the_Future_of_Health_Council_Report.pdf.

Zeltner, B. 2019. "Walmart to Send Employees to Cleveland Clinic for Heart Care." *The Plain Dealer*. Updated January 12. www.cleveland.com/healthfit/index.ssf/2012/10/wal-mart_to_send_employees_to.html.

CHAPTER

2

EXTERNAL ENVIRONMENT

Learning Objectives

1. Define the ways in which the external environment influences the operation of the healthcare delivery system.
2. Explain the healthcare triangle and demonstrate how it relates to management of healthcare organizations and the function of health information technology (HIT).
3. Describe the interdependent challenges of cost, quality, and access currently facing the US healthcare system.
4. Analyze the implications of the cost, quality, and access challenges for the management of HIT.
5. Assess the relative importance of evidence-based management, organizational change, and international comparisons in the current and future management of healthcare delivery organizations.
6. Describe a justification for government intervention in business generally and specifically in healthcare.
7. List five major types of government intervention into the healthcare business and explain the need for government to invest in healthcare information management and HIT.
8. Describe the eight components of the administrative simplification portion of the Health Insurance Portability and Accountability Act.
9. Analyze why privacy and security are vital and why HIT has a key role in protecting them.
10. Assess the intent and impact of key healthcare regulations: the Health Information Technology for Economic and Clinical Health Act, the 21st Century Cures Act, the Medicare Access and CHIP Reauthorization Act, the Food and Drug Administration Safety and Innovation Act, and the Patient Protection and Affordable Care Act.
11. Describe HIT leadership's role in responding to healthcare legislation.
12. Assess how well healthcare system challenges and their implications align with healthcare information system priorities.

Overview

As chapter 1 indicates, the future of health information technology (HIT) is now. While the bulk of this textbook addresses management challenges with HIT, some of the greatest challenges faced today are motivated by factors external to the healthcare organization. These external challenges and responses to them can no longer be ignored or placed with someone outside of HIT. This chapter looks at some key elements of the external environment and how that environment influences the healthcare delivery system overall and healthcare informatics in particular. The external environment, government intervention and investment, and healthcare leadership's responses all qualify as external factors. In this chapter, we discuss three aspects of the external environment in detail.

First, we examine the external environment that has both direct and indirect impacts on healthcare organizations and HIT within the organization. Second, this chapter justifies the role of government in HIT and details specific key healthcare legislation. While not an exhaustive list of those impacts, its goal is to provide HIT leadership with the awareness of, tools for, and strategic vision of the potential effects of healthcare legislation on HIT business practices. Understanding why government gets involved will assist you in responding to legislation and anticipating future actions. Also, there have been a number of attempts to "fix" healthcare with specific legislation. These attempts, positive and negative, have direct effects on HIT.

Third, HIT leadership roles in managing through the external environment and government regulation merits direct discussion. Leaders must understand those roles today and anticipate roles in the future. This section presents an action plan for HIT leadership.

External Environment

The external environment's influence appears in two related sections: The Healthcare Triangle and Impact of External Environment on Health Information Technology. Efforts to address the interrelated challenges of this triangle (cost, quality, access) occupy much of healthcare leadership's and researchers' time and energy. Much research has been done on each of the three elements, and we briefly introduced the challenges in chapter 1. Despite these efforts, however, we are still far from identifying a solution to problems caused by any of the three sides of the triangle. Controlling costs, improving quality, and expanding access will continue to represent external challenges to healthcare delivery and HIT management in the years to come.

The impact will foster the rise of evidence-based management, healthcare organizational changes, and international comparisons. By using evidence for decision-making in a more direct way, clinical and administrative healthcare leaders will need more intensive and more timely information from the HIT system.

The Healthcare Triangle

By presenting the three main challenges—cost, quality, and access—facing the healthcare delivery system as an interrelated triangle (see exhibit 2.1), we are suggesting that efforts to achieve goals in any one of the areas will necessarily have an impact on the other two. For example, costs can be controlled, but not without resultant reductions in access to care or in quality of care. The challenge is to find ways to achieve goals in the three areas that are satisfactory to all participants. Who pays for care? Who might have limited or no access to care? Who might suffer from less-than-satisfactory quality of care? The answers are often different groups of people. The political considerations in finding a solution are substantial—as was evident in the debate surrounding the healthcare reform legislation passed by the Obama administration, a debate that continued to be a major focus during and long after the 2012 presidential election. That debate became even more focused after the 2016 election with concerted efforts to roll back many aspects of the Obama-era reforms.

More recently, there has been a recognition that the healthcare triangle may ignore stress in the provider community. Krisberg (2018) suggests that the burden of providing healthcare to many with a high

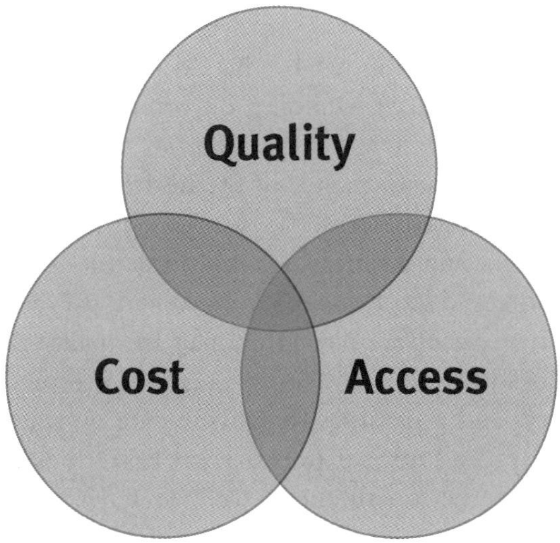

EXHIBIT 2.1
The Healthcare Triangle: Interrelations Among Cost, Quality, and Access

EXHIBIT 2.2
The Healthcare Quadruple Aim

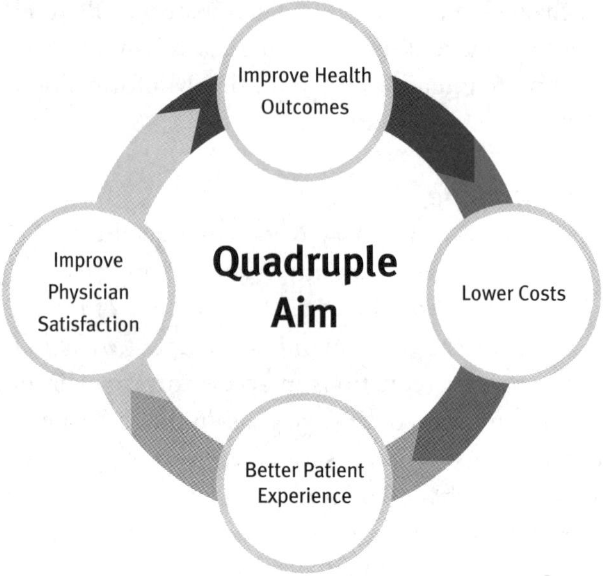

level of quality has resulted in burnout of physicians, nurses, and other providers. Along with others, Krisberg suggests adopting the quadruple aim (see exhibit 2.2) to formally recognize provider stress (Sikka, Morath, and Leape 2015). While this recognition does not alter the fundamental challenges that meeting conflicting goals generates, it adds to the complexity of solutions.

The study of how we measure healthcare systems' performance in these three or four areas keeps government agencies, foundations, and consultants busy. An effective way to organize the key elements of the triangle comes from work funded by the Commonwealth Fund (Radley, McCarthy, and Hayes 2016). Building on prior work by the Commonwealth Fund (2006), the new work, *Rising to the Challenge*, presents a scorecard assessing the performance of the healthcare system in over 300 communities in the United States. The assessment looked at performance from 2011 to 2014 using 33 measures in 4 dimensions: access, avoidable hospital utilization and cost, healthy lives, and prevention and treatment. The last two dimensions roughly map to quality. Exhibit 2.3 lists these dimensions and the 33 measures. Healthcare organizations will be required by payers and regulators to provide data on some of these measures, which will put additional pressure on HIT. It is no surprise that this has extended to the fourth aim as well (Stefanacci 2018), with more to follow.

EXHIBIT 2.3
Dimensions and Measures Used to Assess Healthcare System Performance

- Access
  - Adults aged 19–64 uninsured
  - Children aged 0–18 who are uninsured
  - At-risk adults without a doctor visit
  - Adults who went without care because of cost in past year
- Quality
  - Home health patients with a hospital admission
  - Medicare 30-day hospital readmissions per 1,000 beneficiaries
  - Short-stay nursing home residents with a 30-day readmission to the hospital
  - Long-stay nursing home residents with a hospital admission
  - Potentially avoidable ED visits among Medicare beneficiaries per 1,000 beneficiaries
  - Medicare admissions for ambulatory care–sensitive conditions, aged 75 and older
  - Medicare admissions for ambulatory care–sensitive conditions, aged 65–74
  - Total reimbursements per enrollee (aged 18–64) with employer-sponsored insurance
  - Total Medicare (Parts A and B) reimbursements per enrollee
- Healthy lives
  - Breast cancer deaths per 100,000 female population
  - Colorectal cancer deaths per 100,000 population
  - Adults who smoke
  - Adults with poor health-related quality of life
  - Infant mortality, deaths per 1,000 live births
  - Adults who are obese
  - Suicide deaths per 100,000 population
  - Mortality amenable to healthcare
- Prevention and treatment
  - Home health patients who get better at walking or moving around
  - 30-day mortality
  - Nursing home residents given an antipsychotic medication
  - Elderly patients who received a contraindicated prescription drug
  - Elderly patients who received a high-risk prescription drug
  - Hospital safety composite score
  - Adults with age-appropriate vaccines
  - High-risk nursing home residents with pressure sores
  - Home health patients whose wounds healed after an operation
  - Hospital discharge instructions for home recovery
  - Adults with a usual source of care
  - Patient-centered hospital care

Source: Data from Radley, McCarthy, and Hayes (2016).

Interestingly, the Commonwealth studies report a wide range of scores across individual measures and locations. Overall, more of the measures increased than decreased, with uninsurance rates, 30-day mortality following surgery, and quality of nursing home care doing well. Variation across locations and within states was substantial. For example, adults who went without care because of cost varied from 31 percent in McAllen, Texas, to 6 percent in Waterloo, Iowa. On the other hand, home health patients whose wounds healed after surgery ranged from 96 percent in Providence, Rhode Island, to 78 percent in Anchorage, Alaska. Within states, premature deaths from treatable conditions varied from 64 deaths per 100,000 in Traverse City, Michigan, to 142 deaths per 100,000 in Dearborn, a Detroit suburb.

The point to notice, however, is that for each of these indicators, the performance data are key, which means that completing a report card for the Commonwealth Fund, a government payer, or an external rating agency will require increased efforts by those responsible for HIT. The consideration of system performance measures will influence the HIT and organizational leadership to collect, analyze, and report a broader range of data than usual. They may have to identify that data for the patients they treat and for the potential patients in their service areas. While much of these data come from traditional sources (e.g., infant mortality rates, childhood immunization rates), other measures are relatively new to most hospital systems (e.g., adults with age-appropriate vaccines). Many of these indicators are based on population characteristics and are not usually items that individual organizations take the responsibility for collecting (e.g., adults with a usual source of care, or even hospital discharge instructions for home recovery).

Measuring performance is not the only approach to addressing the healthcare triangle. Other analysts have looked at combinations of factors as well. Baicker and Chandra (2004) examined the interrelationships among quality of Medicare beneficiaries' care, physician workforce, and spending. They found that states with greater spending actually had lower quality outcomes and that the composition of the physician workforce played a role in outcomes. Having more primary care physicians tended to direct spending to more effective services and thus resulted in more desirable outcomes.

Similarly, Yasaitis and colleagues (2009) reported on the link between quality of care and intensity of spending at the hospital level. They found that the relationship was mostly nonexistent and, if significant, was mostly negative. Other examinations have had similarly mixed results. Epstein and Newhouse (1998) found that Medicaid expansion had minimal impact on medical outcomes for mothers and babies. The expansion of care to dependents aged up to 26 had positive impacts on reduction in preterm birth and adequate prenatal care but no impact on cesarean delivery, low birth rate, or neonatal intensive care admissions (Daw and Sommers 2018). When looked at overall, however, expansion of coverage (access) has generally improved access to and utilization of services, self-reported health, and some health outcomes. While there is limited empirical evidence, some suggests savings at the state level, but more than likely, improving access resulted in increased costs (Antonisse et al. 2019).

HIT plays a central role in providing quality care, as explained in this book, and has the potential to improve efficiency and effectiveness. While it cannot solve efficiency and effectiveness problems, it serves as an important tool for government leaders and leaders of healthcare delivery systems in their efforts to find solutions. A challenge, as we will see in later chapters, is that technology can also impose burdens and added stress on providers.

Healthcare Costs

Healthcare costs continue to grow unabated. The government estimates that total national health spending reached over $3.6 trillion in 2018 and consumed about 17.7 percent of the US gross domestic product (GDP) (see exhibit 2.4). This spending has been increasing steadily in the past 50 years (from $27.2 billion in 1960) and is expected to exceed $4.0 trillion in 2020 (Centers for Medicare & Medicaid Services [CMS] 2019). To put the magnitude of this number into context, exhibit 2.5 presents the data over time—from 1960 to 2020, including projections for 2020—on a per person (per capita) basis. In 2018, the United States spent $11,174 per person on healthcare, compared with the $146 spent per person in 1960; by 2020, we are expected to spend $12,069 per person. Exhibit 2.4 also shows health spending per capita and as a percentage of GDP for the same period (1960–2018). Healthcare expenditures are taking an ever-increasing portion of the goods and services produced in the United States, rising from only 5.2 percent of GDP in 1960 to 17.7 percent in 2018.

Exhibit 2.6 analyzes the annual growth in healthcare spending by decade, from the 1960s through 2020, using data from exhibit 2.4. Healthcare spending increased faster than the GDP in all periods presented, although not always by the same amounts. These data suggest that regardless of good or bad economic times, Republican or Democratic presidents, and other factors, the result has been the same: The national health expenditure (NHE) continues to grow faster than the GDP—the measure of the output of goods and services for the economy as a whole.

Exhibit 2.7 looks at the aggregate data in detail, using the same data on which exhibit 2.4 was based. It displays the spending by major healthcare delivery categories for 2018. Hospital services represented the largest single category of spending at 32.7 percent, followed by physician services at 19.9 percent, prescription drugs at 9.2 percent, and nursing home care at 4.6 percent. It is interesting that research and construction (or "investment")

EXHIBIT 2.4

Aggregate National Health Expenditures and Select Economic Indicators: Selected Calendar Years 1960–2018

Type of Expenditure	1960	1970	1980	1990	2000	2010	2015	2018
				Amount in Billions				
National health expenditures	27.2	74.6	255.3	721.4	1,369.2	2,593.2	3,199.6	3,649.4
Investment	2.5	7.5	19.9	47.3	83.3	142.7	154.1	174.4
Health consumption expenditures	24.7	67.0	235.5	674.1	1,285.9	2,450.5	3,045.5	3,475.0
Personal healthcare	23.3	63.1	217.0	615.3	1,161.5	2,191.4	2,710.2	3,075.5
Hospital care	9.0	27.2	100.5	250.4	415.5	822.3	1,034.6	1,191.8
Professional services								
Physician and clinical services	5.6	14.3	47.7	158.4	288.2	512.6	631.2	725.6
Other professional services	0.4	0.7	3.5	17.3	36.6	69.9	87.8	103.9
Dental services	2.0	4.7	13.3	31.6	62.1	105.9	118.8	135.6
Other health, residential, and personal care	0.4	1.3	8.4	23.8	63.9	129.1	164.5	191.6
Home health care	0.1	0.2	2.4	12.5	32.3	71.6	89.2	102.2
Nursing care facilities and continuing care retirement communities	0.8	4.0	15.3	44.7	85.0	140.5	158.1	168.5
Retail outlet sales of medical products								
Prescription drugs	2.7	5.5	12.0	40.3	121.0	248.4	317.1	335.0
Durable medical equipment	0.7	1.7	4.1	13.8	25.2	39.9	48.6	54.9
Other nondurable medical products	1.6	3.3	9.8	22.4	31.6	51.3	60.2	66.4
Government administration	0.1	0.7	2.8	7.2	17.1	30.2	42.8	47.5
Net cost of health insurance	1.0	1.9	9.3	31.6	64.2	153.2	206.7	258.5
Government public health activities	0.4	1.4	6.4	20.0	43.0	75.7	85.8	93.5
US population (in milions)	186	210	230	254	282	309	320	327
GDP (USD, billions)	542.4	1,073.3	2,857.3	5,963.1	10,252.3	14,992.1	18,224.8	20,580.2
CMS Personal Health Care Price Index, 1982–84 = 100	22.3	34.0	74.8	162.8	260.8	388.4	446.8	484.7
CPI	29.6	38.8	82.4	130.7	172.2	218.1	237.0	251.1
GDP implicit price deflator, chain weighted 2012 base year	16.1	21.0	41.2	61.9	75.7	93.1	104.8	110.6
NHE percent of GDP	5.0%	7.0%	8.9%	12.1%	13.4%	17.3%	17.6%	17.7%

Note: CMS = Centers for Medicare & Medicaid Services, CPI = consumer price index, GDP = gross domestic product, NHE = national health expenditure, USD = United States dollars.

Sources: Data from CMS (2019); US Bureau of Labor Statistics (2019).

EXHIBIT 2.5
Per Capita NHE and NHE's Share of GDP, 1960–2020

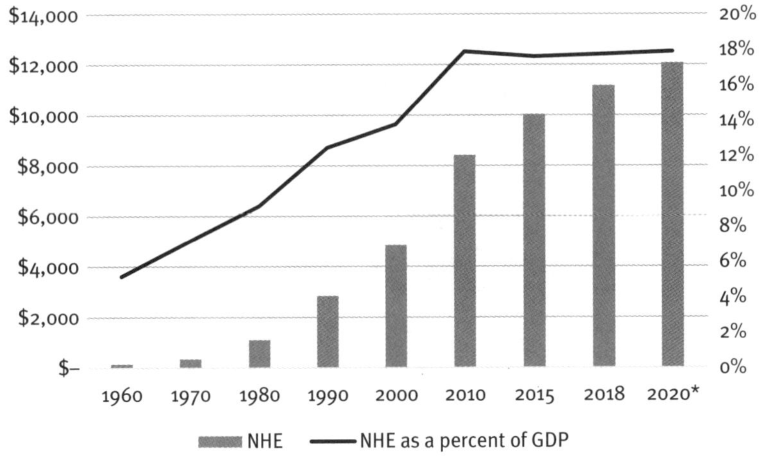

* Projected.
Source: Data from CMS (2019).

EXHIBIT 2.6
Annualized Growth Rates for NHE and GDP, 1960–2020

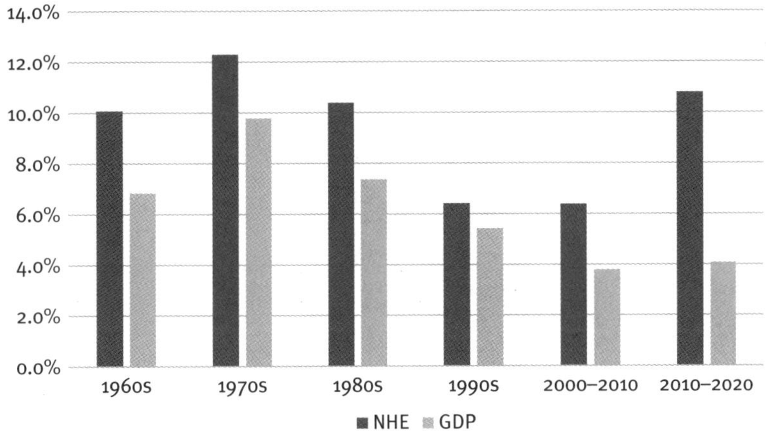

Source: Data from CMS (2019).

constituted a substantial portion of spending at 4.8 percent. While these categories vary over time, they tend to remain stable for short periods. For example, exhibit 2.8 presents the same NHEs breakdown by category—but for 2010. The big differences in this eight-year period (2010–2018) are a decline in the proportion of spending on nursing home care, investment, and prescription drugs (small). Looking at a longer period, exhibit 2.9 presents the same breakdown for 1980. In this 38-year period, hospital services declined substantially, as did nursing home services and investment. Prescription drug spending increased from 4.7 percent of the total in 1980 to 9.2 percent in 2018.

EXHIBIT 2.7
NHE by Major Service Category, 2018

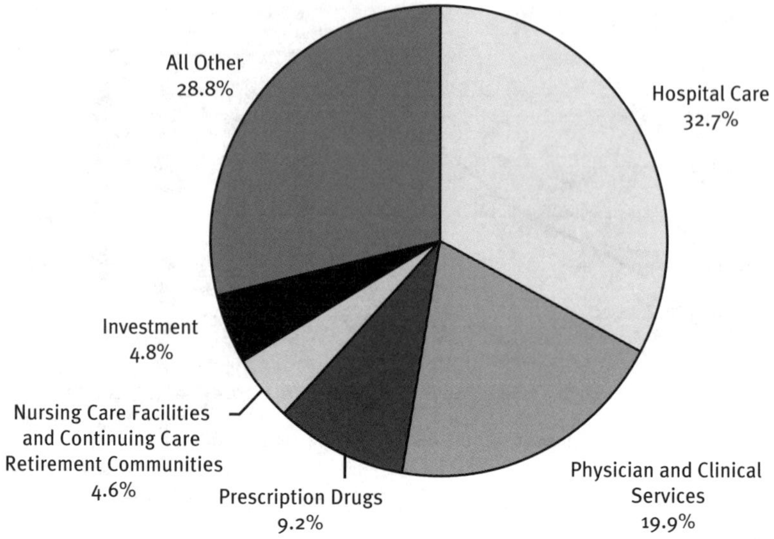

Source: CMS (2019).

EXHIBIT 2.8
NHE by Major Service Category, 2010

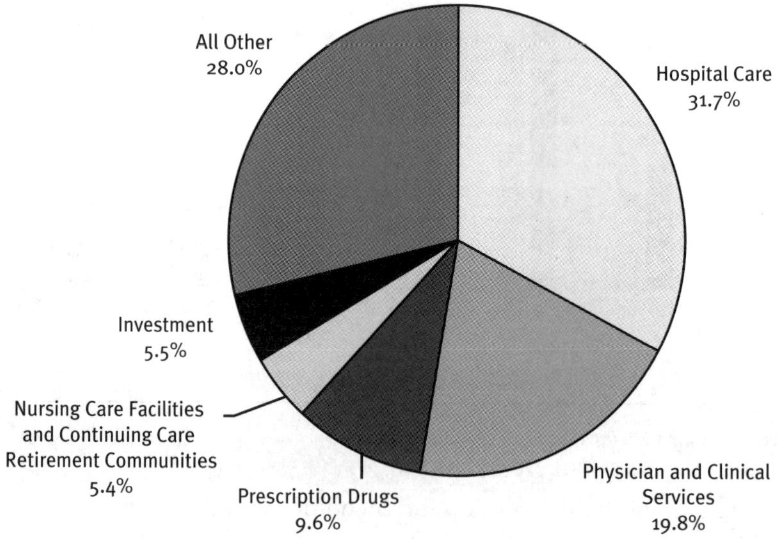

Source: CMS (2019).

Another way to look at this is in terms of spending per year. Exhibit 2.10 presents the annual spending changes for select major healthcare expense categories, for NHE in total, and for GDP from 2010–2018 and the 2000–2010 decade. For the overall period, NHE increased at an annual

EXHIBIT 2.9
NHE by Major Service Category, 1980

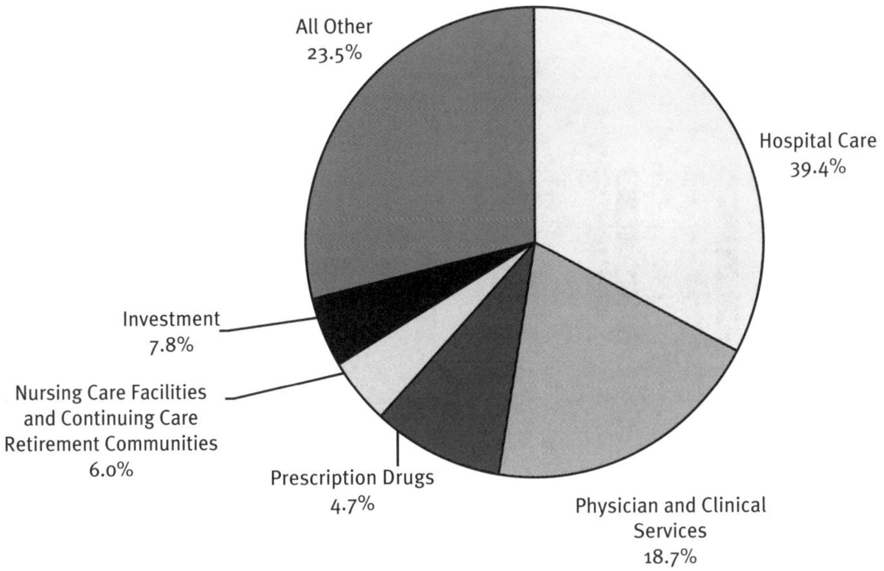

Source: Data from CMS (2019).

rate of 4.2 percent per year from 2010 to 2018 but 6.4 percent from 2000 to 2010. In the later period, hospital services spending rose more than the aggregate, at 4.6 percent, as did physician services at 4.3 percent, while prescription drugs, nursing home services, and investment all increased less per year than the aggregate at 3.7 percent, 2.3 percent, and 2.5 percent, respectively. NHE increased on average a little faster than GDP for the period. For the earlier decade, hospital services and prescription drug expenditures increased more than the overall average at 6.8 percent and 7.2 percent, respectively. In this period, physician services and nursing home expenditures increased less than the overall at 5.8 percent and 5.0 percent, respectively. Investment increased less than the overall increase in health expenditures in the decade at 5.4 percent but much more than in the 2010–2018 period.

To put all of this in perspective and get a better understanding of the factors that contributed to these overall changes in NHE, you can decompose these overall changes into key component parts. Decomposition helps to determine the true magnitude of this overall change in healthcare spending and to aid in seeking solutions. The data in exhibit 2.4 form the basis of the decomposition of overall health expenditure changes. Exhibit 2.11 is a summary of the decomposition results for the 2010–2018 period and for the 2000–2010 decade. Many factors contribute to this overall result, including the following:

EXHIBIT 2.10
Annual Changes in Major Categories, NHE and GDP, 2010–2018 and 2000–2010

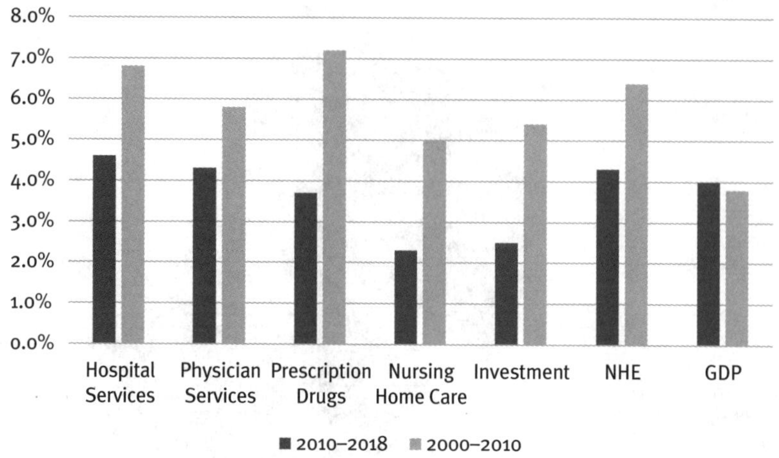

Source: Data from CMS (2019).

EXHIBIT 2.11
Decomposition of Annual NHE, 2000–2010 and 2010–2018

	2010–2018		2000–2010	
	Percentage of Total	Annual Percentage Change	Percentage of Total	Annual Percentage Change
Population	16.4%	0.7	14.1%	0.9
Inflation	42.3%	1.8	37.5%	2.4
Healthcare prices	23.8%	1.0	25.0%	1.6
Real GDP	61.9%	2.6	21.9%	1.4
Residual	−45.2%	−1.9	0.1%	0.2
National health expenditures		4.2		6.4

Source: Data from CMS (2019).

2010–2018

The US population grew by about 0.7 percent per year in this period. Therefore, health spending per capita increased only 3.5 percent (4.2 percent – 0.7 percent) per year during the period. Population growth accounted for 16.7 percent of overall NHE increases if you assume that everyone received an equal portion of the increase.

Inflation for the economy as a whole (measured by the Consumer Price Index) was 1.8 percent per year during the period. Therefore, real or inflation-adjusted health spending per capita went up 1.7 percent per year (4.2 percent [NHE] – 0.7 percent [population] – 1.8 percent [inflation]). Overall inflation increases accounted for 42.9 percent of health spending increases during this period. Of this remaining 1.7 percent per year, a substantial portion can be attributed to price increases for healthcare goods and services relative to general inflation.

The medical care component of consumer prices climbed 2.8 percent during the 2010–2018 period. This increase was 1.0 percent (2.8 percent [medical care prices] – 1.8 percent [inflation]) more rapid than the overall inflation. Higher medical care prices accounted for 1.0 percent per year of the remaining real per capita increase of 1.7 percent per year, leaving a 0.7 percent annual increase unaccounted. Relative medical care price increases accounted for 23.8 percent of overall health spending increases. The remaining 0.7 percent per year may be the result of two potential categories. One part represents greater spending due to increases in income, and the other part is residual. The residual would be interpreted as the quality and quantity of healthcare services not measured in other ways.

If you assume that health spending goes up at least as rapidly as income does, then real income increases should account for some of the 0.6 percent remaining. Real income (GDP adjusted for inflation) rose 2.6 percent per year during the period (4.4 percent [GDP] – 1.8 percent [inflation]). Real GDP increases accounted for more than the remaining increase in healthcare expenditures (0.7 percent). It appears that income increases did not account for much of healthcare expenditure increases during this period and the residual must, in fact, be negative. The implication is that once we account for population, general inflation, and healthcare price increases, very little can be attributed to the population becoming wealthier, increases in quantity of services provided, or increases in quality.

2000—2010

During this decade, the US population grew by about 0.9 percent per year. Therefore, health spending per capita increased only 5.5 percent (6.4 percent – 0.9 percent) per year during the period. Population growth accounted for 14.1 percent of overall NHE increases if you assume that everyone received an equal portion of the increase.

Inflation for the economy as a whole (measured by the Consumer Price Index) was 2.4 percent per year during the 2000–2010 period. Therefore, real or inflation-adjusted health spending per capita went up 3.1 percent per year (6.4 percent [NHE] – 0.9 percent [population] – 2.4 percent [inflation]). Overall inflation increases accounted for 37.5 percent of health spending increases during this period. Of this remaining 3.1 percent per year, a substantial portion can be attributed to price increases for healthcare goods and services relative to general inflation.

The medical care component of consumer prices climbed 4.0 percent during the 2000–2010 period. This increase was 1.6 percent (4.0 percent [medical care prices] – 2.4 percent [inflation]) more rapid than the overall inflation. Higher medical care prices accounted for 1.6 percent per year of the remaining real per capita increase of 3.1 percent per year, leaving a 1.5 percent annual increase unaccounted for. Relative medical care price increases accounted for 25.0 percent of overall health spending increases. The remaining 1.5 percent per year may be the result of two potential categories. One part represents greater spending due to increases in income, and the other part is residual.

If you assume that health spending goes up at least as rapidly as income does, then real income increases should account for some of the 1.5 percent remaining. Real income (GDP adjusted for inflation) rose 1.4 percent per year during the decade (3.8 percent [GDP] – 2.4 percent [inflation]). Real GDP accounted for about 21.9 percent of the total increase in healthcare expenditures. Together these four factors (population, prices in the economy, healthcare prices, income) almost completely account for the increase in total expenditures for the decade. The residual of 0.1 percent represents increases in quantity; quality of services did not change during the decade.

The preceding decomposition of causes represents more than just an interesting exercise. As underlying causes of expenditure increase change, different solutions will arise. As we have seen in these two periods, less of overall change results from expanding quantity of services or increases in quality. Especially in the most recent period, it appears that quantity and quality have decreased. These outcomes, if they continue, will affect how HIT leadership must collect and report key data. Decomposition also indicates that in aggregate, change results from a complex mix of price increases overall, medical care price increases, and greater income. Cutting services further will not control expenditure increases; we must look at prices and perhaps the mix of services being delivered for solutions. This finding is further evidence that the external environment has a major impact on the healthcare system.

As our cost analysis suggests, healthcare expenditure growth will likely continue into the future; this trend is supported by federal government projections (see exhibit 2.12). This analysis also indicates that not all of the healthcare cost problem can be attributed to healthcare prices or utilization, but both contribute substantially to it. National healthcare spending in total, per capita spending, and NHE as a percent of GDP are all expected to continue to increase. However, cost analyses look backward and do not address the underlying socioeconomic factors that drive increases in spending in a more fundamental manner (Thorpe 2005). Among these factors are modifiable "population risk factors such as obesity and stress," although Thorpe (2005, 1436) points out that rising disease prevalence and new medical

EXHIBIT 2.12
National Health Expenditures and Selected Economic Indicators, 2015 and Projected to 2027

Item	2015	2020	2025	2027
National health expenditures (in billions)	$3,199.6	$4,031.1	$5,344.8	$5,963.2
Gross domestic product (in billions)	18,224.8	22,535.2	28,217.6	30,755.4
CMS Personal Health Care Price Index, chain weighted 2012 base year	103.7	112.5	128.4	135.9
Consumer Price Index (CPI-U)—1982–1984 base	237.0	263.5	299.6	315.4
US population (in millions)	320	334	347	353
National health expenditures (per capita)	$10,018	$12,087	$15,396	$16,907
National health expenditures as a percentage of gross domestic product	17.6%	17.9%	18.9%	19.4%

Source: Data from CMS (2019).

treatments account for much of the increase as well. In addition, as we will see with healthcare reform efforts, many individuals with limited or no access to healthcare services may begin to participate as a result of expanded insurance coverage. If that persists, healthcare expenditures should continue to increase.

Quality of Care

According to the Institute of Medicine's (IOM's) 1999 landmark report, *To Err Is Human*, medical errors are a leading cause of adverse health consequences in hospitals (see chapter 1). The IOM followed up this study with a 2001 blueprint, *Crossing the Quality Chasm*, designed to help healthcare organizations fix the delivery system. The notion that quality in healthcare matters did not begin with these IOM studies, however. Most quality considerations for healthcare trace their origins to Avedis Donabedian.

Donabedian, through his vast body of work, conceptualized quality as a function of structure, process, and outcome—first in an article titled "Evaluating the Quality of Medical Care" (Donabedian 1966) and later and more formally in the classic book *The Definition of Quality and Approaches to Its Assessment* (Donabedian 1980). His work became a foundation that continues to influence how we think about measurement and improvement of quality. He addressed many of the practical concerns regarding access to and use of patient clinical record data to measure and improve quality. In one of his later books, *An Introduction to Quality Assurance in Health Care*, Donabedian (2002) provided a guide to the many complex processes necessary for quality improvement. In his early work, he questioned access to and completeness of information in the traditional medical records (before the electronic health record [EHR]) and noted the challenges posed by physician record keeping. He even raised the notion of using direct observation, as opposed to paper records, as a means of collecting reliable, valid, and unbiased data. This innovative thinking occurred before the advent of most of the EHR technologies that occupy our time today, and it continues to be an important consideration, as a recent review of the evidence on the reliability and validity of quality measures suggests that more HIT work will be forthcoming in this regard (Chan, Fowles, and Weiner 2010). We urge you to read Donabedian's literature, including his 1988 article "The Quality of Care: How Can It Be Assessed?"

Davis and colleagues (2004) reported on the measurement of six domains of quality just from the perspective of the patient:

1. *Patient safety*—patient-reported medical error with serious health consequences
2. *Patient-centeredness*—patient assessment of quality of physician care, especially regarding involvement of the patient in care decisions
3. *Timeliness*—patient-reported waiting time for hospitalizations, elective surgery, and physician appointment
4. *Efficiency*—patient-reported coordination of care
5. *Effectiveness*—patient-reported ability to follow up on care ordered by the physician
6. *Equity*—patient-reported influence of income on ability to receive care

Combining the foundation of quality from Donabedian, the challenges regarding medical errors from the IOM, and the concept of patient-perceived domains from Davis and colleagues led to the conceptualization of quality of care in terms of a more comprehensive set of measures. The Agency for Healthcare Research and Quality assists providers and researchers in navigating the complex and expanding quality measurement space through its quality indicators website (https://qualityindicators.ahrq.gov). This comprehensive source of information on quality metrics includes resources such as webinars, presentations, and tool kits. The source collects and provides documentation for thousands of potential metrics and contains helpful classification schemes, as well as archives of prior versions and a log of changes.

Further, Davis and colleagues (2004) reported some of the problems with quality and the variability in the level of quality. Doing something about quality requires identifying a methodology and training people to monitor, assess, and improve specific aspects of quality of care. This has led to the formation of a host of associations, programs, and sources that have the common goal of organizing healthcare professionals around the task of improving quality or some aspects of service delivery in the US healthcare system (see exhibit 2.13). All of these initiatives rely on the HIT function to provide data.

To demonstrate how vital information management is to the future, Senator Max Baucus (D-Montana, retired) advocated for two basic reforms to be implemented to improve the system (Baucus 2005). First, the way that providers are paid must be changed to a system that encourages value and efficient, effective, patient-centered care. Second, more spending on (i.e., investment in) information technology is needed. Baucus asserted that these changes would result in a more transparent and value-based healthcare system. His insightful thinking about fundamental needs for reform of the healthcare system were on target—some of his ideas appeared in the Patient Protection and Affordable Care Act (ACA) of 2010.

Since the early days of HIT, the literature has presented evidence of HIT's positive impact on quality. In a systematic review, Buntin and colleagues (2011) reported that 92 percent of the literature found HIT provided positive or mixed benefits. Among Buntin and colleagues' many findings is that research that examined specific information technology tools was less likely to demonstrate positive results than research that explored comprehensive information technology systems. The evaluation methodology suggests that this should not have been the case. More research on

EXHIBIT 2.13
Major Healthcare Quality Improvement Organizations

- Agency for Healthcare Research and Quality: www.ahrq.gov
- Ambulatory Care Quality Alliance: www.aqaalliance.org
- Physician Consortium for Performance Improvement: www.thepcpi.org
- American Society for Quality: www.asq.org
- Institute for Healthcare Improvement: www.ihi.org
- Institute of Medicine: www.iom.org
- The Joint Commission: www.jointcommission.org
- Leapfrog Group: www.leapfroggroup.org
- National Association for Healthcare Quality: www.nahq.org
- National Committee for Quality Assurance: www.ncqa.org
- National Initiative for Children's Healthcare Quality: www.nichq.org
- National Quality Forum: www.qualityforum.org

this topic is needed to fully understand the role of HIT in quality of care. Appari and colleagues (2012) conducted a large-scale study of US hospitals and found that institutions that adopted HIT had patients who displayed significantly greater likelihood of adherence to recommended medications (for acute myocardial infarction, heart failure, pneumonia, surgical care) than patients of non-HIT adopters. Appari and colleagues looked separately at all computerized physician order entry and electronic medication administration record systems. This study suggests HIT's positive impact on quality because adherence to recommended medications is a necessary element in overall quality-of-care improvement.

The complexity of systematically measuring and evaluating HIT impacts makes the studies that do exist somewhat unsatisfying, however. HIT's effect on outcomes is difficult to identify immediately because several steps occur between the implementation and use of an HIT system and the final clinical outcome; the best system in the world will not work if the operators (physicians) do not use the system correctly. Thus, many studies instead examine the intermediate outcomes, such as adherence to practice guidelines, rather than the patient outcome. For example, Jamal, McKenzie, and Clark (2009) found that most studies (14 out of 17 they reviewed) demonstrated evidence of improved compliance with guidelines but essentially no positive impact on patient outcomes. Similarly, Black and colleagues (2011) found little evidence of HIT's positive impact on quality when they examined a host of systems, including clinical decision support and distance technologies.

Despite substantial progress in measurement and improvement of care, serious caveats exist. Baron (2007) suggests that information technology may not be an easy answer to improvement despite its substantial promise. For example, an EHR's failure to adequately structure information means that retrieving and using vital patient data will be difficult for users. In addition, in many ambulatory care settings, neither teams nor resources exist to implement improvement initiatives despite the availability of good data.

On the positive side, however, there are empirical studies that document and demonstrate the positive role of HIT on quality (Collins Higgins et al. 2015). Examples from primary care suggest that, even in an environment that has traditionally been less cutting-edge, HIT provides benefits. Similarly, a comprehensive review of technology and its role in improving patient safety found many positive impacts (Alotaibi and Federico 2017). Specifically, they examined 12 distinct technologies for evidence of positive influence on patient outcomes. These were not uniformly found to be positive because not all had been subject to rigorous clinical trials, but the influence was generally positive:

- *Electronic physician orders and e-prescribing.* Significant findings for reduction of medication errors and adverse drug reactions but only when paired with clinical decision support.

- *Clinical decision support.* Mixed outcomes when examined alone depending on type of support system.
- *Electronic sign-out and hand-off tools.* Tends to improve process, reduce omissions of critical information, and reduce hand-off times.
- *Bar code medication administration.* Results positive, though based only on observational studies.
- *Smart pumps.* Fixed with hard limits, tended to be positive, but the only rigorous study found no impact.
- *Automatic medical dispensing tools.* Appear to reduce medication errors in critical care settings.
- *Retained surgical item prevention technology.* Insufficient evidence of value.
- *Patient electronic portals.* May improve outcomes in disease awareness, preventive care, and self-management; broader value uncertain.
- *Telemedicine and synchronous telemedicine.* Adds apparent value but limited study of value beyond describing impact on process.
- *Remote patient monitoring.* Appears to reduce medication errors and other common negative outcomes.
- *Electronic incident reporting.* Generally integrated into the EHR; has some positive effects.
- *Overall EHR.* Strong evidence of improvements in guidance adherence, reduction in medication errors, and reduction in adverse drug reactions.

Access to Care

In addition to its quality-of-care challenges, the US healthcare system suffers from myriad problems related to poor access. If you cannot pay for diagnosis, much less treatment, lack of access may contribute to poor outcomes. Despite significant progress with the uninsured (see exhibit 1.1), a substantial number of people remain uninsured, and as of 2018, the number rose once again (Keith 2019). As with quality, the concept of access can be addressed in many ways, making full understanding and viable solutions difficult (American College of Healthcare Executives 2016; US Department of Health and Human Services [HHS] 2020). This type of challenge exists because the uninsured are not a uniform group. Some details about personal characteristics of the uninsured population include the following (Tolbert et al. 2019):

- Most uninsured (77 percent) are from low-income families with at least one working member.
- Their primary reason for lack of insurance is that they cannot afford it (45 percent).

- Uninsured people are likely to have difficulty paying medical bills.
- Over half of uninsured are in families making more than 200 percent of federal poverty level.
- Ten states have over 10 percent of their population uninsured, while nine states have less than 7 percent uninsured.

One type of access problem may arise from people living in remote, rural parts of the country that do not have healthcare facilities and personnel close by. "Close by" can apply to distance or travel time. Crowding also can present an access barrier. If available facilities are underdeveloped to meet the needs of the local population, crowding can result. Other access barriers stem from the interrelated issues of lack of insurance, fear of public programs, literacy, cultural competency, transportation, and many more (see DeVoe et al. 2007; Lazar and Davenport 2018; Syed, Gerber, and Sharp 2013). For this discussion, we primarily consider the financial aspects of access challenges.

Many residents in the United States have no health insurance, making obtaining care a cost-prohibitive undertaking. The number of uninsured fell from its high in 2010 of 48.2 million (18.2 percent of the population) to a low of 28.2 million in 2016 (10.4 percent). The number of uninsured has increased again to 30.1 million in 2018 (11.1 percent). The National Health Interview Survey details other dimensions of lack of access (National Center for Health Statistics 2019). One thing is certain—US residents consistently rank access at or near the top of "the most urgent" healthcare-related concerns, as reported by the Gallup organization (Saad 2009). Progress has been slow.

People without access to care are, generally, those without insurance. Because they do not have a usual source of care, the uninsured consistently exhibit behaviors that contribute to poor health outcomes, which ironically often end in a higher overall cost. Specifically, those without insurance (Families USA 2012)

- use the emergency department as their regular source of care,
- obtain few (if any) health screenings and preventive care,
- often delay or completely forgo medical services,
- are typically sicker and may die earlier than those with insurance, and
- pay more for medical care.

More recent analyses of the uninsured by the Kaiser Family Foundation, done after efforts to address this challenge, reveal a surprisingly similar profile. Compared to those with employer-sponsored care or those with government insurance, the uninsured were more likely to lack a consistent source of care, postpone seeking care because of cost, go without care because of cost, and put off purchasing prescription drugs because of costs (Garfield, Orgera, and Damico 2019).

Problems of the uninsured are systemwide challenges, but they manifest in clinical care, and thus HIT, directly. A number of studies have demonstrated that lack of insurance and variations in the type of insurance have a negative impact on the stage of diagnosis and care for patients with cancer (Bradley et al. 2008; Farkas et al. 2012; Halpern et al. 2007). Other views exist, however, because the uninsured are not uniform; in fact, many of them could pay for insurance, pay for care, and receive substantial healthcare (O'Neill and O'Neill 2009). The challenges of insurance, access to care, and cost and quality outcomes are at the center of the ACA, which is discussed in more detail later in this chapter.

The bottom line is that as solutions to access-to-care barriers for uninsured individuals emerge, the US healthcare system will face a capacity problem. With improved access, more people (perhaps 25–30 percent of the population) will gain meaningful access to basic care and insurance. This increase will strain the public health and emergency systems, on which many Americans rely (Book 2005, 579).

Impact of External Environment on Health Information Technology

A host of external factors related to cost, quality, and access will influence healthcare delivery organizations. Importantly, each factor has direct implications for HIT. These include direct cost, quality, and access remedies; growth and development of evidence-based management; organization change; and international comparisons.

Direct Cost, Quality, and Access Remedies

The real issue, however, is whether the growth of cost genuinely constitutes a problem. Are we getting value for this investment in healthcare goods and services? Many studies explore this problem and propose solutions, including a 2010 IOM report titled *The Healthcare Imperative: Lowering Costs and Improving Outcomes*. Any review of the literature will demonstrate that identification of and solutions to cost increases dominate the published articles, and these studies (e.g., Cutler, Rosen, and Vijan 2006) suggest that investments in healthcare have been relatively cost-effective overall.

Improving quality requires greater accuracy, reliability, and timeliness of clinical information at the individual patient level (Metzger, Ame, and Rhoads 2010). As quality improvement efforts take hold, organizations will need to be able to collect and share information across components of their systems. Identification of best practices involves sharing of information across units and institutions. Further, delivery organizations will increasingly be required to provide access to high-quality care to meet the needs of patients in their communities.

These may not be patients in the traditional sense; thus, reliably obtaining information about them is essential. Sources, validation, and security of this information will pose future challenges to HIT. Organizations must adopt greater standards of transparency in reporting quality and cost information (Aron and Pogach 2009). However, if the challenges of improving quality from HIT investments prove too great a barrier, as we have observed, the likelihood of sharing information across systems is in doubt.

Similarly, access involves a number of challenges that HIT must address. First, expanding access to 30–50 million more people strains delivery systems and HIT's ability to collect, monitor, and report across a host of environments. Second, by nature, many of the currently uninsured are challenging to serve. Often, they have different, more complex acute and chronic medical problems than those with insurance. On average, they are less likely to have a high education level, positive home environment, and nutritional history or prior medical records at a healthcare facility. These make the newly insured less likely to comply with forms and paperwork or general medical treatment. Gathering data and validating data are, thus, more difficult.

From a cost perspective, access and quality further increase cost pressures. Efforts at reducing duplicate tests and procedures, eliminating fraud and abuse, reducing excess administrative costs, and redesigning processes all entail HIT involvement. While there is great prospect, macrolevel studies of large systems do not support operational changes from HIT that influence either cost of care or quality (Agha 2014).

Growth and Development of Evidence-Based Management

As defined in chapter 1, evidence-based medicine is a systematic approach to diagnosis and treatment that encourages the physician to formulate questions and seek answers from the best available published evidence. As we seek solutions to cost, quality, and access challenges, all participants seek evidence to make better decisions. The past two decades have witnessed a corresponding increase in the emphasis on evidence-based management —the management application of the evidence-based medicine concept (Kovner, Fine, and D'Aquila 2009; Pfeffer and Sutton 2006; Walshe and Rundall 2001). In fact, Kovner, Fine, and D'Aquila's book *Evidence-Based Management in Healthcare* suggests that this topic has become mainstream in the training of healthcare leaders. However, we can expect many of the challenges associated with evidence-based medicine to arise for evidence-based management as well.

While experience, judgment, intuition, and a good sense of the political environment are still critical skills, administrative decision-making increasingly relies on information. While some may discount the value of information in the management process—stating that management is still more an art than a science—at the other end of the spectrum are the technocrats, who argue that management and information are inseparable and that all management decisions need to be completely rational and based entirely on an analysis of comprehensive information. The resulting revision in the method of managerial decision-making that relies more on data is part of the culture of healthcare organizations (Center for Healthcare Organization and Implementation Research 2006). This new culture relies heavily on organizational information systematically gathered, stored, analyzed, and reported by a wide array of health informatics professionals.

The most obvious example of the potential value of evidence-based management is in reducing the high levels of variation in management (and clinical) practices observed across healthcare delivery organizations. Over the last 40 years, a growing body of evidence regarding variation in care points to the problems that variations generate (Wennberg and Gittelsohn 1973). The investigations and evidence have mounted, and Gawande (2009) wrote an article that clarifies the evidence and importance of these variations. If we manage patients and organizations without valid, reliable information, then healthcare costs rise and quality falls (Fisher, Bynum, and Skinner 2009; Fisher et al. 2003). The remaining question is, Does management employ evidence in decision-making? Some empirical evidence (Guo et al. 2017) provides limited support. Healthcare leaders seem more likely to adopt evidence in management decisions in larger institutions with more employees and if their attitude toward evidence-based management is positive. The precise nature of the sources of evidence make this and other studies problematic, but advances continue to be made.

Organizational Change

Restructuring healthcare delivery organizations might be considered as a response to addressing challenges in the healthcare triangle. Consequently, the chief information officer (CIO) must stay aware of change, advise on organization responses, and plan for IT support. The stress of the evolving environment has been a major driver of organizational change along a number of dimensions (Bigalke, Copeland, and Keckley 2011) that include some key elements:

- Securing information from physicians, hospitals, and post-acute providers regarding safety, quality, and healthcare outcomes
- Employing scientific evidence for recommended treatment protocols
- Facilitating coordination of care across entities with greater investment in information technologies
- Actualizing consumer decision-making by providing choices in type of care and location of care delivery

Each of these strategies involves the use of information technology in new ways; they currently strain HIT operations and will continue to generate strain in the future. Securing information poses particular technical and political challenges for HIT, as it entails gathering information from multiple sites. These data are collected from entities that are separate geographically, culturally, and by ownership. Interoperability is a necessary step in enabling that to happen, and even the government recognizes that true interoperability is a work in progress, as evinced by the dynamic nature of the information on the HealthIT.gov site (see www.healthit.gov/topic/interoperability for current information and resource links).

Much of what is envisioned in today's healthcare reform appears similar to the managed care initiatives pushed as a solution to cost issues in the early 1970s. Back then, organizations responded to the growth of managed care by consolidating (Cuellar and Gertler 2003), purchasing medical practices (Morrisey et al. 1996), and improving efficiency and effectiveness (Enthoven and Toller 2005). Managed care, which flourished in the 1990s, was designed to help contain costs by providing financial incentives to squeeze out inefficiency in the delivery system. However, another way to contain costs is not just to provide care but to truly make the system more efficient. Much of the growth of managed care did not arise from consumers' preference for the delivery model. People selected managed care options to avoid paying the higher premiums charged by alternative insurance plans (Gilmer and Kronick 2005). Consumer backlash to managed care arose because of fear of restrictions on access to care. This sentiment was fueled by physicians, who did not support managed care because its plans placed limitations on the delivery of care and reduced physician reimbursement (Ginsburg 2005). Health maintenance organizations, in particular, came under heavy criticism from consumers and physicians. The political battle over the Patient's Bill of Rights, which was developed in response to the managed care restrictions, is a reflection of these consumer and physician concerns. Whether ongoing efforts at health reform can avoid the problems of the managed care era is open to speculation.

The managed care movement did not end with the criticisms we mentioned. Accountable care organizations (ACOs), bundled payments, and other elements of healthcare reform legislation suggest that basic tenets of managed care survived—but under different terminology. Some form of assigning responsibility to providers for the full continuum of care, rather than for individual units of service, will be part of the healthcare future. For HIT, the implications are staggering. Collecting, storing, retrieving, and analyzing patient data across this continuum require increases in the amount of data and changes in the types of data needed (e.g., inpatient, outpatient, rehabilitation, prescription drug). Furthermore, as stated, these data will come from separate entities. Leaders of HIT must become more strategic in assessing many data-related options and meeting the changing needs of their organization.

International Comparisons

The threat or opportunity posed by healthcare delivered outside of the organization or outside of the country must be identified and planned for. Although international threats were briefly addressed in the medical tourism section in chapter 1, their implications were not fully analyzed.

A potential fundamental change in the healthcare landscape might come from an international comparison of outcomes, costs, and efficiency. Again, a growing body of evidence suggests that the US healthcare system does not measure up to international comparisons across a host of dimensions:

- *Overall.* Patient perspectives suggest that the US system does not compare favorably with almost any similar country (Commonwealth Fund 2020; Peter G. Peterson Foundation 2019; Peterson-KKF 2020). Many metrics are reported but two are vital. First, satisfaction, as indicated by easy-to-understand explanations by a provider, found the United States at 89.5 percent—much lower than the Netherlands at 96.9 percent or even the United Kingdom at 90.5 percent but better than France at 83.7 percent (Peterson-KKF 2020). Second, overall satisfaction with the healthcare system, as measured by agreement with the statement "our health care system has so much wrong with it that we need to completely rebuild it," came in at 23 percent (9 percent said yes in Canada, 7 percent in the United Kingdom, and 4 percent in Australia).
- *Outcomes.* Most of the comparisons of outcomes point to problems in the US system. The Commonwealth Fund's (2020) International Comparisons presents a broadly consistent set of comparisons. The US performs at or near the bottom among all of the countries profiled for most measures. For example, avoidable deaths for conditions amenable to healthcare had the United States at 112 per 100,000 patients, while the United Kingdom was at 85. Switzerland (the lowest) had 55 deaths, Canada had 78, and Australia had 62. The position of the United States was poor with the exception of breast cancer five-year survival rates, for which it was at or tied for the top.
- *Access.* Access is poorer in the United States. We discussed lack of insurance earlier in the chapter, but even for other measures, the United States performs poorly relative to other developed countries. For example, wait time, as measured by the percentage of patients who can get an appointment the next day, was 51 percent for the United States, only slightly better than Canada at 43 percent and Sweden at

49 percent. The top performers were Netherlands at 77 percent and Australia at 67 percent (Peterson-KKF 2020). Similarly, the percentage of adults reporting at least one of three access problems was 40 percent in the United States versus 34 percent in New Zealand and 9 percent in the United Kingdom (Schoen and How 2011). The three access problems indicated in the report were not getting care because of cost, not filling prescriptions because of cost, or skipping prescription doses because of cost.
- *Efficiency.* In terms of efficiency, the United States scored worse than other countries across a number of measures. For example, the percentage of adults who went to the emergency department (in the previous two years) for a condition that could have been treated by a primary physician was 26 percent for the United States versus 21 percent for Canada (the next highest) and 6 percent for Germany (the lowest among the reported countries) (Schoen and How 2011).
- *Expenditures.* Health spending was highest in the United States as we saw earlier in the chapter. In 2018 or the closest year available to the data analysts, the United States spent much more than any other country in total and, more important, per capita. For the comparison year, the US spent $11,172 per person, much more than the next closest country, Switzerland, at $7,317. Both countries were far above the next highest, Germany, at $5,986, and the United Kingdom only spent $4,070 per person (Peterson-KKF 2020).

International comparisons may present a competition challenge for US healthcare delivery. If medical tourism—generally defined as travel across national borders to access healthcare either not readily available in the home country or available at lower cost in the destination country—increases, it might directly address some challenges of the healthcare triangle. According to the website of Medical Tourism Corporation (www.medicaltourismco.com) and the scant literature on the topic (Dalen and Alpert 2019), the benefits of medical tourism are that it enables people to

- save on medical costs;
- avoid wait times for medical services;
- gain access to skilled providers; and
- enjoy concierge services, such as destination activities, during recovery.

These benefits are not fully documented as of 2020, but the competitive threat of medical tourism and its potential advantages exist. Much is still being considered, including exploring medical tourism as a potential revenue stream (Fottler et al. 2014), but the extant data on volume, growth, and financial return are insufficient to make robust predictions about the long-term impact on the healthcare industry. (For an interesting overview of these issues, see Wharton School [2011].) What we do know is that at least some of the results from the United States' adverse performance in international comparisons may arise from less-than-adequate use of HIT in its healthcare system (Anderson et al. 2006). Anderson and colleagues document that while delivery organizations in the United States employ fewer resources (e.g., beds, nurses, physicians) per capita, they spend more than twice as much as other Organisation for Economic Co-operation and Development countries.

Major funding organizations have begun to provide international comparisons for all to follow. The Commonwealth Fund, for example, provides a comprehensive set of data for dozens of countries that span many of the cost, quality, and access issues discussed in this chapter. Tikkanen (2018) provides a comprehensive analysis of multinational healthcare spending stratified by several variables, including percent of GDP, source of healthcare spending, spending by type (e.g., hospital, physician, drugs), specific disease treatment costs, long-term care spending, supply comparisons (e.g., physicians, nurses), number of procedures, and select social determinants of health. These estimates suggest potential reasons the United States lags the rest of the developed world in cost, quality, and access measures. However, they also point to a great potential for improvement with the assistance of a concerted HIT leadership and management.

Government and Healthcare

Government's Role in Health Information Technology

Three questions must be asked in assessing the role of government in HIT:

1. Why does the government (at any level) get involved in healthcare or any business practice? Is there justification for government intervention?
2. If yes, how much and what types of intervention are justified?
3. What triggers those interventions?

The superficial answer to these questions is that the government recognizes the challenges that the healthcare field faces regarding cost, quality, and access to care. Further, the government has an obligation to intervene to provide access to high-quality, affordable care to all residents.

Justification for Government Intervention

The generic argument for government intervention is that the marketplace does not perform its normal function of optimizing resource-production efficiency and resource-allocation decision-making as classical economics theory suggests (Santerre and Neun 2004). As a result of the market's failure, government can—and some say should—intervene to fix the problem. Key reasons for intervention include problems with public goods, externalities, imperfect consumer information, and monopoly. Public goods are those that producers cannot easily exclude people from consuming, and consumption by one person does not reduce the availability for others to consume. A classic example is national defense, but medical research that leads to cures for disease is another. Externalities are costs or benefits related to a market action that parties not related to the transaction incur. For example, cigarette smoking may impose costs on those not involved in the decision to smoke. Imperfect information may give rise to government involvement in markets because people are concerned that profit-seeking businesses may take advantage of people's inability to make informed choices. In each of these cases, the market does not reliably provide the optimal quantity.

If the market fails to produce a good or service for any of these reasons, government is empowered to intervene in the public interest. Generally, the "fix" is to develop and implement policies that approximate what the market solution would generate, if possible. For healthcare, that intervention is justified because of asymmetric information between purchasers and providers and significant uncertainty about future need for services (Arrow 1963; Poterba 1996). However, some have argued that government interventions are designed to benefit those special interests that influence politicians rather that society as a whole (Blumenthal 2006; Feldstein 2015; Goldsmith, Blumenthal, and Rishel 2003; Kleinke 2005; Taylor et al. 2005).

Examples of the range of government intervention are included in exhibit 2.14. Correcting externalities has been one of the major reasons for government intervention. The Health Insurance Portability and Accountability Act (HIPAA), described later in this chapter, can be considered an intervention to force a market solution that would not occur without direct government support. Funding for medical research is a more traditional example of this type of intervention and is briefly described as it relates to funding for HIT. The other categories in the exhibit are not directly relevant to this book but are still worthy of note.

A significant amount of research in HIT has been funded by the federal government. A primary source of this funding for research and demonstration projects comes from the National Library of Medicine (NLM, www.nlm.nih.gov). The importance of the NLM to current initiatives and emerging features of HIT make it a major change agent. NLM aims to become a

EXHIBIT 2.14
Types of Government Market Intervention

Purpose	Government Initiative
Provide public goods	Funding of medical research
Correct for externalities	Tax on alcohol and cigarettes
Impose regulations	Federal Drug Administration
Enforce antitrust laws	Limit hospital mergers
Sponsor redistribution programs	Medicare and Medicaid
Operate public enterprises	Veterans Administration hospitals

Source: Reprinted from Feldstein (2001). Used with permission from Health Administration Press, Chicago.

platform for biomedical discovery and data-powered health. Enabling biomedical research, supporting healthcare and public health, and promoting healthy behavior constitute the NLM (2020) mission. Three pillars support this mission: "(1) innovating, building, and sustaining an open ecosystem for health information, biomedical data, and scientific scholarship, (2) optimizing user experience and use of our data, literature, and information resources, and (3) assuring a diverse and growing data-savvy biomedical workforce and data-ready users of NLM resources."

NLM enables open science and scholarship by ensuring that all constituents can find, access, and share all research objects (digital and nondigital). HIT leadership should be familiar with NLM funding priorities. Exhibit 2.15 presents the primary functions of the NLM. Assisting healthcare organizations

EXHIBIT 2.15
Primary Functions of the National Library of Medicine

- Acquiring, organizing, preserving, and providing free online access to scholarly biomedical literature from around the world.
- Providing access to biomedical and health information across the country in partnership with the over 6,400 members of the National Network of Libraries of Medicine.
- Serving as a leading global resource for building, curating, and providing sophisticated access to molecular biology, genomic, clinical trial, toxicological, environmental health and other types of biomedical data, including those from high-profile, trans-NIH [National Institutes of Health] initiatives.
- Conducting research and development on biomedical communications systems, methods, technologies, and networks and information dissemination and utilization among health professionals, patients, and the general public.
- Funding advanced biomedical informatics and data science research and serving as the primary supporter of pre- and post-doctoral research training in biomedical informatics and data science at 18 U.S. universities.

Source: Reprinted from NLM (2020).

with developing the data systems to support both their clinical operations and health services research is a major portion of the agency's charge. Using the justification for government intervention argument, the government funds these (and other) crucial activities because it believes that private organizations will not spend sufficiently on them. Further, the findings from these efforts will benefit the entire US healthcare system by enabling the development and testing of new technologies and infrastructure support.

Government Intervention in the Healthcare Field

For most industries, the government largely allows the market to determine costs, efficiency, quality, availability, and firm survival. With the exception of enforcing property rights and legal contracts, the government's role is minor.

Healthcare is different from other industries, however. The government gets involved in healthcare—and, by extension, HIT—because the government has a broad obligation to protect the health and welfare of the population. That obligation extends beyond ensuring that markets function and property rights are enforced (Feldstein 2015). Finding that the health of the population is at risk makes intervention to improve patient safety vital. Evidence that this risk is real comes from a series of prestigious studies, such as the IOM's 1999 and 2001 reports. Further, published estimates that nearly 50 million people are uninsured and many more are underinsured (DeNavas-Walt, Proctor, and Smith 2012) bring another call for government intervention. Lack of insurance affects the health of the population because this lack may actually lead to preventable morbidity and mortality (a negative health outcome), which in turn cost the US healthcare system more than $65 billion per year (Ayanian et al. 2000; IOM 2003).

As discussed earlier, healthcare costs have been rising rapidly both in absolute terms and relative to the GDP. These increases in cost are largely paid by governments; thus, budget considerations drive government interest as well. In 2017, 38.1 percent of total healthcare expenditures were paid by Medicare and Medicaid alone (CMS 2019). All levels of government have a major stake in payment rates. The conclusion is that quality, access, and cost provide a justification of the government's role in healthcare and thus in HIT. Attempts of government to accomplish this objective are mixed, and much of the political debate over healthcare reform centers on the appropriate role of government. For example, while expanding access was the goal of the ACA (discussed later), the legislation tried to overcome market forces by forcing insurers to offer insurance in costly markets and tried to force people to purchase insurance that they did not think that they needed (Cangero 2017).

Government and Business Practice

Given that government intervention can be justified, how much and what types of intervention are warranted? With respect to HIT, patient information privacy and security are the major foci of government intervention. The argument is that social interest in having patient healthcare information protected cannot be left to individual providers. Good business practice dictates that much of what comes under the guise of government intervention should be followed irrespective of the regulations. As addressed in detail in the next section, HIPAA has, among other features, enhanced privacy regulation. Because healthcare delivery organizations are responsible for the health and welfare of their patients, it only makes sense to adopt strict privacy standards even in the absence of government regulation. Therefore, information system managers in healthcare facilities must develop policies and procedures to protect the security of information contained in automated systems throughout the organization.

Government can extend into healthcare business practices in a number of potential ways. Goldsmith, Blumenthal, and Rishel (2003) argue for the need for government-sanctioned and government-supported standardization of, at least, communication protocols and nomenclature. Without a direct government role, healthcare organizations will adopt technology slowly and in a haphazard fashion. Blumenthal (2006) provides three business arguments justifying government intervention. First, no compelling business case exists for investment in HIT. Better performance is not routinely rewarded in healthcare, and, in fact, poor performance and providing more services generate greater revenue. The savings from implementing HIT do not go to providers but rather insurers and others. Second, for real system benefits to be seen, all components of the fragmented US healthcare delivery system must participate. Without this participation, benefits are incomplete. Interoperability among providers is a necessary step for true sharing to occur, and government needs to impose common communication standards. Third, fraud and abuse regulations do not allow physicians to receive subsidies from hospitals. Blumenthal (2006) makes a strong case for the failure of the market to achieve the desired results, and thus for the government to become more actively involved. HIT leadership must be aware of specific government interventions to manage their organization effectively.

The bottom line is that government has intervened in healthcare markets in significant ways, such as through HIPAA, the Health Information Technology for Economic and Clinical Health (HITECH) Act, and the ACA. The issue with regard to HIT intervention is still somewhat open, but a growing body of evidence suggests that HIT investment will have positive results (Buntin et al. 2011). Economic recovery funding through the HITECH Act implicitly assumes that this investment is good for quality and potentially for cost savings.

Specific Healthcare Legislations

Health Insurance Portability and Accountability Act

As an example of legislation that has had far-reaching effects on HIT, HIPAA has no equal. Begun as a mechanism to ensure that individuals could retain access to health insurance when they changed jobs (portability) (Flores and Dodier 2005; Schmeida 2005), HIPAA also contains a second provision called *administrative simplification* that has far greater impact (Assistant Secretary for Planning and Evaluation 1996; CMS 2020a): "The Administrative Simplification provisions of the Health Insurance Portability and Accountability Act of 1996 (HIPAA, Title II) required the HHS to establish national standards for electronic healthcare transactions and national identifiers for providers, health plans, and employers. It also addressed the security and privacy of health data. As the industry adopts these standards for the efficiency and effectiveness of the nation's healthcare system, the use of electronic data interchange will improve."

As this general provision indicates, HIPAA anticipated the development of electronic record keeping in healthcare. The healthcare field was not able internally to develop the standards and rules governing these new technologies for collecting, storing, and transmitting health information (another example of potential market failure mentioned earlier). Many realized that strict government controls would have to be put in place to enable healthcare providers to develop systems that met internal needs and facilitated the transfer of information across institutions (Blumenthal 2006; Goldsmith, Blumenthal, and Rishel 2003; Kleinke 2005). The electronic medium also raised concerns with security and privacy that the government felt it should address. In simple terms, administrative simplification involved setting standards, mandating health plan and provider compliance, and establishing privacy elements (CMS 2020a).

The complete text of HIPAA's Summary of Administrative Simplification Provisions is provided in exhibit 2.16. Each of the five provisions presented in the exhibit is important because of what it implies. While the translation of these broad provisions to policy details has evolved incrementally since the passage of HIPAA in 1996, the details emerge as a result of negotiations among all interested parties. Exhibit 2.17 shows the eight components of the administrative simplification provisions that were promulgated to meet the five provisions listed in exhibit 2.16.

The HIPAA overview reveals specific details of these standards and the timing of their implementation (CMS 2020a). Steps to achieving the goals of improving patient quality and enhancing efficiency through the use of electronic records were developed in stages. The first step was to make employers obtain a national identification number for healthcare

EXHIBIT 2.16
HIPAA's Summary of Administrative Simplification Provisions

Standards for electronic health information transactions. Within 18 months of enactment, the Secretary of HHS is required to adopt standards from among those already approved by private standards developing organizations for certain electronic health transactions, including claims, enrollment, eligibility, payment, and coordination of benefits. These standards also must address the security of electronic health information systems.

Mandate on providers and health plans, and timetable. Providers and health plans are required to use the standards for the specified electronic transactions 24 months after they are adopted. Plans and providers may comply directly, or may use a health care clearinghouse. Certain health plans, in particular workers compensation, are not covered.

Privacy. The Secretary is required to recommend privacy standards for health information to Congress 12 months after enactment. If Congress does not enact privacy legislation within 3 years of enactment, the Secretary shall promulgate privacy regulations for individually identifiable electronic health information.

Pre-emption of State Law. The bill supersedes state laws, except where the Secretary determines that the State law is necessary to prevent fraud and abuse, to ensure appropriate state regulation of insurance or health plans, addresses [*sic*] controlled substances, or for other purposes. If the Secretary promulgates privacy regulations, those regulations do not pre-empt state laws that impose more stringent requirements. These provisions do not limit a State's ability to require health plan reporting or audits.

Penalties. The bill imposes civil money penalties and prison for certain violations.

Note: Provisions in the original legislation have been modified by subsequent legislation, including the ACA.

Source: Reprinted from CMS (2020a).

EXHIBIT 2.17
Eight Major Components of HIPAA Administrative Simplification Provisions

1. Employer-identifier standard
2. Enforcement
3. National provider-identifier standard
4. Security standard
5. Transaction and code sets standard
6. Place-of-service codes for HIPAA transactions
7. Health insurance reform for consumers (HIPAA Title I)
8. Medicaid HIPAA administrative simplification

Source: Data from CMS (2020a).

transactions. Next, providers were required to have a commonly determined standard identifier—the National Provider Identifier (NPI). These rules set the stage for creating a regional or national data set of electronic information transmission by uniquely identifying the payer source and the provider. This seems insignificant when viewed from within a healthcare organization because they have always used unique numbers to identify patients and to keep patient records distinct. The NPI was novel when applied across organizations, however. The timing of the NPI mandate is current in relation to this discussion in that after May 23, 2007, "healthcare providers may only use their NPIs to identify themselves in standard transactions" (CMS 2020a).

Transactions and code set standards warrant additional commentary because they are vital to the effective implementation and use of the electronic record. The precise definition of these standards is also still in flux. According to CMS (2020a),

> Transactions are activities involving the transfer of healthcare information for specific purposes. Under the Health Insurance Portability & Accountability Act of 1996 (HIPAA), if a healthcare provider engages in one of the identified transactions, they must comply with the standard for that transaction. HIPAA requires every provider who does business electronically to use the same healthcare transactions, code sets, and identifiers. HIPAA has identified ten standard transactions for Electronic Data Interchange (EDI) for the transmission of healthcare data. Claims and encounter information, payment and remittance advice, and claims status and inquiry are several of the standard transactions. Code sets are the codes used to identify specific diagnosis and clinical procedures on claims and encounter forms. The HCPCS [Healthcare Common Procedure Coding System], CPT-4 [Current Procedural Terminology] and ICD-9 [International Classification of Diseases] codes with which providers are familiar, are examples of code sets for procedures and diagnoses.

This generic statement gives rise to an array of specific rules designed to enable organizations to collect data in a consistent manner. Unless everyone uses a common nomenclature for defining all clinical and administrative terms, there will be no capacity to communicate. *Interoperability* is the term that describes the goal to its fullest extent. To assist providers and others in this pursuit, CMS (2020a) provides information on their website that can be easily accessed and applied. In addition, CMS makes resources available to assist organizations in dealing with issues appropriate to their particular need. For example, there are resources organized by provider type and guidance topics, as well as broad categories such as administrative simplification, legislation, and regulations.

The Need for Information Privacy and Security

Without question, HIT incorporates sensitive information about patients and employees, financial and proprietary information about business units, and many other types of information that should be maintained securely with privacy controls. HIPAA has placed special emphasis on data security and privacy, and the implications of safeguarding privacy to HIT leadership are expansive.

To give some idea of the nature and extent of ongoing privacy and security issues, the *HIPAA Journal* (2018) documents, describes, and reports healthcare breaches. As of December 27, 2018, 351 data breaches involving 500 or more healthcare records were reported to the Department of Health and Human Services (Office for Civil Rights). The number of breaches did not increase much from 2017, but the number of records involved (more than 13 million) nearly doubled (from more than 5 million the year before). Eighteen breaches involved over 100,000 records and of these nine providers, three were health plans, and six were business associates. The challenges come from all directions. Further, 12 of the 18 breaches stemmed from hacking, while four involved unauthorized access, and one each for improper disposal and theft. Information security is a real challenge for HIT professionals. An examination of some of the major breaches that occurred in 2018 demonstrates the diversity:

- AccuDoc Solutions is a billing company that operates the online payment system used by a network of 44 hospitals in North Carolina, South Carolina, and Georgia. While the databases viewed could not be downloaded, the breach occurred over a seven-day period and involved the records of 2,652,537 patients.
- A UnityPoint Health hack originated as a phishing attack from multiple email accounts on March 14–April 3. A trusted executive's email account was spoofed, and several employees responded to the messages and disclosed their email credentials. The protected health information (PHI) of 1,421,107 individuals was compromised.
- The Employees Retirement System of Texas operated a flawed portal enabling outsiders to view the PHI of members after logging into the portal. Attributed to a coding error, as many as 1,248,263 individuals' PHI was potentially viewed by other health plan members.
- The California Department of Developmental Services experienced an office break-in that compromised information of employees, contractors, job applicants, parents of minors in the system, and the PHI of more than 500,000 patients.
- Tennessee-based MSK Group, PC, a network of orthopedic medical practices, determined that hackers accessed portions of their network

over multiple months. Hackers may have viewed or copied PHI and insurance information of over 500,000 patients.

- A division of CNO Financial Group, Inc., disclosed that hackers accessed their systems for about three and a half months starting at the end of May. Potentially, these hackers stole the personal information of over 500,000 individuals.
- Health Management Concepts discovered hackers installed ransomware on their servers and paid the attackers to unlock the encrypted files. Subsequently, the organization inadvertently provided the hackers with a file that contained the PHI of 502,416 individuals.
- St. Peter's Surgery & Endoscopy Center in New York disclosed that malware had been installed on one of its servers that compromised the PHI of 134,512 patients. The malware was discovered the same day it was installed.

Needless to say, ensuring the security of clinical information systems must be a top priority for healthcare leaders and HIT managers alike. The term *clinical information systems* encompasses the following types of health and healthcare records:

- *Patient care systems* include information technology used in the course of providing care, services, or treatments, such as order entry and results reporting; EHRs; and lab, pharmacy, and radiology systems. Data contained in these systems—including medical histories, medication lists, physician orders, diagnoses, treatment plans, and test results—are extremely private and thus should be accessible only to those involved in care delivery. Breach of security in this instance has legal and ethical ramifications for the healthcare delivery organization.
- *Public health information systems*, according to Stahl (2003), "support disease prevention and surveillance programs. Protecting public health requires the acquisition and storage of health-related information about individuals. Public health benefits sometimes conflict with threats to individual privacy. Individuals concerned about privacy who avoid clinical tests and treatments may endanger the health of others in the community." For example, a person with a sexually transmitted infection may opt to not test for or report the presence of the infection, which could then lead to the spread of the disease (Gostin, Hodge, and Valdiserri 2001). A security breach of public health information systems could lead to a person or groups facing discrimination in employment or insurance eligibility.
- *Medical research information systems* are repositories of medical diagnoses, health conditions, disease data, risk factors, and other health-related details culled from patient records. The purpose of such a system

is to enable clinical researchers and other investigators to understand disease risks, patterns, and contributing factors observed in a patient population. Lau and Catchpole (2001) emphasized the importance of respecting the patients' privacy rights as well as protecting the information contained in these systems by restricting access and use to authorized personnel.

Organizations must first attain compliance with HIPAA standards by doing the following:

- Developing a task force with appropriated charge.
- Installing a new compliance office or function dedicated to managing HIPAA-related challenges or assigning the responsibility to an existing office or function (e.g., CIO, medical records, risk management) to address or prevent issues (Marietti 2002).
- Using information system software designed by a vendor to meet the specific purpose, needs, and concerns identified by the organization. In this way, adhering to HIPAA guidelines helps repair existing programs, but some in-house work is required to ensure the applications interface with one another (Wilson and McPherson 2002).
- Implementing changes to some business processes and procedures. Marietti (2002, 55) projected that "80 percent to 85 percent of HIPAA compliance issues will depend on adjusting human behavior."
- Monitoring specified rules for misconceptions and legal rulings on operations (Litton 2017) such as the following:
  - Use of PHI for operational purposes is permitted as long as external entities are not involved in the delivery of care.
  - Phone number is not protected, but if it was collected as part of the patient intake, it becomes part of protected information.
  - If physicians leave an active practice, protected information does not automatically go with them.
  - Selling a practice provides limited allowances for the disclosure of protected information if done as a means of evaluating the practice.
  - Protected information can be shared with family members without permission under select crisis situations.

Following are some of the ways healthcare delivery organizations have maintained HIPAA standards of compliance (Stericycle 2017):

- Appointed a subject matter expert who reviews and updates policies, monitors compliance, and provides education

- Crafted relevant policies
- Observed how policies play out in practice
- Provided timely and appropriate education

Findings from studies of the HIPAA regulations have emerged. First, the immediate impact has been on the research community. Evidence suggests that HIPAA compliance makes recruitment and retention of subjects into research projects more difficult (Wipke-Tevis and Pickett 2008). Second, some specific examples now exist regarding how process improvements (e.g., automated access verification) can assist organizations to demonstrate compliance (Hill 2006). Third, the change process is still incomplete because privacy and security rules are being revised and updated frequently. The current status tries to establish protection of the privacy of subjects while at the same time giving researchers defined access to information with which to conduct vital research. Under select circumstances, investigators can use PHI from patients, but doing so is not a minor endeavor. There must be documentation that the internal review board has approved the request to use this information. Their decision must satisfy three criteria:

> 1. The use or disclosure of protected health information involves no more than a minimal risk to the privacy of . . . individuals;
>
> . . .
>
> 2. The research could not practicably be conducted without the waiver or alteration; and
> 3. The research could not practicably be conducted without access to and use of the protected health information. (HHS 2017)

A number of studies have examined the impact of privacy rules on healthcare organizations, giving rise to a set of inappropriate responses related to privacy (Upham and Dorsey 2007). Some concerns center on the application of privacy rules to other activities or innovations in healthcare. For example, in 2007, Paul Tang, then the chair of the board of the American Medical Informatics Association, indicated that EHR software vendors often included contract provisions that required providers to violate patient privacy standards (Conn 2007). Similarly, in the wake of mass tragedies, access to the perpetrator's health record often is cited as a reason to relax privacy constraints. Peel (2007) discussed this issue in the context of the Virginia Tech shooting in April 2007, in which a student killed 32 people. Peel concluded that relaxing privacy constraints was not likely to have prevented these events.

In 2012, James Holmes opened fire at an Aurora, Colorado, movie theater, killing 12 and injuring about 50 people. Prior to the shooting, Holmes was reportedly being seen by a mental health specialist at the

University of Colorado, where Holmes was a student (Meyer and Ingold 2012). The specialist contacted a university threat-assessment team but did not invoke a "72-hour psychiatric hold" because Holmes was leaving the university. Under pressure from news sources that were trying to piece together the events that led up to the tragedy, the University of Colorado released thousands of emails related to Holmes. However, the university did not make available any records or documents related to the crime or Holmes's mental health status (Meyer and Ingold 2012). As consumers continue to provide information over the internet, the collection, availability, and security of their data will remain a major concern (Nelson 2006).

At the level of information sharing across organizations was a study commissioned by the California Healthcare Foundation to look at privacy from the perspective of developing regional health information organizations (RHIOs). The study was trying to determine what needed to be done at the systems level to facilitate RHIO development. It resulted in a number of findings and substantial recommendations on developing and implementing security policies for RHIOs. The analyses identified the following four key questions that must be addressed to develop privacy policies (Rosenfeld, Koss, and Siler 2007):

1. Who will have access to patient information?
2. Which information will be accessible?
3. What are acceptable purposes of patient information exchange?
4. What circumstances justify patient information exchange?

In addition, the study reported a number of common elements that are important to consider in developing privacy policies across organizational entities, including the following:

- Privacy policies are local.
- Organizations participating in the RHIO influence the privacy policies.
- Privacy policies need to be developed early and revisited often.
- Work on privacy policies is ongoing.
- Privacy policies are unique to the environment.
- Building consensus on privacy policies takes time.
- The consumer role in privacy policy development is limited.

HIPAA was not the first effort by the government to assure the public that the privacy of an individual's medical information would be secure. The Privacy Act of 1974 established key provisions to protect the privacy of patients (CMS 2020a). Enacted before the conception of EHRs prevalent today, the legislation protected all patient records with "personal identifiers" (e.g.,

Social Security number). Under the Privacy Act, every patient can access and, if necessary, correct their individual records, and it generally prohibits disclosure of these records—but that right applied only to records maintained by federal agencies.

The individual's right to genetic privacy was also addressed in Oregon's Genetic Privacy Act of 1995, which provides legal protection for medical information, tissue samples, and DNA samples. Harris and Keywood (2001, 415) pointed out that individuals "have a powerful interest in genetic privacy and its associated claim to ignorance"; however, "any claims to be shielded from information about the self must compete on equal terms with claims based in the rights and interests of others." Further, Cummings and Magnusson (2001, 1089) stated that "as genetic privacy legislation is developed and enacted at state and federal levels, the needs of individuals must be balanced with the needs of institutions and of research in the larger context of societal needs."

Currently, the ACA has increased the rigor of the HIPAA rules by requiring a unique health plan identifier and establishing standards and rules for financial transactions.

Health Information Technology for Economic and Clinical Health Act

President Obama signed the American Recovery and Reinvestment Act (ARRA) in February 2009. This comprehensive stimulus package was designed to address the 2007–2009 economic crisis. ARRA contains many provisions, including tax relief (federal); unemployment benefit expansion; social welfare spending; and spending for specific sectors such as energy, education, and healthcare. The healthcare spending is also diverse, allocating funds or subsidies for Medicaid, health research and construction, benefits for the newly uninsured, prevention and wellness, and research on the effectiveness of healthcare treatments, among many other provisions.

A major part of ARRA is called the Health Information Technology for Economic and Clinical Health (HITECH) Act. It is designed to promote the expansion of the EHR because of its perceived social benefits. A total of about $22 billion was allocated to the HITECH Act, with the bulk ($19.2 billion) devoted directly to EHR adoption. An additional $2 billion went to the Office of the National Coordinator for Health Information Technology (ONCHIT 2011) to support the agency's varied activities for promoting information exchange, training health professionals for information technology, and enhancing interoperability. ONCHIT is the body responsible for implementing the incentives for EHR use and establishing an HIT Policy Committee and an HIT Standards Committee. These committees are charged with developing recommendations for adopting health information infrastructure and standards for information exchange, respectively (HealthIT.gov 2020).

Adoption of Electronic Health Records

From a broad social perspective, and consistent with our earlier justification for government intervention, the benefits of the meaningful use of EHRs include the following:

- Complete and accurate information
- Better access to information
- Patient empowerment

One can argue whether the government or private sector is better at realizing these goals, but some opine that the benefits of sharable electronic information accrue to society at large and thus cannot be fully captured by any private provider or organization. Consequently, investing in this public good can be warranted. The evidence now, however, points to a positive and statistically significant impact on the adoption of EHRs as a result of the HITECH Act. In fact, examining adoption rates before and after the implementation of the incentive to attain meaningful use, Adler-Milstein and Jha (2017) found that adoption rates went from 3.2 percent per year to 14.2 percent per year for hospitals subject to the incentives. For hospitals not receiving the incentives, the adoption also increased, but by much less.

Meaningful Use

The HITECH Act provided the authority to make changes that can improve healthcare quality, safety, and efficiency through the use of EHRs and the exchange of electronic health information. ONCHIT has released regulations to define appropriate standards for the certification of EHR technologies and the means by which providers could receive financial incentives to adopt and use those systems (see www.healthit.gov/topic/certification-ehrs/certification-health-it for specifications and www.healthit.gov/topic/federal-incentive-programs/MACRA/merit-based-incentive-payment-system for rewards). An example of one of the many features of the HITECH Act is the Meaningful Use provision, which offered incentives to organizations that adopted and implemented EHRs. The underlying assumption is that EHRs can provide benefits to providers and patients. The benefits may not be realized, however, without sufficient intensity of use. Consequently, CMS developed a set of standards called *Meaningful Use*. These standards allowed hospitals and individual providers deemed eligible to obtain incentive payments by meeting specific criteria; the incentives for adoption by clinical professionals were substantial. While important to the process that led us to our current place, Meaningful Use incentives are no longer available. The goals of meaningful use remain but are now a part of the Merit-Based Incentive Payment System (MIPS) that we discuss below.

Although the Meaningful Use framework is gone, the underlying elements still exist. For example, providers were required to attain levels or stages of Meaningful Use, and the government specified specific core measures that defined attainment of any stage. The HIT requirement for Meaningful Use was clearly detailed in stage 1. Eligible providers needed to report providing all 15 core measures, a choice of 5 out of 10 menu objectives, and 6 clinical quality measures. By stage 3, the required reporting had evolved to 8 core areas of capacity as detailed in exhibit 2.18.

The implementation of stage 3 was supposed to span from 2015 to 2017. Because a new administration was elected during that time, Meaningful Use changed substantially. The Meaningful Use program, now "Promoting Interoperability," eliminated many quality measures (39 in total), including a structural safety measure, the Safe Surgery Checklist. A number of measures were removed that directly assessed the quality of patient care (Boskey 2020). It will take some time to determine whether these changes impact quality of care.

Currently, MIPS and its many components have largely replaced Meaningful Use for reporting. The goal of MIPS and its components are the same with regard to using information technology to improve patient care (HealthIT.gov 2019).

21st Century Cures Act

The 21st Century Cures Act (Food and Drug Administration 2018) was passed into law on December 13, 2016. While aimed more at clinical care, it has an indirect impact on HIT. The act expanded the ability of the Food and Drug Administration (FDA) to speed products and services to market. The concern was that the review process inhibited the dissemination of innovations and advances of potentially life-saving technology. Specifically, it aimed formally to bring the perspectives of patients into the review and approval process. Innovations such as regenerative medicine advanced therapy and breakthrough devices can now reach patients more rapidly.

For HIT, this pace implies a more rapid expansion of clinical diagnostic and therapeutic tools coming online and expansion of use of the tools. Further, because many of these advances are less established, clinicians and investigators will apply greater monitoring and scrutiny of subjects, side effects, and outcomes. Clinicians will apply these fast-tracked applications only to specific types of patients through highly restricted protocols. Further, some of these more rapid applications will not be effective, thus information technology departments will be required to set up warnings should they be withdrawn or modified.

Medicare Access and CHIP Reauthorization Act of 2015

The Medicare Access and CHIP Reauthorization Act (MACRA) also had an impact on HIT. The legislation first and foremost ended the sustainable growth rate formulas. This historic item had the potential to

EXHIBIT 2.18
Stage 3 Core Measures for CMS Meaningful Use

1. Protect Electronic Patient Health Information (ePHI) created or maintained by the Certified EHR Technology (CEHRT) through the implementation safeguards. Meaningful use stage 3 added a requirement to conduct or review security risks and update encryption as necessary. This must include a risk analysis, implementation of updates and rectification of flaws.
2. Electronic Prescribing: Providers must submit 60+ percent of prescriptions electronically and hospitals and others must transmit at least 25 percent of medication orders electronically.
3. Implement Clinical Decision Support: Five clinical decision support applications and both drug-drug and drug-allergy interactions must be implemented.
4. Use Computerized Provider Order Entry: At least 60 percent of orders for medication, laboratory and diagnostic imaging must use computerized provider order entry.
5. Provide Patient Health Information: Most (80 percent) of unique patients must be given timely online information that they can download or transmit. Further, patient-specific education resources must be made available to no less than 35 percent of unique patients.
6. Patient Engagement and Care Coordination: Extensive use of electronic health record to fully engage patients with 10 percent viewing, downloading or transmitting health information, 25 percent receiving electronic messages, and 5 percent of patient generated data must be integrated into record.
7. Health Information Exchange (HIE): More than half of patient transitions and referrals must receive an electronic summary record from the host provider, 40 percent of receiving providers must incorporate summary into patient health record and for 80 percent of transitions, referrals received and new patients the provider must perform a clinical information reconciliation for medication, allergies and the current problem list.
8. Public Health and Clinical Data Registry Reporting: Provider must submit data to public health agency or clinical data registry for the following: immunization, syndromic surveillance, case reporting, public health registry, clinical data registry and electronic reportable laboratory results.

Source: Hayes (2015).

reduce payment to physicians and had been put off for a long time. Ending the program may have reduced stress in the C-suite, but it did not directly impact information technology. MACRA also authorized the Quality Payment Program as part of a move to reward quality over volume (CMS

2020b). Generally, this change shifted the emphasis to the data collected on patients and forced greater linkages among quality metrics, patient characteristics, and patient resource utilization. Under the program, CMS created the Advanced Alternative Payment Models (APMs) and MIPS. APMs reward providers for high-quality and efficient care of Medicare patients if selected to participate in an APM. The decisions to receive the incentive and enter the program create a demand for timely and accurate information, which in turn affects HIT. MIPS similarly set up a structure to reward providers for quality outcomes. Together, these spawned a host of related legislation and program initiatives aimed at the same objective. Exhibit 2.19 presents key legislative and program-sponsored initiatives from the CMS website.

Food and Drug Administration Safety and Innovation Act of 2012

In a slightly different direction, the Food and Drug Administration Safety and Innovation Act of 2012 has had substantial repercussions on HIT. This legislation ordered ONCHIT, the Federal Communications Commission, and the FDA to propose a "strategy and recommendations on an appropriate, risk-based regulatory framework for HIT, including medical mobile applications, that promotes innovation, protects patient safety, and avoids regulatory duplication." The resulting report from these three agencies (ONCHIT 2014) presents an outline of progress, impediments, and a plan for going forward. It is likely that these agencies working together will become the source of HIT operational changes in the years ahead. The specifics will unfold with time but the goal remains constant.

EXHIBIT 2.19 Timeline of Value-Based Programs

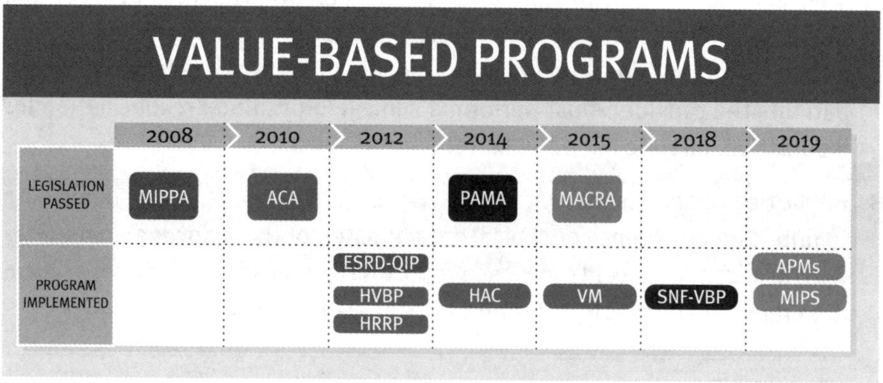

Notes: ACA = Affordable Care Act; APMs = alternative payment models; ESRD-QIP = End-Stage Renal Disease Quality Incentive Program; HACRP = Hospital-Acquired Condition Reduction Program; HRRP = Hospital Readmissions Reduction Program; HVBP = Hospital Value-Based Purchasing Program; MACRA = Medicare Access and CHIP Reauthorization Act of 2015; MIPPA = Medicare Improvements for Patients and Providers Act; MIPS = Merit-Based Incentive Payment System; PAMA = Protecting Access to Medicare Act; SNF-VBP = Skilled Nursing Facility Value-Based Purchasing Program; VM = Value Modifier or Physician Value-Based Modifier (PVBM).
Source: CMS (2020b).

Specific priorities developed and presented in this report include the following:

- Promoting the use of quality management principles
- Identifying, developing, and adopting standards and best practices
- Leveraging conformity assessment tools
- Creating an environment of learning and continual improvement (ONCHIT 2014)

Further, their approach focuses on minimizing regulatory intervention by building capacity in the private sector and creating a culture of continuous improvement in the use of HIT. In their words, they propose to rely on "ONC[HIT]-coordinated activities and private sector capabilities." As an example, development of a culture of safety and quality supplants the need for added oversight by the FDA. The industry can capitalize on the culture of safety, employ internal testing and certification, and implement tools for developing a transparent learning environment that strives for continual HIT improvement. These nice words imply that the onus of healthcare quality and safety will fall on those in the field using the technologies for patient care. While less regulation generally garners approval by industry, with less regulation comes more responsibility.

Affordable Care Act

No single legislation in the past several years represents the government's attempt to address a host of social problems in healthcare more than the ACA. Signed on March 23, 2010, HR 3590 and the accompanying HR 4872 (Health Care and Education Reconciliation Act of 2010) proposed historic changes to the US healthcare delivery and financing system. Designed to expand coverage, the ACA contains a host of provisions with both short-term and far-reaching implications. Because of its size, however, most individuals and groups tend to focus only on the provisions important to them. It has since become a text with extensive detail (McLaughlin 2015). Further, the Kaiser Family Foundation (2013) issued a comprehensive overview designed to assist all readers to fully understand the scope of the legislation.

- Expand coverage
  - Individual mandate for all citizens to have insurance
  - Most employers required to offer insurance
- Expand public programs
  - Income-based expansion of public programs, but Supreme Court ruled that states could opt out
  - Expand Children's Health Insurance Program

- Premiums and cost sharing
  - Premium credits and subsidies provided to limit insurance cost for low-income individuals, figured as proportion of income
- Tax changes related to health insurance or financing health reform
  - Tax on individuals with no insurance
  - Limit flexible spending accounts to $2,500
  - Increase threshold for itemized deductions to $10,000
  - Increase Medicare Part A contribution to 2.35 percent of income
  - Tax on high-cost health insurance
  - Fees on pharmaceutical companies and health insurance companies
- Health insurance exchanges
  - Established by state or by federal governments
- Benefit design
  - Define essential benefits necessary in insurance offering
- Changes to private insurance
  - Create high-risk pools
  - Establish medical loss ratios for insurers
- Cost control
- Investment in quality
  - Patient-Centered Outcomes Research Institute funds further research
  - Bundled payments
  - Medical malpractice reform
- Prevention and wellness
- Long-term care
- Miscellaneous investments
  - Workforce training
  - Public health and disaster preparedness

Many of the ACA features cause stress for HIT, but the following deserve special mention. First, ACOs assign responsibility (accountability) to the organization for patients who may not obtain all or even most of their care from the host organization (Kaiser Permanente 2012; Miller 2009). Finding the patient, effectively exchanging information with other providers, and ensuring the privacy and confidentiality of that information outside of organizational boundaries are a challenge. That information is exchanged both ways, so even if the institution is not sponsoring an ACO, it may be asked to provide clinical information on select patients.

Second, pay-for-performance initiatives demand greater linkages between provider cost and clinical performance than is customary (Rosenthal and Camillus 2007; Rosenthal and Dudley 2007). Management across organizational boundaries is put to the test as clinical (chief medical officers and chief nursing officers) and financial (chief financial officers) leaders demand accurate and timely data for evaluation, improvement, and contracting purposes (see chapter 4).

Third, expansion of covered lives is taxing to HIT in a number of ways. Having more patients can be a minor stressor, but (depending on current capacity) sufficient volume growth might require added facilities. In addition, at least some new patients are likely to be unfamiliar with the delivery system and thus less compliant with completing forms and documentation necessary to manage the care process. Further, some added patients may be "sicker" and may present new problems to the clinicians, testing the provider's documentation, coding quality, and select systems in unforeseen ways.

Fourth, as Gawande (2010) pointed out, there is a host of pushback efforts to the ACA as there was to Medicare and Medicaid decades before, which emphasizes Gawande's argument that "the battle for health-care reform has only begun." More than any individual ACA feature causing concern for HIT leadership, the timing of implementation is highly uncertain. Planning for an unknown future makes life difficult for HIT management, but that may justify the salary that HIT leadership receives.

As a current example, challenges to the ACA have been fought in the courts. Musumeci (2020) summarizes this nicely. In essence, a number of states challenged the ACA based upon the constitutionality of the individual mandate or the provision that everyone must acquire health insurance or pay a fine (called the shared responsibility payment). Further, they argued that if the individual mandate is unconstitutional, then the entire law is unconstitutional because of severability (one provision brings down the entire law). The individual mandate was held to be constitutional by the Supreme Court in 2012, but severability was not determined. There are a number of detailed elements in this argument, but that is the core.

Subsequent to the 2012 Supreme Court decision, Congress passed the Tax Cuts and Jobs Act in 2017, which set the shared responsibility payment to zero. The government cannot extract payment from individuals who do not have insurance. That change made the individual mandate unconstitutional. Consequently, 18 state plaintiffs, along with two individuals, are asking the court to declare the entire ACA unconstitutional. Defending the ACA are 17 states, led by California and the US House of Representatives. The Supreme Court is due to hear arguments in fall 2020 and to hand down a decision in spring 2021.

Health Information Technology Leadership Roles

While government involvement through HIPAA, the HITECH Act, and the ACA may seem difficult for information technology specialists to fully understand, it is particularly baffling for those outside of HIT. The consequence of this difficulty is that HIT leadership (e.g., CIO, CEO) is required to understand, anticipate, and explain the impact of these legislations. They must be prepared for new government regulations and policies, and changes to existing regulations and policies, by developing and then implementing a number of activities and programs, including comprehensive environmental scanning and organizational education, information security policies and procedures, disaster preparedness and recovery planning, and information privacy and confidentiality protection.

Environmental Scanning and Organizational Education

The first responsibility of HIT leadership is to understand fully the operational and resource implications of all legislations. Internally, the team must understand what it must do differently as a result of the law and determine what extra staffing, expertise (consultants), hardware and software, and time are needed. The six steps for this activity are as follows:

1. Determine the breadth and scope of impending or current legislation
2. Assess current organizational readiness for the impact
3. Perform a gap analysis within the organization
4. Recommend strategies to meet legal and regulatory changes
    a. Develop staffing and critical expertise needed to address changes
    b. Specify hardware and software needs
    c. Estimate total financial implications of the recommendations
5. Identify clinical and other resources in the organization that are necessary to meet the standards
6. Outline a timeline for implementation with key dates and milestones

Naturally, HIT departments may encounter difficulty in effectively accomplishing these tasks once the legislation is in place and the deadlines are looming. Consequently, HIT leadership should be constantly monitoring the horizon for proposed legislation to get a head start on planning for its passage. To do this, HIT leadership should be engaged with those responsible for legislative affairs within the organization (if such a role exists). Getting a heads-up from this source is vital. State and national associations—such as the Healthcare Information and Management Systems Society, American College of Healthcare Executives, Healthcare Financial Management Association, and the American Hospital Association, among many others—are good sources of these early data.

A body of literature is available as well that documents the many and varied impacts of HIPAA, the HITECH Act, and the ACA. It is important for HIT leadership, either directly or through surrogates, to monitor and stay up-to-date on this literature. For example, Houser, Houser, and Shewchuk

(2007) use the nominal group technique (NGT) for gathering information regarding the impact of HIPAA privacy rules on the release of patient information. "The NGT approach is a consumer-oriented formal brainstorming or idea-generating technique that is assumed to foster creativity and to be particularly effective in helping group members articulate meaningful disclosures in response to specific questions" (Houser, Houser, and Shewchuk 2007, 2).

Because the nature of legislation can be highly complex, HIT leadership should be prepared to educate senior leadership on the implications of these regulatory interventions. Senior leadership includes the CEO, as well as the chief operating officer (if the organization has that position), chief medical officer, chief nursing officer, and chief financial officer. Generally, the person responsible for strategic planning, the head of the legal department, the head of human resources, and the head of development should be educated also in HIT-related legislative matters.

Information Security Policies and Procedures

Healthcare organizations must establish enterprise-wide standards to maintain data security and protect the privacy and confidentiality of information, particularly patient records. Data security involves two essential elements: (1) protecting against system failures or external catastrophic events, such as fires, storms, deliberate sabotage, and other destructive acts of humans and nature that could result in critical information being lost; and (2) controlling access to computer files by unauthorized personnel.

Disaster Preparedness and Recovery Planning

The HIT steering committee must ensure that effective data backup and recovery procedures are implemented at all processing sites throughout the organization. Critical data files should be copied to removable disk packs or tapes and stored in a secure location away from the processing sites, preferably in a different building. The CIO should develop a data backup plan for approval by the steering committee. The plan should specify which files require duplication and how often backup procedures should be conducted. Recovery procedures to be used if catastrophic events occur should also be included.

The need for disaster planning has been justified by numerous well-publicized natural and human-initiated disasters, including hurricanes, floods, wildfires, and mass shootings. All types of disasters stress local healthcare systems from a service continuity perspective, and HIT often is compromised, but is a key resource in disaster management. Disaster plans must be implemented, tested periodically, and refined. Testing of the plan provides training for employees and helps identify shortcomings in technology and procedures before they need to be used. A disaster plan document, in both digital and hard media, should be developed and stored at the healthcare facility, at an off-site storage location, and at the homes of key employees who are involved in recovery procedures (Vecchio 2000). Covid-19's spread throughout the world provided an evolving and substantial challenge. Healthcare facilities in China were overwhelmed—a situation that is likely to occur in the United States and other countries as well (Jacobs and Fink 2020).

Consultants can be used to assist in disaster planning and recovery. For example, IRM International offers a disaster recovery program that includes four phases: assessment, documentation consolidation, disaster plan development, and testing and refinement. See www.irminternational.com/rptcard.html for a disaster recovery report card that rates disaster planning readiness.

In addition, data can be lost through computer viruses, which are increasingly prevalent and destructive. Each computer program should be inspected by virus protection software every time the program is run. Acquisition of software should be subject to central review and approval, and particular care must be exercised to ensure that software downloaded from the internet or obtained over networks is scanned and proven to be virus free. All incoming email messages should be scanned for viruses, and employees should be trained not to open suspicious files attached to an email, text, or any other electronic communication.

Information Privacy and Confidentiality Protection

As suggested in the earlier discussion related to HIPAA, the HITECH Act, and the ACA, protecting information privacy and confidentiality should be a major concern of HIT leadership. A comprehensive information security policy should include three elements: (1) physical security, (2) technical controls over access, and (3) management policies that are well known and enforced in all organizational units (Stahl 2003) (see exhibit 2.20).

The specifics of these three major aspects of information security evolve over time, but the fundamental areas of vulnerability and concern remain. Because of the expanding role of government in incentivizing and supporting HIT adoption, some useful tools now exist in the open domain. ONCHIT 2015 is a comprehensive document that spells out the reasons for

EXHIBIT 2.20 Components of Information Security

Physical Security	Technical Safeguards	Management Policies
Hardware	Passwords	Written security policy
Data files	Encryption	Employee training
	Audit logs	Disciplinary actions for violations

and steps to develop privacy and security safeguards. It is vital to understand why privacy and security matter, your responsibilities, and patient rights, and to realize how existing regulatory rules shape your actions. ONCHIT provides a seven-step guide:

1. Lead your culture, select your team and learn.
2. Document process, findings, and actions.
3. Perform security risk analysis (see www.healthit.gov/topic/privacy-security-and-hipaa/security-risk-assessment-videos).
4. Develop an action plan.
5. Manage and mitigate risk.
6. Attest meaningful use.
7. Monitor, audit, and update your security plan.

The report also contains links to many other supportive resources.

Understanding the processes of information privacy and confidentiality is a necessary step to successful implementation at the systems level. While the past decade offers many examples of how individual systems have accomplished these goals, evidence indicates that many organizations are still not compliant with basic security standards (Kwon and Johnson 2013). Some in the healthcare field have called for systematic incentives from the healthcare field or from insurers to induce organizations to adopt privacy and security technology (e.g., Lang 2006). Despite substantial improvements, however, violations of basic privacy rights by hospitals and other providers are still a challenge (Hiltzik 2012). For an up-to-date list of privacy rule violations and settlements, see www.hhs.gov/ocr/newsroom/index.html.

Summary

Change is occurring rapidly in healthcare. While much of that change will be internal to the technologies and processes in healthcare delivery organizations, much will be derived from forces external to the organization and even external to the United States. Major forces of change that have a direct impact on the application of HIT include the healthcare triangle or specific challenges with healthcare costs, quality, and access. The impact of these forces is seen in the growth of evidence-based management for decision-making, the need for healthcare organizational change, and greater emphasis on international comparisons for performance assessment.

Because these market changes influence such a vital component of the US economy and the private sector has not fully addressed the challenges, the government has intervened in a number of ways. Many regulations and policies affect all aspects of healthcare delivery, but this chapter focused on HIPAA, HITECH, 21st Century Cures, MACRA, the FDASIA, and the ACA. Each of these interrelated items of healthcare policy and regulation have direct and indirect effects on those responsible for managing HIT. These pieces of legislation are also in flux as political forces continue to push back or extend their original intent. These environmental trends present challenges to healthcare leaders overall, but to HIT leadership particularly. Addressing the healthcare triangle must involve improved access to and use of health information and HIT. These challenges involve not only internal operational responses but also the need to interface with organizations and agencies outside of the host institution. Hospitals, physician practices, and other elements of the provider network must learn to gather, store, retrieve, and analyze information more efficiently. Organizational leaders are learning to use data as evidence in making decisions; thus, they will demand more reliable and valid data, presented in understandable formats and in a timely manner. Further, information from external organizations (regionally and nationally) will need to be integrated and made available to those clinical and administrative decision makers as the decision frameworks expand. Finally, comparisons and competition from international providers may enlarge the scope of the information required.

Web Resources

A number of organizations (through their websites) provide more information on the topics discussed in this chapter:

- The American Health Quality Association (www.ahqa.org) is a national membership organization that promotes and facilitates fundamental changes designed to improve the quality of healthcare.
- The American Society for Quality (http://asq.org/index.aspx) is a global organization that focuses on using tools and ideas to make the world better.
- The Agency for Healthcare Research and Quality has a vast quantity of publications and research related to HIT, quality and safety, and other key topics (www.ahrq.gov/programs/index.html?search_api_views_fulltext=&field_program_topics=14176).
- The Commonwealth Fund (www.commonwealthfund.org/topics) has the broad charge to "enhance the common good." Its mission is to improve access, quality, and efficiency in the healthcare system with special emphasis on low-income people, the uninsured, members of racial and ethnic minorities, young children, and the elderly. You will

find details of healthcare reform efforts related to the ACA and updates on efforts to repeal this legislation.

- The Henry J. Kaiser Family Foundation is a leader in health policy analysis and communication dedicated to providing a trusted, independent analysis of key policy issues. While it has many key agenda items, cost and coverage are central to its work. Its research is a great source of data and analysis. Its website, www.kff.org, includes a great deal of information on the impact of the ACA.
- The Health and Medicine Division (HMD), a part of the National Academies of Sciences, Engineering, and Medicine that was formerly the IOM (www.nationalacademies.org/hmd/About-HMD.aspx), is an independent, nonprofit organization that provides authoritative advice to decision makers and the public on healthcare issues. With a strong clinical focus, IOM has specific initiatives in coverage and access to care as well as quality and patient safety.
- The National Quality Measures Clearinghouse (www.qualitymeasures.ahrq.gov/index.aspx) is a source of comprehensive information on quality measures for healthcare.
- The Office of the National Coordinator for Health Information Technology (ONCHIT) (www.healthit.gov/) is a primary source of all information related to HIT.
- The Robert Wood Johnson Foundation (www.rwjf.org/en/about-rwjf.html) is a large philanthropic organization devoted to the public's health. Among its many topics are cost, quality, and access to care (www.rwjf.org/en/our-focus-areas/focus-areas/health-systems.html). They also have a focus on healthcare leadership (www.rwjf.org/en/our-focus-areas/focus-areas/health-leadership.html).
- The US Department of Health and Human Services' "HIPAA for Professionals" (www.hhs.gov/hipaa/for-professionals/index.html) contains many resources related to HIPAA, including links to legal and regulatory information.

Discussion Questions

1. Why do national concerns about the cost and quality of care, and access to care, affect those responsible for managing information systems in healthcare institutions?
2. What information would you assemble for healthcare leadership in your organization to monitor healthcare cost, quality, and access? Would that differ if you worked in a hospital versus a physician practice or other organization?

3. What organizational challenges do you anticipate with the changes necessary to control cost, improve quality, and expand access in your organization?
4. How much synthesis of external information will be necessary for effective evidence-based management? Who is best able to provide that synthesis?

References

Adler-Milstein, J., and A. Jha. 2017. "HITECH Act Drove Large Gains in Hospital Electronic Health Record Adoption." *Health Affairs* 35 (8): 1416–22.

Agha, L. 2014. "The Effects of Health Information Technology on the Costs and Quality of Medical Care." *Journal of Health Economics* 34: 19–30.

Alotaibi, Y., and F. Federico. 2017. "The Impact of Health Information Technology on Patient Safety." *Saudi Medical Journal* 38 (12): 1173–80.

American College of Healthcare Executives. 2016. "Access to Healthcare." Revised November. www.ache.org/about-ache/our-story/our-commitments/policy-statements/access-to-affordable-healthcare.

Anderson, G., B. Frogner, R. Johns, and U. Reinhardt. 2006. "Health Care Spending and Use of Information Technology in OECD Countries." *Health Affairs* 25 (3): 819–31.

Antonisse, L., R. Garfield, R. Rudowitz, and M. Guth. 2019. "The Effects of Medicaid Expansion under the ACA: Updated Findings from a Literature Review." Kaiser Family Foundation. Published August 15. www.kff.org/medicaid/issue-brief/the-effects-of-medicaid-expansion-under-the-aca-updated-findings-from-a-literature-review-august-2019.

Appari, A. E., E. Carian, E. Johnson, and D. Anthony. 2012. "Medication Administration Quality and Health Information Technology: A National Study of US Hospitals." *Journal of the American Medical Informatics Association* 19: 360–67.

Aron, D., and L. Pogach. 2009. "Transparency Standards for Diabetes Performance Measures." *Journal of the American Medical Association* 301: 210–12.

Arrow, K. 1963. "Uncertainty and the Welfare Economics of Medical Care." *American Economic Review* 52: 941–73.

Assistant Secretary for Planning and Evaluation. 1996. "Health Insurance Portability and Accountability Act of 1996. Summary of Administrative Simplification Provisions." US Department of Health and Human Services. Published August 21. https://aspe.hhs.gov/report/health-insurance-portability-and-accountability-act-1996/summary-administrative-simplification-provisions.

Ayanian, J. Z., J. S. Weissman, E. C. Schneider, J. A. Ginsburg, and A. M. Zaslavsky. 2000. "Unmet Health Needs of Uninsured Adults in the United States." *Journal of the American Medical Association* 284 (16): 2061–69.

Baicker, K., and A. Chandra. 2004. "Medicare Spending, the Physician Workforce, and Beneficiaries' Quality of Care." *Health Affairs.* Accessed January 7, 2020. www.healthaffairs.org/doi/full/10.1377/hlthaff.w4.184.

Baron, R. 2007. "Quality Improvement with an Electronic Health Record: Achievable, but Not Automatic." *Annals of Internal Medicine* 147: 549–52.

Baucus, M. 2005. "Looking at the U.S. Healthcare System in the Rear-View Mirror." *Health Affairs.* Accessed January 7, 2020. www.healthaffairs.org/doi/full/10.1377/hlthaff.W5.544.

Black, A., J. Car, C. Pagliari, C. Anandan, K. Cresswell, T. Bokum, B. McKinstry, R. Procter, A. Majeed, and A. Sheik. 2011. "The Impact of eHealth on the Quality and Safety of Health Care: A Systematic Overview." *PLoS Medicine* 8 (1): e1000387.

Blumenthal, D. 2006. *Health Information Technology: What Is the Federal Government's Role?* Published March 1. www.commonwealthfund.org/publications/fund-reports/2006/mar/health-information-technology-what-federal-governments-role.

Book, E. L. 2005. "Health Insurance Trends Are Contributing to Growing Healthcare Inequality." *Health Affairs.* Accessed January 7, 2020.

Bigalke, J., W. Copeland, and P. Keckley. 2011. "I'm OK, You're OK . . . But Will We Be All Right?" *DeLoitte Review.* Accessed February 21, 2020. www2.deloitte.com/content/dam/insights/us/articles/im-ok-youre-ok-but-will-we-be-all-right-innovations-in-addressing-health-care-reform/US_deloittereview_Im_Okay_Youre_Okay_But_Will_We_Be_All_Right_Jul11.pdf.

Boskey, E. 2020. "An Overview of Meaningful Use Stage 3: The Final Phase of Electronic Health Incentives." Verywellhealth. Updated on January 30. www.verywellhealth.com/meaningful-use-stage-three-4589798.

Bradley, C., D. Neumark, L. Shickle, and N. Farrell. 2008. "Differences in Breast Cancer Diagnosis and Treatment: Experiences of Insured and Uninsured Women in a Safety Net Setting." *Inquiry* 45 (3): 323–39.

Buntin, M., M. Burke, M. Hoaglin, and D. Blumenthal. 2011. "The Benefits of Information Technology: A Review of the Recent Literature Shows Predominantly Positive Results." *Health Affairs* 30 (3): 464–71.

Cangero, T. 2017. "Government Intervention in Health Insurance Falls Short." American Institute for Economic Research. Published June 9. www.aier.org/article/government-intervention-in-health-insurance-falls-short.

Center for Healthcare Organization and Implementation Research. 2006. "A Paradigm Shift for Managers and Researchers: Evidence-Based Management." Accessed December 28, 2007. www.colmr.research.va.gov/mgmt_research_in_va/framework/evidence.cfm.

Centers for Medicare & Medicaid Services (CMS). 2020a. "Regulation and Guidance." Updated February 11. www.cms.gov/Regulations-and-Guidance/Regulations-and-Guidance.

———. 2020b. "What Are the Value-Based Programs?" Updated January 6. www.cms.gov/Medicare/Quality-Initiatives-Patient-Assessment-Instruments/Value-Based-Programs/Value-Based-Programs.

———. 2019. "NHE Historical and Projections 1960–2027." Modified February 26. www.cms.gov/Research-Statistics-Data-and-Systems/Statistics-Trends-and-Reports/NationalHealthExpendData/NationalHealthAccountsProjected.html.

Chan, K., J. Fowles, and J. Weiner. 2010. "Electronic Health Records and Reliability and Validity of Quality Measures: A Review of the Literature." *Medical Care Research and Review* 67 (5): 503–27.

Collins Higgins, T., J. Crosson, D. Peikes, R. McNellis, J. Genevro, and D. Meyers. 2015. "Using Health Information Technology to Support Quality Improvement in Primary Care." Mathematica Policy Research. Published March. https://pcmh.ahrq.gov/page/using-health-information-technology-support-quality-improvement-primary-care.

Commonwealth Fund. 2020. "International Health Care System Profiles." Accessed March 13. https://international.commonwealthfund.org.

———. 2006. *Why Not the Best? Results from a National Scorecard on U.S. Health System Performance.* Published September 1. www.commonwealthfund.org/publications/fund-reports/2006/sep/why-not-best-results-national-scorecard-us-health-system.

Conn, J. 2007. "IT Guru Says Some E-vendor Contracts Violate Privacy." *Modern Healthcare.* Published July 19. www.modernhealthcare.com/article/20070719/INFO/70719007/it-guru-says-some-e-vendor-contracts-violate-privacy.

Cuellar, A., and P. Gertler. 2003. "Trends in Hospital Consolidation: The Formation of Local Systems." *Health Affairs* 22 (6): 77–87.

Cummings, L. A., and R. Magnusson. 2001. "Genetic Privacy and Academic Medicine: The Oregon Experience." *Academic Medicine* 76 (11): 1089–93.

Cutler, D. M., A. B. Rosen, and S. Vijan. 2006. "The Value of Medical Spending in the United States, 1960–2000." *New England Journal of Medicine* 355 (9): 920–27.

Dalen, J. E., and J. S. Alpert. 2019. "Medical Tourists: Incoming and Outgoing." *American Journal of Medicine* 132 (1): 9–10.

Davis, K., C. Schoen, S. Schoenbaum, A. M. Audet, M. Doty, and K. Tenney. 2004. "Mirror, Mirror on the Wall: Looking at the Quality of American Healthcare through the Patient's Lens." Published January. Commonwealth Fund. www.commonwealthfund.org/sites/default/files/documents/___media_files_publications_fund_report_2004_jan_mirror__mirror_on_the_wall__looking_at_the_quality_of_american_health_care_through_the_patients_lens_davis_mirrormirror_683_pdf.

Daw, J., and B. D. Sommers. 2018. "Association of the Affordable Care Act Dependent Coverage Provision with Prenatal Care Use and Birth Outcomes." *Journal of the American Medical Association* 319 (6): 579–87.

DeNavas-Walt, C., B. Proctor, and J. Smith. 2012. *Income, Poverty, and Health Insurance Coverage in the United States: 2011.* Washington, DC: US Census Bureau.

DeVoe, J. E., A. Baez, H. Angier, L. Krois, C. Edlund, and P. A. Carney. 2007. "Insurance + Access ≠ Health Care: Typology of Barriers to Health Care Access for Low-Income Families." *Annals of Family Medicine* 5 (6): 511–18.

Donabedian, A. (ed.). 2002. *An Introduction to Quality Assurance in Health Care*. New York: Oxford University Press.

———. 1988. "The Quality of Care: How Can It Be Assessed?" *Journal of the American Medical Association* 260: 1743–48.

———. 1980. *The Definition of Quality and Approaches to Its Assessment*. Ann Arbor, MI: Health Administration Press.

———. 1966. "Evaluating the Quality of Medical Care." *Milband Memorial Fund Quarterly* 44 (3): 166–206.

Enthoven, A., and L. Tollen. 2005. "Competition in Health Care: It Takes Systems to Pursue Quality and Efficiency." *Health Affairs*. Accessed January 4, 2008. http://content.healthaffairs.org/cgi/content/abstract/hlthaff.w5.420.

Epstein, A., and J. Newhouse. 1998. "Impact of Medicaid Expansion on Early Prenatal Care and Health Outcomes." *Health Care Financing Review* 19 (4): 85–99.

Families USA. 2012. *Dying for Coverage: The Deadly Consequences of Being Uninsured*. Published June. https://familiesusa.org/wp-content/uploads/2019/09/Dying-for-Coverage.pdf.

Farkas, D., A. Greenbaum, V. Singhal, and J. Cosgrove. 2012. "Effect of Insurance Status on the Stage of Breast and Colorectal Cancers in a Safety-Net Hospital." *American Journal of Managed Care* 18 (2): SP65–70.

Feldstein, P. J. 2015. *Health Policy Issues: An Economic Perspective*, 6th ed. Chicago: Health Administration Press.

Feldstein, P. J. 2001. *The Politics of Health Legislation: An Economic Perspective*. Chicago: Health Administration Press.

Fisher, E., J. Bynum, and J. Skinner. 2009. "Slowing the Growth of Health Care Costs—Lessons from Regional Variation." *New England Journal of Medicine* 360: 849–52.

Fisher, E., D. Wennberg, T. Stukel, D. Gottlieb, F. Lucas, and E. Pinder. 2003. "The Implications of Regional Variations in Medicare Spending. Part 1: The Content, Quality, and Accessibility of Care." *Annals of Internal Medicine* 138: 273–87.

Flores, J. A., and A. Dodier. 2005. "HIPAA: Past, Present, and Future Implications for Nurses." *Online Journal of Issues in Nursing* 10 (2): 5.

Fottler, M.D., D. Malvey, Y. Asi, S. Kirchner, and N. A. Warren. 2014. "Can Inbound and Domestic Medical Tourism Improve Your Bottom Line? Identifying the Potential of a U.S. Tourism Market." *Journal of Healthcare Management* 59 (1): 49–63.

Garfield, R., K. Orgera, and A. Damico. 2019. "The Uninsured and the ACA: A Primer—Key Facts About Health Insurance and the Uninsured Amidst Changes to the Affordable Care Act." Kaiser Family Foundation. Published January 25. www.kff.org/report-section/the-uninsured-and-the-aca-a-primer-key-facts-about-health-insurance-and-the-uninsured-amidst-changes-to-the-affordable-care-act-how-does-lack-of-insurance-affect-access-to-care.

Gawande, A. 2010. "Now What?" *New Yorker*. Published March 29. www.newyorker.com/talk/comment/2010/04/05/100405taco_talk_gawande.

———. 2009. "The Cost Conundrum." *New Yorker*. Published May 25. www.newyorker.com/magazine/2009/06/01/the-cost-conundrum.

Gilmer, T., and R. Kronick. 2005. "It's the Premiums, Stupid: Projections of the Uninsured Through 2013." *Health Affairs.* Accessed January 7, 2020. www.healthaffairs.org/doi/full/10.1377/hlthaff.W5.143.

Ginsburg, P. B. 2005. "Competition in Healthcare: Its Evolution Over the Past Decade." *Health Affairs (Millwood)* 24 (6): 1512–22.

Goldsmith, J., D. Blumenthal, and W. Rishel. 2003. "Federal Health Information Policy: A Case of Arrested Development." *Health Affairs (Millwood)* 22 (4): 44–55.

Gostin, L. O., J. G. Hodge, and R. O. Valdiserri. 2001. "Informational Privacy and the Public's Health: The Model State Public Health Privacy Act." *American Journal of Public Health* 91 (9): 1388–92.

Guo, R., S. Berkshire, L. Fulton, and P. Hermanson. 2017. "Use of Evidence-Based Management in Healthcare Administration Decision-Making." ResearchGate. Published July. www.researchgate.net/publication/317117840_Use_of_evidence-based_management_in_healthcare_administration_decision-making.

Halpern, M., J. Bian, E. Ward, N. Schrag, and A. Chen. 2007. "Insurance Status and Stage of Cancer at Diagnosis Among Women with Breast Cancer." *Cancer* 110 (2): 403–11.

Harris, J., and K. Keywood. 2001. "Ignorance, Information, and Autonomy." *Theory of Medical Bioethics* 22 (5): 415–36.

HealthIT.gov. 2020. "Health Information Technology Advisory Committee (HITAC)." Updated March 9. www.healthit.gov/hitac/committees/health-information-technology-advisory-committee-hitac.

———. 2019. "Meaningful Use: Meaningful Use and the Shift to the Merit-Base Incentive Payment System." Updated October 22. www.healthit.gov/topic/meaningful-use-and-macra/meaningful-use.

Hill, L. 2006. "How Automated Access Verification Can Help Organizations Demonstrate HIPAA Compliance: A Case Study." *Journal of Healthcare Information Management* 20 (2): 116–22.

Hiltzik, M. 2012. "Her Case Shows Why Healthcare Privacy Laws Exist." *Los Angeles Times.* Published January 4. www.latimes.com/health/la-xpm-2012-jan-04-la-fi-hiltzik-20120104-story.html.

HIPAA Journal. 2018. "Largest Healthcare Data Breaches of 2018." Published December 27. www.hipaajournal.com/largest-healthcare-data-breaches-of-2018.

Houser, S., H. Houser, and R. Shewchuk. 2007. "Assessing the Effects of the HIPAA Privacy Rule on Release of Patient Information by Healthcare Facilities." *Perspectives in Health Information Management* 4 (1): 1–11.

Institute of Medicine (IOM). 2010. *The Healthcare Imperative: Lowering Costs and Improving Outcomes.* Washington, DC: National Academies Press.

———. 2003. *Hidden Costs, Value Lost: Uninsurance in America.* Washington, DC: National Academies Press.

———. 2001. *Crossing the Quality Chasm: A New Health System for the 21st Century.* Washington, DC: National Academies Press.

———. 1999. *To Err Is Human: Building a Safer Health System.* Washington, DC: National Academies Press.

Jacobs, A., and S. Fink. 2020. "How Prepared Is the U.S. for a Coronavirus Outbreak?" *New York Times.* Published February 29. www.nytimes.com/2020/02/29/health/coronavirus-preparation-united-states.html.

Jamal, A., K. McKenzie, and M. Clark. 2009. "The Impact of Health Information Technology on the Quality of Medical and Health Care: A Systematic Review." *Journal of Health Information Management* 38 (3): 26–37.

Kaiser Family Foundation. 2013. "Summary of the Affordable Care Act." Published April 25. www.kff.org/health-reform/fact-sheet/summary-of-the-affordable-care-act.

Kaiser Permanente. 2012. *Building ACO Foundations: Lessons from Kaiser Permanente's Integrated Delivery Model: Case Study.* Danvers, MA: HealthLeaders Media Rounds.

Keith, K. 2019. "Uninsured Rate Rose in 2018, Says Census Bureau Report." *Health Affairs.* Published September 11. www.healthaffairs.org/do/10.1377/hblog20190911.805983/full.

Kleinke, J. D. 2005. "Dot-Gov: Market Failure and the Creation of a National Health Information Technology System." *Health Affairs (Millwood)* 24 (5): 1246–62.

Kovner, A. R., D. J. Fine, and R. D'Aquila. 2009. *Evidence-Based Management in Healthcare.* Chicago: Health Administration Press.

Krisberg, K. 2018. "Concerns Grow About Burnout, Stress in Health Care Workers: New Demands Adding to Burden." *Nation's Health* 48 (8): 1–15.

Kwon, J., and M. E. Johnson. 2013. "Security Practices and Regulatory Compliance in the Healthcare Industry." *Journal of the American Medical Informatics Association* 20 (1): 44–51.

Lang, R. D. 2006. "Patient Safety and IT: A Need for Incentives." *Journal of Healthcare Information Management* 20 (4): 2–4.

Lau, R. K., and M. Catchpole. 2001. "Improving Data Collection and Information Retrieval for Monitoring Sexual Health." *International Journal of STD and AIDS* 12 (1): 8–13.

Lazar, M., and L. Davenport. 2018. "Barriers to Health Care Access for Low Income Families: A Review of Literature." *Journal of Community Health Nursing* 35 (1): 28–37.

Litton, E. 2017. "Top 5 Common HIPAA Mistakes to Avoid in 2018." Fox Rothschild LLP. Published December 28. https://hipaahealthlaw.foxrothschild.com/2017/12/articles/business-associates/top-5-common-hipaa-mistakes-avoid-2018.

Marietti, C. 2002. "HIPAA: Blueprint for Privacy and Security." *Healthcare Informatics* 19 (1): 55–60.

McLaughlin, D. B. 2015. *The Guide to Healthcare Reform: Readings and Commentary.* Chicago: Health Administration Press.

Metzger, J., M. Ame, and J. Rhoads. 2010. "Hospital Quality Reporting: The Hidden Requirements in Meaningful Use." Computer Sciences Corporation. Accessed

June 20, 2012. http://assets1.csc.com/health_services/downloads/CSC_Hospital_Quality_Reporting_Hidden_Requirements.pdf.

Meyer, J., and J. Ingold. 2012. "Source: Psychiatrist Rejected Offer to Put James Holmes on Psych Hold." *Denver Post.* Accessed March 15, 2013. www.denverpost.com/2012/12/05/source-psychiatrist-rejected-offer-to-put-james-holmes-on-psych-hold./

Miller, H. 2009. *How to Create Accountable Care Organizations.* Center for Healthcare Quality and Payment Reform. Published September 7. www.chqpr.org/downloads/HowtoCreateAccountableCareOrganizations.pdf.

Morrisey, M., J. Alexander, L. Burns, and V. Johnson. 1996. "Managed Care and Physician–Hospital Integration." *Health Affairs* 15 (4): 62–73.

Musumeci, M. 2020. "Explaining Texas v. U.S.: A Guide to the Case Challenging the ACA." Kaiser Family Foundation. Published January 28. www.kff.org/health-reform/issue-brief/explaining-texas-v-u-s-a-guide-to-the-case-challenging-the-aca.

National Center for Health Statistics. 2019. "Early Release of Selected Estimates Based on Data from the 2018 National Health Interview Survey." Centers for Disease Control and Prevention. Reviewed May 30. www.cdc.gov/nchs/nhis/releases/released201905.htm#2.

National Library of Medicine (NLM). 2020. "National Library of Medicine (NLM): Mission Statement." Updated January 21. www.nih.gov/about-nih/what-we-do/nih-almanac/national-library-medicine-nlm.

Nelson, S. 2006. "Privacy and Medical Information on the Internet." *Respiratory Care* 51 (2): 183–87.

O'Neill, J., and D. O'Neill. 2009. *Who Are the Uninsured? An Analysis of America's Uninsured Population, Their Characteristics, and Their Health.* Washington, DC: Employee Policy Institute.

Office of the National Coordinator for Health Information Technology (ONCHIT). 2015. "Guide to Privacy and Security of Electronic Health Information." US Department of Health & Human Services. Published April. www.healthit.gov/sites/default/files/pdf/privacy/privacy-and-security-guide.pdf.

———. 2014. "FDASIA Health IT Report: Proposed Strategy and Recommendations for a Risk-Based Framework." US Food and Drug Administration. Published April. www.fda.gov/media/87886/download.

———. 2011. *Federal Health Information Technology Strategic Plan, 2011–2015.* Washington, DC: US Government Printing Office.

Peel, D. 2007. "Will Violating Privacy Prevent Mass Murder?" *Modern Healthcare.* Accessed January 4, 2008. http://modernhealthcare.com/apps/pbcs.dll/article?AID=/20070427/FREE/70426007.

Peter G. Peterson Foundation. 2019. "How Does the U.S. Healthcare System Compare to Other Countries?" Published July 22. www.pgpf.org/blog/2019/07/how-does-the-us-healthcare-system-compare-to-other-countries.

Peterson-KKF. 2020. "Health System Tracker." Accessed March 13. www.healthsystemtracker.org/dashboard.

Pfeffer, J., and R. I. Sutton. 2006. "Evidence-Based Management." *Harvard Business Review* 84 (1): 62–74, 133.

Poterba, J. 1996. "Government Intervention in the Markets for Education and Health Care: How and Why?" In *Individual and Social Responsibility: Child Care, Education, Medical Care, and Long-Term Care in America*, edited by V. Fuchs, 277–308. Chicago: University of Chicago Press.

Radley, D. C., D. McCarthy, and S. L. Hayes. 2016. *Rising to the Challenge: The Commonwealth Fund Scorecard on Local Health System Performance*, 2016 ed. New York: Commonwealth Fund.

Rosenfeld, S., S. Koss, and S. Siler. 2007. "Privacy, Security, and the Regional Health Information Organization." California Health Care Foundation. Published June. www.chcf.org/wp-content/uploads/2017/12/PDF-RHIOPrivacySecurity.pdf.

Rosenthal, M., and J. Camillus. 2007. *How Four Purchasers Designed and Implemented Quality-Based Purchasing Activities: Lessons from the Field.* Agency for Healthcare Research and Quality Pub. No. 07-RG008. Washington, DC: AHRQ.

Rosenthal, M., and A. Dudley. 2007. "Pay for Performance: Will the Latest Payment Trend Improve Care?" *Journal of the American Medical Association* 297 (7): 740–44.

Saad, L. 2009. "'Most Urgent U.S. Health Problem' Still Access to Healthcare." Gallup. Published November 23. www.gallup.com/poll/124460/urgent-health-problem-access-healthcare.aspx.

Santerre, R. E., and S. P. Neun. 2004. *Health Economics: Theories, Insights, and Industry Studies.* Mason, OH: Thompson South-Western.

Schmeida, M. 2005. "Health Insurance Portability and Accountability Act of 1996: Just an Incremental Step in Reshaping Government." *Online Journal of Issues in Nursing* 11 (1): 7.

Schoen, C., and S. How. 2011. "National Scorecard on U.S. Health System Performance, 2011, Chartpack." Accessed June 20, 2012. www.commonwealthfund.org/~/media/Files/Publications/In%20the%20Literature/2006/Sep/U%20S%20%20Health%20System%20Performance%20%20A%20National%20Scorecard/955_Schoen_nat_scorecard_US_hlt_sys_performance_co%20pdf.pdf.

Sikka, R., J. Morath, and L. Leape. 2015. "The Quadruple Aim: Care, Health, Cost and Meaning at Work." *BMJ Quality & Safety* 24: 608–10.

Stahl, M. J. (ed.). 2003. *Encyclopedia of Health Care Management.* Thousand Oaks, CA: SAGE Publications.

Stefanacci, R. 2018. "Targeting the Quadruple Aim Through Clinical Pathways." *Journal of Clinical Pathways* 4 (2): 33–35.

Stericycle, Inc. 2017. *Key Strategies for Maintaining HIPAA Compliance.* Published November 29. www.stericycle.com/knowledge-center/info-sheet/maintaining-hipaa-compliance.

Syed, S. J., B. S. Gerber, and L. K. Sharp. 2013. "Traveling Towards Disease: Transportation Barriers to Health Care Access." *Journal of Community Health* 38 (5): 976–993.

Taylor, R., A. Bower, F. Girosi, J. Bigelow, K. Fonkych, and R. Hillestad. 2005. "Promoting Health Information Technology: Is There a Case for More-Aggressive Government Action?" *Health Affairs (Millwood)* 24 (5): 1234–45.

Thorpe, K. 2005. "The Rise in Healthcare Spending and What to Do About It." *Health Affairs* 24 (6): 1436–45.

Tikkanen, R. 2018. *Multinational Comparisons of Health Systems Data, 2018.* Commonwealth Fund. Published December 3. www.commonwealthfund.org/publications/other-publication/2018/dec/multinational-comparisons-health-systems-data-2018.

Tolbert, J., K. Orgera, N. Singer, and A. Damico. 2019. "Key Facts About the Uninsured Population." Kaiser Family Foundation. Published December 13. www.kff.org/uninsured/fact-sheet/key-facts-about-the-uninsured-population.

Upham, R., and A. Dorsey. 2007. "Living Day to Day with HIPAA Privacy: The Top 10 Most Inappropriate Responses Overheard in the Healthcare Workplace." HIPAAdvisory. Accessed January 4, 2008. www.hipaadvisory.com/action/privacy/daytoday.htm.

US Bureau of Labor Statistics (BLS). 2019. "Inflation and Prices." Accessed May 14. www.bls.gov/data/#prices.

US Department of Health & Human Services (HHS). 2020. "Access to Health Services." Accessed March 13. www.healthypeople.gov/2020/topics-objectives/topic/Access-to-Health-Services.

———. 2017. "Research." Revised December 18. www.hhs.gov/hipaa/for-professionals/special-topics/research/index.html.

US Food & Drug Administration. 2018. "21st Century Cures Act." Published March 19. www.fda.gov/regulatory-information/selected-amendments-fdc-act/21st-century-cures-act.

Vecchio, A. 2000. "Plan for the Worst Before Disaster Strikes." *Health Management Technology* 21 (6): 28–30.

Walshe, K., and T. G. Rundall. 2001. "Evidence-Based Management: From Theory to Practice in Healthcare." *Milbank Quarterly* 79 (3): 429–57.

Wennberg, J. E., and A. M. Gittelsohn. 1973. "Small Area Variations in Health Care Delivery." *Science* 183: 1102–8.

Wharton School. 2011. "Healthy Business: Will Medical Tourism Be India's Next Big Industry?" University of Pennsylvania. Published June 2. https://knowledge.wharton.upenn.edu/article/healthy-business-will-medical-tourism-be-indias-next-big-industry.

Wilson, K. J., and C. E. McPherson. 2002. "It's 2002: How HIPAA-Ready Are You?" *Health Management Technology* 23 (1): 14–15, 20.

Wipke-Tevis, D. D., and M. A. Pickett. 2008. "Impact of the Health Insurance Portability and Accountability Act on Participant Recruitment and Retention." *Western Journal of Nursing Research* 30 (1): 39–53.

Yasaitis, L., E. Fisher, J. Skinner, and A. Chandra. 2009. "Hospital Quality and Intensity of Spending: Is There an Association?" *Health Affairs* 28 (4): w566–72.

CHAPTER

3

LEADERSHIP: THE CASE OF THE HEALTHCARE CHIEF INFORMATION OFFICER

Learning Objectives

1. List job duties and analyze functional responsibilities of senior healthcare leadership and the chief information officer (CIO).
2. Identify key knowledge, skills, and attributes of the CIO position.
3. Describe the typical priorities of contemporary CIOs.
4. Prepare and assess an organizational chart for the health information technology department or area of a healthcare organization.
5. Illustrate future challenges faced by healthcare CIOs.

Overview

This chapter discusses the leadership, human resources, and management expertise required to make effective use of information and the health information technology (HIT) infrastructure in healthcare organizations. Senior management of HIT departments must plan for and implement HIT to meet today's information needs (which have administrative, clinical, and operational applications), anticipate tomorrow's information needs, and ensure a smooth transition between current and future HIT. While doing so, these leaders confront rapidly evolving hardware and software capabilities and ever-changing government interventions—both of which shift the rules that influence the collection, transmission, storage, retrieval, and dissemination of healthcare information. Furthermore, the network interconnectedness of biomedical equipment and devices brings further complexity and need for effective HIT leadership.

While it is difficult to master all or even most of these complex HIT tasks, senior HIT leadership must, however, understand the associated challenges in sufficient detail to effectively manage technology experts as well as clinical and business operational content experts. Consequently, this chapter details the functional responsibilities of chief information officers (CIOs); the organization, staffing, and budgeting of the HIT department; and the organizational challenge of outsourcing or multisourcing HIT functions. It concludes with a brief examination of future trends related to the role of the CIO and the HIT leadership team.

Today's Health Information Technology Management

Determining what area of leadership is responsible for the management of information technology (IT) in the healthcare organization has always been a key responsibility of the CEO and the governing board. In the early years of IT in healthcare, many organizations assigned information management responsibility to the chief financial officer (CFO), reflecting the high priority the organization reserved for accurate and timely financial information generally and patient billing particularly.

Because of the increasing importance of clinical information systems, the need to integrate those with administrative and financial information systems, regulatory reporting requirements, and the use of information in strategic planning and decision support, most healthcare organizations have, for many decades now, assigned HIT to a separate executive-level position—the CIO. This shift has led to the publication of a host of books concentrating on the CIO and their evolving role (e.g., Broadbent and Kitzis 2005; DuBois 2017; Heller 2013; Smaltz et al. 2005).

The Senior Management Role

A discussion of the roles that HIT management play begins with the active engagement of the senior executives in the organization. In the literature of organizations that successfully manage information technologies (Alreemy et al. 2016; Blitstein 2012; Ellis 2018), some common characteristics emerge and are summarized in exhibit 3.1.

Many of the characteristics on this list contribute to the success of organizational IT endeavors, and this list reinforces the important role of the CIO

EXHIBIT 3.1
Characteristics of Organizations That Successfully Manage IT

1. Effective IT governance with active stakeholder involvement and active management support
2. Adequate financial support
3. Organizational culture that embraces enterprise governance of IT
4. Strategic alignment between IT and the business/clinical enterprise
5. Effective IT staffing management
6. An effective IT organizational structure
7. Conformity with external/regulatory compliance requirements
8. Effective IT project management
9. IT organization focused on business and clinical benefits

and other senior leaders. In order for HIT governance to be effective (item 1), the focus of governance must be on overall organizational objectives and performance goals rather than simply on considerations of HIT's internal operations. Senior executives must actively design, lead, and regularly review HIT governance. Similarly, in effective organizations, senior management creates culture that expects active management involvement (item 3) not only in strategic decisions but also in technology decisions that have strategic implications (item 4). Conflicting goals have become the norm in complex organizations and, if not handled appropriately, may lead to various problems in the institution.

While it has always been important to appropriately staff and structure the IT function (items 5 and 6), the convergence of social media, mobile applications, analytics, and cloud computing have created an intensely complex operating environment for HIT departments. New roles such as chief analytics officer and chief digital officer are emerging at some healthcare organizations, creating potentially fragmented HIT management and oversight, as well as possible conflicting organizational goals. Contemporary healthcare organizations that have created these roles must pay particular attention to ensuring that clear charters and explicitly articulated roles and responsibilities are established under a single governance framework to increase alignment and produce desired outcomes. At a fundamental level, successful HIT governance must provide the right incentives and rewards in the organization and assign ownership and accountability for each function. In healthcare, incentives are important to foster synergy between and among operating units. Likewise, accountability for HIT design, implementation, and performance must be firmly assigned at the CEO, CIO, or board committee level (Information Systems Audit and Control Association 2017; Zahreddine 2019). With these considerations, the selection of the CIO leader is vital. Because excellent HIT performance depends on all organizational components working together smoothly, those who are accountable for these components must possess a broad view of the organization; that is, no leader can protect their turf. Organizational leaders (other than the CIO) must be aware that they, too, contribute to IT governance, and all must understand the symbiotic relationship between HIT and the organization's overall strategic direction (item 3).

Building on these ideas is a practice-oriented book aimed at helping CIO leaders achieve success—*The CIO Edge: Seven Leadership Skills You Need to Drive Results* (Waller, Rubenstrunk, and Hallenbeck 2010). The book identifies seven leadership skills that support the need for CIOs to have management skills as opposed to purely technical skills; these leaders do the following:

1. *Commit to leadership.* Success depends on the ability of the CIO to fully embody the role people play in success. Consequently, the CIO does not just "talk" the leadership mantra but "walks" or adopts behaviors consistent with leadership.

2. *Lead differently.* The point of this characteristic is to not abandon the core analytical approach to problem solving but to make sure that the current processes are collaborative in nature.
3. *Embrace the "softer" side.* This tired rhetoric has a grain of truth in that leaders should become open and caring, acting as mentors for others. This approach may involve empowering those around you to grow professionally. Key to this are not just words but also actions.
4. *Forge the right relationships.* Because HIT is still largely a people, not a technology, function, the leader must devote time and effort on managing relationships. As discussed later in this chapter, those relationships connect you not just with direct reports but also with other leaders inside the organization, as well as vendors and suppliers outside the organization.
5. *Communicate effectively.* What a successful leader says and does are constantly being watched for signs of commitment and direction. The ability to effectively communicate at all times and in all manners is essential.
6. *Inspire others.* Getting people to go the extra mile to meet goals requires more than reminding them to do a good job. A leader must learn to inspire employees and convince them to believe firmly that they are working on something grander than their immediate set of tasks. Working for a greater good is inspiring and often is vital to success.
7. *Build people.* Professional development for your employees serves as the greatest success for the organization. It breeds high performance in the short run and helps to generate the future leaders of the organization.

To make these traits a reality, a solid and mutually supportive relationship between the CEO and the CIO is essential. The gap between these institutional leaders pervades a host of environments. The challenges arise from poor communication as well as misaligned goals between the organization and IT, diverse education and training, and basic lack of understanding of the environment each leader faces (Hütter, Arnitz, and Riedl 2017).

Functional Responsibilities of the Chief Information Officer

Information systems can be useful to management, provided the process for planning, designing, installing, and operating such systems is itself well managed. The CEO, CIO, and other senior managers of a healthcare organization must assume the responsibility for planning and controlling the development of effective information systems to serve their needs. These tasks cannot be delegated to technical personnel if information processes are to be truly supportive of high-quality patient care and managerial decision-making. In today's competitive environment, information is essential for strategic planning, cost and productivity management, continuous quality improvement, innovation, and program evaluation purposes. Important senior management responsibilities are summarized in exhibit 3.2.

EXHIBIT 3.2
Senior Management Responsibilities

- Management must insist on a careful, governance-guided planning process that precedes all major decisions related to the installation of HIT. A master plan for HIT development should be created and updated at least once a year. The master plan should be dynamically linked to the strategic plan of the healthcare organization and should guide all specific implementation decisions.
- Management must employ a user-driven focus throughout the development process. Active involvement of personnel from all segments of the healthcare organization is essential. This participation should begin with a definition of information requirements before the organization considers acquisition of hardware and software. It should continue through all phases of analysis, design, HIT evaluation and selection, and implementation.
- Management must take the responsibility for recruiting competent personnel for the design and operation of HIT. Consideration should be given to recruitment of a CIO to serve as a member of the senior management team. When outsourcing is used, careful selection of vendors and contract negotiations with the assistance of legal counsel should precede the awarding of contracts for software, equipment, or services.
- Managers at the corporate level must establish policies and procedures to ensure integration of data files or interfacing among individual information systems for tracking patient flows, consolidating cost and financial data, monitoring quality of care, and evaluating individual products and services. Interoperability of data among individual systems is an absolute necessity in complex healthcare organizations, particularly those involving subsidiary units and central corporate management.
- Management personnel at all levels must adhere to legal and ethical obligations to maintain security of HIT and to protect the confidentiality of patients, human resources, and other sensitive information.
- The design of individual computer applications must be carried out by an interdisciplinary project team. HIT personnel will take the lead on technical analysis and design activities. Representatives of user departments should help guide the specification of system requirements and evaluate the technical design plans of the HIT analysts.
- Management should be involved in all major design projects to ensure congruence with organizational goals and objectives, and it should insist on a user-driven system focus rather than a technology-driven focus.
- Once a project team has been organized, careful systems analysis should precede any implementation decisions. Shortcuts in the systems analysis phase will inevitably lead to problems later in the process.
- Managers must ensure that the preliminary design specifications for individual computer applications are in harmony with the master plan for information systems.

(continued)

EXHIBIT 3.2
Senior Management Responsibilities *(continued)*

- Detailed system specifications must be established before any implementation activities take place. These specifications should be reviewed formally and approved by all relevant user departments and by management before proceeding with the next steps in system development.
- Throughout the analysis, design, and implementation phases of a project, management must require careful scheduling of all activities and should receive periodic progress reports as the project proceeds.
- Managers must ensure thorough training of all personnel involved in the implementation phase of the new HIT.
- No computer application should be put into operation without first carrying out a comprehensive system test. The testing should cover all phases of system operation, including computer programs and procedures, personnel training, user satisfaction, ability of the system to meet original objectives, information security, and accuracy of the initial cost estimates.
- Provisions must always be made for adequate maintenance after an application is operational. Maintenance procedures are essential to correct operational errors, to make system improvements, and to facilitate changes necessitated by shifts in organizational needs.
- Management must make certain that HIT is periodically audited and that all systems are formally evaluated once they are installed and operating normally.

The person assuming these responsibilities, the CIO, must have broad corporate and system understanding and also must have the ability to lead teams of technical experts responsible for complex IT. Typically reporting directly to the CEO (or chief operating officer [COO] in some large organizations), the CIO has two important duties: (1) to assist the senior management team and governing board in using information effectively to support strategic planning and management and (2) to provide management oversight and coordination of information processing and telecommunications systems throughout the organization.

The range and scope of specific CIO job responsibilities flow from the senior management duties. The scope can be defined in a number of ways, but the job's common parameters are synthesized from job descriptions and from leading healthcare search firms (including hrVillage.com, Community Clinics Initiative, WittKeifer, Healthcare Recruiters International, Heidrick & Struggles, Korn Ferry International, and Tyler & Company). The range and scope generally include the following:

- Enterprise-wide planning
- Leadership
- Management oversight
- Human resources management
- Financial management

Notice from this list that technical expertise is not mentioned as a separate responsibility. While the successful CIO cannot be ignorant of healthcare information systems and communication systems, they do not generally become directly involved in the details of software development or hardware design. At the same time, some degree of technical competence is crucial for the CIO to manage an organization's HIT functions effectively. Generally, the CIO must provide a vision for healthcare technology for the organization and leadership for developing and implementing HIT initiatives throughout the institution—from the boardroom to the clinical suites and in between. Many HIT initiatives are often designed to improve the cost-effectiveness of clinical and administrative functions, enhance the quality of healthcare services, and support business development. All initiatives assist the organization in navigating the constantly changing, competitive marketplace.

The CIO leads in planning and implementing enterprise information systems to support all aspects of both distributed and centralized clinical and business operations. Exhibit 3.3 provides a select list of knowledge, skills, and abilities of CIOs. Notice that a significant portion of the skill set and demonstrated abilities extends beyond the traditional HIT domain. This breadth does not imply that those with significant technical expertise cannot become the next CIO. Many paths lead to a leadership position in IT, and technical expertise provides as good a path as any other. However, moving to the C-suite, as the CIO title implies, does require a skill set beyond technical expertise.

Recently, Healthcare Information and Management Systems Society (HIMSS) released a report on the priorities of IT leaders in healthcare provider organizations, information garnered from responses to HIMSS's comprehensive survey. Exhibit 3.4 displays the ten key priorities for the next two years identified in the survey (HIMSS 2019).

EXHIBIT 3.3
Select Knowledge, Skills, and Abilities of CIOs

- Collaboration
- Understanding the nature of the health system
- Formulation of HIT components of the health system strategic plan
- HIT strategic business and market planning
- HIT needs analysis
- Organization's HIT strengths and weaknesses
- HIT culture
- State-of-the-field assessment
- Technology assessment
- Evaluation, adoption, and implementation standards
- HIT policy development

Source: Data from Applied Health Informatics Learning and Assessment (2020).

EXHIBIT 3.4 Ten Key Priorities of HIT Leaders: HIMSS Survey

Priority*	Hospital	Non-acute	All Providers
1. Cybersecurity, privacy, and security	5.81	5.43	5.69
2. Improving quality outcomes through health information and technology	5.28	5.13	5.23
3. Clinical informatics and clinician engagement	5.24	4.90	5.14
4. Culture of care and care coordination	4.92	4.94	4.93
5. Process improvement, workflow, change management	5.03	4.61	4.90
6. User experience, usability, and user-centered design	4.86	4.94	4.88
7. Data science/analytics/clinical and business intelligence	4.91	4.33	4.73
8. Leadership, governance, strategic planning	4.90	4.18	4.68
9. Safe information and technology practices for patient care	4.62	4.67	4.63
10. Health information exchange, interoperability, data integration and standards	4.62	4.22	4.50
N = 232 healthcare provider information and technology leaders			

* Based on a 1-to-7 scale, where 1 = "not a priority" and 7 = "essential priority."

Source: Data from HIMSS (2019).

Interestingly, digital health—or, more precisely, consumer and patient engagement and digital health—did not make the top ten list. However, via their various consulting engagements, the authors have observed a marked increase in interest in healthcare provider organizations' desire to enhance their relationships with their patients via mobile and digital applications that patients can access from their personal mobile devices. We suspect that in future HIMSS surveys, digital health will become a higher priority.

Characteristics of a Successful Chief Information Officer

The CIO must possess a good understanding of the healthcare environment and clinical care processes, be an experienced manager, and have sufficient understanding of IT to ensure that HIT is properly planned and implemented. Consider the following complex elements of the role:

- As discussed in chapters 1 and 2, the external environment and government policy have a direct impact on HIT. The CIO must monitor these activities, understand their implications, and prepare IT and organizational structures to respond to these trends.
- As part of the executive team, the CIO must understand the business of healthcare (i.e., the clinical, business, and administrative operations) and how they interact in order to intelligently discuss issues with the organization's leadership.
- The HIT function involves an array of individuals with diverse backgrounds. The CIO must be adept at communicating with and motivating this heterogeneous group.
- Technical knowledge is important for a CIO because the staff responsible for the technical aspects may have limited respect for a leader who is not conversant with actual and potential technical challenges.

In addition, the CIO must ensure that all HIT internal systems work properly. As a simple example, pharmacy systems (whether stand-alone or integrated) must operate continuously; otherwise, the organization will be unable to control dangerous drugs (particularly narcotics) or to manage drug ordering and inventory, drug distribution to patients, storage and retrieval of drug information, construction of patient drug profiles, the organization's formulary, and the generation of charges for billing (see chapters 8 and 9).

CIO success depends on many factors that are both internal and external to the leader's areas of influence. According to HIMSS (2012), six key factors are the responsibility of IT executives. These are not success factors per se, but they are factors that the CIO must be capable of handling or supporting:

- Delivering the value of HIT investments
- Alignment with overall business strategy
- Assistance in optimizing business and clinical processes
- Organizational performance management improvement
- HIT department management improvement
- Process change management improvement

Each factor received 83 percent or higher positive responses from HIMSS's survey respondents.

Organization of the Health Information Technology Department

The organizational structure of the HIT department should be guided by the institution's strategic objectives or plans and HIT strategic plan. Thus, the CIO must be aware of where they fit into the broader organizational framework and how best to structure internal operating responsibilities. With respect to reporting relations, the pervasive nature of HIT management and the key role that HIT leaders and managers play in achieving the organization's strategic initiatives suggest that the CIO should report directly to the CEO. Whereas at the turn of the century only about 37 percent of CIOs reported to the CEO, by 2018, 51 percent of CIOs reported to the CEO, 28 percent reported to the CFO, 17 percent reported to the COO, and the remaining 4 percent to others (Kark, Shaikh and Brown, 2018). In a recent survey of 44 life sciences and healthcare CIOs, 50 percent of CIO respondents said they report to the CEO, while 30 percent report to the COO, and 9 percent report to the CFO. The remaining 11 percent report to the board of directors. A recent College of Healthcare Information Management Executives (CHIME 2013) survey of 91 healthcare IT leaders found similar reporting relationships, with 51.6 percent of CIOs reporting to the CEO, 23.1 percent reporting to the CFO, and 16.5 percent reporting to the COO.

Irrespective of the CIO's reporting relationship, Smaltz and colleagues (2006) found that when the CIO is a formal member of the senior executive team (e.g., the executive committee of the organization)—and thereby is constantly engaged in discussions, dialogue, and strategic direction setting (Hütter, Arnitz, and Riedl 2017)—they are perceived by their C-suite peers as being more effective than CIOs who have no formal placement in the senior executive team.

As mentioned, the CIO oversees a broad range of functions, so the organizational chart must be sufficiently complex to capture that scope of responsibility fully. Organizations have not standardized the range of services reporting to the CIO; thus, organizational charts look different from one institution to the next. The size and complexity of tasks to be carried out by a central HIT department are affected by a number of factors, including the following:

- Degree of centralization or distribution of HIT throughout the organization
- Use of applications developed in-house
- Use of packaged software or contracts with application service providers
- Extent to which functions and tasks are outsourced to contractors

Despite this variety in organizational approaches, a fairly typical HIT department organizational chart for a hospital or health system can be presented along with typical functions (see exhibit 3.5). Often the complexity of contemporary hospitals or health systems necessitates a chief medical information officer (CMIO) taking responsibility for the structured relations between HIT and the clinical staff. In 2012, 36 percent of survey respondents indicated that they employ a CMIO (HIMSS 2012). In smaller hospitals, these same functions in exhibit 3.5 exist but are often staffed with director-level roles with smaller overall staffs. In large healthcare organizations and systems, these division directors often have substantial staffs, whereas in midsize organizations, a single person might occupy two or three of these functional positions as well as fill other job responsibilities. In small facilities, one staffer might be responsible for all of these functions. No matter who fulfills the position, the CIO and related functions typically exist.

It is important to note that actual titles vary. For instance, the role of the chief technology officer (CTO) could alternatively have any of the following common titles depending on the healthcare organization's size, human resources titling norms, and culture:

- Deputy CIO, Technology
- Director, Technology
- Manager, Technology

Looking further into the organizational structure of the HIT department reveals that, beyond the first level of reporting relations, it has even more layers. Exhibit 3.6 depicts the chart of the chief technology officer division. Such a technology division typically consists of three major components:

EXHIBIT 3.5 Organizational Chart of an HIT Department in a Large Organization

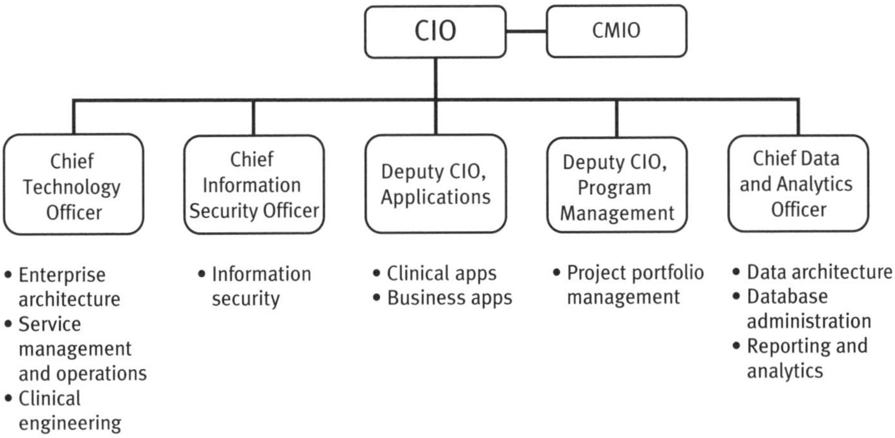

EXHIBIT 3.6 Sample Organizational Chart of the Chief Technology Officer

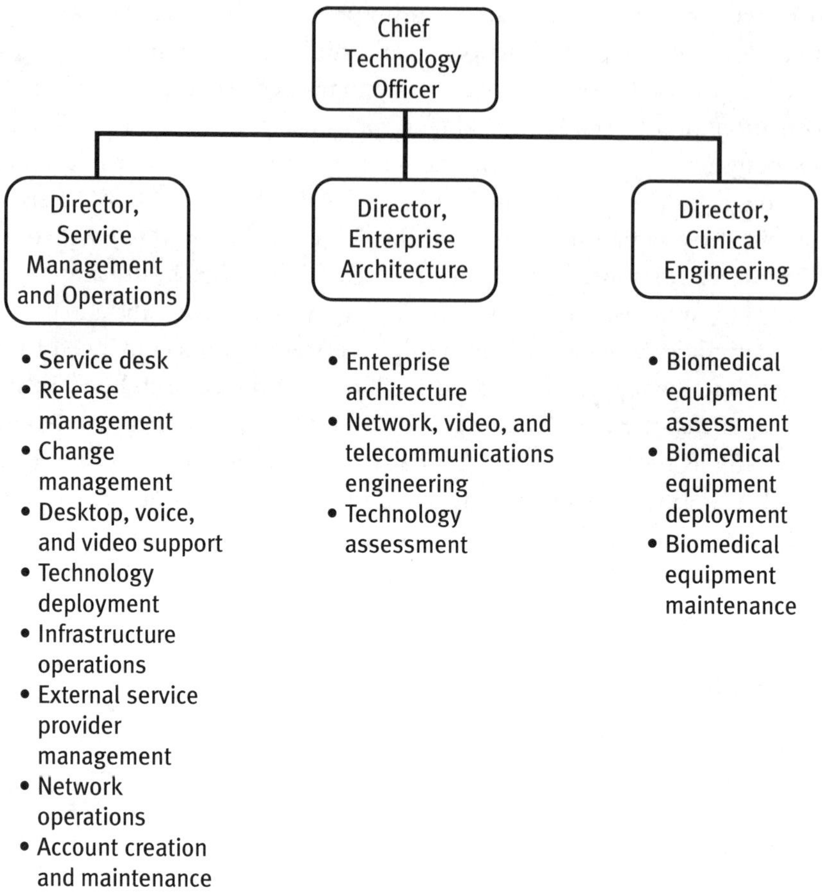

enterprise architecture; service management and operations; and, more recently, clinical engineering.

As the complexity of HIT has increased over the past two decades, the enterprise architect function has emerged with responsibility for creating and maintaining accurate architectural plans that are continually leveraged for planning and engineering any desired changes to existing HIT applications or service providers. Enterprise architects also plan and engineer the implementation of new HIT applications or service providers.

Service management and operations, which is covered in more detail in chapter 6, provides a host of support and operational services such as the service desk; desktop, voice, and video support; release management; change management; infrastructure and network operations; technology deployment; and account creation and maintenance. The service desk handles all incidents that end users report and tracks the incident through to resolution. Desktop, voice, and video support are specialized services to help end users with any incidents related to their end user devices—their telephones or video teleconferencing and recording equipment. Release management plans and provides support services whenever new releases of any kind (e.g., applications, devices) are needed. Change management oversees the logistical planning for any refashioning of the various components of HIT infrastructure and applications. With the continued migration of on-premise data centers to external service providers, infrastructure operations have become more complex. They now often require continued support services to ensure that both on-premise and externally provided data center services are running optimally. Network operations are concerned with the secure and effective operation of the organization's internet services—hardwired and wireless. Technology deployment focuses on effectively implementing new HIT technologies (e.g., laptops, telephones, video monitors) and assisting with helping end-user departments in activities such as office relocation. Account creation and maintenance is a never-ending need, as new employees arrive and separating employees depart, to ensure that secure access to the HIT environment is effectively maintained.

The clinical engineering function is responsible for biomedical equipment implementation and maintenance. As a result of the increased network capabilities of most biomedical equipment, many hospitals and health systems have moved the clinical engineering function to operate within the CTO's division.

Aside from these typical organizational structures, two other characteristics are important to note:

1. Most organizations, as we cover in more detail in chapter 4, reported having an HIT steering committee. The role of this committee is to provide strategic direction for HIT decisions. Specifically, it tends to provide strategic approval for HIT decisions, be involved in budgetary decisions, and play a role in vendor selection. The committee is generally viewed as something that improves HIT operational and strategic effectiveness and that links the HIT department to potential and actual end users; small organizations are less likely to have this linkage function.
2. In many organizations, some HIT staff report to directors of other departments (outside of the HIT department) and not directly to the CIO. Typical examples are IT support staff that report to the primary ancillary department chiefs in radiology, pharmacy, and the laboratory. More recently, separate functions for analytics and digital health are emerging that dwell outside of the HIT department and may report to a chief analytics officer or chief digital officer, respectively. Mary Finlay, the program director of Harvard University's T. H. Chan

School of Public Health, notes that "the role of CIO is evolving. The new technology leader needs to be able to move away from managing technology under his or her complete [authority] to partnering with other leaders throughout the enterprise" (Ellis 2018). This complexity necessitates a leadership and governance model that promotes coordination, standards, and efficiency. HIT governance will be explored in more detail in chapter 4.

Staffing of the Health Information Technology Department

Given the organizational structure and responsibilities of the HIT department, each section must be staffed appropriately. Selecting the individuals with the necessary skills and expertise is the next task of the CIO. Even the best structure cannot be successful without optimal staffing. Naturally, from the CIO's perspective, matching the skills and expertise of direct reports to their areas of responsibility is most important, but staff selection and assignment as well as other staffing decisions should be based on the design of the HIT unit. Generally, the directors or managers reporting to the CIO should have more technical and operational knowledge, experience, and expertise in their assigned areas than the CIO. Leadership must be able to count on these individuals to plan, design, and implement the best technology solutions or operational processes for their area. For example, the health information security division should be headed by an experienced and certified information security professional.

The approach to organizing and staffing the HIT department depends on the complexity of the organization. For example, an integrated delivery system composed of multiple facilities is much more complex than a single facility, requiring a larger and more intricate HIT function. Further, as a matter of culture, some systems are highly centralized, with all HIT planning and development carried out by a corporate IT staff. In other, less complex systems, more responsibility may be delegated to operational units. Whatever the approach, the organizational structure must facilitate reliable, safe, and secure electronic information collection, storage, and use, to the benefit of almost every business and clinical workflow throughout the enterprise.

Staffing for HIT has grown rapidly in recent years, both at HIT vendors and provider organizations. HIMSS (2019) reports workforce increases from the previous year were at 62 percent for HIT vendors and 42 percent for provider organizations. While only 16 percent of HIT vendors reported no changes in workforce size, 31 percent of provider organizations reported no growth. Furthermore, the HIMSS study suggests that staffing challenges (filling vacant positions with qualified candidates) continue to have a negative impact on HIT projects in 48 percent of healthcare provider organizations. As such, the importance of effective HIT staffing cannot be overemphasized for contemporary healthcare CIOs.

Budgeting the Health Information Technology Department

Budgets for HIT have increased over the past two decades. They were considered low compared to other fields at the turn of the century but now are considered to be slightly above the median—though still well below other information-intensive industries such as banking and financial services (CEB 2015). Between 2012 and 2016, Hall and colleagues (2016) found that healthcare provider IT spending as a percentage of overall revenue grew from 3.9 percent to 4.3 percent. Viewed through another lens, IT spending as a percentage of operating expenses also grew modestly from 4.1 percent to 4.6 percent over that same period. "While revenue may be subject to external-market-based volatilities, business operational expense typically remains much more consistent and predictable year over year. Therefore, it better reflects the overall business investment strategy. Typically, organizations with a greater level of IT investment relative to operating expense view IT as a strategic enabler, and this can improve business performance and productivity levels" (Hall et al. 2016).

The budget increases for HIT are likely to continue as workforce shortages drive labor costs up and as technology advancements lead to more opportunities for expanded and enhanced services. Despite the emphasis on hardware and software, however, labor costs continue to be the key driver of HIT costs. Hall and colleagues (2016) report that HIT personnel costs, along with outsourced services (which often have the effect of offsetting personnel costs), make up 58 percent of contemporary HIT budgets. As with overall increases in salaries that affect HIT budgets, CIO salaries have increased. Exhibit 3.7 presents the average and median salaries for CIOs overall, for CIOs in various work settings, for CIOs with different educational training, and for CIOs working in different regions of the country. As shown in the exhibit, the "average" CIO in all settings made about $235,806 in 2018—up from $151,000 in 2006 (CHIME 2020). The size and complexity of the organization tends to have an influence on CIO salaries in 2018 and is reflected in exhibit 3.7.

Outsourcing and Multisourcing Health Information Technology Functions

With the ascendance of cloud computing (i.e., the practice of using a network of remote servers hosted on the internet to store, manage, and process data, rather than a local server or a personal computer [Lexico 2019]) and the continued focus on operational cost control, many healthcare organizations are considering outsourcing portions of their HIT functions as an alternative to in-house staffing (Monegain 2013). The decision to outsource entails

EXHIBIT 3.7 Salary for CIO by Type of Organization, Education, and Region, 2018

Category	Average Salary, 2018
Overall	$235,806
Type of organization	
CIO—Hospital/acute care facility	$243,035
CIO—Stand-alone hospital < 25 beds	$136,183
CIO—Academic health center	$287,385
CIO—Children's hospital	$309,028
Education/Degree	
MD	$381,688
PhD	$220,076
Master's degree	$236,724
Bachelor's degree	$206,535
Technical certificate	$207,000
Associate's degree	$172,360
High school diploma	$121,500
Region	
Pacific	$262,272
Northeast	$231,122
Southeast	$228,125
Midwest	$238,710
Mountain	$186,125
South Central	$238,275

Source: Data from CHIME (2020).

purchasing the services from an external vendor or a contractor rather than hiring the staff and producing the service in-house. This decision between "making" and "buying" your services must be seriously considered as the complexity of HIT increases. Traditionally, the term *outsourcing* has been associated with a contract for facilities management. More recently, however, the term is used in a broader context to denote contracting with the best-qualified company to meet a specific information systems objective. This may involve *multisourcing* to a number of different vendors as well as outsourcing to a single vendor.

Some of the major potential benefits of outsourcing include the following five:

1. Reduction of in-house staffing requirements
2. Smaller investment in capital equipment

3. More flexibility in meeting changing requirements and adopting new technology
4. Reduction in the time required to implement new applications
5. More predictable cost structure, particularly if fixed-price contracting is employed

Outsourcing is not without potential dangers and risks to the organization and to the CIO leading the outsourcing initiatives; they include the following four:

1. Heavy dependence on vendors, with the possibility that a critical contractor might exit the market or change business direction
2. High costs associated with vendor fees
3. Employment of contractors who do not understand the operation and culture of healthcare organizations
4. Misaligned incentives between the vendors' own profit motive and the health system's goal of reducing costs

Hensley (1997) describes some of the time-tested principles that careful leaders should adhere to as they outsource. He emphasizes the importance of weighing the cultural fit with the vendor; suggests that outsourcing be part of a long-term strategy (not just a quick fix); recommends good reference checking; and recommends looking for staying power among vendors being considered. Further, Hensley states that healthcare organizations should not outsource the things they do best, should not become obsessed with short-term savings, and should not negotiate such favorable terms in a contract that a business partner is put out of business. To address the dynamic between a need for stable information processing environments and innovation, Su, Levina, and Ross (2016, 82) suggest an innovative IT outsourcing model that combines a select few—but key—outsourcing partners to create stability while leveraging "a dynamically changing and unrestricted number of smaller contracts with other suppliers to deliver specific value propositions beyond the capabilities of the key partners."

A survey by Waller, Rubenstrunk, and Hallenbeck (2010) reveals the top three reasons for outsourcing HIT services, according to survey respondents:

1. Expertise of vendor: 90 percent
2. Cost savings: 63 percent
3. New service: 9 percent

In addition, between 27 percent and 34 percent of respondents indicated that they outsource EHR management, patient surveys, and help desk functions. *Modern Healthcare* magazine conducts an outsourcing survey as well. The top outsourcing firms, based on size of the client base, reported a 13 percent gain in the number of clients in 2011 (Kutscher 2012). However, IT ranked seventh in terms of money spent by organizations on outsourcing.

Davis (2015), citing a Black Book Market Research study of 1,030 hospital CIOs, 243 CFOs and other financial executives from 266 hospitals, and business managers from 1,400 non-acute facilities, found that 74 percent of health systems with more than 300 beds are leveraging HIT outsourcing to some degree. The figure is even greater (81 percent) for provider organizations under 300 beds. While HIT outsourcing has had some historical perceptions of underperformance relative to expectations, the Black Book Market Research study found that 84 percent of respondents who were using some form of outsourced HIT services were satisfied and reported that their expectations were being met. For those who encountered issues, respondents suggested the problems could have been mitigated by choosing a more suitable vendor, preparing more accurate budgets, establishing more realistic expectations, and monitoring performance more effectively.

In an updated survey of 807 hospital CIOs, IT leaders, and CFOs, representing 244 inpatient facilities and 789 physician practices, Black Book Market Research (2017) found the following:

- Of respondents, 82 percent had either signed HIT department outsourcing contracts since the third quarter of 2016 or are in the process of vendor selection.
- The key area fueling the growth of outsourcing is infrastructure, where respondents noted a need for "better and secured IT facilities."
- The biggest demand for outsourced services was in the area of cybersecurity, with nearly 44 percent of hospitals and 35 percent of physician groups outsourcing all security application needs as of the third quarter of 2017.
- The primary motives for seeking outsourced services were to achieve a positive return on investment (81 percent), immediate access to key skill sets (73 percent), and access to needed technology (71 percent).
- As of the second quarter of 2017, 91 percent of hospital organizations noted that they were at or near achieving their expected return on investment.
- Of vendor firms providing the outsourced services, 41 percent "met expectations."
- Of respondents, 39 percent noted that vendor firms providing outsourced services had "fallen below expectations."

- Only 10 percent were thought to exceed expectations.
- Of the 69 outsourcing vendors represented in the survey, 17 that had been rated "superior" in 2015 were "slipping" in 2017.
- Seventy-seven percent of the dissatisfaction stemmed from outsourcing vendors with limited experience in the healthcare provider setting.

Doug Brown, a managing partner at Black Book, suggests that "doing business with firms with insufficient health care experience that are not knowledgeable of current industry issues, such as compliance, cybersecurity, value-based revenue changes and interoperability, is extremely risky. The successful client/vendor relationship depends (on) health care provider experience to ensure efficient connectivity between IT, clinical care and business workflows" (Black Book Market Research 2017).

In short, HIT outsourcing and multisourcing are expected to continue to be an important option for contemporary CIOs and leadership teams, despite mixed reviews with regard to achieving expected benefits. The collective HIT outsourcing experience of healthcare organizations suggests that by selecting vendor partners with healthcare experience, articulating expectations more comprehensively, establishing more realistic budgets that can be tuned to changes in the healthcare organization's needs, and actively and continuously managing the performance of the outsourcing vendor firm, healthcare organizations can reduce some of the risk that has historically been attributed to HIT outsourcing arrangements.

Evolving Role of the Chief Information Officer

At the risk of stating the obvious, the *I* in CIO stands for "information." Yet for decades it has been suggested that CIOs gravitated more toward the technical and tactical aspects of the senior HIT executive's role. Phoenix Children's Hospital CIO David Higginson suggests that "in the '80s and '90s, it was kind of a plumber-type person who got the network working, got the servers running, got the emails going, and that was their job. . . . Next, in the 2000s, [CIOs] got into having great big budgets and being tasked by the organization to 'go make this thing happen.' I think a lot of CIOs today did really well in that project management, system implementation–type field" (Sullivan and Miliard 2018).

As of 2020, the *I* in CIO is finally becoming more operative. Today and in the near future, innovation and leveraging data are becoming ever more important (see chapter 11). "We're moving toward more of an information science. . . . All that effort and all that money we've spent getting data into the system—now what are we going to do with it? The potential role for the CIO is to be the digital transformation person who's going to understand what's going on with business and then apply technology to get something out of it" (Sullivan and Miliard 2018). Sam Hanna of George Washington School of Public Health further suggests that "gone are the days of tactical and project management expertise. . . . To be effective, the role requires transformational thinking, real-world innovation experience, and the ability to connect multiple pieces of strategy, technology, and people together for better sustainable outcomes" (Sullivan and Miliard 2018).

Increasingly, new roles outside of the CIO's department are being established to focus on innovation and information science. Titles such as chief innovation officer, chief data and analytics officer, or chief digital officer are being created to focus fully on these needs. Doug Brown of Black Book suggests that "the successful CIO is adapting to be the orchestrator of multiple IT support functions, not the IT purchase decision-maker. . . . The new CIO must make sure he or she is recognized as the go-to person for help on integrating technologies, ensuring they meet corporate policies and getting the right price, rather than [as] the leader of complex vendor selections for specific business units. However, the broad distribution of decision-making power around the acquisition, deployment and management of digital technology is a huge challenge for CIOs because business units want independence" (Raths 2019). This statement suggests even more diligence and use of effective enterprise architecture approaches to integrating technologies and service providers will be needed in the future, as well as the use of effective governance in making these types of decisions.

Regardless of whether or not innovation and/or analytics remains under the CIO's direction, contemporary and future CIOs must ensure that the healthcare organization is able to nimbly innovate and appropriately leverage data and information to the benefit of the healthcare organizations that they serve.

Summary

This chapter discussed the leadership, human resources, and management expertise required to make effective use of HIT infrastructure in healthcare organizations. The organizational position of the CIO has evolved over the years and is now a separate, executive-level role. This elevation is a result of the growing importance of clinical systems, regulatory reporting requirements, and the use of information in strategic planning and decision support.

Today, regardless of reporting relationship, the CIO is generally a formal member of the senior leadership team (e.g., the executive committee of the organization) and primarily assists the team in using information effectively, providing management of information processing and telecommunications in the organization. The required skills of the CIO include enterprise-wide planning, leadership, management oversight, human resource management, and financial management.

The HIT department's organization has also evolved over the years. However, this department's specific functions and associated organizational structures vary widely according to the size and complexity of the organization. In large, complex organizations, CTO and CMIO roles may exist. Most HIT departments have one or more steering committees to assist in providing strategic direction. One added complexity of the CIO role is that many organizations have information systems staff members who report to operational units outside of the HIT department.

To manage the HIT business unit, the evolving role of HIT will force the CIO to work upward with the CEO and board, horizontally with other hospital leaders, and internally with staff members. The functions and roles outlined for HIT leadership exist even in small organizations that do not have individuals with those assigned tasks. The functions must be managed in small institutions, as in large organizations, but individuals with other non-HIT roles often assume the responsibilities for these functions.

Key priorities for the coming decade include innovation around digital health, analytics, cybersecurity, enterprise architecture, and HIT governance.

Web Resources

A number of organizations (through their websites) provide more information on the topics discussed in this chapter:

- *American College of Healthcare Information Administrators (ACHIA, www.achca.org)*. A subunit of the American Academy of Medical Administrators, ACHIA is a personal membership organization for information managers with special focus on continuing education and research in healthcare information administration.
- *American Health Information Management Association (AHIMA, www.ahima.org)*. AHIMA is a personal membership organization of information professionals who specialize in the use and management of clinical information.
- *American Medical Informatics Association (AMIA, www.amia.org)*. The term *medical informatics* is used to describe the science of storage, retrieval, and optimal use of biomedical information for problem-solving and medical decision-making. AMIA is a personal membership

organization of professionals interested in computer applications in biomedicine.

- *Applied Health Informatics Learning and Assessment (www.nihi.ca/hi)*. This comprehensive website details the competencies necessary for CIOs and other HIT leadership. Here, you can view the challenge faced by the CIO or other leader, a detail of the smaller roles necessary to meet that challenge, an assessment of the importance of this role, and even suggestions for how to gain the experience necessary for the job. See www.nihi.ca/hi/ahimacroroles.php?id=1&Menu%20ItemID=5.
- *College of Healthcare Information Management Executives (CHIME, https://chimecentral.org)*. CHIME is a personal membership organization of CIOs in the healthcare field. CHIME provides professional development and networking opportunities for its members.
- *Healthcare Information and Management Systems Society (HIMSS, www.himss.org)*. HIMSS is a personal membership organization representing professionals in clinical systems, information systems, management engineering, and telecommunications. HIMSS provides professional development opportunities to its members through publications and educational programs.
- *HIT and quality improvement training, Health Resources and Services Administration, US Department of Health and Human Services (www.hrsa.gov/library/health-information-technology)*. This website is rich with information, fundamental data, research studies, and manpower assessments related to HIT.

Discussion Questions

1. Why are clinical, business, and operational acumen more important for healthcare CIOs today than in past years?
2. What factors can increase the size and complexity of the HIT organizational structure?
3. What factors are contributing to the need for even more effective HIT governance?
4. Why is the relatively new HIT function of enterprise architecture important?
5. In organizations where not all HIT functions report to the CIO, what are some approaches to ensure alignment of HIT purchase decisions with the healthcare organizations' strategy?

6. With the increase in the use of external service providers (e.g., cloud-based data centers, externally provided applications), what are some of the challenges that CIOs and HIT departments must address in order to successfully leverage these options? What are some of the risks associated with these options?

References

Alreemy, Z., V. Change, R. Walters, and G. Wills. 2016. "Critical Success Factors (CSFs) for Information Technology Governance (ITG)." *International Journal of Information Management* 36 (6): 907–16.

Applied Health Informatics Learning and Assessment. 2020. "IT Leader (ITL)." Accessed May 1. www.nihi.ca/hi/ahimacroroles.php?id=1&MenuItemID=5.

Black Book Market Research. 2017. "IT Outsourcing by Hospitals and Medical Groups Continues to Boom, Fewer Vendors Meeting Expectations." Updated September 27. https://blackbookmarketresearch.newswire.com/news/it-outsourcing-by-hospitals-and-medical-groups-continues-to-boom-fewer-19957143.

Blitstein, R. 2012. "IT Governance: Bureaucratic Logjam or Business Enabler? Business Technology Strategies." *Executive Update* 15 (10): 1–3.

Broadbent, M., and E. Kitzis. 2005. *The New CIO Leader: Setting the Agenda and Delivering Results.* Boston: Harvard Business School Press.

CEB. 2015. *Key Findings from the IT Budget Benchmark: 2015–2016.* Accessed December 18. http://docs.media.bitpipe.com/io_10x/io_102267/item_465972/CEB%20IT%20Budget%20Benchmark%202015-16_MFV.pdf.

College of Healthcare Information Management Executives (CHIME). 2020. "Executive Salary Survey." Accessed February 24. https://chimecentral.org/salary-survey-download.

———. 2013. "CIO and CMIO Reporting Relationships." Published August 29. https://chimecentral.org/chime_member_surveys/cio-and-cmio-reporting-relationships.

Davis, J. 2015. "Health IT Outsourcing: A Rising Priority." *Healthcare IT News.* Published November 24. www.healthcareitnews.com/news/health-it-outsourcing-rising-priority.

DuBois, J. 2017. *Six-Word Lessons to Think Like a Modern-Day CIO: 100 Lessons CIOs and Tech Leaders Must Embrace to Drive Business Velocity.* Bellevue, WA: Pacelli Publishing.

Ellis, L. D. 2018. "The Changing Role of Health IT Leaders: Positioning for Success Moving Forward." T. H. Chan School of Public Health, Harvard University. Published March 19. www.hsph.harvard.edu/ecpe/changing-role-health-cio-leaders.

Hall, L., S. Futela, D. Badlani, and E. Stegman. 2016. "IT Key Metrics Data 2017: Key Industry Measures: Healthcare Providers Analysis: Current Year." Gartner. Published December 12. www.gartner.com/en/documents/3524820/it-key-metrics-data-2017-key-industry-measures-healthcar.

Healthcare Information and Management Systems Society (HIMSS). 2019. "2019 HIMSS Leadership and Workforce Survey." Published February. www.himss.org/2019-himss-leadership-and-workforce-survey.

———. 2012. *23rd Annual HIMSS Leadership Survey: Senior IT Executive Results.* Chicago: Published February 21. https://documents.pub/amp/document/2012-final-leadership-survey-with-cover.html.

Heller, M. 2013. *The CIO Paradox: Battling the Contradiction of IT Leadership.* Brookline, MA: Bibliomotion.

Hensley, S. 1997. "Outsourcing Moves into New Territory." *Modern Healthcare* 27 (2): 39–43.

Hütter, A., T. Arnitz, and R. Riedl. 2017. *On the Nature of Effective CIO/CEO Communication: Evidence from an Interview Study.* Springer Briefs in Information Systems. Cham, Switzerland: Springer International Publishing.

Information Systems Audit and Control Association. 2017. "Survey: Strong Tech Governance Drives Improved Business Outcomes." Published October 2. www.isaca.org/why-isaca/about-us/newsroom/press-releases/2017/survey-strong-tech-governance-drives-improved-business-outcomes.

Kark, K., A. Shaikh, and C. Brown. 2018. "Who's the Boss? Trends in CIO Reporting Structure." *CIO Insider.* Published May 3. www2.deloitte.com/us/en/insights/focus/cio-insider-business-insights/trends-in-cio-reporting-structure.html.

Kutscher, B. 2012. "Expertise on Call." *Modern Healthcare.* Published September 1. www.modernhealthcare.com/article/20120901/MAGAZINE/309019954/expertise-on-call.

Lexico. 2019. "Cloud Computing." Accessed December 13. www.lexico.com/en/definition/cloud_computing.

Monegain, B. 2013. "Health IT Outsourcing Demands Rise." *Healthcare IT News.* Published August 6. www.healthcareitnews.com/news/health-it-outsourcing-demands-rise.

Raths, D. 2019. "Healthcare CIOs Face New Pressures and Novel Opportunities." *HealthTech.* Published March 4. https://healthtechmagazine.net/article/2019/03/healthcare-cios-face-new-pressures-and-novel-opportunities.

Smaltz, D., J. Glaser, R. Skinner, and T. Cunningham III (eds.). 2005. *The CEO-CIO Partnership: Harnessing the Value of Information Technology in Healthcare.* Chicago: Healthcare Information and Management Systems Society.

Smaltz, D., V. Sambamurthy, and R. Agarwal. 2006. "The Antecedents of CIO Role Effectiveness in Organizations: An Empirical Study in the Healthcare Sector." *IEEE Transactions on Engineering Management* 53 (2): 207–22.

Su, N., N. Levina, and J. W. Ross. 2016. "The Long-Tail Strategy for IT Outsourcing." *MIT Sloan Management Review* 57 (2): 80–89.

Sullivan, T., and M. Miliard. 2018. "Meet the Modern Healthcare CIO: A Business Leader That Is Casting Off Their Traditional IT Role." *Healthcare IT News.* Published March 29. www.healthcareitnews.com/news/meet-modern-healthcare-cio-business-leader-casting-their-traditional-it-role.

Waller, G., K. Rubenstrunk, and G. Hallenbeck. 2010. *The CIO Edge: Seven Leadership Skills You Need to Drive Results.* Boston: Harvard Business School Publishing.

Zahreddine, M. 2019. "What Is IT Governance and Why Does it Propel Massive Growth?" *Forbes.* Published June 7. www.forbes.com/sites/forbestechcouncil/2019/06/07/what-is-it-governance-and-why-does-it-propel-massive-growth/#d57c9e823f38.

CHAPTER

4

HEALTH INFORMATION TECHNOLOGY GOVERNANCE AND DECISION RIGHTS

Learning Objectives

1. Define *governance* as it applies to health information technology (HIT) and describe its primary purpose.
2. Summarize the five major components of HIT governance.
3. Explain why charter, representation and decision rights, and accountability are vital to a governance plan.
4. Explain why HIT strategic planning has become more important for healthcare organizations.
5. Describe the major elements of a healthcare organization's planning effort.
6. Assess the major elements of an HIT strategic plan.
7. Describe systems theory and explain why it is vital to HIT governance and planning.

Overview

The competitive advantage that successful health information technology (HIT) governance may bestow has become the center of much discussion and even some debate. Smaltz, Carpenter, and Saltz (2007) and Kloss (2015), among many others (Broadbent and Kitzis 2005; Glaser 2002; Weill and Ross 2004), conclude that effective governance and expanding decision rights, inherent in HIT leadership, are essential for organizational success. The discussion of what *governance* and *decision rights* mean and how these concepts have evolved in healthcare organizations is a major portion of this chapter. Such emphasis on governance does not imply that the more traditional HIT strategic planning is either unimportant or out of date. Planning is still vital and is an important part of HIT governance.

Today, more than in the past, successful HIT governance and planning must address challenges from outside HIT operations. Broad questions that need to be addressed include these: What is HIT governance? What does *data governance* mean? Who is involved in governance processes? How are participants in governance processes held accountable? How does transparency in the organization influence governance? How does the governance model differ from historical HIT strategic planning? What changes must be made in organizations to transform HIT functions to a corporate asset?

This chapter first presents an overview of HIT governance with a key discussion of charter, representation, accountability, and strategic planning. It then outlines strategic planning in healthcare organizations from the perspective of an integrated governance model. Topics covered include organizing an HIT strategic planning effort, the importance of system integration, the basics of systems theory, and management control and decision support systems.

Background of Health Information Technology Governance

Information systems in many healthcare organizations evolved piecemeal, rather than from a carefully controlled planning process. Specific requirements for capturing, storing, and retrieving data when needed were developed on an ad hoc basis as new programs and services were added. As a result, the same data were captured repetitively, files were duplicated, and information was not always available when needed. Analysts recognized that if an HIT planning process was not in place, priorities for developing individual computer applications were often established by the exigencies of the moment.

The broader corporate perspective suggests that governance is the way in which owners and managers of an organization manage the *agency problem*—the fundamental conflict of interest imposed by delegating operational authority to managers who do not own the resources managed (Denis 2001). Managers want to keep their job of running the business and thus may become risk averse in their decisions to minimize the chance that they will have a bad outcome that would cost them their employment. This risk aversion does not maximize returns to the owners. The owners want to make sure the business operates in such a way as to maximize its well-being, which means long-run profit in the business world and quality, reputation, or size for healthcare organizations. In any event, the challenge facing the owners or the governing board is how best to ensure that management makes the right decisions. Two solutions to this agency problem are bonding and monitoring.

Bonding is developing contracts that reward managerial behavior that leads to positive outcomes or penalize managerial behavior that leads to negative outcomes; incentive-based compensation is one method of bonding.

Monitoring, on the other hand, refers to owners closely observing managerial behavior to ensure managers behave as desired. Both bonding and monitoring strategies have costs. The complexity of the HIT functions being managed are so great that monitoring has a minimal chance of being successful in today's HIT world. Likewise, the weak link between the activities of the HIT leaders and the outcomes that owners desire make bonding strategies questionable. These strategies are made even more problematic during periods of rapid change. Specifying contracts and monitoring activity pose challenges in a changing environment.

HIT priorities have changed to focus on integration of systems across multiple facilities, automation of patient records, and improved decision support for clinicians and managers. Achieving these complex objectives requires a careful planning process to develop a functional, scalable, and flexible information architecture that facilitates data exchange and provides users real-time, remote access to information from any location.

This chapter covers three closely related topics that, while separate, must be considered together. First, we outline HIT governance with a discussion of purpose, then discuss governance for leadership, then present a governance plan. Second, we highlight how to organize an HIT strategic planning effort with some useful examples. Finally, we discuss system integration as a necessary component to governance and planning.

Purpose

HIT governance helps the organization make business decisions accurately and in a timely manner. With that benefit in mind, many have attempted to define the purpose and scope of HIT governance (e.g., Butler 2013; Data Governance Institute 2020a; Kloss 2015, 2013; Lutchen and Collins 2005; Sambamurthy and Zmud 1999; Weill and Ross 2004).

Haseley and Brucker (2012) present a compelling case for strict HIT governance review criteria. Following the IT Process Institute's guidelines, they propose five domains, or focus areas, that have meaning to all HIT processes (Haseley and Brucker 2012, 56):

> *Strategic alignment*—Maximize opportunities for the business use of IT while providing transparency and assurance that IT objectives are being achieved. This includes defining the IT value proposition, determining the linkage between business and IT plans and increasing managerial effectiveness.
>
> *Risk management*—Address legal and regulatory compliance needs and understand and manage key operation risks. This includes determining risk appetite and tolerance, assessing IT risk awareness and identifying risk exposures.
>
> *Resource management*—Appropriately align IT capabilities with business needs, including optimizing IT resources, optimizing knowledge and aligning capabilities.

Performance measurement—Utilize real-time data to continuously improve IT delivery. Approaches include measuring strategy implementation, reporting and the application of operational and strategic metrics.

Value delivery—Optimize return on IT investments by executing on the IT value proposition, meeting business requirements and verifying the integrity and accuracy of information.

Another, similar approach to purpose has been proposed in broad terms by Levy (2018). Differences mostly exist with regard to the level of granularity.

- *Ensure data availability.* The best systems with current technology are ineffective if the end users don't find the data easy to locate and use. Departments cannot own data; thus, governance must transcend the organization. In addition, with large, unstructured data storage, all users must understand what data are to be used and how best to process them. Availability requires that data schemes are applied consistently across organizational divisions.
- *Ensure consistency.* When leaders in your organization address problems using different data sets, they are likely to reach different conclusions. The resulting confusion and stress impede operational performance. All users must have access to consistent, reliable data, in order to facilitate valid comparisons and conclusions. Governance across the organization by a team of executives, managers, and data stewards with both the knowledge and vested authority ensure that all follow consistent rules.
- *Keep or delete data.* The risks of data hoarding are the same as those of physical hoarding. Servers and storage devices often fill up with unimportant, redundant, or just old data. This impedes the location of vital information and creates an opportunity for users to capture and use extraneous information. As much as one-third of the data stored is estimated to be unimportant. Often data not required for other reasons can be discarded quite quickly. Walmart uses only four weeks of transaction data, for example. Data governance provides rules for what must be kept and what can be discarded or archived.
- *Analyze and report issue resolution.* Effective organizational metrics and the data used to generate the metrics rely upon consistency across the organization. This includes recorded standards and definitions so that everyone understands the meaning from a common point. Business analytics provide useful information as long as they are fed the same data with the same definitions. Problems that arise are usually not the fault of the technology employed but misapplication of the tools and data used. Replacing basically sound systems will not solve the problem

but improved data governance can bring greater benefit, bring it much faster and at less cost.

- *Ensure security and compliance.* Consequences for noncompliance with data regulations can be enormous, especially where protected health information (PHI) from patients is concerned. Defining how its data are acquired, stored, backed up, and secured against accidents, theft, or misuse may enable the organization to avoid these consequences. Achieving secure data management and maintaining compliance with laws and regulations incorporates effective audits and controls to ensure that the procedures are followed. Beyond the formal control mechanisms, education and awareness campaigns will facilitate compliance with increasing user access to self-service solutions.

Governance for Leadership

The domains listed above from either scheme do not translate directly to the operational needs of HIT leadership. If you synthesize the information from Menning and Carpenter (2005); Smaltz, Carpenter, and Saltz (2007); and Herman, Scalzi, and Kropf (2011), you find the primary operational components of HIT governance necessary to achieve the key domains. These operational components are listed in exhibit 4.1 and discussed in more detail in the following sections.

Consistent (and Consistently Applied) Health Information Technology Strategy

HIT should support the strategic goals, objectives, and priorities of the organization it serves. As healthcare organizations have become more sophisticated, they use information more effectively to position themselves strategically in the environment where they operate (Austin, Trimm, and Sobczak 1995, 27; Shortliffe 2005).

As mentioned, hospitals and other healthcare organizations historically employed information technology (IT) to support day-to-day operations. Increasingly, healthcare managers are recognizing the role of information systems in increasing market share, supporting quality assessment and

EXHIBIT 4.1
Components of HIT Governance

1. Consistent (and consistently applied) HIT strategy
2. Alignment of HIT strategy with organizational strategy
3. Well-developed HIT infrastructure, architecture, and policies
4. Well-managed HIT project priorities and investments in HIT infrastructure
5. Documented HIT value or benefits to enhance accountability

improvement, and adding value to the organization. To accomplish these strategic objectives, the HIT plan must be consistently applied across the multiple operating units of an organization. Creating consistent applications in an environment that has grown piecemeal and that consists of employees who do not report directly to the chief information officer (CIO) presents a challenge.

HIT strategic planning has grown over the years, evolving into a field that has finally been given its due. In 1996, 35 percent of the respondents to the Healthcare Information and Management Systems Society's seventh annual leadership survey (HIMSS 1996) indicated that their organizations did not have an HIT strategic plan. By January 2002, that number went down, with only 8 percent of the responding organizations admitting that they lacked such a plan (HIMSS 2002). By 2005, the question of having an HIT strategic plan in place was left out of that year's survey and was replaced by a question of whether the plan was an integrated component of the organization's overall strategic plan (46 percent responded yes) or was integrated in content but stood as a separate plan (44 percent responded yes) (Scottsdale Institute and HIMSS Analytics 2005). In 2012, 48 percent of respondents to the 23rd annual survey indicated that their HIT strategic plan was a component of the organizational strategic plan, while 37 percent of respondents reported that the two plans were separate but integrated in content. Only 7 percent of respondents indicated that the HIT plan was not aligned, and 7 percent reported that the organization did not have an HIT strategic plan (HIMSS 2012, figure 19).

Planning is now a part of the culture for HIT. The question remains—Has the drive for consistency had an impact on how HIT priorities evolve? Only indirect evidence on this question exists, but if we consider HIMSS survey data for 2018, priorities remain relatively consistent for hospital IT respondents from 2017 to 2018 (HIMSS 2018, table 6). While some change occurred, the top priority remained the same in both years (patient safety). The second priority in 2018 (privacy, security, and cybersecurity) was third in 2017, and the fifth priority in 2018 (process improvement, workflow, and change management) was also fifth in 2017. The second priority in 2017 (electronic health records [EHRs]) fell to eighth place in 2018, and the fourth priority in 2018 (data analytics and clinical and business intelligence) rose from ninth in 2017. The decline in the EHR's priority ranking was probably a result of progress in improving these technologies by system vendors. Likewise, data analytics and clinical and business intelligence have been made more acute as evolving technologies open new opportunities.

The vendor or consultant portion of that same survey (HIMSS 2018, table 7) reveals similar consistency over this short time. Interestingly, the top priority for 2018, data analytics and clinical and business intelligence, was ninth in 2017, reflecting the rise in opportunities for this application. Others in the top five were consistent, however.

Alignment of Health Information Technology Strategy with Organizational Strategy

The HIT strategic plan must be closely aligned with the strategic plan of the organization. The issue of alignment has been an integral part of the HIT planning mantra for years (see Ward and Griffiths 1996). Aligning HIT strategy with the overall organizational strategy requires (1) a consistently applied HIT plan and (2) the recognition by HIT leadership of the importance of the interrelationships among HIT, the rest of the organization, and the external environment. Moreover, Stacey and Skinner (2005) argue that alignment involves three essential elements for success. First, an alignment of purpose must be in place. HIT leadership and organizational leadership must agree that they are trying to achieve the same ends. Second, both sets of leaders must agree to work jointly to develop goals and tactics to meet those ends. Third, they must agree to share the responsibility and accountability for achieving the ends. In the words of Stacey and Skinner (2005, 41), "We're in this together." These references may be dated, but looking at more recent work (*Healthcare Business & Technology* 2017) reveals that the core points continue to apply.

Because business objectives change over time, the HIT plan should be reviewed frequently to ensure it remains in alignment with current organizational strategy. Implementing an aligned plan is much more difficult than stating the need for alignment. To assist leaders in achieving strategic alignment, the following six questions must be addressed by the CIO and organizational leadership together from the perspective of the organization:

1. What does the organization do?
2. Whom does the organization do it to or for?
3. Where does the organization do it?
4. When does the organization do it?
5. Why does the organization do it?
6. How does the organization do it?

Well-Developed Health Information Technology Infrastructure, Architecture, and Policies

Healthcare organizations must make choices and set priorities for their information systems. The plan should identify the major types of information required to support strategic objectives and establish priorities for installation of specific computer applications, the architecture on which the systems function, and the detailed rules that drive HIT operations.

To meet strategic objectives and develop high-priority applications, the healthcare organization must develop blueprints for its HIT infrastructure. This process involves making decisions about hardware configuration (architecture), network communications, degree of centralization or decentralization of computing facilities, and types of computer software required to support the network.

HIMSS attempts to determine current and future HIT use and adoption through its annual leadership surveys. Although the wording of survey questions evolves over time, they are similar enough to note the following shifts in focus since 2000:

- Early 2000s: system connectivity is key
  - High-speed networks
  - Intranets
  - Wireless information systems
  - Client and server systems
- 2012: infrastructure emerges as a top priority
  - Servers and virtual servers
  - Mobile devices
  - Desktops and virtual desktops
  - Security systems
  - Storage and backup
  - Wired and wireless networks
  - Cloud computing
  - Telemedicine
- 2018: system utility and applications take the forefront
  - Patient safety
  - Privacy security and cybersecurity
  - Process improvement and workflow
  - Data analytics and clinical and business intelligence
  - Clinical informatics and clinical engagement

The update for 2018 (HIMSS 2018) revealed some additional changes in priorities for hospitals. The focus of the survey changed slightly, addressing the question, What are your top priorities? Please note that framing of the question differed from prior years, so outcomes are less comparable over time. Interestingly, the same question was asked of vendors and consultants, revealing the differing focus of the two groups:

- Data analytics and clinical and business intelligence
- Health information exchange, interoperability, and data integration
- Improving quality outcomes through HIT
- Privacy security and cyber security
- EHRs

After the infrastructure and architecture are developed, the HIT steering committee (see the section titled Organizing Health Information Technology Strategic Planning Effort) should oversee the development of a set of enterprise-wide policies that govern the design, acquisition, and operation of information systems throughout the organization. Important policies needed by every organization include data security policies; data definition standards; policies governing the acquisition of hardware, software, and telecommunications network equipment; and policies on use of the internet.

Data Standardization

As discussed, system integration is an important element of HIT strategic planning in healthcare organizations. Most computer applications must include the ability to share information with other systems. This requirement has come to the attention of many operations and research organizations in healthcare (Observational Health Data Sciences and Informatics 2020). For example, a laboratory results reporting system must be able to transfer information for storage to the EHR. Electronic data exchange cannot occur without some level of standardization of data structures. For this reason, healthcare organizations should consider developing a *data dictionary*—a tool or list that specifies or defines the format of each data element and the coding system (if any) associated with that element. For example, the data dictionary might define the data element "date of birth" as follows:

> Date of birth—Eight-digit numeric field with three subfields:
> Month—two digits ranging from 01 to 12
> Day—two digits ranging from 01 to 31
> Year—four digits ranging from 1850 to 2100

In this example, notice that the range of the subfield for year is designed to accommodate historical records of patients with birth dates that go backward to the mid-nineteenth century and forward to the end of the twenty-first century.

In addition to data compatibility among information systems within the organization, there is a growing need to facilitate the exchange of information among health systems, government and private insurance companies, medical supply and equipment vendors, and other entities. A number of projects have been initiated to develop voluntary, industry-wide standards for electronic data interchange in the healthcare field. Examples of these projects include the following:

- The American National Standards Institute (ANSI; www.ansi.org) X.12 Group works on specifications for transactions involving the processing of health insurance claims.
- The Health Industry Business Communication Council (www.hibcc.org/about-hibcc/overview) works to provide common coding of supplies, materials, and equipment.
- Health Level Seven (HL7, version 3; www.hl7.org) is a standard for healthcare electronic data transmission. It is now marketed as HL7 International.
- The Healthcare Information Technology Standards Panel (HITSP; www.hitsp.org) received a contract from the US Department of Health & Human Services (HHS) to support a new collaborative effort to harmonize HIT standards.

The HL7 project, initiated in 1987, is a voluntary effort by healthcare providers, hardware and software vendors, payers, consultants, government groups, and professional organizations. The broad goal is developing a cost-effective approach to system connectivity by developing standards for clinical and administrative data. As with other standards-developing organizations certified by ANSI, HL7 develops messaging specifications that enable organizations to exchange clinical and administrative data; it has been working on improving these specifications since 1987. Version 3 of HL7 embodies a new approach that addresses many of the weaknesses of earlier versions and encompasses messaging, component specifications, structured document architecture, and more. Even earlier versions provided a coherent set of standards for messages, component interfaces, and documents that all users can embrace (Beeler 2001). The technology and applications update continuously and expand in scale and scope (Levin 2019).

The federal government has continued to support the creation and adoption of HL7 and other data exchange standards. As a part of the presidential initiative on consolidated health informatics, HHS and the departments of Defense and Veterans Affairs announced the adoption of HL7 messaging standards along with prescription drug, imaging, and other standards in 2003 (georgewbush-whitehouse.gov 2020). These standards enable the federal agencies to share information and improve coordination of care. Similarly, in 2004, five additional standards related to information exchange were announced (georgewbush-whitehouse.gov 2020).

In addition to these voluntary efforts at industry-wide data standardization are the mandatory electronic data standards and standard transaction formats for claims processing, which were established by the Health Insurance Portability and Accountability Act (HIPAA) of 1996. Providers are required to follow these standards to receive reimbursement from Medicare, Medicaid, and other health insurers. As a means of addressing growing mandatory standards, "HITSP [brings] together a wide range of stakeholders to identify, select, and harmonize standards for communicating data throughout the healthcare spectrum" (ANSI 2005). Under a contract from the Department of Health & Human Services and the sponsorship of ANSI, HIMSS, the Advanced Technology Institute, and Booz Allen Hamilton (a strategic partner), HITSP attempts "to accelerate the adoption of health information technology and the secure portability of health information across the United States" (AHRQ 2005). The purpose of HITSP is to develop a generally accepted "set of standards specifically to enable and support 'widespread interoperability, accurate use, access, privacy and security of shared health information'" (ANSI 2005).

HITSP is designed to function with public and private partnerships that have the potential to access much of the healthcare community. If successful in getting healthcare software developers and users to adopt these standards, it will buoy the Nationwide Health Information Network initiative for the United States called for by former President George W. Bush in Executive Order #13335, which established the Office of the National Coordinator for Health Information Technology (ONCHIT).

The challenge of achieving data standards to enable organizations to share data internally and externally is a work in progress. Mostly concerned with the external challenge, the ONCHIT has continually updated information regarding the status, requirements, and progress of health data standardization. The standards and technology sections of the Office of the National Coordinator (ONC) are a valuable starting point for keeping current (see www.healthit.gov/topic/standards-technology/health-it-standards). While constantly changing, common information initiatives include the following:

- Federal Health Architecture (www.healthit.gov/hitac/committees/health-information-technology-advisory-committee-hitac) seeks to coordinate data exchange and reporting requirements across federal agencies responsible for delivery and support of healthcare.

- Interoperability Portfolio (www.healthit.gov/topic/interoperability) is the central repository of current standards development and setting.
- Standards (www.healthit.gov/topic/standards-technology) works to ensure that a functional infrastructure is in place to support the adoption of HIT throughout the country.
  - Scientific Initiatives (www.healthit.gov/topic/scientific-initiatives) leverages scientific information to support biomedical and health services research.
  - Usability and Provider Burden (www.healthit.gov/topic/usability-and-provider-burden) works to ease the burden of use by both patients and providers as technology has become pervasive.
- International Health IT Collaborations (www.healthit.gov/topic/international-health-it-collaborations) aims to assemble the planning and coordination being done with providers and systems abroad so that US HIT standards are not at odds or incompatible with HIT systems from other countries.

Despite these ongoing efforts, data standards still present major challenges. Panangala and Jansen (2013) published an assessment of the potential for the Department of Defense and the Veterans Health Administration to merge health information across active service and retired service member systems. They suggest that significant challenges exist; currently, the original goal of creating a single medical record for all service-connected personnel is being replaced by improved interoperability between the systems. Furthermore, health information exchanges (HIEs) are not progressing as quickly or easily as hoped (Kellerman and Jones 2013). HIE has not been stalled exclusively because of data standards, but Kellerman and Jones's analysis indicates that a major impediment is the failure to specify a standard structure and format of data exchanged or the definition of the terms used.

As part of the HIT strategic planning process, the steering committee should study requirements for data interchange, including HIPAA mandates, and should develop a policy on data standardization for the organization. For example, many hospitals and integrated delivery systems (IDSs) are specifying that all software purchased from vendors must meet an industry standard protocol such as HL7.

Hardware and Software Standards

Healthcare organizations need to develop a number of technical policies related to information systems. Most of these are highly technical and should be drafted by the CIO or the director of information systems operations. However, the HIT steering committee should oversee the creation of a broad set of policies related to the acquisition of computer hardware, software, and network communications equipment for the organization.

The steering committee must determine whether the organization will require central review and approval of all computer hardware and software purchases. Such items are often the budgetary authority of individual organizational units, but compelling reasons exist for central review and approval, regardless of cost, including the following five:

1. Central review and approval helps ensure compatibility with enterprise-wide data standards, such as HL7.
2. Central review and approval of personal computer purchases can ensure that data terminals and workstations use a common operating system, such as Windows.
3. Central review and purchasing of generalized software provides cost advantages through the acquisition of site licenses for multiple users of common packages (e.g., word processing, spreadsheets, database management).
4. Central review and approval ensures that hardware and software are of a type that can receive technical support and maintenance from the HIT staff.
5. Central review and approval can help prevent illegal use of unlicensed software in the organization.

In addition, the HIT steering committee should approve the network communications plan for the enterprise. A variety of network configurations are possible, and the network plan must be compatible with the overall HIT development plan for the organization.

Well-Managed Project Priorities and Investments in Infrastructure

The HIT function must also effectively oversee the purchase and implementation of HIT infrastructure consistent with the needs of the organization. The specialized knowledge and skills of HIT staff and the growing complexity of the underlying technology make this overseer role vital to the success of HIT operations. The use of technology has made information available and accessible to clinical and administrative staff across the organization, but the infrastructure on which software and other applications operate in the systems through which data are transmitted remains the domain of HIT. While end users are vital considerations in the priority-setting process, governance of HIT requires HIT leadership to manage effectively the priorities among alternative investment options (Menning and Carpenter 2005). This management includes items directly from the HIT strategic plan; for example, as outlined by Stacey and Skinner (2005, 44), a hospital had to change all of its human resources, finance, patient accounting, and other support services information systems to enable integration with the rest of the health system and investments that arise episodically (a good example was Y2K considerations; see Wilson and McPherson [2002]).

Documented Health Information Technology Value or Benefits to Enhance Accountability

The final purpose of HIT strategic planning is to provide data for estimating the budget and resources required to meet the objectives and priorities established through the planning process. Planning is the basis for developing operating and capital budgets for HIT in the organization. The importance of this purpose has increased as CIOs report the need to obtain value from existing HIT (Glaser and Garets 2005) and the move from value preservation to value creation (Kark 2018). Turisco (2000, 13) called for value management in justifying HIT investments: "There is a growing demand for ensuring that . . . HIT investment practices and processes not only justify the large cash outlays, but track and realize the value. . . . Values can only be realized through measurable business changes supported by the business units."

The Center for Information Technology Leadership published a number of articles arguing that greater documentation of HIT value is essential (e.g., Johnston, Pan, and Middleton 2002). This "call to the field" identified three dimensions from which to derive HIT value: financial, clinical, and organizational. With this direction, a host of studies have emerged to address all or some of these dimensions (see Buntin et al. 2011; Encinosa and Bae 2011; Menachemi et al. 2006; Rahimi and Vimarlund 2007). Despite some success in specific applications such as decision support (Stenner, Chen, and Johnson 2020), the field has yet to demonstrate value in a consistent and significant manner (Rudin et al. 2014). The financial return on these investments is addressed in more detail in chapter 12.

The financial dimension is the most obvious source of value, consisting of cost reductions, revenue enhancements, and productivity gains. Clinical enhancements seek evidence of HIT's impact on service delivery (e.g., adherence to protocols) and clinical outcome indicators. Organizational enhancements include stakeholder satisfaction improvements and risk reduction. In all cases, Johnston, Pan, and Middleton's (2002, 1) fundamental point is that healthcare executives currently must rely on "anecdote, inference, and opinion to make critical HIT decisions." The evidence is still mixed, but some studies show the value of HIT when applied to specific technologies such as computerized physician order entry (CPOE) (e.g., Johnston et al. 2003; Koppel et al. 2005; Yu et al. 2009), clinical decision support (Stenner, Chen, and Johnson 2020), and information exchange and interoperability (e.g.,

Walker et al. 2005). In addition, positive results have been observed when applied in small group practices (Miller et al. 2005) and among primary care physicians (Pizziferri et al. 2005) and when tangible and intangible financial benefits are examined (Simon and Simon 2006). At this point, diverse research has not yet achieved a consensus on the financial or clinical value of HIT.

Governance Plan

Developing a governance plan for the organization is not an easy task. HIT professionals and executives would agree with the purpose, but getting support and engagement proves to be a challenge. Major efforts by respected organizations have struggled with this for years. The Data Governance Institute (2020a; 2020b) provides the structure for what follows, although others have contributed (Butler 2013; Kloss 2015, Kloss 2013). The Data Governance Institute website provides more details (www.datagovernance.com). It is a substantial resource with many important sources that will be used in this text. The site is divided into two parts: Data Governance Basics and the DGI Framework. Basics include an introduction to the process, definition of governance, goals and principles, governance and stewardship, quality roles and responsibilities, and a data governance glossary. The framework provides a comprehensive set of processes to follow to implement data governance.

Charter

A broad definition of HIT data governance is the place to start our discussion of charters. Healthcare data governance defines decision rights and accountabilities for all information-related processes. It uses established models that limit who can take what actions with what information, and when they can take that action, under what circumstances that action can be taken, and what methods can be employed in that action. Organizations need a plan for handling data in a consistent manner throughout the organization. The charter ensures safe handling, done in compliance with regulations, and enables the organization to derive maximum value from information to improve business performance. The charter requires a formalized set of goals, guiding principles, and benefits from the perspectives from someone outside of the organization.

Goals

Goals of data governance may vary but typically include the ability to do the following:

- Enable better decision-making
- Reduce operational friction

- Protect the needs of data stakeholders
- Train management and staff to adopt common approaches to data issues
- Build standard, repeatable processes
- Reduce costs and increase effectiveness through coordination of efforts
- Ensure transparency of processes (Data Governance Institute 2020d)

Guiding Principles

Organizations must establish the principles derived from their specific environment. Some organizations heavily consider the politics involved in data governance, while others focus on data ownership, adequately apportioned accountability, recognition of data stakeholders, assignment of data stewardship, and developing data standards. Data governance principles help stakeholders come together to resolve the types of data-related conflicts that are inherent in every organization. A typical list from the Data Governance Institute (2020d) includes the following:

- *Integrity.* Data governance participants will practice integrity with their dealings with each other; they will be truthful and forthcoming when discussing drivers, constraints, options, and impacts for data-related decisions. The key staff need to be fully trusted as handlers of organization information as they negotiate rules for data collection, reporting, and sharing among various stakeholders.
- *Transparency.* Data governance and stewardship processes will exhibit transparency; it should be clear to all participants and auditors how and when data-related decisions and controls were introduced into the processes. Transparency can be a difficult principle to handle because not everything can be fully transparent, but key representatives should be included for all major decisions.
- *Auditability.* Data-related decisions, processes, and controls subject to data governance will be auditable; they will be accompanied by documentation to support compliance-based and operational auditing requirements. Again, the balance must be between sufficient documentation for external and internal reviewers to follow versus too much time and energy expended for needless efforts. Full ability to audit process also supports the transparency principle.
- *Accountability.* Data governance will define accountabilities for cross-functional data-related decisions, processes, and controls. Finding data overview shortcomings will benefit the organization. It is likely that for some elements, no person or segment has established accountability

or, even more likely, several segments have redundant accountability. In either case, resolving this will improve data and operational management.

- *Stewardship.* Data governance will define accountabilities for stewardship activities that are the responsibilities of individual contributors, as well as accountabilities for groups of data stewards. Formally assigning someone responsibility enhances accountability.
- *Checks and balances.* Data governance will define accountabilities in a manner that introduces checks and balances between business and technology teams, as well as between those who create and collect information, those who manage it, those who use it, and those who introduce standards and compliance requirements. Conflicts and internal stress arise when competing users and functions vie for control of aspects of organizational data. The data governance function should manage these potentially significant challenges.
- *Standardization.* Data governance will introduce and support standardization of enterprise data. While not everything can or should be standardized, widespread standardization supports efficient and effective business, clinical, and IT projects.
- *Change management.* Data governance will support proactive and reactive change management activities for reference data values and the structure and use of master data and metadata. While managing data changes becomes central for the data governance function, if, when, and how that change occurs present a necessary function. Building in the process for that change will effectively smooth these functions over time.

These principles and others you might introduce for your particular environment help stakeholders unite to resolve inherent data-related conflicts in the organization. As you move forward, consider the importance of external or neutral viewpoints regarding your data governance efforts. Individuals who provide such feedback can help you modify your vision and develop approaches to the following:

- Developing a value statement
- Preparing a roadmap
- Planning and funding the function
- Designing the structure
- Deploying necessary resources
- Governing the process
- Monitoring, measuring, and reporting the outcomes.

Benefits

The data governance process will enable the organization to decide how best to manage data, realize value, minimize complexity, manage risk, and ensure compliance with legal and regulatory requirements. In all cases, for complex organizations, leadership will not always make resilient and appropriate decisions without the guidance of a data governance plan. The plan provides guidance for developing effective rules that are then followed to address a range of exceptions that may arise.

Representation and Decision Rights

A full understanding of the representation and decision rights in an organization involve addressing five key issues derived primarily from the Data Governance Institute (2020a).

Issue 1: Data Governance Participants

All data stakeholders should be involved in data governance. In healthcare organizations, clinical areas, finance, planning, human resources, and operations should collaborate with IT because they all have a direct interest in how data are created, collected, processed and manipulated, stored, made available for use, or retired. In reality, stakeholders delegate routine implementation activities essential for data governance to data management teams. However, sometimes these decisions require groups of stakeholders to engage through an established process, as discussed in the section on Accountability.

Issue 2: Data Governance Definitions

Data governance means "the exercise of decision-making and authority for data-related matters." More specifically, data governance is "a system of decision rights and accountabilities for information-related processes, executed according to agreed-upon models which describe who can take what actions with what information, and when, under what circumstances, using what methods" (Data Governance Institute 2020c).

When people refer to data governance, however, they might be talking about

- organizational bodies;
- rules;
- decision rights (how we "decide how to decide");
- accountabilities; or
- monitoring, controls, and other enforcement methods.

Data governance programs can differ significantly, depending on their primary focus, but every program will have essentially the same three-part mission.

Specifically, the program should be designed to make, collect, and align rules; to resolve issues; and to monitor and enforce compliance while providing ongoing support to data stakeholders.

Issue 3: Need for Data Governance

Organizations can survive with informal data governance when they are small, systems are not complicated, horizontally functioning groups do not need an enterprise perspective, and regulation and contractual requirements do not call for formal governance. Few organizations fall into these categories, and thus a formal data governance structure is called for. The framework for data governance enables stakeholders to think and communicate about highly complex and sometimes ambiguous concepts. Management makes better decisions with the full stakeholder participation that a formal framework supports rather than organizational placement.

Issue 4: Location of Data Governance Programs

Each organization has a choice of the best place to locate the data governance team. Options include business operations, IT, compliance and privacy, or data management. Success relies upon senior-level commitment and support and full engagement by major stakeholder groups.

Issue 5: Operations of Data Governance

As mentioned earlier in the chapter, the process of building data governance has a number of steps, including setting priorities for focus; developing a set of value statements; establishing a roadmap for action; obtaining buy-in from stakeholders; implementing the roadmap; and setting up processes to monitor, measure, and report findings. These steps sound easy, but experience indicates that it is best to focus initially on discrete issues to achieve some success, then expand the scale and scope of activities through cycles of effort.

These five steps, culled from the Data Governance Institute (2020a) framework, provide a broad overview of the process. They beg questions of how much governance is required for a particular organization and how to determine the organization's readiness to begin the process. Generally, the extent should be as little as needed to meet stated goals, but professionals charged with this task should realize that the size and complexity of the organization will expand over time. Having a robust governance process in place should enable you to function effectively in that future world. Readiness will be come apparent, should business units or senior management not become fully involved. These elements are essential to moving forward.

Accountability

Data or rights to data governance do not reside with individuals or particular groups, but with the organization as a whole. Having said that, accountability requires you to establish a clear assignment of responsibilities to implement data governance processes. Further, accountability must be assigned and maintained at different levels. At the implementation level, a formal office assigned the primary tasks of driving data governance programs must be defined and charged. Within the data governance structure, a number of key individuals have responsibility and accountability for specific aspects of data governance.

The Data Governance Office

While many methods can accomplish this balance between ownership and responsibility, most suggest establishment of a data governance office (DGO). If a formal DGO structure is not developed, there must be individuals assigned to and responsible for all of the DGO functions. (For an interesting summary of the DGO in the context of the University of Pittsburgh Medical Center, see the case study from the Advisory Board [Aranow 2014]).

The central role of the DGO demonstrates its value to organizing and implementing your data governance plan. Among other functions, the DGO does the following:

- Manages your data governance activities
- Keeps track of data stakeholders and data stewards
- Coordinates other key disciplines (compliance, privacy, security, architecture, data quality)
- Collects and aligns policies, standards, and guidelines from key stakeholder groups
- Facilitates and coordinates data analysis and issue analysis projects
- Collects metrics and success measures and reports on them to data stakeholders
- Provides centralized communications for governance-led and data-related matters
- Maintains governance records

Couture (2018) provides a clear testimonial to the role of the DGO: "A data governance office is a great area to coordinate and ensure the continuation of a data quality management process. . . . Without a data governance program, it's difficult to find anyone to 'own' the ongoing process to ensure continued high-quality data."

Assigned Roles

As previously mentioned, designating roles and responsibilities is an essential part of any data governance strategy. There are many ways to configure this and many roles to consider. At a minimum, you need four primary roles (Walton 2013):

1. *Data owner:* This person should be a director or executive with full accountability for one or more types of data. They formulate appropriate solutions to data quality issues using advice from both business and technical data stewards.
2. *Business data steward:* As the key individual with deep content knowledge in their domain, this person determines optimal solutions and is responsible for determining strategies for data quality, data definitions, and business rules regarding data quality transformation and aggregation.
3. *Technical data steward:* This role uses data profiling tools to identify data quality issues and develops and implements fixes. They act with the oversight and approval of the data owner.
4. *Gatekeeper:* This individual ensures that identified data quality issues are logged, assigned, and tracked until resolved.

While everyone agrees that accountability is a vital element, there are multiple mechanisms for achieving this outcome. The management of data and data governance processes can be assigned formally or distributed. Assigned responsibility gives individual or specific teams that level of ownership. In fact, they can be termed *data owners.* This strategy is particularly useful for compliance and access management purposes. These data owners are given the right to decide who can have access to enterprise data. This approach works as long as the creation-to-acquisition-to-collection paths of data elements are uncomplicated.

More likely, however, a process with distributed control proves more effective. Because data flows throughout the organization and may impact many business and technical processes, it appears in large numbers of reports, data feeds, and information products. The distributed approach has a number of vital steps. The path that the data takes from intake to use needs to be documented. After documentation, data stewards or content experts become accountable for a set of these elements. The complex system has significant hurdles, including effort expended to document data flow, overwork resulting from accountabilities assigned, and the time and effort devoted to management and coordination of the many responsible individuals. Also, the process often requires a more seasoned person to intervene with challenges as they arise. Employees may feel that needless complexity has been added, but the overall outcome is improved.

Organizing a Health Information Technology Strategic Planning Effort

The development of information systems in a modern healthcare organization is a complex task involving major capital expenditures and significant staff commitments if the systems are to function properly. Developing a consistent, integrated master plan for information systems is essential. To exclude this critical planning activity would be analogous to beginning a trip without knowing precisely the destination, the method of transportation, the route or directions to the destination, the time frame of arrival or departure, and the budget or allowance for the trip. While we would not do this as individuals, organizations continue to move directly into the acquisition of computer systems without any kind of master plan. This section provides guidelines for organizations that have yet to create, organize for, or implement an HIT strategic plan or for anyone hoping to update their current plan. While there is content specific to HIT, the broad strategic planning effort forms the core. With the general planning background in place, HIT strategic planning is the process of identifying and assigning priorities for the application of IT as an organization executes its business plans and achieves its strategic goals and objectives. This historical definition, which might have been seen as many as ten years ago, does not sound much different from the definition of HIT governance. Despite the similarities between the two definitions, there are subtle differences in regard to the importance of the external focus of HIT orientation. Many have analyzed HIT governance issues from theoretical and applied perspectives, and much conceptual work has been done, as discussed in the earlier sections titled Governance for Leadership and Governance Plan.

The importance of HIT strategic planning has increased as healthcare organizations have grown in size and complexity and IT has become increasingly sophisticated. Aside from assigning management to coordinate an orderly planning process, HIT governance also requires managers to expand their reach beyond HIT operations to ensure that IT is used to support the strategic priorities of the organization effectively (Herman, Scalzi, and Kropf 2011; Kloss 2013; Menning and Carpenter 2005; Weill and Ross 2004). For example, discussions among and about CIOs often center on topics such as mergers, acquisitions and divestitures, and other strategic options for the organization (as opposed to internal operational issues and new technology).

In 2001, Gabler pointed out that governing boards and senior managers of healthcare organizations were increasingly concerned about the business value of investments in IT and wanted assurances that information systems would deliver strategic benefits to the enterprise. Today, as a continuing response to demands that emerged two decades earlier, HIT strategic planning has assumed a higher priority. Fortunately, the federal government has provided some resources to assist. These resources include an overview of the process and a toolkit to evaluate your progress toward planning objectives (ONCHIT 2020a, 2020b, 2020c).

General Approach

The CEO should take direct responsibility for organizing the planning effort. As discussed, appropriate governance creates an environment in which the board of trustees assigns responsibility, authority, and accountability to the CEO—thus, the impetus for action rests with the CEO. Many structures have been proposed for this planning effort, ranging from highly centralized to informal (Menning and Carpenter 2005). Naturally, the level of sophistication of this structure depends on the size and complexity of the organization and the nature of the environment in which it operates.

Because the CEO often does not have the expertise or time to develop the HIT plan, an HIT steering committee should be formed with representatives from major units of the organization that contribute to and benefit from HIT functions (see Watts 2017). This committee should include representatives from senior management, the medical staff, nursing, finance, human resources, planning and marketing, facilities, clinical support services, and IT. The steering committee needs to be driven by a mission with authority and scope of activity defined, a charter defining the roadmap of action, appropriate staffing, and a focus on collaboration and communication (i.t.Toolkit 2020).

The committee should be directed by a senior manager—preferably the CIO if such a position has been established. HIT strategic planning is primarily a managerial, not a technical, duty. A suggested organizational chart for the planning effort is shown in exhibit 4.2. The HIT steering committee usually has subcommittees that manage discrete aspects of the steering committee's responsibilities. Specific tasks of subcommittees differ according to local needs, but the following are the three components that subcommittees typically address:

1. *Priorities for new and replacement systems.* The identification and planning for new and, importantly, replacement applications serve to determine the scope of user needs.
2. *Specifications for IT infrastructure.* Technology infrastructure specifications must be created by the most technically proficient members of the steering committee.
3. *Capital and operating budgeting.* The budget group is essential to keeping the scale and scope of technology needs under control.

EXHIBIT 4.2
Suggested Organizational Chart for HIT Strategic Planning

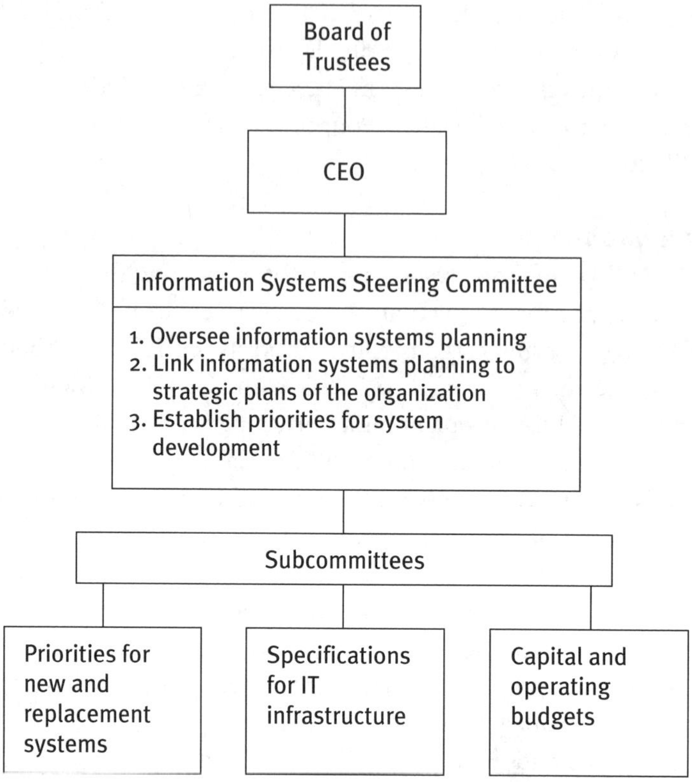

Steering committee composition includes senior staff in HIT as well as representatives from the key constituencies across the organization. Additional personnel from the organization and technical consultants can be appointed members of specific subcommittees as needed. The chairs of the subcommittees usually come from the steering committee.

Consideration also should be given to use of outside consultants if additional technical expertise is needed in the planning process. Except for the largest, most organizations cannot employ all of the specialized technical expertise necessary to make quality, informed decisions about IT. Consequently, hiring these experts is a necessity, but consultants should be chosen carefully. In general terms, an IT consultant should have the characteristics of any consultant hired in a business (White and White 2014). These characteristics include character, solid experience, creative problem-solving skills, communication skills, and interpersonal skills.

They should possess technical knowledge of systems analysis and computer systems and should be well informed about healthcare organizations. Consultants must be independent practitioners—not associated with any equipment manufacturer or firm that sells software. When hiring independent consultants, executives must be sure that the consultants have no bias or stand to benefit from the decisions made, especially in cases when the organization lacks the in-house expertise to validate consultants' recommendations. Finally, consultants should be familiar with the latest technological developments but must be able to resist the temptation to push for applications that are too close to the leading edge.

Lohman (1996) suggested that the following factors be considered in selecting an information systems consultant; this advice is still valid more than 15 years after publication:

- *Independence and objectivity.* The consultant should exclusively focus on the interests of the client.
- *Healthcare expertise.* The consultant should have an understanding of healthcare business and clinical issues.
- *Resources.* The consultant should have sufficient breadth and depth of resources to complete the assignment without "on-the-job training."
- *Effective personality.* The consultant should have an appropriate mix of character traits and skills.

Kushan (2016) recommends healthcare leaders assess the potential consultant in the following dimensions:

- Relevant Experience. Make sure that your consultant is not just an experienced consultant but has particular expertise for the applications you are pursuing.
- Cultural Fit. The consultant must work closely with staff and senior leadership to determine if the cultural fit is strong for your candidate.
- Communication Skills. The consultant must demonstrate the ability to communicate in oral and written forms to all levels of staff and to senior leadership.

Consultants should be used as sources of technical information and as facilitators of the planning process; they should not be employed to do the planning. Planning must be the responsibility of knowledgeable managers and users of information within the organization itself. Consultants can be of most assistance by advising those on the steering committee of the functionality specifications of the technology or systems being considered and the system-level consequences of an action or decision. Before using a consultant's "off-the-shelf" planning product, ensure that the planning methodology is compatible with the organization's culture and strategic priorities.

Boyd (2005) presents an interesting set of reasons for and against outsourcing HIT. Although his discussion is more in the context of outsourcing fundamental HIT functions, the reasoning applies in the case of hiring consultants to advise the steering committee. Simply put, organizations should outsource to take advantage of the capacity and expertise of the external resource and reduce the fixed costs of having added expertise in-house.

The CEO should ensure that staff members participating on the steering committee are provided sufficient release time from their normal duties so that they can participate fully in the planning efforts. Release time estimates should be drawn up in advance, and formal written notification of this time should be provided to all involved. Senior management and the board of trustees should be prepared to allow a significant number of the institution's staff to carry out this important task.

As stated, the CIO should chair the steering committee, if the CIO position has been established. Reporting directly to the CEO or chief operating officer, the CIO serves two important functions: (1) assisting the senior management team and governing board in using information to support strategic planning and management and (2) providing management oversight and coordination of information systems and telecommunications throughout the organization. See chapter 3 for a full description of the role of the CIO.

Elements of a Health Information Technology Strategic Plan

Exhibit 4.3 lists seven major elements that should be included in the HIT strategic plan, each of which is discussed in this section.

Statement of Corporate or Institutional Goals and Objectives

The HIT strategic plan should begin with a review and concise statement of major organizational goals and objectives for the three- to five-year planning period. HIT goals and objectives should be aligned with the strategic objectives of the organization. For example, if reduction of medical errors is a major priority, then this goal should be reflected in the priorities for HIT development, paying particular attention to medical records, clinical protocols, clinical decision support systems, and incident reporting. If diversification and expansion of the market service base are strategic objectives, then information systems should focus on utilization analysis and forecasting, analysis of changes in the demographic profile of the service market, and analysis of resource requirements for new service development. If an urban medical center has placed priority on expansion of ambulatory care services, but HIT priorities continue to focus on inpatient services, then the organization has a serious problem of goal displacement.

EXHIBIT 4.3
Elements of the HIT Strategic Plan

1. Statement of corporate/institutional goals and objectives
2. Statement of HIT goals and objectives
   a. Management information needs
   b. Critical success factors
   c. Information priorities
3. Priorities for the applications portfolio
   a. Clinical applications
   b. Management/administrative applications
   c. Electronic networking and e-health
   d. Strategic decision support
4. Specification of overall HIT architecture and infrastructure
   a. Level of distribution
   b. Network architecture
   c. Data location (from central data warehouse to total data distribution)
   d. Integration via internet
   e. Database security and control requirements
5. Software development plan
   a. Commercial packages
   b. In-house development
   c. Contract software development
   d. Application service providers
   e. Combinations of the above
6. HIT management and staffing plan
   a. Central information systems staffing and control
   b. Limited central staffing in support of department-level HIT staff
   c. Outsourcing
   d. Combinations of the above
7. Statement of resource requirements
   a. Capital budget (e.g., for hardware, software, network communication equipment)
   b. Operating budget (e.g., for personnel, supplies, consultants, training)

Critical success factors are often used in defining information requirements and HIT goals during the planning process (Rockart 1979; Ward and Griffiths 1996). Variations on the approach have been adopted. Kuperman and colleagues (2006) used a "requirements-driven" approach for quality improvement, identifying data warehousing and clinical encounter documentation as the critical factors that would lead to improved patient quality. Similarly, Johnson (2005) used a continuous cycle of assessment, prioritization, and scheduling to allocate scarce HIT resources optimally. Senior management must define these requirements for HIT, but executives often have difficulty with specifying needs for information. By pointing out the critical areas in which things must go right for the organization to flourish, senior managers assist the HIT planning team in determining information requirements and setting priorities for system development. Formal analyses have demonstrated the alignment of goals of HIT usually related to quality improvement and even in primary care applications (Higgins et al. 2015). Further, strong evidence of impact on throughput and financial outcomes also exists (AlHazme et al. 2016). Effectively communicating goals among the C-suite officers of the organization is critical to success.

Statement of Health Information Technology Goals and Objectives

Objectives should be as specific as possible and should flow from a review of strategic priorities and an analysis of deficiencies and gaps in current information processes. The CIO and other members of the steering committee should consult a good text or how-to book on strategic planning at this stage so that goals and objectives are well specified (Ginter, Duncan, and Swayne 2018). Avoid general statements of objectives such as "information systems for Metropolitan Health System should be designed to improve the quality of care and increase the efficiency of system operations." Such statements are self-evident and nonfunctional as far as planning is concerned. Rather, a detailed list of objectives should be established that will provide specific targets against which future progress can be measured and systems can be evaluated. Examples of specific objectives might include the following:

- Information systems for the health plan should be designed so that all records from the master patient index file are available online to all physicians in the plan.
- Information systems for the clinic should be designed so that all diagnostic test results are available online within two hours after the tests have been completed.
- Information systems should be designed so that information on inpatient and outpatient activity by major diagnostic categories is reported to corporate management on a monthly basis, with reports indicating the health system's share of the total services provided in the market area.
- Disease management protocols for the ten highest-volume chronic conditions should be available online and should be used to provide automatic reminders to all physicians practicing in the hospital.
- If the organization is a university-affiliated health system, information systems should expand the university's current infrastructure to meet optimally the ongoing needs of the institution in the areas of research, education, patient care, and community service.
- Support the institution's IT users through the formation of a service center.

These goals and objectives then provide the pool from which the organization must derive its set of key priorities.

Priorities for the Applications Portfolio

Healthcare organizations cannot acquire all the systems they need in any given year. The statements of corporate and HIT objectives aid the steering committee in preparing a priority list of applications to be acquired. The list, in turn, is essential in planning how limited resources can be used to have the greatest impact on strategic priorities. Chapter 9 provides a comprehensive discussion of application opportunities.

The applications list should consider the needs of all major functional areas of the healthcare organization, such as finance, human resources, resource utilization and scheduling, materials management, facilities and project management, and office automation. Both new and replacement systems should be considered, and the need for major changes to existing systems should be reviewed as well. Applications should be ranked in the recommended sequence for implementation, and items on the applications priority list should be linked to specific organizational strategies. If an HIT steering committee determines that financial control is the most pressing organizational problem, the development of a new financial information system might assume highest priority.

Many healthcare organizations have initiated programs of business process reengineering to achieve operational efficiency through dramatic improvement in core processes used in the organization. The pay-for-performance movement sponsored by government and business has heightened the urgency of process improvement (Rosenthal et al. 2006). This broad movement makes clear not only the importance of HIT but also the direct involvement of HIT applications in every aspect of delivery systems (Petersen et al. 2006). Many of these reengineering projects involve development of new information systems, and these should be considered by the HIT steering committee in developing the applications priority list.

After the priority list has been completed, the steering committee should report preliminary results back to the CEO and board of trustees. The statement of objectives and priority list should be carefully reviewed and modified as necessary to make sure that together they reflect the positions of senior management and the board.

Specification of Overall Health Information Technology Architecture and Infrastructure

Specification of overall systems architecture is a critical task in the planning process (see chapter 5). In short, the plan must specify an overall architecture and infrastructure, including the following:

1. *The degree to which computing is centralized or decentralized throughout the organization.* Opinions differ about the degree to which computing should be centralized or decentralized in healthcare organizations (DeFord and Porter 2005). Carr (2003) argues that HIT no longer matters in obtaining a competitive advantage for healthcare organizations because IT is such an integral part of all aspects of healthcare delivery that no one organization benefits more than its competitors. DeFord and Porter (2005) argue convincingly, however, that IT infrastructure as one part of overall HIT is still valuable and benefits from centralization. In their opinion, centralized information technology does the following:
    - Reduces variability
    - Improves security
    - Reduces human resource requirements
    - Enhances flexibility
    - Reduces procurement costs
    - Reduces total cost of ownership
    - Improves end-user satisfaction
    - More effectively and efficiently aligns HIT to business needs

    Proponents of decentralization, on the other hand, claim that decentralization places control of information systems back where it belongs—in the hands of users. It fosters innovation in system design and develops increased user interest and support. Local flexibility is maintained, and the frustrations of lengthy programming and processing backlogs at a central facility are avoided. Analysts often indicate that neither is best and the decision rests with the particulars of the organization (Staheli 2015). However, a consistent downside of centralization rests in the inability of individual units to control their own operations, especially those units that are strong financially and have the ability to work in a decentralized framework.
2. *The network architecture that specifies how computers and workstations are linked together through communication lines and network servers.* Chapter 5 includes a detailed description of alternative network architecture configurations. Data distribution plans help determine which type of network architecture should be employed by the healthcare organization. Alternatives range from creation of large, centralized (enterprise-wide) data warehouses to complete distribution of data in which each organizational unit on the network maintains its own database.
3. *The manner in which data are stored and distributed throughout the organization, including database security and control requirements.*

Many healthcare organizations, particularly IDSs, have moved toward a combination of approaches to data distribution. For example, the IDS might develop a centralized data warehouse containing a master patient index and computerized records for all patients in the system. Individual organizations in the IDS (e.g., hospitals, ambulatory care centers) might maintain their own data files for patient appointments, employee records, inventory control, budgeting, and financial management. The telecommunications network supporting the system is designed to facilitate electronic exchange of information so that patient records are accessible at all treatment sites and financial information can be transmitted to corporate offices on a periodic basis. In addition to describing the network architecture, the plan should specify how the infrastructure supports related activities such as audio, video, and wireless communications; document imaging; and radiographic imaging.

4. *The manner by which individual applications are linked so that they can exchange information.* Interoperability is discussed fully in chapter 1, but briefly, it is a key strategic consideration that affects all clinical and administrative components of the delivery system.

Regardless of the approach followed for data distribution and system integration, data standards are required. Data security and protection of information confidentiality are discussed in chapter 5. The subcommittee that reviews HIT architecture and infrastructure must include competent technical staff or consultants working closely with representatives of management, the medical staff, and other major HIT users.

Software Development Plan

The HIT strategic plan should specify procedures for software development. In the early days of healthcare computing (1960s to 1980s), most hospitals and other healthcare organizations employed a staff of computer analysts and programmers to develop computer applications in-house. Today, most healthcare organizations rely primarily on software packages purchased from commercial vendors. A wide array of software products are available; see, for example, the annual resource guide published by the Healthcare Innovation Group (which is available online at www.hcinnovationgroup.com). This source presents a vast listing of companies, including a brief description of the company, its product categories, and contact information.

Use of application service providers (ASPs) is another alternative for software acquisition that has grown in popularity among healthcare organizations. An ASP is a vendor that contracts with a healthcare organization to provide access to and use of applications on a subscription basis on an off-site server. Many large healthcare organizations and IDSs use combinations of these software development options. Commercial software may be combined with tailor-made programs developed by in-house staff, particularly programs that support database management and electronic communications across the network. ASPs may be used for selected applications by smaller units affiliated with the enterprise.

The ASP has been somewhat replaced or expanded through managed service providers (MSPs). This expanded service has evolved from the 1990s and now has a strong presence in middle-tier firms. Observers estimate that its market doubled between 2014 and 2019. Reasons to adopt are similar to those articulated for ASPs: to improve efficiency and reliability of IT operations (56 percent); to enhance security and compliance (38 percent); and to manage all IT infrastructure and services remotely (Hogan 2017).

Management and Staffing Plan

The HIT strategic plan should specify the management structure for information systems. Most healthcare organizations still employ an in-house staff for information system operation and management, even if all or most software is purchased from commercial vendors or leased from ASPs, or if services are outsourced to MSPs.

Decisions must be made on the extent to which technical personnel are centralized or distributed among the major user departments of the organization. An increasing number of organizations are outsourcing all or some of their information-processing functions to contractors who provide on-site system implementation and management services.

Centralized staffing offers the advantages of economies of scale and reduction in the number of technical personnel to be employed. Decentralized staffing brings systems management closer to the user and offers the potential for increased support and user involvement in system development and operation.

Outsourcing HIT functions allows the healthcare organization to get out of the IT business through contracting with experts in the field. However, the costs of outsourcing may be high and may tend to generate too much distance between users and technical systems specialists.

Statement of Resource Requirements

The final element of the HIT plan identifies the resources required to carry out the plan. The capital budget should include five- to ten-year projections for the cost of computer hardware, network and telecommunications equipment, and software. The operating budget includes costs for personnel, supplies and materials, consultants, training programs, and other recurring expenses. Both budgets should be updated annually, and the timing of their preparation should be coordinated with the overall organizational budget cycle.

Although the IT budgets of healthcare organizations lag those of other information-intensive industries, the *23rd Annual HIMSS Leadership Survey* reported in 2012 that budgets increased in an attempt to keep pace with developing technology. Seventy-five percent of the survey respondents indicated that their budgets definitely or probably would increase in the current year, and only 7 percent expected their budgets to decrease (HIMSS 2012). Since this time, however, the outlook for IT budgets—at least for hospitals—appears to be declining. Data from the 2018 Annual HIMSS Leadership Survey (2018, 14) demonstrate that fewer respondents expect budgets to increase:

Year	Percent Increase	Percent Decrease	Percent Unchanged
2016	65%	7%	21%
2017	57%	18%	17%
2018	24%	43%	21%

Note: Some individuals did not respond or did not have an estimate.
Source: Adapted from HIMSS (2018).

The planning process is the subject of many other books, but to round out our discussion here, we provide a generic planning methodology adapted from Glaser (2002) in exhibit 4.4. This plan starts with the necessary gathering of information to review existing organizational strategies with senior management and middle management. The goal is to identify information systems needs by contrasting existing resources with the requirements that will meet users' expressed needs. Glaser suggests that much of the information gathering should be done by external consultants.

Once the gap between needs and capabilities is determined, the next step is to delineate information systems alternatives. These alternatives will require key implementation steps to be specified, followed by estimates of resource requirements and timelines for implementation. Finally, the full plan with recommendations is presented to management.

Review and Approval of the Health Information Technology Strategic Plan

The HIT plan should include an overall schedule, detailing the target dates for implementation. Although cost estimates and target dates are preliminary at this point, they assist management and board members in evaluating the

EXHIBIT 4.4
Generic HIT Strategic Planning Methodology

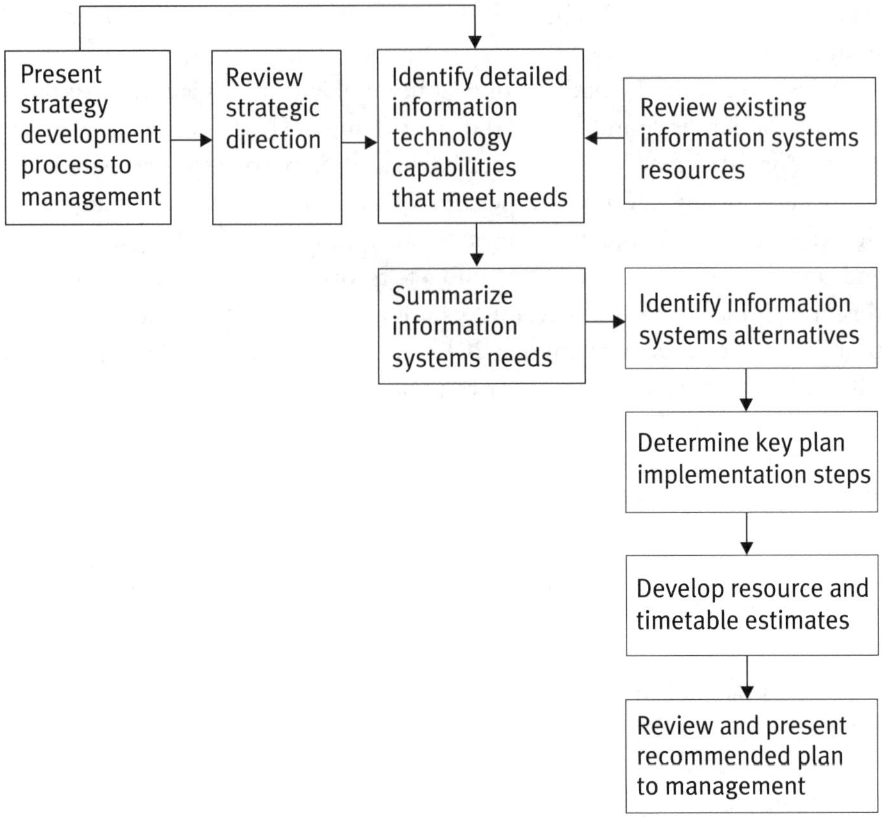

Source: Glaser (2002). Adapted with permission of John Wiley & Sons, Hoboken, New Jersey.

magnitude of organizational commitments required to implement the recommended set of alternatives.

After the HIT steering committee has approved the plan, it should be presented to executive management and the governing board for their review and approval prior to implementation. The written plan should be submitted to management in advance of a formal presentation and discussion session.

As with any plan, the HIT strategic plan must be a dynamic instrument that is reviewed periodically and updated regularly. At least once a year, the steering committee should review progress in meeting the original criteria set forth in the plan, and the plan should be changed as necessary. This review process is essential for the steering committee to monitor progress in completing goals (or any related barriers) and to report that status to HIT leadership. If problems arise or should the environment change dramatically, the committee may put forward a suggestion that the organization change strategic direction.

End-User Computing

A problem that many healthcare organizations face is what to do about dissatisfaction among organizational units whose information systems needs are not identified as priorities in the HIT strategic plan. End-user computing strategies offer one potential solution to this problem.

Many employees have become sophisticated in their computer use. Powerful personal computers with user-friendly software and user-oriented programming tools have helped to facilitate end-user computing—some users no longer require the services or resources of the central HIT department.

End-user computing most often involves use of departmental software packages purchased from vendors (e.g., laboratory, pharmacy, radiology systems) or leased from an ASP. In some cases, computer-literate users may write programs to meet specialized needs in their departments. For example, end users at an outpatient clinic in a large medical center may create and maintain a database of companies that provide medical supplies for the clinic.

End-user computing offers the potential to expand the base of HIT development and overcome issues that arise when a low priority is assigned to certain applications that are nevertheless viewed as important to units within the organization. End-user computing must be approached cautiously, however. Most activities in healthcare organizations are interrelated, and computer applications must be able to exchange information for efficient operations (see the next section on standards and policies). If a departmental system can stand alone, management might authorize acquisition, provided that department funds are available and the system is developed in accordance with the HIT strategic plan and enterprise-wide standards and policies. If the system needs to exchange information with other units of the organization, central control and planning are needed before the end-user department is authorized to acquire the system. *Data compatibility*—use of common codes and data definitions for electronic information exchange across the organization—should be mandatory (see the following section).

Health Information Technology Strategic Planning for Integrated Delivery Systems

IDSs must consider the need for integration of information systems across institutions as well as for individual organizational units. Such integration is particularly critical in vertically integrated organizations, where patients may progress and seek treatment at various organizational units such as clinics, surgical centers, acute care hospitals, substance abuse centers, and skilled nursing facilities. Information systems must be patient centered to aggregate data from the various medical care units and track patients throughout the healthcare delivery organization. At the same time, corporate system management must recognize that different types of facilities (e.g., hospitals, ambulatory care centers and clinics, nursing homes, home health agencies) have their own distinct information requirements. Corporate policy must provide mechanisms for specialized information systems to meet the needs of individual units.

Information systems for an IDS must be able to provide comparative financial data for management to allocate resources efficiently to individual units. Such an ability is especially critical when healthcare costs are paid on a capitation basis. Corporate management will need to carefully monitor how patient care dollars are being spent across units for actuarial risk analysis. The IDS also needs special information for the purposes of market research and analysis of competitor services. Physician performance in various components of the system must be monitored as well.

At the technical level, information systems for an IDS may require standardization of coding and data definition for all organizational units—for example, a common chart of accounts for financial reporting. If such an approach is not feasible, then complex data conversion tables are required to facilitate electronic data exchange. To serve corporate management information needs and operational support requirements of each medical care unit, IDSs need to strike a balance between centralized data management and local control of data processing.

In recent years, hospitals have merged to form corporate systems, medical centers have acquired community hospitals and brought them into their organizations, and some corporate systems have sold or divested some of their existing facilities. These mergers and changes in ownership can create special problems with respect to information systems at the individual facilities.

If the corporate system has highly centralized information processing through a corporate data center and acquires a new facility, it needs to draft a special HIT plan to bring the new unit into the central system while allowing it to continue to use its current hardware and software to support ongoing operations. If computing in the corporate system is decentralized at the facility level, the newly acquired facility may not have compatible hardware and software. Conversion programs may be required to convert data from these legacy systems to meet corporate reporting requirements. Unique information-processing problems usually result from these mergers, acquisitions, and joint ventures. Management at both the corporate and institutional levels must be prepared to address these problems as the plans for organizational change are developed.

Data Warehouses

Many health systems are developing data warehouses to serve the needs of facilities in their systems. As has happened for many IT applications, industry experts provide guidelines for what works, in a practical sense, for developing data warehouses ahead of formal research evidence. Johnson (2017) outlines a five-step approach to effective establishment of data warehouses in an organization that should look much like the steps to success for other processes, as well:

1. *Obtain leadership commitment to outcomes improvement.* While this sounds trivial, data warehouses require a sustained commitment of time and resources with limited payback in the short run. Key senior leaders and probably an outside vendor must clearly receive informed support.
2. *Build team.* The involvement of key data architects, business intelligence developers, and data stewards or content experts provides the breadth and depth of expertise to implement a workable system.
3. *Partner with IT.* The data warehouse team needs support from the organization's information systems department to implement the plan fully. This group of stakeholders includes systems administrators to manage software, operations programmers to maintain the network and servers, and a database administrator to support data infrastructure.
4. *Generate interest and buy-in.* Dashboards and education ensure that all potential users (especially clinical users) begin to understand the value and importance of the capacity being developed.
5. *Maintain support.* As the system develops, existing applications become routine, and conflicts among competing extensions can cause a decline in functionality.

Breen and Rodrigues (2001, 87) present an interesting case study on development of a data warehouse and conclude, "Successful implementation of a data warehouse involves a corporate treasure hunt—identifying and cataloging data. It involves data ownership, data integrity, and business process analysis to determine what the data are, who owns them, how reliable they are, and how they are processed."

The Cleveland Clinic, based in Ohio, has extended its efforts to report quality indicators by using its administrative and clinical data repository of patient data to aggregate and report physician indicators of quality. At the clinic's locations, advanced-practice nurses (APNs) provide primary care to patients in the ambulatory setting, but the data are traditionally linked to the primary care provider and not to the nurse. The extension is to link patient information assembled via its EHR to the APN managing the patient. In this way, quality outcomes can be reported for this vital provider group, demonstrating APNs' contribution to patient care (Kapoor et al. 2006).

Even the federal government has developed the data warehouse concept for collection, storage, and dissemination of the vast quantity of healthcare data it manages. For example, the website of the Department of

Health and Human Services' Office of the Chief Technology Officer (see https://healthdata.gov/content/about) has information from nearly 4,000 healthcare-related data sets from across government agencies. This repository enables users to select vast quantities of health information by topic (e.g., health behavior, disabilities), geography (e.g., state), or initiative (e.g., Healthy People 2020, County Health Indicators). Similarly, the Healthcare Data and Analytics Association (www.hdwa.org) was created to facilitate the use of health data to control costs, improve quality, and improve patient satisfaction and quality.

Importance of System Integration

The What

Certain background concepts are important to an understanding of the effective application of IT in healthcare organizations. These concepts include general systems theory, which is the basis of the key principles of management related to the development and operation of information systems, including the need for change management in adapting systems to the organizational culture.

Systems Theory

Systems theory is the foundation on which the development of information systems is based. Healthcare managers should have a general understanding of this theory to determine how information systems function in their organizations, particularly in using information for management control. Scientists have completed considerable research on systems and how they function in all phases of society. Interest in general systems theory developed in the post–World War II period. Initial research efforts were focused primarily on the physical sciences, with the study of strategic military weapons systems, systems for space exploration, and automated systems of all kinds to reduce manual labor and improve the overall quality of life.

In the 1960s, attention shifted to the application of systems theory to the social sciences, including organizational theory and management. Although much of this work is highly theoretical and of interest to those involved primarily in research, some general discussion of systems theory is a useful background for understanding management control systems in healthcare delivery and for setting forth principles of information systems analysis and design.

The systems approach is important because it concentrates on examining a process in its entirety, rather than focusing on the parts, and relates the parts to each other to achieve total system goals. Management control requires that performance be compared against expectations and that feedback be used to adjust the system when performance goals are not being met.

Systems analysis is a fundamental tool for the design and development of information systems. It is the process of studying organizational operations and determining information systems requirements for a given application. Systems analysis employs concepts from general systems theory in analyzing inputs, processes, outputs, and feedback to define requirements for an information system. The remainder of this section presents a general overview of systems theory and its application in healthcare organizations.

A variety of systems compose the functioning of healthcare organizations. These systems can be categorized into three groups: mechanical systems, human systems, and human–machine systems. *Mechanical systems* are an integral part of the physical plant, serving such purposes as heating and cooling; monitoring temperature, pressure, and humidity; and supplying chilled and heated water. Most of the essential functions of a healthcare organization are carried out through *human systems*—organized relationships among patients, physicians, employees, family members of patients, and others. Many of these human systems are formally defined. For example, nursing care is provided in accordance with a scheduled set of predetermined protocols and procedures, and nursing service personnel are trained and supervised in the proper execution of this system of care. Many things also happen through informal relationships, which often become well defined and known to those in the organization. Thus, certain activities get accomplished by "knowing the right person" or sending informal signals to key individuals about actions that need to be taken. Because of the development of modern IT, many systems fall into the third category of *human–machine systems*. These are formally defined systems in which human effort is assisted by various kinds of automated equipment. For example, computer systems have been developed to monitor the vital signs of critically ill patients in intensive care units of hospitals or medical centers continuously.

HIT falls into the second and third categories of this simple taxonomy; that is, information systems are either human systems or human–machine systems designed to support operations. Information systems that operate without any type of machine processing of data are referred to as *manual systems*. Although much of this book deals with computer-aided information processing, most of the principles set forth here—particularly those dealing with systems analysis and design—apply equally to the manual systems for information processing.

A healthcare organization can be described in a systems context as well. Exhibit 4.5 is a systems diagram for a healthcare organization; it shows the relationships among and between various inputs and environmental factors as these factors influence the provision of services to the community. In this context, mechanical, human, and human–machine systems constitute elements (or subsystems) of the conversion process.

EXHIBIT 4.5
The Healthcare Organization as a System

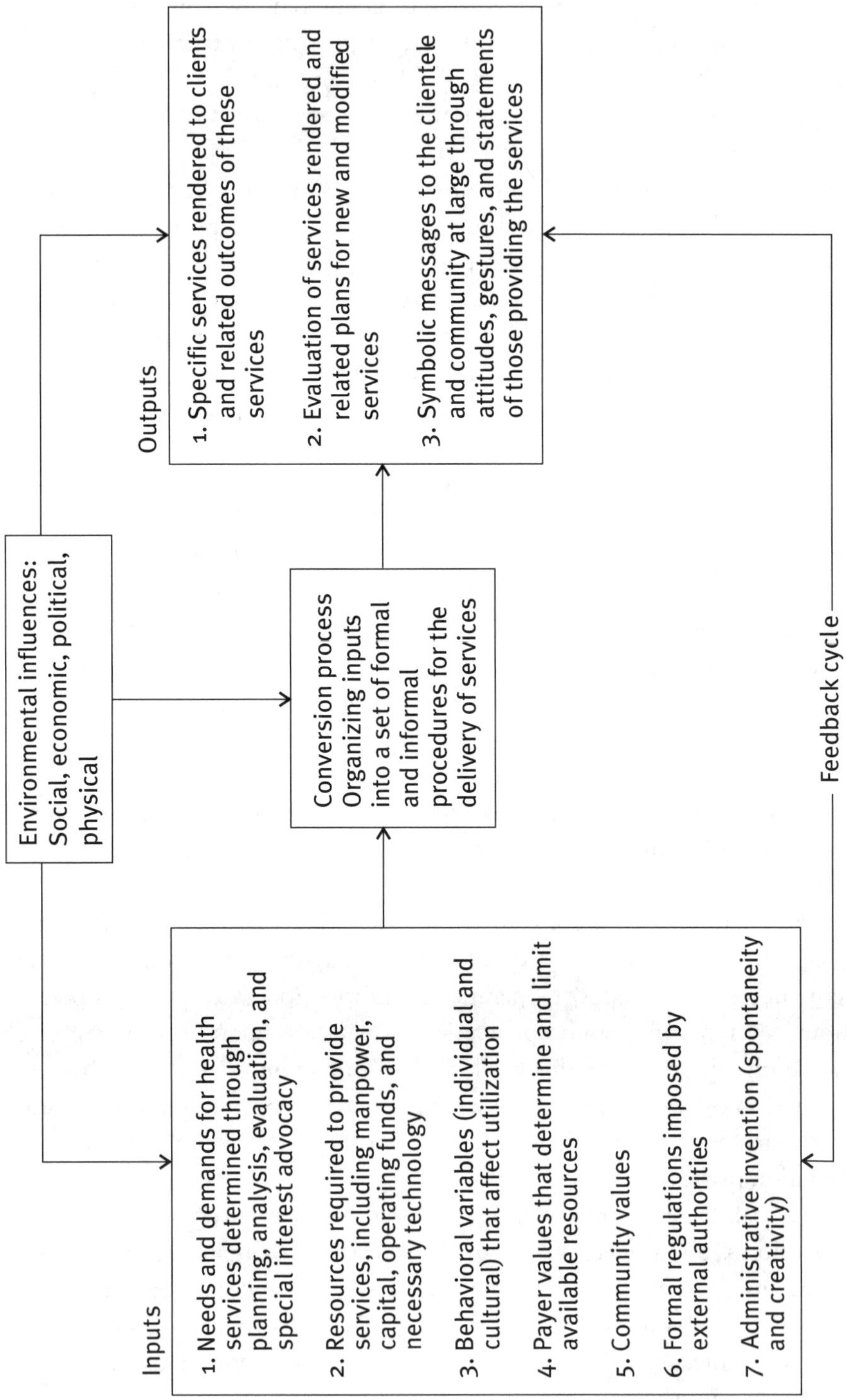
Inputs
1. Needs and demands for health services determined through planning, analysis, evaluation, and special interest advocacy
2. Resources required to provide services, including manpower, capital, operating funds, and necessary technology
3. Behavioral variables (individual and cultural) that affect utilization
4. Payer values that determine and limit available resources
5. Community values
6. Formal regulations imposed by external authorities
7. Administrative invention (spontaneity and creativity)
Environmental influences: Social, economic, political, physical
Conversion process Organizing inputs into a set of formal and informal procedures for the delivery of services
Outputs
1. Specific services rendered to clients and related outcomes of these services
2. Evaluation of services rendered and related plans for new and modified services
3. Symbolic messages to the clientele and community at large through attitudes, gestures, and statements of those providing the services
Feedback cycle

Systems Characteristics

Certain basic concepts explain what systems are and how they function:

- *A system must have unity or integrity.* A system must be viewed as an entity in its own right; it has a unity of purpose—the accomplishment of a goal or function. A system must have an identity and must have describable boundaries that allow it to be defined without reference to external events or objects.
- *Systems at work in healthcare organizations are, mostly, very complex.* The intricate web of complex relationships that constitute most social systems often makes describing the simple cause-and-effect relationships among individual system components difficult. System complexity is often described as a by-product of a system being more than the sum of its parts.
- *Complex systems are further defined by their hierarchical structure.* Large systems in healthcare organizations can be divided into several subsystems, and these subsystems in turn are subject to further subdivision in a nested format. For example, the patient care component of an IDS is composed of several subsystems—diagnostic, therapeutic, rehabilitative, and so forth. Each of these subsystems can be further delineated by a series of smaller systems. The network of systems and subsystems of a patient care system has a nested structure (see exhibit 4.6).

EXHIBIT 4.6
Healthcare Organization Systems Network

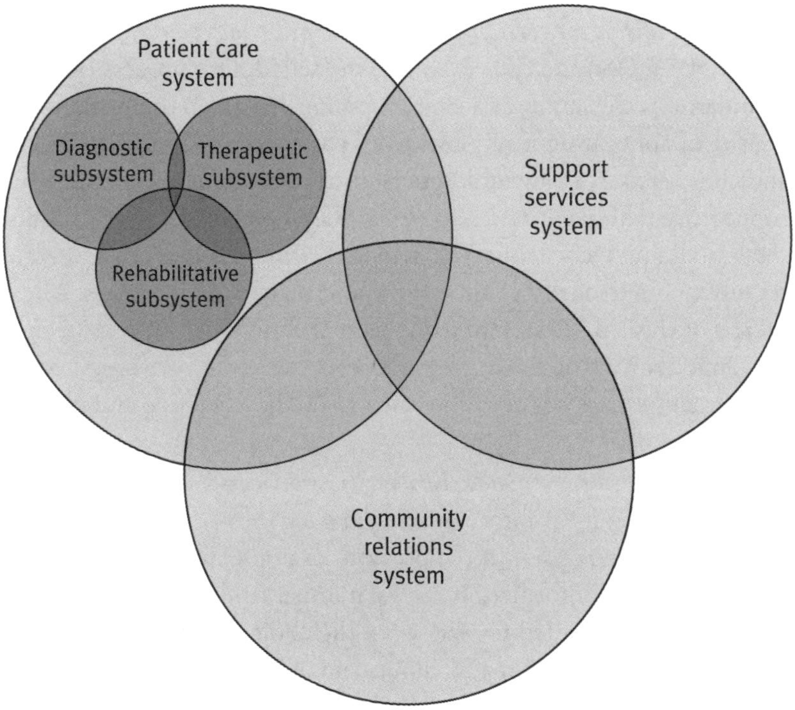

- *Although most organizational systems are dynamic and subject to frequent change, they nonetheless must possess some stability and equilibrium.* The system must continue to function in the face of the changing external environment in which it operates. To accomplish this, procedures must be sufficiently generalized to accommodate a variety of situations that could develop. Complex systems must be self-adapting and must include control functions that are continuous and automatic. When the system can no longer adapt to changing requirements or external environment, it no longer functions as a system—a breakdown has occurred.
- *Systems can be either deterministic or probabilistic.* In a deterministic system, the component parts function according to completely predictable or definable relationships. Most mechanical systems are deterministic. On the other hand, a human systems or human–machine systems (including an information system) is probabilistic because all of its relationships cannot be perfectly predicted. In healthcare organizations, for example, most clinical systems are subject to fairly extreme fluctuations in the quantity and nature of the demand for patient services. Systems theory, then, provides a perspective—a way of viewing not just the parts and not just the whole but the spectrum of relationships of the parts in the context of the entire system's unity of purpose.
- *The simplest of all systems consists of three essential components: one or more inputs, a conversion process, and one or more outputs* (see exhibit 4.7). Consider, for example, the scheduling process of an ambulatory care center as a simple system. *Inputs* to the system consist of appointment requests from patients; physician schedules; and clinic resources, including personnel, treatment rooms, and supporting materials. The *conversion process* comprises a set of actions: the scheduling clerks collect information from patients, match patient requirements to available time slots, and make appointments. The *output* of this simple system is the patient scheduled for service in the clinic. Note that the output becomes the input for several other functional systems of the clinic, such as medical records and patient accounting.
- *Most systems involve feedback. Feedback* is a process by which one or more items of output information feed back into and influence future inputs (see exhibit 4.8). In the previous example, feedback is in the form of adjusted information on the number of time slots available as the patient is scheduled for service in the clinic. In other words, each time an appointment is made, input data on times available are revised and updated.

- *Systems are either open or closed.* A *closed system* is completely self-contained and is not influenced by external events. In an *open system*, the components of the system exchange materials, energies, or information with their environment (see exhibit 4.9); that is, an open system influences and is influenced by the environment in which it operates. All closed systems eventually die (cease to function as a system). Only open systems that adjust to the environment can survive as systems in the long term.

Environmental Factors in Open Systems

Healthcare systems, with the exception of certain purely mechanical systems in the physical plant, fall into the category of open systems. Human or human–machine systems in healthcare organizations are influenced by a variety of environmental factors (sometimes referred to as *exogenous factors* or *variables*) that are important to consider in understanding how a system functions. These environmental factors fall into four broad categories: social, economic, political, and physical.

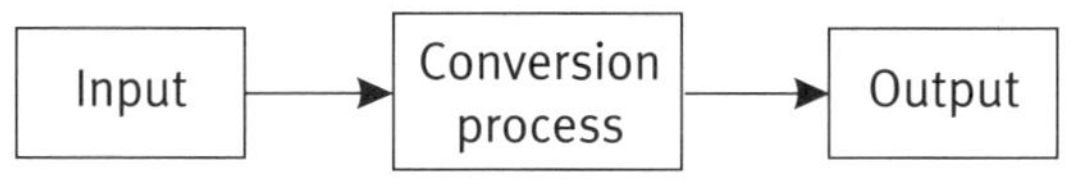

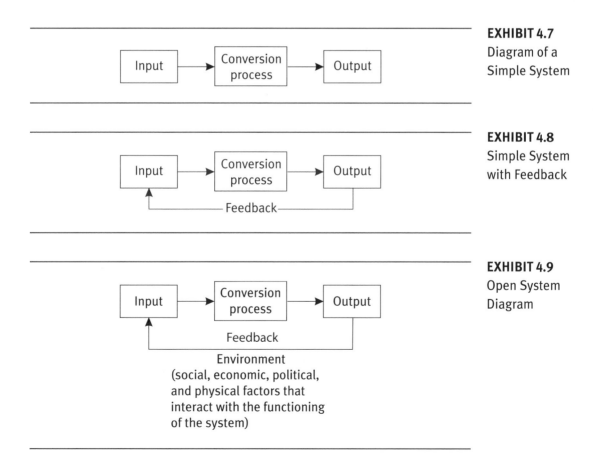

EXHIBIT 4.7
Diagram of a Simple System

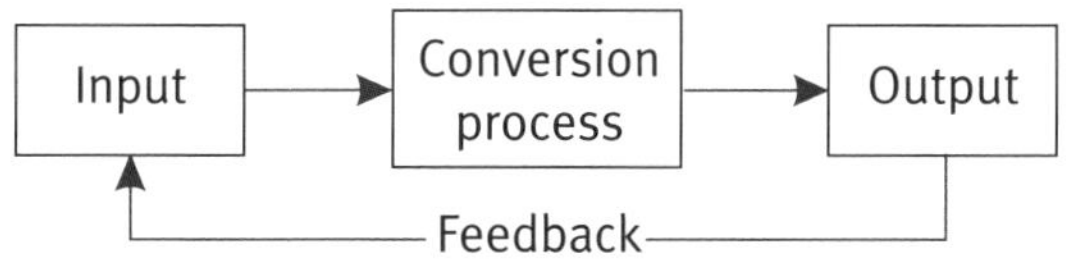

EXHIBIT 4.8
Simple System with Feedback

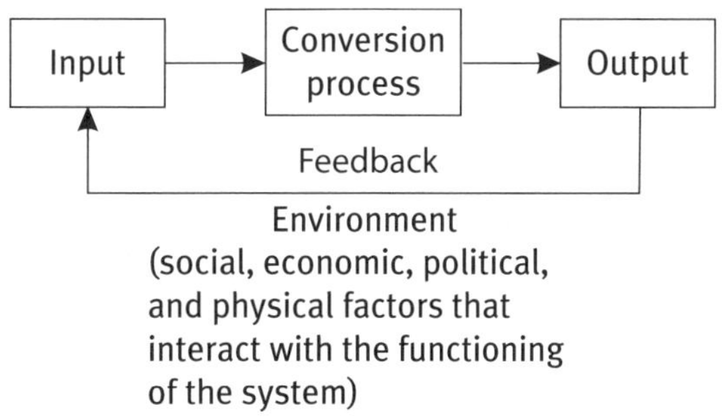

EXHIBIT 4.9
Open System Diagram

Healthcare systems are influenced by *social factors*—characteristics of individuals and groups of people involved in the transactions that organizations undertake. Social factors affect patient behavior and patterns of service utilization. Informal patterns of behavior develop among employees, and these have definite effects on the way operating systems function. The organizational roles played by physicians and other health professionals interact with the formal functioning of healthcare systems. Social factors are important determinants of system functioning, and systems analysts need to be well versed in the art of human-factors engineering when designing systems.

A second major category is *economic factors*. Systems are directly dependent on the availability of resources, and fluctuations in the local and national economy influence both demand and resources. It is well known, for example, that patients often defer elective procedures during a recession. Healthcare systems are also affected by *political factors*, the third category. A variety of special interest groups place competing demands on healthcare organizations, and systems are influenced by both community politics and organizational politics. These political realities must be considered in the analysis and design of any system for the institution. The *physical factor* constitutes the fourth and final category that affects organizational systems. This tangible environment refers to the amount of space available and the way in which system components relate physically to each other.

Cybernetic System

A cybernetic system is self-regulating (Weiner 1954). Feedback in a cybernetic system is controlled to adjust the future functioning of the system within a predetermined set of standards. The following are added to the system components to enable automatic control:

1. A sensor continuously gathers data on system outputs.
2. Data from the sensor are fed into a monitor to continuously match the quantity or quality (or both) of performance with the standards—predetermined expectations of system performance.
3. Error signals from the monitor are sent to a control unit, whose purpose is to automatically modify inputs and conversion processes to bring the functioning of the system back into control.

The most often cited example of a cybernetic system is a thermostat for the automatic heating and cooling of a building. The sensor unit continuously measures ambient temperature and sends signals to the monitor, which compares the current temperature with the preset standards. Through the control process, automatic correction signals are sent back to the heating and cooling units to keep their temperature within control limits.

Bielecki and Nieszporska (2019) provide a current and extensive overview of a variety of health systems models and demonstrate the value added of a cybernetic perspective for analyzing the "pathology" inherent in each of the models. The systems span the range from the a simple US healthcare system with insurance engagement; a German model with centralized funding but health funds operating as insurers; a fully centralized model of healthcare provision, such as Poland; and a hypothetical participatory model. Cybernetic analysis clearly identifies conflicts and inefficiencies in each model.

Management Control and Decision Support Systems

Organized systems in healthcare organizations should be designed as cybernetic systems, which have built-in formal management controls. The inputs include the demand for services by patients and their representatives (e.g., family members) and the resources required to provide the services (e.g., labor, materials, capital, technology). The conversion process consists of actions taken by employees and other clinicians aided by formal procedures, informal patterns of functioning, equipment, and management. The outputs include the services rendered and the specific outcomes or impact of the services provided.

Management control in a cybernetic system is presented in exhibit 4.10. The sensor continuously gathers data on the quantity, quality, and

EXHIBIT 4.10
Cybernetic Management Control System for a Healthcare Organization

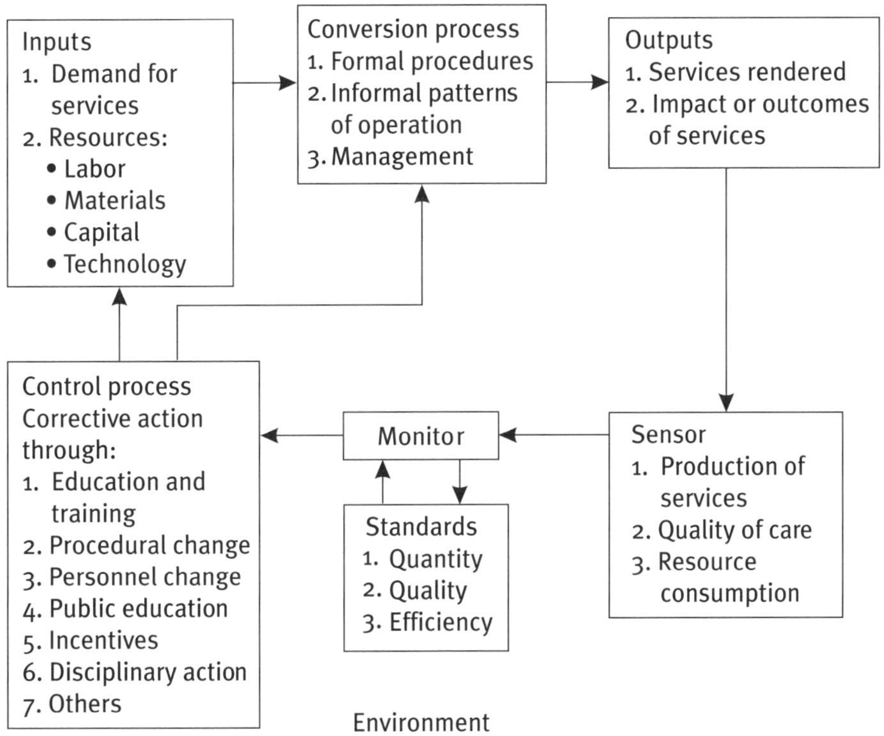

other characteristics of the services rendered as well as the resources consumed in the provision of these services. Data from the sensor (i.e., management reports) are monitored against the established standards of quantity (production and service goals), quality of care, efficiency of the service process, and patient outcomes. When standards are not met, a control process is activated to initiate necessary changes and improvements. The control process contains several components, including education and training of personnel, community or public education, reengineering of the care process, personnel changes to improve service, employee incentives, disciplinary action, and many others.

A key component in management control systems is the establishment of standards for performance and quality control. This task is not easy, requiring considerable effort and thoughtful planning from managers and professional personnel practicing in or employed by the healthcare organization. Standards can be developed or emerge in a number of ways. First, the administrative or medical authority in the institution may take the lead in the process. Second, the standards may be the result of negotiations and subsequent agreement between employees and supervisors. Third, the organization may conduct empirical studies of previous performance, using industrial engineering techniques, to determine the best standards to follow. Fourth, in certain areas of operation, standards are mandated by external regulations, legal requirements, or accrediting agencies.

Whatever the approach to or circumstances of establishing standards, healthcare organizations must realize standards are essential to effective management control. Standards prevent management control from operating on an ad hoc basis, and they require careful management planning, continual review and revision, and frequent reinforcement through incorporation into the formal employee reward system.

Consider as an example the operation of a centralized clinical laboratory in an IDS that can be described as a cybernetic system with planned controls built into the system for quality assurance and performance control purposes. Exhibit 4.11 is a schematic diagram of the functioning of the laboratory in cybernetic system terms.

System inputs include scheduled demand (i.e., laboratory tests planned, ordered, and scheduled in advance) and unscheduled demand (i.e., tests required to be processed on an emergency basis). Resource inputs include technical personnel in the laboratory, materials and equipment used in the testing process, and related technology. The conversion process consists of those formal and informal organizational actions related to collecting specimens; conducting laboratory tests; and reporting results to appropriate points in the hospitals, outpatient clinics, and other service units of the IDS. System outputs include the test reports sent back to clinicians ordering the

EXHIBIT 4.11
Clinical Laboratory as a Cybernetic System

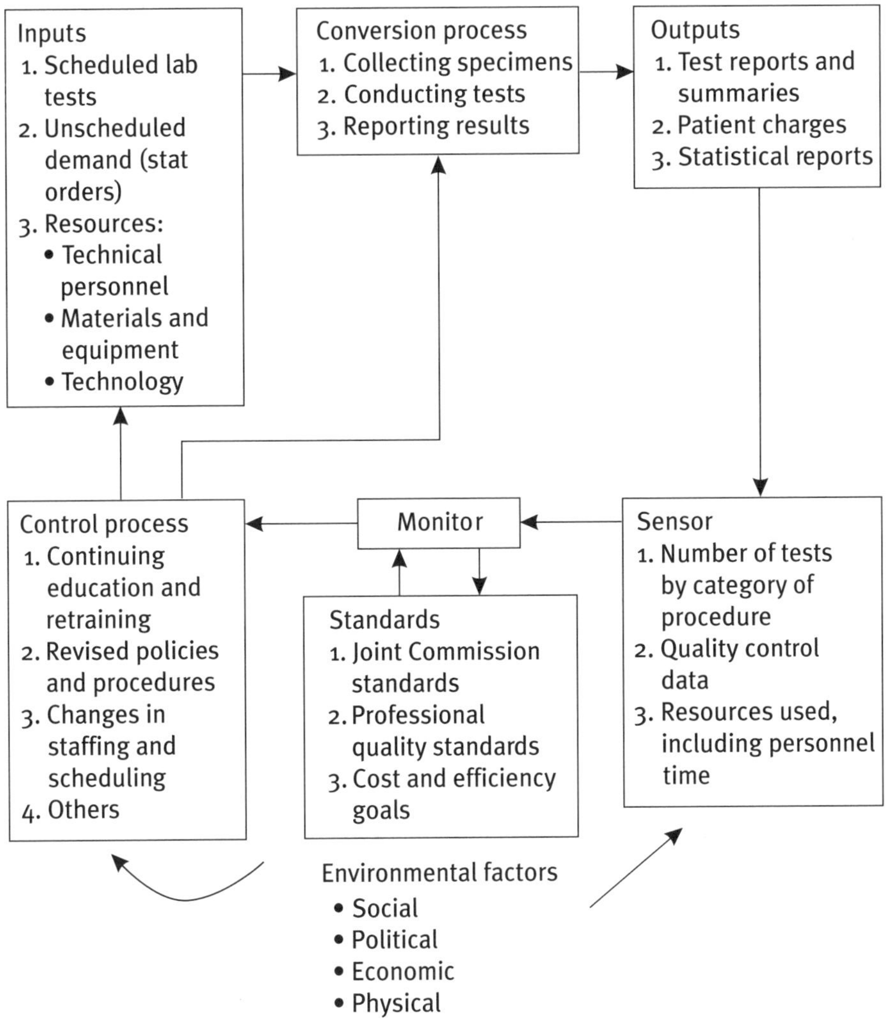

tests, charges for services transmitted to the patient accounting department for billing purposes, and various statistical reports.

Cybernetic components for management control are also included. The sensor component is the management reporting system of the laboratory by which data on the number of tests conducted by various categories, quality control data, and records of resources consumed (including personnel time of laboratory technicians) are collected and recorded. These data are used by laboratory managers who monitor actual performance against predetermined standards, including those established by accrediting and oversight agencies, professional standards of quality established by the chief pathologist and medical staff, and cost and efficiency (productivity) goals established jointly by the administrative and medical personnel in the organization. When standards are not met, corrective actions are initiated, including activation of continuing education and retraining; revision of operating policies and procedures, including recalibration of test equipment if necessary; and change in staffing patterns and scheduling. The laboratory operates overall as an open system influenced by several contextual or environmental factors, including the physical environment of the laboratory facility, current economic conditions of the IDS, social and political factors related to personnel interaction in the laboratory, and advancement of technology.

Useful Information for Management Control

Any management control system is information dependent. Information requirements permeate the system diagrams presented in the preceding exhibits. For healthcare programs to be properly managed, information is needed about each of the major system components.

Input information must be collected to monitor continuously both scheduled and unscheduled demand as well as the resources consumed in the provision of services. Operational procedures must be constantly observed through information on exceptions, error rates, system malfunctions, and similar performance measures on a management-by-exception basis. Output information on the quantity and quality of services rendered must be matched with information on related outcomes of the specific services provided. In addition, the effective manager must keep in close contact with the environment in which their department or institution functions. Environmental information—such as demographic characteristics of the service population, previous utilization patterns, services offered by other organizations, and recent changes in community values—is essential to this task. An effective information system is designed with these kinds of management information needs in mind.

What, then, are the attributes of information that are useful for management control in the delivery of healthcare? Some of the more important characteristics of effective management information are listed in exhibit 4.12 and explained as follows:

- *Information must contain information, not just raw data.* Data must be intelligently processed in accordance with predesigned plans before they become information useful to management or operating personnel.
- *Information must be relevant to the purposes for which it is to be used and must be sufficiently sensitive.* This kind of information enables distinction among similar or competing variables and meaningful comparisons for operating managers. Many information systems provide data that are so aggregated that they provide no meaningful indicators for management

planning or control purposes. Overall hospital cost per patient day is a good example. By contrast, separating costs into fixed and variable components and allocating variable costs by diagnostic groupings and level of care provide more useful information to management.
- *Information must be unbiased.* This means information must not be collected or analyzed in such a way that it becomes a self-fulfilling prophecy.
- *Information should be comprehensive.* In this way, all elements or components of a system are visible to those responsible for administering that system.
- *Information must be timely.* It must be presented to users in advance of the time when decisions or actions are required. Many information systems produce beautifully prepared reports that are completely useless because of their failure to meet operational time requirements.
- *Information should be action oriented.* It should be designed to aid the manager directly in the decision process rather than merely present passive facts about current operations. For example, information from an inventory control and materials management system should include direct indicators of when specific items need to be reordered rather than just data on current numbers in stock.
- *Information systems should have the goal of producing uniform reports.* This way, performance indicators can be compared over time—both internally against previous performance and externally against the experience of similar organizations or competitors.
- *Information must be performance targeted.* It must be designed and collected in reference to predetermined organizational goals and objectives.
- *Information should be cost-effective.* The anticipated benefits of having the information available should be worth the costs of collecting and processing that information.

EXHIBIT 4.12
Characteristics of Useful Management Information

- Information—not data—driven
- Relevant and sensitive
- Unbiased
- Comprehensive
- Timely
- Action oriented
- Uniform (for comparative purposes)
- Performance targeted
- Cost-effective

The Why

Why is system integration one of the most important objectives of HIT strategic planning? Healthcare delivery involves a wide range of providers. Much of that care used to be given primarily in a hospital or in a physician's office, but today, care is provided in many settings by many providers. Getting these diverse groups to coordinate care is a challenge because of geographic and organizational separation. For optimum care, organizations must become highly interconnected.

The foremost challenge in realizing this highly interconnected ideal is getting the disparate units in the organization to communicate with one another and share clinical information. To make diagnostic and treatment decisions, clinicians need information that is generated by several different departments (e.g., radiology, pathology). Connecting clinical and financial information is essential for effective management and strategic decision support. The government has a useful but abstract framework for understanding exchange (see www.healthit.gov/topic/health-it-and-health-information-exchange-basics/what-hie). In their framework, there are three primary forms of health information exchange:

1. *Directed exchange* supports coordinated care by sending and receiving "secure information" electronically among care providers.
2. *Query-based exchange* allows a provider to request and obtain health information on a patient from other (external) providers. The request comes from a core provider and often arises as a result of unplanned care.
3. In *consumer-mediated exchange*, health information from multiple providers is made available to patients to aggregate and control.

Internal communication and sharing of information is only half the battle, however. The concept of system integration has expanded from the need to connect internally to the need to connect externally across organizations (Markle Foundation 2004). Healthcare organizations need to link to outside institutions or providers for both business and regulatory reasons. The federal government's mandate for interoperability has raised the urgency for system integration and has led to the establishment of the Certification Commission for Health Information Technology (CCHIT). CCHIT is charged with creating standards of communication for healthcare organizations, and the idea behind such government standards is to force vendors to develop software that meets interoperability requirements. In addition, connectivity must include the organization's business partners and all other providers in an integrated delivery network. For example, exhibit 4.13 presents a schematic diagram of the information requirements for a truly integrated healthcare delivery system (Markle Foundation 2012).

EXHIBIT 4.13

Information Requirements for an Interconnected Network

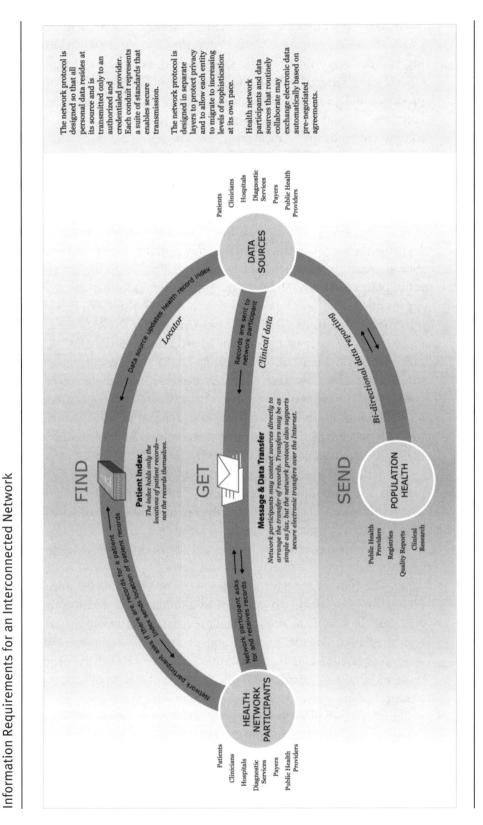

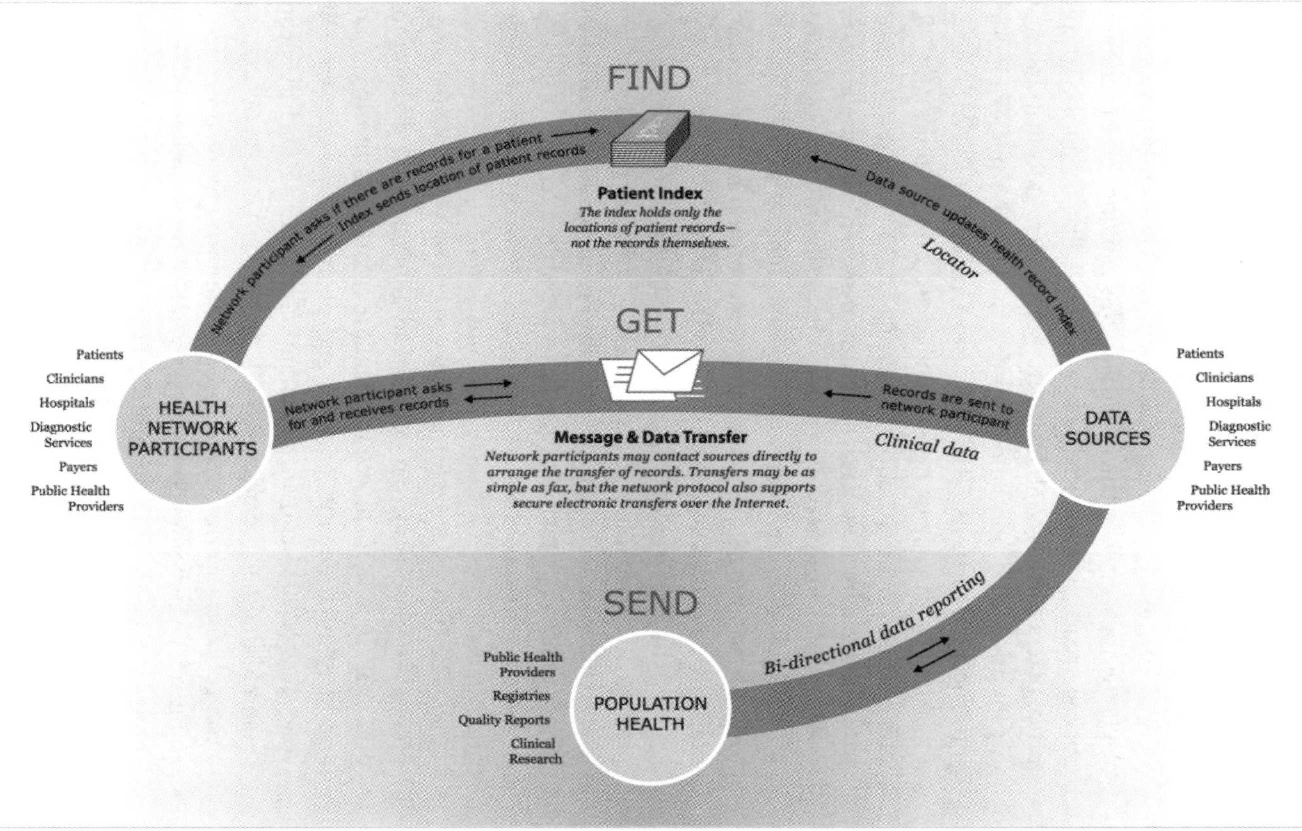

The network protocol is designed so that all personal data resides at its source and is transmitted only to an authorized and credentialed provider. Each conduit represents a suite of standards that enables secure transmission.

The network protocol is designed in separate layers to protect privacy and to allow each entity to migrate to increasing levels of sophistication at its own pace.

Health network participants and data sources that routinely collaborate may exchange electronic data automatically based on pre-negotiated agreements.

Source: Figure 3.13: ©2012, Markle Foundation. This was originally published as part of the *Markle Connecting for Health Common Framework: Resources for Implementing Private and Secure Health Information Exchange*. Reprinted with permission.

Oas (2001) states that system integration has been slow in coming to healthcare. Information systems developed in the 1980s focused on billing and business office functions. Most of these systems contained limited clinical information. In the 1990s, emphasis shifted to automation of clinical processes and provision of access to clinical data to individuals across the enterprise. Seamless integration and information sharing are essential in today's environment. However, much has yet to be done to achieve this ideal. Former CCHIT chair Mark Leavitt has indicated that two-member entities in the healthcare field have a limited ability to exchange information (Robeznieks 2006), and the final CCHIT chair, Karen Bell, implied that this exchange ability was still limited as of 2012.

Hochman, Garber, and Robinson (2019) argue that information exchange broadly has failed and suggest a more concentrated and mandatory approach is warranted. They contend that a minority of physicians in office practice have the ability to transmit patient information outside of their organization, and only one in three can integrate this external information into their EHR. In its 2018 report to Congress, ONCHIT comments, "As of 2015, 96 percent of non-federal acute care hospitals and 78 percent of office-based physicians adopted certified HIT. As a result, most Americans who receive care now have their health data recorded electronically. However, this information is inaccessible across systems and appropriate end users in the market in ways that can generate value. End users also lack modern tools for accessing information that are common in other industries but are not widely available in health care" (ONCHIT 2018, 8).

Achieving system integration requires careful front-end planning prior to the selection and acquisition of computer hardware and software. The technical aspects of data and software integration are discussed in chapters 8 and 9. The planning processes described in this chapter are essential in ensuring that systems are connected for information sharing across the organization.

The business case for integration stems from the vital impact of comprehensive information on clinical and administrative decision-making. The potential for CPOE to reduce medical errors rests firmly on HIT capacity and integrated medical, nursing, and pharmacy systems (see Hillestad and colleagues [2005] and Johnston and colleagues [2003] for general discussions and findings regarding CPOE, as well as Yu and colleagues [2009] for a comprehensive review). Strategic growth through full use of joint inpatient, ambulatory, and physician practices relies on seamless information flows among and between these entities. Finally, the movement to regional health information networks requires access to and sharing of clinical and financial information among organizations. Investment in the capacity of organizations to share clinical and financial information is occurring in an era of significant cost constraints for healthcare and HIT.

Summary

HIT governance has expanded in scope and importance along with the growth of the integrative role of HIT. Healthcare organizations that successfully implement HIT must have a governance structure that effectively (1) develops (and consistently applies) a consistent HIT strategic plan; (2) aligns HIT strategy with organizational strategy; (3) develops HIT infrastructure, architecture, and policies; (4) sets and manages HIT project priorities and investments in HIT infrastructure; and (5) documents HIT value or benefits to enhance accountability.

A successful HIT strategic plan includes (1) a statement of corporate or institutional goals and objectives; (2) a statement of HIT goals and objectives; (3) priorities for the applications portfolio; (4) specification of overall HIT architecture and infrastructure; (5) a software development plan; (6) an HIT management and staffing plan; and (7) a statement of resource requirements. The planning process should be guided by an enterprise-wide HIT steering committee, whose membership is composed of representatives from senior management, medical staff, nursing staff, finance, human resources, planning and marketing, facilities, and clinical support services. The CIO should chair the steering committee (if the healthcare organization has established a chair position).

System integration—the ability of information systems to communicate with one another and share information—is essential. Integration can be achieved through a number of alternative network architecture configurations, including a terminal–host system, client and server computing, file and server architecture, peer networks, and grid and cloud computing. In addition, the strategic planning process should include the development of major institutional policies related to HIT. The steering committee should oversee policies related to data security, privacy, and confidentiality; data standardization; acquisition of hardware, software, and telecommunications network equipment throughout the enterprise; and use of the internet.

An understanding of general systems theory is useful in designing and developing management control systems and in obtaining the kinds of information required to enable such control systems to function effectively. Healthcare systems are open systems, and as such they are influenced by the environment in which they function and exchange information. Key environmental factors include social, economic, political, and physical elements that influence system performance. Healthcare systems are also considered cybernetic systems if they include formally planned components that introduce automatic control into the systems. Cybernetic components include sensors to gather data continuously on current system functioning, monitors to compare these data against predetermined standards, and control elements to change inputs or process (or both) when system function is out of control. Management control systems in healthcare organizations can be designed according to the principles of cybernetic systems.

Healthcare delivery viewed in a systems context is information dependent. Effective information for management control purposes has several important characteristics, including dependence on information (not data), relevance and sensitivity, objectivity, comprehensiveness, timeliness, action orientation, uniformity, performance targeting, and cost-effectiveness. Good information systems are developed with these characteristics constantly on the minds of those charged with their design and implementation.

Suggested Readings

Wayland, M. S., and W. G. McDonald. 2015. *Strategic Analysis for Healthcare Concepts and Practical Applications.* Chicago: Health Administration Press.

Harris, J. 2017. *Healthcare Strategic Planning*, 4th ed. Chicago: Health Administration Press.

Harrison, J. 2016. *Essentials of Strategic Planning in Healthcare*, 2nd ed. Chicago: Health Administration Press.

Web Resources

A number of organizations (through their websites) provide more information on the topics discussed in this chapter.

The following are consulting organizations with experience and expertise in healthcare information technology:

- Accenture (www.accenture.com/us-en/services/health/health-consulting) provides a wide range of management and healthcare IT solutions.
- CentraForce Health (centraforcehealth.com) provides consulting and management support in information technology.
- CharlesRiver Advisors (www.charlesriveradvisors.com) consults on a wide variety of HIT issues and specializes in helping organizations assess, select, and implement appropriate technologies.
- The Healthcare Innovation Group website (www.hcinnovationgroup.com) contains a vast array of vendors organized by function.
- Klas Consulting (klasresearch.com/best-in-klas-ranking/healthcare-management-consulting/2019/313) consults with IT and other professional in the healthcare space.

Understanding the Status Board

The status board monitor is located on the wall in the waiting area. You can track the patient on this board using their case/patient number. Names are not displayed for privacy reasons. The number is given to you in the Ambulatory Surgery Unit.

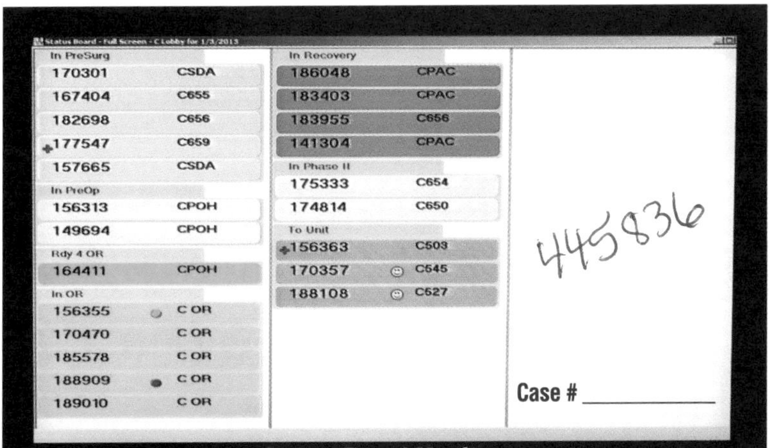

Status Board Monitor

In PreSurg	The patient is in Ambulatory.
In PreOp	The patient is in the Pre-Op Room, being prepared for surgery.
Rdy 4 OR	The patient is ready for surgery.
In OR	The patient is in the Operating Room. = Surgery started. 8:30 = Surgery finished. 9:38
In Recovery	The patient is recovering in the Recovery Room.
Surgery Holding	The patient is being transferred to the next department.
In Phase II	For outpatient surgeries, the patient is back in Ambulatory.
To Unit	For inpatient surgeries, the patient is in their room on one of the units in the hospital. = Ready for visitors. = Added patient for surgery.

NOTE: Patient's room number is displayed to the right of the case number.

If you have any questions, please ask the waiting area volunteer or front desk receptionist.

What to Expect from... Covenant HealthCare Surgical Services

Support from family and friends is important for patients awaiting surgery. This guide will assist you, so you know what to expect during your wait. Following these points will help you better understand the surgical path.

Ambulatory – 3RD FLOOR HARRISON

You may wait with the patient while they are in the Ambulatory Unit.

Pre-Op

From ambulatory, the patient will be moved to a Pre-Op Room. They will usually be in Pre-Op for about one (1) hour.

You will be directed to the waiting area in the main Lobby on the first floor. Please check in with the waiting area volunteer for further instructions.

If you leave the main waiting area, please let the volunteer know. When you return to the waiting area, please check-in with the volunteer.

Cafeteria and vending machines are located on the first floor.

Surgery / Operating Room

The patient's surgery is scheduled for 68 hour(s) / minutes

Surgery does not begin as soon as the patient enters the Operating Room. Preparation times vary and could be longer or shorter than expected.

You will be given an update by an operating room nurse if the surgery takes longer than two (2) hours.

Post-Surgery / Recovery

Outpatient surgery:

You will be notified once the patient returns to the Ambulatory Unit. You may then return to Ambulatory to be with them.

Inpatient surgery:

You will be notified when the patient enters the Recovery Room. When the patient is in their room and ready for visitors, the waiting room volunteer will be called and will let you know. Please limit visitors to two (2) people at a time.

Discharge

When the patient is discharged, they will need a responsible adult to transport them home.

more info on back ▶

If you have questions while you wait, please let the volunteer in the waiting area know and they will contact someone from the surgical floor.

COVENANT HealthCare

Extraordinary care for every generation.

The following are web resources regarding data standards and healthcare data sets:

- The American National Standards Institute's X.12 Group (ANSI; see www.ansi.org) works on specifications for transactions involving the processing of health insurance claims.
- Department of Health and Human Services Office of the Chief Technology Officer (see https://healthdata.gov/content/about) has vast arrays of data sets related to healthcare that are available and accessible to the public.
- The Environmental Protection Agency (EPA; http://enviro.epa.gov) maintains Envirofit, another federal source for data warehousing.

The following provide guidance on governance issues and templates:

- Data Governance Institute (http://www.datagovernance.com) is the principal source of information on data governance for healthcare organizations.
- Erwin: The Data Governance Company: https://erwin.com/blog/healthcare-data-governance
- EHR Intelligence: https://ehrintelligence.com/news/data-governance-best-practices-for-healthcare-health-it
- Varonis, Inc.: www.varonis.com/blog/data-governance-in-healthcare
- KPMG on data governance: https://assets.kpmg/content/dam/kpmg/xx/pdf/2018/06/data-governance-driving-value-in-health.PDF
- HealthIT.gov provides broad overview of governance and planning activities at www.healthit.gov/playbook/pddq-framework/data-governance/governance-management and even tools for evaluating organizational performance at www.healthit.gov/playbook/pddq-framework/worksheet.
- HL7 (www.hl7.org is a standard for healthcare electronic data transmission.

For diverse examples of HIT strategic plans, including guidelines and templates available from associations and vendors, see the following:

- Centers for Disease Control and Prevention strategic plan: www.cdc.gov/od/ocio/docs/CDC-IT-StrategicPlan2017-2021.pdf
- CEB CIO Leadership Council strategy: https://img.en25.com/Web/CEB/CEB_CIO_-_IT_Strategy_on_a_Page.pdf

- CIO Index strategic planning template: https://cioindex.com/reference/it-strategy-template
- The Joint Commission (www.jointcommission.org) is an accreditation organization that provides guidelines for information management planning and broader strategic planning as a part of its overall accreditation standards (by subscription).
- University of South Florida IT strategic plan 2018–2022: www.usf.edu/it/documents/informationtechnologystrategicplan022018submittedbot.pdf
- Harvard University IT strategic plan: https://huit.harvard.edu/files/huit/files/final_2018_itstrategicplan.pdf
- Indiana University School of Medicine strategic plan 2018–2022: https://medicine.iu.edu/about/strategic-plan

Discussion Questions

1. With the change in the definition of HIT governance, why is the external focus of HIT orientation important?
2. What factors should be considered when developing a consistent HIT strategy?
3. Should the HIT strategy be developed with the HIT department in mind and then aligned with the organizational strategy, or should the HIT strategy be developed with the organizational strategy in mind? Why?
4. Why is data standardization becoming increasingly important in healthcare?
5. Several reasons for central review and approval of software and hardware standards are presented in the chapter. In what other ways could central review and approval assist the organization?
6. What factors and concepts should be included in a master plan for information systems development?
7. What would be the functions of the members of the HIT steering committee, such as senior management, medical, nursing, finance, human resources, facilities, and clinical support services staff? Why is having all these organizational areas represented on the steering committee important?
8. There are several reasons to prefer centralized computing over decentralized computing, and vice versa. Which would you prefer, and why?
9. What are your opinions on end-user computing? What are its advantages and disadvantages?

10. What is the importance of data warehouses or clinical data repositories?
11. Give five examples of simple systems and include the input(s), conversion process, and output(s) in your answer. Ensure that some feedback is included in your examples.
12. Why do closed systems eventually die, while open systems continue to be upgraded and modified?
13. Find examples of the use of cybernetic systems in healthcare, other than the examples provided in the chapter.
14. What challenges does system integration present between and among healthcare organizations? What are the solutions to these problems?

References

Agency for Healthcare Research and Quality (AHRQ). 2005. "Electronic Newsletter." Published October 14. https://archive.ahrq.gov/news/enews/enews181.htm.

AlHazme, R. H., S. S. Haque, H. Wiggin, and A. M. Rana. 2016. "The Impact of Health Information Technologies on Quality Improvement Methodologies' Efficiency, Throughput and Financial Outcomes: A Retrospective Observational Study." *BMC Medical Informatics and Decision Making* 16: 154–65.

American National Standards Institute (ANSI). 2005. "New Healthcare Information Technology Standards Panel Formed Under Contract from DHHS." Published October 6. www.ansi.org/news_publications/news_story.aspx?menuid=7&articleid=1054.

Aranow, M. 2014. "Data Governance Is Key to UPCMS's $100-Million Investment." Advisory Board. Published June 18. www.advisory.com/research/health-care-it-advisor/research-notes/2014/data-governance-is-key-to-upmcs-100-million-dollar-bet.

Austin, C. J., J. M. Trimm, and P. M. Sobczak. 1995. "Information Systems and Strategic Management." *Health Care Management Review* 20 (3): 26–33.

Beeler, G. W. 2001. "The Crucial Role of Standards." *Healthcare Informatics* 18 (2): 98–104.

Bielecki, A., and S. Nieszporska. 2019. "Analysis of Healthcare Systems by Using Systemic Approach." *Complexity* 2019. Published April 21. https://new.hindawi.com/journals/complexity/2019/6807140.

Boyd, J. 2005. "The Grass Is Greener? Outsourcing and the Merits of Marriage." In *The CEO–CIO Partnership: Harnessing the Value of Information Technology in Healthcare*, edited by D. Smaltz, J. Glaser, R. Skinner, and T. Cunningham III. Chicago: Healthcare Information and Management Systems Society.

Breen, C., and L. M. Rodrigues. 2001. "Implementing a Data Warehouse at Inglis Innovative Services." *Journal of Healthcare Information Management* 15 (2): 87–97.

Broadbent, M., and E. Kitzis. 2005. *The New CIO Leader: Setting the Agenda and Delivering Results.* Boston: Harvard Business School Press.

Buntin, M., M. Burke, M. Hoaglin, and D. Blumenthal. 2011. "The Benefits of Information Technology: A Review of the Recent Literature Shows Predominantly Positive Results." *Health Affairs* 30 (3): 464–71.

Butler, M. 2013. "Keeping Information Clean: New Information Governance Efforts Challenge HIM to Sort Out Dirty Data." *Journal of AHIMA* 84 (11): 28–31.

Carr, N. 2003. "It Doesn't Matter." *Harvard Business Review* 81 (5): 41–49.

Couture, N. 2018. "Data Governance: The Start of Something Wonderful." *CIO*. Published August 23. www.cio.com/article/3300119/data-governance-the-start-of-something-wonderful.html.

Data Governance Institute. 2020a. "The Basic Information." Accessed January 29. www.datagovernance.com/the-basic-information.

———. 2020b. "The DGI Data Governance Institute Framework." Accessed January 31. www.datagovernance.com/dgi-data-governance-framework.

———. 2020c. "Definitions of Data Governance." Accessed January 31. www.datagovernance.com/adg_data_governance_definition.

———. 2020d. "Goals and Principles for Data Governance." Accessed January 31. www.datagovernance.com/adg_data_governance_goals.

DeFord, D., and D. Porter. 2005. "To Centralize or Decentralize? That Is the Question." In *The CEO–CIO Partnership: Harnessing the Value of Information Technology in Healthcare*, edited by D. Smaltz, J. Glaser, R. Skinner, and T. Cunningham III. Chicago: Healthcare Information and Management Systems Society.

Denis, D. 2001. "Twenty-Five Years of Corporate Governance Research . . . and Counting." *Review of Financial Economics* 10 (3): 191–212.

Encinosa, W., and J. Bae. 2011. "Health Information Technology and Its Effects on Hospital Costs, Outcomes, and Patient Safety." *Inquiry* 48 (4): 288–303.

Gabler, J. M. 2001. "Linking Business Values to IT Investments." *Health Management Technology* 22 (2): 76–77.

georgewbush-whitehouse.gov. 2020. "Consolidated Health Informatics." Accessed January 8. https://georgewbush-whitehouse.archives.gov/omb/egov/c-3-6-chi.html.

Ginter, P. M., W. J. Duncan, and L. E. Swayne. 2018. *Strategic Management of Health Care Organizations*, 8th ed. Hoboken, NJ: Wiley.

Glaser, J. 2002. *The Strategic Application of Information Technology in Health Care Organizations*, 2nd ed. San Francisco: Jossey-Bass.

Glaser, J., and D. Garets. 2005. "Where's the Beef? Part 1: Getting Value from Your IT Investments." In *The CEO–CIO Partnership: Harnessing the Value of Information Technology in Healthcare*, edited by D. Smaltz, J. Glaser, R. Skinner, and T. Cunningham III. Chicago: Healthcare Information and Management Systems Society.

Haseley, S., and J. Brucker. 2012. "Assessing IT Governance: Considerations for Internal Audit." *Journal of the Association for Healthcare Internal Auditors* 31 (2): 54–58.

Healthcare Business & Technology. 2017. "2017 Trends: Aligning Health IT with Business Strategy." Published January 24. www.healthcarebusinesstech.com/2017-trends-healthcare.

Healthcare Information Management Systems Society (HIMSS). 2018. *2018: HIMSS U.S. Leadership and Workforce Survey.* Accessed January 30, 2020. www.himss.org/sites/hde/files/d7/u132196/2018_HIMSS_US_LEADERSHIP_WORKFORCE_SURVEY_Final_Report.pdf.

———. 2012. "2012 HIMSS Leadership Survey." Published February 21. s3.amazonaws.com/rdcms-himss/files/production/public/HIMSSorg/Content/files/2012FINAL%20Leadership%20Survey%20with%20Cover.pdf.

———. 2002. *Thirteenth Annual HIMSS Leadership Survey.* Chicago: HIMSS.

———. 1996. *Seventh Annual HIMSS Leadership Survey.* Chicago: HIMSS.

Herman, D., G. Scalzi, and R. Kropf. 2011. *Managing Health IS Supply and Demand: IT Governance Remains a Top Organizational Challenge.* IT Governance Best Practices. Wheat Ridge, CO: Aspen Systems, Inc.

Higgins, T. C., J. Crosson, D. Peikes, R. McNellis, J. Genevro, and D. Meyers. 2015. *Using Health Information Technology to Support Quality Improvement in Primary Care.* Agency for Healthcare Research and Quality. Published March. https://pcmh.ahrq.gov/sites/default/files/attachments/Using%20Health%20IT%20Technology%20to%20Support%20QI.pdf.

Hillestad, R., J. Bigelow, A. Bower, F. Girosi, R. Meili, R. Scoville, and R. Taylor. 2005. "Can Electronic Medical Record Systems Transform Health Care? Potential Health Benefits, Savings, and Costs." *Health Affairs* 24 (5): 1103–17.

Hochman, M., J. Garber, and E. Robinson. 2019. "Health Information Exchange After 10 Years: Time for a More Assertive, National Approach." *Health Affairs.* Published August 14. www.healthaffairs.org/do/10.1377/hblog20190807.475758/full.

Hogan, P. 2017. "Managed Service Providers: How Do They Benefit Businesses?" Business 2 Community. Published May 24. www.business2community.com/tech-gadgets/managed-service-providers-benefit-businesses-01847576.

i.t.Toolkit. 2020. "The Four Keys to Successful Project Steering Committees." Accessed February 27. www.ittoolkit.com/articles/project-steering-committees.

Johnson, P. 2017. "A 5-Step Guide for Successful Healthcare Data Warehouse Operations." Health Catalyst. Published April 11. www.healthcatalyst.com/a-five-step-guide-to-healthcare-data-warehouse-operations.

Johnson, W. 2005. "The Planning Cycle." *Journal of Healthcare Information Management* 19 (3): 56–64.

Johnston, D., E. Pan, and B. Middleton. 2002. *Finding the Value in Healthcare Information Technologies.* Boston: Center for Information Technology Leadership.

Johnston, D., E. Pan, B. Middleton, J. Walker, and D. Bates. 2003. *The Value of Computerized Provider Order Entry in Ambulatory Settings.* Agency for Healthcare Research and Quality. Accessed January 30, 2020. https://digital.ahrq.gov/sites/default/files/docs/page/CITL%20ACPOE%20Executive%20Preview_0.pdf.

Kapoor, R., J. Fuchs, C. Lutz, and A. Jain. 2006. "A Model for Extending Physician-Specific Process Measures to the Advanced Practice Nurses." *AMIA Annual Symposium Proceedings* 975.

Kark, K. 2018. "IT Spending: From Value Preservation to Value Creation." Deloitte Insights. Published March 12. https://deloitte.wsj.com/cio/2018/03/12/it-spending-from-value-preservation-to-value-creation.

Kellerman, A., and S. Jones. 2013. "What Will It Take to Achieve the As-Yet-Unfulfilled Promises of Health Information Technology?" *Health Affairs* 32 (1): 63–68.

Kloss, L. L. 2015. *Implementing Health Information Governance: Lessons from the Field.* Chicago: AHIMA.

Kloss, L. L. 2013. "Leading Innovation in Enterprise Information Governance." *Journal of AHIMA* 84 (9): 34–38.

Koppel, R., J. P. Metlay, A. Cohen, B. Abaluck, A. R. Localio, S. E. Kimmel, and B. L. Strom. 2005. "Role of Computerized Physican Order Entry Systems in Facilitating Medication Errors." *Journal of the American Medical Association* 293 (10): 1197–203.

Kuperman, G., A. Boyer, C. Cole, B. Forman, P. Stetson, and M. Cooper. 2006. "Using IT to Improve Quality at New York-Presbyterian Hospital: A Requirement-Driven Strategic Planning Process." *AMIA Annual Symposium Proceedings* 2006: 449–53.

Kushan, D. 2016. "Tips for Selecting a Health Care Consultant." HealthcareIS. Published August 3. www.healthcareis.com/blog/tips-for-selecting-a-healthcare-it-consultant.

Levin, D. 2019. "What is HL7?" Datica. Published April 18. https://datica.com/blog/what-is-hl7.

Levy, E. 2018. "Why You Should Already Have a Data Governance Strategy." Sisence. Published June 6.www.sisense.com/blog/why-you-should-already-have-data-governance-strategy/.

Lohman, P. 1996. "Measure Consultant's Objectivity and Character Before Contracting." *Health Management Technology*, July, 31.

Lutchen, M., and A. Collins. 2005. "IT Governance in Healthcare Setting: Reinventing the Healthcare Industry." *Journal of Healthcare Compliance* 7 (6): 27–30.

Markle Foundation. 2012. *Markle Connecting for Health Common Framework: Resources for Implementing Private and Secure Health Information Exchange.*

———. 2004. *Achieving Electronic Connectivity in Healthcare: A Preliminary Roadmap from the Nation's Public and Private-Sector Healthcare Leaders.* Published July. www.markle.org/publications/956-achieving-electronic-connectivity-healthcare.

Menachemi, N., J. Burkhardt, R. Shewchuk, D. Burke, and R. Brooks. 2006. "Hospital Information Technology and Positive Financial Performance: A Different Approach to Finding an ROI." *Journal of Healthcare Management* 51 (1): 40–58.

Menning, W., and R. Carpenter. 2005. "Who's Minding the Store? Effective IT Governance." In *The CEO–CIO Partnership: Harnessing the Value of Information Technology in Healthcare*, edited by D. Smaltz, J. Glaser, R. Skinner, and T. Cunningham III. Chicago: Healthcare Information and Management Systems Society.

Miller, R. H., C. West, T. M. Brown, I. Sim, and C. Ganchoff. 2005. "The Value of Electronic Health Records in Solo or Small Group Practices." *Health Affairs* 24 (5): 1127–37.

Oas, B. 2001. "Integration: Organizations Streamline the Business of Healthcare by Joining Disparate Systems." *Healthcare Informatics* 18 (2): 58–60.

Observational Health Data Sciences and Informatics. 2020. "Data Standardization." Accessed January 30. www.ohdsi.org/data-standardization.

Office of National Coordinator for Health Information Technology (ONCHIT). 2020a. "Data Governance." US Department of Health & Human Services. Accessed January 28. www.healthit.gov/playbook/pddq-framework/data-governance/governance-management.

———. 2020b. "Evaluate your Organization." US Department of Health & Human Services. Accessed January 28. www.healthit.gov/playbook/pddq-framework/worksheet.

———. 2020c. *2020–2025 Federal Health IT Strategic Plan*. US Department of Health & Human Services. Accessed January 28. www.healthit.gov/sites/default/files/page/2020-01/2020-2025FederalHealthIT%20StrategicPlan_0.pdf.

———. 2018. *2018 Report to Congress*. US Department of Health & Human Services. Accessed January 30. www.healthit.gov/sites/default/files/page/2018-12/2018-HITECH-report-to-congress.pdf.

Panangala, S. V., and D. J. Jansen. 2013. *Departments of Defense and Veterans Affairs: Staus of the Integrated Electronic Health Record (iEHR)*. Washington, DC: Congressional Research Service.

Petersen, L. A., L. D. Woodard, T. Urech, C. Daw, and S. Sookanan. 2006. "Does Pay-for-Performance Improve the Quality of Health Care?" *Annals of Internal Medicine* 145 (4): 265–72.

Pizziferri, L., A. Kittler, L. Volka, M. Honourb, S. Guptaa, S. Wang, T. Wang, M. Q. Lippincott, Q. Lia, and D. W. Bates. 2005. "Primary Care Physician Time Utilization Before and After Implementation of an Electronic Health Record: A Time-Motion Study." *Journal of Biomedical Informatics* 38: 176–88.

Rahimi, B., and V. Vimarlund. 2007. "Methods to Evaluate Health Information Systems in Healthcare Settings: A Literature Review." *Journal of Medical Systems* (5): 397–432.

Robeznieks, A. 2006. "Leavitt Surveys Road to Interoperability." *Modern Healthcare*. Published October 30. www.modernhealthcare.com/article/20061030/INFO/61030014/leavitt-surveys-road-to-interoperability.

Rockart, J. F. 1979. "Chief Executives Define Their Own Data Needs." *Harvard Business Review* 57 (2): 81–84.

Rosenthal, M., B. Landon, S. L. Normand, R. Frank, and A. Epstein. 2006. "Pay for Performance in Commercial HMOs." *New England Journal of Medicine* 355: 1895–902.

Rudin, R., S. Jones, P. Shekelle, R. Hillestad, and E. Keeler. 2014. "The Value of Health Information Technology: Filling the Knowledge Gap." *American Journal of Managed Care* 20 (Special Issue): esp1–8.

Sambamurthy, V., and R. Zmud. 1999. "Arrangements for Information Technology Governance: A Theory of Multiple Contingencies." *MIS Quarterly* 23 (2): 261–90.

Scottsdale Institute and HIMSS Analytics. 2005. *Healthcare Leaders Report: The Changing Lanscape of Healthcare IT Management and Governance*. Chicago: HIMSS Analytics.

Shortliffe, E. 2005. "Strategic Action in Health Information Technology: Why the Obvious Has Taken So Long." *Health Affairs* 24 (5): 1222–33.

Simon, S. J., and J. Simon. 2006. "An Examination of the Financial Feasibility of Electronic Medical Records (EMRs): A Case Study of Tangible and Intangible Benefits." *International Journal of Electronic Healthcare* 2 (2): 185–200.

Smaltz, D., R. Carpenter, and J. Saltz. 2007. "Effective IT Governance in Healthcare Organisations: A Tale of Two Organisations." *International Journal of Healthcare Technology and Management* 8 (1–2): 20–41.

Stacey, R., and R. Skinner. 2005. "Crystal Balls: The Elusive Art of Business and IT Strategic Alignment." In *The CEO–CIO Partnership: Harnessing the Value of Information Technology in Healthcare*, edited by D. Smaltz, J. Glaser, R. Skinner, and T. Cunningham III. Chicago: Healthcare Information and Management Systems Society.

Staheli, R. 2015. "Healthcare Reporting: Centralized vs. Decentralized." Health Catalyst. Published April 30. www.healthcatalyst.com/healthcare-reporting-centralized-vs-decentralized.

Stenner, S. P., Q. Chen, and K. B. Johnson. 2020. "Impact of Generic Substitution Decision Support on Electronic Prescribing Behavior." *Journal of the American Medical Informatics Association* 17 (6): 681–88.

Turisco, F. 2000. "How to Justify the Investment: Principles for Effective IT Value Management." *Health Management Technology* 21 (3): 12–13.

Walker, J., E. Pan, D. Johnston, J. Adler-Milstein, D. Bates, and B. Middleton. 2005. "The Value of Health Care Information Exchange and Interoperability." *Health Affairs.* Accessed January 8. www.healthaffairs.org/doi/full/10.1377/hlthaff.W5.10.

Walton, J. 2013. "Data Governance Best Practices for Healthcare, Health IT." *EHR Intelligence*. Published July 2. https://ehrintelligence.com/news/data-governance-best-practices-for-healthcare-health-it.

Ward, J., and P. Griffiths. 1996. *Strategic Planning for Information Systems,* 2nd ed. New York: John Wiley and Sons.

Watts, S. 2017. "What Is an IT Steering Committee? IT Steering Committees Explained." BMCBlogs. Published November 20. www.bmc.com/blogs/it-steering-committee.

Weill, P., and J. Ross. 2004. *IT Governance: How Top Performers Manage IT Decision Rights for Superior Results.* Boston: Harvard Business School Press.

Weiner, N. 1954. *The Human Use of Human Beings: Cybernetics and Society.* Garden City, NY: Doubleday Anchor.

White, D., and P. White. 2014. "The 5 Essentials of Choosing a Consultant." *Entrepreneur.* Published November 4. www.entrepreneur.com/article/238710.

Wilson, K. J., and C. E. McPherson. 2002. "It's 2002: How HIPAA-Ready Are You?" *Health Management Technology* 23 (1): 14–15, 20.

Yu, F., N. Menachemi, E. Berner, J. Allison, N. Weissman, and T. Houston. 2009. "Full Implementation of Computerized Physician Order Entry and Medication-Related Quality Outcomes: A Study of 3364 Hospitals." *American Journal of Medical Quality* 24: 278–86.

PART

II

OPERATIONAL EFFECTIVENESS

CHAPTER

5

HEALTH INFORMATION TECHNOLOGY INFRASTRUCTURE, STANDARDS, AND SECURITY

Learning Objectives

1. Define and use in context the technical terms related to information technology architecture and infrastructure.
2. Distinguish between the hardware and software components of an information system and provide illustrative examples.
3. Discuss basic telecommunication concepts.
4. Describe data storage options, discussing considerations, advantages, and concerns associated with each option.
5. Discuss data transaction types subject to electronic data interchange regulations.
6. Identify data standards organizations with influence in the healthcare sector.
7. Discuss provisions of the Health Information Portability and Accountability Act Privacy and Security Rules.

Overview

Infrastructure, broadly defined, consists of all components of an enterprise's information technology (IT) resources, including not only physical elements such as hardware and other equipment, networks, and data centers, but also software, operational and governance policies, and contractual relationships with vendors and partners. This superficial definition does not convey the scope of a typical system's components or the complexity of designing and managing a dynamic conglomerate that enables the enterprise to conduct its myriad business and clinical activities. These activities must be compliant with extensive government and industry regulations, incorporate numerous technologies, and ensure that clinical services are safe and effective. And all this has to happen under value-based business models driven by third-party payment regulations that constrain revenue enhancement opportunities.

While designing and managing the inherent complexities of information systems are mercifully the purview of a team of IT specialists, healthcare managers need conceptual understanding of system components, network structures, standards and regulations, security risks, and trending issues in health information technology (HIT). A basic level of knowledge is essential to effective participation in HIT budget development, negotiating system contracts, ensuring regulatory compliance, and assessing enterprise risk associated with information system policies and practices. As noted in chapter 1, managers, clinicians, and technicians possess differing bodies of knowledge relative to operational needs, system use, and technical design, and all viewpoints need to inform decisions about the enterprise information system.

Our world has become "connected" in the literal sense of the word. Approximately 95 percent of Americans own a cell phone, and most (77 percent) are smartphone users (Pew Research Center 2019). These smartphones provide constant personal communication opportunities through email, texts, and social media; instantaneous access to a seemingly infinite amount of information via the internet; and numerous apps to manage daily life activities. Things that once could be accomplished only at a hardwired desktop computer can now be done via a smartphone while riding a bus or standing on a beach. This ubiquitous connectivity exists in business computing as well. Information technology in healthcare enterprises, once deployed primarily as stand-alone applications in individual operating units such as the human resources department and the business office, is now conceived as a seamless integrated system of physical and virtual connections to devices that provide access to the full range of information needed for business and clinical operations—but a system that is secure and protected from unauthorized access. In fact, because of Bluetooth and other wireless technologies, very few data devices, even personal devices, used in a healthcare enterprise are not connected (or capable of connecting) to the enterprise information system.

The basic system components of first-generation computers (input, processing, then output) remain relevant, but the ways in which these actions occur have become more numerous and more sophisticated than were possible even five to ten years ago, as each generation of technology eclipses the last more quickly than previous generations evolved. This so-called law of accelerating returns (Kurzweil 2001) suggests that learning from one innovation informs future innovations for faster development, generating an exponential rate of return with regard to human-created technology.

Computing advancements are an excellent demonstration of this law. Computers entered our world in 1946 with the Electronic Numerical Integrator and Computer and its vacuum tube technology (Rosen 1969), moved through second and third generations (transistors and integrated circuity) in the 1950s and 1960s, and had evolved to a fourth generation (microchips) by the early 1970s. Innovations in the second two generations decreased computer size, increased processing capacity and speed, and improved the user interface. Because these innovations also made computer technology more affordable, these advancements significantly increased the use of computers for business applications. However, the innovations of the fourth generation have literally integrated computing and its technology into our daily lives. The ability to network computers and devices, the emergence of the internet and World Wide Web, and the increasing cost-effectiveness of computers for personal use converged to spur innovation in technology and applications at an unprecedented pace.

One result of this rapid innovation and explosion of applications for healthcare is that the "schematic" of an enterprise information network has become more difficult to illustrate graphically as system components become increasingly distributed remotely and virtually, and third-party entities become major contributors to the governance of the information infrastructure. Thus, recognizing that actual infrastructure components will continue to evolve as new and improved technologies emerge at an increasing pace, this chapter will describe currently employed configurations, technology trends, and emerging HIT issues that healthcare managers should be conversant in and that should enable them to continue learning as their enterprise systems evolve in response to continued innovation, business needs, and regulatory guidelines.

Information System Components

The most basic tangible elements of an information system are hardware, software, data storage, and connections among the system components, each of which can be further categorized and described in terms of their functionality and integration. Simplistically, a computing system comprises these components:

- Input devices
- Processing unit
- Output devices
- Primary storage and secondary storage
- Communication devices

The communications devices create connections that enable the computer to interact with other computers or devices, either in or outside the organization. The ability to connect multiple devices that work collaboratively to complete a work process gives rise to the concepts of networking and telecommunications.

Computer hardware, the physical components and devices configured into an information system, comprises input and output devices, processing units, and storage media. Computer hardware spans incredibly broad spectrums of size and function. Some devices are small enough to be held in and manipulated with one hand. For example, a large segment of the general population enjoys personal computing with such devices as a tablet, notebook computer, or smartphone (or a smartwatch), and even these devices may be used for data capture, data processing, and output, and connect wirelessly to the internet or other devices.

A typical outpatient healthcare organization will have at least basic servers, which can store text files, and other servers may contain radiological or other diagnostic images. In a large integrated delivery network composed of multiple hospitals and outpatient facilities, the norm is more likely a dedicated floor or building filled with numerous servers with specified functions such as web servers that connect users to web pages, mail servers for storing email and email account information, and dozens of other file servers. Many diagnostic machines are computers that analyze clinical samples, process data, and produce reports. At the upper extreme of the computing spectra are large and powerful supercomputers.

Hardware is useless without programming or application software, which allow computers to perform specific functions. Software includes system operating instructions and applications that perform tasks, such as nursing documentation or billing. Applications to support healthcare enterprise computing are addressed later in chapters 8 and 9.

A key point for managers to remember is that software and hardware decisions must be made in tandem; one cannot be considered independently of the other. For example, a software application used by physicians may require a large amount of cache storage or a high processing speed to operate effectively, both of which are hardware factors. Healthcare managers need an understanding of basic software concepts to be knowledgeable participants in the complex processes of selecting, implementing, and testing software to maximize the value of their HIT investments. Knowledge needs include an understanding of the purpose and functionality of clinical, business, and communication application software; an awareness of the distinction between integrated and interfaced systems; a recognition of the role of system management software; and a general comprehension about programming languages and language translators.

Data storage options range from small independent devices (such as a thumb drive that you might use to store and transport a PowerPoint presentation) to large data warehouses that store millions of discreet clinical data elements, accessible by approved users in diverse locations simultaneously. Each storage option has unique security issues, some attributable to physical characteristics (e.g., small size that allows easy theft), and other risks that emerge from how and by whom the data are accessed. Physical and virtual connections, which transform independent devices into an integrated network, are arguably the most complex and dynamic of these components. Let us consider these components by looking at their functionality.

Input: Capturing the Data

The power of an information system can be realized only when data and programs have been entered for processing and information is generated for the user. System designers can select from among multiple input options to meet the organization's needs for speed, accuracy, and cost-effectiveness for a given application. As technology advances, new modes of data input emerge, but few have become obsolete.

Although the keyboard remains a frequently used input device, healthcare organizations have found that other input devices are especially suitable for specific applications. For example, scanning devices provide an efficient and accurate means for tracking many types of inventory items, locating paper documents, and even identifying patients via bar code technology. Medical supplies, pharmaceuticals, and patient identification bands may be tagged with bar codes or graphical markings that perform several functions when scanned and recognized by the computer software. For example, a medical supply item or drug may be removed from current inventory, charged to a patient's account, and scheduled for inventory replacement with one simple scanning process. In addition, the computing skills and time constraints of the staff members who will enter the data may be a consideration in choosing the input approach. For commonly performed tasks such as medication orders, busy clinicians often respond better to data-entry options that are highly automated, such as prepopulated entries chosen from a drop-down menu, rather than to keyboard entry, which requires some skill, allows for more errors, and perhaps takes more time than is desirable.

Physicians may order diagnostic tests or medications simply by touching the monitor screen where a list of options is displayed. While discrete data are preferred for reporting purposes, scanning handwritten documents may make the information available to more users much sooner than if the document is audiorecorded and transcribed through keyboard entry. Scanned graphical material, such as electrocardiogram reports, can be accessed online by users in multiple locations, unlike hard copies stored in a single location, which requires users to travel to the storage location or the document to travel to the user.

Selection of the best input device for a given application should consider both efficiency and accuracy criteria. While speed of input provides user convenience, which is important to time-pressured clinicians, speed should not be gained at the expense of data quality, patient safety, and information confidentiality. Clinicians must be able to trust the accuracy of electronic data, and the quality and resolution of captured images must be adequate for visual recognition and interpretation of clinical data.

In the early phases of healthcare computing, data entry typically occurred at centralized locations, such as nursing stations or dictation rooms. Today, information systems are designed to facilitate data capture at the point of care, such as the patient's bedside or in other diagnostic or treatment areas. Often, data are captured concurrently with patient examination and treatment (point of care), through voice recorders, medical scribes, or digitally enhanced diagnostic devices. Areas such as the emergency department may use medical scribes, individuals who observe treatment and document clinician dictation and diagnostic test data in real time. Data also may be entered using computer workstations in or near the patient's room or by using a portable or handheld device that connects the user to the electronic health record (EHR) system. This ability to perform point-of-care data capture is mandated by regulations specific to reimbursement by Medicare that require hospitals to implement Certified Electronic Health Record Technology (CEHRT). Exhibit 5.1 summarizes commonly used data input devices.

Processing: Converting Data to Information

The hardware components of even the most powerful supercomputer cannot by themselves produce output that is of value to the healthcare manager, because they need a detailed set of instructions that describe, step by step, the tasks that must be performed to achieve a desired objective. This detailed set of instructions is known as a *program*, and programs are collectively referred to as *software*.

Although for many people software is equated with user applications (either general purpose or function specific), computer software also includes operating systems, utilities, programming languages, software development tools, and language translators. The *operating system* (OS) is the interface between the human user and the computer, managing the functioning of the software and hardware. Most people are familiar with the Microsoft Windows OS or the Apple iOS for personal computers, and Linux, which is open source. *Utilities* software performs general processing, computational functions, or system maintenance functions. Virus scanning and encryption are examples of utility software.

All software—application, operating system, or utility—consists of a detailed set of instructions describing the specific steps the computer is to perform. Processing instructions are communicated to the central processing unit (CPU) in a structured programming language, which has evolved over time from binary code (0, 1) to instructions resembling spoken language. Examples of programming languages include BASIC, COBOL, and Java, all of which have rules and context frameworks. Despite the number and type of programming languages in existence, the objective of all languages from the

EXHIBIT 5.1
Input Devices

Device	Description	Advantages	Disadvantages
Keyboard	Device containing a panel of "keys," including alphabetic and numeric characters and special function keys	Familiar, inexpensive, rapid entry (when done by skilled users on full-sized boards)	Poor keying skills result in data-entry errors; smaller boards on handheld devices may be difficult to use.
Pointing device (mouse, joystick, rollerball, light pen, touch screen)	Device that controls the screen cursor (locus of data entry); the pointer may be a finger or a special device	Easy to use, rapid data entry	Precision in pointing is required to avoid data-entry errors.
Scanning device (bar code reader, optical mark/character reader)	Device that captures data by reading differences in light reflection between the mark and the white space	Rapid data entry, good error control, useful in tracking systems	Limited amounts of data are captured; most data cannot be manipulated after entry.
Handwriting recognition device	A stylus or other device used to write data on touch-sensitive screen; may be optical scan of writing on paper	Familiar skill, no training required	Handwriting must be intelligible.
Image capture/video input (computed tomography, magnetic resonance imaging, webcam, digital camera)	Device that captures digital images, which are then stored in a system-defined format	Particularly useful in telehealth and diagnostic applications	Devices are relatively expensive; image resolution must be precise for diagnostic and other healthcare applications; file size can be very large.
Voice input technology	Microphone used to enter data and instructions; software program converts spoken language to machine language by digitizing sound waves	Technical skills not required	Devices are relatively expensive; machine must "learn" user's voice pattern and pronunciation; vocabulary must be built.

user's perspective is simple. The overarching goal is to communicate with the computer in some prescribed format so that useful output can be generated. Whereas skilled programmers may find reward in creating complex code, for the nonprogrammer user, the satisfaction of this communication process lies in the output created, not in the communication process itself.

The progression of programming languages can be tracked through successive generations, with each generation improving the computer–human interface. The evolutionary goal is to achieve ***natural language*** input, whereby the user is able to give verbal commands to a computer as easily as communicating with another—or as easily as you tell Alexa or Siri via your tablet or smartphone to add an item to your grocery list or play a specific song! A ***language translator*** program would convert natural language statements into the binary number commands a computer understands. The technology necessary to recognize spoken words, interpret their content, transform them into a set of procedures, and translate this sequence into machine commands is complex and has not been perfected. While various voice-recognition applications are available for business or personal use, acceptance for medical applications is not universal, although innovation continues apace.

Software issues are important for healthcare managers to understand for a number of reasons. First, although most healthcare organizations do little in-house development of software, the manager must be a knowledgeable participant in software acquisition. Managers must acknowledge that the quality of available software is variable, and in some cases software purchased at significant expense fails to meet expectations.

Second, all software must be appropriately licensed and used only as specified by the license. Users may want to install personal applications on facility computers. While these issues can be controlled to a large degree by system security configurations, policies should be in place that emphasize the organization's strong stance on exclusive use of legally licensed software and facility ownership.

Third, managers should be aware of the rapid evolution of software versions. Operating systems and application software are constantly being revised. Generally, upgrades to major systems come with a cost, and sometimes that cost will exceed the value of the improved functionality, if the current version is meeting their needs. In other cases, the vendor might actually cease to support a given version, thereby forcing the user to upgrade. Again, knowledgeable participation by the manager is valuable in making upgrade decisions.

Finally, and perhaps most important in the current technology environment, the manager must understand the challenges created by the need for interfaces that link disparate software packages and system components.

Upgrading one module of an interfaced system may require extensive modification of the interface as well. Increasingly, there is a need to connect facility applications with those hosted by other providers in the continuum of care or with enterprise partners. A simple example is the electronic transfer of a patient prescription to an external pharmacy, a procedure that may contribute to patient satisfaction.

For stand-alone computers, the CPU is where the actual "computing" takes place. The speed and power of the CPU greatly influence the computer's capabilities, and each generation of computer technology has increased the processing capability while reducing the size of the processing component. An important by-product of processor evolution has been the increased speed of processing. Thus, processors are now smaller, faster, handle more volume, and cost less than their predecessors. You will recall we are now in the fourth computer generation (microprocessors embedded in microchips), enabling very small devices to have exceptional computing capacity.

Distributed processing, combining multiple processors either in one computer or across multiple networked computers, increases processing speed and computing power even further. A single computer may be configured to employ more than one CPU, but a more typical option is to connect multiple computers into a network. A local area network (LAN), sometimes referred to as an *intranet*, connects computers and peripheral devices, usually within a defined entity, such as a building or organization. The connections may be hardwired or wireless, or a combination. The intent of a LAN is to share resources such as software or output devices, facilitate data transfer among users, and provide internet connection.

A *wide area network* (WAN) extends this connectivity to a larger geographic region using multiple telecommunication networks. WANs may be private, such as those restricted to a business enterprise, or public, connecting many networks (LANs) together. The internet is a worldwide WAN. In today's world of "big data" and all-pervading connectivity, distributed processing (or distributed computing) takes on a complex reality. Simplistically, distributed computing systems' components cross multiple networks, and resources and information can be shared among an infinite number of users through communication linkages. The internet is embedded in our social and economic structures such that we take this extreme degree of connectivity for granted as the way we do business and manage personal affairs. A very large volume of healthcare business and information transfer is conducted via the internet. The relative ease with which data move across the internet and its widespread acceptability are undeniable. However, the inherent open access that supports this convenience is not without risk, as data security is a significant challenge that must be addressed when designing internet-based business processes.

Output: Making Information Available for Decisions

Accurate, comprehensive data are required to produce the information clinical and administrative decision-makers need, and the ability to access the information at the time it is needed is crucial. The actual work performed by the computer system is of little value until it is produced (output) in a usable format accessible to the user, such as in print or as a screen image, digitally for additional processing, or in audio or spoken form. An important goal of the IT industry is to make both data entry and retrieval as simple as possible.

Types of output of particular value to healthcare managers include visual displays, printed documents, and audio (including voice) output. The oldest and still most widely used form of displaying output from an information system is a video display screen, typically called a *monitor* for stand-alone devices or a *screen* on a handheld device. Technology has advanced from small monochrome screens into large (or very small), high-resolution liquid crystal displays (LCDs) that can be enabled for data entry by touch, thus serving as both an input device and an output device. These sophisticated monitors can display images at resolutions high enough to support clinical diagnosis and treatment. Where processing devices have evolved to smaller sizes, monitors have moved in the opposite direction for desktop and conference room use. LCD monitors come in more than a dozen sizes and vary in resolution and pixel density. Two or more monitors can be connected to a single computer to allow simultaneous viewing of data from multiple applications. Although most users prefer larger, higher-resolution monitors, purchasing decisions should be based in part on the applications to be used on the system and the data to be displayed on the monitor. For example, monitors to be used for image display need higher resolution than do monitors used for text processing. Individuals who are coding medical diagnoses and procedures may need multiple monitors, or very large split-screen monitors, to access multiple applications simultaneously. If the processing output is intended to meet the needs of a mobile user, the built-in screen in a smartphone or other handheld device serves that purpose. Again, the resolution and image quality needed must be considered when determining the type of device to host the application.

Printers, too, have developed extensively from the early devices that were similar to typewriters, except they printed on track-fed continuous paper rolls. Today's color laser printers are capable of reproducing artwork, photographs, and detailed diagnostic images. These machines can print in a variety of sizes and on multiple grades of paper, cardstock, and other media. Most recently, the addition of three-dimensional printers, designed to add material layer by layer to create a three-dimensional object, are used in medicine. These "built" items may be models of organs created from a patient's imaging data, assistive devices such as hand splints, or other items from an ever-growing list of possibilities. Photocopying machines now multitask as printers, and high-resolution printers are available for lease or purchase at acceptable costs. In fact, for many low-end printers, the cost of color ink cartridges compared with printer cost may cause a user to question whether the printer is the disposable item. Key printer characteristics to consider in lease and purchase decisions include memory capacity, print resolution, and print speed. Networking and wireless technology enable a single printer to service multiple computers and the many users who may share access to those computers. Thus, as with monitors, decisions about printer selection can be based on users and applications served rather than on cost alone.

As technology has enabled digitization of sound with good quality, audio output has become a more viable option in clinical technology applications. When digital text is converted to understandable speech by voice synthesis, an ordinary telephone can be used to access healthcare information. For example, a physician needing a patient's diagnostic test results could use a telephone to call the laboratory or radiology system and hear the results read by a voice synthesizer. Clinicians also can listen to body sounds, such as breathing or heartbeat, from distant locations using a telephone or other audio-transmitting devise. This ability allows expert consultation without patient travel or monitoring of homebound patients with chronic conditions. Collectively, these types of applications are referred to as telehealth, or mHealth.

Storage: Archiving for Active Use or Mandated Retention

Important decision factors for selecting or designing data and information storage for healthcare enterprises are volume, physical security, disaster recovery, and expansion planning. These points are discussed briefly here, but the savvy manager will use a just-in-time approach to explore relevant issues and available options in greater detail when the need to apply these concepts is relevant to the job.

Operational definitions for primary and secondary storage have evolved from early computing days when *primary storage* meant the data were stored on the computer's internal drive for access by the CPU, and *secondary* meant data were stored on external media. Currently, *primary storage* is the label attached to those repositories used for transactional data that are frequently accessed for business and clinical purposes, and *secondary storage* refers to repositories with an archival orientation for data accessed infrequently or not at all. Thus, the distinction between primary and secondary storage is based on data access or use frequency rather than the storage medium or the storage location. Data may be archived for anticipated future uses, such as clinical or business research or trend analysis. Data also may be archived to comply with state or federal mandates to retain business and clinical records for specified periods. Most healthcare organizations have a record-retention schedule that specifies the length of time categories of records must be kept and the date such records can be destroyed as part of their data governance plan. Unfortunately, considering the costs and challenges of data storage and the risks of unauthorized access, many organizations opt to retain records indefinitely rather than implement the destruction schedule (Houser, Slovensky, and Wang 2017).

The goal for data utility, efficiency, and cost-effectiveness is to capture data once and store it in a single location, and to have the data from that location available as needed by any application or user. Replicating data for storage in multiple locations is undesirable for several reasons. First, capturing or inputting the data multiple times is an unnecessary expense. Each unique data capture or entry has an associated expense. If it costs $1 in personnel time to enter a birth date, and every patient's birth date is entered three times, with an annual inpatient census of 100,000, $200,000 would have been spent on the two unnecessary birthdate entries. Second, multiple captures or inputs create opportunities for increased data errors, as every entry poses independent risk of error. Third, if differing data formats are used, the data may not aggregate correctly when files are merged across applications. Data stored in multiple locations may change as data are manipulated, updated, or edited for differing purposes by the various users—which can pose legal risks if the appropriate data are not accessed in response to a specific inquiry. Thus, drawing data from one location may not inform decisions in the same way as drawing the "same" data from another location.

Key issues with regard to data storage include data classification, media used, location, cost, and security. Data classification assists in data management by categorizing data into types that have similar requirements for selected attributes, perhaps for security, regulatory compliance, or processing needs. Storage options, discussed in the following section, are numerous, but should be deliberately chosen to meet access and security needs. While decisions about type, location, and control of data storage are important from financial and data security perspectives, the real value of the repository—and thus the pivotal decision factor—lies in the accessibility and utility of the data housed inside.

Storage Options

The actual storage required for captured and archived data in a healthcare enterprise is massive, and the associated costs are a significant component of the total HIT cost equation. How much storage required for a given application is dependent on the type and volume of data captured, access and retrieval requirements, and retention requirements. For example, are data in text or nontext format? The size of image files and other nontext files is a significant contributor to the total volume of archival storage space required, as nontext data require significantly more storage space (*Journal of AHIMA* 2011).

Many other questions must be posed to inform decisions about storage needs. For diagnostic images, how many procedures are performed in a year? How many years must original images be maintained? Must the diagnostic image and the clinical interpretation be maintained in the same file? Must previous diagnostic data be accessible for comparison with current diagnostic tests? Must the data be accessible in real time for an extended period, or can the data be archived quickly with minimal access requirements? These and other questions are paramount to establishing system data storage requirements.

In addition to nonvolatile storage options (those that retain data permanently), cache or active memory storage requirements for data that require rapid access and manipulation in real time can be extensive. When evaluating certain types of systems, cache capacity can become the determining factor in selecting one vendor product over another. For application-specific parameters, such as cache requirements for image viewing, including clinician users on the product evaluation and selection team is extremely important. If a technology solution does not produce quality data that can support clinical decision-making, the solution is insufficient. With issues of clinical adequacy, patient safety, and patient satisfaction, product cost is rarely the deciding criterion.

Perhaps the simplest and most controllable electronic data storage option is *on-premise hardware-based storage*, where data are housed on hard disks in arrays of network servers. While the technical points are beyond the intent of this discussion, the types of drives used in the array are determined by the type of data stored (structured or unstructured), with hybrid arrays addressing both cost and performance needs. A disk array is scalable, providing data storage and access for connected devices in the enterprise network. *Off-premise storage* may refer to a remote data center owned and managed by the enterprise, or a hosted solution outsourced to a vendor that provides data management services to meet enterprise needs. Generally, off-premise storage configurations will resemble those used on premise; the service is just in a location remote to users. However, this situation is changing as more enterprises adopt cloud storage or hybrid solutions of physical servers and cloud storage.

Cloud storage refers to an off-premise, distributed storage model where data are stored on the internet, generally through a contractual fee-for-service arrangement with an external vendor. The cloud service may be private or public. A *private cloud* is based on an IT infrastructure dedicated to a single enterprise, and offers greater security and control than a shared, public cloud service such as Amazon Web Services or Google Cloud. The technology may be owned and controlled by the enterprise, or a vendor may provide dedicated network resources under a lease or contract arrangement. Healthcare enterprises, whose dynamic computing requirements are coupled with stringent security regulations, may find that private clouds meet those dual needs. A *public cloud* allows distribution of data over internet servers shared among multiple users. These virtual servers are accessed through an online interface. One advantage of public cloud service is that costs may be scaled by usage volume rather than a fixed price for the service. Data also may be distributed across multiple cloud providers for geographic benefits or to segregate data with differing access or security needs.

Storage Expansion Planning and Data Governance

It is a certainty, equally as profound as death and taxes, that the volume of data produced by healthcare enterprises will only increase. The corollary of that certainty is that data integrity and privacy and security regulations for archived health information will not lessen. Technology capabilities will continue to evolve, the types of data that can be captured will expand, and the storage media employed will change. All of these changes will occur rapidly and successively. A continuing challenge for information resource managers will be to ensure that previously archived data and information can be migrated to emerging storage media with no loss of data integrity, irrespective of current IT infrastructure.

The inevitable and constant acquisition and production of data in healthcare enterprises necessitates managing data purging and destruction as well as ensuring adequate storage capacity for archived data. As storage costs for many options have lessened, some managers have found it easier to expand storage capacity than to design and manage a data governance plan. This avoidance technique results in a circular information lifecycle model with no "death" (deletion or destruction) component (Houser, Slovensky, and Wang 2017). A robust approach to information governance is needed and should encompass organizational policies, business and clinical procedures, technology and infrastructure, and a well-defined accountability framework (Empel 2014).

From a financial perspective, one might consider that unimpeded growth will soon subsume more of an enterprise's IT budget than can be reasonably allocated to managing a vast amount of data that has no value to patient care or to business operations. Resources encumbered to manage data resources should be based on sound judgments that ensure accessibility of useful and reliable information to meet business, clinical, and analytical needs (Willig 2015). Thus, healthcare enterprises need to make deliberate distinctions between data that have ongoing utility or must be retained for regulatory compliance, and data that are retained as a result of insufficient data governance. However, selective archiving and destruction of data should be based on legal and regulatory guidelines to ensure defensible disposal (FTI Consulting 2015).

A well-documented data governance plan is important to ensure that data are maintained in accordance with business and clinical needs, securely protected to maintain patient privacy and meet regulatory requirements, and properly destroyed at the terminal point of their life cycle. The American Health Information Management Association (AHIMA) offers assessment tools and an information governance model created specifically for healthcare. Information about the model and assessment tools is available on their website at www.ahima.org.

Disaster Planning and Data Recovery

Not only are healthcare enterprises accountable for protecting all medical and patient identification data maintained and used in the facility, they also must maintain a secure but accessible copy of these data in an off-site location in case information resources are damaged or destroyed by disaster. This obligation, required by the Health Information Portability and Accountability Act (HIPAA) Security Rule's Administrative Safeguards (Snell 2015), increases the secondary storage requirements imposed by the clinical and administrative operational needs of the enterprise. Information about IT disaster recovery plans and links to planning resources are available at www.ready.gov, an official website of the Department of Homeland Security.

Communication: Network Connectivity and Interoperability

Historically, two general approaches have been available for acquiring and implementing application software in a healthcare organization—integrated and interfaced. In the first approach, all modules required to satisfy the organization's computing needs are purchased from a single vendor. Typically, these modules have been designed to work with one another so that data transfer among modules proceeds smoothly. This type of system is known as an *integrated* information system. Epic (www.epic.com), Cerner (www.cerner.com), and Siemens Healthineers (www.siemens-healthineers.com) are well-known vendors of integrated healthcare system solutions for all types of organizations.

By contrast, each of the required modules could be purchased from the vendor thought to be the leader in that particular application area—or one that offers a unique feature valued by the enterprise. Historically, these high-performing applications were referred to as "best of breed," and one might argue that following this approach contributed significantly to the challenges of moving legacy systems toward interoperability. Although a given module might work well for its particular application area, connecting the module to other modules for data sharing could be problematic. For example, the data contained in one module could be incompatible with the data format of other modules. The data formats or the vocabulary used could differ between the two systems. Something as simple as the way a date is recorded (e.g., 01–31–20 versus 2020–01–31) can prevent data from transferring or being matched correctly. Often, the solution is the development of an *interface*, which acts as a bridge between the two modules and which, for example, translates the data format into one that the receiving module can interpret, process, and store.

While these concepts remain conceptually relevant in an organization, the current computing environment in which healthcare enterprises operate requires not only connectivity among components of the internal enterprise information system but exchange of information between computers across industry networks with little intervention on the users' behalf (generally referred to as *interoperability*). Electronic health information must be transmitted by the collecting provider organization to third-party payers, other providers involved in the care of the patient, compliance and oversight agencies, the patient, and other business and clinical partners and stakeholders. The process of data transfer among various networks and systems, called *electronic data interchange* (EDI), requires that data are stored in standard formats, or are translated between sender and receiver, and that agreed-on communication protocols ensure data integrity after the transfer. The 21st Century Cures Act defines interoperability as "the ability to exchange and use electronic health information without special effort on the part of the user and as not constituting information blocking" (Office of the National Coordinator for Health Information Technology 2019).

In healthcare, EDI standards were mandated under HIPAA and include very specific data formats for exchanging billing information between covered entities. The EDI standards apply to all HIPAA-covered entities for the following transaction types (CMS 2017):

- Claims and encounter information
- Payment and remittance advice
- Claims status
- Eligibility
- Enrollment and disenrollment
- Referrals and authorizations
- Coordination of benefits
- Premium payment

Full interoperability has been difficult to achieve through collaborative efforts of consortia and interest groups, partly because early information systems were designed to be fully proprietary, ensuring more market share for vendors. There remains a lack of agreed-on standards that would ensure a uniform exchange and processing of clinical and financial information between providers. Because interoperability between systems remains elusive, legislation and government regulations have been necessary to maintain forward momentum. In 2016, the Centers for Medicare & Medicaid Services (CMS) retitled its EHR Incentive Program as the Promoting Interoperability Program and began requiring use of CEHRT by eligible hospitals in 2019. These certified EHRs require easier exchange of certain elements of a patient's record between healthcare providers.

Recognizing that not all barriers to full interoperability are technical, the US Department of Health & Human Services (HHS) drafted the Trusted Exchange Framework and Common Agreement to support national network-to-network information exchange. In draft stage at the time this chapter was written, the final rule and current requirements will be available at www.hhs.gov.

Data Standards Organizations and Regulatory Bodies

EDI is more efficient and reliable if the data were created in accordance with a standard that makes data formats and definitions compatible. The American National Standards Institute, the National Information Standards Organization, the Organization for the Advancement of Structured Information Standards, and the Public Health Data Standards Consortium are examples of organizations and consortia working toward consensus standards for information products and services. Compliance with such accepted industry standards is an important criterion to apply when evaluating vendors' products. Current information about the standards organizations and their active initiatives is available on their websites, which are in the Web Resources section at the conclusion of this chapter.

There are several federal regulatory agencies that enforce HIT legislation and influence best practices in the sector. Some of the higher-profile agencies are presented in exhibit 5.2. Regulatory compliance generally, and information and data reporting specifically, is an extremely important and complex responsibility for healthcare organizations. Many organizations have delegated accountability for this responsibility to a chief compliance officer (CCO), generally an attorney with special training and experience in healthcare law and regulation. This person will have a staff who build and maintain the regulatory body of knowledge needed to protect the organization, develop and maintain relevant policies, prepare and submit regulatory reports, conduct risk assessments, and train clinicians and staff about compliance issues and appropriate practices. Some CCOs achieve recognition as a certified professional compliance officer, an exam-based designation by the American Academy of Professional Coders (www.aapc.com).

EXHIBIT 5.2
HIT Regulatory Agencies

Entity	Authority	Purpose
Health Information Technology Advisory Committee (HITAC)	21st Century Cures Act, P.L. 114-255 Federal Advisory Committee Act (FACA), P.L. 92-463, as amended, 5 U.S.C. App. 2	Recommends to the National Coordinator for Health Information Technology certain policies, standards, implementation specifications, and certification criteria relating to the implementation of a health information technology infrastructure, nationally and locally, that advances the electronic access, exchange, and use of health information.
Office of National Coordinator for Health Information Technology (ONCHIT)	HITECH Act of 2009 21st Century Cures Act of 2018	Responsible for advancing connectivity, interoperability, and usability of HIT. Oversees conditions of certification and trusted exchange framework.
ONCHIT HITECH Programs	American Recovery and Reinvestment Act (ARRA)	Supports nationwide implementation of HIT, including the State Health Information Exchange Cooperative Agreement Program, regional extension centers to assist primary care providers in adoption and meaningful use of EHRs, and the Workforce Development Program to train healthcare workers in new health information technologies.
Office for Civil Rights	Department of Health & Human Services	Enforces federal civil rights laws; conscience and religious freedom laws; HIPAA Privacy, Security, and Breach Notification Rules; and the Patient Safety Act and Rule, which together protect fundamental rights of nondiscrimination, conscience, religious freedom, and health information privacy.
Cybersecurity and Infrastructure Security Agency (CISA)	Cybersecurity and Infrastructure Security Agency Act of 2018	Communicates cybersecurity and infrastructure security knowledge and practices for federal network protection, cyberprotection, infrastructure resilience, and emergency communications.

Privacy, Physical Security, and Cybersecurity

The healthcare sector has experienced a major evolution—most health information and patient medical records are now online and connected across providers and health systems, and medical professionals enjoy significant advances in medical and information technology. However, as the healthcare field continues to expand its reliance on digital technologies, organizations face increasing concerns about safeguarding the privacy and security of information and the corollary of cybersecurity threats. Unfortunately, the technology advances that allow valuable, legitimate uses that improve business operations and clinical services also provide cybercriminals and recreational hackers with tools to breach systems and wreak havoc. EHRs, discussed in chapter 8, are a prime target for cyberattacks because of the extensive personal information they contain and the potential such data have for financial advantage.

Data breaches—generally, any unauthorized access to information—are a significant threat for healthcare enterprises, posing both reputational and financial risks. The HIPAA Breach Notification Rule, enacted under the Health Information Technology for Economic and Clinical Health (HITECH) Act of 2009, requires that breaches resulting in exposure of 500 or more individual records must be reported by the healthcare organization to HHS's Office for Civil Rights (OCR). Guidelines for submitting notice of a breach are available on the HHS website. For the year 2018, the OCR received notice of 351 data breaches involving exposure of more than 13 million health records—a significant increase over 2017, when 5.1 million records were exposed in 359 breaches (Donovan 2018a; *HIPAA Journal* 2018). The Ponemon Institute, an independent research firm that explores issues related to personal and business information, conducted interviews with more than 2,200 data protection and compliance professionals across 17 industries and identified 477 companies that experienced a data breach in the previous year (Ponemon 2018). With the caveat that healthcare organizations comprised only 1 percent of the sample, their findings calculate the average cost of a data breach to be $3.86 million, approximately $148 per record stolen. In addition, the financial penalties that covered entities could incur as a result of a data breach were outlined under the HIPAA Omnibus Rule, which became final in 2013. Because data breaches can be intentional (neglecting to manage known security risks) or unintentional (processes and technology were in place to prevent a network intrusion, but a sophisticated hacker gained access anyway), CMS defines a tiered approach to penalties that may be incurred by an offending covered entity.

Research reports such as these limited examples, coupled with high-profile media releases about individual security incidents, compel healthcare executives to consider information security a high priority in strategic planning and resource allocation. The reputational impact of a data breach that has been determined to stem from negligence and inadequate policies and procedures cannot be quantified, but the financial impact of the incident certainly can.

Privacy

An individual's right to general privacy is protected by the Fourth Amendment to the US Constitution. More specifically, individuals' right to privacy of their health information is protected by HIPAA and the modifications to HIPAA made via the HITECH Act, along with later amendments. These laws are the most significant and comprehensive legal protections that exist for health information generally, and electronic health information specifically. The laws have multiple accompanying rules; two notable for this discussion are the Privacy Rule and the Security Rule. Detailed summaries and current information about these rules are available at www.hhs.gov.

The HIPAA Privacy Rule, enforceable for all entities since 2004, is binding on any healthcare provider, health plan, or covered entity that transmits health information electronically. The Privacy Rule ensures protection of individual health records through national standards and governs disclosure and use of the information. The Privacy Rule references personal health information (PHI), sometimes described as "protected health information," which is defined as "individually identifiable health information held or transmitted . . . in any form or media, whether electronic, paper, or oral" (OCR 2003). Electronic PHI is referred to by some sources as ePHI. The OCR, which oversees HIPAA enforcement, holds healthcare organizations accountable for protecting PHI under penalty of financial fines and loss of access to federally funded insurance programs, such as Medicare and Medicaid (OCR 2003).

Despite the significant burden engendered by HIPAA rules, notably with regard to the Privacy Rule, few changes were made between 2013 and 2019. One example of burdensome administrative requirements is that organizations must obtain written confirmation from patients that they were given a copy of the organization's privacy practices. Only limited changes are under consideration in 2019, with a focus on regulations that hinder efforts to provide coordinated care across multiple organizations (*HIPAA Journal* 2019a; *HIPAA Journal* 2019b), such as requirements for patient authorization to release PHI to a transfer entity.

The Security Rule supports the Privacy Rule by defining technical and nontechnical standards for archiving or electronic transfer of PHI. The intent of these rules is to allow entities some flexibility in designing policies and procedures to create, store, receive, and transmit PHI electronically, but to safeguard against inadvertent disclosure or unauthorized access to PHI in storage or during transfer. Because a significant proportion of the data maintained by a healthcare enterprise is classed as PHI, compliance with these security regulations is not a trivial matter. The rule requires that organizations address security issues with administrative, physical, and technical safeguards; with policies and procedures; and by management of contractual business relationships.

Current issues that might drive future changes to the Security Rule include efforts to increase national system interoperability and reduce information blocking by covered entities through rules proposed by CMS and ONC in 2019. Because laws and regulations are subject to change, the practice community regularly verifies current requirements at authoritative websites such as www.hhs.gov and www.cms.gov.

Physical Security

Simply speaking, security in this context means to protect information resources—personnel, hardware, communication devices, and so on—from harm, theft, destruction, or other compromise of the integrity of data or infrastructure. Protecting the physical security of the enterprise information system requires a portfolio of approaches that range from management policies (such as specifying an individual's system access rights) to hardwired security features (such as a fire wall) to physical measures such as requiring a code or passkey to enter an off-site server facility. Ensuring the physical security of data and information system components is essential for compliance with regulatory and legal requirements in addition to the need to safeguard access to the information that flows through the system.

Physical security of health information and technology resources arguably was easier before the connectivity era. Paper records could be stored in locked file cabinets in a locked room with access control. The computer room could be locked and accessible only to HIT personnel and authorized administrators. Early secondary storage media increased the security risk only slightly, as centralized storage areas could be protected with similar approaches. The strategic management approach at this time consisted of well-defined policies to guide operational practices, coupled with consistent monitoring and stringent enforcement of the policies.

In today's computing environment, the sheer volume of computing devices distributed across the enterprise, portable storage options, mobile device access, number of authorized users, and many other variables converge to make physical security a complex challenge at best. However, well-defined policies, consistent monitoring, and policy enforcement remain pivotal success tactics.

Many healthcare organizations have a high-level position titled chief information security officer (CISO) or something similar. This individual is responsible for developing and enforcing policies and practices to anticipate and mitigate risks to the security of the information system in its entirety—the physical components, the information in the system, strategic relationships, and so on—as well as ensuring compliance with security regulations germane to the enterprise. In addition to regulatory compliance and physical protection, the CISO must be prepared to safeguard against financial and reputational threats to the enterprise resulting from HIT or data security incidents.

The Administrative Safeguards provisions of the HIPAA Security Rule mandate specific security measures, generally implemented across the enterprise as policies and procedures. The categories of requirements include the following (Snell 2015):

- Security management processes—includes risk management and risk analysis
- Assigned responsibility for security—is typically a designated CISO
- Workforce security—ensures access for job performance; removes access from terminated employees
- Management of information access—ensures access on a need-to-know basis
- Security awareness and training—ensures compliance with policies and procedures
- Security incident procedures—reports structure; manages response
- Contingency plans—prepares for disaster; develops backup and recovery procedures
- Evaluation—monitors to adjust to environmental or operational changes that affect security
- Business associate contacts and other arrangements—is similar to business associate agreements related to Privacy Rule, but specific to ePHI

Managing information security requires a team of skilled personnel who work together to manage all facets of the security conundrum, and who are committed to monitoring changes in regulations and industry best practices. These individuals collectively need knowledge and experience in the technical aspect of HIT security, current privacy and security regulations and compliance requirements, interpersonal and communication skills, and data management skills.

Cybersecurity

Cybersecurity, or protection of internet-connected information systems, poses complex and pervasive challenges to protecting the information resources of an enterprise, not the least of which is the dynamic nature of the threats. Much like biological viruses, computer viruses and other forms of cyberattacks mutate and evolve to avoid destruction from approaches deployed by organizations to protect the security and integrity of an information system. All connected elements of the system, from an employee smartwatch that autodownloads email from an external vendor to a cloud network that hosts a large data warehouse (and everything in between), are vulnerable to cyberattack. Thus, all elements of the system, and all nonenterprise devices that connect, must be considered in designing security protocols to protect the enterprise information resources.

End-point devices, including employees' personal devices such as laptops, tablets, and smartphones or smartwatches, can put an enterprise information system at risk without any deliberate intent on the part of the user.

Cyberthreats and cybersecurity incidents receive immediate media attention and often are reported in the news in an inflammatory style. Sometimes, a very important aspect of the CISO's job is managing the public perception that information privacy and the security of that information is a top priority of the healthcare enterprise. In the aftermath of a security incident, it is important for the CISO, the enterprise CEO, and other top administrators to be coached by communications and legal experts in managing public statements and responses to public inquiries. The focus must remain on mitigating patient harm first, then organizational harm second.

Monitoring cyberthreat activity is important. Most CISOs and their staffs participate in professional networks and have trusted information websites or other sources to stay abreast of recent and emerging threats and how other organizations are responding to those threats. Accessing this type of information is a critical tool, along with managing system and network updates, monitoring network activity for aberrant access, and employing security approaches such as antimalware and antivirus software.

Cyberhygiene, adherence to good security practices for internet-connected components, can help protect devices from outside attack. Regular device and system monitoring and maintenance activities should be procedural, and oversight should be specifically assigned to accountable personnel. Minimal hygiene factors include the following:

- Maintain documentation of current system components and connections
- Ensure backup of critical data to secure but accessible storage, ideally off-line
- Designate storage options by data type (e.g., sensitive, clinical, research, business) to ensure coverage by appropriate security protocols
- Maintain current versions of antivirus and antimalware software
- Maintain current updates of software to ensure currency of security elements
- Enforce policy for regular strong password changes
- Limit access and user rights to system components on need-to-know basis

Many organizations have migrated to two-factor authentication (2FA), which requires entering a strong password and a second code provided by SMS text or a security token to access a system. While many users consider this inconvenient and inefficient, it is a strong deterrent to unauthorized access. In a survey of more than 1,300 senior healthcare executives, more than 25 percent of respondents said they had been victims of a cyberattack, with losses exceeding $1 million for 70 percent of the organizations. About half of the executives responded to the incident by implementing 2FA to control remote access (Donovan 2018b).

Internet of Things

In 2017, the Information Security Forum, a nonprofit organization that produces research data on information security and risk management, released a report on the threat horizon through 2019. The report suggests that "cybercriminals will increasingly focus their ransomware efforts on smart devices connected to the Internet of Things (IoT)" (Olavsrud 2017)—and they rank this problem among their top nine. Ransomware, a malicious software, encrypts a computer or computing system to deny access or control by the owner until a ransom is paid. The virus often attacks the system through a phishing email, a bogus message that seeks to gain user information to access desired systems such as financial or healthcare data repositories, or infected websites.

Beazley Breach Response Services, a specialist insurer, reported that healthcare is the field most targeted for ransomware attacks. In fact, ransomware accounted for 47 percent of their 2018 data breach claims (Beazley 2018). After ransomware, accidental disclosure was the second most common source of breaches at 20 percent. In addition to an increased number of data breach claims filed with Beazley relative to 2017 numbers, the ransom amount demands have increased, as high as $2.8 million. Ransomware attacks can be even more challenging because of issues in the malware itself or unskilled hackers. Either may result in fatal corruption of compromised data or an inability to decrypt data despite payment of the ransom. In many cases, backups have been compromised before the primary data were captured by the attackers; thus, the ransom demand has added power.

The *Internet of Things* is the entirety of devices and objects with unique identifiers that transmit data over the internet without an intermediary person or device. Based on machine-to-machine communication principles, the IoT is a network of smart devices, including medical devices, numbering in the billions. Some estimates suggest IoT growth will exceed 75 billion devices by 2025, powered by 5G mobile technology (Statista Research Department 2020). Device examples include sensors implanted in the body that transmit biomedical data such as glucose levels or heart rate, smart home applications such as automated temperature control, and geolocation chips in animals. IoT attacks are a major risk, as security is not robust on many devices, and exploiting one vulnerability engenders access to data produced by many other devices, including the types of personally identifiable data that cybercriminals seek. As "wearables" and other real-time data-capturing devices become more pervasive in healthcare, and more organizations adopt mHealth as a service delivery approach, security risks associated with the IoT will become higher priority.

Health Information Technology Legislation and Regulations

In addition to ongoing and pervasive amendments to HIPAA and related legislation, notably laws that apply to Medicare, several other laws are notable for their impact on HIT. Exhibit 5.3 provides a summary of legislative intent and key provisions of selected laws that mandate HIT practices. As discussed previously, compliance with evolving regulations and reporting requirements is a complex, challenging, and dynamic responsibility for all healthcare organizations. Monitoring legislative and regulatory updates should be the purview of a team of skilled staff.

EXHIBIT 5.3
Summary of Key Legislation

Law	Intent	Additional Information Source
Health Insurance Portability and Accountability Act (HIPAA) of 1996, P.L. 104-191	Improve portability and continuity of health insurance coverage; combat waste, fraud, and abuse; regulate privacy and security	www.hhs.gov/hipaa/index.html
Health Information Technology for Economic and Clinical Health (HITECH) Act of 2009	Promote HIT, including EHRs and health information exchange	www.healthit.gov/hitac/committees/health-information-technology-advisory-committee-hitac
Food and Drug Administration Safety and Innovation Act (FDASIA) of 2012 (Section 618)	Set risk-based regulatory framework for HIT, including mobile applications	www.healthit.gov/sites/default/files/fdasiahealthitreport_final.pdf
Patient Protection and Affordable Care Act (ACA) of 2010, P.L. 111-148	Simplify administrative processes; establish operating rules for transactions; provide unique identifiers for health plans; set standards for electronic funds transfer and claims attachments	www.healthcare.gov/glossary/patient-protection-and-affordable-care-act/
Medicare Access and CHIP Reauthorization Act (MACRA) of 2015	Change physician payment models and provide funding for technical assistance	https://qpp.cms.gov/
21st Century Cures Act of 2018, P.L. 114-255	Amend HITECH Act; clarify HIPAA Privacy Rule; advance interoperability; promote medical product development	www.congress.gov/bill/114th-congress/house-bill/6

Summary

A robust HIT infrastructure, which comprises all components of an enterprise's IT resources—physical elements, software, policies, and contractual relationships—is complex, dynamic, and essential to a healthcare organization's survival. Technology supporting the clinical environment of the hospital has evolved such that the notion of the "state of the art" is a moving target as advancements and innovations accelerate. The business environment, with its changing payment models and shifting power relationships, requires organizations to be nimble and able to respond quickly to achieve financial incentives and avoid penalties. The need to exchange information with business partners, payers, patients, and other providers compel organizations to strive to achieve the full system interoperability goal set by the federal government.

The healthcare environment is a complex configuration of opportunities to provide high-quality patient care with available technologies, coupled with extensive risks inherent in using those same technologies. The concept of opportunity versus risk can also be applied to IT. The convenience of digital and wireless technologies has increased the complexity of managing the physical security of information resources and the information itself. Arguably, the greatest challenge to ensuring security and privacy of health information is protecting against malicious, invasive attacks by individuals or groups for personal financial gain or notoriety.

Leaders, managers, and HIT professionals will be challenged to design, maintain, and protect the organization's information resources in a volatile environment—one that is constantly changing as a result of technology advancement, regulatory expansion, and constrained business models. Building and supporting a team with the needed skill mix, who are guided by a good strategic plan and governance framework, will be key success factors.

Web Resources

A number of organizations (through their websites) provide more information on the topics discussed in this chapter:

- The American Health Information Management Association (www.ahima.org) was established in 1928. AHIMA is the recognized leadership and advocacy group for health information professionals, promoting the "advancement and use of health data and information for the delivery of quality healthcare worldwide."

- The American National Standards Institute (www.ansi.org) serves as "the voice of the U.S. Standards and conformity assessment system." ANSI "oversees creating, promulgation, and use" of standards in many fields, including healthcare.
- Centers for Medicare & Medicaid Services (www.cms.gov) is an agency of the HHS that administers Medicare and other federally funded health programs. This federal government website available to the public provides extensive information about the agency, regulations, guidance, and research data, among other topics.
- The Cybersecurity and Infrastructure Security Agency (www.us-cert.gov) is an official website of the Department of Homeland Security. It was authorized by the Cybersecurity and Infrastructure Security Agency Act of 2018 to provide cybersecurity and infrastructure-security knowledge and practices to enable risk management and protect the nation's information resources. Specific priorities include federal network protection, cyberprotection, infrastructure resilience, and emergency communications.
- The HHS maintains a public-facing government website, www.hhs.gov, that provides information on laws and regulations in addition to HHS programs and services. An extensive index is available to aid searches.
- The National Information Standards Organization (www.niso.org) is a US-based, nonprofit standards organization accredited by ANSI that "identifies, develops, maintains, and publishes technical standards to manage information in today's continually changing digital environment."
- OASIS (www.oasis-open.org) functions as a nonprofit consortium whose goal is to drive "development, convergence and adoption of open standards for the global information society."
- The Office of the National Coordinator for Health Information Technology (www.healthit.gov) exists to support the adoption of HIT and nationwide health information exchange to improve healthcare.
- Health Level Seven (HL7) (www.hl7.org) is a leading healthcare standard-developing organization. HL7 is working as a coordinating agent for various active standard-setting groups.

Discussion Questions

1. Differentiate between primary and secondary data storage, providing examples.

2. Suggest how the use of a patient ID bracelet containing a bar code representation of the patient's ID and a bar code scanner can lead to improved quality of care in a hospital.
3. Distinguish between an interfaced system and an integrated system. Provide some examples in which one model would provide an advantage over the other.
4. Describe some important applications of electronic data interchange in the healthcare field.
5. How does mobile computing differ from wireless communication?
6. How do data standards organizations contribute to quality of healthcare?
7. Why is the Internet of Things considered an extreme security risk to personal health information?
8. Define cybersecurity and discuss system vulnerabilities that pose threats.
9. What is the purpose of a data governance plan?
10. Differentiate the requirements posed by the HIPAA Privacy Rule and HIPAA Security Rule.
11. Discuss barriers to achieving full interoperability in HIT data sharing.

References

Beazley. 2018. "Beazley Breach Insights October 2018." Published November 1. www.beazley.com/news/2018/beazley_breach_insights_october_2018.html.

Centers for Medicare & Medicaid Services (CMS). 2017. "Transactions Overview." Published July 26. www.cms.gov/Regulations-and-Guidance/Administrative-Simplification/Transactions/TransactionsOverview.html.

Donovan, F. 2018a. "Healthcare Continues to Bear the Brunt of Ransomware Attacks." *Health IT Security*. Published October 31. https://healthitsecurity.com/news/healthcare-continues-to-bear-the-brunt-of-ransomware-attacks.

———. 2018b. "Healthcare Data Presents Lucrative Target for Cyberattackers." *Health IT Security*. Published September 7. https://healthitsecurity.com/news/healthcare-data-presents-lucrative-target-for-cyberattackers.

Empel, S. 2014. "Way Forward: AHIMA Develops Information Governance Principles to Lead Healthcare Toward Better Data Management." *Journal of AHIMA* 85 (10): 30–32.

FTI Consulting. 2015. *The Information Governance Guide for Compliance Professionals*. Accessed February 3, 2020. http://static.ftitechnology.com/docs/toolkits/IG-for-Compliance-Teams-Toolkit.pdf.

HIPAA Journal. 2019a. "Expected HIPAA Updates and HIPAA Changes in 2019." Published January 31. www.hipaajournal.com/hipaa-updates-hipaa-changes.

———. 2019b. "New HIPAA Regulations in 2019." Published March 4. www.hipaajournal.com/new-hipaa-regulations.

———. 2018. "Largest Healthcare Data Breaches of 2018." Published December 27. www.hipaajournal.com/largest-healthcare-data-breaches-of-2018.

Houser, S. H., D. J. Slovensky, and L. Wang. 2017. "Information Governance for Analytics Support: Remember the Life Cycle Component." *Journal of the American Health Information Management Association* 88 (6): 38–40.

Journal of AHIMA. 2011. "Practice Brief: Managing Nontext Media in Healthcare Practices." *Journal of AHIMA* 82 (11): 54–58.

Kurzweil, R. 2001. "The Law of Accelerating Returns." Published March 7. Kurzweil Network. www.kurzweilai.net/the-law-of-accelerating-returns.

Office for Civil Rights (OCR). 2003. "Summary of the HIPAA Privacy Rule." US Department of Health & Human Services. Revised May. www.hhs.gov/sites/default/files/privacysummary.pdf.

Office of the National Coordinator for Health Information Technology. 2019. "Interoperability." Reviewed May 9. www.healthit.gov/topic/interoperability.

Olavsrud, T. 2017. "9 Biggest Information Security Threats Through 2019." *CIO.* Published March 28. www.cio.com/article/3185725/9-biggest-information-security-threats-through-2019.html.

Pew Research Center. 2019. "Mobile Fact Sheet." Published June 12. www.pewinternet.org/fact-sheet/mobile.

Ponemon Institute. 2018. "2018 Cost of a Data Breach Study: Global Overview." IBM Security. Published July. www.ibm.com/downloads/cas/861MNWN2.

Rosen, S. 1969. "Electronic Computers: A Historical Survey." *Computing Surveys* 1 (1): 7–36.

Snell, E. 2015. "A Review of Common HIPAA Administrative Safeguards." *Health IT Security.* Published July 17. https://healthitsecurity.com/news/a-review-of-common-hipaa-administrative-safeguards.

Statista Research Department. 2020. "Internet of Things (IoT) Connected Devices Installed Base Worldwide from 2015 to 2025 (in Billions)." Published February 19. www.statista.com/statistics/471264/iot-number-of-connected-devices-worldwide.

Willig, J. H. 2015. "The Many Lives of Data." In *Handbook of Healthcare Management*, edited by M. D. Fottler, D. Malvey, and D. J. Slovensky. Cheltenham, UK: Edward Elgar Publishing.

CHAPTER

6

HEALTH INFORMATION TECHNOLOGY SERVICE MANAGEMENT

Learning Objectives

1. Articulate the impact that unplanned work has on the health information technology (HIT) department.
2. Identify a number of different process improvement frameworks that could be applied to the management of the HIT department and the advantages and disadvantages of each approach.
3. Describe ITIL management practices and their interrelationships.
4. Articulate why the configuration management database is critical to the service management practices.
5. Describe what service-level agreements are and why they are important to the HIT department.
6. Describe some of the reasons given for HIT service continuity plan failures.

Overview

A consistent area of focus throughout a healthcare manager's career, regardless of responsibility, is the constant effort to achieve efficient, cost-effective operations. While it is certainly true that all healthcare managers will continually be asked to think more strategically, a focus on the strategic aspects of the job at the expense of the operational aspects is a sure recipe for failure. Debra Walker, former chief information officer (CIO) of Goodyear Tire & Rubber Company, provides a framework for how to think about the effective management of a health information technology (HIT) department for both operational effectiveness and strategic impact. She suggests that the HIT department must master three levels of services. The base level provides a robust and reliable infrastructure for the organization, which is covered in chapter 5. The second level, which builds on the base level, provides excellent HIT services, which is the focus of this chapter. Walker characterizes the third level by noting that "if [the HIT department] achieves those two things, then

[it] gets the credibility that allows [it and the CIO] to play in the third level: partnering with the business to do the very high value-added activities and create competitive advantage" (Field 1998).

Why Health Information Technology Service Management Matters

The assertion that the more tactical or operational elements of HIT services are critical to strategic HIT value delivery is consistently reinforced in a number of academic studies (Agarwal and Sambamurthy 2002; Kaplan and Harris-Salamone 2009; Melendez, Dávila, and Pessoa 2016; Smaltz, Sambamurthy, and Agarwal 2006; Watson, Pitt, and Kavan 1998). Much in the same way that Maslow's (1970) hierarchy of needs applies to human psychology, if lower-level operational HIT needs (e.g., reliable infrastructure, consistent and effective HIT support services) are not being met, the CEO may wonder whether the CIO and the organization can be effective in delivering the higher-level strategic HIT needs of the institution.

Ironically, only the most progressive organizations are adopting best practices in HIT service management, while many HIT departments continue to rely on informal, "seat of the pants," error-prone processes (Hoerbst et al. 2011; Melendez, Dávila, and Pessoa 2016). This leads to reactive firefighting in HIT departments, when formal, proactive approaches would be more effective. Recent studies suggest that one of the most accurate indicators of HIT departmental effectiveness in delivering quality services is the percentage of unplanned work in which the department is engaged. *Unplanned work* is any activity in the HIT organization that cannot be mapped to an authorized project, procedure, or change request. While unplanned work can never be entirely eliminated from the HIT department, Kim (2006) suggests that the nature of the unplanned work is very different for high- and low-performing HIT departments. In Kim's study, low-performing HIT departments' unplanned work includes the following:

- *Failed change.* The production environment is used as a test environment, and the customer is the quality assurance team.
- *Unauthorized change.* Engineers do not follow the change management process, making mistakes harder to track and fix.
- *No preventive work.* Failing to conduct preventive work makes repeated failures inevitable. Mean time to repair may be improving, but without root-cause analysis, the organization is doomed to fix the same problems over and over.

- *Configuration inconsistency.* Inconsistencies in user applications, platforms, and configurations make appropriate training and configuration mastery difficult.
- *Security-related patching and updating.* Inadequate understanding and inconsistency of configurations make applying security patches extremely dangerous.
- *Too much access.* Too many people have too much access to too many HIT assets, causing preventable issues and incidents.

In contrast, Kim (2006) found that high-performing HIT departments have very different types of unplanned work, which include the following:

- Product failures
- Release failures
- Human errors

The key difference between low- and high-performing HIT departments is that high-performing HIT departments put in place holistic controls and processes that cut horizontally across the HIT department, whereas low-performing HIT departments often operate in vertical function-based silos with little to no formal crossfunctional controls or processes. Interestingly, the Sarbanes-Oxley Act, passed by Congress in 2002, now mandates that holistic and formal controls be established for all for-profit organizations (Congress.gov 2002). However, these controls are not mandated for not-for-profit organizations, which make up the majority of the healthcare delivery field. As such, many HIT departments will continue to have high levels of costly, unplanned work as a result of poor adoption rates of leading organizations' process frameworks that include, but are not limited to, the HIT process improvement frameworks outlined in exhibit 6.1.

Sundaresan (2020) notes that "while transforming a typical IT organization into an efficient service delivery organization is difficult, companies that don't make the transition face loss of competitiveness, while the IT organization faces loss of credibility, influence and most importantly impact." Kim (2006) illustrates this sentiment via the following scenario, adapted for our healthcare purpose:

> Suppose someone changes an IT asset [such as releasing a seemingly small software patch to a major enterprise application such as an electronic health record (EHR)], but the change fails catastrophically due to lack of preproduction testing and change management authorization. The failed change results in an "all hands on deck" situation for the IT operational staff; IT drops planned work to remedy

EXHIBIT 6.1
HIT Process Improvement Frameworks

Information Technology (IT) Process Improvement Framework	Description
Capability Maturity Model (CMM)	An IT process improvement framework best suited to process improvements surrounding the application development and maintenance domains. The model is based on five levels of maturity (Gartner 2001): Level 1: Initial—no repeatable processes Level 2: Repeatable—requirement-identification process, policy compliance, and basic project management are all in place Level 3: Defined—application-development processes are well defined, as are applications training and coordination processes Level 4: Quantitatively managed—precise measurement, forecasting, and predictability are added; seeks to reduce process variation resulting from unique events Level 5: Optimized—continual process improvement efforts at reducing common cause–process variation are added; describes what characterizes an organization at each level but does not describe how to get there
Control Objects for Information Technology (CoBiT)	An IT governance, oversight, and process audit framework linked to the Sarbanes-Oxley Act's corporate financial reporting compliance law. CoBiT is made up of five principles (Information Systems Audit and Control Association 2020): 1. Meeting stakeholder needs—ensures alignment of stakeholder needs with underlying processes and practices

	2. Covering the enterprise end to end—ensures a comprehensive approach to IT management 3. Applying a single integrated framework to guide IT governance and oversight activities 4. Enabling a holistic approach—ensures a deliberate and systematic focus on enablers such as processes, organizational structure, information, principles, policies, etc. 5. Separating governance from management—ensures a clear distinction between governance/oversight activities (e.g., policy and direction setting) and management activities (e.g., planning, building, running, and monitoring processes) Like the CMM, CoBiT tends to describe what characterizes an organization that has solid internal control mechanisms in place but does not offer how-to descriptions.
International Organization for Standardization (ISO) 9000	Also from manufacturing, ISO 9000 requires that organizations become accredited or registered, thereby assuring customers that the organization adheres to ISO quality assurance standards. One criticism of ISO 9000 is that it requires a great deal of administrative overhead to employ ISO 9000 standards and become registered.
ITIL (formerly known as the IT Infrastructure Library)	A mature IT governance and best-practice framework focused on value creation through IT services. It guides practitioners to consider the entire IT service value chain, offers IT best practices, IT guiding principles, governance guidelines, and a continuous improvement focus. It prescribes 14 specific general IT management practices, 17 specific IT service management practices, and 3 technical management practices (Axelos 2019). ITIL is well suited to organizations whose CIO or IT leader is championing IT practice improvements. As opposed to some other process/practice improvement models, ITIL provides high-level how-to guidance.

> the results of the changes. The service disruption causes an incident that takes four hours to repair and involves 25 IT staffers from all functional roles: application developers, QA [quality assurance] workers, database administrators, network and systems administrators, and security. Lost IT staff productivity is the first cost of this episode of unplanned work.
>
> Unplanned work also comes at the cost of planned project work. In this case, the application developers and QA staffers are taken from the critical path of an important patient satisfaction project, and the project completion date slips one week. In addition, to address this project delay, IT has to employ a team of contractors longer.
>
> The costs continue to mount. While the IT staff works to restore service, [physicians and nurses] call the service desk to find out why they can't access their [patient's information in the EHR]. Because of the large [EHR user] base, [hundreds of users] call the service center. The excess calls require the service center to activate the overflow call center, which costs tens of thousands of dollars. Revenue is also disrupted because [the delay in EHR-related workflows causes delays in admitting, transfer, and discharging patients in a timely manner].
>
> Downtime and IT project resource costs run in the thousands of dollars; service center costs, lost revenue and the delayed IT project costs are in the tens of thousands. . . . Now that this single rogue change affects [the revenue cycle], costs increase almost exponentially. . . . [The impact on the revenue cycle for a large hospital can easily run into the hundreds of thousands of dollars in either lost revenue (workflow disruptions cause a bed to not be available to admit a new patient when needed) or delayed revenue or decreased margins (patient discharged beyond normal length of stay).]
>
> And, there is one more extremely high cost of unplanned work. Any of those late projects, which are getting even further delayed, had some ROI that the [organization] attached to it. So, every moment of unplanned work delaying that project has a quantifiable opportunity cost.

The scenario is all too common in most hospital and healthcare delivery organizations. As such, doing nothing to improve these broken HIT processes will make it increasingly difficult for the CIO and the HIT department to take on the even more challenging strategic HIT issues facing the healthcare field. It is beyond the scope of this text to expand on each of the various HIT process improvement frameworks listed in exhibit 6.1. While each has its own advantages and disadvantages, ITIL is an HIT value creation framework that is well suited to agile business alignment efforts led by the CIO or HIT leader and department (Foederer 2018). As opposed to some of the other process improvement models, ITIL provides high-level "how-to" guidance via its many generic ITIL process flow diagrams and descriptions.

The Information Technology Infrastructure Library

While Control Objects for Information Technology (CobiT) (see exhibit 6.1) can be thought of as a framework for *what* sorts of things an HIT department should consider having in place, ITIL can be thought of as a framework of *how* HIT department practices should be interlinked to gain optimum proactive HIT service management. The Information Technology Infrastructure Library (now simply referred to as ITIL) was originally created by the Office of Government Commerce (OGC) in the United Kingdom; as of 2013, it is curated by Axelos, a joint venture created between the UK Cabinet Office and Capita, a private firm (Axelos 2020). It is intended to be a holistic framework for incorporating guiding principles, governance, management practices, and a continual improvement focus on delivering value to its stakeholders through a service value chain (see exhibit 6.2). Furthermore, it describes and provides guidance for HIT general management practices, service management practices, and technical management needs of an organization (see exhibits 6.3 and 6.4). Arguably, current HIT operating budget levels—which typically average 2–3 percent of operating expenses in community hospitals and 4 percent across all health-delivery organizations (Hall et al. 2016; Potter et al. 2013)—may make full adoption of the entire ITIL framework challenging. By this we mean that ITIL requires organizations to dedicate some of their resources toward putting in place the more proactive ITIL practices. However, the low operating budget levels of HIT departments in the healthcare sector mean that most do not perceive that they have the slack resources needed to break out of their reactive, firefighting mode.

EXHIBIT 6.2
The ITIL Service Value System

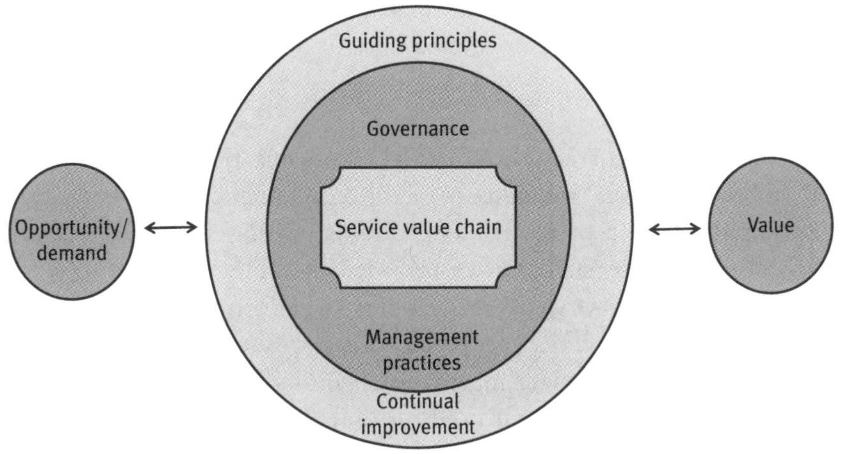

Source: Adapted from Axelos (2019).

By comparison, the financial services industry expends 5–7 percent on HIT operating budgets (Potter et al. 2013) and, not coincidentally, is a robust adopter of both the CobiT and ITIL frameworks.

HIT services in most healthcare organizations will, out of necessity, most likely require more proactive approaches with the increasing use of technology solutions in mission-critical areas of clinical and business operations, such as an electronic health record (EHR) with clinical decision support (CDS) and computerized physician order entry (CPOE). The ITIL service value system is particularly well suited to HIT departments that seek to create value to their stakeholders by continually improving their service delivery and support via more proactive, holistic, and integrated HIT services (Foederer 2018). In short, ITIL provides a framework of best-practice guidance for IT service management and has been widely implemented, both in the United States and abroad. While a comprehensive review of ITIL is beyond the scope of this text (the ITIL foundation reference is over 200 pages), we will provide a brief description of each practice in exhibit 6.3 and a more in-depth focus on some of the key ITIL service management practices in exhibit 6.4.

While all of the ITIL practices outlined in exhibits 6.3 and 6.4 are important to the effective operation and value delivery of the HIT department, we will next focus on some of the key highlighted ITIL service management practices and how they are interrelated.

ITIL Service Management Practices

All of the HIT service practices are heavily interrelated and should be put in place with forethought. Exhibit 6.5, for example, provides some insight into how some of the key practices, such as the service desk, incident management, problem management, change management, release management, and configuration management, are interrelated.

Service Desk

Almost all hospitals or healthcare delivery organizations provide a "help desk" or "service desk," which users call or access online to obtain assistance with computer-related problems. This desk is possibly the most misunderstood and underappreciated service provided by the HIT department. Best practices in providing services for incidents (when malfunctions occur that require HIT support services to repair) are discussed later in the chapter. Here, the healthcare manager must recognize that because the service desk provides such wide exposure into the customer-interfacing operations of the HIT department, it becomes—for better or worse—one of the main ways that healthcare executives and managers throughout the organization gauge

EXHIBIT 6.3
ITIL General Management Practices

ITIL Version 4	Practices	Description
General management practices	Architecture management	Provides an understanding of all the different elements (business architecture, service architecture, information systems architecture, technology architecture, and environmental architecture) that make up an organization and how those elements interrelate, enabling the organization to effectively achieve its current and future objectives.
	Continuous improvement	Provides guidance on aligning the organization's practices and services with changing business needs through the ongoing identification (all improvement initiatives are registered in Continual Improvement Register) and improvement of services, service components, practices, or any element involved in the products and services.
	Information security management	Provides guidance on protecting the information (which includes confidentiality, integrity, and availability of information, as well as other aspects of information security such as authentication and nonrepudiation) needed by the organization to conduct its business.
	Knowledge management	Provides guidance on maintaining and improving the effective, efficient, and convenient use of information and knowledge across the organization.
	Measurement and reporting	Provides guidance on good decision-making and continuous improvement by decreasing the levels of uncertainty.
	Organization change management	Provides guidance on managing the human aspects of the changes.
	Portfolio management	Provides guidance on ensuring that the organization has the right mix of programs, projects, products, and services to execute its strategy within funding and resource constraints.

(continued)

EXHIBIT 6.3
ITIL General Management Practices *(continued)*

ITIL Version 4	Practices	Description
	Project management	Provides guidance on ensuring that all projects in the organization are successfully delivered (covered in detail in chapter 10). This is achieved by planning, delegating, monitoring, and maintaining control of all aspects of a project and keeping the motivation of the people involved.
	Relationship management	Provides guidance on establishing and nurturing the links between the organization and its stakeholders at strategic and tactical levels.
	Risk management	Provides guidance on ensuring that the organization understands and effectively handles risks.
	Service financial management	Provides guidance on supporting the organization's strategies and plans for service management by ensuring that the organization's financial resources and investments are being used effectively.
	Strategy management	Provides guidance to formulate the goals of the organization and adopt the courses of action and allocation of resources necessary to achieve those goals.
	Supplier management	Provides guidance to ensure that the organization's suppliers and their performance are managed appropriately to support the seamless provision of quality products and services.
	Workforce and talent management	Provides guidance to ensure that the organization has the right people with the appropriate skills and knowledge and in the correct roles to support its business objectives.

Source: Adapted from Service Desk Academy (2019).

EXHIBIT 6.4
ITIL Service Management and Technical Management Practices

ITIL Version 4	Practices	Description
Service management practices	Availability management	Provides guidance to ensure that services deliver agreed levels of availability to meet the needs of customers and users.
	Business analysis	Provides guidance to analyze a business or some element of it, define its associated needs, and recommend solutions to address these needs and/or solve a business problem, which must facilitate value creation for stakeholders.
	Capacity and performance management	Provides guidance to ensure that services achieve agreed and expected performance, satisfying current and future demand in a cost-effective way.
	Change control/management	Provides guidance to maximize the number of successful IT changes by ensuring that risks have been properly assessed, authorizing changes to proceed, and managing the change schedule.
	Incident management	Provides guidance to minimize the negative impact of incidents by restoring normal service operation as quickly as possible.
	IT asset management	Provides guidance to plan and manage the full life cycle of all IT assets to maximize value, control costs, manage risks, support decision-making about purchase, reuse, and retirement of assets, and to meet regulatory and contractual requirements.
	Monitoring and event management	Provides guidance to systematically observe services and service components, and to record and report selected changes of state identified as events.
	Problem management	Provides guidance to reduce the likelihood and impact of incidents by identifying actual and potential causes of incidents, and managing workarounds and known errors.
	Release management	Provides guidance to make new and changed services and features available for use.

(continued)

EXHIBIT 6.4
ITIL Service Management and Technical Management Practices *(continued)*

ITIL Version 4	Practices	Description
	Service catalog management	Provides guidance to provide a single source of consistent information on all services and service offerings, and to ensure that it is available to the relevant audience.
	Service configuration management	Provides guidance to ensure that accurate and reliable information about the configuration of services, and the configuration items that support them, is available when and where it is needed.
	Service continuity management	Provides guidance to ensure that the availability and performance of a service is maintained at a sufficient level in the event of a disaster.
	Service design	Provides guidance to design products and services that are fit for purpose, fit for use, and that can be delivered by the organization and its ecosystem.
	Service desk	Provides guidance to capture demand for incident resolution and service requests. It should also be the entry point and single point of contact for the service provider with all of its users.
	Service-level management	Provides guidance to set clear business-based targets for service performance, so that the delivery of a service can be properly assessed, monitored, and managed against these targets.
	Service request management	Provides guidance to support the agreed quality of a service by handling all predefined, user-initiated service requests in an effective and user-friendly manner.
	Service validation and testing	Provides guidance to ensure that new or changed products and services meet defined requirements.
Technical management practices	Development management	Provides guidance to move new or changed hardware, software, documentation, processes, or any other component to live environments.
	Infrastructure and platform management	Provides guidance to oversee the infrastructure and platforms used by an organization.
	Software development and management	Provides guidance to ensure that applications meet internal and external stakeholder needs, in terms of functionality, reliability, maintainability, compliance, and auditability.

Source: Adapted from Service Desk Academy (2019).

EXHIBIT 6.5
Key ITIL Service Management Practice Interrelationships

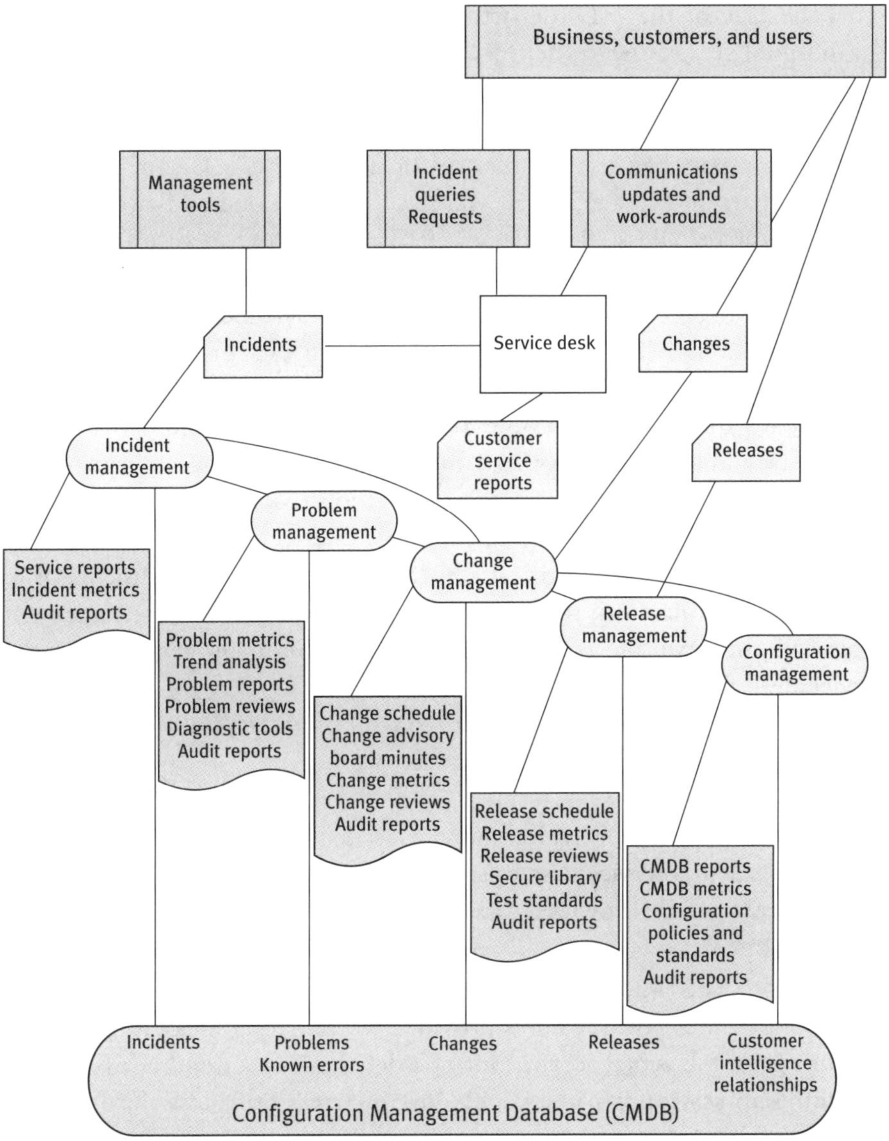

Source: © Crown Copyright material reproduced with the kind permission of the United Kingdom Office of Government Commerce and the Controller of Her Majesty's Stationary Office (HMSO); © Copyright itSMF®, 2001.

the effectiveness of the HIT services delivered. Therefore, it behooves CIOs and HIT department managers to ensure that the leading customer service practices are in place. The service desk is a highly visible, demanding function in the HIT department, and underestimating its importance, high profile, and the skills and repeatable processes required to perform the service desk duties well can severely hinder an organization's ability to deliver quality IT services (Tang and Todo 2013).

For most of the users of computer resources, the help desk represents the face of the HIT department. While some of the employees of the hospital or healthcare delivery organization have the opportunity to interact with the other service delivery teams in the HIT department, statistically almost *all* employees, at some point in their tenure, will have a need to contact and use the services of the help desk. Gartner Research suggests that, on average, users will place between one and two calls per month to the help desk (Potter et al. 2013). This does not necessarily mean that each and every user will call the help desk at least once a month (e.g., a single user may place six calls in one month and six more the next month to the help desk, while another may not place a call for a year or more). Because many help desks address not only malfunctions or incidents but also how-to questions, over time a user can average 1.1 to 1.6 calls per month. In addition, as exhibit 6.4 indicates, a second source of incidents comes from HIT operational management tools that can monitor the HIT infrastructure. When certain thresholds are met (e.g., central processing unit [CPU] capacity on a critical server reaches 75 percent, disk space in the storage area network reaches 85 percent capacity), these management tools will automatically trigger an incident that initially gets sent to the service desk for action.

Hospital or healthcare delivery organizations typically have one of three different types of HIT service desks:

1. *Decentralized.* This is typical of many academic medical centers, where often a central service desk exists, but historically many departments have retained their own HIT staff to deal with incidents in their departments.
2. *Virtual.* This is a new form of service desk whereby a single contact phone number or website is provided for initiating incidents; however, the actual services may be delivered by a number of different service providers, including internal staff and a third-party provider.
3. *Centralized.* A pool of resources, typically within the HIT department, provides centralized service desk support.

While there are pros and cons for each type of HIT service desk, the key feature that all three must put in place to optimize service support is an integrated view of all incoming incidents. This view not only facilitates a coordinated resolution of the incident but also ensures that trends across the enterprise can be spotted and more proactive approaches can be applied to prevent incidents in the first place (as opposed to simply reacting to them each time they recur).

Incident Management

The goal of incident management is to minimize the negative impact of an uplanned interruption of service or reduction of quality of a service by restoring normal service operation as quickly as possible (Axelos 2019). In most organizations with a central service desk function, all incidents are channeled through the service desk. Typically, central HIT service desks are organized to provide three levels of support.

1. *First-level support services.* All incidents initially come to the individuals who staff the first-level support services. These individuals typically log the call or request into a "trouble ticket" or "incident management" database so that incidents can be tracked from start to finish. In addition, members of the first-level support staff are typically trained to handle most routine, recurring incidents such as resetting a user's password, assisting with routine office-automation software, and answering how-to questions. When HIT service desk technicians are armed with service desk tools that allow remote control of a user's desktop device, organizations can expect 65 percent resolution on the first call into the first-level support technicians. With increased training and access to a knowledge base of symptoms and resolutions, first-call resolution rates above 80 percent can be obtained (Rumberg 2011).
2. *Second-level support services.* Incidents that cannot be addressed by the first-level support technicians because they require greater expertise and training or require that a technician physically go to the user's location are handed off to dedicated desktop or field-support technicians for resolution.
3. *Third-level support services.* Incidents that are routed to third-level support are typically the most difficult and unusual problems and often require deep root-cause analysis and reengineering of the application or system affected.

Exhibit 6.6 depicts a sample workflow diagram showing how incidents may flow through the various levels in a service desk.

In this example of a typical organizational central HIT service desk, the end user can either call in an incident, a request, a problem, or a question (IRPQ) or, for a nonurgent IRPQ, simply open an incident report via the service desk's web-based incident portal application. In either case, first-level service desk technicians will initially address the IRPQ and attempt to resolve it on the spot. In this example, the service desk technicians also have access to an ITIL best practice—configuration management database (CMDB), which is covered later in this chapter. In short, this is essentially a knowledge store of solutions, answers, and temporary fixes (SATs) as well as a knowledge store

EXHIBIT 6.6
Sample IT Service Desk Workflow

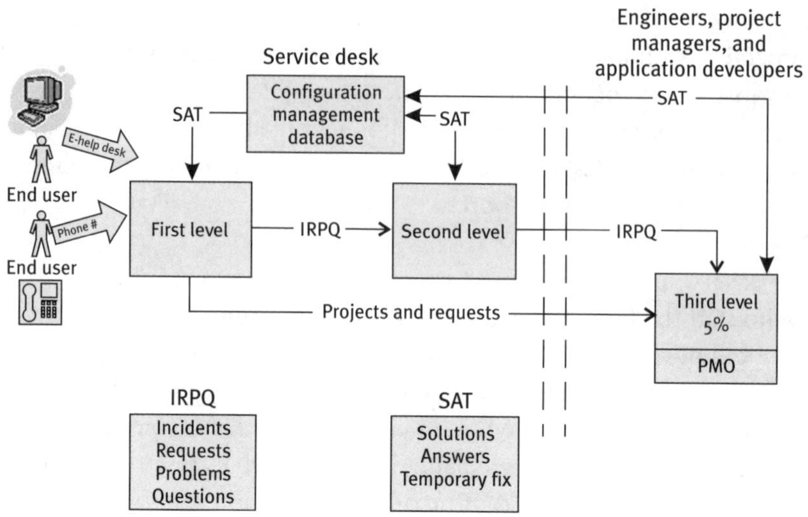

Note: IRPQ = incident, request, problem, or question; PMO = program management office; SAT = solution, answer, or temporary fix.

for system configuration settings that first-level technicians can use to potentially expedite the resolution of an end user's incident. However, if the first-level service desk technician cannot immediately resolve it, the IRPQ gets escalated to a second-level service desk technician. Finally, for organizations that have implemented a portfolio or program management office (PMO), as outlined in chapter 10, often the service desk becomes the "front door" for requesting new HIT projects—which, as exhibit 6.6 suggests, get escalated immediately to the PMO.

Second-level HIT service desk technicians make use of the CMDB and may create new knowledge in it when they discover a permanent solution or find a reliable temporary workaround or fix to a recurring problem. As the exhibit indicates, when second-level service desk technicians cannot resolve the issue, the IRPQ is then moved to the third-level service desk technicians, who typically are members of the organization's HIT network engineering, server administration, or applications development group. There, root-cause analysis occurs, along with efforts to engineer a permanent solution to the IRPQ. Ideally, first- and second-level service desk technicians should be able to find SATs 95 percent of the time, while third-level service desk technicians should be needed for only 5 percent of IRPQs.

Without a disciplined, effective front door approach to all trouble calls and requests for services, the HIT department can quickly become swamped with requests that circumvent the service desk process. Also, without the integration with some of the other ITIL processes (e.g., change management, release management, configuration management, all discussed later in this chapter), the service desk can be seen as largely ineffective. Ciccolini and McDermott (2005) suggest that

> in many cases, the front-line service desk acts as little more than an answering service, logging incidents and forwarding them to a more senior IT person [second- or third-level support technicians] for resolution. Further, service desks often lack the information needed to address end-user incidents—particularly those that involve proprietary applications. The under-utilization of front-line service desks poses both cost and credibility problems for IT organizations. Incident resolution costs (and indirect opportunity costs) increase as cases are passed on to more senior IT specialists. Business users suffer from productivity declines and perceptions of IT often sour as customers fail to see their issues being addressed in a timely fashion.

Best practices in incident management to overcome these costs and productivity declines include the following:

- Insisting that all users employ the service desk as the front door for submitting all IRPQs
- Using effective automated service desk tools such as telephony to track phone metrics (e.g., average time a customer is on hold) and service desk management software to log and track all incidents through to resolutions
- Ensuring that service desk technicians have access to an effective CMDB, which serves as an effective knowledge base of system configuration settings, upcoming changes to the infrastructure, upcoming new releases, known problems and errors, resolutions, and workarounds
- Ensuring that service desk technicians have access to service-level management data (covered later in this chapter)

One of the most important functions of the service desk—in addition to quickly finding a resolution to an incident and returning users to productivity—is providing data to spot trends that require a root-cause analysis and a more permanent resolution. For instance, in tracking monthly incident metrics, the HIT manager spots the same incidents recurring each month. As exhibit 6.5 indicates, these recurring incidents become the input to the next HIT service support process—problem management.

Problem Management

The goal of problem management is "to reduce the likelihood and impact of incidents by identifying actual and potential causes of incidents and managing workarounds and known errors" (Axelos 2019).

With incident management, the primary goal is to restore service to end users as quickly as possible. This often results in temporary workarounds or Band-Aid solutions to allow the end user to use whatever HIT asset is needed to perform their job. Problem management, on the other hand, is focused on determining the underlying root cause or causes of incidents to ensure that the problem will not reemerge. Many healthcare organizations use a root-cause analysis approach in their process improvement activities. Root-cause analysis should not be a foreign concept, as The Joint Commission (2020) requires root-cause analysis to be conducted to get to the underlying causes of sentinel events that occur in healthcare settings. Furthermore, the National Aeronautics and Space Administration uses root-cause analysis routinely to determine underlying causes of spacecraft system malfunctions. These same root-cause analysis processes are applied by leading HIT departments as a means of providing world-class HIT support services. While there are numerous approaches to conducting a root-cause analysis, a simple approach is composed of the following four elements:

1. *Data collection.* HIT department analysts collect all known information about a particular problem from myriad sources, which include but are not limited to the incident management database, the configuration management database, and change control logs.
2. *Causal factor charting.* Analysts create a flowchart of events, configuration settings, and other known facts that created the problem. This charting process often identifies gaps in knowledge that require more data collection to investigate the problem. Therefore, the data collection and causal factor charting should be viewed as iterative processes that work in tandem. In addition, it is not uncommon for multiple contributing causes to problems to exist.
3. *Root-cause identification.* After all of the potential contributing causes have been identified in a flowchart, analysts identify the underlying root causes for the problem.
4. *Recommendation generation and implementation.* Based on the particular root causes, people from the HIT department with the relevant skill sets are gathered to generate ideas about resolving the identified root causes, select the "best" recommended solution or solutions, and develop and implement the plan (this typically involves the change management process discussed next).

Healthcare organizations with formal problem management processes in place can expect to see a reduction in the number of overall incidents that are generated, a decrease in average time to resolve incidents, and an increase in customer satisfaction over time.

Change Management

To administer needed changes effectively to the *HIT infrastructure*—broadly defined as any HIT application or architecture component—organizations generally defer to a change review committee or change advisory committee. This committee is made up primarily of HIT personnel from all of the various teams in the HIT department, along with key users from business and clinical areas. The typical representation in such a group includes but is not limited to the following:

- Network engineer or architect
- Server or hardware engineer or architect
- Key application analyst
- Support center manager
- Nurse manager
- Business office manager
- Physician (as needed for changes that involve physician workflow)
- Vendor representative (as needed when changes affect a vendor-supplied application or hardware device)
- Third-party consultant and other technical expert (as needed)

This group meets as often as necessary to manage upcoming changes proactively. Typically, organizations have a means of dealing with both urgent and routine changes. Urgent changes follow a fast-track approach, such as quickly rolling out the latest virus-protection signature files to all end-user devices after an organization is hit with a new virus. Routine changes include those for which lead times are known and can be planned in a less hurried manner, such as adding disk-encryption software to all end-user devices, which can be planned far in advance and rolled out in a measured way.

As exhibit 6.5 indicates, requests for changes can come from the business or clinical units (e.g., request to interface two preexisting applications that have not previously been interfaced), can come from incidents, or can stem from a problem management process that has recommended changes to alleviate root causes to identified problems. Also, change management processes must ensure that ongoing changes are documented in the organization's CMDB.

Release Management

The purpose of release management processes is to ensure that either new software or new hardware being added to a live environment has been built and tested in such a way that it is put into service without causing negative effects (described earlier in this chapter). For instance, as part of the healthcare organization's testing of a new version of a mission-critical application, an HIT manager discovers that the software will run only on hardware with an upgraded operating system and upgraded hardware memory. In this case, the decision is made to release this new version of software as part of a package that includes an upgrade of its associated hardware. Organizations without rigorous release management practices suffer from disruptions in service resulting from unplanned work.

The full release management practice, as outlined by Axelos (2019), includes the following value chain activities, all of which are tied to the CMDB at a minimum (as it is the definitive knowledge source for documenting changes to all HIT resources):

- Plan: policies, guidance, and timelines for releases are driven by the organizational strategy and service portfolio. The size, scope, and content of each release must be planned and managed
- Improve: new or changed releases may be required to deliver improvements and these should be planned and managed in the same way as any other release
- Engage: the content and cadence of releases must be designed to match the needs and expectations of customers and users
- Design and transition: release management ensures that new or changed services are made available to customers in a controlled way
- Obtain/build: changes to components are normally included in a release and delivered in a controlled way
- Deliver and support: releases may impact on delivery and support. Training, documentation, release notes, known errors, user guides, support scripts, etc. are provided by this practice to facilitate service restoration

In essence, the release management process requires explicit and deliberate coordination and communication mechanisms to be evident in and beyond the HIT department. Release management processes are closely tied to both change management and configuration management. In the past, when putting these ITIL processes in place, leading organizations were advised to centralize oversight of the change, configuration, and release management processes (Farah 2005; OGC 2005) and to tie this centralized oversight closely to the project management process identified in chapter 10. However, contemporary HIT operating models tend to incorporate multiple cloud service providers external to the healthcare organization, which itself is increasingly characterized by more autonomous business units as it pursues direct-to-consumer, digital health offerings. These realities require much more adaptive and agile approaches to change, configuration, and release management.

Configuration Management

A common feature of almost all hardware and software is the ability to manipulate its configurations. Examples of configuration settings can be simple (such as the screen saver that can be selected on a personal computer) or complex (such as the automatic fail-over settings for adding CPU capacity, for instance, to a virtual server environment). Most hospitals and integrated hospital delivery networks use a hundred or more different applications and dozens of different hardware platforms. Thus, maintaining comprehensive knowledge of the configuration settings on each becomes an important task for HIT departments that want to avoid all of the reactive, unplanned work that results when new changes or releases are introduced without knowledge of their impact on preexisting configurations. Configuration management processes focus on the identification, recording, and reporting of HIT components to include software versions and the interrelationships between the components (Axelos 2019).

Configuration management includes the following five subprocesses:

1. *Planning.* This entails high-level outline planning and detailed three- to six-month planning that address envisioned additions to the hardware or software environment that likely will have an impact on configuration settings of one or more of the HIT assets in the healthcare organization.
2. *Identification.* This explicitly identifies configurable components of the HIT infrastructure and documents their ownership and the interrelationships between them. Examples include but are not limited to servers, network components, software licenses, desktops, and computer facilities.
3. *Control.* This ensures that no change is enacted in the HIT infrastructure without appropriate documentation validating that the possible affected configuration items have been adequately tested prior to implementation.
4. *Status accounting.* This ensures accurate reporting of the configuration setting of all of the items that make up an organization's HIT infrastructure throughout their life cycle.
5. *Verification and audit.* This involves routinely auditing the documentation that exists on configuration items to ensure accuracy.

One tool that can facilitate the configuration management process is the CMDB. As noted in exhibit 6.6, the HIT service support management practices (incident management, problem management, change management, release management) can have an effect on HIT asset configuration settings. As such, a single CMDB used by the entire HIT department can provide a powerful means of dynamically and agilely documenting change states in asset configurations as well as serving as an up-to-date tool to plan changes and releases.

The ITIL service management practices in exhibit 6.6 were largely focused on establishing a rigorous, interconnected set of operational methodologies. In exhibit 6.7, we focus on tactical methodologies that ensure that services meet the HIT department's customer expectations.

Service-Level Management

The purpose of service-level management is to proactively review, with the HIT department's customers, the value of the services being delivered. Service-level management is typically operationalized via the establishment of service-level agreements (SLAs) between the HIT department and specific sets of customers. The requirements for successful SLAs include the following (Axelos 2019):

- The SLA must be related to a defined "service" in the service catalogue; otherwise they are simply individual metrics without a purpose, that do not provide adequate visibility or reflect the service perspective
- The SLA should relate to defined outcomes and not simply operational metrics. This can be achieved with balanced bundles of metrics, such as customer satisfaction and key business outcomes
- The SLA should reflect an "agreement," i.e. engagement and discussion between the service provider and the service consumer. It is important to involve all stakeholders, including partners, sponsors, users, and customers
- The SLA must be simply written and easy to understand and use for all parties

Some HIT departments do not enter into SLAs at all; hospital users simply get whatever service the HIT department is able to provide. Others enter into SLAs whereby the HIT department specifies the terms or conditions of the services it is able to provide within specified periods without any input from its customers. Both of these examples (no SLAs and SLAs dictated by the HIT department) are suboptimal practices that do not align HIT service delivery expectations with the drivers of the hospital's business. High-functioning HIT departments, on the other hand, take the time with all of their major customers to negotiate and agree on specific service-level expectations at a given cost. Typically, HIT departments with more resources can be more responsive. Often, however, hospital budgets limit the amount of dollars available for the delivery of HIT services. For this very reason, it becomes paramount that HIT managers put in place SLAs with their customers. The

EXHIBIT 6.7
Additional Key ITIL Service Management Practice Interrelationships

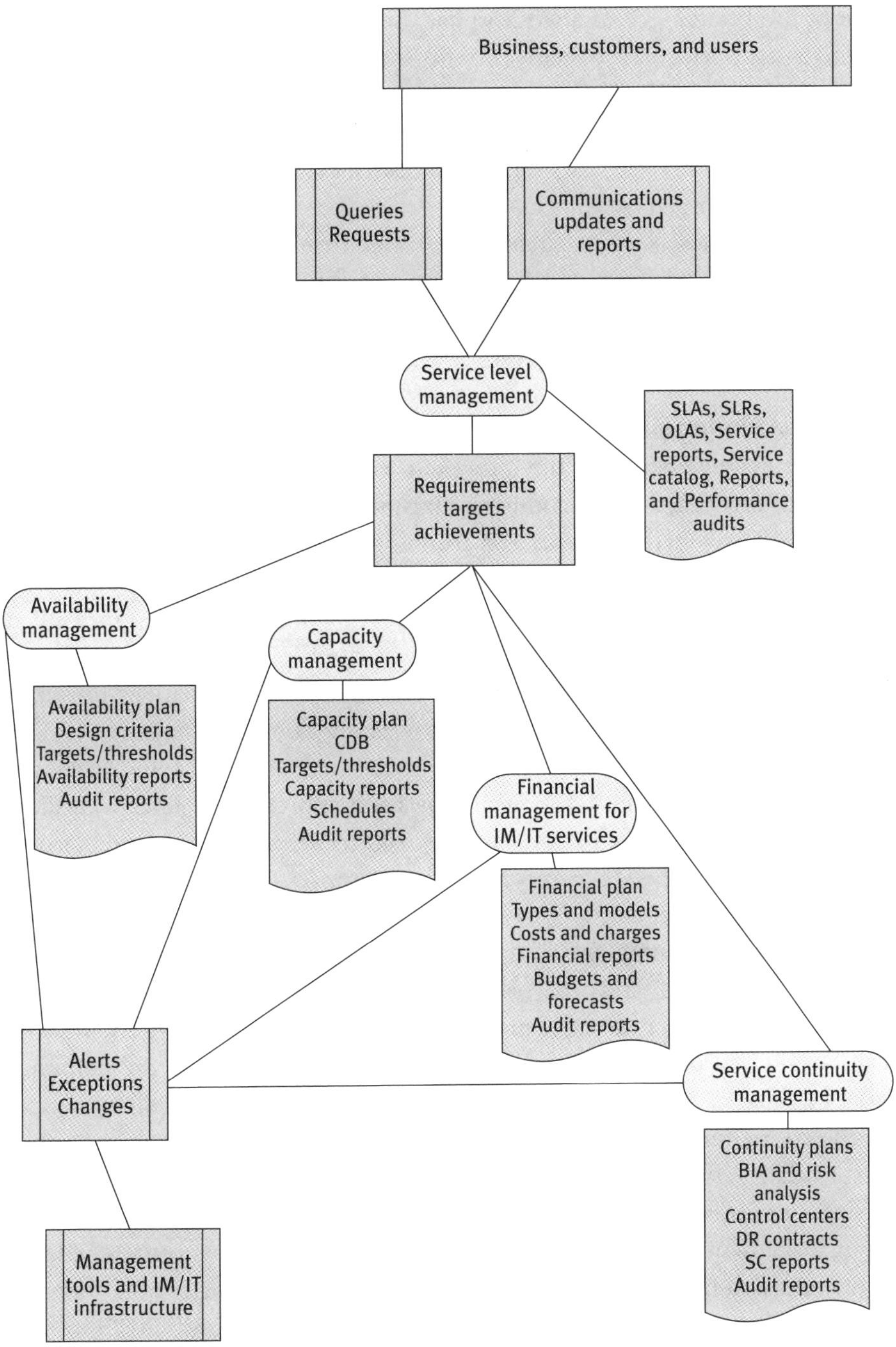

purpose of these agreements is not only to set realistic expectations (in the case of the budget-constrained hospital) but also to work together continually to assess performance relative to the SLA and make adjustments (perhaps by increasing the HIT budget to attain higher service levels).

Another important component of service-level management is the development of a service catalog, which describes all of the HIT services that the healthcare organization's customers can expect to receive from the HIT department. These service catalogs can range from simple brochures detailing the services and means of accessing the services to fully web-enabled dynamic service catalogs that link to various applications that serve as entry points to numerous HIT services.

Capacity Management

Capacity management is "the process used to ensure the IT capacity is capable of meeting current and future business needs in a cost-effective fashion. In capacity management, the planning and implementation involved, unlike other management areas, are proactive in nature rather than reactive" (Technopedia 2014). Specifically, first, capacity management is an explicit process to create a better understanding of the business and clinical needs for computer resources (such as the impact that adding a patient portal to a preexisting EHR system will have on existing computer resources). This analysis of the organization's changes in business goals and approaches is largely outward-looking. Changes in goals and approaches might necessitate changes in the hardware or software environment that supports the business and clinical processes. The second focus of capacity management is more inwardly focused, whereby CPU performance, disk space utilization, growth of applications running on computer resources, growth of users accessing computer resources, and network traffic patterns are constantly monitored so that HIT managers are able proactively to address potential problems that can be forecasted as a result of rigorous monitoring. As such, the definitive goal of capacity management is to predict and implement needed changes in the computer resources of an organization consistently and accurately to ensure that sufficient capacity exists in the computing resources for unimpeded business and clinical operations. Organizations that do not have capacity management processes in place experience high amounts of unscheduled downtime and high costs associated with mitigating the impact of unforeseen computer resource upgrades needed to restore capacity (Robb 2017).

Availability Management

Availability management is closely related to capacity management in its focus on ensuring that computer resources are available when users need them. Availability management typically consists of the following five components:

1. *Availability*—the percentage of agreed-on service hours that a particular computer resource or service is available for use (e.g., the service center is available for taking trouble calls from 7:00 a.m. to 7:00 p.m.)
2. *Reliability*—the prevention of malfunctions and the ability to keep services and computer resources operational (e.g., by using backup power distribution units, power-related failures are mitigated)
3. *Maintainability*—the ability to restore services or computer resources back to normal operations quickly (e.g., an effective service center that can quickly resolve incidents and restore computer resources to an operational state)
4. *Serviceability*—the ability of external contractors to augment internal HIT department resources to service parts of the HIT infrastructure (e.g., an effective escalation process whereby vendor specialists can be called in to help resolve vendor-specific hardware or software issues)
5. *Security*—the implementation of appropriate access controls to ensure continued services (e.g., the ability to accurately restore user passwords for bona fide employees when such a need arises)

The availability management practice focuses on measuring system downtime, network downtime, average time it takes to resolve an incident, and other metrics that describe periods when systems and services are not available to users. These metrics then become the internal benchmarks with which HIT managers assess improvements in availability of computer resources.

Financial Management for Health Information Technology Services

While considered a general management practice in the new ITIL version 4 reformulation, effective and tightly coupled financial management of IT resources is imperative for all aspects of the HIT operation, but especially for the ITIL practices of service-level management, availability management, capacity management, and service continuity management depicted in exhibit 6.7. Many small HIT departments do not set up a distinct function to manage holistically the finances associated with providing HIT services. As healthcare institutions continue to automate an increasing number of their operational processes, and as the complexity of managing computer resources increases as a result of this significant growth in automation, the need to manage HIT effectively as a business in and of itself will also continue to grow (Chou 2016). In fact, all healthcare organizations, and particularly medium-to-large organizations with more than 100 HIT employees, will typically have a senior manager who oversees the HIT department finances and reports directly to the CIO (McGowan

2018). Typical functions associated with the financial management of HIT services include, but are not limited, to the following:

- Creation of the annual HIT budget and management of that budget to ensure annual expenditures do not exceed the budgeted amounts
- HIT asset procurement management to ensure purchased items are within the budget and to seek maximum volume discounting on purchases
- Creation of the schedule of costs and oversight of charge-back processes and receipt of funds from customers
- Vendor management to seek vendor discounts continually and manage relations with vendors
- Oversight of antifraud policies and procedures, such as Sarbanes-Oxley Act compliance (particularly true for for-profit healthcare organizations)

As noted in exhibit 6.7, the finances required to provide a given level of HIT services are driven by the clinical and business needs of the healthcare organization. As the need for responsiveness goes up, so does the need for additional finances to support these higher service-level targets. Likewise, organizations' attempt to increase the number of HIT development initiatives they wish to undertake during a budget cycle typically will also drive up the funding levels needed to support increased simultaneous development efforts. Thus, it is critical to negotiate definitive SLAs with all of the customers of the HIT department to ensure that adequate funding needs can be identified. Often, cutting back on HIT budgets forces organizations to remove resources that had previously been assigned to providing HIT services. In these situations, it is paramount that HIT leaders renegotiate SLAs to ensure that misunderstandings about service-level expectations can be avoided. The old adage "you get what you pay for" holds particularly true in providing HIT services to healthcare organizations. To avoid a mismatch in customer expectations, fully understanding the service-level constraints of given levels of funding is important to the effective financial management of HIT services.

Service Continuity Management

While HIT service interruptions resulting from unforeseen downtime are fairly well understood, expected, and largely routinized, major service interruptions resulting from natural disasters such as earthquakes, hurricanes, or fires typically require a very different response. HIT service continuity management is the process for restoring the healthcare organization's HIT services as quickly as possible after a service interruption (Axelos 2019). Examples of devastating impacts on healthcare operations were plentiful in the New Orleans area following Hurricane Katrina in 2005. Some healthcare operations, such as Charity Hospital, simply ceased to exist as a result. As noted earlier, healthcare delivery organizations' poor financial health often makes it difficult to invest adequately in HIT services such as continuity plans. While it is not uncommon for organizations to have continuity plans, in the event of a real disaster or major disruption in service, the execution of these plans often fails. Clarke (2004) refers to such plans as "symbolic plans" or "fantasy plans." He notes, "symbolic [continuity] plans are the ones that are a charade. They're touted as workable but, in fact, they're not based on actual expertise or experience and, by definition, they overpromise. . . . [Furthermore,] symbolic plans can create a dangerous false sense of security" (Clarke 2004, 21–22).

To ensure that the HIT department has workable HIT service continuity plans in place, Axelos (2019) suggests that the organization undertake a business impact analysis whereby the senior leadership team identifies the business and clinical processes that are absolutely critical to the functioning of the enterprise. For instance, a performance reporting application may not be essential, but the admissions, discharges, and transfers and billing applications will likely be considered critical. The business impact analysis also assesses the following (US Department of Homeland Security 2015):

- Lost revenue
- Delayed revenue
- Increased expenses (e.g., overtime labor, outsourcing, expediting costs)
- Regulatory fines
- Contractual penalties or loss of contractual bonuses from suppliers or partners
- Customer or partner dissatisfaction, damaged credibility, or defection
- Delay of new business plans

After the business impact analysis is completed, a risk assessment is conducted to assess the extent to which a healthcare organization is vulnerable to different potential threats. For instance, a hospital in Lubbock, Texas, has a higher likelihood of sustaining damage from a tornado than a hospital in Vancouver, British Columbia. After assessing the business impacts as well as the potential risks and their likelihood of occurrence, an HIT service continuity strategy is developed. The key elements of this strategy should describe the following:

- Implementation of the strategy.
- Arrangements made for standby recovery locations, either via contracts with third-party vendors specializing in disaster recovery hosting services or via reciprocal support agreements with other organizations.

- Risk-reduction measures (while the organization cannot do much about being located in a tornado alley, for example, identifying a need to move the computer room from the basement of the building because it is in a flood zone is certainly something that can be accomplished to reduce risk).
- Detailed step-by-step procedural checklists to restore service levels.
- Timeline for testing the plan in a realistic manner (e.g., periodically simulating a disaster and invoking the standby contracts to bring up one or more of the critical applications at an alternate location). This is an important element of service continuity planning, as it overcomes Clarke's (2004) criticism of symbolic plans and ensures that the organization has a tried-and-tested approach to restore critical HIT-dependent business processes.

As a framework of information technology service management practices, ITIL continues to evolve and be refined. From its start in the 1980s, through multiple iterations and reconceptualizations—including its most recent publication of ITIL edition 4 (Axelos 2019)—when implemented effectively, it is particularly well suited to the contemporary cloud-based, multisourced environment (Goldberg, Satger, and Fromm 2016) that more and more HIT departments are gravitating toward.

Summary

Healthcare administrators have long recognized the need for efficient and effective operations throughout the healthcare enterprises that they lead. However, because few senior executives have come from HIT backgrounds, the internal workings of the HIT department have often been a "black box" to senior leadership. In this chapter, we opened the HIT department black box and presented a number of key operational and tactical practices that, when managed in a loose, informal manner, will create costly, unplanned work that limits the resources available for new strategic initiatives. To maximize efficiencies and effectiveness, many healthcare enterprises are adopting frameworks to enhance their internal operations.

A number of frameworks were presented here, including the ITIL framework, which Foederer (2018) suggests is best suited for HIT department-led agile business alignment efforts. ITIL categorizes HIT department practices into three: (1) general management practices, which includes service financial management; (2) service management practices, which include incident management, problem management, change management, release management, configuration management, service-level management, capacity management, availability management, and services continuity management; and (3) technical management practices. As more and more healthcare enterprises are becoming automated, demands on professional HIT department services will continue to increase. HIT departments that have implemented, or are implementing, formal practice improvement frameworks like ITIL will create greater efficiencies and thereby leverage HIT resources toward more strategic initiatives and value delivery. ITIL continues to evolve and is now in its fourth edition as it addresses contemporary digital business operating environments.

Web Resources

A number of organizations (through their websites) provide more information on the topics discussed in this chapter:

- Axelos, a joint venture between the United Kingdom Cabinet Office and Capita, an outsourcing firm, curates ITIL content and maintains the official ITIL website at www.axelos.com/best-practice-solutions/itil.
- IT Service Management Forum International (www.itsmfi.org/default.aspx) is an international member organization that promotes best practices in information technology service management.
- IT Service Management Forum US (www.itsmfusa.org/default.aspx) is the US chapter of the IT Service Management Forum International and acts as a member organization to promote and share best practices in information technology service management.

Discussion Questions

1. Why does unplanned HIT work increase costs?
2. Identify some process improvement frameworks that are applicable to an HIT department. What are the advantages and disadvantages of each?
3. Describe at least five HIT service management practices and how they are interrelated.
4. What is a CMDB, and why is it an important component of HIT service management?
5. What is an SLA, and why is it an important component of HIT service management?

6. List some of the reasons given for HIT service continuity plan failures.
7. Why would an IT practice framework like ITIL need to continue to evolve over time?

References

Agarwal, R., and V. Sambamurthy. 2002. "Principles and Models for Organizing the IT Function." *MIS Quarterly Executive* 1 (1): 1–16.

Axelos. 2020. "About Axelos." Accessed February 21. www.axelos.com/about-axelos.

———. 2019. *ITIL Foundation*, ITIL 4 edition. London: Axelos Limited.

Chou, D. 2016. "Are You Managing Your Department Like a Business?" *CIO*. Published June 27. www.cio.com/article/3088745/are-you-managing-your-department-as-a-business.html.

Ciccolini, C., and M. McDermott. 2005. "Leveraging the ITIL Service Support Framework." ITSM Watch. Published December 18. www.itsmwatch.com/itil/article.php/3348501/Leveraging-the-ITIL-Service-Support-Framework.htm.

Clarke, L. 2004. "What's the Plan?" *Harvard Business Review* 82 (6): 21–22.

Congress.gov. 2002. "H. Rept. 107-414: Corporate and Auditing Accountability, Responsibility, and Transparency Act of 2002." Published July 30. www.govinfo.gov/content/pkg/PLAW-107publ204/pdf/PLAW-107publ204.pdf.

Farah, J. 2005. "Taking the Complexity Out of Release Management." *CM Crossroads.* Published December 5. www.cmcrossroads.com/article/taking-complexity-out-release-management.

Field, T. 1998. "Shop Talk: Goodyear's Debra Walker on Leveraging Business-Side Experience in IS." *CIO* (11) 16: 80.

Foederer, M. 2018. "ITIL Update—the High-Performing IT Organization." Axelos. Published May 21. www.axelos.com/news/blogs/may-2018/itil-update-the-high-performing-it-organization.

Gartner. 2001. "Describing the Capability Maturity Model." Accessed February 6. http://suraj.lums.edu.pk/~cs564a05/Resources/CMM.pdf.

Goldberg, M., G. Satger, and H. Fromm. 2016. "Adapting IT Service Management for Successful Multi-Sourcing Service Integration." Association for Information Systems. Published September 12. https://aisel.aisnet.org/ecis2016_rp/186/.

Hall, L., S. Futela, D. Badlani, and E. Stegman. 2016. "IT Key Metrics Data 2017: Key Industry Measures: Healthcare Providers Analysis: Current Year." Gartner. Published December 12. www.gartner.com/en/documents/3524820/it-key-metrics-data-2017-key-industry-measures-healthcare.

Hoerbst, A., W. Hackl, R. Blomer, and E. Ammenwerth. 2011. "The Status of IT Service Management in Health Care—ITIL in selected European Countries." *BMC Medical Informatics and Decision Making* 11 (76).

Information Systems Audit and Control Association. 2020. "COBIT: Effective IT Governance at Your Fingertips." Accessed March 10. www.isaca.org/resources/cobit.

Information Technology Service Management Forum (itSMF). 2001. *IT Service Management.* Version 2.1.b. London: Office of Government Commerce.

Joint Commission. 2020. "Framework for Root Cause Analysis and Corrective Actions." Accessed March 7. www.jointcommission.org/-/media/tjc/documents/resources/patient-safety-topics/sentinel-event/rca_framework_101017.pdf.

Kaplan, B., and D. Harris-Salamone. 2009. "Health IT Success and Failure: Recommendations from Literature and an AMIA Workshop." *Journal of the American Medical Informatics Association* 16 (3): 291–99.

Kim, G. 2006. "Unplanned Work Is Silently Killing IT Departments." *Computerworld.* Published April 10. www.computerworld.com/article/2563263/unplanned-work-is-silently-killing-it-departments.html.

Maslow, A. 1970. *Motivation and Personality,* 2nd ed. New York: Harper and Row.

McGowan, B. 2018. "CIOs Reveal Their Most Essential IT Financial Management Principles." *CIO.* Published February 27. www.cio.com/article/3257786/cios-reveal-their-most-essential-it-financial-management-principles.html.

Melendez, K., A. Dávila, and M. Pessoa. 2016. "Information Technology Service Management Models Applied to Medium and Small Organizations: A Systematic Literature Review." *Computer Standards and Interfaces* 47: 120–27.

Office of Government Commerce (OGC). 2005. *Best Practices for Service Support,* 10th impression. London: Office of Government Commerce.

Potter, K., J. Guevara, J. McGittigan, L. Hall, and E. Stegman. 2013. "IT Metrics: IT Spending and Staffing Report, 2013." Gartner Research. Published February 1. www.gartner.com/en/documents/2324316/it-metrics-it-spending-and-staffing-report-2013.

Robb, D. 2017. "Data Center Strategy: Tips for Better Capacity Planning." Data Center Knowledge. Published May 24. www.datacenterknowledge.com/archives/2017/05/24/data-center-strategy-tips-for-better-capacity-planning.

Rumberg, J. 2011. "Metric of the Month: First Contact Resolution." MetricNet. Accessed March 8. www.thinkhdi.com/~/media/HDICorp/Files/Library-Archive/Insider%20Articles/First%20Contact%20Resolution.pdf.

Service Desk Academy 2019. "ITIL and Service Management: ITIL V4 Practices." Published July 8. https://servicedeskacademy.com/itil-v4-practices.

Smaltz, D., V. Sambamurthy, and R. Agarwal. 2006. "The Antecedents of CIO Role Effectiveness in Organizations: An Empirical Study in the Healthcare Sector." *IEEE Transactions on Engineering Management* 53 (2): 207–22.

Sundaresan, V. 2020. "Optimizing IT Service Delivery." CIO Update. Accessed February 6. https://cioupdate.com/optimizing-it-service-delivery.

Tang, X., and Y. Todo. 2013. "A Study of Service Desk Setup in Implementing IT Service Management in Enterprises." *Technology and Investment* 4 (3): 190–96.

Technopedia. 2014. "Capacity Management." Technopedia. Published September 11. www.techopedia.com/definition/30454/capacity-management.

US Department of Homeland Security. 2015. "Business Impact Analysis." Ready. Published December 11, 2015. www.ready.gov/business-impact-analysis.

Watson, R., L. Pitt, and C. Kavan. 1998. "Measuring Information Service Quality: Lessons from Two Longitudinal Case Studies." *MIS Quarterly* 22 (1): 61–79. https://en.wikipedia.org/wiki/ITIL#Problem_management.

CHAPTER

7

HEALTH INFORMATION TECHNOLOGY SELECTION AND CONTRACT MANAGEMENT

Learning Objectives

1. Describe the steps in the health information technology (HIT) selection process.
2. Articulate why it is important to clarify objectives prior to engaging in HIT selection.
3. Describe the request for proposal (RFP) and how it is used in HIT evaluation and selection.
4. Describe vital features that an organization should include when negotiating and crafting contract terms and conditions.
5. Articulate the purpose of an HIT total-cost-of-ownership analysis.
6. Describe potential evaluation criteria that a HIT selection committee can use to evaluate RFP submissions by HIT vendors.
7. Articulate the purpose of a benefits realization assessment.

Overview

When he saw a large wooden horse at the gates of Troy, presumably left as a peace offering by the Greek army, the Trojan priest Laocoön coined the now-famous saying, "Beware of Greeks bearing gifts." As the mythology tells us, the Trojans ignored Laocoön's warning and accepted the gift horse, which resulted in the fall of Troy (Phrase Finder 2011). Clearly, this Trojan horse analogy is entirely too strong for health information technology (HIT) vendors; it is nevertheless prudent for healthcare managers to play modern-day Laocoön when working with any outsider whose interests and risk profile may not be aligned with those of the organization. To be sure, failed information technology (IT) implementations can sometimes be attributed to poor execution on the part of the hospital or health system project team. Although this chapter is not about failure to execute scenarios, it does focus attention on how to establish productive relationships with potential HIT vendors.

Mike Murphy, president and CEO of Sharp Healthcare in San Diego, once commented, "I have been disappointed that many of the products are not really ready for prime time when they are sold" (Smaltz et al. 2005). Similarly, David Hoidal, while CEO of the University of Alabama at Birmingham Health System, noted that "it's disappointing that the lack of functionality that cuts across multiple applications leaves healthcare system like ours to bear the cost and the burden of making everything work together" (Smaltz et al. 2005). These anecdotal insights from leading CEOs suggest that having a sound HIT selection process with contract management is instrumental in making informed HIT investment decisions. This chapter focuses on the crucial HIT selection process and contract management function.

The Health Information Technology Selection Process

For many healthcare providers, selecting and implementing a new enterprise information system can be one of the most costly and high-risk investments they will make over the course of many years. Especially in the case of an enterprise electronic health record (EHR), revenue cycle, or enterprise resource planning (ERP) solution, the capital and ongoing operational investment can run into hundreds of millions of dollars, and the system itself will have a direct impact on the daily lives of staff, clinicians, administrators, and (most important) patients and their families. These core systems are long-term investments, so a lot of fear and uncertainty are associated with the selection process because it is an activity that occurs infrequently but has far-reaching consequences.

The good news is that HIT selection is relatively straightforward, and the guidelines and principles of a well-managed HIT selection process apply equally well to the process of selecting a departmental solution (such as a pharmacy information system) and an enterprise EHR. The primary activities in an HIT selection process are as follows:

- Clarification of the objectives
- Formation of the HIT selection governance structure and processes
- Establishment of a HIT selection plan
- Education: Understanding the marketplace
- Down-selection: Narrowing the field
- Documentation of the requirements: Developing the request for proposal (RFP)
- Conducting detailed product demonstrations
- Completion of other due diligence activities
- Final selection
- Contract negotiations
- Benefits realization

Clarification of the Objectives

As with any organizational management decision, the first step is to document the problems that the organization is trying to solve with the new HIT or define the opportunities that the organization will be able to pursue because of the investment in a new HIT. This step addresses what the great philosopher and baseball legend Yogi Berra once said: “You’ve got to be careful if you don’t know where you’re going, because you might not get there” (Berra and Kaplan 2003, 39).

For instance, the organization can develop a set of requirements that address known problem areas with current applications or processes. Even more important, once the organization has created this initial list of needs, it must vet these requirements to understand which ones truly are must-have capabilities and which ones are less important. Too often, the organization becomes enamored of a new technology or popular product without knowing the purpose for the HIT. Technology should always be implemented to support the achievement of a desired process or outcome. Key questions for which an organization should have clear answers include the following:

- Is the HIT required to meet a regulatory mandate?
- What aspects of the organization’s strategic business plan will it support?
- Will it help to drive business growth or support service-line development?
- Will it enhance patient safety and quality outcomes?
- Will it improve the flow of clinical, financial, or operational information across the enterprise?

Ideally, the objectives for the HIT must be clearly identified and agreed on before any products are reviewed. A project charter that lists these objectives, the expected benefits, the main project participants, the participants’ roles and responsibilities, and the process for monitoring project progress is an excellent tool to support communication and buy-in. The project charter’s objectives can be the basis for a return-on-investment analysis, which is required for the approval of capital investment in many organizations.

Formation of the Health Information Technology Selection Governance Structure and Functions

One of the most difficult tasks in HIT implementation is achieving the desired level of adoption in the organization. An excellent way to lay the foundation for enthusiastic adoption is to bring all the stakeholders to the table as early as possible, obtain their endorsement of the objectives, and then ensure their active participation in the selection process. This leads to a shared sense of ownership in the result as well as a better-educated and better-prepared user population. Note here that the HIT department should almost never be seen as the main driver of the HIT selection. Having executive-level sponsorship for the project and highly visible leadership by members of the intended user population (be they physicians, nurses, pharmacists, or others), with the IT department providing support to the process in the background, is ideal. Also important is to establish a project organizational governance structure that ensures strong and ongoing sponsorship, effective management and oversight, and sufficient involvement of operational staff so that all requirements are properly defined and evaluated. A hierarchical structure works well, where operational work groups perform the bulk of the analysis, feeding the information up to a selection committee for decision-making. In some cases, it may be appropriate to seek the assistance of an external consultant with expertise in the specific technology and vendor marketplace to help guide the process and provide subject matter expertise. An example organizational governance structure is provided in exhibit 7.1.

Most organizations have a preexisting executive committee that can serve in the executive oversight role. Under that committee, typically an HIT selection committee composed of representative stakeholders is formed. For instance, if the technology is a pharmacy system, the committee membership could comprise the pharmacy director or vice president (VP), the finance director or VP, the chief nurse, the chief medical information officer, one or two representatives from the medical staff, the IT applications director, and other key stakeholders of the potentially affected workflow areas. On the other hand, if the system is an enterprise EHR, then the HIT selection committee must have much broader stakeholder representation. For efficiency, establishing functional work groups for focused activities is often useful. For example, the HIT selection committee may form an ancillary services work group to develop requirements for the ancillary modules of the EHR, while a decision support work group might work on developing requirements and evaluating vendor responses for order set development, alerts and reminders, and so on. Finally, external consultants sometimes augment the process in organizations that prefer to have a consultant who has broad experience in running an HIT selection process.

Establishment of a Health Information Technology Selection Plan

Another best practice is to develop a HIT selection plan and timeline that are not only efficient but also realistic. If the process is rushed to meet an aggressive deadline, decisions may need to be made too quickly—and this can result in errors or omissions and in members of the selection team feeling left out of the process or forced into a solution they were not ready to accept. Some tasks in the selection process can be very time intensive, so it is important to ensure that selection team members understand or are conscious of the time

EXHIBIT 7.1

Sample HIT Project Organization: Roles and Responsibilities

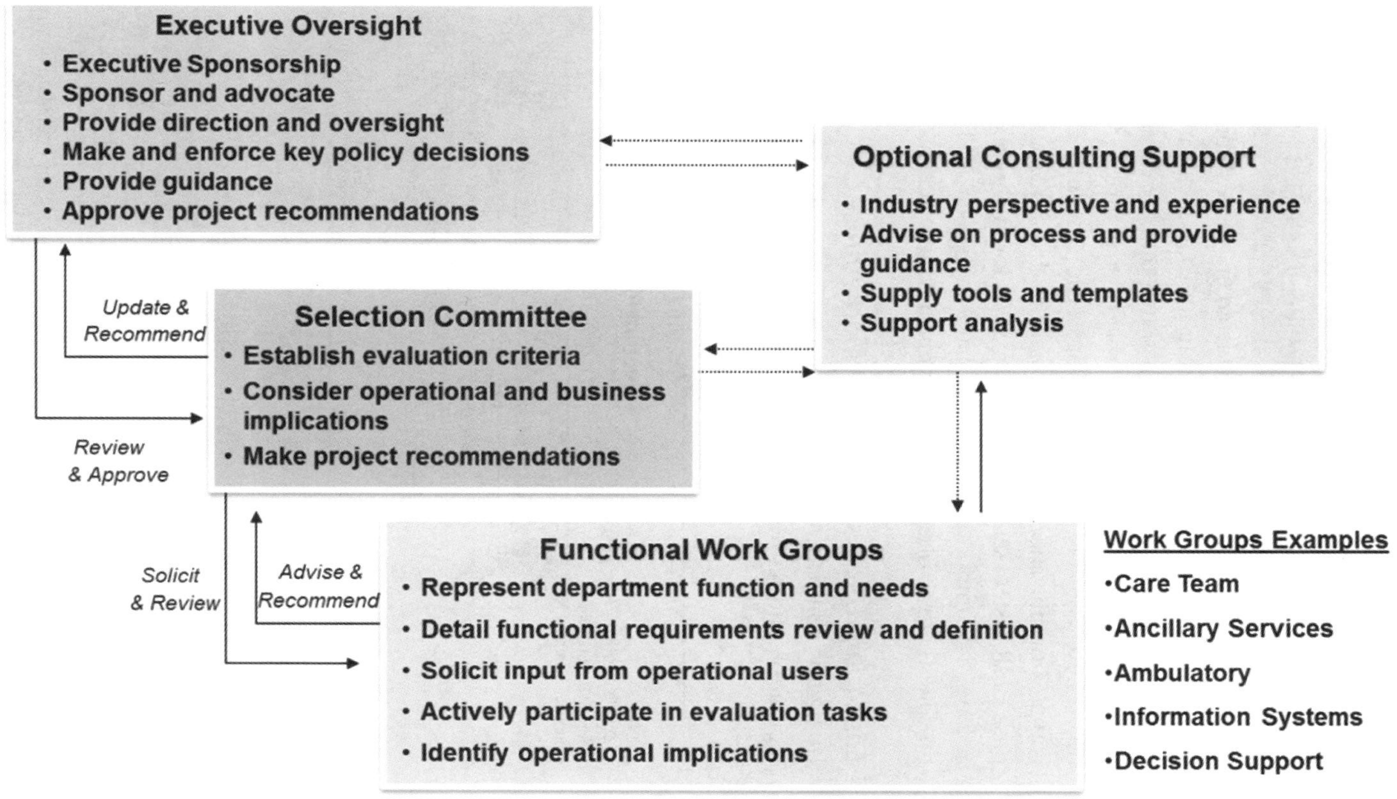

Executive Oversight
• Executive Sponsorship
• Sponsor and advocate
• Provide direction and oversight
• Make and enforce key policy decisions
• Provide guidance
• Approve project recommendations
Optional Consulting Support
• Industry perspective and experience
• Advise on process and provide guidance
• Supply tools and templates
• Support analysis
Update & Recommend
Review & Approve
Selection Committee
• Establish evaluation criteria
• Consider operational and business implications
• Make project recommendations
Solicit & Review
Advise & Recommend
Functional Work Groups
• Represent department function and needs
• Detail functional requirements review and definition
• Solicit input from operational users
• Actively participate in evaluation tasks
• Identify operational implications
Work Groups Examples
•Care Team
•Ancillary Services
•Ambulatory
•Information Systems
•Decision Support

Source: Reprinted from material in "The Vendor Selection Process" by Paul Murphy, 2011, Encore Health Resources White Paper, Houston, Texas, pp. 1–12. Used with permission.

commitment required of them, the time impact of competing projects and responsibilities, and specific calendar events (such as public holidays and summer vacations). Equally important is to match the selection project timeline to the complexity of the HIT being evaluated and the committed availability of the selection team members, both at the functional work group level and the HIT selection committee level. Organizations should anticipate activities that will require extra time to coordinate and plan (such as product demonstrations) and prepare early. An example of an HIT selection work plan is provided in exhibit 7.2.

The HIT selection plan depicted in the exhibit outlines a 17-week intended process for the steps leading up to, but not including, the contract negotiation and beyond. This plan assumes that the organization has no delays in forming the HIT selection governance structure and functions, the stakeholders are available and can participate on schedule, and so forth. In large, complex organizations with many stakeholders undertaking a complex enterprise EHR system selection, selecting a vendor of choice could easily take twice as long. The important point is to have an explicit HIT selection plan with a timeline that the organization thoughtfully develops and attempts to follow.

Education: Understanding the Marketplace

In highly competitive markets with many quality products, the vendors' reputation and services may represent the biggest differentiator between one

EXHIBIT 7.2
Sample HIT Selection Work Plan

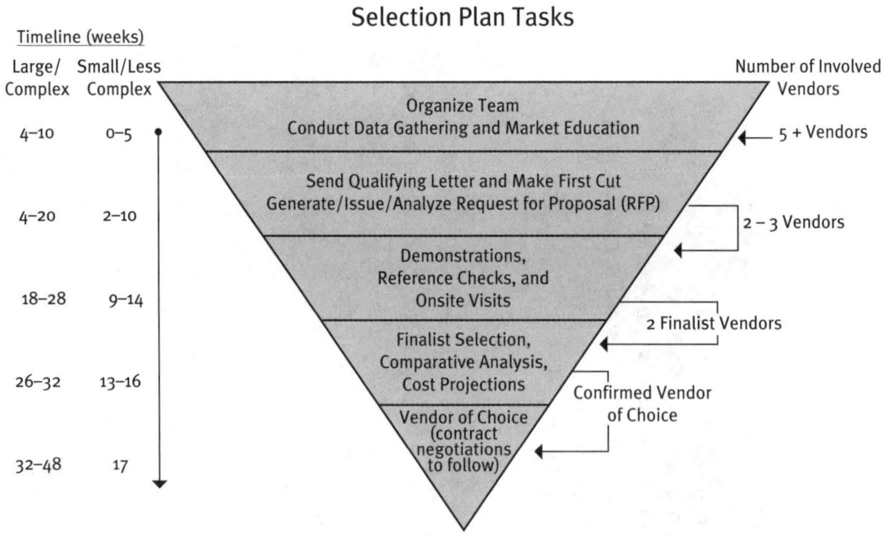

Source: Adapted from material in "The Vendor Selection Process," by Paul Murphy, 2011, Encore Health Resources White Paper, Houston, Texas, pp. 1–12. Used with permission.

HIT and another. HIT selection committee members typically conduct some initial data gathering on the leading vendors in the marketplace to find out details such as the following:

- How long has the vendor been in business?
- What is the vendor's reputation for providing customer support during implementation and ongoing maintenance?
- How much effort will the vendor put into product development and enhancement?
- What is the vendor's business plan?
- How has the vendor performed financially over the past several years?

If the vendor is financially or organizationally unstable, it may not be able to adequately support an organization or continue to invest in the quality of the product. In the HIT marketplace, vendor acquisitions are common, and the new owner may not provide the level of service given by the original vendor.

A number of subscription-based sources are available for assessing HIT functionality and the extent of a vendor's installed base for its products (number of units actually in use). The first is Gartner (www.gartner.com), a consulting firm that specializes in providing market research in the IT industry. Many healthcare organizations' IT departments maintain subscription services to Gartner, which also tracks the HIT industry specifically. For instance, for EHR applications, Gartner tracks, by vendor, the level of sophistication of various EHR capabilities, such as the following:

- Clinical data repository
- Privacy
- Interoperability
- Controlled medical vocabulary
- Workflow
- Clinical decision support
- Clinical documentation
- Display
- Order management (computerized physician order entry)
- Knowledge management
- Continuum of care

Furthermore, Gartner tracks the number of implementations of various vendors' EHR components.

Another source for assessing the extent of installed base of various vendors' EHR offerings is the HIMSS Analytics database (www.

himssanalytics.com). This information is generally free to healthcare organizations that are willing to submit their own data regarding their particular installed base of various products. Furthermore, because the HIMSS Analytics database tracks organizational demographic information (e.g., number of beds, adjusted patient days), it can create peer-comparison reports that can be used to benchmark peers running similar financial or clinical application suites.

Finally, KLAS Enterprises (www.klasresearch.com) provides another source for doing research on HIT products. Regardless of a healthcare manager's tolerance for risk, the acquisition of most HIT is an expensive endeavor—one that requires particular due diligence with respect to narrowing the field, negotiation, and contracting.

Down Selection: Narrowing the Field

Down selection is the term for narrowing down an initial set of vendors to just a few finalists. Often, there are many potential suppliers of a product; some may be industry veterans with tried-and-tested solutions, while others may be newcomers with exciting new technologies but a short track record. It is usually not possible or even desirable to do a full and detailed evaluation of every potential vendor and product. To use time and resources efficiently, it is best to narrow the field of vendors as quickly as possible to the top two or three candidates before engaging in very detailed, time-consuming analysis. Think of this initially as a process of elimination rather than a process of selection. Weed out the obvious misfits so that the HIT selection committee can focus on the leaders. An effective way to narrow the field is to establish a list of selection criteria that match the organization's objectives closely. Following are some criteria that are often used:

- Essential product functionality
- Existing client base for the HIT
- Ability to integrate with other HIT
- Technology platform
- Vendor reputation and financial health
- Cost to acquire and implement
- HIT usability

The selection team may apply a percentage weighting to each of the selection criteria so that everyone understands the relative importance of functionality versus cost versus technology and so on. This weighting will prove highly valuable in the final selection as it provides an objective way to score the finalist vendors.

If a very large number of vendors exist in the marketplace, it can be useful to write a short *qualifying letter* that requires each vendor to indicate its ability to comply with basic, objective selection criteria—for example, the vendor must have existing clients that are similar to the organization, or the vendor must hold desired certifications such as the Centers for Medicare & Medicaid Services' Meaningful Use certification for EHRs. This qualifying letter helps to quickly eliminate outliers with the minimum of effort.

Documentation of the Requirements: Developing the Request for Proposal

During the initial stages of the HIT selection process, high-level objectives and knowledge gained by the HIT selection committee members during the marketplace education stage are used to down select to a few key vendors. Some organizations spend a great deal of time developing lists with hundreds or even thousands of functional requirements for the HIT, to which the vendors are then required to respond. This effort is time consuming for both the selection team and the vendors and can provide limited value (the vendor responses also take a lot of work to review). Often, it is better to think "bigger picture" and then create an RFP or, alternately, a request for information (RFI) that contains fewer than 100 questions addressing the primary functions and features desired by the organization. The RFP or RFI is a formal notice—often issued by an organization's purchasing department—that the organization is interested in purchasing a particular type of HIT product. If the selection team is unsure of the features available in the current market, the team may invite one or two vendors to provide a high-level demonstration of their products as a form of education before creating the RFP.

The RFP should be divided into sections addressing different aspects of the HIT and vendor. It should begin with a few paragraphs that inform the vendors about the organization and its objectives for the HIT selection, followed by a series of questions about the vendor, the product it is proposing, the functionality offered, underlying technology, associated services, comprehensive costs, and any other relevant information that will help the selection team make a decision. The work groups should participate in drafting questions in their areas of expertise. The RFP questions should require the vendor to explain key aspects of the proposed solution rather than merely give a simple yes-or-no response. For example, instead of "Does your system include medication ordering?" the question should be "Describe medication orders functionality, including related decision support and any features designed to enhance patient safety." Typical RFP sections are illustrated in exhibit 7.3.

EXHIBIT 7.3
Sections in a Typical Request for Proposal

Information Category	Details Sought
Corporate overview	Vendor corporate history, size, organization, financials
Client base	Current client base using relevant products, geographic spread, clients similar to the organization
Healthcare reform and regulatory compliance	Meaningful use compliance plan, support of quality measures reporting, interoperability support for medical home
Product availability	Products matching required functions (e.g., inpatient, ambulatory, clinical, administrative, technical, reporting), date released, Office of the National Coordinator for Health Information Technology certification status, delivery and support models
Interface availability	Interfacing approach, relevant experience
Technology platform	Use of current, industry-standard technologies
Preliminary and ongoing costs	One-time and ongoing costs, including hardware, software licensing, implementation, training, support, and subscriptions
Implementation and support approach	Phasing, resource requirements (vendor and organization), ongoing support services
Development direction, unique attributes	Future product and technology plans, alignment with organizational vision, market differentiators

According to mThink (2003), HIT selection committee members should ensure that

> vendors account for all costs, such as implementation and maintenance, and don't overlook hidden costs for items such as training and infrastructure costs (wireless, mobile devices, etc.). Here is a list of common expenses:
>
> - Hardware
> - System software (e.g., operating system, database licensing, etc.)
> - Vendor software
> - Interfaces
> - Conversions
> - Ongoing licensing [and] maintenance

- Increased staff needs
- Networking
- Peripherals (printers, PCs, bar code readers, handheld devices)
- Training
- Facility renovation to accommodate hardware and training.

Some organizations provide a separate spreadsheet form in which the vendors are required to list costs by category, along with other distinguishing information (National Learning Consortium 2012). This practice helps to ensure that all the costs are identified and can be compared across the vendors' price quotes. Comparing vendor costs should be "apples to apples," carefully separating one-time costs (e.g., licenses, implementation services, training services) from ongoing costs (e.g., annual maintenance, subscriptions) and ensuring that the functionality being included matches across the quotes.

In addition, the RFP should include detailed instructions for vendor responses, including the format for response, dates of submission, and rules for communication. It is important to limit vendor communications to a small number of people on the selection team so that the process can be properly managed and to ensure that all vendors receive the same information. In the selection process, it is a best practice to inform the vendors that the responses documented in their RFP and quotes will be attached to the final contract as a commitment. This helps to set the vendors' expectations that they will be held accountable to their RFP promises and prevents rework during the negotiation. Analysis of the RFP responses and how well they match the HIT selection criteria helps to determine which vendors are asked to continue to the next step—conducting detailed product demonstrations.

Conducting Detailed Product Demonstrations

Detailed product demonstrations are usually one of the most time-consuming steps in the selection process. Demonstrations for an enterprise EHR can take more than a full day per vendor and require the attendance of many key personnel. For this reason, it is best to use the information from the qualifying letter and RFP to eliminate all but the top two or three vendors before inviting them for demonstrations. A formal agenda for the product demonstrations is helpful, as it sets the expectation that all vendors follow the same approximate sequence and show equivalent functions and features. Paul Murphy, formerly of Encore Health Resources (a firm that specializes in assisting hospitals with HIT selection processes), suggests that organizations should avoid very detailed scripts, as these may force the vendor into a workflow that does not match the design of their HIT and will confuse the audience. Scripted demonstrations tend to take much longer to prepare for and conduct. A simple evaluation document that outlines the major requirements outlined in the RFP will allow HIT selection committee members to record their observations easily. This ability is vital to performing an objective comparative analysis.

Completion of Other Due Diligence Activities

The term *due diligence*, in the context of this chapter, means the effort to educate oneself when evaluating options available for purchase. To round out the selection process, talking to existing users of the finalist vendors' products is always valuable. Using an evaluation form for these reference calls is also recommended. If the organization can afford it, it should conduct site visits with a select group of representatives from the selection team. Many selection committees create a clear agenda for the site visit and share it with the host before traveling to the site. Site visits are also an opportunity to forge relationships with other organizations that can become great sources of advice and assistance during the implementation process and beyond.

Toward the end of the process, ensure that any questions left unanswered from the RFP, demonstrations, and reference checks are addressed through additional meetings with the finalist vendors. It is often valuable for the technical team at the provider organization to meet directly with technical representatives from the vendors to understand the details of the system infrastructure and technical support requirements more fully.

If the vendors were asked to supply cost quotes during the RFP, the selection team should review these proposed prices again and ask the vendor to confirm the total quoted costs. Frequently, new costs are introduced during due diligence. As a result, creating a total-cost-of-ownership (TCO) analysis prior to final HIT selection is often helpful in understanding the expenses an organization is likely to incur. A sample TCO for an EHR project appears in exhibit 7.4.

The intent of the TCO analysis is to uncover not only the fees payable to the HIT vendor but also any additional third-party software fees. A TCO analysis is also important because it allows the organization to gain an understanding of its own staff costs because subject matter experts from the current staff often are assigned full-time to the project and will need to be filled with new or temporary hires; these often-significant costs have historically been underestimated in large HIT projects. Many organizations build in a budgetary reserve of 5–15 percent of the anticipated TCO to cover any unforeseen costs (e.g., a hospital acquisition midway through HIT implementation, which would increase licensing and implementation costs).

EXHIBIT 7.4
Sample Ten-Year Total Cost of Ownership for Typical EHR Software

Products	FY06	FY07	FY08	FY09	FY10	FY11	FY12	FY13	FY14	FY15	Total
Capital Based License fees											
Volume Based Software Licenses											
Chunk 1 (350K Visits)											
25% at Signing	$$$,$$$										$$$,$$$
20 % at Delivery	$$$,$$$										$$$,$$$
5 % on final workflow walkthru		$$,$$$									$$,$$$
5 % on integrated testing kickoff		$$,$$$									$$,$$$
25 % on First Live Use (FLU)		$$$,$$$									$$$,$$$
10% FLU + 90 Days			$$$,$$$								$$$,$$$
10% FLU + 12 months			$$$,$$$								$$$,$$$
Chunk 2 (up to 500K Visits)			$$$,$$$								$$$,$$$
Chunk 3 (up to 750K Visits)			$$$,$$$	$$$,$$$							$$$,$$$
Chunk 4 (up to 850K Visits)				$$,$$$	$$$,$$$						$$$,$$$
Oncology Module	$$$,$$$		$$$,$$$								$$$,$$$
Third Party Database	$$,$$$	$$,$$$	$$$,$$$	$$$,$$$	$$$,$$$						$,$$$,$$$
Addl Vendor One Time Products	$$,$$$	$$,$$$									$$,$$$
Third Party One Time Products		$$,$$$									$$,$$$
Interfaces (Live)											
25% at Signing	$$,$$$										$$,$$$
25% at Delivery		$$,$$$									$$,$$$
25 % at FLU		$$,$$$									$$,$$$
25% at FLU + 90		$$,$$$									$$,$$$
Medication Interfaces (Phase II)			$$,$$$								$$,$$$
Capital Based Implementation Fees											
Implementation (Base)	$$$,$$$	$$$,$$$									$$$,$$$
Implementation (Oncology)		$$,$$$	$$$,$$$								$$$,$$$
Implementation (Interfaces)		$$$,$$$									$$$,$$$
Post-Live Activities	$$,$$$										$$,$$$
Project Team Training	$$$,$$$	$$,$$$									$$$,$$$
Estimated Travel	$$$,$$$	$$$,$$$									$$$,$$$
Rollout			$$$,$$$								$$$,$$$
Capital Based Hardware Fees											
Hardware Environment											
AIX Servers		$$$,$$$					$$$,$$$				$,$$$,$$$
SAN		$$$,$$$	$$$,$$$	$$,$$$			$$$,$$$	$$$,$$$	$$,$$$		$$$,$$$
Test/Training Server	$$,$$$					$$,$$$					$$,$$$
Clarity RDBMS Server	$,$$$					$,$$$					$,$$$
Crystal Enterprise Server		$$,$$$	$$,$$$				$$,$$$	$$,$$$			$$,$$$
Print Server		$,$$$					$,$$$				$$,$$$
Patient Portal Server		$$,$$$					$$,$$$				$$,$$$
Citrix Servers	$$,$$$	$$$,$$$	$$$,$$$			$$,$$$	$$$,$$$	$$$,$$$			$$$,$$$
Citrix Server Optional				$$$,$$$					$$$,$$$		$$$,$$$
Blade Enclosure		$$,$$$	$$,$$$	$$,$$$			$$,$$$	$$,$$$	$$,$$$		$$$,$$$
Citrix Licenses	$$,$$$	$$,$$$	$$,$$$	$$,$$$		$$,$$$	$$,$$$	$$,$$$	$$,$$$		$$$,$$$
Training/Implementation for AIX		$$,$$$					$$,$$$				$$$,$$$
SQL Enterprise Licenses	$$,$$$					$$,$$$					$$,$$$
Citrix Administrator		$$$,$$$					$$$,$$$				$$$,$$$
Citrix Technical Training	$$,$$$										$$,$$$
Network Infrastructure Upgrades	$$,$$$	$$$,$$$	$$$,$$$			$$,$$$	$$,$$$	$$$,$$$			$,$$$,$$$

(continued)

EXHIBIT 7.4

Sample Ten-Year Total Cost of Ownership for Typical EHR Software *(continued)*

Operating Based Software Fees (Maintenance and Subscription Fees)											
Volume Based PP Chunk 1 (350)		$$,$$$	$$$,$$$	$$$,$$$	$$$,$$$	$$$,$$$	$$$,$$$	$$$,$$$	$$$,$$$	$$$,$$$	$,$$$,$$$
Yearly Support - Optional			$$,$$$	$$$,$$$	$$$,$$$	$$$,$$$	$$$,$$$	$$$,$$$	$$$,$$$	$$$,$$$	$,$$$,$$$
Oncology			$$$,$$$	$$$,$$$	$$$,$$$	$$$,$$$	$$$,$$$	$$$,$$$	$$$,$$$	$$$,$$$	$,$$$,$$$
Third Party dB - Required	$,$$$	$$,$$$	$$,$$$	$$,$$$	$$,$$$	$$,$$$	$$,$$$	$$,$$$	$$,$$$	$$,$$$	$$$,$$$
Third Party dB - Optional			$$,$$$	$$,$$$	$$$,$$$	$$$,$$$	$$$,$$$	$$$,$$$	$$$,$$$	$$$,$$$	$,$$$,$$$
Third Party Maintenance Fees		$$,$$$	$$,$$$	$$,$$$	$$,$$$	$$,$$$	$$,$$$	$$,$$$	$$,$$$	$$,$$$	$$$,$$$
Vendor Consulting On Hand		$$,$$$	$$,$$$	$$$,$$$	$$$,$$$	$$$,$$$	$$$,$$$	$$$,$$$	$$$,$$$	$$$,$$$	$,$$$,$$$
Patient Portal Software		$,$$$	$$,$$$	$$,$$$	$$,$$$	$$,$$$	$$,$$$	$$,$$$	$$,$$$	$$,$$$	$$$,$$$
Interface Maintenance		$$,$$$	$$,$$$	$$,$$$	$$,$$$	$$,$$$	$$,$$$	$$,$$$	$$,$$$	$$,$$$	$$$,$$$
Subscription Applications	$0	$$,$$$	$$,$$$	$$,$$$	$$,$$$	$$,$$$	$$,$$$	$$,$$$	$$,$$$	$$,$$$	$$$,$$$
Operating Based Additional EMR Staffing											
Clinical Applications IS Team	$$$,$$$	$$$,$$$	$$$,$$$	$$$,$$$	$$$,$$$	$$$,$$$	$$$,$$$	$$$,$$$	$$$,$$$	$$$,$$$	$,$$$,$$$
Oncology Specific IS Team		$$$,$$$	$$$,$$$	$$$,$$$	$$$,$$$	$$$,$$$	$$$,$$$	$$$,$$$	$$$,$$$	$$$,$$$	$,$$$,$$$
Other IS Staff		$$$,$$$	$$$,$$$	$$$,$$$	$$$,$$$	$$$,$$$	$$$,$$$	$$$,$$$	$$$,$$$	$$$,$$$	$,$$$,$$$
Core Trainers	$$,$$$	$$$,$$$	$$$,$$$	$$$,$$$	$$$,$$$	$$$,$$$	$$$,$$$	$$$,$$$	$$$,$$$	$$$,$$$	$,$$$,$$$
End User Trainers - Initial		$$$,$$$	$$$,$$$	$$$,$$$							$$$,$$$
End User Trainers - Addtl.			$$$,$$$	$$$,$$$	$$$,$$$	$$$,$$$					$,$$$,$$$
Onsite Support Personnel - Initial		$$$,$$$	$$$,$$$	$$$,$$$	$$$,$$$	$$$,$$$	$$$,$$$	$$$,$$$	$$$,$$$	$$$,$$$	$,$$$,$$$
Onsite Support Personnel - Addtl.				$$$,$$$	$$$,$$$	$$$,$$$	$$$,$$$	$$$,$$$	$$$,$$$	$$$,$$$	$,$$$,$$$
Total Spend	**$,$$$,$$$**	**$,$$$,$$$**	**$,$$$,$$$**	**$,$$$,$$$**	**$,$$$,$$$**	**$,$$$,$$$**	**$,$$$,$$$**	**$,$$$,$$$**	**$,$$$,$$$**	**$,$$$,$$$**	**$$,$$$,$$$**
Required and Optional Split of Costs											
Total Required	$,$$$,$$$	$,$$$,$$$	$,$$$,$$$	$,$$$,$$$	$,$$$,$$$	$,$$$,$$$	$,$$$,$$$	$,$$$,$$$	$,$$$,$$$	$,$$$,$$$	$$,$$$,$$$
Total Optional	$0	$0	$$$,$$$	$,$$$,$$$	$,$$$,$$$	$$$,$$$	$$$,$$$	$$$,$$$	$$$,$$$	$$$,$$$	$,$$$,$$$
Capital and Operational Split of Costs											
Total Capital	$,$$$,$$$	$,$$$,$$$	$,$$$,$$$	$,$$$,$$$	$$$,$$$	$$$,$$$	$,$$$,$$$	$$$,$$$	$$$,$$$	$$$,$$$	$$,$$$,$$$
Total Operational	$$$,$$$	$,$$$,$$$	$,$$$,$$$	$,$$$,$$$	$,$$$,$$$	$,$$$,$$$	$,$$$,$$$	$,$$$,$$$	$,$$$,$$$	$,$$$,$$$	$$,$$$,$$$

Legend:

$,$$$	Thousands
$$,$$$	Tens of Thousands
$$$,$$$	Hundreds of Thousands
$,$$$,$$$	Millions
$$,$$$,$$$	Tens of Millions

Notes:

1. For confidentiality reasons, real dollar figures could not be used.
2. This 10-year total cost of ownership model is from a 5-hospital, 1000+ bed academic medical center with 700+ physicians.
3. The total estimated operational spend over the 10-year period is 75% of the total spend, while the capital spend is only 25% of the total spend.

Final Selection

It is helpful to return to the original selection criteria and rate each of the finalist vendors against each of these weighted criteria based on all the findings from the activities performed by the selection committee. Much of the scoring is subjective, but the selection criteria help the selection team to make decisions regarding the pros and cons of each solution and weigh those decisions in an objective way. While evaluation and selection criteria can vary across healthcare organizations, exhibit 7.5 provides a high-level sample to guide the HIT selection committee.

Once the final vendors are ranked (e.g., first preference, second preference), identify the vendor of choice (pending contract negotiations). In this way, the first-place vendor is aware that the organization has a second option, and thus the vendor may be more willing to negotiate the terms more favorably to close the deal.

Contract Negotiations

A well-conducted selection process should set the stage for a streamlined negotiation. By clearly identifying the expectations for the products being purchased or licensed and working through the pricing and implementation support elements of the RFP response, the selection team will already have laid out many of the terms that are of highest priority in the contract negotiations prior to the actual formal discussions.

As a general guideline, the most productive contract negotiations are those in which all parties are committed to developing an agreement that is fair, that clearly sets out expectations for the implementation project and subsequent support relationship, that provides legal and financial protection

EXHIBIT 7.5
HIT Evaluation Criteria and Weighting

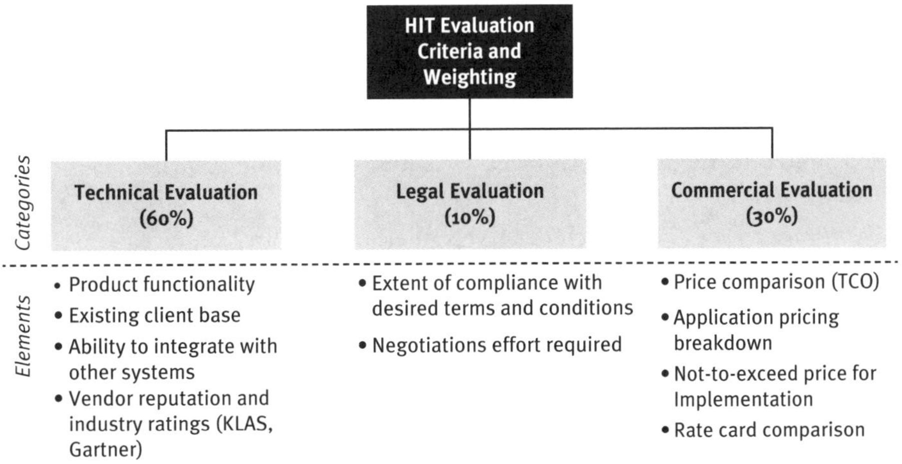

to the purchaser, and that establishes a relationship based on mutual respect and collaboration. Organizations that take a combative stance or adopt an aggressive, no-compromise attitude during the negotiations must recognize that contract negotiations are the first step in a new business relationship that may continue for many years; they may find this negative approach unproductive in the long term.

The first step in negotiations is to identify the members of the negotiations team, which include senior executives who have the authority to make financial commitments on behalf of the organization, management-level members of the selection committee who understand the product and its intended functionality, a representative from the organization's purchasing department, and the organization's legal counsel.

Contract negotiations should be treated as a project in itself, with designated negotiation committee members, documented goals and objectives, and a timeline and meeting schedule that includes internal review sessions between the negotiating meetings. In most cases it is necessary to hire legal counsel, who will take the lead in managing the legal aspects of the contract negotiation. Because legal counsel can be expensive, especially for an organization that is not large enough to have an internal legal professional, the discussion may be put on hold until all or most of the business terms have been resolved.

Before the first negotiation session with the vendor, the internal negotiating committee should meet to agree on the negotiating strategy, which includes the issues that are most important (e.g., better pricing on software licenses, additional implementation resources, better support services). Naming a primary spokesperson during the negotiating meetings as well as an individual to be responsible for handling communications between meetings creates clarity, prevents confusion about the most current status of issues, and helps prevent conflicts. Another efficient practice is to have the negotiating team prospectively vet and gain agreement on which items are of the highest priority, which items the organization will be unwilling to compromise on, and which items are open for negotiation and can therefore be used as bargaining chips. Some items that an organization should pay particular attention to when negotiating and crafting terms and conditions include but are not limited to the following (Chesney 2005; O'Connor 2005):

- *Project scope.* Scope includes levels of effort, resource requirements, timing, costs, and deliverables. Areas that vendors are keenly sensitive to include the potential for endless customizations. Recognize that vendors, like buyers, will want to minimize their risk by limiting customizations. Seek to strike a mutually agreeable balance.
- *Consequences of nonperformance.* These might include requiring the vendor to provide additional resources at no additional cost to mitigate

nonperformance, giving the organization the right to a set sum of money for liquidated damages, or giving the organization the right to withhold payments. Because much of an EHR or ERP implementation requires large-scale workflow reengineering, recognize that vendors will not want to take on the risk that the organization cannot make decisions regarding changes in the workflow.

- *Personnel commitments.* Clearly specify the personnel by name, and retain the right to be involved in personnel selection should changes be required during the project. Establish the expectations regarding on-site work versus off-site work; redesigning workflows using an automated tool typically requires vendor expertise on-site for a large portion of the effort.
- *Project management methodology.* This identifies, among other things, governance and decision rights, change processes, escalation processes for problem resolution, testing and acceptance criteria, expectations regarding standard meetings, and regular project-performance reporting expectations.
- *Payment terms.* Most vendors will want to link payment terms to measured time intervals. The healthcare organization should link payment terms to explicit deliverables that involve demonstrated, stable, functional use of the product. It should also specify limits in increases in ongoing maintenance and support costs, ensuring that those ongoing costs are indexed to the negotiated price and *not* a "book" price—list the price of the application, which averages in the range of 18–22 percent of the negotiated price.
- *Site of litigation.* This site should be the location in which the organization is located. While litigation is clearly something to be avoided, should it become necessary, specifying the site up front, when the organization's legal counsel is better positioned to address it, is ideal.
- *Vendor's accounting cycles.* Attempt to negotiate on price at the end of an accounting quarter—or, even better, an accounting year. Sometimes, particularly for publicly traded vendor organizations, substantial discounts may be offered during these windows of opportunity.

To start the process of contract negotiations, it is customary for the negotiating team to obtain a copy of the vendor's standard contract for the products and services being proposed and to identify any issues in the contract that are important to address, such as some of the items noted in the preceding list. These issues may be entered into an *issues matrix*, which may be sent to the vendor in advance of the first meeting so that the vendor is prepared to discuss alternatives at the outset. Examples of typical categories and items found in an issues matrix include the following:

- *Scope Definition*
  - Software, hardware
  - Interfaces and conversions
  - Professional services
  - Custom development items
  - Service support levels
- *Business Terms*
  - License term, renewal, termination
  - Upgrades and enhancements
  - Future products and services
  - Risk-sharing terms
  - Pricing and discounts, payment terms
  - Implementation work plan
- *Legal Terms and Conditions*
  - Acceptance terms
  - HIT performance and response times
  - Regulatory compliance
  - Governing law
  - Indemnity, warranties, and remedies
  - Assignment
  - Intellectual property and confidentiality
  - Liability

Include space to record negotiating positions, relevant dates, contract identifiers, and status. An example of a one-page negotiations issues matrix is provided in exhibit 7.6.

Using the issues matrix as the primary tool to track progress, the negotiating team can conduct several rounds of meetings to work through the issues on the list and agree on the terms. During meetings, stay focused and adopt a tone of collaborative problem solving. It is always appropriate to call a short time-out to discuss an item in private (e.g., if a new issue is raised and the team needs to agree on the organization's position). It is normal to compromise on certain items in order to "win" on priority issues; this is where the advance discussion and planning will help to keep the selection process moving forward.

In negotiating the terms of an HIT implementation, a best practice is to seek payment terms that tie payments to achievement of milestones (rather

EXHIBIT 7.6
Sample Negotiations Issues Matrix

Discussion Topic	Our Position	Vendor Response	Cross-reference to Contract Section	Date Discussed	Current Status (Open, In Process, Resolved)
License	The license to use the software should be perpetual.				
Term	Customer will consider entering into a 7–10 year term for support.				
Scope of use	The agreement would include the entire enterprise, as well as future sites. The list of sites is: • [insert list]				
Products	The following products are included in the base deal: *Clinical* • [insert product names] *Revenue cycle* • [insert product names] *Departmental* • [insert product names] The following products should be considered options to be purchased in the future: • [insert product names]				
Pricing	Provide best and final pricing by: • Application				

than regular calendar payments), as this encourages the vendor to activate the product in the desired time frame and reduces risk for the purchasing organization. Many organizations seek to establish risk-sharing arrangements, where the vendor may receive higher payments if it accomplishes certain tasks or outcomes ahead of schedule and, conversely, may be penalized financially if it falls behind schedule. Risk-sharing arrangements such as this ensure that each party has "skin in the game"; however, note that this also places a burden on the purchasing organization to hold up its end of the agreement to provide resources and make decisions as required to accomplish the desired results.

Because the contract with the vendor will include costs and services for implementation of the new HIT, it is usually best to draft a preliminary implementation plan to make sure that both parties have a shared understanding of the resources and timeline, including the achievement of major milestones. At the conclusion of contract negotiations, the team can create an internal communication document for senior leadership that summarizes the business deal, key terms and conditions, concessions received, and other risk-mitigation agreements.

Remember the importance of clearly defining the project scope up front, such as levels of effort, resource requirements, timing, costs, and deliverables. If the organization has a professional project management office, the HIT project will have built-in performance measurements and updates. However, if the organization has not yet made an investment in comprehensive project management methodologies, it should at the very least ensure that someone in the organization (not someone from the vendor's firm) is tracking progress on full-time equivalent resource consumption, project timelines and milestones, and other costs and deliverables. To gain fully the contracting benefit of having specified these items in the terms and conditions of the contract, the organization must demand regular project-performance updates with the members of the vendor team.

Benefits Realization

An often overlooked but incredibly important part of the HIT selection process is that, at some point after the new HIT goes into productive use, the organization must conduct a formal benefits realization assessment to see whether the vision behind the investment has been achieved. The best approach for accomplishing this is to collect baseline information (e.g., length of stay, readmission rates by diagnosis-related group, overtime hours by staff type) in the areas of performance the organization hoped to improve with HIT; then, about 12 months after the new HIT goes into production, the organization can measure the same performance indicators and compare the two sets of data. This is a powerful step that can provide valuable lessons and validation to the board of directors or senior leadership team—they may learn that the HIT investment made is actually reaping the benefits envisioned.

Summary

The selection of HIT by an organization, particularly those technologies that affect a large portion of operational functions, is a process that requires rigorous due diligence and systematic, participative decision-making. In this chapter, we provided a framework for conducting an HIT selection process that includes the following activities:

- Clarification of the objectives
- Formation of the HIT selection governance structure and process
- Establishment of an HIT selection plan
- Education: Understanding the marketplace
- Down selection: Narrowing the field
- Documentation of the requirements: Developing the request for proposal
- Conducting detailed product demonstrations
- Completion of other due diligence activities
- Final selection
- Contract negotiations
- Benefits realization

The key to increasing the chances of having a successful outcome to an HIT selection process is to provide sufficient resources for it, like any other formal process, and to include the key stakeholders throughout the organization. The organization must ensure that these stakeholders are active participants in both the due diligence and the decision to move forward with a vendor of choice.

Web Resources

A number of organizations (through their websites) provide more information on the topics discussed in this chapter:

- Gartner (www.gartner.com/en/products) provides subscription-based research notes on IT that covers a full spectrum—from technical to IT-based business processes.

- HIMSS Analytics (www.himssanalytics.org) provides data and analytic expertise.
- KLAS (www.klasresearch.com) provides ratings of healthcare technology that help organizations make informed decisions.
- HealthIT.gov (www.healthit.gov/resource/request-proposal-rfp-template-health-information-technology) provides RFP information, templates, and a sample.

Discussion Questions

1. What are the major activities that make up the HIT selection process?
2. What are some examples of functional work groups and the types of work that they might accomplish in support of a HIT selection project?
3. Why is it important to create an HIT selection plan at the outset of an HIT selection endeavor?
4. What is down selection, and why is it an important step in the HIT selection process?
5. What is an RFP, and what is its purpose?
6. What are some of the typical sections that make up an RFP?
7. What is a total cost of ownership, and why is it important to estimate prior to making a HIT selection?
8. What are some of the important items that an organization should consider when going into contract negotiations with a vendor?
9. What is a benefits realization assessment?

Note

Portions of this chapter have been reprinted and/or adapted from *The Executive's Guide to Electronic Health Records* by Detlev H. Smaltz and Eta Berner (Health Administration Press, 2007) and from an unpublished 2011 work by Paul Murphy, strategy advisory service leader at Encore Health Resources. Material from Paul Murphy's work—"The Vendor Selection Process" (July 2011) and "Selection Process Exhibits" (July 2011)—is used with permission of Encore Health Resources.

References

Berra, Y., and D. Kaplan. 2003. *What Time Is It? You Mean Now? Advice for Life from the Zennest Master of Them All.* New York: Simon and Schuster.

Chesney, J. 2005. "IT Contracts, Negotiation, and Outsourcing: Let's Make a Deal." Presentation at the Seminar in Healthcare Administration Executive Program, University of Alabama at Birmingham, Birmingham, AL, January 14.

mThink. 2003. "Selecting a Clinical IT Vendor." Accessed April 2, 2013. http://mthink.com/dev/mthink/content/selecting-clinical-it-vendor.

Murphy, P., 2011. "The Vendor Selection Process." Encore Health Resources working papers. Houston, TX, July 11.

National Learning Consortium. 2012. "Request for Proposal (RFP) Template for Health Information Technology." Published March 31. www.healthit.gov/sites/default/files/request-for-proposal-template-for-health-information-technology.docx.

O'Connor, K. 2005. "Minimize Large-Scale IT Project Risk Through Effective Contracting Strategies." *Journal of Healthcare Information Management* 19 (2): 16–18.

Phrase Finder. 2020. "Beware of Greeks Bearing Gifts." Accessed February 12. www.phrases.org.uk/meanings/beware-of-greeks-bearing-gifts.html.

Smaltz, D., R. Branzell, D. Hoidal, M. Murphy, S. Spooner, R. Stacey, and M. Waldrum. 2005. "The CEO–CIO Relationship: A Roundtable Discussion." In *The CEO–CIO Partnership: Harnessing the Value of Information Technology in Healthcare*, edited by D. Smaltz, J. Glaser, R. Skinner, and T. Cunningham III, 99–110. Chicago: Healthcare Information and Management Systems Society.

CHAPTER

8

APPLICATIONS: ELECTRONIC HEALTH RECORDS

Learning Objectives

1. Define the term *electronic health record* (EHR).
2. Understand the key capabilities of a robust EHR.
3. Discuss the benefits of a robust EHR.
4. Name some of the key cost categories associated with the purchase and implementation of an EHR.
5. Describe the Electronic Medical Record Adoption Model.
6. Describe some of the criteria that both individual providers and hospitals need to meet to earn incentives for meaningfully using an EHR.

Overview

There has been an evolution of the terms used to describe a digital version of a medical record. Currently, *electronic health record* (EHR) is the most commonly used term to describe "a longitudinal electronic record of patient health information generated by one or more encounters in any care delivery setting. Included in this information are patient demographics, progress notes, problems, medications, vital signs, past medical history, immunizations, laboratory data, and radiology reports and images. The EHR automates and streamlines the clinician's workflow. The EHR has the ability to generate a complete record of a clinical patient encounter, as well as supporting other care-related activities directly or indirectly via interface; including evidence-based decision support, quality management, and outcomes reporting" (Healthcare Information and Management Systems Society [HIMSS] 2019). A key component of this definition is the ability to record patient information generated in *any* care delivery setting. In other words, the EHR should provide caregivers with the ability to communicate patient information collected from across organizational boundaries. Regardless of where care was delivered, the EHR is designed to gather that information for a full, longitudinal, detailed view of a patient's medical history.

The term *electronic medical record*, or EMR, describes a single healthcare practice or health systems digital patient record. A simple way to remember the distinction between EMRs and EHRs, if you think about the term "medical" versus the term "health." An EMR is a narrower view of a patient's medical history, while an EHR is a more comprehensive report of the patient's overall health. Here are a few more ways EMRs and EHRs differ:

- An EMR is mainly used by providers for diagnosis and treatment.
- EMRs are not designed to be shared outside the individual practice [or health system].
- EHRs are designed to share a patient's information with authorized providers and staff from more than one organization.
- EHRs allow a patient's medical information to move with them to specialists, labs, imaging facilities, emergency rooms and pharmacies, as well as across state lines. (USF Health, 2020)

In the past, terms like the *computer-based patient record* (CBPR or CPR) were used and should be viewed as less robust versions of what today has evolved into the EHR.

Components of an Electronic Health Record

Dick, Steen, and Detmer (1997) published an Institute of Medicine (IOM) report titled *The Computer-Based Patient Record*, which articulated the key features of the contemporary EHR. Later, HIMSS Analytics expanded on the original key components and features of an EHR that Dick and his colleagues suggested (Garets and Davis 2006) and developed the eight-stage (0–7) EMR Adoption Model (EMRAM), depicted in its current iteration in exhibit 8.1. It originally covered features of an EMR. While the definitive distinguishing features were added to the EMRAM, HIMSS Analytics never bothered to change the service-marked (SM) name of its adoption model. So while we cover the EMRAM in detail in this chapter, the EMRAM fully describes the capabilities of a full EHR to include the ability to share patient data across organizational boundaries. In addition, in 2018, HIMSS Analytics released updated criteria that added security criteria. These eight stages not only have become the de facto international standard description of the key components of a complete EHR, but also, with the addition of the stages of adoption of these key components and features, have provided a means of tracking the degree of EHR adoption throughout the industry and around the world.

EXHIBIT 8.1
EMRAM

Stage	Cumulative Capabilities
7	Complete EMR; External HIE [health information exchange]; Data Analytics, Governance, Disaster Recovery, Privacy and Security
6	Technology-Enabled Medication, Blood Products, and Human Milk Administration; Risk Reporting; Full CDS [clinical decision support]
5	Physician documentation using structured templates; Intrusion/ Device Protection
4	CPOE with CDS, Nursing and Allied Health Documentation; Basic Business Continuity
3	Nursing and Allied Health Documentation; eMAR; Role-Based Security
2	CDR; Internal Interoperability; Basic Security
1	Ancillaries—Laboratory, Pharmacy, and Radiology/Cardiology Information Systems; PACS; Digital non-DICOM image management
0	All Three Ancillaries Not Installed

Source: HIMSS Analytics (2020). Used with permission from HIMSS Analytics.

The following sections provide a brief overview of each of the key components of a hospital-based EHR (primarily in the context of the EMRAM) and some key components of an outpatient EHR (primarily in the context of the Outpatient EMRAM). However, these key components are applicable in other healthcare delivery settings.

Ancillary Systems

The ancillary systems component of an EHR includes automated information systems to support workflow in the laboratory, medical imaging, and pharmacy departments. In the laboratory department, for instance, these automated systems capture results from various laboratory test devices and automatically pull them into an automated stand-alone laboratory information system or an EHR module that physicians and other caregivers can access to obtain their patients' test results. Similarly, in the medical imaging department, automated systems may provide results of radiologic and cardiologic exams to the physicians who ordered them. In the pharmacy department, they manage the process of dispensing and delivering drugs to patients.

Picture Archiving and Communication Systems

Picture archiving and communication systems (PACS) capture and store digital medical images, such as X-ray images, CT (computerized tomography, or "CAT") scans, MRI (magnetic resonance imaging) scans, and other medical diagnostic images. They also have the ability to allow caregivers from across the organization to access those images electronically. Contemporary EHRs provide a means to make PACS images available to caregivers outside of the imaging departments. Ideally, physicians can access actual images associated with the results they are viewing in the EHR by clicking on a context-aware link (one that sees what the physician is trying to do and brings up relevant links that can help) to the associated images. This capability improves usability of the EHR.

Document Imaging

Many healthcare providers make copies of paper records that are either generated in their own care setting or that patients bring with them from another care setting (e.g., clinic, hospital). Making these images of paper records available through the EHR is another capability that helps ensure providers have as much information available as possible as they assess and care for patients. DICOM (digital imaging and communications in medicine) is "a standard used for the electronic communication of medical images and associated information" (HIMSS 2019). Non-DICOM images are captured electronically but do not use DICOM for electronic communications. These non-DICOM images can be scanned paper documents (e.g., memos, copies of reports, photos) and other electronic files (e.g., .pdf, .jpeg, .txt). For example, many hospitals operating on an EHR are still documenting resuscitations, commonly referred to as *code blue events*, on paper. The information on this paper may be relevant to future clinical decisions and therefore should be scanned into the patient's EHR so that it is easily accessible when needed.

Clinical Data Repository and Internal Interoperability

The clinical data repository (CDR) collects data from a variety of information systems and makes the data available to physicians and other caregivers in a unified view of each of their respective patients. It is "a structured, systematically collected storehouse of patient-specific clinical data" (HIMSS 2019). While CDRs from different EHR vendors may differ slightly, they typically aggregate data from ancillary systems such as lab results, pathology reports, and medical imaging reports, as well as pharmacy data and other data relating to the patient (e.g., demographics; admission dates; transfer dates, if applicable; discharge dates; diagnosis codes). This aggregation requires internal interoperability between the various systems. Data about a patient should be securely and appropriately exchanged intra-organizationally (i.e., across all inpatient, outpatient, ancillary, and complementary care settings). This internal interoperability requires the use of a controlled medical vocabulary (CMV).

Controlled Medical Vocabulary

CMV is a capability used to standardize information for purposes of capturing, storing, exchanging, searching and analyzing data in a consistent manner. A CMV addresses the many needs and limitations of healthcare's information infrastructure; examples are as follows:

- Reducing ambiguity that is inherent in normal human languages (e.g., "heart attack," "myocardial infarction," and "MI" may mean the same thing when describing a patient condition but represent different conditions to a computer coding that information)
- Making the exchange of information consistent between different providers, care settings, researchers, and others, even at different points in time
- Overcoming differences in medical information recording from one place to another
- Summarizing medical information (in a consistent manner)
- Allowing symbolic manipulation of data (searches for specific analyses)
- Providing automated reasoning (clinical decision support)

Some common CMVs include the following:

- *Systematized Nomenclature of Medicine-Clinical Terms (SNOMED-CT).* "SNOMED CT provides the core general terminology for the electronic health record and as of 2019 contains more than 349,000 active concepts with unique meanings and formal logic-based definitions organized into hierarchies. When implemented in software applications, SNOMED CT can be used to represent clinically relevant information consistently, reliably and comprehensively as an integral part of producing electronic health records" (SNOMED International 2020).
- *Logical Observation Identifiers Names and Codes (LOINC).* LOINC is a universal code system for identifying laboratory and clinical observations (Regenstrief Institute 2020).
- *Unified Medical Language System (UMLS).* "The UMLS integrates and distributes key terminology, classification and coding standards, and associated resources to promote creation of more effective and interoperable biomedical information systems and services, including electronic health records" (National Library of Medicine 2019).
- *Current Procedural Terminology (CPT).* CPT offer doctors and healthcare professionals a uniform language for coding medical services and procedures to streamline reporting and increase accuracy

and efficiency. It is also used to report medical, surgical, radiology, laboratory, anesthesiology, genomic sequencing, and evaluation and management services under public and private health insurance programs (Connelly 2020).

- *International Classification of Diseases (ICD).* The ICD was begun in 1893 by the International Statistical Institute and was entrusted to the World Health Organization (WHO) when it was established in 1948. ICD is the diagnostic classification standard that enables the identification of health trends and statistics globally and supports clinical and research purposes. It defines the universe of diseases, disorders, injuries, and other related health conditions in a comprehensive, hierarchical fashion. The system makes it easier to monitor the incidence and prevalence of diseases, observe reimbursements and resource allocation trends, and keep track of safety and quality guidelines. The ICD also enumerates deaths, symptoms, reasons for an encounter, factors that influence health status, and external causes of disease. The most common version in use today is ICD-10; ICD-11 was released in June 2018 to allow countries around the world to begin implementation preparation activities, but it will not be required for official data reporting purposes until 2022 (WHO 2018).

In short, the main value of a CMV is in providing a means for health-related information systems—particularly, EHRs and EHR component modules—to become semantically interoperable.

Nursing and Allied Health Professional Documentation

Contemporary EHRs have the ability to document vital signs, flow sheets (particularly relevant clinical data recorded over time to assess a patient's condition), nursing assessments, nursing notes, and care plans. They also can keep a comprehensive record of all medications that have been administered to the patient. Physicians and nurses are not the only clinical disciplines to care for and document patient information. Documentation from allied health professionals is often considered part of the legal medical record. These professionals include respiratory therapists, occupational therapists, physical therapists, dieticians, and, in some organizations, clergy, along with others who contribute to the collection of a patient's documented health status; they all need a means to add to the EHR.

Electronic Medication Administration Record

HIMSS (2019) defines the *electronic medication administration record* (eMAR) as an electronic record-keeping system that documents when medications are given to a patient during a hospital stay. Used in conjunction with technologies such as bar codes, quick response (QR) codes, radio frequency identification (RFID) tags, or other near field communication (NFC) technologies, eMAR helps to promote a safer medication administration process by automating "five rights" checks (i.e., right patient, right medication, right dose, right route, right time). This EHR module is intended to generate an alert when any of these five rights are violated.

Computerized Practitioner Order Entry

Computerized practitioner order entry (CPOE) is also referred to as *computerized provider order entry*, *computerized physician order entry*, and *computerized patient order entry*. HIMSS (2019) defines CPOE as "an order entry application specifically designed to assist practitioners in creating and managing medical orders for patient services and medications. This application has special electronic signature, workflow, and rules engine functions that reduce or eliminate medical errors associated with practitioner ordering processes." An earlier definition (HIMSS 2020) further described the CPOE application, indicating, "The system then transmits the order to the appropriate department, or individuals, so it can be carried out. The most advanced implementations of such systems also provide real-time clinical decision support such as dosage and alternative medication suggestions, duplicate therapy warnings, and drug-drug and drug-allergy interaction checking."

Both the Health Information Technology for Economic and Clinical Health (HITECH) Act of 2009 and employer advocacy groups share the goals of improving quality of care and reducing the cost of care via incentives to healthcare practitioners who adopt CPOE. The Leapfrog Group, for example, is a continually growing coalition of *Fortune* 500 companies that promotes CPOE, which research data have shown to reduce the possibility of adverse drug events (Reckmann et al. 2009). Hospitals that have CPOE are promoted to the employees of Leapfrog Group companies as safer hospitals with fewer medical errors that come with having a CPOE capability. This push from Leapfrog, and federal legislation mandating increased patient safety (e.g., the HITECH Act), has prompted growing interest in CPOE adoption. Remember, however, that CPOE alone is unlikely to realize the proposed benefits—unless the technology is coupled with an EHR with the foundational features discussed in this chapter. CPOE must also be linked to at least basic clinical decision support (CDS) that provides advice on appropriate drug ordering, such as alerts for drug–drug interactions, drug–allergy interactions, dose range checks, cumulative dosing checks, drug–lab interactions, drug–food interactions, duplicate orders, and drug–disease interactions.

Physician Documentation

Physician documentation that was produced and managed as a paper record—such as progress notes, consult notes, discharge summaries, problem lists, and diagnosis list maintenance—can now be entered and maintained electronically in the EHR. Not only should the EHR support direct entry of data by physicians, but it also should support structured data entry, which necessitates a defined vocabulary (as noted previously). This requirement does not mean that physicians need to be taught a new language to use the system—rather, the database that underlies the record should be structured. There have been some attempts to use mechanisms to process actual spoken or written natural language, but these have not been as successful in gaining full EHR benefits in the way that structured data have. What is needed, if unstructured input is going to be allowed, is a mechanism to link from the dictated language to the structured language—that is, *natural language processing* (NLP), which continues to make progress as a technology. HIMSS (2019) defines NLP as "a subfield of artificial intelligence that helps computers understand, interpret and manipulate human language. NLP draws from many disciplines, including computer science and computational linguistics, in its pursuit to fill the gap between human communication and computer understanding."

At this writing, NLP is not yet a fail-safe means of leveraging practitioner input for direct patient care decisions, although it is an excellent means of conducting medical research, such as the ability to identify, extract, and categorize information found in clinical narrative text (Al-Haddad et al. 2010; Terry 2012). However, templates for recording patient information have been used with some success. Indeed, using structured templates for routine types of care (e.g., a template for adult-acquired pneumonia) provides the added benefit of enabling real-time evaluation and management coding, which can have a huge impact on expediting billing and consequently reducing accounts receivable days. Structured documentation allows the EHR to leverage CDS systems (CDSSs) by triggering the appropriate recommendations or advice alerts for treating the patient.

Clinical Decision Support and Clinical Decision Support Systems

CDS has been defined in a variety of ways. Garg and colleagues (2005, 1,223), in a review of CDSSs and their effects on practitioner performance and patient outcomes, say, "CDSSs are information systems designed to improve clinician decision making. Characteristics of individual patients are matched to a computerized knowledge base, and software algorithms generate patient-specific recommendations." HIMSS (2019) defines CDS as "the use of automated rules based on clinical evidence to provide alerts, reminders, clinical guidelines, and other knowledge to assist users in healthcare delivery." Furthermore, HIMSS (2019) defines CDSS as the application that uses these preestablished rules and guidelines to trigger alerts and treatment suggestions.

Most major EHR system vendors have CDSS capabilities; that is, they can generate a variety of alerts and reminders, such as drug–drug and drug–food adverse effects, as well as checking for conflicts in drug–lab orders. A more advanced CDSS also has the ability to supply evidence-based medicine protocols (e.g., order sets that have been shown in the medical body of literature to have the best statistical outcomes for patients with specific diagnoses or conditions). These advanced CDS capabilities provide easy access to any local or remote subscription-based knowledge sources, such as Ovid, the Medline medical literature database, and national or local clinical guidelines. The most advanced CDSS also can provide guidance—in the form of variance and compliance alerts— for all clinical activities related to clinical protocols and outcomes (HIMSS Analytics 2020; Middleton et al. 2004).

Key CDSS implementation considerations that in the past were determined locally with input from the clinical staff include

- the choice of which alerts and reminders to include,
- the manner in which alerts and reminders are delivered to the clinician, and
- the circumstances under which clinicians are allowed to override the alerts and reminders.

Too-frequent alerts with only minimal justification result in what has been termed *alert fatigue*, which not only generates complaints from clinicians but also results in frequent overrides and ignoring of even the most important alerts. For instance, many medication knowledge bases that can be purchased to be integrated with the EHR to provide alerts for drug–allergy interactions produce an alert for the specific drug as well as for any drugs in that class—even if patients have already taken the related drugs with no ill effects. Furthermore, alerts are triggered by elements in the EHR; that is, if the clinician had originally included, for instance, an allergy to aspirin when the patient said aspirin upset her stomach, but the clinician never changed the entry when he realized this was not a "real" allergy, then the alert will be triggered anyway. Conversely, if the system is set up so that a blank allergy field suggests that the patient is *not* allergic to anything, when in fact the empty field only means that allergies have not yet been assessed or the documentation is incomplete, unsafe medication orders may not generate an alert. For these reasons, determination of how to implement the CDSS functions of the EHR is definitely too important to leave to the HIT staff. There should be significant involvement by providers during the design phase of the CDSS implementation.

Managing the effectiveness of a CDSS requires deliberately approaching it from a governance perspective. A common success characteristic among organizations that have successfully achieved stage 7 of the EMRAM is the establishment of a governance committee whose purpose is to oversee thoughtfully and guide the CDSS and the alerts and reminders it generates. This multidisciplinary committee (e.g., physicians, nurses, pharmacists) works together to establish the CDSS guiding principles most appropriate to its organization, then works together to implement those principles according to the *rules engine*, the "if–then" directions used by the CDSS. The committee works together to review every alert built into the system with the goal of preventing alert fatigue (e.g., determining when an alert should trigger and for whom, determining override rules and procedures) and monitoring each alert's effectiveness through an appropriate alert override management program. This focused, governance-based approach helps organizations optimize the CDSS.

The US Department of Health & Human Services' Office of the National Coordinator for Health Information Technology (ONCHIT) has emphasized CDS, especially in regard to *e-prescribing*—the transmission of prescriptions electronically from clinician to pharmacy. As part of the national effort, the American Medical Informatics Association (AMIA) developed what has been called a road map for CDS. This road map suggests that while CDS tools are promising, much has yet to be done to realize their full potential—particularly in the following three areas (Ford, Menachemi, and Phillips 2006):

1. Applying the best clinical knowledge, available when needed
2. Achieving high adoption of CDS and effective use
3. Continuous improvement of clinical knowledge and CDS methods

Since the AMIA call to action, CDS adoption was reported at nearly 73 percent, yet Wright and colleagues (2016) found that 93 percent of chief medical information officers had experienced CDS malfunctions; the study concludes that CDSS malfunctions occur commonly and often go undetected. While Osheroff and colleagues (2005) suggest a phased implementation of CDS accompanied by input from physicians, as well as a responsive feedback-and-modification process as the CDS capabilities of the EHR are implemented, it is clear from Wright and colleagues' findings that better methods are needed to detect and prevent these malfunctions. Training and ongoing support for physicians on what the alerts mean and how to respond to them are considered essential.

Technology-Enabled Medication, Blood Product, and Human Milk Administration

Technology-enabled identification of patients and products administered to patients at the bedside is often referred to as "bar code scanning" because bar codes are the dominant technology used; however, it may also include a number of other technologies, such as QR codes, RFID, or other NFC tools.

A best practice medication administration process is typically called *closed-loop medication administration* or *end-to-end medication administration*. The closed-loop, technology-enabled bedside identification may be used for medication and blood product administration, and it may also be used for human milk (mother's expressed breast milk) feeding, especially if the milk is kept in communal storage.

By scanning the patient and the product (medication, blood, milk), the system is able to positively identify both, enabling it to perform the necessary matches between the product and the patient. In the case of medications, the system should be able to verify the five rights. The closed loop also includes CPOE with CDS for error checks. Medication administration is documented and tracked using the eMAR, which is linked to the pharmacy and CPOE applications. For blood product administration documentation and tracking, the blood bank system is also linked to the EHR; for breast milk distribution, an administration documentation module or application is linked to the CPOE application. The closed-loop process obviously requires that the component parts (CPOE, CDSS, eMAR, blood transfusion system, human milk administration system) be in place and integrated with the EHR and is vital for achieving higher levels of patient safety (Smaltz and Berner 2007).

Technology-Enabled Blood Specimen Collection

In addition to using NFC technologies to enable the end-to-end medication administration process, NFC could also be used to create a closed-loop process for blood specimen collection. At the bedside, hospitals are able to positively identify the patient and the technology-enabled (i.e., bar code, QR code, RFID tag) test tube before collecting blood from the patient. This precaution helps to ensure a positive match between the patient and the blood specimen before the specimen is collected and leaves the patient's bedside. It also enables the laboratory to scan the specimen on delivery to automate the receiving process before performing the ordered tests, and it helps ensure accurate matching of the sample to the patient throughout the sample testing and reporting process.

Medical Device Integration with the Electronic Health Record

The healthcare field increasingly demands integration of data from medical devices directly into the EHR without manual intervention. Some of the demand can be attributed to recent government regulations and financial pressures. It is becoming easier to integrate or interface medical devices with EHRs thanks to improvements in standards being pushed by organizations such as Integrating the Healthcare Enterprise (IHE) (www.ihe.net) that are working to improve "interoperability between different healthcare IT devices and systems through the coordination of established standards. . . . New monitors and ventilators are LAN aware (wired, wireless, or both), and manufacturers are engineering standards-based communication capabilities directly into firmware. Because the output of these devices is highly sought-after data, these device types were the first to have this built-in functionality. Manufacturers are now expanding this communication capability to other devices, such as smart pumps and smart beds" (McGeath 2014). Just as with other newly introduced technologies, security becomes more challenging as more and more devices are connected to a hospital's network. McGeath states, "With the added exposure of built-in communications, manufacturers must now think through the security and how to ensure against the threat of hackers."

A key EHR standard included in the HIMSS Analytics EMRAM criteria for achieving stage 7 is that all hospital intensive care units are supported by a direct interface between bedside vital signs monitors and the EHR. Hospitals must clearly understand the role of nursing in verifying data received from these vital signs monitors before they are permanently recorded in the patient's EHR.

Data Analytics

This title has many synonyms: enterprise data warehousing, clinical analytics, business analytics, clinical informatics, quality and efficiency analysis, analyt ics, and so on. EHRs should have the ability to provide advanced reporting to analyze patterns of clinical data to improve quality of care and patient safety, as well as care efficiencies. As the amount of data and information grows with the use of an EHR, it becomes more critical for a hospital to have an effective analytics program that covers the enterprise wherever analyses may occur, including, but not limited to, clinical, financial, and operational analytics activities. An analytics program requires supporting technology and infrastructure with analytics tools to convert information into knowledge and wisdom. Sources of the data may include the primary clinical system, ancillary systems other than the primary clinical system, and other nonclinical systems such as revenue cycle, supply chain, and so on.

The saying "garbage in, garbage out" still holds true. A data quality assurance process is a must-have to ensure data are properly cleaned and ready before they are released for analysis. This may require the use of several applications and platforms from multiple vendors involved in sourcing clinical, financial, and other data that require an extract, transform, and load (ETL) process. An organization should be able to identify easily all of its sources of data and how to apply the ETL process to activate or transform and standardize these data. This need for standardization is where a CMV comes in handy in terms of applying the methodologies needed to achieve common nomenclature and data standards.

Data governance is an important aspect of data analytics. A clearly defined data governance strategy includes the identification of dataset owners or custodians responsible for establishing the data definitions needed to help ensure data accuracy and completeness.

To be successful at analytics, the organization should have a data-driven culture—meaning that its data and analysis tools are available to operational, clinical, and business area analysts and leadership at all levels to enable data-driven decision-making on a regular basis. Hospitals must use analytics to find opportunities for improvement and drive insights supporting those improvements. The key point is that analytics is used to identify a problem to be resolved and is used to direct decision-making toward resolution and improvement. The organization needs to do more than just monitor a set of key performance measures and indicators; it must use analytics to gain insights and improve ongoing clinical, business, and operational activities. While clearly an important element of the EMRAM, the brief overview on analytics provided in this chapter will be further expanded in chapter 11.

Health Information Exchange

ONCHIT believes that health information exchange (HIE) capability is essential to both providing the best possible care for patients and driving down the overall cost of high-quality care at a national level (Williams et al. 2012). Contemporary EHRs should have the basic ability to send and receive data about relevant patients electronically and securely. ONCHIT is working to establish standards for accomplishing this in a more unified, consistent manner. Note that data about a patient should be able to be securely and appropriately exchanged not only intraorganizationally but also interorganizationally (i.e., across distinct, legal, organizational boundaries).

Interorganizational exchange can be enabled through the use of a continuity of care record (CCR) or through consolidated clinical document architecture (C-CDA) documents, which are standards for creating and transmitting structured summary data among providers and between providers and patients. Information exchange is often accomplished through engagement with private and public HIE entities. The receipt of patient information through a bidirectional information exchange may be incorporated into the hospital's EHR and incorporated into the EHR's CDS engine.

Information Technology Governance

EHR governance addresses the process of assessing, prioritizing, and implementing suggested system enhancements. Gartner defines *IT governance* as the processes that ensure the effective and efficient use of IT in enabling an organization's goals and objectives, including processes by which organizations ensure the effective evaluation, selection, prioritization, and funding of competing IT investments; oversee their implementation; and extract (measurable) business benefits. *IT demand governance* is a business investment decision-making and oversight process and is a business management responsibility. IT supply-side governance (how IT should do what it does) is concerned with ensuring that the IT organization operates in an effective, efficient, and compliant fashion, and it is primarily a chief information officer (CIO) responsibility (Gartner 2012). Generally for healthcare organizations, IT governance also includes a predictable, identifiable method by which the voices of the clinicians are heard. Designing the right governance structure involves clearly defining each committee, the reporting relationship, mission statements of the committees, the qualifications of the committee chairs (title and discipline), and the ways in which the board can connect with the patient care activities.

Disaster Recovery and Business Continuity

Accompanying the healthcare field's dependence on IT is a rise in its emphasis on disaster recovery and business continuity strategy. A paperless EHR environment presents an enormous risk to the healthcare organization from prolonged downtime; therefore, there must be a redundancy plan that addresses data and their supporting hardware and networks.

However, a plan is only as good as the paper it is written on, so organizations must periodically test these redundancies to ensure they work when needed. Downtime processes must be clearly defined for both planned and unplanned pauses, and they must include the communication process (e.g., how caregivers receive updates and instructions related to downtime procedures and status updates). Staff taking care of patients in the nursing units, or in ancillary departments, must understand and periodically practice these procedures to ensure proficiency and minimize chaos during a break in service. Hospitals should use tools that enable a local computer or protected workstation to provide access to patient summary reports that include at least patient allergies, medications, a list of problems and diagnoses, and most recent lab results, so they can continue providing safe care to the patients. Over a prolonged power outage, the designated downtime computer should connect directly to a printer supported by an uninterruptable power source (battery backup) or plugged into an emergency circuit. Updating these clinical summaries frequently helps to ensure that clinicians have easy, quick access to the most recent, relevant information needed to support clinical decision-making.

Security and Access

Health organizations must protect the confidentiality and integrity of the patient information collected, processed, and stored in a healthcare organization's information system. The system must be able to track, in a rigorous way, who all have accessed the record. This essential function aligns the evolution of the EHR with the original Health Insurance Portability and Accountability Act (HIPAA) legislation and the HITECH Act extensions to HIPAA (i.e., more rigorous requirements related to protecting personally identifiable patient information). While timely access, both on-site and remote, by a wide range of providers needs to be unequivocally guaranteed, unauthorized access must be prevented. Healthcare organizations must find the right balance between access and security.

HIMSS (2019) defines information security as "a set of strategies for managing the processes, tools, and policies necessary to prevent, detect, document, and counter threats to digital and non-digital information. Information security responsibilities include establishing a set of business processes that will protect information assets regardless of how the information is formatted or whether it is in transit, is being processed, or is at rest in storage." It also deals with the protection and maintenance of data confidentiality, integrity, availability, and accountability. The tools used to enable information security capabilities may include encryption, firewalls, single sign-on, spam and spyware filters, antivirus and antimalware applications, intrusion detection and prevention systems, mobile device management, and so on.

The need for information security increases as an organization moves toward a paperless medical record infrastructure to protect patient information and the information assets of the organization. Creating the right overall approach to privacy and security across the network infrastructure to the point of care becomes increasingly sophisticated in an IT-dependent healthcare organization.

Basic Security

Basic considerations for a sound security strategy start with establishing certain policies that address security and privacy requirements. These policies should not be written and then forgotten; they should be reviewed and updated on a regular basis. In addition, a training program to include annual refresher training must be established to ensure employees know about current threats and understand their expected behavior while using the organization's information assets. Such rules might include a physical access policy that describes the requirements for securing the locations of the organization's physical data assets (e.g., computer and server are located in the primary and backup data centers, mobile computing devices in the various patient care areas are secured).

Another important policy to establish is an acceptable use policy. This policy describes what is and is not considered acceptable use of an organization's computer network, including how one might use the internet, email, or mobile devices issued to an employee. HIMSS (2019) defines an acceptable use policy as "guidance to employees and other workforce members regarding the appropriate use of a healthcare organization's information technology resources and data." An acceptable use policy may stipulate constraints and practices with which a user must agree before being granted access to a corporate network or the internet. Many businesses and educational facilities require that employees signify their agreement by signing an acceptable use policy form before being granted a username.

The most common and widely used information protection technologies are antivirus and antimalware software. Antivirus software is "a program specifically designed to detect many forms of malware and prevent them from infecting computers, as well as cleaning computers that have already been infected" (HIMSS 2019).

All computer hardware will eventually fail and need to be replaced. If patient information or other confidential information assets were stored or processed on a failed device, the organization must establish an appropriate policy that describes the requirements and process for destroying the data on those devices, making it impossible for anyone who may take possession of the devices later to recover the information. According to the International Data Sanitization Consortium (2020), *data destruction* means obliterating information housed in digital storage media so that it is completely unreadable and cannot be accessed or used for unauthorized purposes.

One of the best methods for controlling information is to prevent it from being stored on devices apart from the main storage location (i.e., the CDR). For example, many organizations employ technologies that prevent data from being stored on local devices (e.g., laptops; desktop computers; other mobile devices such as smartphones, USB sticks, and CD/DVDs). One can view the information, but the information is prevented from remaining on the local device. However, if an organization needs to store information on a local device, encryption technologies are implemented to render the data on the device unreadable should the device be lost or stolen. For example, the patient summary reports stored on computers used for backup in emergencies should be encrypted and password protected.

Role-Based Access Control

A very common and essential method used by EHRs to implement certain protections and credentialing policies is the use of role-based access control (RBAC). HIMSS (2019) defines RBAC as "a method of regulating access to computer or network resources based on the roles of individual users within an enterprise. Roles are defined according to job competency, authority, and responsibility within the enterprise." For example, the functions of a nurse role in a system will differ from the functions of a physician role (e.g., narcotic medication orders), and RBAC will help ensure each individual role can only perform those functions it is allowed to perform.

Intrusion Detection and Prevention

The theft of electronic medical records is a highly profitable business in the underworld. The value of electronic medical records greatly exceeded that of credit cards and other personal information until around 2016. However, as a result of the number of EHR megabreeches, the black market is saturated with stolen information. Therefore, hackers have resorted to ransomware to increase their profits (Korolov 2016). Ransomware holds its victims hostage by blocking access to computer systems, and the information contained within, until the victim pays a considerable sum. Healthcare organizations' information systems and networks must be protected from these malicious attacks.

One form of protection is an intrusion detection and prevention system (IDPS). According to an article published by the National Institute of Standards and Technology (NIST) (Scarfone and Mell 2007), intrusion detection is defined as the process of monitoring the events occurring in a computer system or network and analyzing them for signs of possible incidents, which are violations or imminent threats of violation of computer security policies, acceptable use policies, or standard security practices. Scarfone and Mell explain the difference between an intrusion detection system (IDS) and an intrusion prevention system (IPS), indicating that an IDS is software that automates the intrusion detection process, and an IPS is software that has all the capabilities of an IDS and can also attempt to stop possible incidents. HIMSS (2019) defines intrusion detection as "detecting actions that attempt to compromise the confidentiality, integrity, or availability of a resource." An IDPS combines the capabilities of both systems into a single solution. But according to another NIST study, a network IDPS is less effective on mobile devices because mobile devices are only sometimes connected to the enterprise network, while at other times they are connected to cellular networks or public wireless networks that are not monitored by the enterprise (US Department of Homeland Security [DHS] 2017).

Mobile Device Security

Healthcare organizations are more frequently incorporating mobile devices into their EHR infrastructure because such tools are small, portable, and always on, allowing instant access to mobile applications displaying patient and other healthcare information. The US Department of Homeland Security published a study in 2017 on mobile device security that defined mobile devices as smartphones and tablets running mobile operating systems. The study (DHS 2017) explained how mobile devices enable anywhere, anytime access to information and services, both for personal use and for business.

However, their small size, powerful computing capabilities, and the increasing amount of personal and business data accessed by and stored on these devices makes them susceptible to loss or theft—and therefore an attractive target for attackers. Therefore, organizations should consider carefully how to protect these devices from would-be attackers. One way to protect the information is to wipe, or erase, a mobile device remotely, should it be lost or stolen. Remote locking is an alternative to remote wiping and is used when the organization does not want to lose the data.

Risk Management and Risk Assessment

Organizational risk management is a critical function of any organization that wants to protect its information assets (i.e., information technology and information systems, including office networks or finance, personnel, or EHR systems). Appropriately managing risk allows the organization to carry out their mission and business functions successfully. Once an organization establishes and implements the security controls it deems necessary to protect its assets adequately, the best way to determine the effectiveness of these controls is to conduct periodic risk assessments. Risk assessment is one of the fundamental components of an organizational risk management program (Joint Task Force Transformation Initiative 2012). According to NIST, "The purpose of risk assessments is to inform decision makers and support risk responses by identifying: (i) relevant threats to organizations or threats directed through organizations against other organizations; (ii) vulnerabilities both internal and external to organizations; (iii) impact (i.e., harm) to organizations that may occur given the potential for threats exploiting vulnerabilities; and (iv) likelihood that harm will occur. The end result is a determination of risk (i.e., typically a function of the degree of harm and likelihood of harm occurring)." Organizational leadership should consider the level of risk it is willing to accept while remembering that a risk accepted by one is a risk shared by many. Knowing the organization's acceptable risk level will help to determine what actions are needed to mitigate the threats and vulnerabilities revealed in risk assessment results that led to exceeding the organization's acceptable risk level.

One note of caution: when discussing information protection in a healthcare organization, it is easy to focus only on protecting patient information. However, healthcare organizations collect, process, and store much more than just patient information (e.g., payroll information, human resources information, proprietary information). Therefore, when conducting risk assessments and working to implement the needed security controls, it is crucial that all of an organization's information assets are considered in the risk management process.

Future Electronic Health Record Components

While not yet included in the EMRAM criteria, HIMSS is already monitoring the pervasiveness of other EHR components. These include anesthesia information systems (AIS), also known as an anesthesia information management systems (AIMS); CPOE-enabled smart infusion pumps; and other biomedical devices.

Anesthesia Information Systems

Fornell (2008) reports that AIMS have become a popular EHR component because "anesthesiologists are the only doctors who diagnose, prescribe, fill the prescription and administer drugs with no checks or balances to prevent mistakes." Just as the technology-enabled closed-loop medication administration process described earlier has been proven to reduce medication errors, AIMS have also been proven to enhance patient safety documentation, as reported by the International Anesthesia Research Society (O'Reilly et al. 2006).

An AIS is defined as "an information system that allows integrated communication with other hospital and provider systems throughout the perioperative period (such as clinical information systems used by nurses, clinical data repositories used by hospitals, and professional billing systems" (HIMSS 2019). HIMSS further describes an AIMS as a specialized EHR that consists of the hardware and software needed to interface with intraoperative monitors and other components of the hospital's main EHR system to capture data throughout the perioperative process. The key benefits of using an AIS include improvements in interoperative workflow, improved compliance and billing support, and improved transitions of care support (Cordtz 2018).

Computerized Physician Order Entry–Enabled Smart Infusion Pumps

Another emerging EHR capability is the CPOE-enabled infusion pump using smart infusion pumps or IV smart pumps that are interfaced directly with the EHR to help reduce medication errors. This particular capability represents the first EHR system component involving a bidirectional information exchange between an EHR and a medical device. For example, a physician enters an IV infusion order into the CPOE component of the EHR. After the order is approved and processed by the pharmacy, the administration details are automatically transmitted to the smart infusion pump when the nurse scans the barcode on the IV bag at the patient's bedside to administer the medication. The pump then sends infusion data back to the patient's EHR, eliminating the need for manual documentation.

While this two-way communication is complex, the effort to achieve this capability has already proven to reduce medication errors associated with

IV infusions. Pettus and Vanderveen (2013) share several real-world examples of patient safety improvements that resulted in a decrease of severe harm. In addition, Russell and colleagues (2015) report reductions in discrepancies between intravenous fluid orders and infusion pump settings. Finally, Miliard (2017) found that a small community hospital not only saved money but also streamlined nursing workflow and improved billing accuracy after implementing this capability.

Unique Components of an Outpatient Electronic Health Record

In addition to most of the EHR components previously described, there are certain components that are well suited for outpatient environments that focus on improving patient engagement. To provide a road map for outpatient EHR adoption, HIMSS Analytics developed another eight-stage (0–7) EMR adoption model in 2012. This model focused on outpatient care settings in which there is an encounter between a caregiver and a patient, and the caregiver is licensed to assess, diagnose, treat, prescribe, and generate orders and documentation. The Outpatient EMR Adoption Model (O-EMRAM) is depicted in its current iteration in exhibit 8.2. Like the hospital EMRAM, O-EMRAM has become the de facto international standard description of the key components of a complete outpatient EHR. Two of the most impactful outpatient EHR capabilities are patient portals, which

EXHIBIT 8.2
Outpatient EMR Adoption Model

Stage	Cumulative Capabilities
7	Complete EMR: External HIE, Data Analytics, Governance, Disaster Recovery
6	Advanced Clinical Decision Support; Proactive Care Management, Structured Messaging
5	Personal Health Record, Online Tethered Patient Portal
4	CPOE, Use Of Structured Data For Accessibility In EMR And Internal And External Sharing Of Data
3	Electronic Messaging, Computers Have Replaced Paper Chart, Clinical Documentation And Clinical Decision Support
2	Beginning Of A CDR With Orders And Results, Computers May Be At Point-Of-Care, Access To Results From Outside Facilities
1	Desktop Access To Clinical Information, Unstructured Data, Multiple Data Sources, Intra-Office/Informal Messaging
0	Paper Chart Based

Source: HIMSS (2020). Used with permission from HIMSS Analytics.

enable greater engagement with the patient, and population health capabilities (e.g., disease registries).

Patient Engagement: Patient Portal

Kish (2012) writes that an engaged patient is the "blockbuster drug" of the century. Patient engagement has increasingly become a universally recognized aspect of solving many of the challenges in healthcare in terms of cost and perceived quality of services received. The major challenge, however, is encouraging patients and providers alike to embrace engagement and achieve its full potential to improve health and care (Dentzer 2013). The Agency for Healthcare Research and Quality (AHRQ) defines *patient engagement* as a "set of behaviors by patients, family members, and health professionals and a set of organizational policies and procedures that foster both the inclusion of patients and family members as active members of the health care team and collaborative partnerships with providers and provider organizations" (Maurer et al. 2012). One of the information technology tools shown to be effective at increasing patient engagement is the patient portal, also referred to as an *electronic personal health record* (ePHR).

Demonstrating patient portal capability is one of the criteria prescribed in the O-EMRAM; in this case, a *patient portal* is defined as "a secure online website that gives patients convenient, 24-hour access to personal health information from anywhere with an Internet connection. Using a secure username and password, patients can view health information such as: recent doctor visits, discharge summaries, medications, immunizations, allergies and lab results. Some patient portals also allow you to securely message your doctor, request prescription refills, schedule non-urgent appointments, check benefits and coverage, update contact information, make payments, download and complete forms, and view educational materials" (HIMSS 2019). In order for ePHRs to be most effective, they should be tethered to a healthcare organization's EHR so that patient information from the EHR such as the problem list, allergies, and lab tests appear in the patient portal for consumption by the patient (Irizarry, Dabbs, and Curran 2015). When an ePHR is tethered to an EHR, it is considered a patient portal. An ePHR that is not tethered to an EHR limits its patient engagement effectiveness because the healthcare organization is not able to initiate patients' involvement in their own healthcare.

Some of the functions provided through an EHR-tethered patient portal may include preregistration or prescheduling of procedures for hospital admissions or outpatient services. Patients could complete the necessary "paperwork" electronically from the comfort of their own homes. The portal may also allow the patient to request an appointment or, in some instances, directly book an appointment on the provider's schedule.

Portals commonly provide easy access for patients or their proxies (e.g., family members, caregivers) to review diagnostic results (e.g., lab results, imaging reports), clinical summaries (i.e., after-visit summaries), medication lists, immunizations, future appointments, and so on. Bill payment services allowing patients to view and pay their bills through the patient portal are another convenient feature. Secure, two-way communications allow patients or their proxies to follow up with their care team as needed. This particular feature has proven helpful for patients, as it may eliminate the need for the patient to make an appointment and show up in person for issues that could be resolved through a simple electronic communication (e.g., request a medication refill, request clarification after a prior visit). It is also helpful to the providers, as it may free up appointment slots for new patients or patients that truly need a face-to-face encounter.

The portal could also provide patients access to education and information resources by including an internet search function or links to web resources that were vetted and approved by the organization as trusted sources of medical information. One advanced feature of some patient portals is an automated reference to education resources based on a new diagnosis or problem. For example, a physician may add a new diagnosis of diabetes to a patient's EHR that triggers the display of a diabetes-related document or a link to a website with information on managing the condition. Some portals also provide automated health maintenance reminders (e.g., immunizations, follow-up exams, blood sugar checks, blood pressure checks).

Population Health Management

EHRs can be useful in helping an organization identify and manage chronic diseases at both the patient and population levels. While a standardized definition for population health management has not yet emerged (Swarthout and Bishop 2017), information systems have the ability to enable various population health management activities. Healthcare organizations can leverage the EHR and other healthcare analytics tools to identify specific disease types that display the highest incidence rates. Many healthcare organizations use their EHR software to implement a bidirectional exchange with external disease registries (e.g., public health communicable disease databases, tumor registries, immunization databases) to assist government authorities in their disease surveillance activities. Information received through a bidirectional patient information exchange can be added to the EHR and, once verified, can trigger the appropriate CDS alerts to providers. For example, notification from an external disease registry of a particular patient's allergy could trigger a drug allergy interaction alert when the physician attempts to order medication.

Healthcare organizations can also establish internal disease registries to drive their own population health improvement activities for subsets of patients diagnosed with chronic diseases (i.e., obesity, congestive heart failure, high cholesterol, hypertension, diabetes, chronic obstructive pulmonary disease). According to the HIMSS O-EMRAM criteria, outpatient clinics must demonstrate how they use their EHR software to target specific disease types and show improvements. Appropriate uses could include leveraging the patient portal to facilitate ongoing communication, education, follow-up, and patient-supplied information (e.g., automated transmission of data from real-time health-monitoring devices such as scales, glucometers, blood pressure cuffs, heart monitors). This information could be fed directly to the EHR and potentially trigger the appropriate proactive alerts to the clinical staff (or case managers) to take action before the patient's condition worsens.

In one particular study, an EHR-driven dashboard helped case managers track patients in their registry who were due for screening tests and immunizations, along with other important quality metrics (McGough et al. 2018). One of the results of this study was an increase in the number of annual wellness visits for providers who used IT tools to perform population health management.

Benefits and Goals

An EHR can increase the efficiency of clinical care processes not only by getting rid of inefficient paper-based documentation but also by reducing the need to search for lost charts, lab data, or other pieces of patient information. An EHR can potentially increase the efficiency of claims processing through use of actual clinical data to provide documentation. Having the data on care processes in electronic form can also help in monitoring patient care settings at the individual level and in using analytical techniques for identifying patterns in the care process. The monitoring can involve both cost-effectiveness and quality.

In the past, bills were generated, risk assessments were conducted, and quality assurance and quality improvement activities were performed based on painstaking *chart abstraction*—the manual process of reviewing paper-based medical records and extracting the pieces of information needed for the particular task at hand. EHRs can introduce possible improvements in both the processes and outcomes of care that would be difficult to accomplish with a paper chart. We discuss those aspects in this section, but first let's look at four benefits of using an EHR that are related to efficiency and performance monitoring.

Benefit 1: Access to Information

One of the most obvious benefits of an EHR is access to information—that is, getting the clinical information when and where it is needed—and round-the-clock access is common for an EHR. Access and communication go hand in hand, because easy access not only makes it convenient for individual clinicians to get the information they need but also improves communication among providers.

Benefit 2: Better Organization of Data

This benefit includes having basic patient data located in a central place so that the data have to be entered only one time. Other efficiency goals include improving the quality of the data in the record by avoiding illegible handwriting and ensuring the completeness and accuracy of the data.

Benefit 3: Claims Processing Efficiency

Though the EHR is a clinical record, clinical data can improve claims-processing efficiency if this information drives the billing process. Data that are accessible in electronic form can ease the process of gathering documentation for claims purposes. In addition, linking the clinical indications to laboratory test orders can improve the accuracy and efficiency of that process.

Benefit 4: Improved Monitoring of Performance

An EHR allows for individual provider profiles of performance as well as aggregate profiles of all providers, something most of the insurance carriers and managed care organizations are already doing. These data can be used by the organization to target quality improvement initiatives. Clinical information stored in a computer-readable and searchable manner can be easily retrieved in multiple ways, unlike paper, microform, or other static storage medium that requires manual data abstraction and processing.

With an EHR, clinical and financial outcomes can be more easily monitored and linked to quality improvement processes; this level of connection is extremely difficult to do with traditional paper records. Wike (2014) has demonstrated that hospitals with more advanced EHR systems are better able to predict mortality rates for most conditions. Individual caregivers can also develop their own profiles of patient behavior so that they can monitor and modify that behavior. Furthermore, individual profiles can provide insight into needed continuing education. Educational activities can be more easily targeted to real clinical needs, not just the practitioner's interests. Finally, a robust EHR's ability to aggregate data across patients provides a means for population-based monitoring and specific disease management.

Stages of Electronic Health Record Adoption

While it is true that some healthcare facilities focused on CPOE (stage 4) even before getting the back-end ancillary systems automated and integrated, it is generally recommended that other systems (stages under 4) be in place and working well before the workflow changes needed for CPOE are undertaken. Exhibit 8.3 shows the stages of adoption of EHR capabilities across the United States as of early 2019.

In January 2018, HIMSS Analytics released a significant update of the EMRAM criteria based on trends observed in EHR adoption since 2005. New criteria added to the model include certain privacy and security capabilities, as previously described in this chapter. It also added criteria for blood product administration, expressed breast milk administration, and blood specimen collection. The original criteria remained in the model. Adding the new criteria resulted in lower EMRAM scores for many organizations—HIMSS Analytics had raised the bar. However, this increase in maturity expectations has helped hospitals address some of the new challenges presented in today's digital healthcare market.

Healthcare organization leaders benefit from using road maps such as the HIMSS Analytics EMRAM for three primary reasons. First, it provides leaders a communications platform via which they can effectively convey the organization's vision and strategy so that it is easily understood by the staff (use of EMRAM matrix graphic helps). Second, this communication fosters a

EXHIBIT 8.3 New 2018 EMRAM Criteria with US Hospitals by Stage

Stage	Cumulative Capabilities	US Hospital Count (as of Feb. 2019)
7	Complete EMR; External HIE; Data Analytics, Governance, Disaster Recovery, Privacy and Security	326
6	Technology-Enabled Medication, Blood Products, and Human Milk Administration; Risk Reporting; Full CDS	2,000
5	Physician documentation using structured templates; Intrusion/Device Protection	Stage 0–5: 3,154
4	CPOE with CDS, Nursing and Allied Health Documentation; Basic Business Continuity	
3	Nursing and Allied Health Documentation; eMAR; Role-Based Security	
2	CDR; Internal Interoperability; Basic Security	
1	Ancillaries—Laboratory, Pharmacy, and Radiology/Cardiology Information Systems; PACS; Digital non-DICOM image management	
0	All Three Ancillaries Not Installed	
		N = 5,480

Source: HIMSS Analytics (2019). Used with permission.

culture in which all rally around the organizational vision and strategy. Third, using EMRAM enables more effective compliance with and preparation for other accreditations, such as those awarded by The Joint Commission, Joint Commission International, and the College of Pathology laboratory accreditations—or even achieving the highest hospital possible safety rating from the Leapfrog Hospital Safety Grade program. Ultimately, the HIMSS Analytics maturity models are proven road maps toward helping organization achieve their EHR, patient safety, clinical outcomes, and operational efficiency goals and objectives.

Many of the organizations that have achieved stage 7 of EMRAM and O-EMRAM have published short case studies to showcase specific benefits realized from their EMR implementations. These case studies can be found on the HIMSS Analytics website at www.himssanalytics.org/resources. In one particular case, Yale New Haven Health was revalidated at both EMRAM and O-EMRAM stage 7 and presented a case study showing significant improvements resulting from a clinical redesign initiative undertaken by the organization. Yale New Haven Health carried out several 90-day rapid-cycle projects with project management, analytics, application team, and clinician resources from across the organization. They sought to achieve patient-centered, evidence-based care improvements through clinical redesign projects that leveraged data from the EHR, used dashboards to collect clinician feedback and promote transparency, and implemented EHR tools such as best practice alerts and order sets. Among the many benefits realized from these projects are a 29 percent reduction in cirrhotic patient care readmissions, a 23 percent reduction in emergency department mortality, and a 39 percent decrease in patient days for children's sickle cell disease (Hsiao 2019). The Yale New Haven Health chief medical information officer, Dr. Allen L. Hsiao, described the organization's culture and attitude toward its EHR like this: "No one asks what's the ROI [return on investment] for the elevators in a hospital, the organization simply can't operate without them. That is where we are now with the EMR." Yale New Haven Health reported many more benefits resulting from its clinical redesign projects driven by their EHR optimization efforts (see exhibit 8.4). Overall, the organization reported an estimated savings from these projects between $50 million and $60 million and ongoing (Hsiao 2019).

Federal Initiatives to Promote the Meaningful Use of an Electronic Health Record

The 1999 landmark report *To Err Is Human*, published by the IOM, suggested that between 44,000 and 98,000 deaths a year in the United States resulted from medical errors (Kohn, Corrigan, and Donaldson 1999). This report heightened the concerns about patient safety by many groups,

EXHIBIT 8.4
Yale New Haven Health EMRAM and O-EMRAM Stage 7 Validation Case Study (2018)

Cirrhotic Patient Care Readmit rate down 29%	**Telemetry (BH)** # pts on telemetry down 24% Telemetry unit LOS down 15%
Children's PICU / RT Overall LOS down 25% PICU LOS down 39%	**Observation Unit (BH)** Observation patient LOS down 27%
Sepsis Redesign Medicine ICU LOS down 11% ED LOS down 14.3% ED mortality down 23%	**Troponin Utilization (BH)** Utilization down 17%
Children's Sickle Cell Patient days down 39%	**Behavioral Intervention (BH)** ALOS down 10%
TPN Utilization % TPN started within 7 days of readmit down 37%	**Observation Unit (BH)** BPA admitted LOS down 15%
PEG Tube Feeding Inpatient LOS down 8%	**Hospitalist Routine Labs** BMP orders down 6%
Medicine Long-Stay Patients Patient days avoided = 1,541	**ED Radiology Utilization** Total ED scan rate down 15%
Surgical Pack Standardization GYN pack costs down 24% PEDI pack costs down 13% Instruments in circulation down 9,480	**Virtual Hospice** Referrals up 25% Inpatient CMO deaths down 30%
ERAS LOS GI/Colon (YNHH) down 13% Total knee (BH) down 19% Total hip (BH) down 24% GYN (BH) down 21%	**ID & Treatment** Patients with delirium ALOS down 10%
Children's Complex (YNHH) Asthma visits down 41%	**COPD / PNA Care (LMH)** PNA ICU patient ALOS down 43%
Opioid Utilization MME per day down 17% Multimodal analgesia administered down 10%	**MRSA Precautions (YNHH)** 10,400 pts taken off MRSA precautions down 61%

Source: Hsiao (2019). Used with permission from Yale New Haven Health.

including healthcare executives, clinicians, health policymakers, and the general public; more important, it captured the attention of the legislative and executive branches of the US government. The report advocated for the increased use of EHRs, CPOE, and CDSSs as means of preventing errors, leading President George W. Bush, in his 2004 State of the Union address, to emphasize the need to computerize patient health records (Bush 2004).

The HITECH Act, which is part of the American Recovery and Reinvestment Act (ARRA) of 2009, gave significant incentives both to hospitals and independent physicians that meaningfully use a certified EHR and imposed penalties on providers for not using a certified EHR by 2015. The intent of these incentives went beyond rewarding the act of implementing an EHR; they were meant to motivate the use of an EHR that results in significant measurable improvements in the quality and affordability of care (Blumenthal and Tavenner 2010).

ONCHIT, working closely with CMS, guided the development of the requirements to certify vendor EHR products. Both the standards of meaningful use and an objective certification process were intended to help buyers of EHRs make more informed decisions and essentially assure buyers that the systems they purchase meet established standards and can work seamlessly with other vendors' systems. In fact, ONCHIT maintains a list of the current certified HIT products for both ambulatory practices and hospitals (ONCHIT 2020).

From calendar year 2011 through calendar year 2017, the original meaningful use incentives and penalties were effective in gaining EHR adoption. Data collected by ONCHIT (2017) note that by 2017, 96 percent of US hospitals had adopted a certified EHR, while 80 percent of physicians had adopted certified EHRs in their outpatient practices. Most recently, federal incentive programs continued to push the meaningful use of certified EHRs through two key new programs:

- Medicare Access and Children's Health Insurance Program Reauthorization Act of 2015 (MACRA) is the current CMS incentive program that encourages health IT adoption. It includes a Quality Payment Program (QPP) that incentivizes physicians to achieve better value and outcomes via two different means:

    1. The Merit-Based Incentive Payments System (MIPS) is a payment approach that incentivizes physician performance in four areas: (1) quality of the care delivered, based on performance measures created by CMS, as well as medical professional and stakeholder groups; (2) improvement activities, such as improvements in measurable care processes, patient engagement, and increase in access to care; (3) promoting interoperability primarily via use of a certified EHR; and (4) reducing the cost of care (CMS 2020).
    2. The Alternative Payment Model (APM) "is a payment approach, developed in partnership with the clinician community, that provides

> added incentives to clinicians to provide high-quality and cost-efficient care. APMs can apply to a specific clinical condition, a care episode, or a population" (CMS 2016).

These programs continue to maintain a laser focus on patient care outcomes as a goal as well as overall cost of care reduction and continue to show significant associative benefits. For instance, from 2015 to 2017, the greatest increase in the use of EHR data occurred for identifying high-risk patients (from 53 percent in 2015 to 68 percent in 2017), identifying care gaps for patients (from 48 percent in 2015 to 60 percent in the same years), developing an approach to query for patient data (from 40 percent to 51 percent), and supporting quality improvement (from 71 percent to 82 percent) (Parasrampuria and Henry 2019). While adoption and meaningful use of an EHR are beginning to show some real benefits, challenges remain including, but not limited to, the EHR user experience and the cost of EHR software.

The Electronic Health Record User Experience Challenge

A lingering obstacle to the use of clinical systems, in particular EHRs with CPOE, has been physician reluctance. Physicians clearly want to do what is in the best interests of their patients' care, but studies have shown that EHRs—particularly CPOE—change work patterns for physicians in significant ways (Morrison and Smith 2000). In fact, there is growing evidence that the EHR may be contributing to physician burnout in the United States. Shanafelt and colleagues (2015) note a rising prevalence of emotional fatigue; more than half of physicians in some disciplines are burned out. Downing and colleagues (2018) suggest that "the number of clinicians leaving the workforce represents a major concern to health care professionals and to the health of the nation. Many factors contribute, but the physician's interaction with electronic health records (EHRs) is especially important now that EHRs have been broadly adopted across the country."

Downing and colleagues (2018) further comment, "Although EHRs have great potential to improve care, they may also have perverse effects. Some studies suggest that US physicians now spend as much time on 'desktop medicine' (interacting with the computer) as they do face-to-face with patients (Sinsky et al. 2016; Tai-Seale et al. 2017). Providers must divide their attention between patients and the EHR, and many believe that this compromises patient–physician relationships (Zulman, Shah, and Verghese 2016). Although few physicians support reverting to paper, there is a growing sense in the medical community that the EHR is driving professional dissatisfaction and burnout." But their underlying conclusion is that the

EHR itself in not the culprit, but rather the burdensome amount and variety of data entry that a physician must accomplish. They suggest that "the highly trained U.S. physician . . . has become a data-entry clerk, required to document not only diagnoses, physician orders, and patient visit notes but also an increasing amount of low-value administrative data" (Downing et al. 2018).

Furthermore, they compare documentation requirements on physicians outside of the United States with those inside the United States, noting that the documentation burden on US physicians is greater by an order of magnitude than their international counterparts. For instance, the authors present data that the average number of keystrokes per outpatient progress note in the United States is more than 4,000, whereas outside of the US, it is 1,246. They conclude that the regulations applied to documentation and billing likely play a larger role than the EHR per se.

While regulatory compliance reform is beyond the scope of this textbook, additional assistance in unburdening physicians and making their EHR user experience more fulfilling is evolving as well. For instance, technological advances in natural language processing (to capture key documentation data as a by-product of the patient–caregiver interaction) as well as artificial intelligence (to use pattern recognition and machine learning to relieve caregivers of some of the more mundane administrative documentation tasks) are beginning to augment EHRs (Natarajan, Frenzel, and Smaltz 2017) and show great promise. Physicians and caregivers look forward to all of these means, plus the use of human scribes, to enhance their user experience and practice medicine at the top of their license—while focused on interacting more with the patient than the EHR.

Costs and Benefits of an Electronic Health Record

Federal legislation and programs clearly have created monetary incentives to adopt EHRs, but it is important to understand both the scope of implementation efforts and the additional benefits that the IOM and HITECH predict. A study by the RAND Corporation published in *Health Affairs* suggests that $81 billion in aggregate could be saved annually as a result of EHR adoption, but some CEOs wonder how much of that actually could accrue to their respective organizations (Hillestad et al. 2005). They certainly are aware of the legislative incentives and penalties associated with adoption of EHRs and are cognizant of consumer and employer empowerment that may increasingly demand EHRs. In addition, mergers and acquisitions have also created a perceived need to consolidate EHRs of the various acquired hospitals and practices onto a single vendor. CEOs continue to be leery of unknowns, including the following (Hillestad et al. 2005):

- Will their organization be able to undergo successfully the significant cultural and workflow process changes needed to achieve benefits?
- Are the vendor's product capabilities real or marketing hype?
- What hidden costs are associated with an EHR project?
- Will the physicians adopt the new EHR-enabled processes and workflows?

In the following sections, we address the costs questions of these CEOs, along with the envisioned benefits of the EHR.

Costs

The cost of EHR software for small practices has declined significantly, but hospital-based EHR software continues to be relatively expensive. While we applaud efforts to release to the public government-developed EHR software, such as the US Department of Veterans Affairs' VistA system, we issue a caution that the actual cost of that software's license is only the tip of the iceberg. An EHR project, because it affects so many workflows and individuals, is really a large-scale organizational and cultural transformation project. The bulk of the costs of an EHR is spent on workflow-reengineering efforts and ongoing support and maintenance. A particularly useful way to assess the long-term costs of an EHR is to develop a ten-year total cost of ownership (TCO) model for the project. All hospitals and healthcare organizations consider purchase price, ongoing maintenance costs, and additional staff requirements, but few of them accomplish a comprehensive assessment of the total costs of the project (Smaltz and Berner 2007).

In addition, while the costs are obviously less for smaller practices, they may still be substantial. Prior to the development of the HITECH Act's meaningful use incentives, some suggested that the financial benefits of the EHR should largely accrue to payers, the health system, and the patients themselves—as opposed to the individual physician (Berner et al. 2006; Doolan and Bates 2002).

Total Cost of Ownership

Exhibit 8.5 provides the one-time and recurring cost components for assessing the TCO of an EHR project. Most of these cost items likely resonate with CEOs, chief operating officers, chief financial officers, and CIOs, but we advocate taking the time to cost out each component over a ten-year period to reduce blind spots and thus assist the organization in making a well-informed decision about its total investment package over time. Exhibit 8.5 also provides a nice outline of some of the elements that an EHR planning team should take into consideration when estimating the total ten-year spending on the project. These include not only the

EXHIBIT 8.5 Components of Total Cost of Ownership of an EHR

Scope Element	One-Time	Recurring
Software and intellectual property	Perpetual software license Content licensing	Term, ASP (application service provider) license; support fees
Timing	Project management Post-live/cutover management	Ongoing support Subsequent improvement phases
People	Implementation • Application • Functional • Infrastructural • Integration • Project management • Sponsorship • Education • Backfill • Vendor and third-party support	Support • Application • Functional • Infrastructural • Integration • Project management • Sponsorship • Education
Process/redesign (logical scope)	People and organizational change needs Third-party support Infrastructure changes	Ongoing support
Infrastructure—technology, facilities	Computing/servers/storage Network Third-party system interfaces End-user devices Fitting out space, moves	Maintenance Refreshment at end of life

obvious one-time charges (such as the purchase of the software licenses for the EHR or the purchase of the hardware on which the software resides) but also the recurring charges (e.g., ongoing operational personnel needed for the care and feeding of the EHR system, personnel needed to provide ongoing training, and personnel needed to provide integration with future applications).

Exhibit 8.6 is a sample ten-year TCO of an outpatient EHR with CDS and CPOE capabilities at a five-hospital, academic medical center with more than 700 physicians and more than 1,000 beds. For confidentiality reasons, the exhibit does not include actual dollar figures but uses appropriate orders of magnitude to give you an itemized perspective of the TCO of an EHR for such an organization.

EXHIBIT 8.6
Sample Ten-Year Total Cost of Ownership for an EHR

Products	FY06	FY07	FY08	FY09	FY10	FY11	FY12	FY13	FY14	FY15	Total
Capital Based License fees											
Volume Based Software Licenses Chunk 1 (350K Visits)											
25% at Signing	$$$,$$$										$$$,$$$
20 % at Delivery	$$$,$$$										$$$,$$$
5 % on final workflow walkthru		$$,$$$									$$,$$$
5 % on integrated testing kickoff		$$,$$$									$$,$$$
25 % on First Live Use (FLU)		$$$,$$$									$$$,$$$
10% FLU + 90 Days			$$$,$$$								$$$,$$$
10% FLU + 12 months			$$$,$$$								$$$,$$$
Chunk 2 (up to 500K Visits)			$$$,$$$								$$$,$$$
Chunk 3 (up to 750K Visits)			$$$,$$$	$$$,$$$							$$$,$$$
Chunk 4 (up to 850K Visits)				$$,$$$	$$$,$$$						$$$,$$$
Oncology Module	$$$,$$$		$$$,$$$								$$$,$$$
Third Party Database	$$,$$$	$$,$$$	$$$,$$$	$$$,$$$	$$$,$$$						$,$$$,$$$
Addl Vendor One Time Products	$$,$$$	$$,$$$									$$,$$$
Third Party One Time Products		$$,$$$									$$,$$$
Interfaces (Live)											
25% at Signing	$$,$$$										$$,$$$
25% at Delivery		$$,$$$									$$,$$$
25 % at FLU		$$,$$$									$$,$$$
25% at FLU + 90		$$,$$$									$$,$$$
Medication Interfaces (Phase II)			$$,$$$								$$,$$$
Capital Based Implementation Fees											
Implementation (Base)	$$$,$$$	$$$,$$$									$$$,$$$
Implementation (Oncology)		$$,$$$	$$$,$$$								$$$,$$$
Implementation (Interfaces)		$$$,$$$									$$$,$$$
Post-Live Activities	$$,$$$										$$,$$$
Project Team Training	$$$,$$$	$$,$$$									$$$,$$$
Estimated Travel	$$$,$$$	$$$,$$$									$$$,$$$
Rollout			$$$,$$$								$$$,$$$
Capital Based Hardware Fees											
Hardware Environment											
AIX Servers		$$$,$$$					$$$,$$$				$,$$$,$$$
SAN		$$$,$$$	$$$,$$$	$$,$$$			$$$,$$$	$$$,$$$	$$,$$$		$$$,$$$
Test/Training Server	$$,$$$					$$,$$$					$$,$$$
Clarity RDBMS Server	$,$$$					$,$$$					$,$$$
Crystal Enterprise Server		$$,$$$	$$,$$$				$$,$$$	$$,$$$			$$,$$$
Print Server		$,$$$					$,$$$				$$,$$$
Patient Portal Server		$$,$$$					$$,$$$				$$,$$$
Citrix Servers	$$,$$$	$$$,$$$	$$$,$$$			$$,$$$	$$$,$$$	$$$,$$$			$$$,$$$
Citrix Server Optional				$$$,$$$					$$$,$$$		$$$,$$$
Blade Enclosure		$$,$$$	$$,$$$	$$,$$$			$$,$$$	$$,$$$	$$,$$$		$$$,$$$
Citrix Licenses	$$,$$$	$$,$$$	$$,$$$	$$,$$$		$$,$$$	$$,$$$	$$,$$$	$$,$$$		$$$,$$$
Training/Implementation for AIX		$$,$$$					$$,$$$				$$$,$$$
SQL Enterprise Licenses	$$,$$$					$$,$$$					$$,$$$
Citrix Administrator		$$$,$$$					$$$,$$$				$$$,$$$
Citrix Technical Training	$$,$$$										$$,$$$

(continued)

EXHIBIT 8.6

Sample Ten-Year Total Cost of Ownership for an EHR *(continued)*

Operating Based Software Fees (Maintenance and Subscription Fees)											
Volume Based PP Chunk 1 (350)		$$,$$$	$$$,$$$	$$$,$$$	$$$,$$$	$$$,$$$	$$$,$$$	$$$,$$$	$$$,$$$	$$$,$$$	$,$$$,$$$
Yearly Support - Optional			$$,$$$	$$$,$$$	$$$,$$$	$$$,$$$	$$$,$$$	$$$,$$$	$$$,$$$	$$$,$$$	$,$$$,$$$
Oncology			$$$,$$$	$$$,$$$	$$$,$$$	$$$,$$$	$$$,$$$	$$$,$$$	$$$,$$$	$$$,$$$	$,$$$,$$$
Third Party dB - Required	$,$$$	$$,$$$	$$,$$$	$$,$$$	$$,$$$	$$,$$$	$$,$$$	$$,$$$	$$,$$$	$$,$$$	$$$,$$$
Third Party dB - Optional			$$,$$$	$$,$$$	$$$,$$$	$$$,$$$	$$$,$$$	$$$,$$$	$$$,$$$	$$$,$$$	$,$$$,$$$
Third Party Maintenance Fees		$$,$$$	$$,$$$	$$,$$$	$$,$$$	$$,$$$	$$,$$$	$$,$$$	$$,$$$	$$,$$$	$$$,$$$
Vendor Consulting On Hand		$$,$$$	$$,$$$	$$$,$$$	$$$,$$$	$$$,$$$	$$$,$$$	$$$,$$$	$$$,$$$	$$$,$$$	$,$$$,$$$
Patient Portal Software		$,$$$	$$,$$$	$$,$$$	$$,$$$	$$,$$$	$$,$$$	$$,$$$	$$,$$$	$$,$$$	$$$,$$$
Interface Maintenance		$$,$$$	$$,$$$	$$,$$$	$$,$$$	$$,$$$	$$,$$$	$$,$$$	$$,$$$	$$,$$$	$$$,$$$
Subscription Applications	$0	$$,$$$	$$,$$$	$$,$$$	$$,$$$	$$,$$$	$$,$$$	$$,$$$	$$,$$$	$$,$$$	$$$,$$$
Operating Based Additional EMR Staffing											
Clinical Applications IS Team	$$$,$$$	$$$,$$$	$$$,$$$	$$$,$$$	$$$,$$$	$$$,$$$	$$$,$$$	$$$,$$$	$$$,$$$	$$$,$$$	$,$$$,$$$
Oncology Specific IS Team		$$$,$$$	$$$,$$$	$$$,$$$	$$$,$$$	$$$,$$$	$$$,$$$	$$$,$$$	$$$,$$$	$$$,$$$	$,$$$,$$$
Other IS Staff		$$$,$$$	$$$,$$$	$$$,$$$	$$$,$$$	$$$,$$$	$$$,$$$	$$$,$$$	$$$,$$$	$$$,$$$	$,$$$,$$$
Core Trainers	$$,$$$	$$$,$$$	$$$,$$$	$$$,$$$	$$$,$$$	$$$,$$$	$$$,$$$	$$$,$$$	$$$,$$$	$$$,$$$	$,$$$,$$$
End User Trainers - Initial		$$$,$$$	$$$,$$$	$$$,$$$							$$$,$$$
End User Trainers - Addtl.			$$$,$$$	$$$,$$$	$$$,$$$	$$$,$$$					$,$$$,$$$
Onsite Support Personnel - Initial		$$$,$$$	$$$,$$$	$$$,$$$	$$$,$$$	$$$,$$$	$$$,$$$	$$$,$$$	$$$,$$$	$$$,$$$	$,$$$,$$$
Onsite Support Personnel - Addtl.				$$$,$$$	$$$,$$$	$$$,$$$	$$$,$$$	$$$,$$$	$$$,$$$	$$$,$$$	$,$$$,$$$
Total Spend	**$,$$$,$$$**	**$,$$$,$$$**	**$,$$$,$$$**	**$,$$$,$$$**	**$,$$$,$$$**	**$,$$$,$$$**	**$,$$$,$$$**	**$,$$$,$$$**	**$,$$$,$$$**	**$,$$$,$$$**	**$$,$$$,$$$**
Required and Optional Split of Costs											
Total Required	$,$$$,$$$	$,$$$,$$$	$,$$$,$$$	$,$$$,$$$	$,$$$,$$$	$,$$$,$$$	$,$$$,$$$	$,$$$,$$$	$,$$$,$$$	$,$$$,$$$	$$,$$$,$$$
Total Optional	$0	$0	$$$,$$$	$,$$$,$$$	$,$$$,$$$	$$$,$$$	$$$,$$$	$$$,$$$	$$$,$$$	$$$,$$$	$,$$$,$$$
Capital and Operational Split of Costs											
Total Capital	$,$$$,$$$	$,$$$,$$$	$,$$$,$$$	$,$$$,$$$	$$$,$$$	$$$,$$$	$,$$$,$$$	$$$,$$$	$$$,$$$	$$$,$$$	$$,$$$,$$$
Total Operational	$$$,$$$	$,$$$,$$$	$,$$$,$$$	$,$$$,$$$	$,$$$,$$$	$,$$$,$$$	$,$$$,$$$	$,$$$,$$$	$,$$$,$$$	$,$$$,$$$	$$,$$$,$$$

Legend:

$,$$$	Thousands
$$,$$$	Tens of Thousands
$$$,$$$	Hundreds of Thousands
$,$$$,$$$	Millions
$$,$$$,$$$	Tens of Millions

Notes:

1. For confidentiality reasons, real dollar figures could not be used.
2. This 10-year total cost of ownership model is from a 5-hospital, 1000+ bed academic medical center with 700+ physicians.
3. The total estimated operational spend over the 10-year period is 75% of the total spend, while the capital spend is only 25% of the total spend.

The real value of developing a ten-year TCO of an EHR or any major project is to force, in an explicit and deliberate manner, an analysis and articulation of all the expenses the organization will incur, not just the initial purchase costs. While not obvious from the example in exhibit 8.6, given that the actual dollars are masked, do note that in most EHR projects, the capital expenditure over the ten-year period is only about 25 percent or less of the total spending. The vast majority—about 75 percent or more—of the expense of an EHR accrues on the operating side of the balance sheet (Smaltz and Berner 2007). For healthcare organizations that are looking to plan beyond the next budget cycle, accomplishing ten-year TCOs for any major investment, let alone an EHR, provides a systematic means of both making an informed decision at the time of purchase and being more able to proactively reduce the project-execution risks of such a complex project.

Benefits

A common reaction by most CEOs, COOs, and CFOs when they become aware of the costs of implementing an EHR is to immediately ask, "Where's the ROI?" Our colleague Dr. John Glaser has a nice analogy that he uses when someone confronts him with that question. He replies with "what's the ROI of a chainsaw?" After letting his questioner ramble on a bit about the inherent efficiencies of chainsaws over axes or the lower number of full-time equivalents needed when employing a chainsaw versus an axe, he comes to their rescue with an obvious, thought-provoking insight: "What if you're making a dress? You'd be hard pressed to find an ROI for chainsaws if the task at hand were to make dresses efficiently." An equally important question follows that: "What if the chainsaw is in the hands of a 10-year old child?" Again, in the hands of a user without the requisite skills or ability to use a chainsaw effectively, the ROI is equally dubious. Glaser's message is clear: Depending on what you want to do with an EHR and who will be using it, the ROI is variable (Glaser and Garets 2005).

First and foremost, EHRs should not be treated as a silver bullet solution for inefficient patient care processes. Rather, an EHR project is an organizational, cultural transformation that happens to have a technological component. The benefits of the project will depend on three elements. First, which processes is an organization willing to reengineer to take on the associated long-standing or ingrained status quos? Second, what is the extent to which an organization is willing to invest in ensuring that the process owners and users are fully engaged and committed to reengineering the EHR-enabled processes? Third, are users being fully trained on the new tools? In other words, proper project execution is paramount to achieving the promise and value of the EHR. Assuming the healthcare organization has the leadership and buy-in as well as the project management prowess to implement an EHR effectively, an organization can expect to accrue a number of benefits from an EHR (see exhibits 8.7 and 8.8) beyond the meaningful use incentives.

EXHIBIT 8.7
Typical Financial Benefits of EHRs

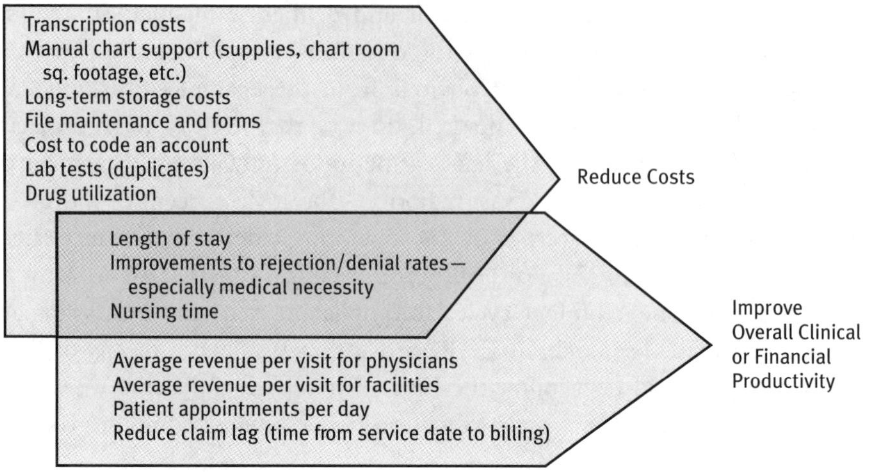

Source: Smaltz and Berner (2007). Reprinted with permission from Health Administration Press, Chicago.

EXHIBIT 8.8
Typical Product Line Benefits of EHRs

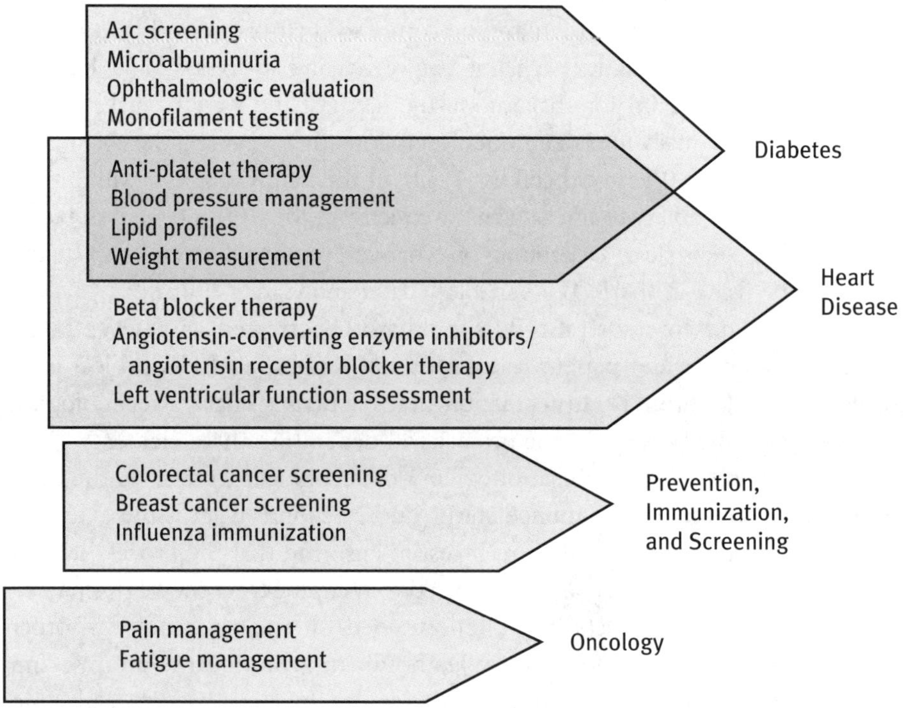

Source: Smaltz and Berner (2007). Reprinted with permission from Health Administration Press, Chicago.

The financial benefits in exhibit 8.7 are fairly self-explanatory and are generally considered when comparing costs with benefits. Not all benefits are strictly financial, although they can be framed in financial terms. The product line benefits in exhibit 8.8 are often overlooked when assessing the positive impact of an EHR. As legislation and payer models begin to reward health maintenance activities, as opposed to health intervention activities, an EHR can—with pinpoint precision—identify patients who need proactive or preventive services such as A1C screenings, immunizations, mammograms, or prostate screenings. EHRs (especially those integrated with CPOE and CDS) have been touted as a key approach to reducing medical errors (Bates et al. 1998; IOM 1999). A number of studies have documented that EHRs have the potential to lead to substantial benefits in patient safety, especially in reducing medication errors. Given that the costs of adverse drug events (ADEs) are enormous, avoidance of ADEs can translate into potential cost savings. Evans and colleagues (1998) found significant savings in length of stay, use of anti-infective agents, and total hospital costs when the advice of a CDS system for antibiotic use was followed. Similarly, Kaushal and colleagues (2006) analyzed the ROI on a CPOE system and estimated a cumulative net savings of $16.7 million dollars to a large academic hospital.

While EHRs can improve efficiency, the efficiencies may not be evenly distributed. An EHR may speed the time between a medication order being placed and the order being received in the pharmacy, but some parts of the overall medication administration process may not be affected by the EHR. An analysis of multiple studies of time savings with electronic documentation systems shows a decrease in documentation time for nurses, but physician time was more variable; in some cases, the time for electronic documentation meant an increase in physician time at the front end (Poissant et al. 2005), but reduced search time for patient records retrieval may compensate for time lost in documentation.

Summary

With federal laws and incentives in place to use an EHR meaningfully, for both individual physicians and hospitals, the stage is set for EHR adoption to continue to rise. Both the federal government and employer advocacy organizations like the Leapfrog Group hope that the meaningful use of an EHR achieves the objectives, originally identified in the IOM report *To Err Is Human,* to prevent unnecessary deaths from healthcare errors, make healthcare demonstrably higher quality, and reduce the overall cost of providing healthcare. Continued work is needed in the area of the EHR user experience, both to reduce unnecessary administrative burden on caregivers and to streamline and optimize EHR-centric workflows for the benefit of both patients and their caregivers.

Web Resources

A number of organizations (through their websites) provide more information on the topics discussed in this chapter:

- The website of the Centers for Medicare & Medicaid Services (CMS; www.cms.gov/Regulations-and-Guidance/Legislation/EHRIncentivePrograms/index.html?redirect=/ehrincentiveprograms/) provides official guidance on CMS EHR incentive programs.
- Healthcare Information and Management Systems Society (HIMSS; www.himss.org/library/ehr) is the largest HIT professional association, and its website provides an overview of EHRs.
- The website of the International Health Terminology Standards Development Organisation (IHTSDO; www.snomed.org/snomed-ct/five-step-briefing) presents information on standard medical nomenclature.
- The website of the Office of the National Coordinator for Healthcare Information Technology (ONCHIT; www.healthit.gov/topic/about-onc) provides guidance on both EHR implementations and incentives for meaningful use of an EHR.

Discussion Questions

1. What are some of the key capabilities of a robust EHR?
2. What is CPOE, and why is it seen as vital to achieving the nation's patient safety and healthcare quality goals?
3. What are some of the benefits of a robust EHR?
4. What are some of the main categories of cost associated with purchasing and implementing an EHR?
5. What are some of the criteria that both individual providers and hospitals need to meet to earn incentives for meaningfully using an EHR?
6. What are some of the challenges of using an EHR that have been articulated and what are some of the promising advances that hope to overcome those challenges?

References

Al-Haddad, M., J. Friedlin, J. Kesterson, J. Waters, J. Aguilar-Saavedra, and C. Schmidt. 2010. "Natural Language Processing for the Development of a Clinical Registry: A Validation Study in Intraductal Papillary Mucinous Neoplasms." *Official Journal of the International Hepato Pancreato Biliary Association* 12 (10): 688–95.

Bates, D., L. Leape, D. Cullen, N. Laird, L. Petersen, J. Teich, E. Burdick, M. Hickey, S. Kleefield, B. Shea, M. Vander Vliet, and D. Seger. 1998. "Effect of Computerized Physician Order Entry and a Team Intervention on Prevention of Serious Medication Errors." *Journal of the American Medical Association* 280 (15): 1311–16.

Berner, E., T. Houston, M. Ray, J. Allison, G. Heudebert, W. Chatham, J. Kennedy, G. Glandon, P. Norton, and M. Crawford. 2006. "Improving Ambulatory Prescribing Safety with a Handheld Decision Support System: A Randomized Controlled Trial." *Journal of the Medical Informatics Association* 13 (2): 171–79.

Blumenthal, D., and M. Tavenner. 2010. "The 'Meaningful Use' Regulation for Electronic Health Records." *New England Journal of Medicine* 363 (6, 5): 501–504.

Bush, G. W. 2004. "Text of President Bush's 2004 State of the Union Address." *Washington Post.* Published January 20. www.washingtonpost.com/wp-srv/politics/transcripts/bushtext_012004.html.

Connelly, J. 2020. "CPT Overview and Code Approval." American Medical Association. Accessed February 17. www.ama-assn.org/practice-management/cpt/cpt-overview-and-code-approval.

Centers for Medicare & Medicaid Services (CMS). 2020. "MIPS Overview." Accessed March 13. https://qpp.cms.gov/mips/overview.

———. 2016. "The Quality Payment Program." Published October 25. www.cms.gov/newsroom/fact-sheets/quality-payment-program.

Cordtz, C. 2018. "9 Key Takeaways on Anesthesia Information Management Systems." *Becker's Hospital Review.* Published February 13. www.beckershospitalreview.com/healthcare-information-technology/9-key-takeaways-on-anesthesia-information-management-systems.html.

Dentzer, S. 2013. "Rx for the 'Blockbuster Drug' of Patient Engagement." *Health Affairs.* Published February. www.healthaffairs.org/doi/full/10.1377/hlthaff.2013.0037.

Dick, R. S., E. B. Steen, and D. E. Detmer (eds.). 1997. *The Computer-Based Patient Record: An Essential Technology for Health Care,* rev. ed. Washington, DC: National Academy Press.

Doolan, D., and D. Bates. 2002. "Computerized Physician Order Entry Systems in Hospitals: Mandates and Incentives." *Health Affairs* 21 (4): 180–88.

Downing, N. L., D. W. Bates, and C. A. Longhurst. 2018. "Physician Burnout in the Electronic Health Record Era: Are We Ignoring the Real Cause?" *Annals of Internal Medicine.* Published July 3. https://annals.org/aim/article-abstract/2680726/physician-burnout-electronic-health-record-era-we-ignoring-real-cause.

Evans, R., S. Pestotnik, D. Classen, T. Clemmer, L. Weaver, J. Orme, J. Lloyd, and J. Burke. 1998. "A Computer-Assisted Management Program for Antibiotics and Other Antiinfective Agents." *New England Journal of Medicine* 338 (4): 232–38.

Ford, E., N. Menachemi, and M. Phillips. 2006. "Predicting the Adoption of Electronic Health Records by Physicians: When Will Healthcare Be Paperless?" *Journal of the American Medical Informatics Association* 13 (1): 106–12.

Fornell, D. 2008. "Understanding Anesthesiology Information Systems." *Diagnostic and Interventional Cardiology*. Published April 8. www.dicardiology.com/article/understanding-anesthesiology-information-systems.

Garets, D., and M. Davis. 2006. "Electronic Medical Records vs. Electronic Health Records: Yes, There Is a Difference." HIMSS Analytics. Updated January 2006. www.aao.org/asset.axd?id=8e9b1f20-0ed6-4d2b-92f8-e28fbaf378ec&t=634962799822530000.

Garg, A., N. Adhikari, H. McDonald, P. Rosas-Arellano, P. Devereaux, J. Beyene, J. Sam, and R. Haynes. 2005. "Effects of Computerized Clinical Decision Support Systems on Practitioner Performance and Patient Outcomes." *Journal of the American Medical Association* 293 (10): 1223–38.

Gartner. 2012. "IT Governance (ITG)." Accessed February 17. www.gartner.com/it-glossary/it-governance.

Glaser, J., and D. Garets. 2005. "Where's the Beef? Part 1: Getting Value from Your IT Investments." In *The CEO–CIO Partnership: Harnessing the Value of Information Technology in Healthcare*, edited by D. Smaltz, J. Glaser, R. Skinner, and T. Cunningham III. Chicago: Healthcare Information and Management Systems Society.

Healthcare Information and Management Systems Society (HIMSS). 2020. "Computerized Provider Order Entry (CPOE) Wiki." Accessed March 17. https://himsscpoewiki.pbworks.com/w/page/10258531/FrontPage.

———. 2019. *Dictionary of Health Information Technology Terms, Acronyms, and Organizations*, 5th ed. Boca Raton, FL: CRC Press.

Hillestad, R., J. Bigelow, A. Bower, F. Girosi, R. Meili, R. Scoville, and R. Taylor. 2005. "Can Electronic Medical Record Systems Transform Health Care? Potential Health Benefits, Savings, and Costs." *Health Affairs* 24 (5): 1103–17.

HIMSS Analytics 2020. "EMRAM: A Strategic Roadmap for Effective EMR Adoption and Maturity." Accessed March 16. www.himssanalytics.org/emram.

———. 2019. "New EMRAM Criteria with U.S. Hospitals by Stage." HIMSS Analytics.

Hsiao, A. L. 2019. "Yale New Haven Health Stage 7 Case Study." Published June 19. www.himssanalytics.org/case-study/yale-new-haven-health-stage-7-case-study.

Institute of Medicine (IOM). 1999. *To Err Is Human: Building a Safer Health System*. Washington, DC: National Academies Press.

International Data Sanitization Consortium. 2020. "Data Sanitization Terminology and Definitions." Accessed February 17. www.datasanitization.org/data-sanitization-terminology.

Irizarry, T., A. D. Dabbs, and C. R. Curran. 2015. "Patient Portals and Patient Engagement: A State of the Science Review." *Journal of Medical Internet Research* (6): e148.

Joint Task Force Transformation Initiative. 2012. "Guide for Conducting Risk Assessments." National Institute of Standards and Technology. Published September. https://csrc.nist.gov/publications/detail/sp/800-30/rev-1/final.

Kaushal, R., A. K. Jha, C. Franz, J. Glaser, K. D. Shetty, T. Jaggi, B. Middleton, G. J. Kuperman, R. Khorasani, M. Tanasijevic, D. W. Bates, and Brigham and Women's Hospital CPOE Working Group. 2006. "Return on Investment for a Computerized Order Entry System." *Journal of the American Medical Informatics Association* 13 (3): 261–66.

Kish, L. 2012. "The Blockbuster Drug of the Century: An Engaged Patient." Health Standards. Published August 28. http://healthstandards.com/blog/2012/08/28/drug-of-the-century.

Kohn, L., J. Corrigan, and M. Donaldson (eds.). 1999. *To Err Is Human: Building a Safer Health System.* Washington, DC: National Academies Press.

Korolov, M. 2016. "Black Market Medical Record Prices Drop to Under $10, Criminals Switch to Ransomware." CSO. Published December 22. www.csoonline.com/article/3152787/black-market-medical-record-prices-drop-to-under-10-criminals-switch-to-ransomware.html.

Maurer, M., P. Dardess, K. L. Carman, K. Frazier, and L. Smeeding. 2012. "Guide to Patient and Family Engagement: Environmental Scan Report." Agency for Healthcare Research and Quality. Published May. www.ahrq.gov/sites/default/files/publications/files/ptfamilyscan.pdf.

McGeath, J. 2014. "Medical Device Integration with EHRs: The Landscape and Outlook for the Future." *Today's Medical Developments.* Published May 29. www.todaysmedicaldevelopments.com/article/tmd0614-medical-device-integration-ehr.

McGough, P., V. Chaudhari, S. El-Attar, and P. Yung. 2018. "A Health System's Journey Toward Better Population Health Through Empanelment and Panel Management." *Healthcare* 6 (2): 1–9.

Middleton, B., G. Christopherson, R. Rocha, and D. Smaltz. 2004. "Knowledge Management in Clinical Systems: Principles and Pragmatics." Paper presented at the International Medical Informatics Association Medinfo Conference, San Francisco, CA, September 11.

Miliard, M. 2017. "How Smart Pump EHR Integration Could Save a Community Hospital $2 Million." Published August 31. www.healthcareitnews.com/news/how-smart-pump-ehr-integration-could-save-community-hospital-2-million.

Morrison, I., and R. Smith. 2000. "Hamster Health Care: Time to Stop Running Faster and Redesign Health Care." *British Medical Journal* 321: 1541–42.

Natarajan, P., J. C. Frenzel, and D. H. Smaltz. 2017. *Demystifying Big Data and Machine Learning for Healthcare.* Boca Raton, FL: CRC Press.

National Library of Medicine. 2019. "Unified Medical Language System." Updated May 23. www.nlm.nih.gov/research/umls.

Office of the National Coordinator for Health Information Technology (ONCHIT). 2020. "Certified Health IT Product List." US Department of Health & Human Services. Accessed March 16. https://chpl.healthit.gov/#/search.

———. 2017. "Health IT Dashboard: HITECH Programs." US Department of Health & Human Services. Accessed February 17. https://dashboard.healthit.gov/apps/health-information-technology-data-summaries.php?state=National&cat9=all+data&cat5=hitech+programs.

O'Reilly, M., A. Talsma, S. VanRiper, S. Kheterpal, and R. Burney. 2006. "An Anesthesia Information System Designed to Provide Physician-Specific Feedback Improves Timely Administration of Prophylactic Antibiotics." *Anesthesia & Analgesia* 103 (4): 908–12.

Osheroff, J. A., E. A. Pifer, D. F. Sittig, R. A. Jenders, and J. M. Teich. 2005. *Improving Outcomes with Clinical Decision Support: An Implementer's Guide.* Chicago: Healthcare Information and Management Systems Society.

Parasrampuria, S., and J. Henry. 2019. "Hospitals' Use of Electronic Health Records Data, 2015–2017." Office of the National Coordinator for Health Information Technology. Published April. www.healthit.gov/sites/default/files/page/2019-04/AHAEHRUseDataBrief.pdf.

Pettus, D. C., and T. Vanderveen. 2013. "Worth the Effort? Closed-Loop Infusion Pump Integration with the EMR." *Biomedical Instrumentation & Technology* 47 (6): 467–77.

Poissant, L., J. Pereira, R. Tamblyn, and Y. Kawasumi. 2005. "The Impact of Electronic Health Records on Time Efficiency of Physicians and Nurses: A Systematic Review." *Journal of the American Medical Informatics Association* 12 (5): 505–16.

Reckmann, M., J. Westbrook, Y. Koh, C. Lo, and R. Day. 2009. "Does Computerized Provider Order Entry Reduce Prescribing Errors for Hospital Inpatients? A Systematic Review." *Journal of the American Medical Informatics Association* 16 (5): 613–23.

Regenstrief Institute. 2020. "LOINC." Accessed February 18. www.regenstrief.org/resources/loinc.

Russell, R., D. Triscari, K. Murkowski, and M. Scanlon. 2015. "Impact of Computerized Order Entry to Pharmacy Interface on Order-Infusion Pump Discrepancies." *Journal of Drug Delivery* 2015: article ID 686598.

Scarfone, K., and P. Mell. 2007. "Guide to Intrusion Detection and Prevention Systems (IDPS): Recommendations of the National Institute of Standards and Technology." National Institute of Standards and Technology. Published February. www.yumpu.com/en/document/read/4935222/nist-sp-800-94-guide-to-intrusion-detection-and-prevention-systems.

Shanafelt, T., O. Hasan, L. Dyrbye, P. Sinsky, D. Satele, J. Sloan, and C. West. 2015. "Changes in Burnout and Satisfaction with Work-Life Balance in Physicians and the General US Working Population between 2011 and 2014." *Mayo Clinic Proceedings* 90 (12): 1600–1613.

Sinsky, C., L. Colligan, L. Li, M. Prgomet, S. Reynolds, L. Goeders, J. Westbrook, M. Tutty, and G. Blike. 2016. "Allocation of Physician Time in Ambulatory Practice: A Time and Motion Study in 4 Specialties." *Annals of Internal Medicine* 165 (11): 753–60.

Smaltz, D., and E. Berner. 2007. *The Executive's Guide to Electronic Health Records.* Chicago: Health Administration Press.

SNOMED International. 2020. "5-Step Briefing." Accessed February 17. www.snomed.org/snomed-ct/five-step-briefing.

Swarthout, M., and M. A. Bishop. 2017. "Population health management: Review of concepts and definitions." *American Journal of Health-System Pharmacy* 74 (18): 1405–11.

Tai-Seale, M., C. W. Olson, J. Li, A. Chan, C. Morikawa, M. Durbin, W. Wang, and H. Luft. 2017. "Electronic Health Record Logs Indicate That Physicians Split Time Evenly Between Seeing Patients and Desktop Medicine." *Health Affairs* 36 (46): 655–62.

Terry, K. 2012. "Natural Language Processing Could Eventually Change Medicine." *FierceHealthcare.* Published February 12. www.fiercehealthcare.com/it/natural-language-processing-could-eventually-change-medicine.

USF Health. 2020. "Differences Between EHR and EMR." Accessed March 12. www.usfhealthonline.com/resources/key-concepts/ehr-vs-emr.

US Department of Homeland Security (DHS). 2017. "Study on Mobile Device Security." Published April. www.dhs.gov/sites/default/files/publications/DHSStudyonMobileDeviceSecurity-April2017-FINAL.pdf.

Wike, K. 2014. "EMR Adoption Reduces Mortality Rates." Health IT Outcomes. Published August 20. www.healthitoutcomes.com/doc/emr-adoption-reduces-mortality-rates-0001.

Williams, C., F. Mostashari, K. Mertz, E. Hogin, and P. Atwal. 2012. "From the Office of the National Coordinator: The Strategy for Advancing the Exchange of Health Information." *Health Affairs* 31 (3): 527–36.

World Health Organization (WHO). 2018. "Classifications." Published June 18. www.who.int/classifications/icd/en.

Wright, A., T. Hickman, D. McEvoy, S. Aaron, A. Ai, J. Andersen, S. Hussain, R. Ramoni, J. Fiskio, D. Sittig, and D. Bates. 2016. "Analysis of Clinical Decision Support System Malfunctions: A Case Series and Survey." *Journal of the American Medical Informatics Association* 23 (6): 1068–76.

Zulman, D., N. Shah, and A. Verghese. 2016. "Evolutionary Pressures on the Electronic Health Record: Caring for Complexity." *Journal of the American Medical Association* 316 (9): 923–24.

CHAPTER

9

APPLICATIONS: MANAGEMENT AND FINANCIAL SYSTEMS

Learning Objectives

1. Describe the components typically included in an enterprise resource planning system.
2. Provide examples of transaction processing applications and discuss how they support financial management.
3. List components of the revenue cycle, describing how various components contribute to cash flow and revenue optimization.
4. Discuss desirable features of an automated enterprise scheduling system.
5. Distinguish between clinical decision support software and executive information systems.
6. Understand the use of computer applications as tools for research and medical education.

Overview

For many years, the healthcare field lagged behind other businesses in the design and implementation of robust information systems. Problems have included undercapitalization of the system development process and the failure of management to oversee system implementation effectively. However, the situation has changed substantially because of heightened competition, increased regulation, and changing payment mechanisms affecting the entire sector. Changes in the delivery and financing of healthcare that began in the late 1980s were pivotal to establishing information management as a key strategic resource in most healthcare organizations. Healthcare managers rely on information systems as essential tools for robust growth, effective competition and, in some cases, survival. In the current healthcare environment, which is evolving toward value-based care and consumerization, the importance of maximizing the contributions of information systems and "digital health tools" cannot be overstated (HIMSS 2019).

Most healthcare organizations began their automated information processing activities with computer systems that supported administrative operations—in particular, financial and accounting systems. While a significant number of healthcare applications serve financial purposes currently, robust clinical information systems are a top priority for most healthcare organizations. Note, however, that clinical information systems not only provide direct support to patient care processes but also populate the data repositories essential for performance measurement, external reporting, cost management, and other organizational accountability activities. Thus, the "ideal" clinical and administrative applications integrate into a comprehensive system that supports the continuum of information needs in an enterprise.

Most early information system applications in healthcare organizations were designed as stand-alone systems, and purchase decisions were based on maximizing desired specific functionality at acceptable costs. In the current environment, however, clinical and administrative applications are integrated, sharing functionality and transferring data across various elements of the enterprise information system as well as exchanging information with systems external to the enterprise. Purchase decision criteria now include interoperability, compliance with data transmission standards, and many other complex factors.

Migrating stand-alone legacy systems into an integrated environment was one of the most difficult challenges health information technology (HIT) teams encountered in constructing systems to meet the rapidly expanding information needs of healthcare enterprises (Gilchrist et al. 2008; Hicken, Thornton, and Rocha 2004; Kraatz, Lyons, and Thompkinson 2010). In fact, some teams concluded that starting from scratch was easier than retrofitting various systems from multiple vintages.

As technologies and system configurations continue to evolve, however, repeated "start-overs" usually are not a realistic option, for several reasons. Purchase and implementation costs of full-scale systems can be prohibitive, although purchase price has become virtually the least important criterion in system selection. Operations and planning are dependent on data and information stored in existing systems, and migrating data archives may be difficult or even impossible. In light of the extent of technology dependence in healthcare organizations, the disruption in service delivery and business operations during a full-system transition could be tremendous. Thus, managers must select system components with forethought for the ability to transition to next-generation products for better interconnectivity and interoperability in both clinical and administrative applications.

Enterprise resource planning (ERP) systems are bundled applications that integrate operational information derived from financial, project management, materials management, and other function-based areas into a robust database used to achieve business management objectives (Oracle.com

2020). These systems connect inventory and facilities management, resource scheduling, accounting and financial management, and other business events in a real-time environment. As with clinical systems, the market for ERP applications emerged from the need to update legacy software. The administrative applications typically incorporated in an ERP include the following:

- Financial information systems
- Human resources information systems
- Resource utilization and scheduling systems
- Supply chain management systems
- Facilities and project management systems
- Office automation systems

Each of these system components is described in this chapter with illustrative examples. Special features of these types of applications designed to meet the needs of nonhospital healthcare organizations, such as physician practices and home health care, are addressed. Additional uses of information systems in healthcare, such as medical research, education, and decision support, are discussed briefly.

Financial Information Systems

The highly competitive and regulated environments in which healthcare organizations operate require timely and accurate financial information that enables managers to monitor and guide operational performance. Managing competing demands for accountability and cost containment while providing high-quality services keeps managers acutely aware of the importance of sound financial management in guiding operational performance. Financial information systems support operational activities such as general accounting, patient accounting, payroll, contract management, and investment management. Financial systems also provide information to management for directing and evaluating organizational performance. Analysis of current and historical information aids in projecting future financial needs of the organization.

Financial information systems require input from transaction-processing systems, external sources, and strategic organizational plans (see exhibit 9.1). Such systems record the organization's routine business activities, collecting information from other administrative subsystems, including payroll, accounts payable, accounts receivable, general ledger, and inventory control. These transactions are the basis for many financial reports required by management. To support effective financial decisions, financial systems

EXHIBIT 9.1
Financial Information System

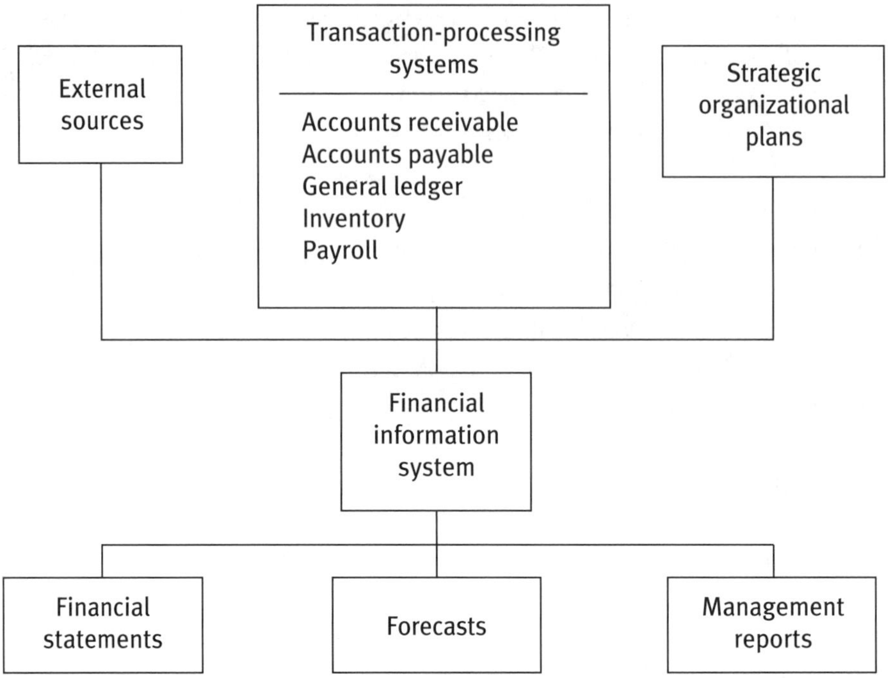

also need external data such as government statistics, inflation rates, and information about the marketplace. An organization's strategic plan should contain financial goals and objectives that help provide the framework for preparation of financial reports.

A fully integrated financial information system brings related information together for planning, monitoring, and control. Individual financial subsystems include the following:

- Payroll preparation and accounting, linked to a human resources information system
- Processing of accounts payable, linked to purchasing and inventory control systems
- Patient accounting, patient and third-party billing, and accounts receivable processing
- Cost accounting and cost allocation of non-revenue-generating activities and general overhead expense
- General ledger accounting
- Budgeting and budget control
- Internal auditing

- Financial forecasting
- Investment monitoring and analysis
- Financial statement preparation
- Financial reporting for operating supervisors, executive management, board members, external regulators, and third-party financing agencies

Developing and maintaining an effective financial information system necessitates the infrastructure of a good accounting system. Sophisticated cost accounting, essential in a negotiated pricing or value-based payment environment, enables the financial information system to generate accurate information on personnel and other physical resources used to deliver services. For services provided under managed care contracts, stakeholders as diverse as providers, managed care organizations, and employers need cost information to help negotiate rates and monitor contract performance. Integrated financial reporting based on a solid cost accounting system provides information for product costing, analysis of labor productivity, inventory control, and examination of the productivity return on capital investments.

Significant proportions of total payments for healthcare services provided are based on either a fixed payment per case (e.g., diagnosis-related groups) or a fixed payment per person per month (i.e., capitation payment systems). For effective management in this environment, a financial information system must have the capability to convert or link cost and net revenue information to multiple units of payment.

A market analysis prepared by the Dorenfest Institute for HIT Research and Education (Dorenfest Institute 2013) for the HIMSS Foundation described the financial management application as "highly saturated" with hospital installation rates for accounts payable, general ledger, and materials management at nearly 100 percent.

Revenue Cycle Management (RCM)

The revenue cycle in healthcare encompasses all business processes and clinical activities associated with generating and receiving revenue through patient care, from preregistration or scheduling through processing payments for services rendered and follow-up on uncollectible accounts (see exhibit 9.2). Although some real-time manual data capture processes are inevitable, almost exclusively the revenue cycle is automated, and data capture, transaction processing, data transmission, and archiving are integrated with the enterprise information system.

Managing the revenue cycle effectively is critical, as this process is the driver for cash flow as well as optimizing the overall income from clinical operations. The goal of revenue cycle management (RCM) is to make the time between service provision and payment for services as short as possible.

EXHIBIT 9.2
Revenue Cycle Components

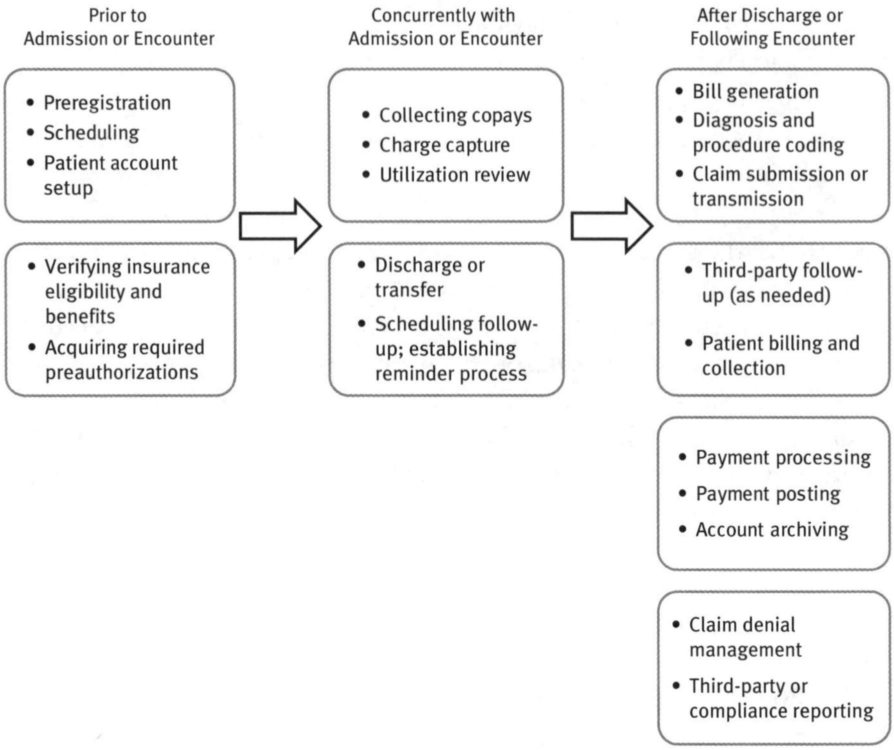

Thus, the efficiency of all business processes associated with generating, submitting, and processing a claim for services provided is paramount to ensuring the effectiveness of the entire RCM system.

The revenue cycle begins with getting a patient in the system to receive services (i.e., registration, service scheduling, account setup). At this point, accurate information capture or entry is critical, as it informs planning and prepping for the clinical services, as well as providing key administrative information that will be used in every step of the process through claim submission and payment processing. Patient identification data and insurance coverage must be accurate and complete to avoid delays in processing eligibility for services or denial of claims. Many insurance companies require preauthorization for some services; thus, the system should be designed to allow time to secure the authorization before the service is scheduled. Because patient satisfaction is a key component of hospital ratings, the efficiency and ease of the patient's engagement in this step in the process is very important. Current data about coverage, copayment, and exclusions for insurance products accepted are essential.

Payment amounts for specific services are driven by several variables. First, there's the charge for the product or service based on the actual cost of resources (e.g., personnel, products, equipment usage) required to deliver the product or service. These billable units are maintained in the chargemaster, a complex database that houses the descriptions of the billable units and the associated codes used to generate a patient bill. The chargemaster serves as the input for the second variable, the negotiated prices charged to third-party payers. These prices vary, sometimes widely, by payer. For example, Medicare has a sophisticated and complex value-based payment model that rewards providers for efficient delivery of care with good outcomes. Other payers may negotiate lower rates for high-volume services or preferred provider designations. Finally, the actual reimbursement, or the amount paid, may differ from the amount billed after application of discounts, penalties, incentives, or uncollectable accounts.

The charges or prices that make up a patient bill are generated from diagnostic and procedure codes that convert large amounts of text-based information to numeric codes derived from one or more approved classification systems, such as the International Classification of Diseases, Current Procedural Terminology, or Systematized Nomenclature of Pathology. Because of the variability in medical language, and the importance of precision and accuracy, coding software is not so much automated as it is assistive to human medical coders. Medical coders are trained health information professionals who play a very important role in RCM. If the correct code is not selected, the reimbursement may not be correct or the claim may be denied pending correction, which affects cash flow. Frequent coding errors, which constitute billing errors, may result in penalties or sanctions from payers.

A key point is that RCM is a dynamic process subject to frequent and profound change as payment regulations and payer contracts evolve. The information systems that support these processes must be dynamic as well. Planned system updates to accommodate changes in the regulations or payer processes must be timely and comprehensive.

Some components of the RCM systems, such as registration, scheduling, and billing, have been utilized for many years, and many healthcare organizations are investing to replace older systems with newer applications that better integrate and improve compliance with federal information technology (IT) initiatives.

As with other business processes in healthcare, RCM can be outsourced to one of many third-party vendors that specialize in this service. Vendors must be vetted for their ability to integrate with the healthcare organization's financial and clinical systems, how they maintain processes compliant with current regulations, their security practices, their approach to managing denied claims, and other sector benchmarks for a robust RCM approach.

Human Resources Information Systems

Employees of a healthcare organization constitute its most important resource. Most organizations spend more than 50 percent of their operating budget on employee salaries and benefits. Thus, a good human resources information system (HRIS) is an important tool to assist managers in personnel planning, staffing, and productivity analysis. The common functions of an HRIS include, but certainly are not limited to, the following:

- Maintaining, updating, and retrieving information from a database of employee personnel records
- Providing automatic position control that is linked to the budget
- Producing labor analysis reports for each operating unit or cost center
- Producing reports used for assessing personnel problems, such as turnover and absenteeism
- Maintaining an inventory of special skills and required certifications of employees
- Producing labor cost allocations with linkage to the payroll system
- Providing information on employee productivity and quality control, assuming that appropriate labor standards have been developed
- Managing employee sick leave, vacation, and other earned time off
- Comparing the organization's compensation and benefit packages with industry norms

Large amounts of data are required to provide these reports and others that may be needed. The HRIS information processing and reporting functions are supported by information drawn from various databases that contain individual employee data, wage and salary records, the organization's job classification structure, benefit packages, employment contracts, and many other related data elements. Actual ownership of the various databases may be distributed among multiple departments. Thus, the structure of the databases is an important factor in data transfer from one element of the system to another.

Although essential for efficient business practices, the availability of computerized employee record files creates a security issue. Because protecting the employee's right to privacy is essential, organizations need to establish software and hardware security systems and set policies for accessing and updating electronic files containing personnel data and information (see chapters 5 and 8 for discussion on data security policies).

In addition to supporting operational work in the human resources department, a well-designed HRIS will produce reports for management planning and control (see exhibit 9.3). For example, HRIS management reports can be used to monitor turnover rates, unfilled positions, labor costs, employee productivity, and utilization of benefits. Attitudes of employees and physicians can be monitored through periodic satisfaction surveys. This survey information, used in conjunction with activity and utilization data, can be an important component of planning changes to benefits provided to employees.

Software applications are used to maintain records related to verifying physicians' and other licensed professionals' credentials and defining practice privileges in the organization, as well as for ongoing evaluation of clinical performance. Credentials and privileging systems are important for monitoring quality standards and for maintaining documentation required by accrediting and regulatory bodies. The task of verifying academic and training credentials and mitigating malpractice exposure is frequently outsourced to a certified credentials verification organization (CVO) such as Professional Credentials Verification Service (www.pcvs.net), which is accredited by the National Committee for Quality Assurance. As for all information system partners and collaborators, accreditation is an important criterion for selection.

Data transmitted by the CVO must be connected to relevant data from the organization's clinical and administrative systems to monitor clinician productivity and conformance to quality standards. Often, health systems must integrate external benchmarks and regulatory agency standards for comparison with actual performance data. Because of the sensitive nature of the data in this system and the specificity of facility accreditation requirements for this function, a stand-alone system often is used to achieve the

EXHIBIT 9.3 Human Resources Information System

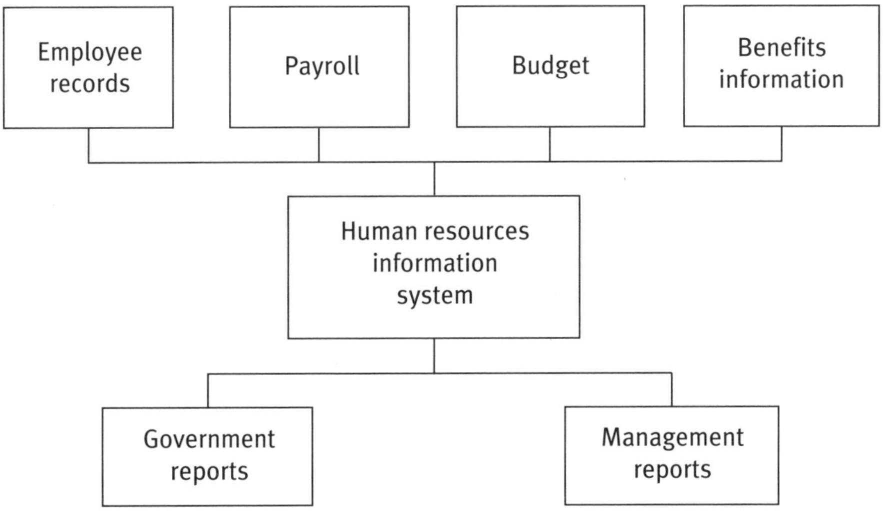

desired functionality and system security. Example applications include MD-Staff (www.mdstaff.com), a cloud-based network that includes background screening, credentialing, and provider management options.

Resource Utilization and Scheduling Systems

Under fixed-price and capitation payment systems, cost containment and efficient resource utilization are pivotal to success. External mandates for utilization review by regulatory agencies and insurance companies are more than balanced by internal drivers for ensuring that resource utilization is optimized. Managers must ensure that services are available when needed and that personnel and technology are efficiently allocated and scheduled. These efficiency needs are met through computerized monitoring and scheduling systems.

Information systems monitor inpatient occupancy rates, clinic and emergency department activity, and utilization of individual service facilities such as the operating suite or diagnostic units. Patient scheduling systems are used for advance booking and scheduling of facilities—both for patient and physician convenience and for efficient (and cost-effective) allocation of resources, particularly staffing. Comprehensive and timely data are essential to monitoring use of expensive diagnostic and treatment technologies in the effort to achieve optimal revenue returns on capital investments.

Advance booking of hospital beds and preadmission systems are particularly useful for situations in which most of the admissions are elective (e.g., a specialized surgical facility). Advance booking also provides time for necessary precertification for managed care patients and others covered by insurance plans that require review and certification of medical necessity for procedures and inpatient admission. Preadmission information systems can be linked to individual physicians' offices as well. Computer programs can project the average length of stay for each elective admission once historical data (including diagnosis, surgical procedure, age of patient, and gender of patient) have been accumulated. After admissions are scheduled and the data are entered into the supporting database, the system calculates projected occupancy levels for each day.

Admissions monitoring and scheduling systems improve staffing and workflow in healthcare organizations. These systems can reduce daily fluctuations in a hospital's census and improve the effectiveness of flexible staffing systems. Acute care general hospitals must maintain an accurate accounting of bed census and occupancy if they are to survive. Census information helps administrators compare projected income against projected budgets. Administrators can also track demands for specific services and adjust staffing levels and scheduling of facilities as demand patterns change.

Computer programs also are available for scheduling operating rooms in hospitals and ambulatory surgery centers. These systems are designed to improve operating room utilization, contain costs, facilitate planning, and aid in scheduling specific surgical procedures for optimal staff utilization. Outpatient clinic appointment and scheduling systems are common in organizations with a large volume of outpatient activity.

Resource utilization and scheduling systems may be designed for use at the department level or for a small entity such as a physician practice, but enterprise-wide scheduling systems that meet multiple objectives are becoming common. These robust integrated systems support fiscal objectives such as balanced schedules, optimal staffing, and management of resources across the enterprise. From a patient perspective, the ability to schedule multiple diagnostic procedures in one session, and perhaps schedule all procedures in a single day, contributes to satisfaction with the encounter experience.

The scheduling system can include modules that capture patient insurance and billing information during the registration process, which can be matched against stored contract data to produce appropriate charge records. Most systems produce automated appointment reminders in a variety of formats, including computer-generated telephone calls, emails, and text messages.

Scheduling systems can be linked with materials management systems to ensure that equipment and supplies are available for scheduled procedures, including initiating the process to transport the supplies to the treatment area. As items are removed from inventory, ordering and restocking procedures are triggered.

Supply Chain Management Systems

Computer systems are invaluable in effective management of supplies and materials, including data exchange with suppliers, automated purchase orders, inventory control, use of bar code devices for encoding supplies and materials, and computerized menu planning and food service management.

In a typical supply chain management system, requisitions for supplies and materials are electronically generated and matched against budgetary authorization for financial control. Reports of overdrafts on supply accounts are transmitted to the appropriate supervisor for follow-up action. Once requisitions are cleared, often using an automated workflow process for sequential authorizations, the system generates purchase orders. Purchase orders can be transmitted electronically to suppliers via established data-exchange protocols. As materials are received, bar coded products can be scanned and matched against an open order file. Automated purchasing systems may include direct linkage to an integrated accounts payable system, and automatic reordering of selected items as inventory is depleted (see exhibit 9.4). Supply chain applications reduce processing costs and obtain materials on a just-in-time basis to minimize the need to carry a large inventory, which avoids storage space costs and prevents losses resulting from expired items.

Detroit Medical Center divides its materials resource management department into several functional areas: linen services, clinical engineering, contract administration, logistics management, procurement, supplier diversity, and systems development (www.dmc.org/vendor). The department communicates with current and potential business associates via a website,

EXHIBIT 9.4 Supply Chain Management System

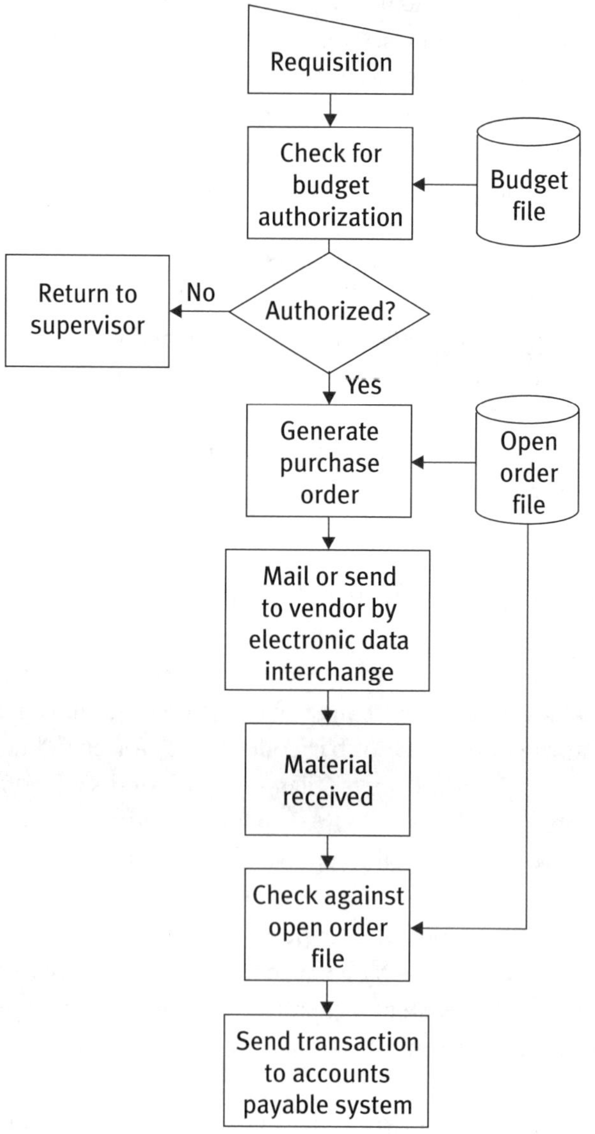

providing information about open requests for proposals, standard contracts and policies, and status on open purchase orders. Some areas of the website are open access, which may generate interest from potential vendors, but areas that store proprietary or contract-related information are protected with a secure login and are accessible only to current business partners.

Coding standards are an important element of automated purchasing and supply chain management systems. Bar codes for all types of medical supplies and pharmaceuticals have become standard and are essential to efficient purchaser–vendor relationships in healthcare.

Computerized menu-planning systems store and analyze data on patients' nutritional and dietary requirements, food items in inventory and their costs, and decision rules for selecting from among alternative menus (see Healing the Body by Stimulating the Appetite). Decision criteria might include patient preferences or visual appearance of food in addition to nutritional adequacy and cost.

Healing the Body by Stimulating the Appetite

UAB Hospital in Birmingham, Alabama, has implemented a novel alternative to routine menu plans for inpatients who want more choice in their meal selections. Patients can order "room service" for delivery to their rooms between 6:30 am and 7:00 pm. Meal choices include breakfast foods, soups, salads, hot and cold sandwiches, pizza, meat-based entrees, and desserts. For the adventurous, a seasonal meal planned by a renowned local restaurateur is available.

Patients with dietary restrictions are flagged in the information system to be automatically connected with a dietary representative who will address their meal requests appropriately. Online menus include designations to aid patients in selecting "heart healthy" foods or those allowed on a diabetic diet.

This meal option is supplemented by nutritional education available on the patient education television channel and with telephone access to a registered dietitian.

More information is available at www.uabmedicine.org/patient-and-visitor-guide.

Facilities and Project Management Systems

Computerized systems help organizations plan, manage, and maintain physical facilities. Examples include preventive maintenance systems, energy management systems, and project scheduling and control systems (particularly useful in new construction and remodeling projects).

Preventive maintenance systems help extend the life of equipment and facilities and reduce costly failures. Routine maintenance can help organizations achieve significant cost savings by preventing repair and replacement costs. Additional benefits accrue, including preventing nonproductive downtime, improving the safety of the workplace, and decreasing the risk of patient or employee injury as a result of equipment malfunction.

Energy conservation is an important cost-saving strategy for healthcare organizations, as it is in all major sectors. Computer applications assist in monitoring routine and peak energy use, providing guiding tactics for reducing consumption. Actual utilization figures can be compared against calculated requirements, and a computer model can be developed to find economies and efficiencies. The energy management system also can be employed to implement the selected tactics, such as automatically lowering or raising room temperatures in areas that are unused at night or on the weekend.

Healthcare organizations frequently are involved in capital construction and major remodeling projects, and computer systems are an extremely useful aid in project management. These project scheduling and control systems typically employ a combination of integrated tools to manage personnel and activity scheduling, labor and materials costs, required resources, and periodic progress reporting. As a key component, these tools are used to document (1) all activities required to complete the project; (2) the relationships of these activities to one another, including those that can be carried out simultaneously and those that must follow a time sequence; and (3) time estimates for completing each activity. These data are used to generate a diagram of activities that shows the critical path (longest time required) for project completion and any opportunities for concurrent or fast-tracked activities. As activities are completed, actual completion times can be entered back into the calculation, and more accurate schedules can be prepared for the remaining work. These systems are excellent tools for dynamic scheduling and control of major projects. More detailed coverage of project management related to HIT is provided in chapter 10.

Office Automation Systems

Office automation helps to coordinate and manage people and workflow, link organizational units and projects, and coordinate work in the organization across levels and functions. Healthcare organizations use a variety of computing tools to carry out general office functions, such as word processing, email, project management, meeting schedules, and personnel calendars for work-related activities. These functions may be conducted using desktop workstations; laptop computers; or a variety of handheld devices, including tablets or smartphones. Use of systems for integrated word and graphic processing, scheduling, electronic filing of documents, and message or document transmission can dramatically improve administrative efficiency and reduce the costs of office operations.

Office systems can link parts of the organization together by scheduling meetings via electronic calendars and emails or texts. Email systems link offices and individuals, allowing electronic files to be forwarded to others or to be archived in a shared storage area for access by members of a work group. Laptops and handheld devices, wireless technology, and the internet have changed the way people work alone or together. Work groups and teams can meet and collaborate from anywhere—in the same conference room or in geographically separated offices—with full access to necessary software programs and organizational files.

This work environment is supported by *groupware*—collaborative software that enables sharing of information via an interactive network (e.g., a virtual workspace). This software–hardware combination not only facilitates real-time interaction among members of the group to improve problem solving and project management but also supports independent work tasks. Audio- and videoconferencing allow real-time interaction among team members. Group members may work asynchronously on project activities while maintaining the integrity of a shared work product. When used effectively, and provided employees are trained to use the electronic tools, the virtual office can be as productive as the traditional office. Typical groupware activities include the following:

- Email and discussion forums
- Teleconferencing
- Interactive videoconferencing
- Relational databases
- Document editing and management, including archiving and version tracking
- Group calendars and scheduling

SharePoint, a Microsoft product, is one example of groupware; Google Apps is another. Many other collaborative software products are available and include both synchronous and asynchronous functionality. Usage may be limited to single functions, such as shared space for document collaboration (Google Docs, Box) or virtual meeting space (Skype, GoToMeeting), or broad-scale integrated products to support the needs of virtual teams, sometimes referred to as computer-supported cooperative work (Grudin 1994).

Information Systems for Nonhospital Healthcare Organizations

As changes to payment models in the 1980s led to changes in delivery models during the 1990s, nonhospital healthcare organizations began implementing information systems to manage clinical services and business operations. Vendors quickly began designing and marketing software products to meet the special information needs of these organizations. Organization types that fall under the nonhospital category include ambulatory clinics; long-term care (LTC) facilities; home health agencies; physician practices; and many others, including retail clinics. Software applications used in these settings typically include multiple modules that meet the organizations' needs for clinical documentation, operations management, and financial management. In the current healthcare environment, these organizations' ability to share information with hospitals, health systems, payers, and regulatory agencies is paramount.

Ambulatory Care Information Systems

Significant components of the healthcare continuum are delivered in outpatient and ambulatory care settings. Information systems that support ambulatory care and assist primary care providers in their practices have become a niche market. The availability of powerful and inexpensive microcomputers and practice management software packages has brought this technology within the reach of even small medical groups and solo practitioners. Meaningful use legislation and incentives to adopt electronic health record (EHR) technology have contributed to the current state, in which more than 70 percent of physicians have adopted certified EHRs (Heisey-Grove and Patel 2015). The EHR was discussed in more detail in chapter 8.

A typical practice management system (Slovensky et al. 2006) includes modules to support such business functions as the following:

- Operations management (e.g., scheduling, reminders, billing, authorizations)
- Services (email, groupware)
- Claims processing
- Document processing, spreadsheets, and databases
- Transcription
- Personnel management
- Inventory management
- Waste management
- Energy management

Clinical applications in medical practices and freestanding clinics include EHRs, prescription management, and disease management resources. Patient applications—an emerging software market—include electronic communication, monitoring, educational resources, and telehealth applications. Various vendor products offer full-service suites or selected modules based on the practice's needs.

Automating practice functions increases operational efficiency and reduces errors in information processing, both of which contribute to patient satisfaction and reduced risk and liability exposure. Automating or using web-based patient communication for services—such as callbacks, prescription renewals, and similar activities—can be helpful as well.

Office practice computers can be linked to local hospitals in addition to serving the management needs of the practice. Many hospitals or integrated delivery systems have developed computer linkages with physician offices to enable clinicians to preadmit patients; order diagnostic tests; and query the patient information system for lab results, progress notes, and other current clinical information. Healthcare organizations use such linkages as incentives to attract physicians to their facilities.

Long-Term Care Information Systems

The LTC sector was a late adopter in implementing computer systems, in part because software vendors were slow to develop products tailored to the needs of nursing homes and continuing care communities. This situation changed as the scope and volume of healthcare delivered in subacute care and post-acute care facilities increased. Typical requirements for LTC systems include census management, initial and periodic resident assessments, documentation of care services provided, documentation of physician orders, nutritional assessments and menu planning in the dietary department, and pharmacy applications.

The ability to communicate clinical information between caregivers and the admitting physician is especially important, as the physician usually is not physically present on a daily basis. Remote access to clinical documentation facilitates timely intervention in an acute episode and contributes to better health outcomes. As with other HIT applications, remote access can be achieved using various computing devices or telephone systems. System security and controlled system access are extremely important.

For LTC facilities that are components of larger integrated delivery systems, electronic sharing of clinical and administrative information with hospitals, clinics, ambulatory care facilities, and other system components is a business essential. Once again, data sharing among the enterprise units and IT strategic partners is a key driver in system design.

Home Health Care Information Systems

Home health care services have expanded rapidly in recent years as an alternative to more costly institutional care. As service volume has increased and the scope of services expanded, information systems have been developed specifically to meet the needs of home care provider organizations.

Many home health agencies use laptop computers and other remote access devices for on-site documentation of patient care and for access to treatment plans and records of previous encounters. Home health nurses and other caregivers enter information at the treatment sites and upload it to the centralized data repository. Relevant data can be accessed during a service visit by any provider. These systems reduce the amount of administrative work needed to document care, allowing nurses and home health aides to spend more time providing patients the care and services they need to achieve desired clinical outcomes.

Electronic devices also can transmit clinical information via telephone lines or the internet for the purpose of routine health monitoring between visits. Patients and family members follow the documented treatment plan, take and record measurements as indicated, and submit data for evaluation by the clinical personnel overseeing their care.

Other Information System Applications in Healthcare

Information systems support most processes in healthcare. While many applications can be categorized by their use for a defined function, many serve the needs of multiple providers and managers in disparate service areas. Clinical information may be combined with administrative information or used for an administrative purpose exclusively. Alternately, administrative information may be applied in the delivery of clinical care.

Websites and patient portals have become essential communication tools for engaging patients in their own care as well as for intrinsic marketing value. It is essential that websites contain current and accurate information and that navigation is intuitive and efficient.

Many healthcare organizations take advantage of the relative ease with which people access the internet via their smartphones to provide information to improve the total patient experience. (See Finding the Way for an example of one app that has helped a wide variety of users.)

Clinical Decision Support Systems

Clinical decision support systems (CDSSs) are designed to assist physicians and other providers in diagnosis and treatment planning. CDSSs fall into two categories: passive and active.

Finding the Way

The University of Alabama at Birmingham (UAB) campus covers more than 100 city blocks and includes dozens of healthcare delivery sites in addition to many academic and administrative buildings. Because UAB Hospital is a tertiary care facility, patients often travel significant distance for care and are unfamiliar with the campus. UAB Medicine Wayfinder is a Bluetooth-enabled app that can be accessed on a smartphone or a computer device. The free app, which has functionality similar to Google Maps, is available on Apple's App Store. In addition to maps and voice directions to clinics and diagnostic sites, the app also offers parking guidance, dining options, and other useful information. Additional information is available at www.uabmedicine.org/wayfinder.

Passive CDSSs use the computer to collect, organize, and communicate clinical data for interpretation and analysis by the physician. They make clinical information, including medical history, physical examinations, and diagnostic tests, more readily available and usable but do not process the information for further analysis. Clinical information systems—such as laboratory, pharmacy, radiology, and other clinical services applications—are examples of passive CDSSs in that they capture clinical data and make them available to caregivers. These applications become more useful to clinicians for decision support when they are fully integrated and can provide complete medical information (both current data and historical information on the patient) through simple, user-friendly access. For example, caregivers could view temperature, heart rate, and blood pressure readings over time to see patterns in relation to medication administration, physical activity, or food ingestion.

Active CDSSs provide direct assistance to the physician in diagnosis and treatment planning. They combine patient-specific data with generalized medical knowledge to reach a conclusion or make a recommendation to the caregiver. These systems may use a branching logic or rule-based structure, or a statistical probability algorithm, to suggest an appropriate diagnostic or treatment response to a clinical condition described by the physician. These systems incorporate validated clinical guidelines and treatment protocols that represent current best practices in clinical medicine.

The types of active CDSSs available include the following three:

1. *Expert systems* contain three major components—knowledge base, patient-specific information, and inference engine. A general knowledge base of medical information, obtained from a panel of experts in a given medical specialty, has been rigorously validated through scholarly

research, clinical practice, and consensus support from the medical community. This knowledge base is matched against patient-specific information retrieved from the healthcare organization's clinical database and may include subjective information as well as objective clinical findings. A rule-based inference engine generates conclusions for consideration by the physician. The system is dependent on the quality of the expert knowledge base and the "reasoning power" of the rules used by the inference engine.

2. *Probabilistic algorithms* employ statistical probabilities, which include a calculated element of randomness, rather than relying solely on knowledge collected from expert human beings. Expert knowledge is based on a combination of academic preparation and experiential learning, and variation may occur in either component of an expert's knowledge base. Extrapolations outside an expert's existing knowledge contribute to experiential learning. While a consensus viewpoint among experts incorporates nonquantifiable variability, a statistical probability allows the decision maker to control the degree of uncertainty tolerated in the system's output.
3. *Clinical reminders and alerts*, incorporated into clinical computer applications, suggest potential medical conditions or other problems that should be given attention in setting treatment plans. Examples include pharmacy information systems that alert the physician to potentially negative interactions between two drugs prescribed for the same patient as well as systems that suggest certain drugs or treatments should not be employed when specific lab results contraindicate their use. This function can also be used to suggest less expensive (but equally effective) alternatives when a high-cost drug has been ordered. Alternative drugs may also be suggested when the prescribed drug has significant risks for certain types of patients.

Computers can aid decision-making by simplifying access to data needed to make decisions, providing reminders and prompts, assisting in order entry, assisting in diagnosis, and reviewing new clinical data to issue alerts when important patterns are recognized. Systems are more likely to be successful when they give patient-specific suggestions, save time, and are incorporated into the regular workflow of the organization. Researchers at the University of Alabama at Birmingham (UAB) found that physicians using a decision-support rule accessed via a handheld device made better prescribing decisions than those who did not (Berner et al. 2006). The study, a randomized controlled trial, examined ordering practices for nonsteroidal anti-inflammatory drugs (NSAIDs). Physicians accessing the rule were more likely to order NSAIDs that were considered "safer" when considering gastrointestinal risk factors.

CDSSs that are well integrated with the enterprise EHR software offer great promise for personalized medicine (Bresnick 2016). Responding to variability among individual patients and applying the ever-increasing body of medical knowledge require information processing on a scale that cannot be achieved by human means. Well-designed systems can process large volumes of knowledge-based data filtered by personal clinical data and even by personal preferences for options among treatment modalities. Patients can be evaluated for risk factors for specific conditions, advised about prevention and early detection strategies, and assessed for probable effectiveness of various treatment options should the condition occur.

Executive Information Systems

The business corollary to CDSSs is the executive information system (EIS). Sometimes referred to collectively as *business intelligence*, EISs include systems designed to access and merge internal and external data into meaningful information reports. Executives identify critical environmental trends and facility performance indicators related to strategic objectives to guide their information capture and analysis. Data to support the EIS may be extracted from clinical and administrative databases serving the healthcare enterprise as well as from public and proprietary data repositories. The information needed from an EIS for decision support generally is not provided by standard reports. Users must be able to select the variables and data sources needed to answer specific questions, so ad hoc reporting capability is essential.

In many analysis scenarios, it is important to begin with general data aggregations and then reduce subsets of the data to increasingly greater detail, a process referred to as *drilling down*. The EIS must support this type of processing through an easily managed user interface. Chapter 11 provides a detailed discussion of the value, indeed, the necessity, of robust analytics capability to ensure the business intelligence and clinical evidence bases are sufficient.

Evidence-Based Medicine and Disease Management Systems

Evidence-based clinical practice guidelines, also referred to as *evidence-based medicine* (EBM), are intended to assist clinicians and healthcare organizations in standardizing decisions about the care of individual patients to achieve cost and quality benefits. Accumulated evidence from clinical research is used to formulate statements of the "right" things to do for patients with a given diagnosis or condition. Ideally, guidelines ensure that patients receive appropriate diagnostic tests and treatments in an efficient and cost-effective manner. Guidelines are assumed to lower treatment costs by avoiding unnecessary tests. Although managed care organizations and health insurers employ such guidelines to make decisions about treatment options, covered services, and other aspects of patient care, practice guidelines are not without significant limitations. Among these limitations are differences in local standards of care, access to recommended technologies, and unique patient characteristics.

While linkages to EBM resources are commonly incorporated in clinical systems for large inpatient facilities or integrated healthcare delivery systems, small clinics or medical practices may rely on independent access to EBM resources via the internet. In these types of primary care settings, the clinician typically is using some component of the office automation system—desktop computer, laptop, or handheld mobile device—for internet access. In this type of environment, convenience is an important factor in determining whether the clinician will seek external information. Research has shown that primary care providers who report using HIT resources as part of their patient encounter routines are likely to conform to evidence-based standards of care (Davis and Pavur 2011). An important caveat to this finding, however, is that providers who used small handheld devices as their primary computing tool did not have the same level of compliance with these standards. As noted in chapter 5, the size of the display screen relative to the output being displayed is an important system design characteristic. The small screens on handheld devices and the difficulty of entering precise input data using an ultracompact keyboard make them a poor choice for this purpose.

Disease management information systems and software products are designed to assist healthcare organizations in designing processes to provide quality care at the most reasonable cost possible. For the most part, they are disease specific and focus on high-volume, high-cost chronic conditions such as asthma, diabetes, and congestive heart failure. The typical approach is to involve patients in self-management of their condition and to create monitoring and feedback processes that encourage compliance with treatment plans. The information system may include capturing blood or urine test data, blood pressure readings, and other clinical information in the patient's home and transmitting it to the healthcare organization via mobile or remote monitoring devices. Communication between patients and providers may be via telephone or the internet. While routine patient monitoring assists in daily decision-making, analyzing aggregated data can guide case managers and physicians in modifying treatment plans for better long-term clinical outcomes.

Computer-Assisted Medical Instrumentation

Virtually every piece of medical equipment used for diagnostic testing and treatment now contains a microprocessor. The processors are used for instrument control, image enhancement, or processing medical data and interpreting the results of the testing or treatment process. Common examples include electrocardiograms, electroencephalograms, and pulmonary function testing. Computer systems interface directly with patient-monitoring devices for continuous surveillance of a patient's vital signs and periodic display of physiological data. These systems are particularly useful in critical care and postsurgical units.

The first step in the process is acquiring data from monitoring equipment attached to the patient and then converting that data for computer processing and display. Data are stored and made available for periodic display or display on demand. Computer programs enhance the measured data through structured analysis of clinical data in accordance with programmed decision rules. Trend data are followed to monitor changes in patient vital signs over time. Patient-monitoring systems can operate at the individual patient bedside, a central station designed to monitor a small number of intensive care beds, or a remote location linked back to the care unit by telecommunication equipment. For example, output from cardiac monitors may be monitored remotely by trained monitoring personnel, who in turn alert caregivers about aberrant readings. Many of these systems also have electronic linkages for transmission of clinical data to the EHR.

Coupling automated patient identification with electronic biomedical devices can produce significant efficiency gains in many routine tasks. UAB Hospital in Birmingham, Alabama, for example, found that using a bar code scanner to read codes on the patient's electronic monitor and armband, and transmitting recorded vital signs to the EHR, resulted in a 92 percent efficiency gain in recording vital signs and decreased the number of errors in documentation significantly (Hicks 2009).

Telemedicine and Telehealth

Telemedicine—now sometimes referred to as telehealth or e-health systems—is the application of computer and communications technologies to support healthcare provided to patients at locations remote from the provider. Telemedicine often involves telephone and online communication between a primary care physician, nurse practitioner, or physician's assistant who is treating patients in a rural area and specialty physicians located at a distant medical center. Audio communications and videoconferencing equipment are used in conjunction with computer access to patient records to establish primary diagnoses or provide expert consultation and second opinions. The systems may employ teleradiology for transmission of medical images for review by specialty physicians. Telemedicine systems can save patients travel time and costs as well as deliver healthcare cost savings to patients and providers.

Telemedicine applications have increased in recent years, resulting in part from the advent of mobile computing, which enabled the deployment of *mHealth*—health-focused applications accessible to the general public. These user-friendly and low-cost applications allow patients to monitor and report health indicators such as blood pressure or blood glucose easily and conveniently. A 2016 Congressional report estimated that "61 percent of healthcare institutions currently use some form of telehealth," including

40–50 percent of hospitals (Mack 2016). The most prevalent uses are remote patient monitoring, communication with patients, and providing counseling for patients with conditions related to cardiovascular disease, diabetes, behavioral health complications, rehabilitation, and respiratory disease (Totten 2016).

However, for traditional telemedicine applications such as specialist consultation or remote diagnostic procedures, many challenges related to reimbursement for remote services, patient privacy protection, and government regulations have been impediments (Thompson 2006). One longtime limiting factor, state licensure of health professionals when the system crosses state or national borders, is being mitigated through the Interstate Medical Licensure Compact Commission (Stewart 2017). Licensure boards in states that pass legislation to adopt the compact agree to share information with other boards to streamline the licensure process. Clinical outcome benefits achieved through various telemedicine applications vary, as do cost savings.

The types of articles published in the *Journal of Telemedicine and Telecare* over the past few years suggest that the number and variety of telemedicine applications continue to increase as technology innovations offer more opportunities. Research on patient satisfaction with telemedicine applications appears to be declining. As computer technology pervades business and social environments, individuals may be more accepting of telemedicine and mHealth applications. Although age is sometimes identified as a barrier to technology acceptance, one nine-month study showed that frail elderly subjects were able to use a web-portal telehealth service to reduce their use of facility-based healthcare (Finkelstein et al. 2011). Subjects needed minimal training to use the web portal, and their self-ratings showed improvement in technology acceptance over the course of the study.

Research involving a US Department of Veterans Affairs cohort showed that patients rated service access and educational components of telehealth programs positively, but they reported frustration with equipment problems and slow responses to requests for assistance (Young et al. 2011). Incorporating routine monitoring of these elements of a telehealth service is pivotal to the long-term success of the service.

The ability to meet data-sharing requirements for telemedicine encounters are emerging as key factors in the sustainability of e-health systems (Ganguly et al. 2009). Telemedicine providers need access not only to clinical data, such as that extracted from an EHR, but also to research findings and other knowledge-based information. Thus, the data exchange protocol must address both standard format data and free-text formats.

Computer Applications in Medical Research and Education

Information systems and medical databases are used extensively to support biomedical education and research. Computerized patient records serve as the basis for epidemiological studies of a variety of diseases and their potential linkages to social and environmental factors. In addition, computers are used to support medical, dental, nursing, and allied health education, using such techniques as computer-aided instruction and patient-management simulation.

Computers are an integral component of most medical research projects. Effective project design requires close collaboration among clinicians, biostatisticians, and information systems specialists. Some research projects would not be possible without the high-speed computational capabilities and data storage capacity of large computer systems. An excellent example is the Human Genome Project, which mapped all the genes of the *Homo sapiens* species. One element of the map detailed all sequences of DNA chemical bases—an astounding three billion pairs. Analytical work of this magnitude is inconceivable without supercomputing capabilities.

Hospitals, medical libraries, and individual clinicians use personal computers to access references to the medical literature and full-text online documents. The most widely used bibliographic databases are available through the National Library of Medicine (www.nlm.nih.gov). Articles from thousands of biomedical journals are indexed, stored in computer files, and available for search and retrieval using standard medical subject headings and keyword searches. The internet is used extensively to retrieve clinical information from a wide variety of specialty databases and sponsored websites.

Computers are an important tool for the education of clinicians. Computer-based education for physicians and other health professionals engages the students actively in the learning process and builds foundational skills in preparation for clinical training. Learning activities range from presentation of information to students via the internet or course management systems to sophisticated simulations of clinical problems. Students are presented initial cues and additional information on request as they proceed through a diagnostic process. Final diagnosis, patient management, and follow-up plans selected by the students are entered, and the system responds with a comparison to the "ideal" solution and critiques the process followed.

Increasingly, computerized mannequins are used to teach clinical skills in a lab environment before health professions students are assigned to healthcare organizations for clinical practice. These mannequins also can be used in continuing medical education as a tool for testing new technologies or exploring procedure innovations.

Summary

Most healthcare organizations began using electronic data processing by developing or purchasing financial information systems. Financial applications remain essential, but from a broader perspective, healthcare organizations use computers and information systems to support not only financial activities but also all administrative operations, including human resources management, resource utilization and scheduling, supply chain management, facilities and project management, and office automation.

As healthcare is delivered frequently in outpatient and nonhospital settings, development of information systems that support the needs of these delivery sites was pivotal to achieving data sharing required for seamless patient care. Typical functions for ambulatory settings include patient scheduling and appointments, electronic medical records and medical management, patient and third-party billing, managed care contract management, and electronic communication with other providers in a network of care. LTC systems support census management, residential care documentation, pharmacy, and other areas of operation in skilled nursing facilities. Home health providers use laptop computers or other remote-access devices to document care at the location where it is provided and to access clinical data from previous encounters. Integration or connectivity between the hospital-based enterprise and these other care sites is pivotal to managing patient information across the continuum of care.

Applications developed to assist physicians and other providers in the delivery of high-quality care include CDSSs and evidence-based medicine programs. These tools aid in diagnosis and treatment planning and comparing treatment plans with established "best practices" using large databases.

Computers have become an integral component of medical equipment for instrument control, image enhancement, and medical data processing. These foundation applications evolved into sophisticated integration of computer and communications technology in telemedicine applications that support patient care at remote locations.

Information systems are used extensively to support biomedical education and research. Automated databases of patient records support epidemiological studies of disease linkage to social and environmental factors. Computer-assisted instruction and patient-management simulation programs support the education of physicians and other health professionals.

Simply stated, no aspect of healthcare delivery or health services management is untouched by computers and information systems. The computer, in its various forms, has become a ubiquitous tool used by clinicians and managers alike. Technological evolution has produced powerful machines whose functions are optimized through the judicious selection of software to meet business and care delivery needs.

Because the healthcare sector became technology-centric through a "natural, inevitable and necessary evolution" (Bowman 2016), many clinicians developed their computing skills through a combination of self-learning and focused training as systems were implemented in their organizations. Thus, a great deal of variability exists among hospital staff with regard to skill levels with the dynamic digital technologies used to manage patient care and operational activities.

Web Resources

A number of organizations (through their websites) provide more information on the topics discussed in this chapter:

- HIMSS (www.himss.org) is a global, not-for-profit organization of approximately 70,000 members that is "focused on better health through information and technology." It provides networking and collaboration forums, sector reports and surveys, as well as education programming and technology resources.
- *Healthcare Informatics* (www.healthcare-informatics.com) is a magazine that provides information about vendors of IT products and information systems management services.
- Healthcare Financial Management Association (HFMA) (www.hfma.org) is a member organization for healthcare finance and business leaders.
- KLAS Enterprises (www.healthcomputing.com/VendorDirectory) offers information about vendors of software, services, and medical equipment.
- The American Academy of Professional Coders (www.aapc.com) is a "training and credentialing organization for the business of healthcare" with special focus on medical billing and coding and clinical documentation.

Discussion Questions

1. Why are administrative systems more evolved than clinical systems?
2. What features of handheld devices make them inappropriate for some medical computing applications?
3. What are the key components of groupware as a resource to the management team?

4. What aspects of clinical applications support quality management and cost-control programs?
5. Describe various functionalities of a pharmacy information system that can aid in reducing medication errors.
6. Distinguish between the logic used in an expert CDSS and systems that employ probabilistic algorithms.
7. What are some ways that HIT contributes to patient satisfaction?
8. Why has HIT development in some segments of the healthcare field, such as long-term care, lagged behind other segments?
9. What challenges do legacy systems pose for enterprise system integration?
10. How are transaction-processing systems employed in financial information systems?
11. What is the purpose of the chargemaster?
12. What are the key functions of a human resources information system?
13. How can centralized scheduling systems contribute to the financial bottom line?
14. List some of the key drivers and some of the challenges of employing telemedicine applications in a healthcare organization.
15. What are the typical elements of a physician practice management system?
16. Describe the basic documentation requirements for an LTC information system. How do these requirements differ from those for the information system used in an inpatient facility?

References

Berner, E. S., T. K. Houston, M. N. Ray, J. J. Allison, G. R. Heudebert, W. W. Chatham, J. I. Kennedy, G. L. Glandon, P. A. Norton, M. A. Crawford, and R. D. Maisiak. 2006. "Improving Ambulatory Prescribing Safety with a Handheld Decision Support System: A Randomized Controlled Trial." *Journal of the American Medical Informatics Association* 13 (2): 171–79.

Bowman, D. 2016. "UPMC's Andrew Watson: Telemedicine a Natural Evolution of Care." *Fierce Healthcare*. Published September 30. www.fiercehealthcare.com/it/upmc-s-andrew-watson-telemedicine-a-natural-evolution-care.

Bresnick, J. 2016. "Precision Medicine, Data Exchange, CDS on New ONC Leader's Agenda." Health IT Analytics. Published August 16. https://healthitanalytics.com/news/precision-medicine-data-exchange-cds-on-new-onc-leaders-agenda.

Davis, M. A., and R. J. Pavur. 2011. "The Relationship Between Office System Tools and Evidence-Based Care in Primary Care Physician Practice." *Health Services Management Research* 24 (3): 107–13.

Dorenfest Institute. 2013. *Annual Report of the U. S. Hospital IT Market.* HIMSS and HIMSS Analytics. Accessed February 20. https://apps.himss.org/cdn/foundation/docs/2013HIMSSAnnualReportDorenfest.pdf.

Finkelstein, S. M., S. M. Speedie, X. Zhou, S. Potthoff, and E. R. Ratner. 2011. "Perception, Satisfaction, and Utilization of the VALUE Home Telehealth Service." *Journal of Telemedicine and Telecare* 17 (6): 288–92.

Ganguly, S., P. Kataria, R. Juric, A. Ertas, and M. M. Tanik. 2009. "Sharing Information and Data Across Heterogeneous E-Health Systems." *Telemedicine and e-Health* 15 (5): 454–64.

Gilchrist, J., M. Frize, E. Bariciak, and D. Townsend. 2008. "Integration of New Technology in a Legacy System for Collecting Medical Data—Challenges and Lessons Learned." *Engineering in Medicine and Biology Society, Conference Proceedings Annual International Conference of the IEEE* 2008: 4,326–69.

Grudin, J. 1994. "Computer-Supported Cooperative Work: History and Focus." *Computer* 27 (5): 19–26.

Heisey-Grove, D., and V. Patel. 2015. "Any, Certified, Basic: Quantifying Physician EHR Adoption Through 2014." Office of the National Coordinator for Health Information Technology. Published September. https://dashboard.healthit.gov/evaluations/data-briefs/quantifying-physician-ehr-adoption.php.

Hicken, V. N., S. N. Thornton, and R. A. Rocha. 2004. "Integration Challenges of Clinical Information Systems Developed Without a Shared Data Dictionary." *Studies in Health Technology and Informatics* 107 (Part 2): 1053–57.

Hicks, J. 2009. "Highlighting Devices." *Modern Healthcare* 39 (26): C8.

Healthcare Information and Management Systems Society (HIMSS). 2019. "Healthcare Trends Forecast: The Beginnings of a Consumer-Driven Reformation." Accessed February 20. www.himss.org/sites/hde/files/d7/u397813/2019_HIMSS PreviewandPredictions.pdf.

Kraatz, A. S., C. M. Lyons, and J. Thompkinson. 2010. "Strategy and Governance for Successful Implementation of an Enterprise-wide Ambulatory EMR." *Journal of Healthcare Information Management* 24 (2): 34–40.

Mack, H. 2016. "HHS Report Outlines Problems, Potential of Telemedicine." MobiHealthNews. Published August 22. http://mobihealthnews.com/content/hhs-report-outlines-problems-potential-telemedicine.

Oracle.com. 2020. "What Is ERP?" Accessed February 20. www.oracle.com/applications/erp/what-is-erp.html.

Slovensky, D. J., J. M. Trimm, R. L. Garrie, and P. E. Paustian. 2006. *Information Management.* Medical Practice Management Body of Knowledge Review 6. Englewood, CO: Medical Group Management Association.

Stewart, M. 2017. "Practicing Telemedicine Across State Borders: New Expedited Licenses Permit Physicians to Expand Practice." University of Arizona. Published May 11. https://telemedicine.arizona.edu/blog/practicing-telemedicine-across-state-borders-new-expedited-licenses-permit-physicians-expand.

Thompson, J. N. 2006. "The Future of Medical Licensure in the United States." *Academic Medicine* 91 (12): S36–39.

Young, I. B., L. Foster, A. Ailander, and B. J. Wakefield. 2011. "Home Telehealth: Patient Satisfaction, Program Functions, and Challenges for the Care Coordinator." *Journal of Gerontological Nursing* 37 (11): 38–46.

PART

III

STRATEGIC COMPETITIVE ADVANTAGE

CHAPTER

10

HEALTH INFORMATION TECHNOLOGY PROJECT PORTFOLIO MANAGEMENT

Learning Objectives

1. Identify some of the primary causes of health information technology (HIT) project failures.
2. Describe the main differences between HIT project management, HIT program management, and HIT portfolio management.
3. Describe the five key processes of project management.
4. Understand how project metrics and portfolio dashboards can facilitate HIT governance.
5. Describe the major roles and functions of the portfolio management office.
6. Identify the actions and changes that are necessary in an organization to reach the synchronized stage.

Overview

Healthcare in the United States now consumes more than 17 percent of the country's gross domestic product and is projected to grow to more than 19 percent by 2027 (Centers for Medicare & Medicaid Services 2020), yet US residents generally do not live longer nor are they healthier than those in other developed nations that spend less than half that amount on healthcare (Papanicolas, Woskie, and Jha 2018). The reality of these statistics, along with the Institute of Medicine's 1999 report (*To Err Is Human*) on preventable deaths in the United States, has energized federal and state governments in ways that will continue to put pressure on healthcare organizations. For example, plans for reduced reimbursement rates will counteract the increasing pressure for a healthy bottom line. Clearly, just by their sheer size—seven-, eight-, or even nine-figure expenditures—electronic health record (EHR) projects (depending on the size of the organization) should automatically create a heightened need for due diligence among healthcare executives; nothing can get an executive fired faster than spending $50 million with nothing to show for that investment.

In their presentation titled "IT Disasters: The Worst IT Debacles and the Lessons Learned from Them" at the American College of Healthcare Executives Congress on Healthcare Leadership, Hunter and Ciotti (2006) provided ample evidence that risks are associated with large-scale health information technology (HIT) projects. While inadequate planning and foresight are problematic in such projects, the single greatest cause of project failure is poor execution (Abouzahra 2011; Hunter and Ciotti 2006). Furthermore, historical studies have suggested that HIT systems may have caused, rather than reduced, medical errors (Han et al. 2005; Koppel et al. 2005) and more recently may contribute to physician fatigue and burnout (Downing, Bates, and Longhurst 2018; Shanafelt et al. 2015). However, a careful reading of these academic articles shows the obvious system design and implementation problems indicating that medical errors are caused by human error, caregiver fatigue and burnout, and workflow process design, and not the HIT itself.

In 2010, studies revealed that 65 percent of HIT projects failed to achieve anticipated benefits (Standish Group 2011). Organizations that fell into the category of the 65 percent who failed to achieve benefits often relied on the collective experience of the individuals who have previously implemented HIT at the organization but typically did not employ disciplined project management methodologies, such as those suggested by the Project Management Institute (www.pmi.org; discussed in more detail later in this chapter). As more and more organizations employ disciplined project management practices, those metrics have started to turn around. A recent Project Management Institute (PMI 2017b) survey of more than 3,200 project management professionals found that only about 31 percent of HIT projects did not meet their goals, while 43 percent still exceeded initial budget estimates, and 49 percent were completed late (see exhibit 10.1).

EXHIBIT 10.1
IT Project Success Statistics

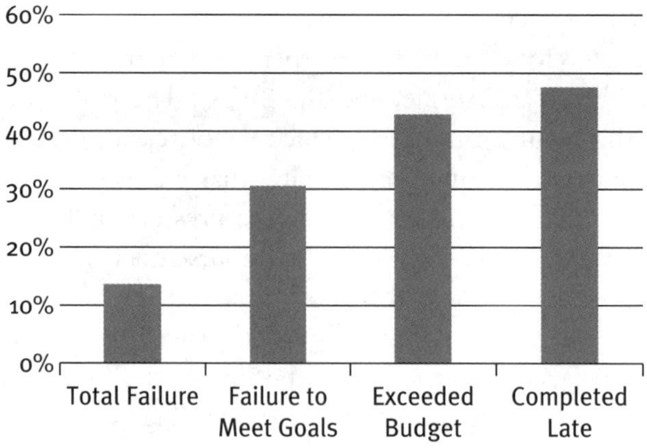

Source: Data from PMI (2017b).

Healthcare delivery is a complex business with incredibly multifaceted, interdependent workflows, yet the field as a whole has been inexplicably slow to adopt professional project management approaches. Organizations that fall into this category typically implement a go-live only to find that large stakeholder groups or key workflows have been overlooked. These organizations must then scramble, after implementation, to reengineer processes that easily could have been proactively addressed had the organization followed disciplined project management methodologies. This chapter provides an overview of HIT project management and encourages healthcare organizations to improve their project success rate by establishing an HIT project portfolio management office.

What Is a Health Information Technology Project Portfolio Management Office?

The following terms and their definitions are used in this chapter to clarify concepts related to portfolio management:

- A *project* is a temporary effort to create a unique product, service, or result (PMI 2017a).
- *Project management* is the application of knowledge, skills, tools, and techniques to project activities in an effort to meet project requirements (PMI 2020).
- A *program* is a group of related, often interdependent projects.
- A *portfolio* is a collection of programs and projects.
- *Portfolio management* encompasses managing the collections of programs and projects in a portfolio. This responsibility includes weighing the value of each project, or potential project, against desired organizational strategic business and clinical objectives. It also encompasses monitoring active projects to ensure adherence to specified objectives and desired outcomes, balancing the portfolio with other investments of the organization, using resources efficiently, and balancing return on investment with risk (PMI 2017a).
- A *portfolio management office* (PMO) is a centralized organization dedicated to improving the practice and outcomes of projects via holistic management of all projects.

While definitions can help distinguish concepts, often the terms *project management office*, *program management office*, *portfolio management office*, and *project portfolio management office* are used interchangeably in the business press. All imply the professional management and oversight of an organization's entire collection of current projects. PMO, however, specifically refers to the activity of providing investment decision support capabilities to an organization's overall HIT governance structure and processes. The term *project management office* or *program management office* does not necessarily mean that decision support capabilities for these investments are in place. Organizations that use the term *PMO* or *project portfolio management office* are intentionally and accurately referring to a more expansive concept, reflecting the methodology's HIT portfolio investment decision support capabilities (Jeffery and Leliveld 2004). In short, effective PMOs are (1) aligned with and serve an organization's strategic governance and investment decision-making processes and (2) practice disciplined project management in the successful execution of the organization's projects. To be consistent, we use the term PMO throughout this chapter. Exhibit 10.2 illustrates how projects, and programs of projects, might interrelate in a typical HIT portfolio.

Individual projects, such as a new inpatient EHR or a new pharmacy system, are grouped into a clinical applications program. Ideally, clinical application projects are led or championed by an influential stakeholder from the clinical leadership of an organization. Likewise, upgrades of an existing financial budgeting system and implementation of a new human resource system are grouped into a business applications program. Business application projects are ideally led or championed by an influential business stakeholder. Purely infrastructure–type projects, such as a network upgrade or implementation of wireless technology, are grouped into an HIT infrastructure program

EXHIBIT 10.2
HIT Portfolio

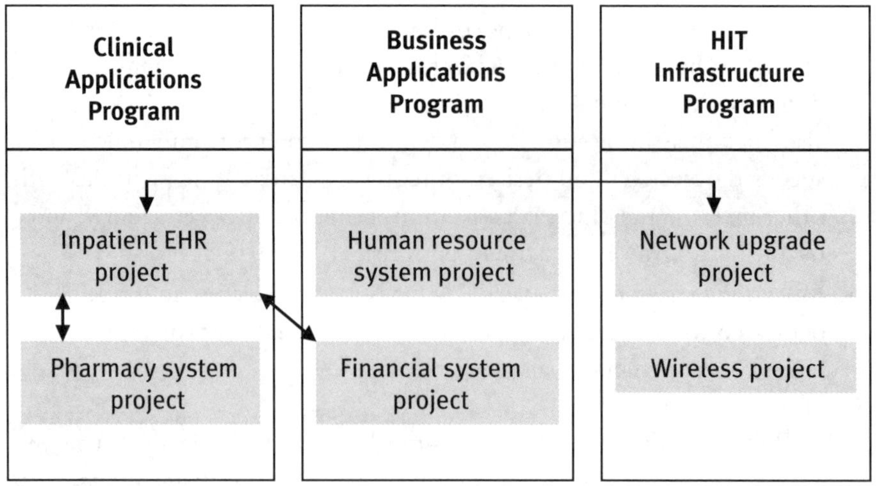

Note: EHR = electronic health record, HIT = health information technology.

championed or led by the chief information officer (CIO) or one of the CIO's key directors. All of the projects in all program groupings then make up the entire HIT portfolio that can be professionally managed via formal HIT portfolio management structures and practices—an HIT PMO.

Why Is a Portfolio Management Office Essential?

As indicated earlier in exhibit 10.1, there continues to be room for improvement with respect to projects meeting intended goals, remaining on budget and on time (PMI 2017b). One of the primary causes of failed HIT projects is a "silo" project management mentality, which occurs when projects are initiated, planned, and fully executed without an effective consideration of their impact on other, preexisting systems or other parallel projects being planned and executed. As indicated in exhibit 10.2, contemporary healthcare applications have significant interdependencies that, if not explicitly and deliberately addressed, can have unintended consequences. Exhibit 10.3 provides real-world examples of unintended consequences of HIT projects that were planned and executed in relative isolation.

While the examples described in exhibit 10.3 may seem to be obvious, common-sense mistakes, they are not uncommon because in reality healthcare delivery organizations have thousands of cross-departmental interrelated workflows that must be considered when embarking on a new HIT project. Exhibit 10.4 depicts sample high-level application interfaces that are in place at a typical academic medical center that is representative of any medium-to-large integrated delivery system. This graphic conveys an incredibly complex web that relies heavily on interfacing applications wherever possible. The sheer volume of interdependencies shown in this exhibit clearly makes a case that individual projects or programs of applications should not be managed in silos but rather in a professional PMO focused on successfully achieving envisioned benefits of particular projects.

In many ways, allowing informal, silo-based project management to occur in a healthcare organization is somewhat like attempting to minimize collisions at an airport without the benefit of a flight control tower. Not incidentally, exhibit 10.4 resembles a typical major airline hub city with flights coming and going from all points on the compass, yet it depicts a real organization's current applications and how each is interfaced and interrelated. This level of interrelatedness strongly suggests the need for a professional control tower to manage HIT projects. An organization's ability to implement large HIT projects successfully and efficiently increases as its project management maturity moves from no professionally managed projects to simple project management to program management and ultimately to portfolio management (PMI 2018).

EXHIBIT 10.3
Examples of HIT Projects That Did Not Follow an HIT Portfolio Management Approach

IT Project	Project Outcome
New Pharmacy System	
The pharmacy director sponsored a new best-of-breed pharmacy system project	The pharmacy system project was expertly managed and implemented on time and within budget. Unfortunately, only after the system was implemented did the pharmacist realize that this new proprietary best-of-breed system could not be reliably interfaced with the hospital's preexisting EHR system, which had built-in computerized physician order entry capability. As such, when a provider entered an order for a pharmaceutical into the EHR, that order had to be printed out in the pharmacy and then reentered into the new pharmacy system. From a pure project management standpoint, the project was successful. From an enterprise portfolio standpoint, however, a very inefficient, labor-intensive workflow was created to overcome the lack of integration that this silo-based project management approach created.
Voice Over Internet Protocol (VOIP) Project:	
A telecommunications director sponsored a switch to digital phone service	The telecommunications director of a large metropolitan hospital system wanted to save millions of dollars annually by switching from a basic traditional phone service model to a VOIP model, whereby the hospital system's existing computer network would be used to provide digital phone service. Unfortunately, the project did not consider the robustness of the existing computer network, which had single points of failure in many of its buildings. The digital phone service was implemented, and soon thereafter, any network outage to one of the buildings affected all phone service for the building. More than an inconvenience, these outages eroded consumer trust and market appeal. Using contingency funds, the hospital system scrambled to redesign its computer network to provide the level of redundancy and reliability needed to ensure digital phone service. Had a portfolio management approach been taken for this project, computer network inadequacies could have been identified up front and computer network upgrades could have been built into the project plan.

Typically, as an organization's HIT project management matures, its overall cost of HIT projects decreases significantly and the success rate of these projects increases substantially. A nonintuitive overall time savings occurs as well, although one would suspect that it would take more time to accomplish the additional work of identifying and tracking interdependencies with other projects across the portfolio of projects. However, this additional

EXHIBIT 10.4
Example of Typical Hospital Application Interfaces

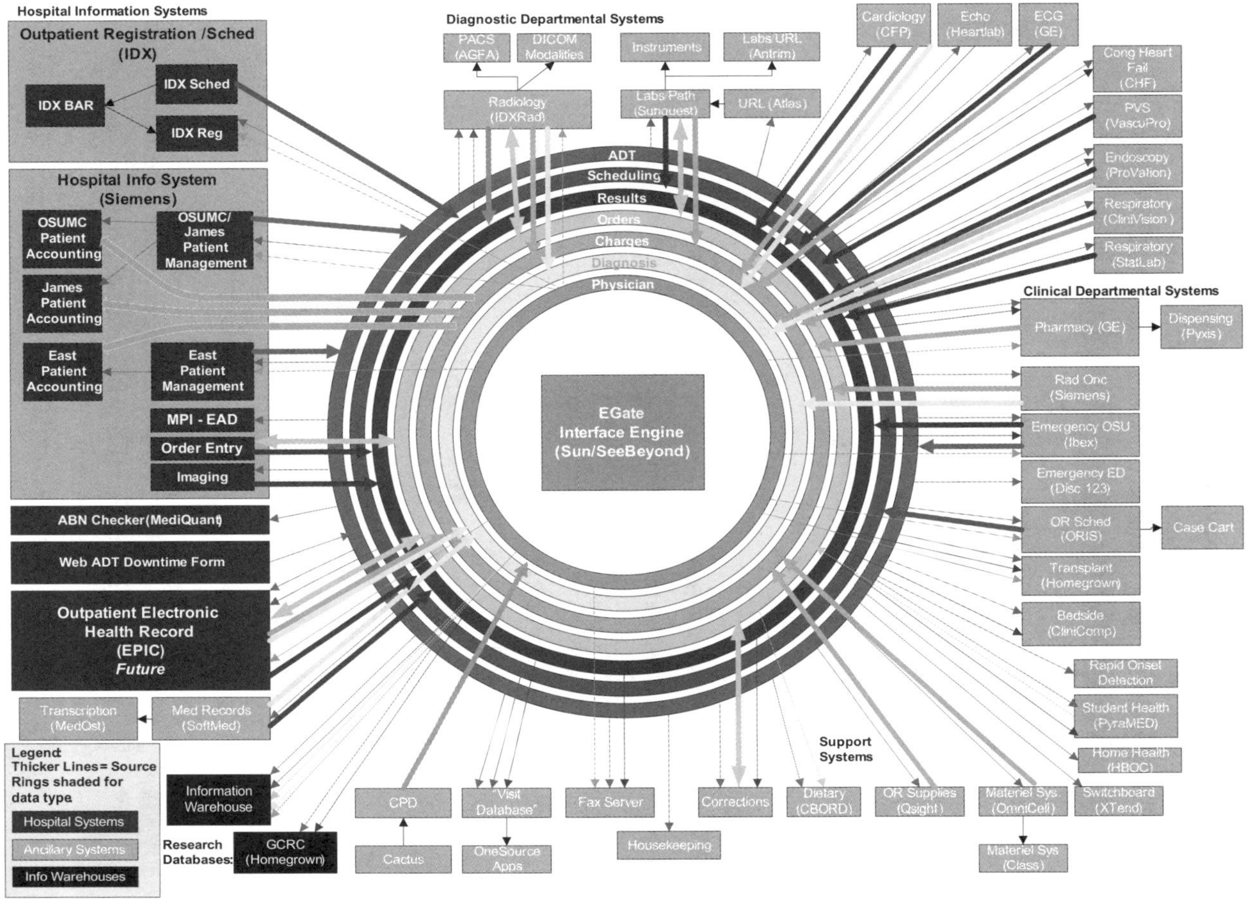

planning time, which is marginal, actually reduces the number of surprises and "gotchas" that occur later when unforeseen interdependencies invariably crop up in projects that are run in a more informal, silo approach, thus decreasing overall project time (Alexander 2015; Hadjinicolaou and Dumrak 2017). One of the main causes of time delays in projects is *scope creep*—when the original agreed-on requirements for a system are continually expanded by the project sponsors. With project management methodologies in place, added or new requirements are collected and saved for a future version of the system so that the original system scope can be implemented in the established time frames.

The next section addresses project management methodologies. Thereafter, managing the collection of projects is discussed, and we reiterate the suggestion that a PMO is a logical organizational response to the increasing HIT complexity in healthcare organizations.

Project Management

Project management entails the following five processes (PMI 2017a):

1. *Project initiation:* launch of a process that can result in the authorization of a new project
2. *Project planning:* definition of the objectives, scope, and plan of action to achieve the desired outcomes
3. *Project execution:* actions to complete the work defined in the project planning process
4. *Project monitoring and controlling:* measurements designed to assess how well a project is being executed per the budget and deliverables as well as to alert project managers to potential corrective actions that might be necessary from time to time
5. *Project closing:* actions to terminate formally all activities associated with the project either by delivering a finished product or by ceasing effort on a canceled project

Professionalizing project management at a healthcare delivery organization means that each HIT project should follow these five key processes. While project management frameworks are important, hiring professionally trained and well-credentialed project managers is equally important. A number of project management credentialing organizations exist, including the PMI, which offers the Project Management Professional (PMP) certification. The PMP certification ensures that an individual has mastered a requisite body of knowledge on project management (see exhibit 10.5 for a list of applicable knowledge areas) and has at least 60 months of project management experience. Furthermore, survey data suggest that increasing the number of individuals in the organization who have professional project management skills and experience and following an explicit HIT project management process framework raise the likelihood that the project will be a success (PMI 2017a); see exhibit 10.6.

EXHIBIT 10.5 Project Management Knowledge Areas

Project Management Knowledge Area	Individuals Must Know How To
Project integration management	Develop project charter Develop project management plan Direct and manage project execution Manage project knowledge Monitor and control project work Perform integrated change control Close project or phase
Project scope management	Plan scope management Collect requirements Define scope Create work breakdown structure Verify scope Control scope
Project schedule management	Plan schedule management Define activities Sequence activities Estimate activity resources Estimate activity durations Develop schedule Control schedule
Project cost management	Plan cost management Estimate costs Determine budget Control costs
Project quality management	Plan quality management Manage quality Control quality
Project resource management	Plan resource management Estimate activity resources Acquire resources Develop team Manage team Control resources
Project communications management	Plan communications management Manage communications Monitor communications

(continued)

EXHIBIT 10.5
Project Management Knowledge Areas (*continued*)

Project Management Knowledge Area	Individuals Must Know How To
Project risk management	Plan risk management Identify risks Perform qualitative analysis Perform quantitative analysis Plan risk responses Implement risk responses Monitor risks
Project procurement management	Plan procurements Conduct procurements Control procurements
Project stakeholders management	Identify stakeholders Plan stakeholder engagement Management stakeholder engagement Monitor stakeholder engagement

Source: Information from PMI (2017a).

Project Management Tools

A number of project management applications are available that provide the automated support to manage projects more professionally. While not intended to be an exhaustive list, the following are applications that Henderson, Stang, and Shoen (2019) rate highly for being able to provide automation to support the five project management processes outlined earlier;

EXHIBIT 10.6
Benefits of HIT PMO

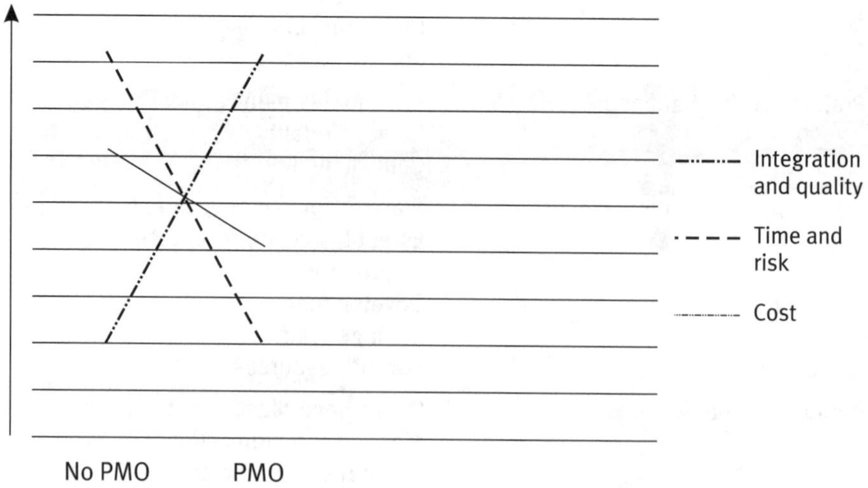

Note: PMO = portfolio management office.

many of these applications also carry the higher-level program and portfolio management capabilities discussed later in this chapter:

- Broadcom: Clarity PPM
- Changepoint: Daptiv PPM and Changepoint
- Microsoft: Project Server, Project Online, Project, Planner, and Teams
- Planview: Enterprise One, PPM Pro, Projectplace, LeanKit, and Spigit
- Planisware: Enterprise and Orchestra

Standardizing HIT operations on a set of project and portfolio management tools provides a common way to establish the processes and business rules that an organization must follow for managing projects. For instance, a healthcare organization's applications group uses one tool (say, Microsoft Project software), the infrastructure group uses a different tool (say, Broadcom's Clarity PPM), and the informatics and analytics group uses no tool at all. Because there is no visibility into the total number of projects going on among these groups, it becomes incredibly difficult to establish standardization of project management processes that is a prerequisite for managing interdependencies between projects; thus, it is difficult to achieve program or portfolio management capabilities.

Entire textbooks have been written on project management (e.g., Coplan and Masuda 2011; Schwalbe 2016) and the tools that support it. For illustrative purposes, we discuss project plans and Gantt charts as examples of key artifacts that are easily developed in most project management and portfolio management tools.

Project Plans and Gantt Charts

All project management applications should have the ability to create a project plan and display it in a way that easily shows task interdependencies. Exhibit 10.7 shows a simple example of a Gantt chart for some tasks in an infrastructure project of a hospital system. This list of tasks is known as a *work breakdown structure* in project management parlance. Note how the interdependencies are clearly visible by the linking arrows that show which tasks must be fully completed before their successor tasks can begin. Other tasks without these interdependencies can be accomplished in parallel (i.e., they have no interdependencies but must nevertheless be accomplished to complete the project). Project management applications have the ability to collapse these tasks—these are all of the tasks that have predecessor (tasks that must be completed before the next tasks can be started) or successor (tasks that cannot begin until certain tasks have been completed) interdependencies—into the critical path of a project (see exhibit 10.8). The reason critical path analysis is important is that it provides a forecast of the shortest possible time in which the overall project can be completed.

EXHIBIT 10.7
Project Plan in Gantt Chart Format

Tasks

Plan and schedule your project's tasks by clicking an item below. Clicking an item displays tools and instructions for completing that step.

Define the project
Define general working times
List the tasks in the project
Organize tasks into phases
Schedule tasks
Link to or attach more task information
Add columns of custom information
Set deadlines and constrain tasks
Identify risks to the project
Add documents to the project
Publish project information to the Web

After planning your tasks, you can go to the Resources area to build your project's team and assign people to tasks.

Gantt Chart

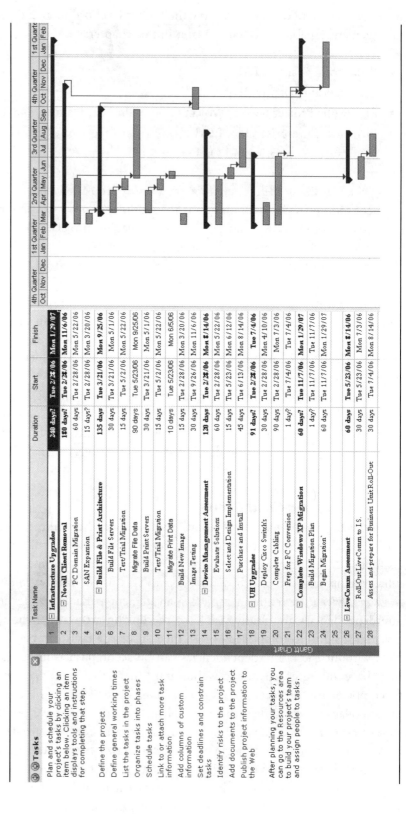

	Task Name	Duration	Start	Finish
1	**Infrastructure Upgrades**	**240 days?**	**Tue 2/28/06**	**Mon 1/29/07**
2	**Novell Client Removal**	**180 days?**	**Tue 2/28/06**	**Mon 11/6/06**
3	PC Domain Migration	60 days	Tue 2/28/06	Mon 5/22/06
4	SAN Expansion	15 days?	Tue 2/28/06	Mon 3/20/06
5	**Build File & Print Architecture**	**135 days**	**Tue 3/21/06**	**Mon 9/25/06**
6	Build File Servers	30 days	Tue 3/21/06	Mon 5/1/06
7	Test/Trial Migration	15 days	Tue 5/2/06	Mon 5/22/06
8	Migrate File Data	90 days	Tue 5/23/06	Mon 9/25/06
9	Build Print Servers	30 days	Tue 3/21/06	Mon 5/1/06
10	Test/Trial Migration	15 days	Tue 5/2/06	Mon 5/22/06
11	Migrate Print Data	10 days	Tue 5/23/06	Mon 6/5/06
12	Build New Image	15 days	Tue 2/28/06	Mon 3/20/06
13	Image Testing	30 days	Tue 9/26/06	Mon 11/6/06
14	**Device Management Assessment**	**120 days**	**Tue 2/28/06**	**Mon 8/14/06**
15	Evaluate Solutions	60 days	Tue 2/28/06	Mon 5/22/06
16	Select and Design Implementation	15 days	Tue 5/23/06	Mon 6/12/06
17	Purchase and Install	45 days	Tue 6/13/06	Mon 8/14/06
18	**UH Upgrades**	**91 days?**	**Tue 2/28/06**	**Tue 7/4/06**
19	Deploy Cisco Switch's	30 days	Tue 2/28/06	Mon 4/10/06
20	Complete Cabling	90 days	Tue 2/28/06	Mon 7/3/06
21	Prep for PC Conversion	1 day?	Tue 7/4/06	Tue 7/4/06
22	**Complete Windows XP Migration**	**60 days?**	**Tue 11/7/06**	**Mon 1/29/07**
23	Build Migration Plan	1 day?	Tue 11/7/06	Tue 11/7/06
24	Begin Migration`	60 days	Tue 11/7/06	Mon 1/29/07
25				
26	**LiveComm Assessment**	**60 days**	**Tue 5/23/06**	**Mon 8/14/06**
27	Roll-Out LiveComm to I.S.	30 days	Tue 5/23/06	Mon 7/3/06
28	Assess and prepare for Business Unit Roll-Out	30 days	Tue 7/4/06	Mon 8/14/06

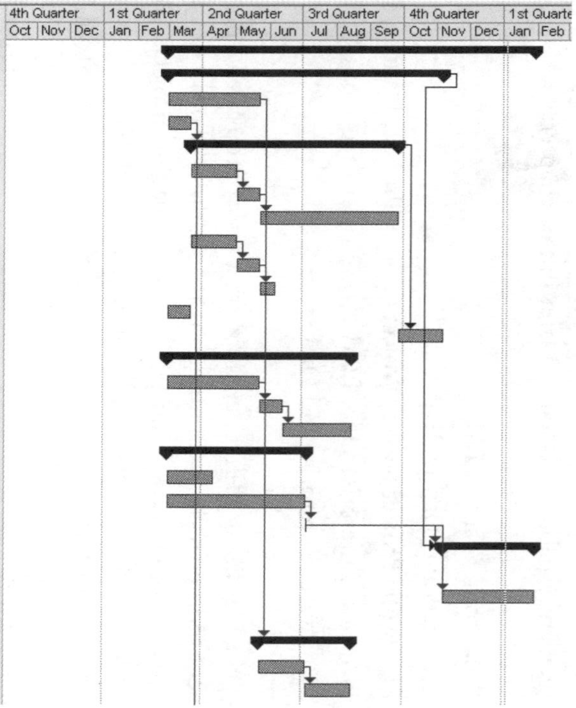

EXHIBIT 10.8
Collapsed Project Plan Gantt Chart Showing Only the Critical Path

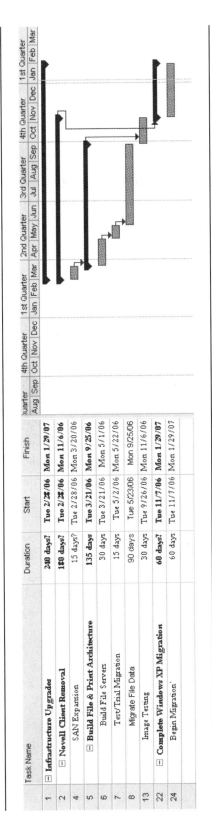

	Task Name	Duration	Start	Finish
1	⊟ **Infrastructure Upgrades**	**240 days?**	**Tue 2/28/06**	**Mon 1/29/07**
2	⊟ **Novell Client Removal**	**180 days?**	**Tue 2/28/06**	**Mon 11/6/06**
4	SAN Expansion	15 days?	Tue 2/28/06	Mon 3/20/06
5	⊟ **Build File & Print Architecture**	**135 days**	**Tue 3/21/06**	**Mon 9/25/06**
6	Build File Servers	30 days	Tue 3/21/06	Mon 5/1/06
7	Test/Trial Migration	15 days	Tue 5/2/06	Mon 5/22/06
8	Migrate File Data	90 days	Tue 5/23/06	Mon 9/25/06
13	Image Testing	30 days	Tue 9/26/06	Mon 11/6/06
22	⊟ **Complete Windows XP Migration**	**60 days?**	**Tue 11/7/06**	**Mon 1/29/07**
24	Begin Migration`	60 days	Tue 11/7/06	Mon 1/29/07

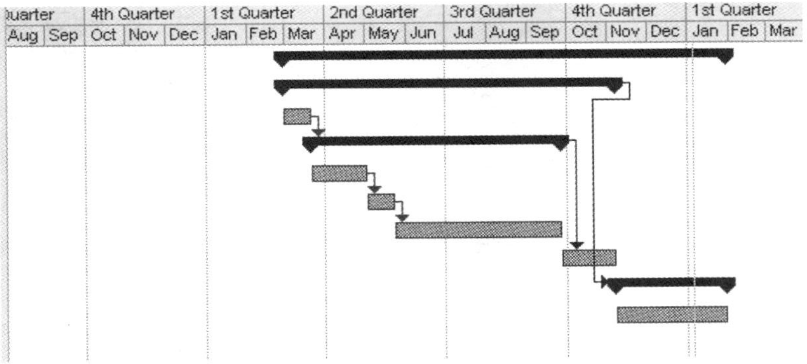

Program Management

As noted earlier, organizations that put in place program management capabilities have moved beyond managing individual projects to managing the interrelationships between projects and preexisting applications and systems. While managing this level of complexity takes slightly longer to plan up front, the extra time expended is recovered during the execution phase of the project in the form of reduced surprises and cost overruns associated with unforeseen interdependencies. In essence, the critical dependency analysis and management depicted in exhibits 10.7 and 10.8 are simply extended beyond a single project to interdependencies that exist within a particular program of projects or even across the HIT portfolio (see exhibit 10.2).

Portfolio Management

Along with the professional project management expertise described in the previous sections, organizations that employ a portfolio management approach also have tightly coupled HIT governance (essentially, making decisions about which information technology to invest in and which not to invest in) with its PMO. In other words, think of project and program management as ensuring that things are done right in a particular project, whereas portfolio management concerns itself with doing the right kinds of projects that align with the organization's overall strategic goals and objectives. This distinction is why a PMO must work hand-in-hand with an organization's HIT governance structure (covered in chapter 4). Illustrating this point is exhibit 10.9, which shows an HIT portfolio of all the projects that are "in flight" at a for-profit healthcare organization. Prior to its annual HIT capital budget process, the particular organization, using the knowledge gained from professionally managing its portfolio of current HIT projects, put together a profile of all of the current HIT projects already in flight and rated them on the basis of value and risk. The organization further labeled each quadrant. The lower left quadrant, which represents low-value and high-risk HIT projects, is labeled "Think Twice (or More)." The upper right quadrant represents HIT projects that are deemed to both be of high value and have low risk associated with implementation; this quadrant is labeled "Ideal." The size of the bubbles in exhibit 10.9 denotes the size in relative dollars of each individual project. Projects are categorized into nondiscretionary projects (e.g., some projects are mandated by law, such as the Sarbanes-Oxley Act) and discretionary projects. Much like an investor reviewing a portfolio of stocks before deciding which to divest and which to add to, an organization developing a graphic such as exhibit 10.9 gains a powerful and succinct decision-support means to evaluate proposed HIT projects.

In addition to decision support, an HIT portfolio management capability also provides regular portfolio status reports to the HIT governance of an organization. For instance, an HIT portfolio dashboard is typically created—sometimes via one of the project and portfolio management applications and

EXHIBIT 10.9
Illustrative HIT Portfolio

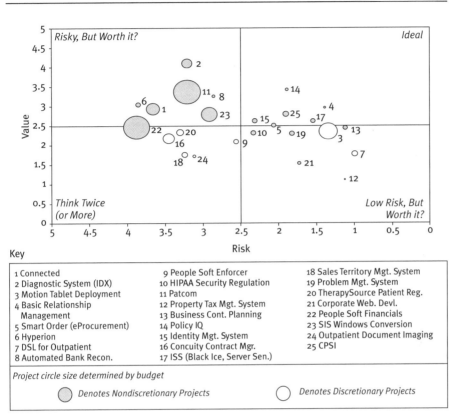

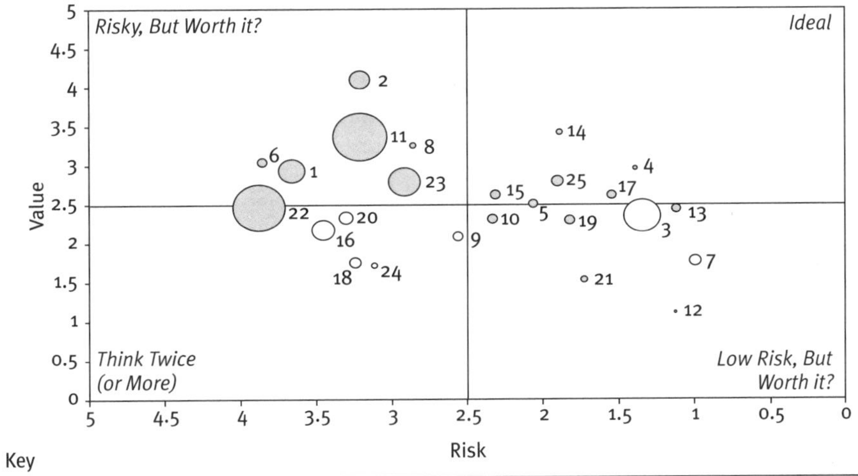

Key

1 Connected
2 Diagnostic System (IDX)
3 Motion Tablet Deployment
4 Basic Relationship Management
5 Smart Order (eProcurement)
6 Hyperion
7 DSL for Outpatient
8 Automated Bank Recon.
9 People Soft Enforcer
10 HIPAA Security Regulation
11 Patcom
12 Property Tax Mgt. System
13 Business Cont. Planning
14 Policy IQ
15 Identity Mgt. System
16 Concuity Contract Mgr.
17 ISS (Black Ice, Server Sen.)
18 Sales Territory Mgt. System
19 Problem Mgt. System
20 TherapySource Patient Reg.
21 Corporate Web. Devl.
22 People Soft Financials
23 SIS Windows Conversion
24 Outpatient Document Imaging
25 CPSI

Project circle size determined by budget

Denotes Nondiscretionary Projects (shaded circle)

Denotes Discretionary Projects (open circle)

Source: Carpenter (2005). Used with permission.

sometimes via an organization's overall quality or other enterprise dashboard tools—to give leadership a view of project progress. Exhibit 10.10 is a sample of one such view, showing all in-flight projects of the organization (listed in exhibit 10.9) grouped by strategic categories that are important to the organization, along with the dollar amounts budgeted for each category. The graph on the left of this exhibit, titled "Portfolio by Category," depicts the monthly expenditures of each project category. The graph on the right of this exhibit, titled "Resource by Category," depicts the amount of full-time equivalent resources being expended on each project category.

While an HIT portfolio dashboard can be set up to provide status along any number of dimensions, its greatest impact comes in providing strategic views of the myriad projects the organization is working on to benefit HIT governance decision-making. In the examples provided in exhibits 10.9 and 10.10, this for-profit healthcare organization is trying to balance strategically the need for greater regulatory compliance with the Sarbanes-Oxley Act and other legislation with the need for revenue growth. Therefore, the dashboard is designed to quickly provide a view within the past three quarters and the

EXHIBIT 10.10
Sample HIT Portfolio Dashboard

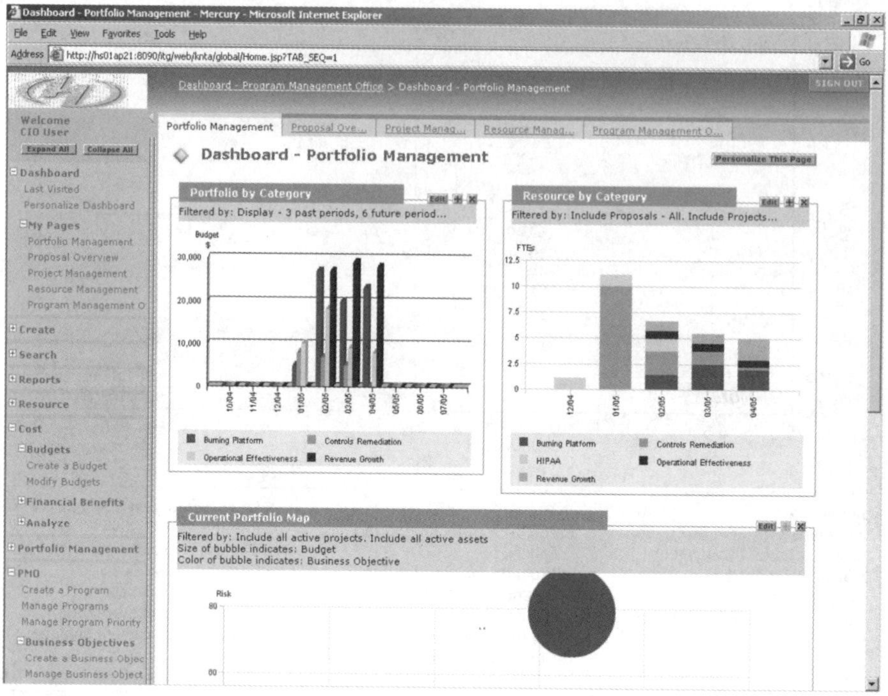

Source: Carpenter (2005). Used with permission.

next six quarters of the amount of money being (or slated to be) invested in compliance-related projects, operational effectiveness projects, and projects the organization hopes will generate increased revenue. While this example is illustrative—not intended to be definitive—this example makes the point that organizations must be able to produce flexible data representations (such as exhibit 10.9) on the entire portfolio of HIT projects to aid their HIT governance bodies. Such data are essential to making informed investment decisions and monitoring progress.

The Portfolio Management Office

Generally, these high-functioning portfolio management capabilities are being formalized in many leading healthcare organizations via the establishment of an HIT PMO. Typically, the functions of a PMO include but are not limited to the following:

- Issuing regular communications to project stakeholders and the rest of the organization regarding progress or status, programs of projects, and the entire portfolio

- Providing authoritative management and oversight of all projects in the portfolio
- Serving as staff support to the HIT governance of the organization, including performing portfolio analyses as requested by HIT governance and recommending HIT investments
- Creating metrics and dashboards to facilitate transparency

These tasks can be accomplished without putting in place a formal PMO, but there is some evidence to suggest that organizations that institute a PMO may have a competitive advantage over those that do not (Caliste 2013). Do note that establishing a PMO is not a quick fix to whatever project management challenge the organization is facing, and it is an effort that likely will take between two and four years to generate significant benefits for the organization. Jeffery and Leliveld (2004), from data derived in their study of 130 *Fortune* 1,000 companies, created the useful IT Portfolio Management Maturity Model, which outlines the four stages of maturity of any organization's portfolio management capabilities. Jeffery and Leliveld refer to these four stages as ***ad hoc***, ***defined***, ***managed***, and ***synchronized***; each stage indicates a higher, more capable PMO function.

In the ad hoc stage, no formal project management capability is in place at all. Projects are managed informally and inconsistently, and project results are equally inconsistent.

In the defined stage, the organization has created a centralized entity to maintain and inventory projects and to manage them centrally. In this stage, applications and infrastructure are well defined and documented.

In the managed stage, the organization has created processes for vetting and rationalizing or ranking projects on the basis of key strategic criteria. Furthermore, investment decisions employ financial metrics to help prioritize projects (e.g., return on investment, return on assets, net present value) and conduct at least annual reviews with business unit leadership on how well the HIT portfolio is aligned with overall organizational strategies.

In the synchronized stage, organizations conduct much more frequent evaluations of the HIT portfolio with business unit leaders and include a consistent assessment of returns versus risks in their project portfolios. Typically, organizations at the synchronized level of HIT portfolio management maturity have created PMO scorecards or dashboards that serve to communicate project status and value transparently. They also consistently conduct post-project benefits realization assessments to see whether benefits envisioned prior to the project's adoption have been achieved.

Since Jeffery and Leliveld (2004) articulated this maturity model, there has been considerable debate in the project management community about the best framework to use for assessing an organization's maturity

(Pasian, Sankaran, and Boydell 2011; PMI 2017a; Zhang, He, and Zhang 2012). Each framework suggests more complex and granular approaches for assessing an organization's project management capabilities. While the debate continues, Jeffery and Leliveld's model continues to provide HIT leaders and professionals with a simple, quick way of assessing the maturity of their organization's HIT portfolio management capabilities.

Summary

This chapter made the case that many HIT projects generally do not achieve the benefits envisioned and that implementing professional portfolio management capabilities is an important first step toward mitigating this project risk. Furthermore, identifying and managing the cross-project interdependencies that a portfolio management approach embodies is an important second step toward mitigating project risk. Finally, implementing an HIT PMO that is tightly coupled with an organization's HIT governance structures and processes and that provides the full complement of capabilities outlined in Jeffery and Leliveld's (2004) IT Portfolio Management Maturity Model represents the greatest return on HIT investments for a healthcare organization.

Web Resources

A number of organizations (through their websites) provide more information on the topics discussed in this chapter:

- Vendors that provide project and portfolio management software include the following:
  - CA Technologies: Broadcom, Clarity Project, and Portfolio Management software (www.ca.com/us/services-support/ca-services/project-portfolio-management-services.html)
  - Changepoint: PPM software (www.changepoint.com)
  - Planview: Project Portfolio Management (www.planview.com/products-solutions/solutions/project-portfolio-management)
  - Microsoft: project software (https://products.office.com/en-us/project/project-and-portfolio-management-software)
- Other website references for project and portfolio management include these:
  - *CIO* magazine, Project Management section (www.cio.com/topic/3198/Project_Management)

- Healthcare Information and Management Systems Society, Project Management Special Interest Group (www.himss.org/project-management)
- The Project Management Institute conference paper on PMOs in healthcare IT organizations (www.pmi.org/learning/library/project-management-office-healthcare-information-technology-8060)

Discussion Questions

1. Discuss some of the primary reasons an HIT implementation project might fail in a healthcare organization.
2. What are the main differences between HIT project management, HIT program management, and HIT portfolio management?
3. What are the five processes of project management?
4. What requirements should be considered when selecting project management tools for an organization?
5. Why are project metrics and portfolio dashboards important to HIT governance?
6. List and describe the major roles and functions of the PMO.
7. Which two project management knowledge areas described in exhibit 10.5 do you consider to be the most important? Why?
8. What actions and changes are necessary in an organization to reach the synchronized stage of maturity of Jeffery and Leliveld's IT Portfolio Management Maturity Model?
9. Even with the development of a PMO, will there be instances in which an HIT venture fails? Explain your rationale.

References

Abouzahra, M. 2011. "Causes of Failure in Healthcare IT Projects." International Conference on Advanced Management Science. Accessed March 11, 2020. https://pdfs.semanticscholar.org/d9f2/fb98c62b4dbd69510d7dffa016de722a6631.pdf.

Alexander, M. 2015. "Planning Is Key to Project Management Success." *CIO*. Published June 10. www.cio.com/article/2932987/planning-is-key-to-project-management-success.html.

Caliste, A. 2013. "The PMO, Maturity, and Competitive Advantage." Paper presented at the PMI Global Congress 2013—North America, New Orleans, LA, October 29, 2013. www.pmi.org/learning/library/project-office-management-competitive-advantage-5843.

Carpenter, R. 2005. "IT Governance." Guest lecture, University of Alabama at Birmingham, Birmingham, AL, January 8.

Centers for Medicare & Medicaid Services. 2020. "National Health Expenditure Projections 2018–2027." Accessed January 15. www.cms.gov/Research-Statistics-Data-and-Systems/Statistics-Trends-and-Reports/NationalHealthExpendData/Downloads/ForecastSummary.pdf.

Coplan, S., and D. Masuda. 2011. *Project Management for Healthcare Information Technology.* New York: McGraw-Hill Company.

Downing, N. L., D. W. Bates, and C. A. Longhurst. 2018. "Physician Burnout in the Electronic Health Record Era: Are We Ignoring the Real Cause?" *Annals of Internal Medicine.* Published July 3. https://annals.org/aim/article-abstract/2680726/physician-burnout-electronic-health-record-era-we-ignoring-real-cause.

Hadjinicolaou, N., and J. Dumrak. 2017. "Investigating Association of Benefits and Barriers in Project Portfolio Management to Project Success." *Procedia Engineering* 182: 274–81.

Han, Y. Y., J. A. Carcillo, S. T. Venkataraman, R. S. Clark, R. S. Watson, T. C. Nguyen, H. Bayir, and R. A. Orr. 2005. "Unexpected Increased Mortality After Implementation of a Commercially Sold Computerized Physician Order Entry System." *Pediatrics* 116 (6): 1506–12.

Henderson, A., D. Stang, and M. Schoen. 2019. "Magic Quadrant for Project and Portfolio Management." Gartner. Published May 21. www.gartner.com/en/documents/3917095/magic-quadrant-for-project-and-portfolio-management.

Hunter, D. P., and V. Ciotti. 2006. "IT Disasters: The Worst Debacles and Lessons Learned from Them." *Healthcare Executive* 21 (5): 8–12.

Institute of Medicine. 1999. *To Err Is Human: Building a Safer Health System.* Washington, DC: National Academies Press.

Jeffery, M., and I. Leliveld. 2004. "Best Practices in IT Portfolio Management." *Sloan Management Review* 45 (3): 41–49.

Koppel, R., J. P. Metlay, A. Cohen, B. Abaluck, A. R. Localio, S. E. Kimmel, and B. L. Strom. 2005. "Role of Computerized Physician Order Entry Systems in Facilitating Medication Errors." *Journal of the American Medical Association* 293 (10): 1197–203.

Papanicolas, I., L. Woskie, and A. Jha. 2018. "Health Care Spending in the United States and Other High-Income Countries." *Journal of the American Medical Association* 319 (10): 1024–39.

Pasian, B., S. Sankaran, and S. Boydell. 2011. "Factors for Designing a Second Generation of Project Management Maturity Models. Paper presented at PMI Global Congress 2011—North America, Dallas, TX, October 22. www.pmi.org/learning/library/second-generation-project-management-maturity-models-6241.

Project Management Institute (PMI). 2020. "What Is Project Management?" Accessed January 14. www.pmi.org/about/learn-about-pmi/what-is-project-management.

———. 2018. *PMI's Pulse of the Profession: 10th Global Project Management Survey.* Accessed January 15, 2020. www.pmi.org/-/media/pmi/documents/public/pdf/learning/thought-leadership/pulse/pulse-of-the-profession-2018.pdf.

———. 2017a. *A Guide to the Project Management Body of Knowledge (PMBOK Guide),* 6th ed. Newtown Square, PA: Project Management Institute.

———. 2017b. *PMI's Pulse of the Profession: 9th Global Project Management Survey.* Accessed January 15, 2020. www.pmi.org/-/media/pmi/documents/public/pdf/learning/thought-leadership/pulse/pulse-of-the-profession-2017.pdf.

Schwalbe, K. 2016. *Information Technology Project Management,* 8th ed. Boston: Cengage Learning.

Shanafelt, T., O. Hasan, L. Dyrbye, P. Sinsky, D. Satele, J. Sloan, and C. West. 2015. "Changes in Burnout and Satisfaction with Work-Life Balance in Physicians and the General US Working Population Between 2011 and 2014." *Mayo Clinic Proceedings* 90 (12): 1600–13.

Standish Group. 2011. *CHAOS Manifesto.* Boston: Standish Group.

Zhang, L., J. He, and X. Zhang. 2012. "The Project Management Maturity Model and Application Based on PRINCE2." *Procedia Engineering* 29: 3691–97.

CHAPTER

11

ANALYTICS

Learning Objectives

1. Describe the difference between traditional analytics and big data analytics.
2. Articulate analytics capabilities that characterize more advanced or mature analytics organizations.
3. Describe different ways that a healthcare organization can establish and structure an enterprise analytics function.
4. Articulate staffing considerations when establishing an enterprise analytics function.
5. Describe typical governance requirements of an enterprise analytics function.

Overview

While there are many technical definitions for the practice of analytics, we provide a more expansive definition that encompasses both the technical practice and the healthcare organizational operationalization of the practice of analytics.

Technical definitions of analytics include the following three (Dictionary.com 2020):

> 1. . . . the science of logical analysis.
> 2. . . . the analysis of data, typically large sets of business data, by the use of mathematics, statistics, and computer software . . .
> 3. . . . the patterns and other meaningful information gathered from the analysis of data.

In an organizational context, such as a healthcare payer or provider organization, analytics are the processes, people, and technology that leverage data to glean information and insights to make sound business, operational, and clinical decisions.

There are generally two useful ways to categorize the practice of analytics in a healthcare organization, outlined in exhibit 11.1.

Historically, traditional and big data analytics often have been deployed separately in isolation from each other. For instance, in many academic medical centers (AMCs), the health system part of the organization

EXHIBIT 11.1 Analytics in a Healthcare Organization

Type of Analytic Capability	Description
Traditional analytics (business intelligence)	• Basic report generation to monitor an organization's clinical and business performance across the entire spectrum of service lines and departments • Generally descriptive and retrospective in nature • More advanced types of traditional analytics often referred to as business intelligence (BI); allows users to reformulate data visualizations quickly (e.g., providing a "drill-down" capability for a specific performance measure that first presents the data at an overall organizational level, then quickly allows a user to drill down to ever-more-specific levels of the organization, such as a specific departmental level or even to individual providers in a particular department) • Typically leverages structured data from various healthcare applications or structured data that were extracted from applications and placed in a data repository (e.g., data mart, enterprise data warehouse) • Leverages analysts adept at writing reports, spreadsheet manipulation, and data visualization
Big data analytics	• An all-encompassing term for any collection of data sets so large and complex that they become difficult to process using traditional data management tools or traditional data processing applications (Press 2014) • Typically leverages advanced parallel processing computing infrastructures • Typically characterized by large (volume), dynamic (velocity), complex, unstructured (variety) data sets that do not lend themselves to traditional enterprise data warehousing technologies and techniques • Leverages data scientists, statisticians, and mathematicians adept at scientifically gleaning meaning from complex data sets

has been leveraging traditional analytics in an effort to continuously improve the performance of the health system. They employ traditional data warehousing approaches—extracting, transforming and loading data from source applications into hierarchical data warehouses—and then build reporting and other data visualizations such as performance dashboards and scorecards. Often the academic and research mission areas of the AMC have focused on big data analytics, leveraging an entirely different set of technologies such as Hadoop and NoSQL (or nonstructured query language) that are not only better able to deal with large, often unstructured data sets but are also able to leverage effectively the parallel processing servers needed to analyze those data sets.

Davenport (2013) suggests that organizations must begin to leverage both of these categories of analytics to gain even more insight and performance improvement. For instance, researchers at an AMC that have been using big data sets may be able to gain even more insight by securely and appropriately linking their big data analytics to traditional data warehouses in the health system component of the organization (albeit via data deidentification protocols to remain compliant with privacy laws). Equally beneficial, the health system can partner with its academic mission area to leverage big data approaches, gaining even more insight into particularly difficult and complex business and clinical operational performance challenges.

While other information-intensive sectors such as financial services or insurance have long leveraged analytics to optimize their business performance, healthcare has lagged in adopting analytics. In a recent study conducted by HIMSS Analytics, Eddy (2019) reports that among 110 senior healthcare leaders surveyed, about a third of those organizations have not yet deployed analytics but plan to do so. Furthermore, only 28 percent of respondents said they were using analytics for effectiveness of care projects, only 22 percent were using analytics for population health, and only 11 percent were deploying analytics for chronic care management (which should be key focus areas for all health systems). Other studies have found similar low analytics adoption and maturity among healthcare organizations (Ginsburg et al. 2018; Landi 2018).

The HIMSS Analytics Adoption Model for Analytics Maturity (HIMSS-AMAM) is a useful framework for further refining analytic capabilities and assessing an organization's level of maturity with respect to analytics adoption.

The HIMSS Analytics Adoption Model for Analytics Maturity

In the early days of electronic health record (EHR) deployment and adoption, HIMSS Analytics was instrumental in pioneering its EMR Adoption Model, which has continued to evolve (see chapter 8). Likewise, HIMSS

EXHIBIT 11.2
HIMSS Analytics Adoption Model for Analytics Maturity

Stage	Cumulative Capabilities
7	Personalized medicine & prescriptive analytics
6	Clinical risk intervention & predictive analytics
5	Enhancing quality of care, population health, and understanding the economics of care
4	Measuring and managing evidence based care, care variability, and waste reduction
3	Efficient, consistent internal and external report production and agility
2	Core data warehouse workout: centralized database with an analytics competency center
1	Foundation building; data aggregation and initial data governance
0	Fragmented point solutions

Source: HIMSS Analytics (2020).

Analytics has championed a similar adoption and maturity model for analytics in healthcare organizations (see exhibit 11.2).

Stage 0

All organizations start their analytics journey at stage 0, with a desire to learn about developing analytics capabilities in response to business demands, market pressures, and the need to develop further insights into the important decisions they make every day.

Stage 1

Organizations are just beginning to accumulate and manage data in centralized locations such as an operational data store or data warehouse supporting historical reference and consolidated access. The main focus of stage 1 is to document and begin execution of an analytics strategy that brings basic data together from appropriate systems of record and then to learn to manage (data governance) and define data so that they can be used and referenced by a broad cross section of analysts.

Stage 2

Data are presented in a formal data warehouse as an enterprise resource (as opposed to a silo-oriented and narrowly used resource) with master data management (MDM) that supports ad hoc queries and descriptive reporting. The enterprise begins advancing data governance while leveraging this environment in support of basic clinical and operational tasks, such as patient registries. All activities should be aligned with the organization's overall strategic goals. Analytic skills, standards, and education are managed through an analytics competency center.

Stage 3

A mastery of descriptive reporting is in place broadly across the enterprise. Varying and different parts of the organization are able to corral data effectively, work with it, and produce historical and current period reporting with minimal effort. Data quality is stable and predictable, tools are standardized and broadly available, and data warehouse access is managed and reliable.

Stage 4

The organization directs analytical data assets, skills, and infrastructure squarely toward improving clinical, financial, and operational program areas, which includes a concerted effort to understand and optimize data by honing analytics resources that support evidence-based care, track and report care and operational variability, and identify and minimize clinical and operational waste.

Stage 5

Organizations show expanded point-of-care-oriented analytics and support of population health. Data governance is aligned to support quality-based performance reporting and bring further understanding of the economics of care.

Stage 6

Stage 6 pushes the organization to mature in the use of predictive analytics and expands the focus on advanced data content and clinical support.

Stage 7

This stage represents the pinnacle of applying analytics to support patient-specific prescriptive care. Healthcare organizations can leverage advanced data sets, such as genomic and biometric data, to support the uniquely tailored and specific prescriptive healthcare treatments of personalized medicine. Organizations can deliver mass customization of care combined with prescriptive analytics.

A number of the capabilities identified in the HIMSS Analytics AMAM, such as MDM and data governance or predictive and prescriptive analytics, will be further articulated later in this chapter. Although at first review of the AMAM, big data appears to be missing, it is actually an essential capability necessary for predictive and prescriptive analytics. As such, it is consistent with thought leadership in the field suggesting that traditional analytics (stages 0–5) should leverage big data analytics (stages 6–7) in order to achieve the highest levels of analytics maturity and organizational performance.

Just as the HIMSS Analytics EMR Adoption Model evolved over time, HIMSS Analytics expects to continue to improve the HIMSS Analytics AMAM. See Web Resources at the end of this chapter for more information.

Building an Analytics Capability in Healthcare Organizations

In the course of researching analytics in the context of both for-profit and not-for-profit companies, Davenport and colleagues (2010) found five basic organizational structuring arrangements, depicted in exhibit 11.3.

In the centralized, consulting, and functional models, a single analytics team provides most of the analytic services to the rest of the organization. The decentralized model, as its name implies, has no corporate oversight or coordination. The center-of-excellence model is a more federated system, according to which each data-consuming functional department has its own analyst group. However, these analysts also belong, in a dotted-line fashion (i.e., in an indirect reporting relationship), to a corporate center of excellence that creates a community of practice and can also double as a program office to help coordinate cross-functional projects. The advantages and disadvantages of each structuring model are presented in exhibit 11.4.

Davenport and his colleagues suggest that "the ideal model ensures that your scarce and valuable analysts (1) are tasked with the most important analytical projects, (2) bring an enterprise perspective to bear, and (3) have ample opportunities for development and job satisfaction. We think the centralized and center of excellence models . . . offer the greatest potential benefit for organizations ready to take an enterprise approach to analytics" (Davenport et al. 2010). It is important to note that Davenport and his colleagues' work ranges across many industries. Unfortunately, healthcare appears to be particularly immature with respect to managing data as a strategic asset. As was the case in Davenport and his colleagues' research, the predominant organizational structure that the authors of this book have found is also the decentralized model. Managers in health systems who believe that their level of data mastery is weak should consider whether a federated, center-of-excellence approach will work as a first step or whether a more centralized model initially needs to be put in place to force change on autonomous business units that may balk at some of the changes that enterprise data management and governance will dictate. Thereafter, perhaps, the health system can evolve to the more federated center-of-excellence model.

Gartner, an information technology (IT) industry research group, advocates that organizations that want to develop more robust enterprise analytics capabilities should consider starting a business intelligence competency

EXHIBIT 11.3
Five Basic Organizational Structuring Arrangements

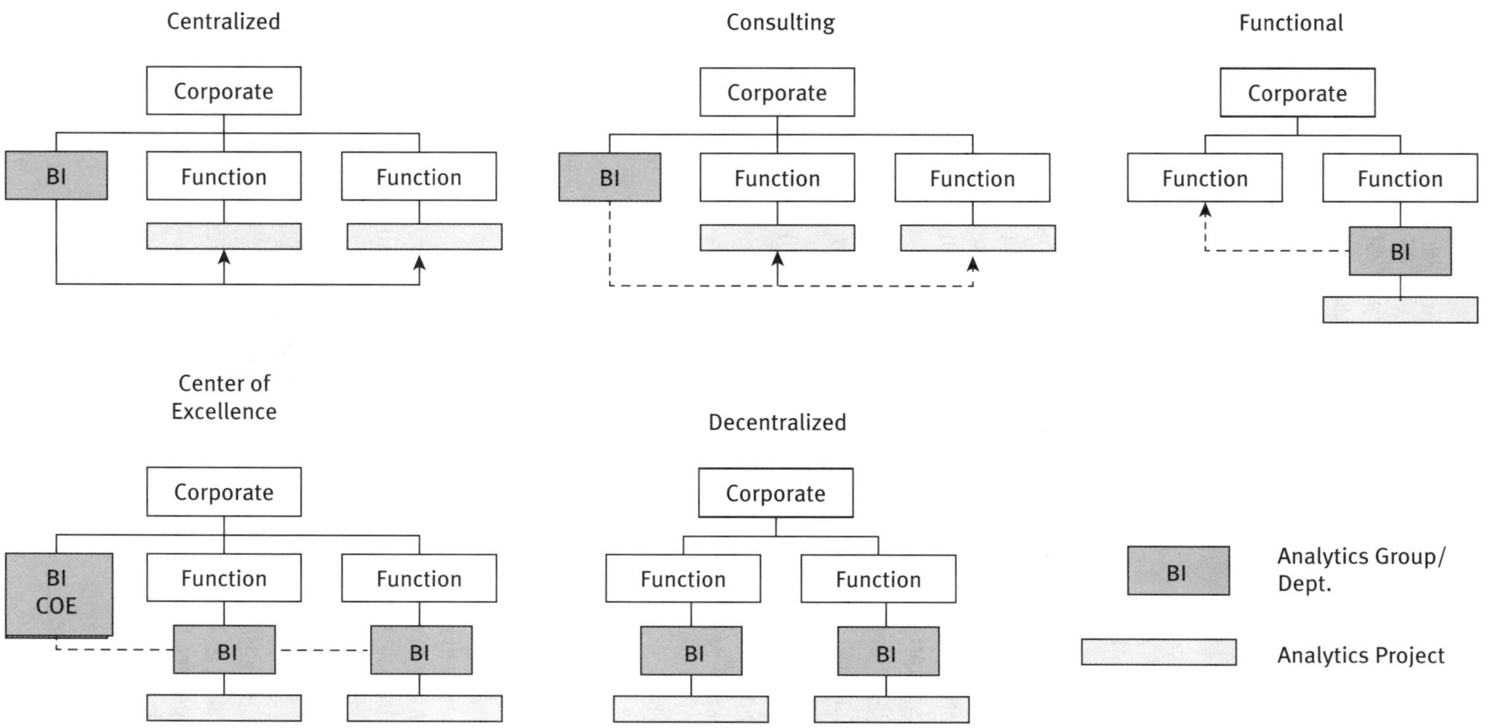

Source: Adapted from Davenport et al. (2010).

EXHIBIT 11.4 Advantages and Disadvantages of Analytics Organizational Structuring Alternatives

Analytics Organizational Structuring Alternatives	Potential Advantages	Potential Disadvantages or Challenges
Centralized (all analyst groups report to one corporate executive as a shared service)	• Easier to deploy analysts on strategic projects • Priorities easier to align with overall organizational goals • Leverages business metadata standardization and economies of learning	• May be seen as an "ivory tower" • May be seen as a bottleneck if governance activities are not transparent and fair
Consulting (same as centralized, only not a shared service; instead departments "hire" analysts for projects in a "pay-to-play" way)	• More market driven; prioritization is simplified, as only projects that departments are willing to pay for are undertaken • Leverages business metadata standardization and economies of learning	• Falters under weak enterprise focus or project selection criteria and/or poor executive leadership • Functional division may attempt to build its own services if costs are high or attention is lacking
Functional (a single analyst group resides in a primary data consumer's department/business unit)	• Negates need for a new central department • Constitutes a lower-cost entry point to assess the analytics readiness of a company	• May be viewed as too parochial by its own functional department or business unit • May lack functional analytics expertise needed by other departments
Center of excellence (community-of-practice program office approach—analyst groups are decentralized but report indirectly to central, corporate program office)	• Provides autonomy of prioritization of analytics projects to each decentralized analyst group • Leverages shared knowledge and experience • Leverages business metadata standardization and economies of learning • Easier to deploy analysts on strategic projects	• Can falter under weak enterprise focus or project selection criteria, particularly in the absence of a formal program office or governance prioritization approach • Can be viewed as a bottleneck if availability of resources is inadequate
Decentralized (analyst groups are associated with their respective functional departments with little or no corporate oversight)	• Provides autonomy of prioritization of analytics projects to each decentralized analyst group	• Difficult to accomplish cross-functional analytics projects • Difficult to set enterprise priorities • Often creates added costs through replication of services • Data standardization may suffer

center or an enterprise analytics function (Buytendijk et al. 2002; Strange and Hostmann 2003). An *enterprise analytics function* is "a cross-functional organizational team that has defined tasks, roles, responsibilities and processes for supporting and promoting the effective use of business intelligence (analytics) across an organization" (Wikipedia 2019). Other names have been used for such an organizational unit, including *analytics center of excellence*, *enterprise analytics department*, *clinical and business intelligence competency center*, or the *analytics competency center*, and various hybrids of these. Regardless of the label given to the team designated to support enterprise analytics, Dresner (2002) suggests the following five main functions of an enterprise analytics program; these functions remain applicable today:

1. Guiding users in self-service to meet their analytic needs, primarily by training them on how to use the data and on how to use analytics tools as a mechanism to access the data and manipulate it. This training allows the enterprise analytics function to have some leverage, instead of having to create every report or query itself
2. Performing ad hoc or complex analysis in conjunction with the business units
3. Overseeing the analytics approach used across the enterprise to ensure it is consistent
4. Coordinating use and reuse of business metadata (e.g., data definitions, source of data) and business rules associated with the data
5. Setting standards for analytic tools that will be used and supported throughout the organization

We turn now to staffing considerations of an enterprise analytics function.

Staffing Considerations for Enterprise Analytics

Regardless of the label an organization gives to the enterprise analytics function, by definition it is charged with supporting and promoting the effective use of analytics across an organization. As such, at a minimum, the individuals that an organization assigns to the enterprise analytics function should possess representative subject matter expertise that spans the key data consumers of the healthcare organization. There are a number of ways that a healthcare organization can go about ensuring that their enterprise analytics function has these representative subject matter experts (SMEs), but the two main methods are depicted in exhibit 11.5.

In option A, the enterprise analytics function is primarily staffed with new hires, though it may use external consultants. In option B, the enterprise

EXHIBIT 11.5 Sample Enterprise Analytics Staffing Options

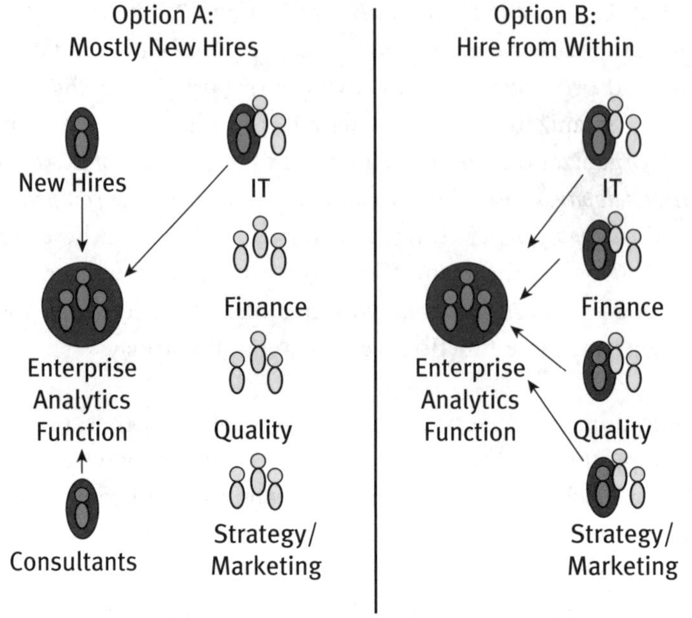

Note: IT = information technology.

analytics function is primarily staffed from resources that already exist in the healthcare organization that are reassigned to the enterprise analytics function. Exhibit 11.5 depicts just a few of the common data consumers in most health systems (e.g., quality department, the finance department). Other functional expertise can come from some of the other data consumer departments, such as strategy, operations, nursing, human resources, or ambulatory practice management. Of course, there are a myriad of hybrid variations of these two basic models. Each of the two basic models has some advantages and some disadvantages highlighted in exhibit 11.6.

In deciding which of the two basic staffing options is best for any given healthcare organization, the following are some of the organizational characteristics that can drive the decision:

- *Full-time equivalent (FTE) growth policy of the healthcare organization.* Organizations that wish to keep their permanent FTE headcount down (i.e., fully burdened salary dollars) may favor leveraging consultants, at least at the outset (option A), or reassigning resources from within (option B)
- *Historical level of trust and cooperation between business units.* In low-trust organizations, leaders in specific functional business units may not want to see their departmental analytic resources reassigned to a corporate enterprise analytics function (option B).

- *Level of analytic expertise in the healthcare organization.* Organizations with few report-writing or analytics skills at their disposal may wish to use new hires or consultants (option A).
- *Level of leadership commitment to an enterprise approach to analytics.* Organizations without demonstrable C-suite-level awareness and commitment to fostering an enterprise approach to analytics will find it difficult to reassign resources from functional departments to the enterprise analytics function (option B).

Typical Roles in an Enterprise Analytics Function

The most important role of the enterprise analytics function is invariably the leader. Depending on which of Davenport and colleagues' (2010) structuring approaches the organization adopts, the level in the organization can be anything from a senior-level position for centralized or center-of-excellence models (e.g., chief analytics officer, chief data and analytics officer) down to a director or manager level in a functional model (e.g., director of analytics,

EXHIBIT 11.6
Advantages and Disadvantages of Staffing Options

Staffing Option	Potential Advantages	Potential Disadvantages or Challenges
Option A (mostly new hires and external consultants)	• Functional/departmental resources and productivity are not affected • Jump starts the program with external expertise • Creates limited disruption to workers in their existing roles and responsibilities	• New hires and consultants won't know the lay of the land and will have a longer learning curve • Functional departments and business units may not trust the efforts of newbies • Requires more resources
Option B (mostly reassign resources from within)	• Enterprise analytics function has organizational knowledge on day 1 • Departments that seeded the enterprise analytics function with their own resources will tend to trust the efforts of the enterprise analytics function (instant credibility) • Process requires fewer resources	• Functional departments may not want to let their best report writers and analysts be reassigned to an enterprise analytics function that they don't directly control • Functional departments may seek to backfill the resources that were reassigned to the enterprise analytics function

director of data and analytics). Given that the enterprise analytics function is, by definition, responsible for supporting and promoting the effective use of analytics across an organization, it is important that the individual recruited to fill this position has a broad understanding of the business of healthcare (both clinical and financial ideally) and a background in data analysis or informatics, regardless of their level. In addition, it is important that this individual have solid "people skills" to help effectively facilitate the kind of cross-functional coordination that is necessary to complete successful enterprise analytic projects. As noted previously, because the healthcare sector is relatively inexperienced at managing data as a strategic asset, there are few seasoned healthcare analytics professionals on the job market. As such, the following are some potential background and experience that a healthcare organization can look to when recruiting for this vital role:

- Nursing, clinical, or medical informaticists typically have a grounding in report-writing and analytics of the clinical and medical domain, so they often make great candidates to lead the enterprise analytics function, particularly if they also have some understanding of the financial domain.
- Biostatisticians are adept at analytics in the medical domain and may also make great candidates for enterprise analytics function leader, particularly as analytics moves from descriptive to predictive.
- Leaders and managers of particular functional department analysts (e.g., manager of financial reporting, or manger of quality analytics) may be excellent for promoting to an enterprise analytics function leadership position, assuming they are open to learning the nuances of data and business rules associated with the other functional areas.
- Vice presidents (VPs), directors, and managers of analytics from other sectors may need to learn some of the nuances of healthcare data and business rules, but they already have a grounding in analytics.

While there is no lack of enterprise analytics function leadership expertise from other sectors, understanding the context of the healthcare provider environment cannot be overstated. One approach that has been suggested is using dyad leadership (Baldwin et al. 2011; Maddox 2019)—that is, in the case of the enterprise analytics function, partnering a seasoned analytics leader who may not have the requisite healthcare background with an influential leader from inside of the healthcare organization. In this manner, the enterprise analytics function that is being led by such a dyad is able to do the following:

- Overcome learning-curve challenges and provide the healthcare organization with a much larger pool of enterprise analytics function

leaders to choose from (e.g., the enterprise analytics leader of the dyad can come from many different fields, not just healthcare)
- More easily navigate the political environment of the healthcare organization (i.e., by ensuring that the functional leader of the dyad is a well-respected, influential member of the organization)
- Over time, create new functional leaders who develop deeper analytics expertise and understanding

When an enterprise analytics leader with a background in healthcare is available, traditional organizational structuring models may suffice, but in the event that an organization is unable to attract such a candidate, the dyad model of leadership should be considered. Exhibit 11.7 provides some additional roles and expertise that should be considered for an enterprise analytics function as an organization continues to increase its analytics capabilities.

These are some of the more typical roles that make up the enterprise analytics function. Of course, the enterprise analytics function relies heavily on the IT organization to maintain the analytics tools and infrastructure of the organization (e.g., maintaining enterprise data warehouse [EDW] servers). For the roles shown earlier, the type and quantity vary from organization to organization. The standard approach is that growth of the enterprise analytics function should be driven by business needs.

Strategic Alignment and Governance

Almost every management book ever written cites effective leadership as an imperative to success, regardless of the topic. Rather than simply stating that effective leadership is vital to establishing a competent analytics capability, we will explore why analytics will be challenged to succeed without leadership. We will also provide pragmatic approaches to engaging leadership in a meaningful way in the effort to advance their healthcare organization's analytics capability. These practical approaches include, but are not limited to, the following:

- Creating tight strategic alignment between analytics projects and the healthcare organization's goals and objectives
- Ensuring that effective, representative governance is in place to prioritize and guide analytic initiatives
- Ensuring that each analytics project always has a named, engaged executive sponsor

We will review each of these in turn.

EXHIBIT 11.7
Typical Roles in an Enterprise Analytics Function

Role	Description
VP/director/manager of the enterprise analytics function	• Typically reports to C-level executive or the executive with responsibility for enterprise-wide business performance management, continuous process improvement, or Lean Six Sigma • Leads efforts to deliver analytics infrastructure and capabilities in support of organizational performance improvement efforts and strategic initiatives; leads an enterprise analytics competency center (a department responsible for analytics strategy, projects, processes, training of end users, and ongoing analytics benefits realization efforts) • In organizations with enterprise data warehouses (EDWs), owns the overall EDW project, ensuring sponsorship and funding are in place • Able to articulate the business problems that will be addressed by the enterprise analytics function or EDW • Is knowledgeable about analytics technology and how it can be applied to solving business problems • Is responsible for tracking return on investment/benefits achieved via various analytics projects • Primary analytics service provider for executives, managers, functional champions, stakeholders, and end users
Enterprise data architect	• Typically reports to enterprise analytics function leader • Is responsible for managing the healthcare organization's overall data architecture, data standardization, data dictionary, and metadata associated with enterprise data (e.g., in maintaining an EDW) • Has an overall understanding of hardware platforms and all software products being used to support analytics projects • Understands relational databases, physical/logical data models, middleware, metadata, and end-user tools • Works closely with business analysts to define data incorporated into logical data model
Data integrator (extraction, transformation, and load developer or data parser)	• Typically reports to enterprise data architect • Writes extraction, transformation, and loading (ETL) scripts and parser scripts (e.g., HL7 parsing) • Adept in graphical user interface–based ETL tools • Focuses on strategic data integration issues, such as data quality/stewardship, real-time/event-based data integration, and crafting a service-oriented vision for data integration

Database administrator	• Creates, tunes, and otherwise maintains the databases associated with the key data repositories used by the enterprise analytics function (e.g., data marts, EDW) • Reports to project manager for task management • Maintains an in-depth knowledge of database technology • Understands physical data models • Is an expert in data structure (including parallel data structure) • Works closely with enterprise data architect
Project manager	• Reports to the enterprise analytics function leader • Understands EDW and analytics project management methodology • Manages the project plan for completeness and timeliness • Manages the resource plan, ensuring the correct individuals are working toward project completion • Reports on project status • Interfaces with both EDW project team and functional stakeholders
Business analyst/data analyst	• Possesses expertise in a particular functional business unit expertise that serves as the point of contact with business users of analytics resources (such as the EDW) • Responsible for training end users on how to navigate enterprise analytics function tools and resources to find information • Run reports and performs analysis • Works closely with business managers to identify requirements
Analytics developer	• Works closely with business analysts/data analysts to develop and publish enterprise reports, dashboards, and scorecards
Data scientist	• Typically trained in statistics or biostatistics • Performs data mining to detect and identify patterns in the data to inform management decision-making • Leverages published predictive models or creates new predictive models and algorithms to inform management decision-making

Strategic Alignment

Contemporary healthcare organizations tend to have more demand for analytic projects (e.g., new report requests, new performance dashboard requests) than resources. Typically, analytic initiatives require the participation of business, clinical, or operational colleagues from other functional departments to properly develop requirements and iteratively assist in completion of analytic projects. These business, clinical, and operational colleagues themselves have a myriad of their own initiatives, setting up a classic theory-of-constraints situation in which the organization is limited by its own resources.

When they are tightly aligned with overall organizational strategic objectives, analytics initiatives tend to be more successful, enjoy greater executive visibility and sponsorship, and get better outcomes. One way to achieve this success is to systematically and deliberately map the healthcare organization's current strategic goals and objectives to analytics opportunities and then allow the resulting document to act as a guiding framework for analytics governance and prioritization decisions. An example of such a strategic analytics alignment document can be found in exhibit 11.8, using some common themes that are representative of many contemporary health systems' overarching strategies. The first column depicts some of these common themes, and the second column describes specific strategic objectives that are typical of many health system's contemporary goals. From these strategic goals and objectives, it is relatively simple to identify key passages that are highly suggestive of a need for data, reporting, and analytics. By articulating potential analytics opportunities that could help the organization achieve those objectives, one can easily create a document similar to the one in exhibit 11.8 that can help guide enterprise business intelligence (BI) project prioritization decisions.

Demands for new reporting and analytics will continue to grow. Organizations that have proactively vetted and achieved buy-in for analytics initiatives should generally support efforts that help advance their overall strategic goals and objectives. They will find a strategic analytics alignment document, such as the one provided in exhibit 11.8, to be an excellent filter through which new analytic requests can be weighed against other requests —an analytics governance process.

Analytics Governance

There are two primary activity areas that require sound, representative governance related to analytics. The first is governance of prioritization and strategic alignment. With high demand for new analytics projects, an appropriate, representative, engaged group of stakeholders from throughout the organization are needed to help guide prioritization with a constant eye on the strategic needs of the organization. In addition, governance related to data standardization and data quality improvements also requires a different

EXHIBIT 11.8
Sample Strategic Analytics Alignment Document

Strategic Focus	Key Strategic Goal Options	Alignment Opportunities
Valued partner to . . .	Physicians: Strive to provide the best possible practice experience for all community physicians, regardless of their affiliation	BI alignment: key performance indicators (KPIs) for physician satisfaction
	Insurers: Strive to become the preferred accountable care partner for health insurers in the region, delivering superior value by lowering the overall cost of care while maintaining top quartile quality of care as measured by a defined set of outcomes metrics (BI alignment opportunity: KPIs by diagnosis-related group's cost of care; KPIs by diagnosis-related group for quality of care)	Analytics alignment: • KPIs for employer and patient satisfaction • Value-based purchasing metrics
	Employers: Strive to become the health system provider of choice for both employers and their employees based on the ability to deliver cost-effective care with high levels of patient satisfaction	
Clinical Signature Program Development	Investments in these programs are expected to deliver achievements that will advance the health system toward preeminence in the following: • Cardiology and cardiovascular surgery (decrease operating room time and resources) • Cancer (expand cancer center to cover all cancer types) • Neurosurgery (increase operating room time and resources) • Transplantation (expand transplant center to include abdominal solid organ transplant and related gastroenterology, renal, and vascular programs)	Analytics alignment: • Automated means to compare baseline program performance with postinvestment performance • KPIs to measure operating room time by signature program, number of cases, and outcomes (e.g., readmissions, hospital-acquired infections)

(continued)

EXHIBIT 11.8
Sample Strategic Analytics Alignment Document (*continued*)

Strategic Focus	Key Strategic Goal Options	Alignment Opportunities
Deliver Greater Value	Maximize value for populations of patients with chronic conditions and increase disease prevention	BI alignment: • Value-based purchasing metrics • Predictive analytics for patients with chronic conditions and readmission prevention
	Maximize value through aggressive targeting of the lowest price point and lowest cost in the region for a hospital-based provider with top-quartile quality (analytics alignment opportunity: correlate quality with cost data to demonstrate)	
Growth	Grow geographically, by natural expansion of existing service areas	Analytics alignment: • Geocode data • Ability to display data geographically
	Grow geographically, by jumps in geography	Analytics alignment: • Geocode data • Ability to display data geographically
	Grow new services	Analytics alignment: external data sources to find new patients
Create Accountability Across the Continuum of Care	Improve the health of the community that the health system serves through the creation of a healthcare alliance with providers that are patient focused	
	Break down traditional barriers and reduce duplication and waste	Analytics alignment: • Population health analytics • ACO-like analytics (leveraging interorganizational data sets to better understand opportunities to reduce duplication and waste)

set of engaged organizational representatives to ensure that the benefit of the data can be maximized.

Typical organizational analytics governance structure, charters, and representation are provided in exhibit 11.9. Typically, most organizations have a standing senior leadership executive committee made up of executives such as the CEO, chief financial officer, chief operating officer, chief medical officer, chief strategy officer, chief information officer, and so on. When organizations make the decision to create an enterprise analytics program, they typically charter a new enterprise analytics steering committee that reports to the senior leadership executive committee.

The enterprise analytics steering committee membership typically consists of vice president–level individuals from the organization's major data consumers. They are charged with ensuring that new requests for projects are properly prioritized and aligned with the organization's strategic goals. They also monitor project progress and oversee any other subcommittee activities, such as data governance.

Some enterprise analytics steering committees also take on tasks related to data governance. But we have found that the work related to data governance requires a different expertise than typically found at the VP level in an organization, and therefore, many organizations create a data governance subcommittee chartered by, and accountable to, the enterprise analytics steering committee.

EXHIBIT 11.9
Typical Organizational Analytics Governance Structure

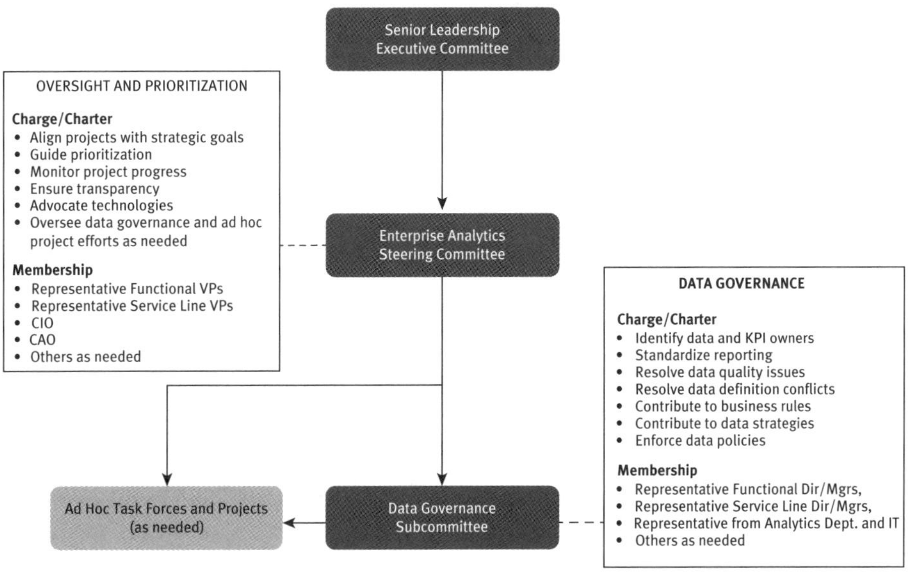

Note: CAO = chief administrative officer, CIO = chief intelligence officer, IT = information technology, KPI = key performance indicator, VP = vice president.

The data governance subcommittee is charged with helping to resolve data definition issues (e.g., What does a "visit" mean in the context of their healthcare organization?); its members help with report standardization (e.g., when an organization has three different reports related to nosocomial infections but they all seem to have different results, the data governance subcommittee often takes on the task of vetting these differences and appropriately reconciling them). Because this type of work requires a much more intimate knowledge of the underlying data related to business, clinical, and operational processes, the data governance subcommittee membership typically includes directors, managers, or supervisors from the primary data-consuming departments throughout the organization to carry out its charge effectively.

By ensuring that representative governance oversees the activities of the new enterprise analytics function (e.g., via an enterprise analytics steering committee) and ensuring that data-literate representatives are engaged in data governance activities, healthcare organizations are poised to advance in their enterprise analytics maturity.

Analytics Project Sponsorship

Along with the governance oversight that we just outlined, appropriate and effective project sponsorship is also vital to analytics projects. Exhibit 11.10 provides a graphical representation of how the analytics governance activities, the enterprise analytics function, and individual projects sponsored by a project champion are conducted in best-practice organizations. At the top, healthcare organization analytics governance has processes in its committee work to vet and select projects. It then hands those down to the enterprise analytics function leader (typically a chief analytics officer) for execution. The enterprise analytics function leader forms individual project teams made up of a business unit champion or sponsor, a team leader drawn from the enterprise analytics function (typically a project manager), and other individuals (e.g., analytics developers) from the enterprise analytics function, along with SMEs from key representative stakeholder departments or business units. For instance, a new analytics project to develop a clinical quality dashboard with some 40 different KPIs may draw relevant SMEs from the quality department (e.g., to provide expertise on the Centers for Medicare & Medicaid Service's clinical quality measures), the emergency department (e.g., to cover expertise on the key performance indicator (KPI) "aspirin upon arrival," a typical quality measure relating to heart attack patients at the emergency department), and perhaps a nursing unit (to cover expertise related to KPIs on patient safety, such as patient falls). This project team is temporary and meets periodically throughout the life of the project; on completion, the project team is disbanded.

Contemporary healthcare organizations suffer from an oversupply of new projects and an undersupply of resources. Without an engaged, committed project champion, enterprise analytics projects can quickly get bogged

EXHIBIT 11.10
Governance and Operations

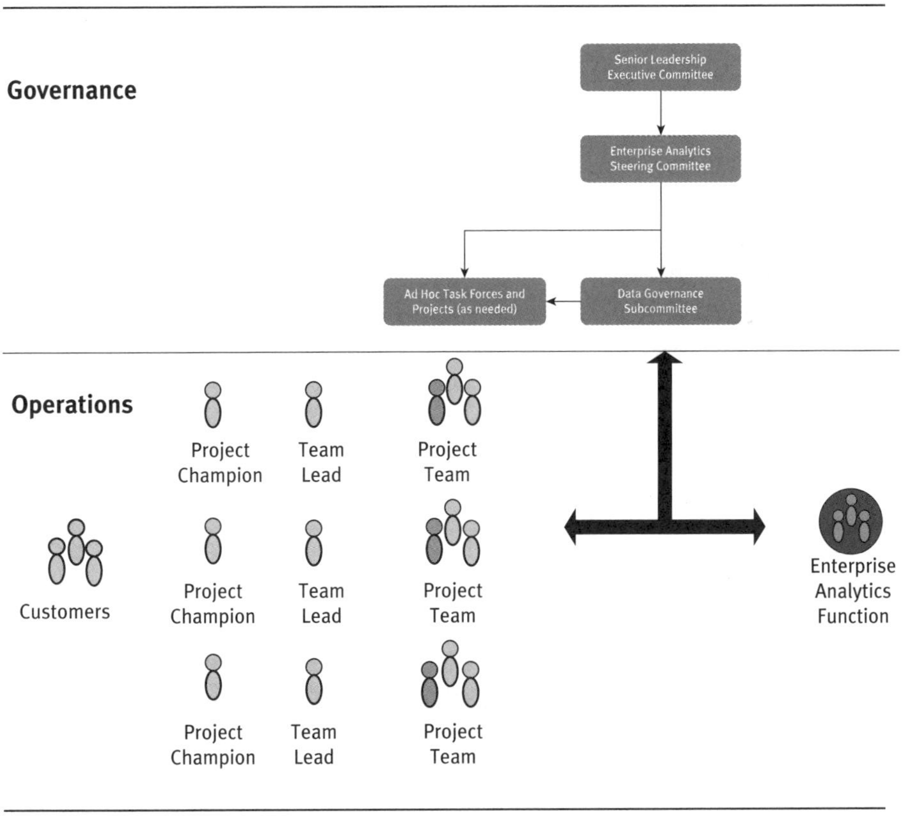

down. By aligning projects to overall strategic objectives, as described previously, and by selecting a project champion who is committed to completion, organizations are much better positioned to achieve value from analytic projects they undertake.

Democratizing Data: Self-Service Analytics

As noted previously, demand for new analytics capabilities (e.g., reports, performance monitoring dashboards and scorecards, predictive models) tends to be greater than the supply of resources able to deliver them in a timely manner. Further exacerbating this situation is the general data illiteracy of many business and clinical employees in healthcare organizations. While these colleagues generally have a deep understanding of the business, clinical, or operational processes that drive their respective parts of the healthcare organization, they are generally ignorant of the underlying data that are generated by those same operations or how to use that data effectively for performance improvement initiatives. To overcome this constraint, leading healthcare organizations, such as Duke Health, are working to increase data literacy throughout the organization. Their efforts will not only reduce the demand on the enterprise analytics function but also serve to democratize the data assets of the organization, allowing rank-and-file clinical, business, and operational staff members throughout to learn appropriately from data in a more self-directed way.

The following is a case study from Duke Health's chief analytics officer, Stephen Blackwelder, which outlines a systematic approach to increasing the data literacy in the healthcare organization and democratizing data for Duke Health's users.

Case Study: Duke Health's Data Prospector Program

With the advent of an enterprise [EHR], health systems have the opportunity to deploy reporting and analytics across their entire organization, anchored by the cache of data collected via the EHR. While mainstream EHR vendors make available a wide range of reports, dashboards, and specialty-topic data marts, health systems typically have a need for at least some customized analytics. The customization may be necessitated by functions such as cost accounting, patient scheduling, and labs management, for example, that are supported by systems outside the EHR. Moreover, the analytics capabilities included with these systems are strongly focused on providing tactical, operational information. Health systems typically create specialized data and reporting structures both to integrate data from disparate sources, as well as to enable generation of strategic insights from enterprise data. Making the available range of data and analytics solutions visible across the organization presents challenges. Users who are unaware of an existing analytics solution are at risk of re-developing a report or data mart themselves, or of purchasing duplicative data or an analytics point solution, risking the creation of disparate and competing "sources of truth."

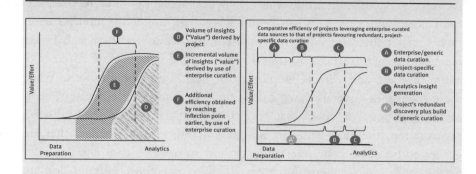

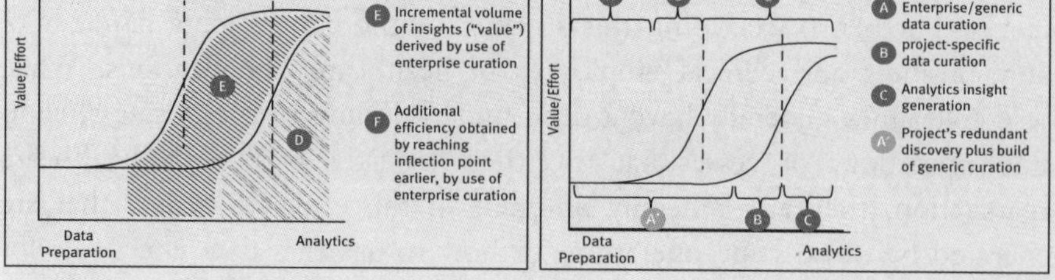

Increasing competition within the healthcare delivery industry drives the need for innovation and strategic differentiation which, in turn, increases demand for—and value of—insights generated by strategic analytics. Analytics projects may be compared on the basis of the value returned to the organization in exchange for the investment of time and effort spent in obtaining and curating data, and in analyzing the data. Value here might reasonably be defined in terms of the volume of insights derived by the project, divided by the effort required to obtain those insights. While obtaining and curating data is a necessary precursor to analytics, these activities alone do not yield insights. Moreover, as illustrated in the figures, due to the greater volume of insights derived from effort devoted to analysis than to curation, projects able to avoid redundant curation return more value and return it sooner, other things being equal, than projects eschewing enterprise-curated data sources. The hypothetical illustration shown assumes that some set of relevant data has already been curated and made available for approved uses, and that some further curation related to specific nuances of the analytics project will be required. At many health systems, a large corpus of curated data is already available for use—improved efficiency can then be gained by making users aware of the resources available so that their data management effort can be focused exclusively on data not already in curation.

Duke Health has implemented a Data Prospector program to help maximize the organization's return on its analytics investments. The program validates which data source a specific project requires, governs data access provisioning, and facilitates compliance audit functions. Importantly, the program also educates users as to what resources are available to them and about how those resources work. Where the curation of data makes sense, the program provides a structure in which data engineering code is documented and catalogued and business definitions and other metadata are added to the enterprise data dictionary.

Analysts in any department seeking programmatic access to enterprise data apply to Data Prospector, including in their application a description of the use case they are seeking to meet by access to the enterprise data warehouse environment. Upon enterprise approval of the use case(s), an applicant will complete a course of training prior to obtaining access to the data.

Data Prospector training components may consist of coursework provided by the EHR vendor on their campus or virtually, as well as coursework created and delivered onsite at Duke. The specific classes needed will vary by requestor and depend upon the user's experience, use case, and

(continued)

the type of data requested. As part of the program, new users are provided with an orientation to the tools and data available, including familiarization with the repository of curated data sources (including the EDW, cubes, data marts, and universes) and available APIs and BI toolsets (both commercial visualization and BI suites as well as Duke-built tools). Not all health system data are equal, and use of protected data—including certain financial data, patient protected health information, and specially protected clinical notes data—are also covered in the training. Standard approaches to designing SQL queries for typical use cases are presented, along with approved methods for versioning and documenting program code. Training in the use of Duke's protected computing environment for research analysis of PHI is available as needed.

Participants are paired with data analysts or developers from the enterprise analytics team as they work through a practical data and/or analytics project related to their use case. This six-week partnership culminates in the participant's sharing their use case with other analysts in a structured presentation. Upon successful completion of a short online examination, the participant's access to the data needed to do their job is confirmed for one year. Access is extended annually on protracted use cases, or with additional approved use cases as appropriate, with annual recertification by exam.

Duke has seen benefits from Data Prospector accruing to analysts, their sponsoring departments and the enterprise more broadly. Analyst participants have found the exercise of documenting their use case to be valuable both in focusing their effort as well as in selling their projects to sponsors. Engagement in the program provides them with an appreciated check against duplicative effort and a confirmation of appropriate data sourcing for their projects. Duke Health and its constituent departments benefit from a clearer understanding of what analytics topics are pursued and of which data are being leveraged and how. Analytics and metrics supporting enterprise strategic goals have become more consistent across groups charged with marketing, planning, and strategy functions.

Enterprise tools introduced to program participants, such as the enterprise data dictionary, documentation of data provenance, and the enterprise repository of reusable SQL code, all benefit from the training and exposure Data Prospector provides. Not least of all, the Data Prospector program has helped reinforce a community of analysts across Duke's variegated analytics landscape.

Source: Reprinted from Blackwelder (2019). Used with permission.

Summary

Contemporary healthcare organizations are all working diligently to try to make sense of their ever-increasing sea of data. They historically have followed a decentralized model in which individual business units or functional departments attempt to address their business intelligence and analytics needs in their respective silos. As organizations attempt to move up the HIMSS Analytics AMAM, outlined in this chapter, the need to structure and organize suggests a need for an enterprise analytics function charged with serving the demands of the whole healthcare organization.

We have presented a number of different structuring arrangements for the enterprise analytics function, along with the advantages and disadvantages of each. Regardless of the structuring approach, it is helpful to align enterprise analytics projects with strategic organizational objectives. Furthermore, to increase the probability of successfully gaining value from investments in the enterprise analytics function, enterprise analytic projects must be sponsored by engaged and committed unit leaders. Indeed, as the volume, variety, and speed at which data are generated by healthcare organizations increases, initiatives that focus on fostering the data literacy of business, clinical, and operational colleagues are vital to democratizing data for self-service users throughout the organization.

Web Resources

A number of organizations (through their websites) provide more information on the topics discussed in this chapter:

- HIMSS Analytics provides an information sheet for its adoption model (AMAM) at www.himssanalytics.org/sites/himssanalytics/files/HIMSS%20Analytics%20AMAM%20-%20web.pdf.

  Businesses looking to improve their clinical and business intelligence can find community and resources with HIMSS at www.himss.org/library/clinical-business-intelligence.
- The home page for the International Institute for Analytics can be found at https://iianalytics.com.

Discussion Questions

1. Distinguish between traditional analytics and big data analytics.

2. What is the advantage of using technologies such as Hadoop and NoSQL for big data analytics rather than typical data warehousing analysis approaches?
3. The HIMSS Analytics Adoption Model is based on a cumulative capability structure. What does this mean?
4. How is achieving stage 7 of the HIMSS Analytics Adoption Model expected to affect clinical care?
5. The authors suggest that healthcare analytics models are "immature" with regard to managing data as a strategic asset. What is the basis for this assertion?
6. What analytics capabilities characterize more advanced or mature analytics organizations?
7. Describe different ways a healthcare organization can establish and structure an enterprise analytics function.
8. What are key staffing considerations when establishing an enterprise analytics function?
9. What are the two primary facets of governance for an enterprise analytics function?
10. What is a common barrier to democratizing data analytics across the enterprise?

Note

Portions of this chapter have previously been published in D. Smaltz, 2014, "Leading and Structuring Analytics Within Healthcare Organizations: The Business Intelligence Competency Center," in *Analytics in Healthcare: An Introduction*, edited by R. Gensinger, Chicago: HIMSS and are used with permission.

References

Blackwelder, S. 2019. "Data Prospector." Working paper, Duke Health, Durham, NC.

Baldwin, K., N. Diminuation, and J. Alexander. 2011. "Health Care Leadership and the Dyad Model." *Physician Executive*, July–August, 66–70.

Buytendijk, F., M. Knox, K. Strange, M. Camm, A. Linden, H. J. Dresner, and T. Friedman. 2002. "The Business Intelligence Competency Center: An Essential Business Strategy." Gartner. Published May 29. www.gartner.com/en/documents/358967/the-business-intelligence-competency-center-an-essential-.

Davenport, T. 2013. "The Rise of Analytics 3.0." International Institute for Analytics. Published July 11. www.iianalytics.com/blog/the-rise-of-analytics-30?rq=Analytics%20 3.0.

Davenport, T., G. Harris, and R. Morison. 2010. *Analytics at Work*. Boston: Harvard Business School Publishing.

Dictionary.com. 2020. "Analytics." Accessed February 27. www.dictionary.com/browse/analytics.

Dresner, H. 2002. "Implementing Business Intelligence to Succeed, Not Fail." Published December 18. www.bus.umich.edu/KresgePublic/Journals/Gartner/research/112200/112204/112204.pdf.

Eddy, N. 2019. "Where Health Systems Are Using Analytics the Most." Healthcare IT News. Published May 2. www.healthcareitnews.com/news/where-health-systems-are-using-analytics-most.

Ginsburg, P. B., A. de Loera-Brust, C. Brandt, and A. Durak. 2018. "The Opportunities and Challenges of Data Analytics in Health Care." Brookings Institution. Published November 1. www.brookings.edu/research/the-opportunities-and-challenges-of-data-analytics-in-health-care.

HIMSS Analytics. 2020. "HIMSS Analytics AMAM: Adoption Model for Analytics Maturity." Accessed February 27. www.himssanalytics.org/sites/himssanalytics/files/image/HIMSS%20Analytics%20AMAM%20Criteria%20sheet.pdf.

Landi, H. 2018. "Study: Healthcare Lags Other Industries in Digital Transformation, Customer Engagement Tech." Healthcare Innovation. Published March 30. www.hcinnovationgroup.com/population-health-management/news/13030021/study-healthcare-lags-other-industries-in-digital-transformation-customer-engagement-tech.

Maddox, W. 2019. "Texas Health's Dyad Leadership Model: Risks and Rewards." *D Magazine*. Published June 10. www.dmagazine.com/healthcare-business/2019/06/the-risks-and-rewards-of-texas-healths-dyad-leadership-model/.

Press, G. 2014. "12 Big Data Definitions: What's Yours?" *Forbes*. Published September 3. www.forbes.com/sites/gilpress/2014/09/03/12-big-data-definitions-whats-yours/#1a25a4ce13ae.

Strange, K., and B. Hostmann. 2003. "BI Competency Center Is Core to BI Success." Gartner. Published July 22. www.gartner.com/en/documents/400976/bi-competency-center-is-core-to-bi-success.

Wikipedia. 2019. "Business Intelligence Competency Center." Edited September 28. https://en.wikipedia.org/wiki/Business_Intelligence_Competency_Center.

CHAPTER

12

HEALTH INFORMATION TECHNOLOGY VALUE ANALYSIS

Learning Objectives

1. Specify why making health information technology (HIT) investment decisions on the basis of realized value rather than on "anecdote, inference, and opinion" leads to better outcomes.
2. Describe five changes that make today's HIT investment decisions more challenging than in the past.
3. Provide examples of HIT costs and outcomes changes that will "always" be adopted and examples that will "never" be adopted.
4. Analyze how the major techniques used for evaluation of an HIT investment differ.
5. List the eight key steps in cost evaluation.
6. Discuss why certain types of HIT applications are less likely to be performed.
7. Describe value realization and total cost of ownership methodologies.

Overview

Up to this point in the book, the discussions surrounding health information technology (HIT) have explicitly recognized that the organization, financing, and delivery of healthcare services are different from those of other goods and services. While we consider this to be fundamentally true, some aspects of healthcare, especially HIT, should adhere to core business processes. HIT can be considered an input into the "production" process, just as inputs of nursing time, allied health staff, medical supplies, and physician services. In that context, the decisions regarding how much and what type of HIT inputs to use should fall under a valuation paradigm. Johnston, Pan, and Middleton (2002) made this point strongly, years ago, in their argument for finding value from HIT.

Firmly establishing value in many healthcare investments has proven to be a challenge, however. Clinical technologies have increasingly been subject to critical valuation, the weighing of benefits received relative to costs incurred, and this notion has taken hold for HIT as well (Buntin et al. 2011; Kark 2018; Rudin et al. 2014; Sanyal et al. 2018; Wiley and Daniel 2006; Wimble and Leroy 2018). Issues related to data collection, methodology, and application make the realization of value from and widespread use of evidence-based management a challenge. The health economics literature is replete with methodologies of cost, cost–benefit, and cost-effectiveness analyses and quality-adjusted life years (e.g., CADTH 2017; Chaudhry et al. 2006; Cusack et al. 2009; Rahimi and Vimarlund 2007; Simon and Simon 2006; Southern California Evidence-Based Practice Center 2006). Most of these studies involve developing the methodology for assessing complex medical applications, and until recently, only a few are applied. Surprisingly, only a few studies look specifically at methods applied to HIT interventions (e.g., Chaudhry et al. 2006; Featherly et al. 2007; Rahimi and Vimarlund 2007; Simon and Simon 2006; Southern California Evidence-Based Practice Center 2006).

Because of the complexity of the problem and the lack of comprehensive data, healthcare executives have largely been forced to make decisions about HIT investments on the basis of cursory evidence at best and instinct or hope at worst. In the words of Johnston, Pan, and Middleton (2002), HIT decisions are often based on "anecdote, inference, and opinion." Inevitably, this approach produces decisions that may not yield the hoped-for benefits. As a result, HIT may fall short in addressing the problems plaguing healthcare. The discipline is making progress, however, with the effectiveness of the technology and improved prospects for future value (Wimble and Leroy 2018).

This is not totally unexpected, however. A host of problems arise from performing these analyses, including the following:

- The need for complex (econometric) techniques rather than straightforward finance and accounting techniques to find meaningful results (Attema, Brouwer, and Claxton 2018; Meyer and Degoulet 2008)
- Indirect measurement of benefits because of the interdependent nature of the production process and because benefits are found in areas not expected (Bower 2005; Encinosa and Bae 2011; Featherly et al. 2007; King et al. 2014)
- Physician and other clinicians' resistance to change once cost data are delivered (Asch 2003; Krousel-Wood et al. 2018; Stammen et al. 2015)
- Indication from the market that some portions of HIT investments are not appropriate (if people do not realize the value, why should we force them to use it? [Loomis et al. 2002])

As organizations struggle to meet patient and community health needs and improve quality with tight budgets, performing a strict value assessment of all investments has become even more important. To give some idea of the magnitude of the issue, healthcare organizations spent approximately $74 billion in 2018 on healthcare technology, up about 10 percent from the prior year. While that seems like a substantial amount in the aggregate, it represents only about 2.8 percent of total revenue for healthcare organizations in 2018. This is a small number, in that context, and it is less than 2014's 3.1 percent (Kass 2017). For 2019, data projections indicate that 71 percent of executives expect spending on healthcare IT to increase by 10 percent or more, while only 8 percent expect a decline. Further, 29 percent of respondents expected a 20 percent increase in spending or more for the year (Padmanabhan 2019). Data from Deloitte suggest that across industries, firms spend about 3.3 percent of revenue on information technology (IT) (Kark 2018).

Barriers to adoption have shifted in recent times. Murphy (2016) reports that factors such as insufficient information technology (IT) transparency, lack of robust interoperability, overt data blocking, and data security needs are the primary faults. In 2012, however, 14 percent of HIT leaders participating in the annual Healthcare Information and Management Systems Society (HIMSS) survey cited financial factors as a barrier to implementing HIT in their organization, a concern second only to adequate staffing—cited by 22 percent of respondents as the top barrier. Both vendor ability to deliver and difficulty in end-user acceptance were named significant barriers as well, selected by 12 percent and 9 percent of respondents, respectively (HIMSS 2012, 24). In recent years, HIMSS leadership surveys do not report comparable data regarding barriers (HIMSS 2018, 2019).

Even as the government and competitive pressures induce healthcare delivery organizations to implement interoperable electronic health records (EHRs) that enable the exchange of information within and across institutions, these organizations must still focus on value creation in addition to the implementation challenges. Providers have come to expect some sort of electronic health information exchange (HIE) as a business necessity. They work in healthcare delivery teams consisting of physicians, nurses, pharmacists, therapists, and others who require a real-time exchange of information. Hospitals have made gains in the interoperability domains of sending and receiving information, but integration of information among providers remains elusive (Holmgren, Patel, and Adler-Milstein 2017). The Health Information Technology for Health and Clinical Health (HITECH) Act established significant incentives to providers that fully implement an HIE, but insufficient data have accumulated to make robust estimates of value.

Supported by the health reform legislation, consumers seek new delivery modes for their care and expect coordination of care across provider segments. Consequently, the ability to assess value will be crucial for the HIT leader of the future, and IT will play a vital role in that value delivery.

This chapter first outlines why the evaluation problem is more complex today because of the systems nature of healthcare delivery. Then, it presents what is known about how HIT investments are analyzed and provides the steps for conducting these analyses. Next, it details value realization as a method to implement evaluation. Last, it presents selected findings from cost-evaluation studies.

Systems Challenges

Despite its costs, HIT is essential in the provision of high-quality care in today's environment. However, technology acquisition is not an all-or-nothing proposition. Questions of scale, scope, application, integration, and timing must be addressed, all of which make the decision complex. Do you wait another year? Do you purchase and install some applications and not others? How do you ensure that the appropriate mix of information technologies is selected? Furthermore, once that set of decisions is made, how do you implement so that costs stay at the expected level and the benefits promised are actually realized? In the face of these questions, some have come to challenge the wisdom of assumed value and even the benefits of HIT investments (e.g., Carayon, Wetterneck Cartmill et al. 2017; Carr 2003; Koppel 2005; Wears and Berg 2005).

If these considerations did not make this problem difficult enough, the interdependence of providers in a healthcare "system" complicates the decision further. As detailed in chapter 2, problems of cost, quality, and access plague those responsible for healthcare delivery. In a general discussion regarding the transformation of the US healthcare system, Adams and colleagues (2006) identify the following five features that make today's challenges different from challenges in the past:

1. Globalization
2. Consumerism
3. Aging and overweight populations
4. Diseases that are more expensive to treat
5. New medical technologies and treatments

To respond successfully to these challenges, Adams and colleagues argue that value decisions must extend beyond an individual organization's considerations to the perspective of society as a whole. For example, medical

Procedure	US ($)	UK ($)	Switzerland ($)	Australia ($)
Appendectomy	15,930	8,009	6,040	3,814
Angioplasty	31,620	7,264	10,066	11,164
Heart bypass	78,318	24,059	34,224	28,888
Hip replacement	29,067	16,335	17,112	19,484
Knee replacement	28,184	18,451	20,132	15,941
Colonoscopy	1,301	3,059	604	372
MRI	1,119	788	503	215
Cesarean section	16,106	NA	9,965	7,901
Normal delivery	10,808	NA	7,751	5,312

Source: Data from Kamal and Cox (2018).

EXHIBIT 12.1
Cost of Select Procedures in Four Countries (USD), 2015

tourism may become common as the financial incentives for care delivered outside of the United States could eventually drive select care overseas (see exhibit 12.1). Identifying this competition and constructing apples-to-apples data will be necessary for senior management to make value decisions. Kaiser Family Foundation has done a credible job of compiling and presenting this and other price- and cost-related international comparisons (Kamal and Cox 2018).

Adams and colleagues' recommendations for successful transformation of the healthcare system include many features, but most important, they argue that there will be different perspectives on value. The US healthcare system will transform from one that emphasizes individual value and cost containment to one with an emphasis on balancing "stakeholder value across dimensions (cost, quality, access, and choice)" (Adams et al. 2006, 42). The latter emphasis will usher in a transformation from the current state of data management to electronic, evidence-based, standard, shared, and interoperable information. This transformation is related to the previously discussed emphasis on population health (Kindig and Stodart 2003).

In the early 2000s, Enthoven and Tollen (2005) recommended addressing cost and quality concerns, rather than introducing competition to the healthcare market. They proposed that healthcare organizations should move away from market changes that foster independent competing business units. In their opinion, to capture potential cost savings and quality improvements, the US government should offer incentives for local and regional markets to form "integrated delivery systems, to provide coordinated, efficient, evidence-based care, supported by state-of-the-art information technology" (Enthoven and Tollen 2005, 420). The expectation was that integrated delivery systems would prove to be a more sustainable delivery model and would address issues of fragmentation (Enthoven 2009). These proposed integrated delivery systems are today's reality, but models are still evolving, and they were not the panacea envisioned, as full interoperability of information exchange and longitudinal health records are yet to be achieved.

Evaluation Problem

At the most fundamental level, business decisions faced by the chief information officer (CIO), and indirectly by the CEO and board of trustees, come down to a challenge of deciding among competing alternatives. The questions they must ask are as follows: Does the investment in HIT increase, have no effect on, or decrease organizational outcomes? Does it increase, have no effect on, or decrease the costs to the organization?

Exhibit 12.2 presents a simple paradigm that can effectively support HIT decisions. The matrix consists of nine cells or potential outcome and cost combinations, and, in some cells, the decision to adopt the technology or not to is straightforward. For example, if adopting the technology results in a reduction in outcomes and an increase in costs (cell 3), most CIOs will not adopt (never). Similarly, if outcomes improve with the new technology and costs are reduced (scenario 7), the decision to adopt is straightforward (always). Combinations of costs and outcomes that place the organization in scenarios 2, 3, or 6 are *never* adopted. Similarly, combinations of costs and outcomes that place the organization in scenarios 4, 7, or 8 are *always* adopted.

The interesting cases involve combinations of costs and outcomes that place the organization on the diagonal in scenarios 1, 5, or 9. For these cases, a methodology must be put in place to more rigorously measure the magnitude of the changes in outcomes and the magnitude of the changes in costs. Formal benefit–cost or cost-effectiveness analyses need to be applied to assess the relative changes for these three cases: both outcomes and costs increase, neither benefits nor costs change, and both benefits and costs decrease.

EXHIBIT 12.2
Technology Cost and Outcome Effect Decision Matrix

	Outcome Effect		
Cost Effect	**Improve**	**No Change**	**Worsen**
Increase	1 ?????	2 Never	3 Never
No change	4 Always	5 ?????	6 Never
Decrease	7 Always	8 Always	9 ?????

Benefit–Cost and Cost-Effectiveness Analyses

A number of studies have documented the use of conventional benefit–cost, cost-effectiveness, or cost–utility analysis in healthcare (Rudin et al. 2014). The discussions that follow are not significantly concerned with differentiating these techniques, as a full history of the concepts is beyond the scope of this book. In simple terms, *benefit–cost analyses* are applied when all aspects of the costs related to a technology and benefits of that technology are measured in monetary terms. The outcome from these analyses might be presented as $3 in benefits for every $1 in cost ($3/$1). The decision calculus then enables leadership to select among alternatives that have the highest ratio.

For many healthcare applications, some of the outcomes or benefits may be difficult or objectionable to put into financial terms. Loss of life, for example, can be quantified in financial terms (Viscusi 2004), but not everyone is comfortable with making those assessments. *Cost-effectiveness analyses* were developed for technologies and resulted in outcomes that could not be quantified (Weinstein and Stason 1977). For example, one might estimate the costs associated with extending life for an additional year. The outcome from these analyses might be presented as $10,000 cost per life year saved ($10,000/life year). In this case, considering alternative technologies, leadership would adopt the technology with the *lowest* cost per life year saved.

Cost–utility analysis extends this measurement challenge even further by recognizing that the quality of life year extended might not always be the same. That realization led to a host of attempts to adjust the life years saved by some notion of the utility, value, or quality of that life (e.g., the findings on the Centers for Disease Control and Prevention's Health-Related Quality of Life website at www.cdc.gov/hrqol/index.htm). For example, if the outcome is an additional year of life, but the patient spends that year in pain or confined to a nursing home bed, the value of that life year might not be as great as nine months of pain-free or fully functional extended life. The key to using any of these formal methods of cost evaluation is to follow some version of the following eight steps (Centers for Disease Control and Prevention 2019; Gold et al. 1996; Rudin et al. 2014).

Steps in Using Cost-Evaluation Methods

Step 1: Identify Study Objectives

While this step may be obvious to many, clearly identifying study objectives may be the most important step in the analysis. Without knowing precisely what the organization desires or what the proposed HIT application or technology is designed to do, the outcomes of the evaluation are meaningless. Essentially, the decision comes down to whether the organization is looking narrowly at the financial benefits and costs associated with the decision or considering broader organizational or social benefits and costs. From the perspective of IT, social costs include those incurred by physicians or others who are not employees of the organization but whose opinions matter to decision makers. An otherwise strong HIT system may fail if the burden on the users is not fully measured.

Step 2: Specify the Alternatives

The relevant alternatives to the proposed technology must be clearly articulated; otherwise, a valid decision cannot be attained. Make the decision relative to the best alternative to ensure that the optimal choice is made. Not using credible alternatives in judging the proposed technology invites the risk of participants losing faith in the outcomes. A common error is to compare a proposed HIT solution with the status quo; the status quo is often not relevant when adopting an EHR, for example. Comparisons should be required among alternative vendors rather than with the current state of health record management.

Step 3: Develop a Framework for Analysis

The analysis framework is often called the *theoretical framework* or *theoretical model*, and one might have a tendency to ignore this step. Developing the framework is important, however, because it puts the technology into the broader systems context and defines how the inputs to the technology are related and how the outcomes are used by the system. It also forces an understanding of how the technology affects the total healthcare delivery system so that the direct and indirect (unintended consequences) costs and benefits to the system can be clearly identified and measured (Han et al. 2005). Returning to the EHR example, the theoretical framework forces a full understanding of how the information flows from the bedside or the physician's office to the electronic record; how that information is stored, catalogued, and retrieved from the record; and what the information's end uses are designed to be. Without that full understanding, crucial components of costs and benefits might be ignored or shortchanged.

Step 4: Measure Costs

Cost assessment is essential to the benefit–cost analysis. The identification and measurement of costs is relatively straightforward for big-ticket items such as direct labor, equipment, and supplies, but fully identifying indirect or opportunity costs associated with the intervention takes more time. The concept of total cost of ownership is an operational device designed to aid in defining and collecting relevant start-up (one time) and recurring costs (Hickman and Kusche 2006; Smaltz and Berner 2007). The EHR might shift some of the burden of data collection, analysis, and reporting. Unless that added burden results in easily measurable increases in time or supply use, it can often be overlooked. Management, in particular, can easily be affected by added data availability. The electronic record facilitates more analysis in an attempt to make better evidence-based decisions. While this may result in benefits associated with better decision-making, it may also result in added time spent understanding the data that are generated. Managers may find they spend more time preparing and poring over reports at the expense of other tasks.

Step 5: Measure Benefits

As with cost identification, good evaluation requires clear identification of all benefits associated with the technology. Ignoring key benefits can clearly lead to underestimating the net effect of technology. Johnston, Pan, and Middleton (2002) argue that many researchers take a narrow view of benefits, or, in their term, *HIT value*. They argue that one should consider organizational, financial, and clinical benefits. Identifying these benefits is facilitated if the framework for analysis is done correctly. A related issue with regard to benefits is that they must be realized and not necessarily speculative, assumed, or hypothetical.

Step 6: Factor in Life Cycle and Discounting

Most HIT projects have a pattern of costs and benefits that varies over the product's life cycle. Typically, costs are incurred early in a project cycle as resources are expended to purchase equipment and hire and train staff. Conversely, the benefits or value to the organization accrue over time. Understanding that cycle with respect to the organization's technology is important for making valid comparisons. Although the CIO or HIT decision-maker may not be as concerned with the timing issue as others in the healthcare organization, the timing of incurred benefits and costs cannot be ignored. In fact, considering alternatives with the same net costs and benefits, one should select that project with the distribution of costs skewed toward the future rather than that project with the distribution of benefits skewed toward the present.

Step 7: Deal with Uncertainty

By the nature of HIT investments, uncertainty exists regarding the estimates of both their costs and their value or benefits. Despite leadership's best efforts, they may find that these estimates are inaccurate. For example, with the EHR, physicians may not readily adopt the new technologies and systems as planned. In these cases, the costs of developing and implementing the system are the same, but the measured benefits are much lower. One never assumes exceedingly high levels of avoidance by the medical staff. If physicians do not adopt, the evaluation of the EHR most likely appears unsatisfactory. To deal with uncertainty, most look at the estimates being used and develop a best-case scenario and a worst-case scenario. For example, in the

EHR example, assume benefits with 80 percent of the medical staff fully participating. To test the best case, estimate benefits with 90 percent medical staff participation (base estimate + 10 percent). To test the worst case, estimate benefits with 70 percent medical staff participation (base estimate – 10 percent). This process is often called *sensitivity analysis.* If performing a sensitivity analysis yields estimates that do not change the overall evaluation of the technology, then confidence has been added to the decision. If, at extreme values, the overall evaluation of the technology changes, return to the framework and assumptions to be certain they are accurate.

Step 8: Consider Equity

This step has its origins in the federal government's use of benefit–cost analysis for evaluating alternative government interventions. However, it has application to individual healthcare organizations as well. Equity considerations require examination of not just what the costs and benefits are for the organization but also who receives those benefits and costs. Again, in the case of the EHR, if the benefits accrue to the institution, its employees, and its patients, but the costs are largely borne by those involved in using the technology (physicians), the EHR strategy is likely to fail (Landro 2003). For social investment decisions, consider compensating those who bear the costs from the gains made in the use of the technology. Healthcare organizations have no way to compensate cost bearers, and legal restrictions may limit their compensation.

Challenges to Evaluation

Despite the prevalence of HIT mechanisms in place in healthcare organizations, much evidence exists that HIT value is not easy to attain or ensure. Early assessments of the "state of the art" (Glandon and Shapiro 1988) suggested that more work was needed in this area. High-profile failures occurred, such as at Cedars-Sinai Medical Center in Los Angeles, which ended its effort to convert to a computerized physician order entry (CPOE) system in January 2003 (Ornstein 2003). The cause of this extreme failure is uncertain. Failure most probably occurs at the implementation stage, although failure of that magnitude may have had many causes.

In the late 1980s, some key findings on reasons for poor evaluations of technology suggested why HIT value did not always ensue from these significant investments. First, much of the technology was selected for the wrong reasons, such as keeping up with the competition. While there might be good reasons to adopt the technology that the competition is using, that alone is not sufficient reason to implement an HIT system or application. Second, knowledge, time, and money prohibited adequate evaluation. The CIO and their managers might have been too busy to spend the time conducting evaluations to determine value from the investment. Third, in many cases, the technology in place was determined to be a poor decision, which might help in future decisions but has no impact on the original decision going forward. This "water under the bridge" argument might keep leaders who are living in the past from investigating prior failures seriously (Glandon and Shapiro 1988).

Related to these items are the following two fundamental impediments to maximizing HIT value:

1. *Documentation*. The comprehensive, reliable data on the clinical or business outcomes related to the technology and the true, full costs associated with selecting, purchasing, and implementing it and with hiring staff and training staff—and so forth—are difficult to obtain, synthesize, and report. It takes time and money to determine whether the value from HIT investments actually exists. More on this issue, called the *total cost of ownership*, is presented in the next section.
2. *Interdependence*. Even if data have been defined and collected, the pervasive nature of the influence of many HIT investments across functional areas in the organization makes determination of value difficult at best. Many systems have both direct and indirect cost and outcome effects across a wide portion of the organization; thus, assigning value to a particular investment is a major undertaking.

Glandon and Buck (1994) identified fundamental challenges to maximizing value from HIT investments effectively. They developed a model of information systems that separates application and function (see exhibit 12.3) and suggests where more rigorous evaluation might exist.

EXHIBIT 12.3 Information Systems by Function and Information Requirement

Information Requirement	**Function**	
	Clinical	**Business**
External systems	Physician recruitment and retention Contracting	Legal actions Cost containment
Administrative systems	Case mix Care planning Patient scheduling	Absence and turnover control Revenue statistics Wage and salary planning Capital spending
Operational systems	Admission, discharge, and transfer Census reporting	Inventory control General ledger Accounts payable

Source: Glandon and Buck (1994). Adapted with permission from SAGE Publications, Thousand Oaks, California.

Assessing and ensuring value at the operational systems level has the greatest chance of success. Investments to improve admissions, discharge, and transfer (ADT) or general ledger applications have a greater chance of clearly linking the technology change to a measurable outcome. The well-defined and limited scope of such application reduces the severity of the measurement challenges. Outcomes at the operational level are generally characterized as intermediate compared with outcomes of the healthcare organization as a whole. For example, ADT outcomes might include time to admit a patient to a bed from the emergency department (ED) as an intermediate outcome. This outcome may depend on the ADT system, but ultimate outcome of patient mortality, morbidity, or satisfaction is less likely to be influenced by the ADT system.

Investments applied to administrative systems are less clear in terms of value assessment. These systems influence the efficiency and effectiveness of institutional operations and often contain some of the quantifiable elements inherent in operational systems. However, they often apply to cross-functional areas within the organization, making their impact more difficult to quantify. In administrative systems, then, it is less clear than in operational systems that outcomes, benefits, and costs are attributable to the new technology. Outcomes for administrative systems are generally intermediate, as are the outcomes for operational applications, but should apply more broadly than operational systems. This outcome has broader impact because medical staff, nursing, ancillary systems, and quality improvement and accreditation preparation all bear costs or benefit from changes in this outcome.

Finally, investments applied to strategic planning have the greatest difficulty with respect to value determination. All of the inputs used in these systems are cross-functional, which implies that data must be gathered from diverse units across the institution and often from outside of the institution. Outcomes are generally final from the perspective of the healthcare organization as a whole; thus, they are very difficult to measure, and attribution is always a challenge. For example, systems to support physician recruitment might be expected to lead to greater market share and improved physician retention. However, many external factors influence these outcomes, leading to greater uncertainty with respect to the value of this type of HIT investment. You might have improved physician recruitment by operating a well-functioning system. However, your market share and physician retention may suffer because a specialty hospital moved into your market and siphoned off key physicians and associated patients. The outcomes are poor from the organization's perspective.

Probably the best example of this type of challenge is with the introduction of the EHR strategy. Smaltz and Berner (2007) outline the interrelated nature of benefits and challenges the EHR system faces. Because an EHR system is not a thing but a comprehensive strategy, it is difficult

EXHIBIT 12.4 Descriptions of EHR Benefits by Category: Demonstration of System Nature of EHR

Category	Subcategory	Example of Impact
Improve efficiency	*Improve efficiency of the clinical patient care–related processes*	
	Access to information	Getting information when and where it is needed
	Organization of the data	Patient data entered one time
	Claims processing	Clinical data drive billing processes
Improve monitoring	*Enables individual provider profiles of performance as well as aggregate profiles*	
Improve clinical processes	*Real-time clinical decision support*	
	Quality improvement	Clinical and financial outcomes can be more easily monitored and linked
	Disease management	Aggregate data across patients

Source: Smaltz and Berner (2007).

to value. It is an "organizational, cultural transformation project that just happens to have a technology component" (Smaltz and Berner 2007, 16). Examination of just the benefits section of an EHR strategy described by these authors reveals how investment in this process spans the organization and creates difficulties in financial documentation. The descriptions in exhibit 12.4 by major benefit category and subcategory demonstrate that benefits are not confined to a single operational unit.

Value Realization

The IT Governance Institute (2006, 5) developed a multipart initiative to support HIT value realization in response to a perceived need for "organizations to optimize the realization of value" from investments (see chapter 4 for more background on HIT governance). The comprehensive framework assists users in measuring, monitoring, and maximizing realized value from HIT investments. Rather than a straightforward, one-step-at-a-time approach, this framework employs a holistic approach to value realization. While not fundamentally different from the benefit–cost analysis and cost-effectiveness analysis methodologies described earlier, this framework is more attuned to HIT leadership's decision-making.

The IT Governance Institute approach starts by asking the following four questions, posed originally by Thorp (2003):

1. *Strategic question: Are we doing the right thing?* Is the investment aligned with a broader business vision, is it consistent with established principles, and does it contribute to the strategic objectives?
2. *Architecture question: Are we doing it the right way?* Is the investment aligned with existing information technology architecture and consistent with ongoing architecture principles?
3. *Value question: Are we getting the benefits?* Do you have a clear understanding of the expected benefits, and do you have a process for realizing the benefits?
4. *Delivery question: Are we getting it done the right way?* Do you have effective and disciplined management, delivery, and change management processes with technical and business resources to deliver the promise of the technology investment?

In the context of these four questions, the Governance Institute uses a three-part strategy to maximize return on HIT investment (the first two elements are described in chapters 4 and 10, and the third is discussed in the following section):

1. *Value governance.* Optimizes the value of an organization's information technology–enabled investments by establishing the governance, monitoring, and control framework; by providing strategic direction for the investments; and by defining the investment portfolio characteristics (see chapter 4).
2. *Portfolio management.* Ensures that an organization's overall portfolio of information technology–enabled investments is aligned with and contributing optimal value to its strategic objectives by establishing and managing resource profiles, defining investment thresholds, evaluating and prioritizing new investments, managing the overall portfolio, and monitoring and reporting on portfolio performance (see chapter 10).
3. *Investment management.* Ensures that HIT investments deliver outcomes at reasonable costs while also managing associated risk.

To accomplish the investment management aspect of obtaining a return on HIT investment, the IT Governance Institute proposes that the organization engage in an eight-step process. In this framework, implementing the investment management process requires detailed information gathering; assessment of benefits, costs, and risks; selection of the investment vehicle; and monitoring outcomes. This process is geared to the corporate environment, as opposed to the government or social perspective. These eight steps by the IT Governance Institute (2006) are outlined in exhibit 12.5 and detailed in the following sections.

EXHIBIT 12.5
Steps in Information Technology Business Case Development

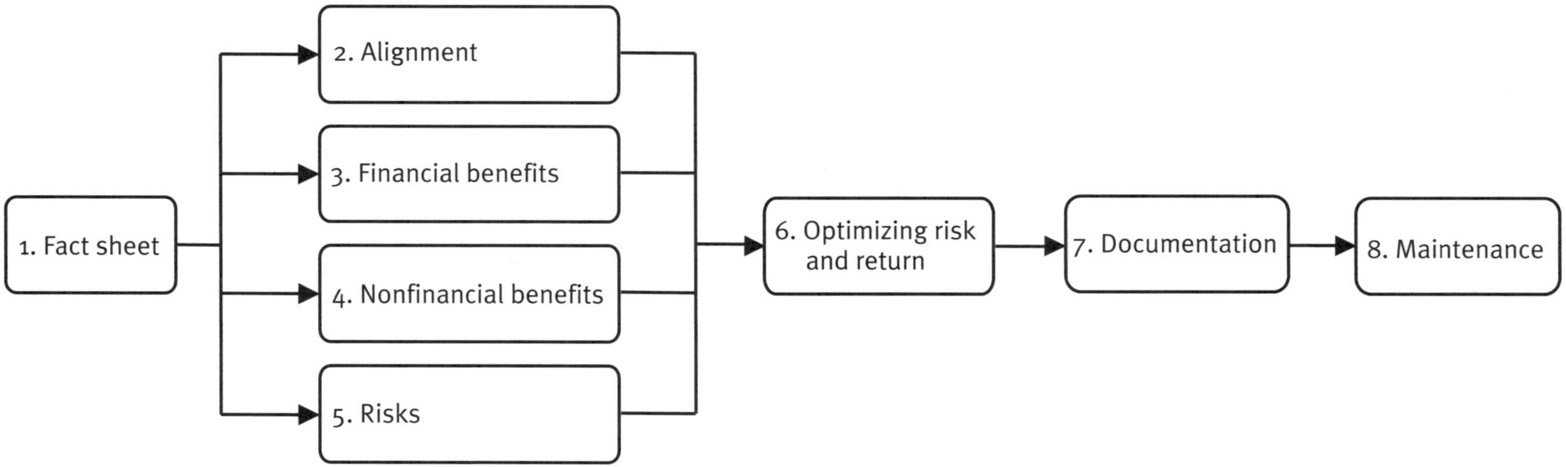

Source: *Enterprise Value: Governance of IT Investments, the Business Case*, IT Governance Institute, © 2006. All rights reserved. Used by permission.

Step 1: Building the Fact Sheet

The first step in the process is to gather all of the information relevant for making the appropriate HIT business decision. The IT Governance Institute provides a model form for collecting the necessary data, but our experience suggests that each organization should implement a collection form that works in its environment. The key point is that no category of information can be ignored. At a minimum, the following categories need to be assembled (IT Governance Institute's equivalent terms are given in parentheses):

- *Congruence (alignment).* The investment must be consistent with documented business strategy (see chapter 4), current HIT management practices, and government regulatory constraints (current and anticipated).
- *Business outcomes.* The investment must deliver an organizational need to achieve intermediate and final outcomes. These outcomes need to be documented and measurable.
- *Financial benefits.* Input for financial benefits should document cost savings, revenue enhancements, capacity and volume growth, and risk mitigation from the investment decision. These include the tangible revenue enhancements or cost reductions in capital, operations, or risk.
- *Indirect benefits (nonfinancial benefits).* As in the benefit–cost assessment, some benefits are not easily quantified in financial terms but must be seriously considered nonetheless.
- *Costs (resources and expenditures).* All categories of equipment, human resources, supplies, consultants, and other resources necessary for the HIT investment must be documented.
- *Sensitivity (risk).* Alternatives that quantify the risk in the investment must be identified. Understanding the best-case and worst-case scenarios for the investment helps the organization select an investment that meets its tolerance for risk.
- *Model (assumptions and constraints).* Understanding how the HIT investment accomplishes the desired outcomes, with associated benefits and costs, helps to determine the reasonableness of the subsequent analyses. The logic of the empirical claims for outcomes, benefits, and costs depends crucially on the assumptions employed. These must be articulated clearly.

Step 2: Alignment Analysis

Investment alternatives abound, necessitating decision-making. The selected option needs to optimize net benefits from the scarce resources available. Alignment helps to ensure that the HIT-related investments support the organization's strategic business objectives. Alignment statements might include direct contribution to the objectives of the current organization or to the broader system or contribution to a future vision for the organization. The investment must also be consistent with existing enterprise architecture. Assuming that this architecture has been selected as a guideline for achieving the current vision, each investment must be chosen carefully so as not to move away from that guideline.

Step 3: Financial Benefits Analysis

To gain acceptance in the healthcare corporate environment, HIT investments must pass conventional financial analysis constraints. Discounting of financial benefits and costs is an essential technique. The final decision requires the project to have a positive discounted net value (positive net present value, or NPV) and perhaps have better NPV than alternative investments, so that the organization selects the best investment.

Step 4: Nonfinancial Benefits Analysis

The nonfinancial aspects of business processes must also be considered, especially in not-for-profit healthcare organizations. Building positive relations with constituencies external to the HIT function may create value for the organization. Alternatively, negative relations can destroy value. Consideration of the external or indirect effects of the investment may not fully offset poor financial considerations but may influence a decision that is otherwise close.

Step 5: Risk Analysis

Not every organization tolerates risk in the same way, and not all investment opportunities carry the same risks. Assessing and documenting these risks in outcomes, financial benefits, and resource use or costs are integral steps in the value-assessment process. Both delivery risk and benefit risk are inherent in any HIT investment. One must ask if the investment delivers on the anticipated business processes, human resources, technology, and organizational changes being proposed. Likewise, the outcomes and financial benefits promised may not, in fact, occur. In simple terms, the HIT investment may not perform as promised. The IT Governance Institute (2006) provides many examples of both delivery and benefit risks.

Step 6: Optimizing Risk and Return

As stated in chapter 10, the program planning office (portfolio management office) must assess and review the HIT investment proposal in the context of other applications and broad business needs. The key is that all proposals have the same sets of information collected and reported and that assessment is done in a comparable manner. The best decision emerges if valid comparisons are made by those with the incentive to maximize value to the organization.

Step 7: Documenting Business Case

Nothing can be more important than transparency in decision-making. Documentation of data and information, assessment techniques, and findings all add to the open framework for decisions. This "open architecture" helps to create the culture of critical assessment that is so important to good decision-making. The tendency to not reveal information as a mechanism to protect those making the decision may lead to poorer outcomes and to greater consequences should those outcomes fail to meet standards.

Step 8: Feedback Mechanism

The single view of HIT investment value as presented by the value-realization effort is a necessary first step for healthcare organizations, but HIT investment needs, organizational priorities, staffing constraints, and other environmental changes occur continuously. The information collected, assumptions made, benefits observed, and costs incurred should be reviewed periodically throughout the life cycle of the investment. While many decisions cannot be undone, midcourse adjustments in investment scale and scope are often possible. If the organization veers off course as a result of an investment, having a feedback mechanism enables the organization to adjust to minimize loss. CPOE provides a good example of the potential value of feedback. Faced with resistance to the widespread adoption of this technology, an organization could apply a temporary solution, implementing it in only some parts of the organization; that is, it could identify clinical areas or key supportive medical staff leaders and implement only in select areas. This narrowing of focus prevents some of the resistance and presents the areas more likely to be successful. Full implementation might occur later, but the costly failure of the entire project could be avoided.

To close this discussion, a number of investigators and thought leaders have found that the methods for realizing HIT value are often difficult to implement. As Johnston, Pan, and Middleton (2002) suggest, HIT investment decisions continue to rely on "anecdote, inference, and opinion" rather than evidence. They argue that HIT leadership must support a comprehensive assessment of value using existing data. Toward that end, Bates and colleagues (2003) propose a set of ten commandments to follow for effective clinical decision support. While specifically designed to make evidence-based medicine a reality, these commandments also enhance HIT value realization. Four of the ten commandments are particularly important for HIT value. They are as follows (Bates et al. 2003):

1. *Be aware that speed is everything.* Providers will not accept a system that does not respond quickly to their inquiries. System design for rapid access appears to be essential for IT effectiveness.

2. *Fit into the user's workflow.* The HIT investment must support the providers' and other users' current practice processes if it is to be readily accepted. They will not use a system that does not fit seamlessly.
3. *Keep in mind that simple interventions work best.* The HIT investment with grand plans to alter the practice of medicine may not be as effective as a simple solution.
4. *Monitor impact, get feedback, and respond.* The feedback mechanism appears to be essential for success. Even the best systems may not integrate in the manner anticipated; thus, being flexible and adaptable may be keys to success.

You should notice at this point how similar the Benefit Cost Analysis section was to the Benefit Realization. While they differ in detail, they both require a systematic and formal set of activities to ensure analyses yield robust results. As Rudin and colleagues (2014) demonstrate, failure in this regard is still common. Their investigations find major challenges with healthcare IT evaluation studies, prompting them to set three primary, simplifying guidelines to use as you read the evaluation literature:

1. Analyses must include measures of both costs related to the technology (including implementation costs) and its benefits. Four of the ten studies they examined did not include either costs or benefits.
2. Analyses must measure the impact over a long enough time frame to be sure to capture the costs and benefits fully. All of the studies they examined were short term.
3. Analyses must recognize that the benefits and even the costs differ with stakeholder preferences. Studies should recognize and report whose perspective is being considered. Only one of the studies considered provided stakeholder perspectives explicitly.

Health Information Technology Value Findings

Impact of Specific Health Information Technology Investments

Many studies have been conducted on specific HIT investment value recognition, but we find that many are not well done and are thus difficult to evaluate concisely. In this section, we feature three groups or ideas as a way of organizing this aspect of the literature. First, we will start with some early studies that applied the growing literature to the health system (Hillstad et al. 2011). This was a time when consideration of large-scale investments in HIT were not accepted without question by all. Second, once we generally believed that HIT was part of the path to the future, we began to examine specific applications in particular settings. A common characteristic of these studies is that they tended to report only narrow analyses of the effects of HIT investments. The desire for academic rigor results in such narrow scope. HIT managers need broader evaluations to make decisions for the organization; therefore, we also report some studies of HIT investment impact on organizations and systems. Third, we look briefly at the remaining challenges in implementing HIT evaluations.

Early Justification of Health Information Technology Investment

If we start with Hillestad and colleagues (2005), we see the early promise from their national simulation of the potential cost savings from HIT investments—specifically, adoption of an electronic medical record (EMR, now referred to as an EHR). Exhibit 12.6, from the Hillestad and colleagues study, suggested that in the near term, savings would possibly total as much as $21.3 billion per year (year 5), more of which was derived from inpatient care than from outpatient care. Once adoption reached the anticipated

EXHIBIT 12.6 Short-Term and Long-Term Annual Cost Savings from HIT, by Selected Major Categories

	Short Term Year 5 (in billions)	Percent of Total	Long Term Year 15 (in billions)	Percent of Total
Outpatient				
Transcription	$ 0.4	1.9	$ 1.7	2.2
Chart pulls	$ 0.4	1.9	$ 1.5	1.9
Laboratory tests	$ 0.5	2.3	$ 2.0	2.6
Drug usage	$ 3.0	14.1	$ 11.0	14.2
Radiology	$ 0.8	3.8	$ 3.3	4.3
Total output savings	$ 5.2	24.4	$20.4	26.3
Inpatient				
Nursing time	$ 3.4	16.0	$ 13.7	17.7
Laboratory tests	$ 0.8	3.8	$ 2.6	3.4
Drug usage	$ 1.0	4.7	$ 3.5	4.5
Length of stay	$ 10.1	47.4	$34.7	44.8
Medical records	$ 0.7	3.3	$ 2.4	3.1
Total input savings	$ 16.1	75.6	$57.1	73.7
Total HIT savings	$ 21.3	100.0	$77.4	100.0

Note: Numbers and percentages do not sum to totals because of rounding.
Source: Hillestad et al. (2005). Used with permission from Project HOPE, Milwood, Virginia.

90 percent, savings could amount to more than $77 billion per year (again, more of this savings was derived from inpatient care). The savings in inpatient care would have come from reductions in length of stay followed by reductions in nursing time. On the outpatient side, most of the savings would have come from reduced and more appropriate drug use.

In addition to these cost savings, benefits or value from HIT investments in the simulation were derived from improved patient safety and health outcomes. Hillestad and colleagues (2005) theorized that the safety benefits of CPOE would be seen at the national level for both inpatient and outpatient care. Inpatient care savings resulting from the elimination of an estimated 200,000 adverse drug events (ADEs) amounted to $1 billion per year once fully implemented. Outpatient care savings resulting from an estimated two million ADEs avoided amounted to $3.5 billion per year. The findings might not be generalizable to other participants because most of the data they used came from studies involving those under age 65. At about the same time, Featherly and colleagues (2007) found that EMR benefits were largely indirect and came from workflow improvements and reductions in medical mishaps.

Near-term preventive care can benefit from HIT intervention as well. Hillestad and colleagues (2005) generated estimates for two vaccination programs (influenza, pneumococcal) and three screening programs (breast cancer, cervical cancer, colorectal cancer). The findings were highly positive from a health outcome perspective and depended heavily on assumptions regarding current compliance rates in the defined population, compliance rates for the specific vaccination and screening programs, and costs. Taking the midpoints of the estimated effects, the simulated pneumococcal vaccination resulted in a median reduction of 21,000 deaths per year (15,000 to 27,000), 2.25 million median bed days eliminated (1.5 million to 3.0 million), and 150,000 median workdays restored (100,000 to 200,000). These effects came at a program cost of about $90 million per year. At the same time, however, the program generated median financial benefits estimated at $750 million per year ($500 million to $1 billion).

Focused Studies

To keep up with what has become a large and growing literature on valuation studies in HIT, it is probably best to rely upon investigators to gather, categorize, and summarize the findings (Buntin et al. 2011; Goldzweig et al. 2011; O'Reilly et al. 2012; Reis et al. 2017). These and others review and summarize the findings of others, often presenting concise comparisons of research methods, study findings, and recommendations. In addition, the Office of the National Coordinator for Health Information Technology (ONCHIT) has a rich website with a host of important information, presented in an organized fashion (ONCHIT 2018). The website includes the following (though it has much more):

- *Health IT and Health Information Exchange Basics.* As the name implies, this section has a great deal of introductory information regarding the EHR, information exchange, and their resultant benefits, among other key topics. Most important, however, it contains a subsection, Case Studies, that presents an ongoing set of detailed descriptions of efforts to implement HIT throughout the country. It also has a subsection, Success Stories, that are more applied and provide discrete examples of HIT use.
- *Health IT in Health Care Setting.* This component of the website delves deeply into specific applications of HIT for you to explore. While not every potential application is included, it has behavioral health, public health, rural health, telemedicine, pediatric care, emergency medical services and emergency preparedness, long-term and post-acute care, and social determinants of care, among other applications.
- *Health IT Resources.* This component contains a host of tools of value to those arguing for value and implementing HIT.
- *International IT Collaboration.* This component hosts a number of specific collaborative efforts coordinated through or with the support of the US government. The content is not specific to valuation, but many innovations in measuring value from HIT have come from and will continue to come from other systems.

The following list contains a sampling of valuation findings organized by key content areas.

1. Electronic health records
   - Electronic prescribing: Devine et al. 2010 (time and motion study); Abramson et al. 2011 (ambulatory prescribing errors); Duffy et al. 2010 (ambulatory medical residency program)
   - Electronic health records: Furukawa, Raghu, and Shao 2010 (greater-capacity EMR related to greater efficiency for California hospitals); Connelly et al. 2012 (EMR data resulted in better outcomes for heart failure patients); Fleming et al. 2011 (cost of implementation and maintenance of EMR in primary care practices in North Texas)
   - Other: Pettit, Zimmerman, Alaniz, and Dorsch 2012 (CPOE evaluation for enoxaparin); Bell et al. 2012 (lab data exchange for HIV); McCormick et al. 2012 (electronic access to lab data);

Stenner, Chen, and Johnson 2010 (generic drug substitution in decision support); Eisenstein et al. 2012 (a study of specific decision-support applications studies found cost increasing)

2. Information access
   - Mobile phones: Quinn et al. 2011 (behavioral modification for blood glucose control)
   - Web: Gustafson et al. 2012 (pediatric asthma); Lau et al. 2012 (influenza vaccine); Ling et al. 2010 (test results at an urban clinic for sexually transmitted diseases); Palen et al. 2012 (online patient access and use of clinical services)
3. Systems technologies
   - Exchange interoperability; Walker et al. 2005 (national model of interoperable exchange); Mäenpää et al. 2011 (five-year follow-up on regional information exchange)

Finally, there are always counter findings to the value of healthcare IT. Carayon, Wetterneck, and colleagues (2017) and Carayon, Du, and colleagues (2017) clearly demonstrate that for some applications (computer-based provider order entry) and locations (ICU), the technologies may introduce errors into the system. Naturally, if outcomes decline and the costs are positive, health systems should not apply the technology (see exhibit 12.2).

Health Information Technology Evaluation Challenges

The challenge in compiling and organizing studies on IT effectiveness hinge on an understanding of the complexities involved in designing the studies. As we examine current studies, we need to classify them to make sense of their application. Not all studies examine the same type of IT, nor do they apply to the same populations. Generalizing individual findings across dimensions is likely inappropriate. A useful paradigm for presentation includes the following elements:

- Type of delivery setting
  - Organization level (e.g., inpatient, outpatient)
  - Kind of organization (e.g., teaching hospital, community hospital for an inpatient setting; physician's office, ambulatory clinic, freestanding surgical center for an outpatient setting)
  - Segment of the organization (e.g., ED, ICU, laboratory)
- Disease application (e.g., high blood pressure, HIV, congestive heart failure)
- Technology studied (e.g., EHR, electronic prescribing, Web-based information)

- Outcome considered (e.g., medication or medical error, readmission, patient satisfaction)
- Patient type (e.g., Medicare, Medicaid, private insurance, male, elderly)

In addition, consistent with the assertion that HIT leadership must reach out to the entire organization in its efforts to invest in HIT, studies have been published that assess the value of HIT investments in terms of their impact on the organization as a whole. Iansiti and colleagues (2005) demonstrate that HIT matters, at least in midsize firms. Their research does not measure the impact of any specific technology intervention or even overall dollars spent. It uses an index of what "IT actually does for a business" to measure impact. Iansiti and colleagues (2005) created an IT scorecard to assess HIT capability in the functional areas of sales and marketing, finance, operations, empowered professionals, and IT infrastructure. They found that greater capability generates business process scalability, which enables firms to do the following:

- Improve process knowledge and standardization
- Streamline operations, allowing the firm to grow without expanding the labor force
- Become flexible enough to take advantage of or respond to new opportunities
- Enhance management's access to critical business indicators used in decision-making

Similarly, Menachemi and colleagues (2006) demonstrate a robust relationship between HIT adoption and hospital financial performance, at least for hospitals in Florida. Their findings suggest that overall and operational improvement followed from IT adoption. This outcome was observed for their categories of clinical, administrative, and strategic IT.

Summary

HIT should adhere to core business processes. In that context, the decisions regarding how much and what types of HIT resources an organization uses should fall under a valuation paradigm. Finding value in any healthcare investment has proven to be a challenge, however, because data collection, methodology, and application make the use of evidence-based management difficult. Because of the complexity of the problem and the lack of comprehensive data, healthcare executives have largely been forced to make decisions about HIT investments on the basis of cursory evidence at best and on the basis of instinct or hope at worst. As a result, HIT may fall short in helping to address the problems plaguing healthcare.

From the perspective of HIT leaders, however, HIT is essential for the provision of high-quality care in today's environment—so they must face the decision to invest in HIT. Many factors make such decisions difficult, including the scaling of IT and the systems nature of IT. For example, technology acquisition is not an all-or-nothing proposition; questions of scale, scope, application, integration, and timing are involved. The interdependence of providers in a healthcare "system" complicates the decision further. Healthcare delivery organizations implement interoperable EHRs to enable the exchange of information across venues while still focusing on value creation.

Early evidence from HIT investment studies indicates that EHRs, HIEs, clinical decision support systems, and a host of other technologies have the potential to improve care and contain or lower costs. However, value has not been identified consistently, and the potential benefits may be less than estimated. Furthermore, not all HIT leaders are yet fully behind HIT implementation. Providers will come to expect electronic information exchange as they increasingly work in teams that require functions in real time. The incentives offered by the HITECH Act encouraged widespread adoption of HIE and other HIT technologies, but impediments still exist. HIT leaders face many barriers to full adoption and remain reluctant to facilitate or implement an HIE.

Business decisions faced by the CIO—and indirectly by the CEO and board—come down to the dilemma of deciding among competing alternatives, leading to the evaluation challenge. The questions that must be asked are whether the HIT investment increases or decreases positive organizational outcomes and whether it increases or decreases costs to the organization. Economists have frameworks for assisting in making these decisions, called benefit–cost analyses, cost-effectiveness analyses, and cost–utility analyses. Further, business models suggest a similar evaluation process for value realization that consists of conceptualizing, capturing, analyzing, and reporting detailed financial and nonfinancial information. In addition, the IT Governance Institute (2006) has developed a detailed value-realization process that can direct HIT leadership to achieve their goals.

A number of challenges hinder the efforts to maximize the value of HIT investments, including lack of proper, detailed documentation of key information and conceptual problems of assigning benefits and costs to a particular investment. These investments garner benefits from and impose costs throughout the organization, thus posing problems of assignment to evaluate uniquely the net effect of any single investment. These effects are now extending even outside of the confines of the traditional organizational entity. Obtaining that data and generating reliable estimates of net value are problematic at best.

Web Resources

A number of organizations (through their websites) provide more information on the topics discussed in this chapter:

- The Advisory Board has prepared an evaluation tool kit for HIT (www.advisory.com/research/service-line-advisor/tools/2015/technology-evaluation-toolkit).
- Agency for Healthcare Research and Quality provides summaries of their funding products in the area of HIT value (https://healthit.ahrq.gov/funding-mechanism/demonstrating-value-health-information-technology).
- Agency for Healthcare Research and Quality has developed a tool kit for practitioners along with other, related evaluation materials (https://digital.ahrq.gov/health-it-tools-and-resources/evaluation-resources).
- The American Hospital Association provides helpful information on HIT evaluation (www.hret-hiin.org/resources/display/health-it-evaluation-toolkit).
- Check out Blue Cross and Blue Shield's Health of America project for a number of healthcare-related topics, including technology (www.bcbs.com/the-health-of-america/topics/healthcare-technology).
- The Center for Information Technology Leadership offers specific HIT intervention evaluations (www.citl.org).
- Centers for Disease Control and Prevention's Health-Related Quality of Life provides quality-of-life measurements (www.cdc.gov/hrqol/index.htm and www.cdc.gov/policy/polaris/economics/index.html).
- Colleaga, an open source network, provides a broad range of HIT evaluation and other information (www.colleaga.org/tools/health-information-technology-evaluation-toolkit).
- The Office of the National Coordinator for Health Information Technology has an expansive and continuously updated website on all aspects of HIT (www.healthit.gov/topic/health-it-and-health-information-exchange-basics/health-it-and-health-information-exchange).
- Large organizations have become sources for healthcare evaluations (see Blue Cross and Blue Shield's Health of America project for more information on many related topics, including technology [at www.bcbs.com/the-health-of-america/topics/healthcare-technology]).

Discussion Questions

1. Explain why obtaining value from HIT investments is so important in today's healthcare environment.
2. How valid and reliable do you think HIT investment decisions are currently? Why?
3. What is the system nature of healthcare, and why does it affect value estimation?
4. What do you think will drive adoption of interoperable EHRs—cost savings or consumer preferences? Why?
5. What is the evaluation problem faced by HIT investment decision-makers? Why does the matrix in exhibit 12.2 help in understanding that problem?
6. Why do we not observe examples of all of the cells in exhibit 12.2?
7. Compare and contrast benefit–cost, cost-effectiveness, and cost–utility analyses. Which do you prefer, and why?
8. List and assess the eight steps in conducting benefit–cost analysis, cost-effectiveness analysis, or cost–utility analysis.
9. What is value realization? In what ways is it similar to and different from economic evaluation techniques?
10. Explain the four questions proposed by the IT Governance Institute and why they are important.
11. Describe how the nature of the HIT investment application affects the quality and nature of the value determination.

References

Abramson, E. L., Y. Barrón, J. Quaresimo, and R. Kaushal. 2011. "Electronic Prescribing Within an Electronic Health Record Reduces Ambulatory Prescribing Errors." *Joint Commission Journal on Quality and Patient Safety* 37 (10): 470–78.

Adams J., E. Mounib, A. Pai, N. Stuart, R. Thomas, and P. Tomaszewicz. 2006. "Healthcare 2015: Win–Win or Lose–Lose? A Portrait and a Path to Successful Transformation." IBM Institute for Business Value. Accessed March 3, 2020. https://issuu.com/jvallejot/docs/healthcare2015-win-win_or_lose.

Asch, D. 2003. "How Physicians React to Cost-Effectiveness Information." *LDI Issue Brief* 8 (9): 1–4.

Attema, A., W. B. F. Brouwer, and K. Claxton. 2018. "Discounting in Economic Evaluations." *PharmacoEconomics* 36: 745–58.

Bates, D. W., G. J. Kuperman, S. Wang, T. Gandhi, A. Kittler, L. Volk, C. Spurr, R. Khorasani, M. Tanasijevic, and B. Middleton. 2003. "Ten Commandments for Effective Clinical Decision Support: Making the Practice of Evidence-Based Medicine a Reality." *Journal of the American Medical Informatics Association* 10 (6): 523–30.

Bell, D. S., L. Cima, D. S. Seiden, T. T. Nakazono, M. S. Alcouloumre, and W. E. Cunningham. 2012. "Effects of Laboratory Data Exchange in the Care of Patients with HIV." *International Journal of Medical Informatics* 81 (10): e74–82.

Bower, A. 2005. *The Diffusion and Value of Healthcare Information Technology*. Santa Monica, CA: RAND Corporation.

Buntin, M., M. Burke, M. Hoaglin, and D. Blumenthal. 2011. "The Benefits of Information Technology: A Review of the Recent Literature Shows Predominantly Positive Results." *Health Affairs* 30 (3): 464–71.

CADTH. 2017. *Guidelines for the Economic Evaluation of Health Technologies: Canada*, 4th ed. Accessed June 2019. www.cadth.ca/dv/guidelines-economic-evaluation-health-technologies-canada-4th-edition.

Carayon, P., T. B. Wetterneck, R. Cartmill, M. A. Blonsky, R. Brown, P. Hoonakker, R. Kim, S. Kukreja, M. Johnson, B. L. Paris, K. E. Wood, and J. M. Walker. 2017. "Medication Safety in Two Intensive Care Units of a Community Teaching Hospital After Electronic Health Record Implementation: Sociotechnical and Human Factors Engineering Considerations." *Journal of Patient Safety*. Published February 28. doi: 10.1097/PTS.0000000000000358.

Carayon, P., S. Du, R. Brown, R. Cartmill, M. Johnson, and T. B. Wetterneck. 2017. "EHR-Related Medication Errors in Two ICUs." *Journal of Healthcare Risk Management* 36 (3): 6–15.

Carr, N. 2003. "IT Doesn't Matter." *Harvard Business Review* 81 (5): 41–49.

Centers for Disease Control and Prevention. 2019. "Cost-Effectiveness Analysis." US Department of Health and Human Services. Updated January 2. www.cdc.gov/policy/polaris/economics/cost-effectiveness.html.

Chaudhry, B., J. Wang, S. Wu, M. Maglione, W. Mojica, E. Roth, S. C. Morton, and P. G. Shekelle. 2006. "Systematic Review: Impact of Health Information Technology on Quality, Efficiency and Costs of Medical Care." *Annals of Internal Medicine* 144 (10): 742–52.

Connelly, D. P., Y. T. Park, J. Du, N. Theera-Ampornpunt, B. D. Gordon, B. A. Bershow, R. A. Gensinger, Jr., M. Shrift, D. T. Routhe, and S. M. Speedie. 2012. "The Impact of Electronic Health Records on Care of Heart Failure Patients in the Emergency Room." *Journal of the American Medical Informatics Association* 19 (3): 334–40.

Cusack, C. M., C. Byrne, J. M. Hook, J. McGowan, E. G. Poon, and A. Zafar. 2009. *Health Information Technology Evaluation Toolkit: 2009 Update*. Rockville, MD: Agency for Healthcare Research and Quality.

Devine, E. B., W. Hollingworth, R. N. Hansen, N. M. Lawless, J. L. Wilson-Norton, D. P. Martin, D. K. Blough, and S. D. Sullivan. 2010. "Electronic Prescribing at the Point of Care: A Time-Motion Study in the Primary Care Setting." *Health Services Research* 45 (1): 152–71.

Duffy, R. L., S. S. Yiu, E. Molokhia, R. Walker, and R. A. Perkins. 2010. "Effects of Electronic Prescribing on the Clinical Practice of a Family Medicine Residency." *Family Medicine* 42 (5): 358–63.

Eisenstein, E. L., K. J. Anstrom, R. Edwards, J. M. Willis, J. Simo, and D. F. Lobach. 2012. "Population-Based Clinical Decision Support: A Clinical and Economic Evaluation." *Studies in Health Technology and Informatics* 180: 343–47.

Encinosa, W., and J. Bae. 2011. "Health Information Technology and Its Effects on Hospital Costs, Outcomes, and Patient Safety." *Inquiry* 48 (4): 288–303.

Enthoven, A. 2009. "Integrated Delivery Systems: The Cure for Fragmentation." *American Journal of Managed Care* 15 (10): S284–90.

Enthoven, A., and L. Tollen. 2005. "Competition in Health Care: It Takes Systems to Pursue Quality and Efficiency." *Health Affairs*. Accessed January 4, 2008. http://content.healthaffairs.org/cgi/content/abstract/hlthaff.w5.420.

Featherly, K., D. Garets, M. Davis, P. Wise, and P. Becker. 2007. "Sharpening the Case for Returns on Investment from Clinical Information Systems." *Healthcare Quarterly* 10 (1): 101–10.

Fleming, N. S., S. D. Culler, R. McCorkle, E. R. Becker, and D. J. Ballard. 2011. "The Financial and Nonfinancial Costs of Implementing Electronic Health Records in Primary Care Practices." *Health Affairs* 30 (3): 481–89.

Furukawa, M. F., T. S. Raghu, and B. B. Shao. 2010. "Electronic Medical Records, Nurse Staffing, and Nurse-Sensitive Patient Outcomes: Evidence from California Hospitals, 1998–2007." *Health Services Research* 45 (4): 941–62.

Glandon, G. L., and T. Buck. 1994. "Cost–Benefit Analysis of Medical Information Systems: A Critique." In *Evaluating Health Care Information Systems: Methods and Applications*, edited by J. Anderson, C. Aydin, and S. Jay. Thousand Oaks, CA: SAGE Publications.

Glandon, G. L., and R. J. Shapiro. 1988. "Benefit–Cost Analysis of Hospital Information Systems: The State of the (Non) Art." *Journal of Health & Human Resources Administration* 11 (1): 30–92.

Gold, M., J. Siegel, L. Russell, and M. Weinstein. 1996. *Cost-Effectiveness in Health and Medicine*. New York: Oxford University Press.

Goldzweig, C. L., A. Towfigh, M. Maglione, and P. Shekelle. 2009. "Costs and Benefits of Health Information Technology: New Trends from the Literature." *Health Affairs* 28 (2): w282–93.

Gustafson, D., M. Wise, A. Bhattacharya, A. Pulvermacher, K. Shanovich, B. Phillips, E. Lehman, V. Chinchilli, R. Hawkins, and J. S. Kim. 2012. "The Effects of Combining Web-based eHealth with Telephone Nurse Case Management for Pediatric Asthma Control: A Randomized Controlled Trial." *Journal of Medical Internet Research* 14 (4): e101.

Han, Y. Y., J. A. Carcillo, S. T. Venkataraman, R. S. Clark, R. S. Watson, T. C. Nguyen, H. Bayir, and R. A. Orr. 2005. "Unexpected Increased Mortality After Implementation of a Commercially Sold Computerized Physician Order Entry System." *Pediatrics* 116 (6): 1506–12.

Healthcare Information and Management Systems Society (HIMSS). 2019. *2019 HIMSS Leadership and Workforce Survey*. Accessed March 25, 2020. www.himss.org/sites/

hde/files/d7/u132196/2019_HIMSS_US_LEADERSHIP_WORKFORCE_SURVEY_Final_Report.pdf.

———. 2018. *2018 HIMSS Leadership and Workforce Survey: Senior IT Executive Results.* Accessed March 25, 2020. www.himss.org/sites/hde/files/d7/u132196/2018_HIMSS_US_LEADERSHIP_WORKFORCE_SURVEY_Final_Report.pdf.

———. 2012. *2012 HIMSS Leadership Survey: Senior IT Executive Results.* Published February 21. https://s3.amazonaws.com/rdcms-himss/files/production/public/HIMSSorg/Content/files/2012FINAL%20Leadership%20Survey%20with%20Cover.pdf.

Hickman G., and K. Kusche. 2006. "Building the EHR Total Cost of Ownership (TCO) Model." Webinar presented by the Healthcare Information and Management Systems Society webinar, Chicago, April 27.

Hillestad, R., J. Bigelow, A. Bower, F. Girosi, R. Meili, R. Scoville, and R. Taylor. 2005. "Can Electronic Medical Record Systems Transform Health Care? Potential Health Benefits, Savings, and Costs." *Health Affairs* 24 (5): 1103–17.

Holmgren, A. J., V. Patel, and J. Adler-Milstein. 2017. "Progress in Interoperability: Measuring US Hospitals Engagement in Sharing Patient Data." *Health Affairs.* Published October. www.healthaffairs.org/doi/abs/10.1377/hlthaff.2017.0546?journalCode=hlthaff.

Iansiti, M., G. Favaloro, J. Utzechneider, and G. Richards. 2005. "Why IT Matters in Midsized Firms." Harvard Business School Working Paper Series No. 06-013. Accessed March 2013. www.hbs.edu/faculty/Publication%20Files/06-013.pdf.

IT Governance Institute. 2006. *Enterprise Value: Governance of IT Investments, the Business Case.* Rolling Meadows, IL: IT Governance Institute.

Johnston, D., E. Pan, and B. Middleton. 2002. *Finding the Value in Healthcare Information Technologies.* Boston: Center for Information Technology Leadership.

Kamal, R., and and C. Cox. 2018. "How Do Healthcare Prices and Use in the US Compare to Other Countries?" Peterson-KFF. Published May 8. www.healthsystemtracker.org/chart-collection/how-do-healthcare-prices-and-use-in-the-u-s-compare-to-other-countries.

Kark, K. 2018. "IT Spending: From Value Preservation to Value Creation." Deloitte Insights. Published March 12. https://deloitte.wsj.com/cio/2018/03/12/it-spending-from-value-preservation-to-value-creation.

Kass, E. M. 2017. "2018 Tech Budgets to Rise about 8.8% for Healthcare Organizations." *Health Data Management.* Published December 27. www.healthdatamanagement.com/news/2018-tech-budgets-to-rise-about-88-for-healthcare-organizations.

Kindig, D., and G. Stoddart. 2003. "What Is Population Health?" *American Journal of Public Health* 93 (3): 380–83.

King, J., V. Patel, E. W. Iamoom, and M. F. Furukawa. 2014. "Clinical Benefits of Electronic Health Record Use: National Findings." *Health Services Research* 49 (1): 392–404.

Koppel, R. 2005. "Computerized Physician Order Entry Systems: The Right Prescription?" *LDI Issue Brief* 10 (5): 1–4.

Krousel-Wood, M., A. B. McCoy, C. Ahia, E. W. Holt, D. N. Trapani, Q. Luo, E. G. Price-Haywood, E. J. Thomas, D. F. Sittig, and R. V. Milani. 2018. "Implementing Electronic Health Records (EHRs): Health Care Provider Perceptions Before and After Transition from a Local Basic EHR to a Commercial Comprehensive EHR." *Journal of the American Medical Informatics Association* 25 (6): 618–26.

Landro, L. 2003. "Doctors Need Incentives to Embrace Technology." Published July 9. www.wsj.com/articles/SB105777796472723600.

Lau, A. Y., V. Sintchenko, J. Crimmins, F. Magrabi, B. Gallego, and E. Coiera. 2012. "Impact of a Web-Based Personally Controlled Health Management System on Influenza Vaccination and Health Services Utilization Rates: A Randomized Controlled Trial." *Journal of the American Medical Informatics Association* 19 (5): 719–27.

Loomis, G. A., J. S. Ries, R. M. Saywell, Jr., and N. R. Thakker. 2002. "If Electronic Medical Records Are So Great, Why Aren't Family Physicians Using Them?" *Journal of Family Practice* 51 (7): 636–41.

Ling, S. B., D. B. Richardson, C. J. Mettenbrink, B. C. Westergaard, T. D. Sapp-Jones, L. A. Crane, A. C. Nyquist, M. McFarlane, R. Kachur, and C. A. Reitmeijer. 2010. "Evaluating a Web-Based Test Results System at an Urban STI Clinic." *Sexually Transmitted Diseases* 37 (4): 259–63.

Mäenpää, T., P. Asikainen, M. Gissler, K. Siponen, M. Maass, K. Saranto, and T. Suominen. 2011. "Outcomes Assessment of the Regional Health Information Exchange: A Five-Year Follow-Up Study." *Methods of Information in Medicine* 50 (4): 308–18.

McCormick, D., D. H. Bor, S. Woolhandler, and D. U. Himmelstein. 2012. "Giving Office-Based Physicians Electronic Access to Patients' Prior Imaging and Lab Results Did Not Deter Ordering of Tests." *Health Affairs* 31 (3): 488–96.

Menachemi, N., J. Burkhardt, R. Shewchuk, D. Burke, and R. Brooks. 2006. "Hospital Information Technology and Positive Financial Performance: A Different Approach to Finding an ROI." *Journal of Healthcare Management* 51 (1): 40–58.

Meyer, R., and P. Degoulet. 2008. "Assessing the Capital Efficiency of Healthcare Information Technologies: An Econometric Perspective." *IMIA Yearbook of Medical Informatics* 1 (17): 114–27.

Murphy, K. 2016. "4 Barriers Limiting EHR Use, Health Information Exchange." *EHR Intelligence*. Published March 21. http://ehrintelligence.com/news/4-barriers-limiting-ehr-use-health-information-exchange.

Office of the National Coordinator for Health Information Technology (ONCHIT). 2018. "Health IT and Health Information Exchange Basics." Accessed December 17. www.healthit.gov/topic/health-it-and-health-information-exchange-basics/health-it-and-health-information-exchange.

O'Reilly, D., J. Tarride, R. Goeree, C. Lokker, and K. A. McKibbon. 2012. "The Economics of Health Information Technology in Medication Management: A Systematic Review of Economic Evaluations." *Journal of the American Medical Informatics Association* 19 (3): 423–38.

Ornstein, C. 2003. "Hospital Heeds Doctors, Suspends Use of Software." *Los Angeles Times.* Published January 22. www.latimes.com/archives/la-xpm-2003-jan-22-me-cedars22-story.html.

Padmanabhan, P. 2019. "Digital and AI Are Top Priorities in 2019, EHR Systems Continue to Dominate IT Spend." DamoIntel. Published January 10. http://damoconsulting.net/wp-content/uploads/2019/09/2019-Healthcare-IT-Demand-Survey-document.pdf.

Palen, T. E., C. Ross, J. D. Powers, and S. Xu. 2012. "Association of Online Patient Access to Clinicians and Medical Records with Use of Clinical Services." *Journal of the American Medical Association* 308 (19): 2012–19.

Pettit, R. S., C. R. Zimmerman, C. Alaniz, and M. P. Dorsch. 2012. "Cost Analysis Before and After Implementation of a Computerized Physician Order Entry Order Form for Enoxaparin." *Pharmacy and Therapeutics* 37 (2): 107–11.

Quinn, C. C., M. D. Shardell, M. L. Terrin, E. A. Barr, S. H. Ballew, and A. L. Gruber-Baldini. 2011. "Cluster-Randomized Trial of a Mobile Phone Personalized Behavioral Intervention for Blood Glucose Control." *Diabetes Care* 34 (9): 1934–42.

Rahimi, B., and V. Vimarlund. 2007. "Methods to Evaluate Health Information Systems in Healthcare Settings: A Literature Review." *Journal of Medical Systems* (5): 397–432.

Reis, Z. S. N., T. A. Maia, M. S. Marcolino, F. Becerra-Posada, D. Novillo-Ortiz, and A. L. P. Ribeiro. 2017. "Is There Evidence of Cost Benefits of Electronic Medical Records, Standards, or Interoperability in Hospital Information Systems? Overview of Systematic Reviews." *Journal of Medical Internet Research* 5 (3): e26.

Rudin, R., S. Jones, P. Shekelle, R. Hillestad, and E. Keeler. 2014. "The Value of Health Information Technology: Filling the Knowledge Gap." *American Journal of Managed Care* 20 (Special Issue): esp1–8.

Sanyal, C., P. Stolee, D. Juzwishin, and D. Husereau. 2018. "Economic Evaluations of eHealth Technologies: A Systematic Review." PLOS ONE 13 (6): e0198112.

Simon, S. J., and S. J. Simon. 2006. "An Examination of the Financial Feasibility of Electronic Medical Records (EMRs): A Case Study of Tangible and Intangible Benefits." *International Journal of Electronic Healthcare* 2 (2): 185–200.

Smaltz, D., and E. Berner. 2007. *The Executive's Guide to Electronic Health Records.* Chicago: Health Administration Press.

Southern California Evidence-Based Practice Center. 2006. "Costs and Benefits of Health Information Technology." Agency for Healthcare Research and Quality. Published April. www.ahrq.gov/downloads/pub/evidence/pdf/hitsyscosts/hitsys.pdf.

Stammen, L. A., R. E. Stalmeijer, E. Patemotte, A. O. Pool, E. W. Driessen, F. Scheele, and L. P. S. Stassen. 2015. "Training Physicians to Provide High-Value, Cost-Conscious Care: A Systematic Review." *Journal of the American Medical Association* 314 (22): 2384–400.

Stenner, S. P., Q. Chen, and K. B. Johnson. 2020. "Impact of Generic Substitution Decision Support on Electronic Prescribing Behavior." *Journal of the American Medical Informatics Association* 17 (6): 681–88.

Thorp, J. 2003. *The Information Paradox: Realizing the Business Benefits of Information Technology.* Toronto: McGraw-Hill Ryerson.

Viscusi, W. 2004. "The Value of Life: Estimates with Risk by Industry and Occupation." *Economic Inquiry* 42 (1): 28–49.

Walker, J., E. Pan, D. Johnston, J. Adler-Milstein, D. Bates, and B. Middleton. 2005. "The Value of Health Care Information Exchange and Interoperability." *Health Affairs.* Accessed March 2. www.healthaffairs.org/doi/full/10.1377/hlthaff.W5.10.

Wears, R. L., and M. Berg. 2005. "Computer Technology and Clinical Work: Still Waiting for Godot." *Journal of the American Medical Association* 293 (10): 1261–63.

Weinstein, M., and W. Stason. 1977. "Foundations of Cost-Effectiveness Analysis for Health and Medical Practice." *New England Journal of Medicine* 298: 716–21.

Wiley, V., and G. Daniel. 2006. *An Economic Evaluation of a Payer-Based Electronic Health Record Within an Emergency Department.* Wilmington, DE: HealthCore, Inc.

Wimble, M., and G. Leroy. 2018. "Health Information Technology: Promise and Progress." *Journal of Health Systems* 7 (3): 161–65.

CHAPTER

13

CONCLUDING COMMENTS: LIKELY TRENDS AND HIGH-IMPACT FACTORS

Learning Objectives

1. List and discuss influencers of likely future changes in the health information technology (HIT) management environment.
2. Describe the likely trend of healthcare cost and associated HIT cost factors.
3. Discuss aspects of "consumerism" that are likely to affect delivery of healthcare and roles that HIT may play in addressing consumer needs and wants for engagement in their healthcare.
4. Define the "five Vs" of big data and the role of the HIT manager in assuring the Vs are optimized in the enterprise information systems.

In the preceding chapters of this book, we made our best effort to document the current status of health information technology (HIT), to explore the most pressing industry issues facing managers and clinicians seeking to optimize information technology (IT), to advocate for IT as an essential tool to improve the quality and safety of healthcare, and to project likely trends in industry evolution. However, our "best efforts" are constrained by the rate of technology change and the complexity of the healthcare industry, which compel us to conclude this book with some suggestions for continuing to explore these fascinating and dynamic topics.

It is our considered opinion that several subject areas should be of continued interest to HIT leaders or aspiring leaders, as they likely will increase the complexity of the HIT management environment. While not an exhaustive list of influencers, regulation, fiscal pressures, evolving business models, growing consumerism and the democratization of healthcare, mHealth, digital health and associated digital apps, and the expansion of analytics capability all can be expected to warrant HIT leaders' attention for some time. Some reliable resources for continued study of these topics are provided in the chapters addressing these topics. A brief summary of some key issues in each area is provided here.

Regulation of healthcare organizations, providers, technologies, research, and so on is arguably a mixed blessing. While oversight and regulation are generally acknowledged as essential for the protection of both business and society, the associated costs and challenges to compliance are almost immeasurable. Despite some attempts at "simplification," notably in the administrative domain, the harsh reality is that not only can we expect the scope of IT regulation to increase, it likely will be dynamic as a result of the rapid rate of innovation and deployment of IT products and services. Thus, compliance professionals will play increasingly important roles on the HIT team, and, evaluating new technologies will require a regulatory compliance assessment as part of the process. From a broader industry perspective, development of new technologies can be facilitated or constrained, depending on prevailing regulatory agencies' current perspectives and the political agendas that influence the agencies.

The cost trend of healthcare moves in only one direction—up. Estimates suggest consistent increases of more than 5 percent annually, and healthcare is expected to consume approximately 20 percent of the gross domestic product by 2026. Thus, the fiscal pressures on the entire healthcare system for cost containment and value will not abate. As technology increasingly contributes to the total cost of healthcare delivery, the pressures to make sound investments will remain and likely will become more important. HIT leaders must adopt value-based business models and ensure that clinical needs for technology-supported diagnosis and treatment are met by engaging clinicians in the design and selection processes. Healthcare, almost always a major issue in national elections, likely will become more important in our volatile political climate as cost, access, and quality challenges engender extreme debate positions.

The concept of consumerism, as defined by *Health Affairs* (Carmen, Lawrence, and Siegel 2019), means that individuals "proactively [use] trustworthy, relevant information and appropriate technology to make better-informed decisions about their health care options in the broadest sense, both within and outside the clinical setting." In essence, it is the democratization of medicine—shifting the expectations that patients or consumers will demand much more transparency and power in decisions that affect their care delivery (Topol 2012). The importance of this concept to the industry is evidenced by the scope of the March 2019 "Patients as Consumers" issue of *Health Affairs.*

Since *information* and *technology* are the driving terms in this definition, HIT leaders must remain informed about current local and national initiatives to ensure public access to needed health and provider information. Also, the ease and effectiveness of the user experience in accessing the healthcare organization's information is of paramount importance. Both the patient portal to access individual information and the public portal to access comparative information are important. Issues associated with effective website design include ensuring compliance with the Health Insurance Portability and Accountability Act and data security in addition to applying robust design principles, including meeting disability accessibility standards.

mHealth, also called *digital health*—health information or services provided using mobile digital technology—is adjunctive to consumerism, as individuals seek to become more involved in their personal healthcare activity and choices. A plethora of mHealth and digital health apps exist, many available directly to consumers at low cost, others intended to be deployed by providers to engage individuals and improve compliance with treatment regimens or improve service accessibility. For those deployed by providers, it is important to keep the focus on how apps improve the workflow or the patient experience, and not on the apps themselves, many of which are likely to have short life spans (innovation in that space comes at a high speed).

A second caveat is to ensure that apps meet the needs of both consumers and providers. While consumers may easily collect health information, such as blood glucose levels or blood pressure trends, with their personal apps, connecting their self-collected data with their provider-owned health record can be quite challenging, if connection is even desired by the provider. Many of the issues associated with health apps used by consumers, either independently or collaboratively with the healthcare organization, fall into the categories of policy and security protection. mHealth and digital health regulation is still evolving—thus, there is more burden on providers to anticipate likely directions of key oversight agencies such as the Federal Communications Commission, the Federal Trade Commission, the Food and Drug Administration, and the Department of Health and Human Services.

The "five Vs" of big data, defined as volume, velocity, variety, veracity, and value, are simplistic words used to convey a complex reality, given that the interactions among the terms is the crucial feature of this amorphous concept. Deriving the potential value from the enormous volume of data created, and ensuring its veracity, impelled analytics to a high-profile field of scholarly inquiry and a high-paying professional career, not only in healthcare but in all domains of society. Analytics inform clinical as well as business decisions, enabling evidence-based medicine and performance- and value-based management of personnel, facilities, and service lines. Each V must be considered in designing and implementing information systems, negotiating vendor business solutions, and in fact, almost every aspect of strategic and operational management of HIT services. As with other facets of the HIT enterprise, trained personnel, appropriate products to run analyses, and policies and procedures to guide analytical practices are essential. Most healthcare organizations elect to use vendor products for analytics and business intelligence, often coordinating multiple applications to enable a range of analytic capability determined by the volume of data and the desired information outcome. Selecting the best products for the organization's analytic needs and recruiting personnel with the desired skill sets are key success factors.

Finally, HIT leaders must contend with the growing desire of business units to exert independence in acquiring and deploying apps and other products, usually to achieve better customer engagement and satisfaction, improve workflow or analytical capacity, or otherwise enhance their bottom-line results. To some extent, this decentralized approach is reminiscent of the "best-of-breed" systems that contributed to the fragmented, redundant, and inefficient information systems IT leaders struggled to integrate in years past. The goal, however, is not to withdraw from the integrated systems used for business and clinical processes, but to use these customer-facing and business utility apps in a complementary manner. Some may be connected to the healthcare organization's systems for data extraction, and others may be stand-alone. Key considerations for the IT leader include much more robust attention to enterprise architecture, assessing security risks for connected systems, managing any desired system integration, and preventing redundancies in data capture and storage.

In the acknowledgments section at the front of the book, we once again expressed our gratitude to Dr. Charles Austin for his vision in initiating a textbook about health information systems that was the first of its kind more than 30 years ago. We appreciate his perseverance in collaborating with Dr. Stuart Boxerman and other colleagues to maintain it as a relevant resource through six editions. This ninth edition is the third edition authored by our team, again with advice and collaboration from many people. As we anticipate our retirements before a tenth edition will be forthcoming, it is our profound desire that one or more individuals with a passion for reporting the then-current status of HIT will ensure continued availability of this long-standing resource for health professions students and working health professionals.

Web Resources

A number of organizations (through their websites) provide more information on the topics discussed in this chapter:

- The website of the Office of the National Coordinator for Health Information Technology (www.healtit.gov/topic/laws-regulation-and-policy/health-it-legislation) summarizes important HIT legislation.

- Health IT Outcomes' website provides access to a white paper on compliance with the HITECH Act (www.healthitoutcomes.com/doc/a-balanced-approach-to-meeting-hit-compliance-0002), as well as suggestions for adapting to future HIT initiatives.
- The *Health Affairs* blog (www.healthaffairs.org/do/10.1377/hblog20190304.69786/full) addresses consumerism and provides links to other relevant sites.
- Since 2005, the World Health Organization Global Observatory for eHealth (www.who.int/goe/en/) has conducted global surveys and produced reports to establish benchmarks in the adoption of necessary infrastructure to support the growth of eHealth.

Discussion Questions

1. Discuss factors that influence the changing role and importance of the compliance officer.
2. Discuss consumerism, and identify several ways that HIT can be used to engage consumers in their healthcare experience.
3. Identify some pros and cons related to decisions to allow business units to deploy apps and HIT products outside the enterprise-centralized HIT structure.
4. What are key factors to consider in establishing an analytics unit as part of the HIT structure in an enterprise?

References

Carmen, K., W. Lawrence, and J. Siegel. 2019. "The 'New' Health Care Consumerism." *Health Affairs.* Published March 5. www.healthaffairs.org/do/10.1377/hblog20190304.69786/full.

Topol, E. 2012. *The Creative Destruction of Medicine: How the Digital Revolution Will Create Better Health Care.* New York: Basic Books.

LIST OF SELECTED ABBREVIATIONS

ACA	Patient Protection and Affordable Care Act
ACO	accountable care organization
ADE	adverse drug event
ADT	admission, discharge, transfer
AHIMA	American Health Information Management Association
AHRQ	Agency for Healthcare Research and Quality
AI	artificial intelligence
AIS/AIMS	anesthesia information systems/anesthesia information management systems
AMAM	Adoption Model for Analytics Maturity
AMC	academic medical center
AMIA	American Medical Informatics Association
ANSI	American National Standards Institute
APM	Advance Alternative Payment Models
APN	advanced-practice nurse
AOE	adverse drug event
ARRA	American Recovery and Reinvestment Act
ASP	application service provider
BI	business intelligence
C-CDA	consolidated clinical document architecture
CCHIT	Certification Commission for Health Infrastructure Technology
CCO	chief compliance officer
CCR	continuity of care record
CDC	Centers for Disease Control and Prevention
CDR	clinical data repository
CDS	clinical decision support
CDSS	clinical decision support system
CEHRT	certified electronic health record technology
CEO	chief executive officer
CFO	chief financial officer
CHIME	College of Healthcare Information Management Executives
CHIP	Children's Health Insurance Program

CIO	chief information officer
CISO	chief information security officer
CMDB	configuration management database
CMIO	chief medical information officer
CMO	chief medical officer
CMS	Centers for Medicare & Medicaid Services
CMV	controlled medical vocabulary
CobiT	Control Objects for Information Technology
COO	chief operating officer
CPOE	computerized physician/provider order entry
CPT	Current Procedural Terminology
CPU	central processing unit
CT	computerized tomography
CTO	chief technology officer
CVO	credentials verification organization
DBMS	database management system
DGO	data governance office
DHS	US Department of Homeland Security
DICOM	digital imaging and communications in medicine
EDI	electronic data interchange
EBM	evidence-based medicine/evidence-based management
EDW	enterprise data warehouse
EHR	electronic health record
EIS	executive information system
eMAR	electronic medication administration record
EMR	electronic medical record
EMRAM	Electronic Medical Record Adoption Model
ERP	enterprise resources planning
ETL	extract, transform, load
FCC	Federal Communications Commission
FDA	Food and Drug Administration
FDASIA	Food and Drug Administration Safety and Innovation Act
FDDI	fiber-distributed data interchange
FTE	full-time equivalent
GAN	global area network
GDP	gross domestic product
HCPCS	Healthcare Common Procedure Coding System
HHS	US Department of Health and Human Services
HIE	health information exchange
HIMSS	Healthcare Information and Management Systems Society
HIPAA	Health Insurance Portability and Accountability Act
HIS	healthcare information system

HIT	health information technology
HITECH	Health Information Technology for Economic and Clinical Health
HITSP	Health Information Technology Standards Panel
HL7	Health Level Seven
HMO	health maintenance organization
HRIS	human resources information system
ICD	International Classification of Diseases
IDPS	intrusion detection and prevention system
IDS	integrated delivery system
IHI	Institute for Healthcare Improvement
IOM	Institute of Medicine
IoT	Internet of Things
IP	internet protocol
IRPQ	incidents, requests, problems, questions
ISDN	integrated services digital network
ISO	International Organization for Standardization
IT	information technology
ITIL	Information Technology Infrastructure Library
KPI	key performance indicator
LAN	local area network
LCD	liquid crystal display
LTC	long-term care
MACRA	Medicare Access and CHIP Reauthorization Act
MDM	master data management
MIPS	Merit-based Incentive Payment System
MPI	master patient/person index
MRI	magnetic resonance imaging
MSP	managed service provider
NCQA	National Committee for Quality Assurance
NFC	near field communication
NGT	nominal group technique
NHE	national health expenditures
NIC	network interface controller/card
NIST	National Institute of Standards and Technology
NLM	National Library of Medicine
NLP	natural language processing
NoSQL	nonstructured query language
NPI	National Provider Identifier
NPV	net present value
NSAIDs	nonsteroidal anti-inflammatory drugs
O-EMRAM	Outpatient-Electronic Medical Record Adoption Model

OCR	Office for Civil Rights
OECD	Organisation for Economic Co-operation and Development
OGC	Office of Government Commerce (United Kingdom)
ONC/ONCHIT	Office of the National Coordinator for Health Information Technology
OS	operating system
PACS	picture archiving and communication system
PC	personal computer
PCP	primary care provider
PDA	personal digital assistant
PHI	personal health information/protected health information
PHR/ePHR	personal health record/electronic personal health record
PMI	Project Management Institute
PMO	portfolio management office/program management office/project management office
PMP	Project Management Professional
PPM	project portfolio management
QPP	Quality Payment Program
QR	quick response code
RAM	random access memory
RBAC	role-based access control
RCM	revenue cycle management
RFI	request for information
RFID	radio frequency identification
RFP	request for proposal
RHIO	regional health information organization
ROI	return on investment
ROM	read-only memory
SAT	solutions, answers, and temporary fixes
SLA	service-level agreement
SME	subject matter expert
SNOMED-CT	Systematized Nomenclature of Medicine—Clinical Terms
SQL	structured query language
TCO	total cost of ownership
VDT	video display terminal
VP	vice president
WAN	wide area network
WHO	World Health Organization
WWW	World Wide Web

GLOSSARY

Administrative information system. An information system designed to assist in the performance of administrative support activities in a healthcare organization, such as payroll accounting, accounts receivable, accounts payable, facility management, intranets, and human resources management.

Algorithm. A step-by-step procedure for performing a task. Computer algorithms consist of logical and mathematical operations.

Analog signal. The representation of data by varying the amplitude, frequency, or phase of a waveform. See also *digital signal.*

Analytics. The science of logical analysis; analysis of large data sets by use of mathematics, statistics, and computer software.

Application service provider (ASP). An organization that contracts with a healthcare facility to provide access to online applications.

Applications program. A program that performs specific tasks for the computer user, such as payroll, order entry, and inventory control.

Arithmetic logic unit (ALU). A computer component that performs the computational and comparison functions. The ALU's speed is a primary consideration for applications involving image processing and other clinical applications.

Artificial intelligence (AI). A discipline that attempts to simulate human problem-solving techniques in a computer environment. See also *expert system.*

Asynchronous transfer mode. A networking technology that segments data into small fixed-length cells, directs the cells to the appropriate destination, and reassembles the data.

Bandwidth. A measure of the data-carrying capacity of a transmission medium. The higher the bandwidth, the larger the volume of data that can be moved across networks.

Bar code. A printed sequence of vertical bars and spaces that represent numbers and other symbols. The code can be read and translated automatically by specially designed computer input devices.

Bar-code scanner. An input device that allows a computer user to scan a bar code and transfer its contents to a computer.

Benefits realization. Determining, during the postimplementation phase of a project, whether goals for health information technology (HIT) investment were achieved.

Bit. A binary digit (0 or 1) that is part of a data byte. In most computer systems, eight bits make up one byte.

Blockchain. A distributed transactional database comprising linked records stored across multiple computers. All participants view, exchange, and store information without a central authority.

Bridge. An interface that connects two or more networks that use similar protocols.

Browser. A software application that enables users to view and interact with information on the World Wide Web.

Bus. (1) The physical network topology in which all workstations are connected to a line directly. (2) Within a computer, the signal path that links the central processing unit with primary memory and with input and output devices.

Byte. The smallest addressable piece of information in a computer's memory, typically consisting of eight bits, used to signify a letter, number, or symbol.

Cache memory. Primarily, short-term storage of data to facilitate high-speed processing. Although most cache data are deleted when the computer is powered down, some data-access tracking and application-specific information may be retained. Some cache memory must be deleted by command.

Client (or server) computing (or architecture). A configuration in which users interact with their machines (called *clients*) and one or more other machines (called *servers*) that store data and do much of the computing.

Clinical data repository. A database that consists of information from various sources of care and from various departments and facilities. The database may represent a longitudinal description of an individual's care.

Clinical decision support system. An application that accesses structured databases of clinical information to aid a clinician provider in defining probable diagnoses or in selecting appropriate diagnostic tests or treatment options.

Clinical (or medical) information system. A system that provides for the organized storage, processing, and retrieval of information to support patient care activities.

Closed system. A completely self-contained system that is not influenced by external events. See also *cybernetic system*, *open system*, *system*.

Cloud computing. Remote access to data storage and processing functions via the internet without use of or concern for the physical location in which the actual processing or storage systems are housed.

Cloud storage. Off-premise, distributed storage model; data are stored on the internet, generally through a contractual fee-for-service arrangement.

Computerized physician (or provider) order entry (CPOE). A process of electronically entering instructions or orders regarding the diagnosis and treatment of patients.

Configuration management database (CMDB). A knowledge store of solutions, answers, and temporary fixes; a knowledge store for system configuration settings that first-level technicians can use to potentially expedite the resolution of an end user's incident.

Connectivity. The capability of information systems to exchange information and data across components and devices.

Controlled medical vocabulary (CMV). Nomenclatures and classification systems of medical terms used to create a standard information infrastructure for capturing, storing, exchanging, searching, and analyzing clinical data.

Cyberhygiene. Adherence to good security practices for internet-connected system components.

Cybernetic system. A self-regulating system that contains the following automatic control components: sensor, monitor, standards, and control unit. See also *closed system*, *open system*, *system*.

Cybersecurity. Protection of internet-connected information systems from unauthorized access.

Data. Raw facts and figures collected by the organization from clinical encounters, empirical observations, or research. Data in and of themselves often have little value and take on meaning only after they are sorted, tabulated, and processed into a usable format (information).

Data breach. Any unauthorized access to information.

Database. A series of records, containing data fields, stored together in such a way that the contents are easily accessed, managed, and updated.

Database management system (DBMS). Software that enables the creation and accessing of data stored in a database.

Data dictionary. A file that contains the name, definition, and structure of all the data fields and elements in a database.

Data field. One piece of information stored in a data record as part of a database. Patient date of birth is one example.

Data governance. A process for ensuring that data are maintained according to business and clinical needs, securely protected to meet privacy and regulatory requirements, and properly destroyed at the terminal point of their life cycle.

Data record. A group of individual fields, corresponding to a real-world entity, that are stored together in a database. Demographic and clinical information captured during a patient encounter is one example.

Data redundancy. A situation in which the same data item appears in several files of a healthcare organization's computer system.

Data warehouse. Collection and organization of data from disparate sources into an integrated, subject-oriented repository to facilitate decision-making.

Decision support system. A system designed to support the decision-making process of an individual or organization through data retrieval, modeling, and reporting. See also *clinical decision support system*.

Deterministic system. A system in which the component parts function according to completely predictable or definable relationships with no randomness present.

Digital signal. The representation of data as a series of on/off pulses (1s and 0s). See also *analog signal.*

Distributed processing. A computer network topology in which the workload is spread out across a network of computers that can be located in different organizational units or geographical locations.

Documentation. Written information that provides a description and overview of a computer program or system and detailed instructions on its use.

Down-selection. Reducing a list of potential vendors to a small number of finalists based on criteria for retention before extensive vetting.

Dumb terminal. A device that can provide input to and display output from a central computer but cannot perform any independent processing.

E-health application. Healthcare software delivered through the internet and related technologies.

Electronic data interchange (EDI). The transfer of structured information between two computers.

Electronic health record (EHR). A system that consists of an individual's medical records from all locations and sources. Stored in digital format, an EHR facilitates the storage and retrieval of individual records with the aid of computers.

Electronic medication administration record (eMAR). An application that tracks medications dispensed to patients and automatically documents them in the electronic health record. Medications may be scanned into the system using barcodes or other electronically readable tags.

Electronic networking. Data exchange between organizations and business partners to facilitate transactions such as billing and insurance or transfer of patients across the continuum of care.

Encryption. The scrambling of an electronic transmission by using mathematical formulas or algorithms to protect the confidentiality and security of communications.

Enterprise resource planning (ERP) system. A bundled application that integrates operational information derived from finance, human resources, materials management, and other function-based areas into a robust database used to achieve business management objectives.

Ethernet. The trade name for a logical network topology used to control how devices on the network send and receive messages. The goal is to prevent "collisions" between two devices attempting to send messages simultaneously.

Evidence-based medicine and evidence-based management (EBM). A movement to explicitly use the most current, best scientific evidence available for managerial or medical decision-making.

Executive information system (EIS). An organized data storage, retrieval, and reporting system that is designed to provide senior management with information for decision-making.

Expert system. A decision support system that can approximate a human decision-maker's reasoning processes. It can assist in reaching a decision, diagnosing a problem, or suggesting a course of action.

Extranet. A private computer network an organization shares with customers and strategic partners using internet software and transmission standards.

Fiber-distributed data interchange (FDDI). A network consisting of two identical fiber-optic rings connected to local area networks and other computers.

Fiber-optic medium. A communication-transmission medium that uses light pulses sent through a glass cable at high transmission rates with no electromagnetic interference.

File (or server) architecture. The physical and logical configuration of the data storage components of a networked system.

Firewall. Hardware and software that restricts traffic to and from a private network from the general public internet network.

Front-end processor. The processor with which application users interact directly. In a client/server network, the front-end processor would correspond to the client.

Gateway. The interface between two networks that use dissimilar protocols to communicate.

Global area network (GAN). Use of wireless technology to extend a computing network beyond the geographic limits of a hard-wired network.

Governance. The way organizational leaders manage the conflict of interest that occurs when operational authority of an entity or unit is delegated to nonowners and used to define decision rights and accountabilities.

Graphical user interface (GUI). A particular interface between the human user and the computer to manage the functioning of the software and hardware that employs icons (graphical symbols on the monitor screen) to represent available operating system commands.

Grid computing. A distributed computing model whereby multiple internet-connected computers emulate a supercomputer.

Groupware. Collaborative software that enables sharing of information via an interactive network.

Hardware. The physical components of a computer system.

Healthcare information exchange (HIE). Smooth and safe coordination or transfer of patient data and information between two or more unrelated and disparate organizations.

Health Information Technology for Economic and Clinical Health (HITECH) Act. A component of the American Recovery and Reinvestment

Act that specifically promotes widespread dissemination and adoption of EHRs through provider incentives.

Health Insurance Portability and Accountability Act (HIPAA). Federal legislation passed in 1996 to make health insurance more portable. The administrative simplification provisions of HIPAA establish standards for electronic transmission of administrative information related to health insurance claims. The privacy protection regulations are designed to limit the nonconsensual use and release of private health information.

Health Level Seven (HL7). A standard for data formatting that helps to facilitate the exchange of data among disparate systems within and across software vendors.

Help desk. Also called *service desk*, a help desk provides in-person, telephone, or email access to trained personnel who can assist IT users in the resolution of equipment malfunctions and incidents or to answer technology-related questions.

Host. A computer to which other, smaller computers in a network are connected and with which it can communicate.

Hub. A hardware device with multiple user ports to which computers and input/output devices can be attached.

Incident management. Processes designed to restore normal operations following a disruption of service.

Information. Data or facts that have been processed and analyzed in a formal, intelligent way so that the results are directly useful to clinicians and managers.

Information Technology Infrastructure Library (ITIL). A framework of how HIT department processes should be interlinked to gain optimum proactive HIT service management.

Input. Data fed into a computer system, either manually (such as through a keyboard or bar-code device) or automatically (such as in a bedside patient-monitoring system).

Integrated services digital network (ISDN). A network that uses a telephone company branch exchange to allow separate microcomputer workstations, terminals, and other network nodes to communicate with a central computer and with each other.

Integrated system. A set of information systems or networks that can share common data files and can communicate with one another.

Internet of Things (IoT). The entirety of devices and objects with unique identifiers that transmit data over the internet without an intermediary person or device. Examples include wearable medical sensors and home environment management systems.

Internet protocol (IP). An addressing scheme that identifies each machine on the internet and is made up of four sets of numbers separated by dots.

Interoperability. The ability of health information systems to effectively transmit and share medical information across organizations.

Intranet. A private computer network contained within an organization that uses internet software and transmission standards.

Legacy system. A computer application designed to meet specific operational needs. Usually developed independent of a broad organizational information management or information technology plan and often is not compatible with newer integrated systems.

Life cycle. The sequence of specification, design, implementation, and maintenance of computer programs. For models of computer hardware, the life cycle is the sequence in market status—development, announcement, availability, and obsolescence.

Local area network (LAN). A computer network enabling communication among computers and peripherals in an organization or group of organizations over a limited area. The network consists of the computers, peripherals, and communication connections, either hardwired or wireless.

Magnetic storage. Online or off-line data storage in which each data character is stored as a 0 or 1 in magnetic form. Magnetic storage includes magnetic disks and tapes.

Mainframe. A large computer system that normally has very large main memories, specialized support for high-speed processing, many ports for online terminals and communication links, and extensive auxiliary memory storage.

Master patient (or person) index (MPI). A relational database containing all of the identification numbers that have been assigned to a patient anywhere in a healthcare system. The MPI assigns a global identification number as an umbrella for all of a patient's numbers, thus permitting queries that can find all appropriate data for a particular patient regardless of where that person was treated in the system.

Meaningful use. Criterion used in incentive programs of the Centers for Medicare & Medicaid Services; payments are made to eligible healthcare providers who demonstrate meaningful use of EHR technology.

Medical device integration. Incorporating data from medical devices into the electronic health record without manual intervention.

Medical tourism. Traveling across country borders for healthcare, including elective and needed surgical procedures, to achieve better quality, lower cost, or more timely services.

mHealth application. Health- and healthcare-related information, tools, and other resources that can be accessed on mobile devices.

Microcomputer. A relatively small computer system in which the microprocessor, main memory, disk drives, CD-ROM, and interface cards and connectors are installed in a small case or box. See also *microprocessor.*

Microprocessor. A CPU contained on a single semiconductor chip.

Middleware. System architecture in which applications are connected to and distributed by networked systems.

Minicomputer. A computer with capabilities somewhere between those of a microcomputer and of a mainframe computer. See also *mainframe*, *microcomputer.*

Modem (modulator/demodulator). A data-communication device that modulates signals from output devices for transmission on a data link and demodulates signals destined for input devices coming from the transmission link.

Multiplexing. The process of combining two or more signals into a single signal, transmitting it, and then sorting out the original signals. The devices that combine or sort out signals are called *multiplexers.*

Multisourcing. Outsourcing information system functions and tasks to a number of different vendors. See also *outsourcing.*

Network. A collection of computer and peripheral devices interconnected by communication paths. See also *local area network*, *wide area network*, *global area network.*

Network computer. A low-cost personal computer that has minimal equipment and is designed to be managed and maintained by a central computing function.

Network configuration. The established connections between the components of a network; the physical and logical topologies.

Network controller. A mini- or microcomputer that directs the communication traffic between the host and the terminals and peripheral devices.

Network interface card (NIC). A plug-in board used in microcomputers and workstations to allow them to communicate with a host computer and other nodes in a local area network.

Open system. A system whose components are exposed to everyone and can thus be modified or improved.

Operating system. A set of integrated subroutines and programs that control the operation of a computer and manage its resources.

Operational management system. A non–patient care information system, such as financial, purchasing, or office automation applications.

Optical disk. A disk in which data are written and read by a laser. Optical disk types include a number of variations of CDs and DVDs.

Output. Any data or information that a computer sends to a peripheral device or other network.

Outsourcing. Delegation of responsibility for specific organizational tasks or functions to an external entity on a contract basis. Examples include software development and accounts receivable collection.

Parallel processing. The use of multiple CPUs linked together generally for the purpose of more efficiently completing complex tasks.

Patient portal. A mechanism by which patients can access a component of the enterprise information system; generally intended to increase patient engagement in the care experience and in the enterprise itself.

Patient Protection and Affordable Care Act (ACA). This 2010 legislation extended HIPAA rules by requiring a unique health plan identifier and by setting standards and rules for financial transactions.

Peer network. A decentralized computing environment in which each computer on the network has either data or some hardware resource that it can make available to the other users on the network.

Peripheral devices. A general term used to refer to input, output, and secondary storage devices on a computer.

Personal health information (PHI). Any health information, in any medium, that can be identified as related to an individual.

Picture archiving and communication system (PACS). A device that provides online storage and retrieval of medical images for transmission to user workstations.

Portfolio. A collection of programs and projects undertaken by an organization.

Portfolio management. The process of selecting and managing the organization's programs and projects, including valuing existing and proposed projects against strategic business and clinical objectives for investment decisions.

Portfolio management office (PMO). A central organization dedicated to improving the practice and outcomes of projects via holistic management of all projects. This includes the professional management and oversight of an organization's entire collection of projects. The terms *PMO*, *project management office*, and *program management office* are used interchangeably.

Primary storage. Internal memory where data to be processed are stored for access by the CPU—or in the broader sense, repositories for frequently accessed transactional data.

Probabilistic algorithm. A decision support system that employs statistical probabilities rather than relying solely on knowledge collected from expert human beings.

Program. (1) An ordered set of instructions that a computer executes to obtain a desired result. (2) A group of related, often interdependent projects being conducted in an organization.

Programming language. A software system that has a specific format, or syntax, used for writing computer programs.

Quadruple aim. A national initiative to improve health outcomes, lower costs of healthcare, improve physician satisfaction, and provide better patient experiences.

Radio frequency identification (RFID). An automatic identification method that relies on storing and remotely retrieving data using devices called *transponders* or *RFID tags*. The RFID tag can be applied to a product, an animal, or a person for the purpose of identification using radio waves.

Random access memory (RAM). Storage that permits direct access to the data stored at a particular address on a computer's hard drive. Data stored in RAM are deleted when the computer is powered off.

Ransomware. A form of malware, or malicious software, that invades a host computer to encrypt the victim's files. The attacker demands a ransom to restore access to the files.

Read-only memory (ROM). Storage that contains permanent instructions or data that cannot be altered by ordinary programming.

Real time. Describes a computer or process that captures data, performs an operation, or delivers results in a time frame that humans perceive as instantaneous.

Registers. High-speed CPU memory; employed during processing activity.

Relational database. A type of database that stores data in individual files or tables, with data items arranged in rows and columns. Two or more tables can be linked for the purposes of ad hoc queries if at least one data item (the "key") is common in each of the tables.

Revenue cycle management. Process encompassing the business and clinical activities associated with generating and receiving revenue through patient care.

Router. A device located at a gateway that manages the data flow between networks. See also *gateway*.

Secondary storage. Various devices and media designed to maintain small or large quantities of data, generally for archival purposes or infrequent access.

Service continuity management. The process for restoring HIT services as quickly as possible after a service interruption.

Service-level agreement (SLA). Contract between an HIT department and specific customers that describes the services to be provided or the deliverable, along with other details.

Software. The programs that control the operation of a computer, including applications, operating systems, programming languages, development tools, and language translators.

Strategic decision support system. System that extracts data from clinical and management information systems and external data sources to enable analyses that support planning, managerial control, and outcomes assessment.

Synching station. A device wired to a computer that allows data to be exchanged between a personal digital assistant and a personal computer so that current data are available on both.

System. A network of components or elements joined together to accomplish a specific purpose or objective. Every system must include input, a conversion process, and output. See also *closed system*, *cybernetic system*, *open system*.

Systems analysis. The process of collecting, organizing, and evaluating facts about information system requirements and processes and the environment in which the system will operate.

Telecommunications. Transmission of information over distances through wired, optical, or radio media.

Telemedicine. Also referred to as *telehealth* and *e-health*, this is a rapidly developing application of clinical medicine that employs communications and information technologies to assist delivery of care (consulting, medical procedures, or examinations).

Terminal. A device consisting of a monitor and keyboard that allows a computer user to perform processing on a host computer directly. See also *dumb terminal.*

Terminal–host system. A centralized computer network configuration in which dumb terminals are connected to a large central host computer (typically a mainframe) and all the computing takes place on the host computer. See also *host*, *mainframe*, *terminal.*

Thin client. System architecture in which most processing is performed on a server remote from the end user or client.

Three-tier architecture. Configuration in which the user interface resides with the client, the relational databases reside on one server, and the application programs reside on a second server. Three-tier system offers faster information processing and distribution than does a two-tier system.

Throughput. The total time span from collection of the first data element to the preparation of the final report in a given system.

Total cost of ownership. A financial measure that incorporates both startup (one-time) and recurring costs associated with technology purchases, such as training costs, costs associated with failure or outage and recovery from security breaches, and other hidden costs.

Transaction processing systems. Application programs that form the bulk of the day-to-day activities of an organization, such as financial, clinical, admissions, and business office systems.

Transmission control protocol/internet protocol (TCP/IP). A collection of data communication protocols used to connect a computer to the internet. TCP/IP is the standard for all internet communication.

21st Century Cures Act. A law, enacted in 2016, intended to accelerate medical product development and bring innovations to market faster.

Two-tier client (or server) architecture. A system in which all back-end functions (database management, printing, communication, and applications program execution) are performed on a single server.

Voice over internet protocol (VOIP). Delivery of voice communication and multimedia sessions via the internet.

Web browser. Software that enables a user to view and interact with information stored on the Web.

Wide area network (WAN). Computer system connectivity over a large geographic region using telecommunication networks.

Workstation. (1) A microcomputer connected to a larger host computer in which some independent processing is performed. (2) A high-end microcomputer with a large amount of primary storage, a fast processor, a high-quality sound card, high-resolution graphics, a CD-RW drive, and in many cases a DVD drive. (3) Any computing device that allows users to input, process, or retrieve data or information necessary to perform their job duties.

INDEX

Note: Page numbers in italics indicate exhibits.

ABOUT THE AUTHORS

Gerald L. Glandon, PhD, was president and CEO of the Association of University Programs in Health Administration (AUPHA) until October 31, 2019. AUPHA is a global network of colleges, universities, faculty, individuals, and organizations dedicated to the improvement of healthcare delivery through excellence in healthcare management and policy education. Its mission is to foster excellence and drive innovation in health management and policy education and promote the value of university-based management education for leadership roles in the health sector. It is the only nonprofit entity of its kind that works to improve the delivery of health services—and thus the health of citizens—throughout the world by educating professional managers at the entry level.

Prior to starting this position in 2013, Dr. Glandon was professor and chair of the Department of Health Services Administration at the University of Alabama at Birmingham (UAB). The department experienced rapid growth during his tenure through expanded enrollment (undergraduate and graduate level), new program development, greater research funding, and international ventures. His primary research interests have been technology evaluation (especially information technology), the economics of aging, patient and physician satisfaction, and assessment of organizational performance. He has received numerous grants as principal investigator and co–principal investigator, including funding from government and private organizations. He has published in such journals as *JAMA*, *Journal of Gerontology: Social Sciences*, *Medical Care*, *Hospital and Health Services Administration*, and *Health Services Research*, as well as numerous books and book chapters. His publications include two editions of this book with Dr. Herb Smaltz and Dr. Donna Slovensky.

Dr. Glandon pursued extensive consulting with academic health centers, external agencies, and organizations. These activities have included process improvement; employee satisfaction assessment and reporting; litigation support; and nursing organization, quality, and cost studies. He has also worked extensively in international health with engagements in Albania, Saudi Arabia, Turkmenistan, Uzbekistan, Yemen, and Kazakhstan. He has both developed and delivered management education in these countries and provided healthcare strategic analysis to ministries of health and individual hospitals. He worked with a team on a report titled "Development of a Comprehensive Health Care Program for the Republic of Kazakhstan" that ended with recommendations regarding public health needs, healthcare delivery, healthcare capital improvement, education and research, administration of the healthcare system, financing and incentives, and budget.

Prior to UAB, he had been program director of the Department of Health Systems Management at Rush-Presbyterian-St. Luke's Medical Center in Chicago. He started his career as a researcher with the American Medical Association and worked as a senior consultant, with InterQual, Inc., and director of research at MediQual, Inc.

Detlev H. (Herb) Smaltz, PhD, LFACHE, FHIMSS, is the founder, president, and CEO of CIO Consult, LLC. He works with healthcare provider and vendor organizations to provide CIO-level professional services, including information technology (IT) strategic planning, business intelligence and analytics strategic planning, analytics competency center planning and implementation, IT and data governance, IT product market placement advice, requests for information and requests for proposal planning and oversight, IT executive and staff coaching and mentoring, IT departmental assessments, IT project portfolio management, office planning and evaluation, and a number of other services designed to maximize IT organizational performance.

In addition to his consulting activities, Dr. Smaltz served as CIO of International Operations at the Cleveland Clinic, as well as CIO of the Ohio State University Wexner Medical Center where, among other highlights, he founded a university technology transfer company, Health Care DataWorks. HCD developed a healthcare business intelligence software company that earned the distinction of a Gartner "Cool Vendor" prior to being acquired in 2015.

Dr. Smaltz has over 30 years of experience in healthcare management, primarily as CIO at organizations of various sizes, including a 20-bed community hospital, a 300-bed tertiary referral medical center, a 1,100-bed academic tertiary referral medical center, a 6,200-bed academic tertiary referral medical center, a five-state region, a seven-country international region, and the corporate headquarters of a $6.2 billion globally distributed integrated delivery system. He is a fellow of the Healthcare Information and Management Systems Society, and he served on the HIMSS board of directors from 2002 to 2005 and as vice chair from 2004 to 2005. In addition, he is a Life Fellow in the American College of Healthcare Executives (LFACHE) and a two-time CIO-100 award recipient.

Donna J. Slovensky, PhD, RHIA, FAHIMA, is professor and senior associate dean for academic and faculty affairs in the School of Health Professions at the University of Alabama at Birmingham (UAB). She holds secondary appointments in the Department of Management in the Collat School of Business, the Graduate School, and the School of Medicine's Center for Outcomes and Effectiveness Research and Education. She is a scholar in the Lister Hill Center for Health Policy, the Center for Interprofessional Education and Simulation, and the Center for Engagement in Disability Health and Rehabilitation Sciences. She is codirector of the Integrated Systems Center in the UAB School of Engineering. She has been on the UAB faculty for more than 40 years, teaching undergraduate and graduate courses in strategic management, quality management, information management, and clinical outcomes evaluation before appointment to her current administrative roles.

Dr. Slovensky earned a PhD in administration-health services with a concentration in strategic management. Her research interests include the strategic use of information resources, mHealth as a product and service delivery model, and team-based learning in health professions education, particularly signature work for honors students. She holds certification as a registered health information administrator and was one of the first individuals to receive recognition as a fellow of the American Health Information Management Association. Dr. Slovensky has consulting experience in a variety of healthcare organizations, including inpatient and ambulatory facilities, home health programs, and physician practices, in addition to consulting with health professions education programs.

Dr. Slovensky is coauthor of *mHealth: Transforming Healthcare*, published by Springer, and was coeditor and contributing author for the focused issue of *mHealth* (an academic journal) titled "mHealth Infrastructure: Issues and Solutions that Challenge Optimal Deployment of mHealth Products and Services." Other scholarship includes serving as coeditor and contributing author for the *Handbook of Healthcare Management*, published by Edward Elgar.